W9-COJ-631

The **Rough Guide** to

Belize

written and researched by

Peter Eltringham

with additional contributions by
Iain Stewart, Rob Coates and John Pirie

ROUGH
GUIDES

NEW YORK • LONDON • DELHI
www.roughguides.com

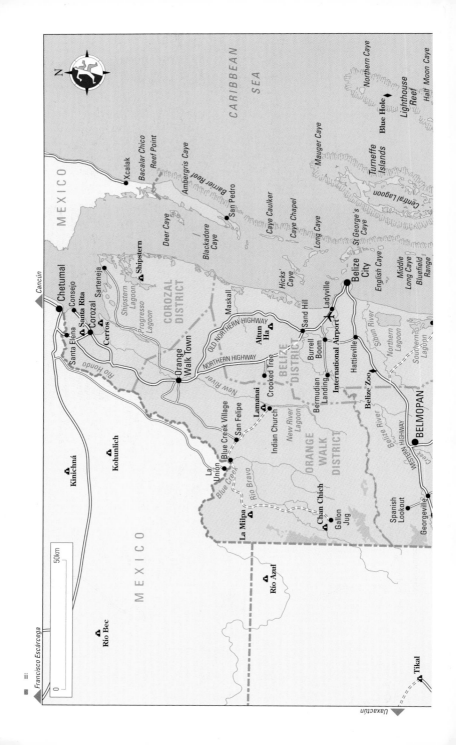

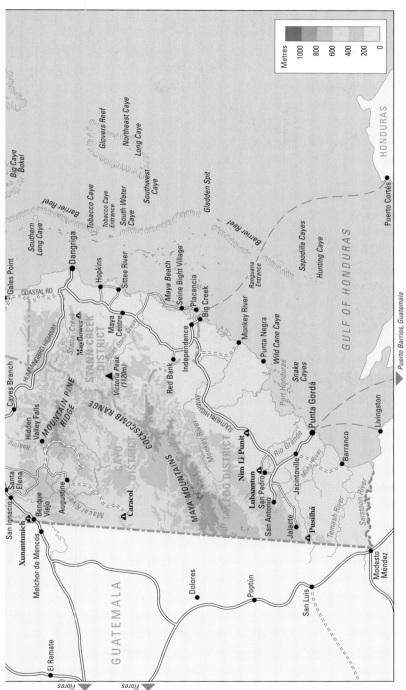

△ River camp, Cockscomb Basin Jaguar Reserve

Introduction to

Belize

Wedged into the northeastern corner of Central America, Belize offers some of the most breathtaking coastal scenery – both above and below water – in the Caribbean. Add to this magnificent landscapes, archeological sites and wildlife to rival any destination in the region, and it's easy to see why the number of visitors to this tiny country increases every year. Despite its small size – roughly that of Wales or Massachusetts – Belize has the lowest population density in Central America, a fact that contributes to its easy-going, friendly and, with the exception of bustling Belize City, noticeably uncrowded character.

Belizean territory comprises marginally more sea than land, and for most visitors it's the sea that's the main attraction. Lying just offshore is one of the country's, and the continent's, most astonishing natural wonders – the dazzling turquoise shallows and cobalt depths of the longest **barrier reef** in the Americas. Beneath the surface, a brilliant technicolour world of fish and corals awaits divers and snorkellers, while scattered along the entire reef like emeralds set in sapphire, a chain of islands, known as **cayes**, protects the mainland from the ocean swell and holds more than a hint of tropical paradise. Beyond the reef lie the real jewels in Belize's natural crown – three of only four **coral atolls** in the Caribbean. Dawn here is a truly unforgettable experience as the red–gold disc of the sun rises over the foaming white reef crest. These reefs and islands, among the most diverse marine ecosystems on the planet, are increasingly under threat; Belize, however, is at the forefront of practical research to develop effective protection for the entire coastal zone, which for visitors means a chance to explore some of the best **marine reserves** in the world.

v

Fact file

• Belize is located at the north-eastern corner of **Central America**, and shares a border with Mexico to the north and Guatemala to the west and south – to the east is the Caribbean Sea. Belize's 22,806 square kilometres of land is roughly equal to that of Massachusetts or Wales and it has a slightly greater area of territorial sea. Over 46 percent of the land in Belize is under some form of legal protection. **Tourism** is now the mainstay of the economy, but agriculture still plays an important role.

• Belize has a bicameral **National Assembly**, consisting of a House of Representatives with 29 members and a 12-member Senate. The government is headed by the **Prime Minister** but, as Belize is a **constitutional monarchy**, the head of state is Queen Elizabeth II, represented in Belize by the Governor-General, who is always a Belizean.

• As of July 2004, Belize's **population** stood at just under 275,000, with an average age of 19 years. Average life expectancy is 67.5 years and the birth rate is 30 births per 1000 people.

• Belize's **national anthem** is "Land of the Free by the Carib Sea", and a recording by schoolchildren is broadcast every morning at 6am on Love FM. The national **animal** is Baird's tapir, the national **bird** is the keel-billed toucan, the national **flower** is the black orchid and the national **tree** is the mahogany tree; you can see all of these at the Belize Zoo (see p.146).

In fact, Belizeans' recognition of the importance of their natural heritage means that the country now has the greatest proportion of protected land (over 40 percent) in the hemisphere. As a result, the densely **forested interior**, with its plentiful natural attractions, including the highest waterfall in Central America and the world's only **jaguar reserve**, remains relatively untouched. The rich tropical forests support a tremendous range of **wildlife**, including howler and spider monkeys, tapirs and pumas, jabiru storks and scarlet macaws; spend any time inland and you're sure to see the national bird, the unmistakable keel-billed toucan. Although it's the only Central American country without a volcano, Belize does have some rugged uplands – the **Maya Mountains**, situated in the south-central region and rising to over 1100m. The country's main rivers start here, flowing north or east to the Caribbean, and forming some of the largest **cave systems** in the Americas along the way. Few of these caves have been fully explored but each year more become accessible to visitors.

In addition to these natural attractions, Belize boasts a wealth of archeological remains. Rising mysteriously out of the forests are the ruins of the **ancient cities** of the **Maya**, the civilization that dominated the area from around 2000 BC until the arrival of the Spanish. Traces of this astonishing culture have been found all over the country; Maya ceremonial artefacts have even been discovered deep in caves. And although only a few sites in Belize have been as extensively restored as the great Maya cities in Mexico's Yucatán pensinsula, many are at least as large, and in their forest settings you'll see more wildlife and fewer tour buses.

Culturally, Belize is as much a Caribbean nation as a Latin one, but with plenty of distinctively Central American features – above all, a blend of races and cultures that includes Maya, Mestizo, African and European. English is the official language – Belize only gained full independence from Britain in 1981 – and Spanish is equally common, but it's the rich, lilting **Creole**, based on English but typically Caribbean, that's spoken and understood by almost every Belizean, whatever their mother tongue.

Belizean art

Whether your artistic tastes range from classic watercolours of Caribbean shores to Picasso-esque abstracts or provocative installations, the Belizean **visual art scene** is bound to have something to suit. With a plethora of galleries springing up across the country, from coastal tourist destinations to towns and inland resorts, you'll find examples of vibrant culture almost everywhere.

Not to miss is the excellent **Image Factory** in Belize City (see p.65), where conceptual artists such as Yasa Musa and Gilvano Swasey have developed their own brands of politically or socially charged work; monthly exhibitions showcase artists from around the country and the region. Another outstanding exhibition is the astonishing **Land-Sculpture Park** of Poustinia (see p.186), with absorbing installations featuring environmental and historical themes in a dramatic forest setting close to the border with Guatemala. A visit to the **Sidewalk Arts Festival** in Placencia (see p.246) would inspire any amateur or avid collector, while **San Pedro** and **Caye Caulker** are now exploding with galleries and artists whose styles may well surprise you in their originality.

A living kaleidoscope

Belize is blessed with mile after mile of glorious coral reef – one of the most amazing and certainly the most colourful ecosystems on earth. The Belize **Barrier Reef** is part of the longest continuous reef system in the Americas, a complex, living wall stretching from just south of Cancún to the Bay Islands of Honduras; beyond the line of the Barrier Reef lie three of only four **coral atolls** in the Caribbean.

The seas off Belize provide the perfect conditions for coral to thrive: a firm foundation, warm, shallow, unpolluted water and strong sunlight. The reef is composed of billions upon billions of coral polyps, the vast majority of which belong to the hard, or stony, corals – the main workforce in reef construction – with hundreds of species in an array of electric colours. The reef provides habitat for over four hundred species of fish and countless other creatures. Other corals include the soft corals, such as sea fans which you'll see gracefully wafting on the sea bed, and the fire corals, equipped (as is all coral) with stinging cells.

Most visitors to Belize will see the reef and its host of amazing creatures at close quarters, on a **snorkelling** or **diving** trip – but always observe the rules outlined in the box on p.111 to prevent damage to the reef. Even if you can't swim it's still worth viewing from the comfort of a glass-bottomed boat.

Where to go

With its wealth of national parks and reserves, numerous small hotels and reliable public transport, Belize is an ideal place to explore independently; even on a short visit you'll be able to take in both the little-visited Caribbean islands and the heartland of the ancient Maya. Almost every visitor will have to spend at least some time in **Belize City**, even if only passing through, as it's the hub of the country's transport system. First-time visitors may be shocked initially by the decaying buildings and the pollution of the river, but it is possible to spend several pleasant hours in this former outpost of the British Empire. In contrast, Belize's capital, **Belmopan**, is primarily an administrative centre, with little to offer visitors. Midway between the two, the **Belize Zoo** is easily the best in Central America and well worth making the effort to visit, to see the native animals close up and learn about the zoo's efforts towards their conservation.

Northern Belize is relatively flat and often swampy, with a large proportion of agricultural land, though still endowed, like everywhere in the country, with Maya sites and nature reserves. **Lamanai**, near Orange Walk, is one of the most impressive Maya sites in the country, while the lagoons at **Sarteneja** (Shipstern Nature Reserve) on the northeast coast and inland at **Crooked Tree** provide superb protected habitats for the country's abundant wildlife, particularly birds. In the northwest, adjacent to the Guatemalan border, is the vast **Rio Bravo Conservation Area**, where hunting has been banned for over a decade, allowing the possibility of close encounters with the wildlife.

The mainland coast is almost entirely low-lying and swampy – wonderful for wildlife, but for swimming and underwater activities you'll need to visit the **cayes**. The largest, **Ambergris Caye**, draws over half of all tourists to Belize, with the tiny resort town of **San Pedro** their main destination; **Caye Caulker**, to the south, is the most popular island for independent travellers. Many of the other cayes are now becoming easier to reach, and organized day-trips are available for divers and snorkellers to the wonderful atolls of the **Turneffe Islands** and **Lighthouse Reef**.

In the west of the country, **San Ignacio** and its environs offer everything the ecotourist could want: Maya ruins and rainforest, rivers and caves and excellent accommodation in every price range. **Caracol**, the largest Maya site in Belize, is now a routine day-trip from here, while the magnificent ruins of **Xunantunich** lie en route to the Guatemalan border. Cross the border and a few hours later you can be in **Tikal**, one of the greatest of all Maya cities.

Dangriga, the main town of the south-central region, is a jumping-off point for visitors to the central cayes and **Glover's Reef**, Belize's most remote atoll – little developed at present but becoming more accessible all the time. Further south, on the coast, the quiet Garífuna village of **Hopkins** sees more visitors every year, while the delightful, relaxed fishing village of **Placencia**, at the tip of a long, curving peninsula, has some of the country's best **beaches**. Inland, at **Maya Center** village, is the road to the **Cockscomb Basin Wildlife Sanctuary** (the **jaguar reserve**) and the

Archeology

In Belize you don't just visit the marvellous **Maya sites** as a tourist – you can participate in digs and attend the annual **Belize Archaeology Symposium** (see p.312) to meet the archeologists themselves and hear first-hand about the amazing new discoveries made here every year. As hieroglyphic inscriptions are unearthed and translated we know the names of ancient cities, their rulers and when they came to power – sometimes even when they were defeated, captured and sacrificed. Major sites have been discovered in areas previously thought to have been virtually uninhabited, such as the rugged terrain at the heart of the Maya Mountains, where deposits of fine clay were mined to create the gorgeous ceramic vessels of the Classic period.

Access to the sites is now much easier, too. The **Tourism Development Project**, a multi-million dollar project to enhance and develop those sites open to the public, has made tremendous progress, and eventually the rough road to **Caracol** (see p.180) will be paved. Most sites also have splendid new museums and visitor centres. Explanatory brochures and leaflets have been updated and tour guides have been trained to offer accurate, high-level information.

trailhead to **Victoria Peak**, Belize's most majestic mountain. Most visitors to **Punta Gorda**, the main town of Toledo District, are on their way to or from Puerto Barrios in Guatemala by boat. Venture inland, however, and you'll come across the villages of the **Mopan** and **Kekchí Maya**, set in some of the most stunning countryside in Belize and surrounded by the country's only true **rainforest**. Here are yet more caves, rivers and Maya sites, including **Lubaantun**, source of the enigmatic Crystal Skull.

When to go

x Belize lies in a **subtropical** latitude, so the weather is always warm by
■ European standards, and often hot and very humid. The immediate climate

is largely determined by **altitude**: evenings in the forests of the Mountain Pine Ridge are generally pleasantly cool, while the lowland jungle is always steamy and humid. On the cayes, the sun's heat is tempered by near constant ocean breezes.

Although Belize has its dry and rainy seasons, you'll find that the sun shines most of the year, while rain can fall in any month. The **dry season** runs roughly from January to April, and the last couple of months before the rains come can be stiflingly hot. During the **rainy season** – officially May to November – mornings are generally clear and afternoons often drenched by downpours; this is when humidity is at its highest. During the heaviest of the rains rural roads can be flooded and journeys delayed, particularly in the south. There's often a break from the rains in August (called the "mauger" season in Belize), and even before then the rain is rarely persistent enough to ruin a holiday. The worst of the rains fall in September and October, which is also the height of the **hurricane season**, when wind speeds can exceed 120kph, though most severe storms follow a track to the north of Belize. If you're out on the cayes you'll need to leave, but rest assured that Belize has an efficient warning system and a network of shelters. The rain can continue into December, a time when **cold fronts**, known locally as "**northers**", are sometimes pushed down from the north – lowering temperatures to 10°C for a couple of days – when you'll be grateful you brought a sweater or jacket. For some really **detailed weather information**, visit Ⓦ www.belizenet.com/weatherix.shtml, where you can follow the links to a satellite picture of the Caribbean.

With all this in mind, the **best time of year** to visit Belize is from late December to March, when the vegetation is still lush and the skies are generally clear. This is also the main tourist season and therefore the priciest time to visit. Plenty of people visit during the summer months, too, a period that's appropriately promoted by the tourism industry as the "**green season**".

Average temperatures, humidity and rainfall in Belize City

	Jan	Feb	Mar	Apr	May	Jun	Jul	Aug	Sep	Oct	Nov	Dec
Max temp (°C)	29	29	30	31	31	31	32	32	32	31	28	28
Min temp (°C)	19	20	21	24	24	23	23	22	22	22	20	20
Humidity (% at 7pm)	89	87	87	87	87	87	86	87	87	88	91	90
Rainfall (mm)	136	64	38	58	108	196	164	172	245	305	226	186
Rainy days	12	7	4	5	7	13	15	14	15	16	12	14

21

things not to miss

It's not possible to see everything that Belize has to offer in one trip – and we don't suggest you try. What follows is a selective and subjective taste of the country's highlights: outstanding natural features, underwater wonders, Maya ruins and distinctive cultural traditions. They're arranged in five colour-coded categories to help you find the very best things to see, do and experience. All entries have a page reference to take you straight into the Guide, where you can find out more.

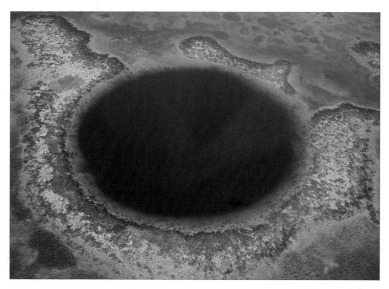

01 **The Blue Hole** Page **138** • On Lighthouse Reef, snorkel or dive the inky depths of the coral-encrusted Great Blue Hole, an enormous circular cavern 300 metres across.

02 **The Museum of Belize, Belize City**
Page **66** • This museum has one of the best collections of painted Maya ceramics and jade jewellery anywhere; a visit here is one of the city's highlights.

03
Carnival
Page **335** • The electrifying energy of Carnival in Belize City is the highlight of the "September Celebrations", which commemorate Independence Day and the Battle of St George's Caye.

04 **Sea kayaking**
Page **238** • For a real "away from it all" adventure, take a sea kayaking trip to the pristine waters of Belize's southern cayes and atolls.

05 **Hiking in the Cockscomb Basin Jaguar Reserve**
Page **239** • In the wild south, the Maya Mountains hold several rewarding trail systems, the best developed of which is in this wildlife sanctuary.

xiii

07 Sailing off Caye Caulker Page 133 • A supremely relaxing way to spend the day is to take one of many sailing trips available from this laid-back island.

06 Caracol Page 180 • The greatest of Belize's ancient Maya cities is gradually revealing its history and becoming more accessible every year.

08 The Belize Zoo Page 146 • Enjoy very close encounters with the animals and birds of Central America at this charming and well-run little zoo.

09 The Macal River Page 167 • Explore the jungle-clad banks of the Macal River as you float through the heart of beautiful Cayo District.

10 Lamanai Page 91 • Over 2000 years ago Lamanai was the largest city anywhere in the Maya world; today, climbing its massive temples is a daunting, though rewarding, objective.

11 Garífuna drumming Page **234** • Listen to the rhythms of Africa pulsating through the Caribbean as the drumbeats of the Garífuna proclaim their unique cultural heritage.

13 Turtles Page **138** • The Half Moon Caye marine reserve allows you to enjoy close encounters with these ancient wanderers of the sea, as they return to the beaches to lay their eggs in the sand.

15 The Mountain Pine Ridge Page **175** • Five Sisters Falls is a perfect place to cool off while exploring this upland area on the route to Caracol.

12 Toucans Page **234** • The unmistakable keel-billed toucan is the national bird of Belize and, though they are found almost anywhere, one of the best places to see them is the village of Sittee River.

14 Tikal Page **198** • Take an overnight trip across the Guatemalan border to visit the truly monumental Maya city of Tikal, set in a magnificent protected rainforest.

16 Ambergris Caye Page **111** • On Belize's largest and most popular island, take a well-deserved break from the hectic day- and night-time activities in and around San Pedro.

17 San Ignacio Page **159** • San Ignacio, the adventure centre of western Belize, also has the best market in the country.

19 Caves Page **154** • Belize boasts many spectacular caves, Actun Tunichil Muknal chief among them. Get here by wading chest-deep through water, and discover Maya artefacts at the end of your journey.

18 The Belize Barrier Reef Page **107** • For sheer spellbinding natural beauty it's hard to beat a trip to the Belize Barrier Reef, the longest in the western hemisphere.

20 Glover's Reef Page **236** • On the best-defined atoll in the Caribbean, comfortable expedition camps offer the opportunity for a "desert island" escape.

21 Lobsterfest Pages **128** & **246** • Caye Caulker and Placencia each celebrate the opening of the lobster season in June with a weekend-long festival, featuring music and dancing – and of course sampling the catch.

Contents

Using this Rough Guide

We've tried to make this Rough Guide a good read and easy to use. The book is divided into six main sections, and you should be able to find whatever you want in one of them.

Colour section

The colour section provides a quick tour of Belize. The **introduction** aims to give you a feel for the place, with suggestions on where to go and when. We also tell you what the weather is like and include a basic country fact file. Next, our author rounds up his favourite aspects of Belize in the **things not to miss** section – whether it's a local festival, an amazing sight or a fun activity. Right after this comes a full **contents** list.

Basics

The Basics section covers all the **pre-departure information** to help you plan your trip. This is where to find out which airlines fly to your destination, what paperwork you'll need, what to do about money and insurance, about Internet access, food, security, public transport, car rental – in fact just about every piece of **general practical information** you might need.

Guide

This is the heart of the Rough Guide, divided into user-friendly chapters, each of which covers a specific city or region. Every chapter begins with a list of **highlights** and an **introduction** that helps you decide where to go. Likewise, introductions to the various towns and smaller regions within each chapter will help you plan your itinerary. We start most town accounts with arrival and accommodation information, followed by a tour of the sights and finally reviews of places to eat and drink, as well as nightlife details. Longer accounts also have a directory of practical listings. Each chapter concludes with **transport** information for that region.

Contexts

Read Contexts to gain a deeper understanding of what makes Belize tick. We include a brief **history**, as well as in-depth essays about the Maya, archeology, ethnic Belize, landscape and wildlife, conservation issues, human rights, music and dance. We also review the best **books** on Belize.

Language

Our Language section has a **Kriol** primer, with phrases, proverbs and publications, as well as enough **Spanish** to get by, especially if you're crossing over to Guatemala.

Small print + index

Apart from a **full index**, which includes maps as well as places, this section covers publishing information, credits and acknowledgements, and also has our contact details in case you want to send in updates or corrections to the book – or suggestions as to how we might improve it.

Map and chapter list

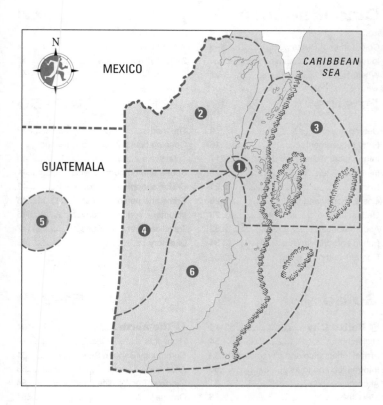

Contents

Contexts   279–348

Language   349–355

Small print + index

371–384

Basics

Basics

Getting there

Getting to Belize is simplest and usually cheapest by air. Belize has no national airline but there are daily scheduled flights to Belize City from the US departure hubs of Dallas, Miami and Houston (each about two and a half hours away) and three times a week from Charlotte, North Carolina; most international flights will pass through here first. There are no flights between Mexico and Belize but Mexico does have excellent, often inexpensive, air connections from the US and Canada (particularly to Mexico City, Cancún and Cozumel), making flying there and continuing overland (see p.15) a relatively inexpensive option. Belize also has a land border and a sea entry point from Guatemala, and there are weekly fast boats from Honduras. Since most international flights to Belize mean a stopover in the US you'll need to ensure your passport (and visa if you need one) will enable you to enter the US if you're not a US or Canadian citizen; for more on this, see "Entry requirements", p.16.

The range of **tours** to Belize gets bigger every year, with specialist companies organizing escorted group trips (often including other countries in the region) to Maya ruins and nature reserves with options of kayaking, biking, diving, bird-watching and the like. If time is short these can be very good value and give you the option of doing things that would be more difficult (or even impossible) to organize on your own, such as expeditions to remote jungle ruins and rivers and sea-kayaking trips. In a group, you'll also have the benefit of expert leaders and emergency back-up. All the tour operators we list have good websites and most also provide detailed information sheets on each trip; many also arrange slide shows so you see what's on offer in advance. The tours are usually led by someone from the company who knows the area, but you'll have a qualified local guide too. Some operate only through the winter period but a few run year-round. Transport varies from local buses to comfortable minibuses, fast launches to light aircraft. **Prices**, where given, are a guide only, and unless stated otherwise the quoted price excludes international airfares, though local flights within Belize are generally included. Some tours also require a local payment for some meals and reserve entry fees. Shop around to see what's on offer; the best, most experienced tour operators offering trips to Belize are listed in the following pages.

Shopping for flights

The price you actually pay for a flight can depend more on when and with whom you book it than on a particular "season". However, prices do rise during the **high season** (December to Easter, especially around Christmas and Easter itself) and, from Europe via the US, during July and August. At these times seat availability can be a problem: selecting a good flight agent, flying mid-week and booking ahead will pay dividends. If you plan to travel around the region you should consider buying an open-jaw ticket, which enables you to fly into one city and out of another. You might also consider combining this with an airpass (see p.10).

Barring special offers, the cheapest of the airlines' published fares is usually an **Apex ticket**, although this will carry certain restrictions: you have to book – and pay – at least fourteen days before departure, spend at least seven days abroad (there's sometimes a maximum stay of three months, though it's usually valid for six months), and you tend to get penalized if you change your schedule. Many airlines offer **youth or student fares** to under-26s. If you qualify, you'll save perhaps eight to fifteen percent more, though these tickets are subject to availability and can have eccentric booking conditions. Round-the-world tickets do not generally include Belize, though you could always build in a visit (at extra cost) if you intend to travel using one of the vast range of such tickets available from the flight specialists.

Despite the rapid advances of the giant Internet travel sites, the **best flight deals** are still found by contacting one of the recommended specialist flight agents, some of whom also offer other travel services such as student fares, insurance and tours. You could also check with a consolidator, who buys up blocks of tickets from the airlines and sells them at a discount, or a discount agent. Another possibility is to check with a courier flight specialist – though courier flights to Belize are rare, you can often get one to Mexico. Most courier companies require you to pay a membership fee and there are often special introductory offers on their websites. If you do this you'll usually need to be flexible about your flight dates and itinerary and be carrying very little luggage.

All airlines and discount flight and travel agents have websites enabling you to book flights and tours online, though you'll often still need to call to finalize your choice. Unfortunately, the airlines' own sites are often confusing and frustrating without necessarily saving you money, though you can sometimes find one-off special deals. Details of recommended flight specialists, travel websites and tour operators are given below, under each "Flights and tours from..." heading.

If you want to combine a visit to Belize with several other destinations in Mexico and Central America in a fairly short time, it's worth checking with a good travel agent about a regional **airpass**. Taca, a group of Central American airlines, and Mexican airlines Aeroméxico and Méxicana offer various airpasses. These aren't as good value as they used to be, since the passes generally no longer include Cancún and Flores, but routes and rules change frequently and some savings can be made. You'll have to purchase a minimum number of pre-booked, pre-paid coupons and generally fly into the region on one of the participating carriers.

Flights and tours from the US and Canada

Three US airlines fly non-stop directly to Belize: American from Miami and Dallas; Continental from Houston and Newark; and US Airways from Charlotte, North Carolina. El Salvador-based Taca also has daily flights from Houston. Together, depending on the day of the week, they have between six and seven daily direct flights to Belize International Airport; from elsewhere in the US, and from Canada, you'll probably have to fly to one of these hubs first. Seat availability can be tight during the high winter season, especially so at Christmas and the New Year. From Canada you can get same-day connections from Vancouver, Toronto and Montréal.

Typical **prices from the US** are around US$470–520 low season/US$530–615 high season from New York; US$640–665/680–730 from Seattle; or US$375–475/475–525 from Houston; taxes can add around another US$85. **From Canada** (Toronto, Montréal and Ottawa) expect to pay from around Can$675 low season/Can$850 high season; from Vancouver, Can$695/995. Flight taxes are around Can$80–100, depending on departure airport and routing.

Airlines in North America

Aeroméxico ☏1-800/237-6639, Ⓦ www.aeromexico.com. Direct flights from many US gateways to Mexico City and Cancún. Tickets can be linked to the "Mexipass" for connections throughout Mexico, and onwards to Central and South America.

American ☏1-800/433-7300, Ⓦ www.aa.com. Two daily non-stops from Miami and one from Dallas to Belize City.

Continental ☏1-800/231-0856, Ⓦ www.continental.com. Two daily non-stops from Houston and a direct flight from Newark on Saturday to Belize City, and many flights to Mexico and all Central American capitals. Alliance with Copa (which has an airpass) of Panamá means good prices flying on that airline into Central America.

Méxicana ☏1-800/531-7921, Ⓦ www.mexicana.com. Frequent flights from Chicago, Denver, LA, New York, San Francisco, Montréal and Toronto to many destinations in Mexico. Tickets can be linked to the "Mexipass" airpass.

Taca ☏1-800/535-8780, Canada ☏1-888/261-3269, Ⓦ www.taca.com. Handles reservations for four of the national airlines of Central America: Aviateca (Guatemala), Nica (Nicaragua), Lacsa (Costa

Rica) and Taca (El Salvador). Taca has daily flights from Houston and Miami to Belize City, and daily flights from many other cities in North America to all Central America capitals. Tickets can be linked to the "Taca Airpass".

US Airways ☎1-800/622-1015, ⓦwww.usairways.com. Three direct flights per week to Belize City from Charlotte, North Carolina, with good connections throughout the US.

North American flight specialists and consolidators

In addition to the flight specialists listed below it's always worth checking a few good general travel websites, such as ⓦwww.cheapflights .com, ⓦwww.expedia.com, ⓦwww.flyaow .com, ⓦwww.travelocity.com and the travel pages on ⓦwww.yahoo.com. The best place to begin an Internet search for flights to Belize and Mexico is eXito's superb website (see below), followed up by a phone call to their expert staff. Additionally, many of the recommended tour operators (see below) can book good-value flights for their clients.

Air Courier Association ☎1-800/280-5923, ⓦwww.aircourier.org. Courier flights and other good airfare and travel deals for members.
Air-tech ☎212/219-7000, ⓦwww.airtech.com. Standby seat broker and courier flights. Very good deals on their website, if you're prepared to be flexible.
eXito ☎1-800/655-4053, ⓦwww.exitotravel.com. North America's top specialists for travel to Belize and Latin America. Website has a particularly useful fare-finder and there's a candid comparison of the merits of various airpasses.
Flightcentre US ☎1-866/WORLD-51, ⓦwww.flightcentre.us, Canada ☎1-888/WORLD-55, ⓦwww.flightcentre.ca. Rock-bottom fares worldwide.
Now Voyager ☎212/459-1616, ⓦwww.nowvoyagertravel.com. Courier flight broker. Check the excellent website first, then call for flight prices, though usually only flights to Mexico, not Belize, are offered.
STA Travel US ☎1-800/781-4040, Canada ☎1-888/427-5639, ⓦwww.sta.com. Worldwide discount travel specialists in student/youth fares and all travel-related services. Offices throughout US, Canada and worldwide.
Travel Cuts ☎1-800/359-2887 or 1-866/416-2887, ⓦwww.travelcuts.com. Foremost Canadian specialists in student/youth fares, IDs, insurance and

other travel services. Dozens of branches throughout Canada, mainly on college campuses.

Organized tours from North America

Adventure Life ☎1-800/344-6118, ⓦwww.adventure-life.com. Specialists in small-group travel and customized itineraries to wilderness areas and nature reserves in Latin America, using the best local and international guides. On the nine-day "Belize Explorer" trip (US$1585), you spend the first couple of days on Glover's Reef, then head inland to the jungle, rivers and caves of Cayo District, finishing up with a trip to Tikal. Or, for US$900, you get six days' sea-kayaking from islands and beaches in southern Belize.
Close Encounters ☎1-888/875-1822, ⓦwww.belizecloseencounters.com. Small company, very experienced in arranging individual itineraries for all budgets to Belize.
Elderhostel ☎1-877/426-8056, ⓦwww.elderhostel.org. A non-profit organization offering upmarket educational programmes for over-55s (companions can be younger). A week studying bottlenose dolphins on the Belize atolls is around US$1900; a fifteen-day visit to Maya sites in Honduras, Belize and Guatemala costs US$2650.
Far Horizons ☎1-800/552-4575, ⓦwww.farhorizons.com. Superb archeologist-led trips to Maya sites in Belize, Guatemala and Honduras. About US$4000 for a nine-day expedition.
Gap Adventures ☎1-800/465-5600, ⓦwww.gap.ca. Canadian company offering a wide range of group trips (some camping) with diving and kayaking in Yucatán, Belize and throughout Central America. Around US$1920 plus US$300 local payment for 22 days in Belize and Tikal, including sea-kayaking and jungle trips in Belize.
International Expeditions ☎1-800/633-4374, ⓦwww.internationalexpeditions.com. Superbly led natural history tours and individual itineraries throughout Latin America, including Belize and Tikal. A ten-day "Reefs, Rainforests and Ruins" trip to Belize and Tikal costs around US$3000.
Island Expeditions ☎1-800/667-1630 ⓦwww.islandexpeditions.com. Vancouver-based company, one of the best going to Belize, running expertly led and superbly equipped sea- and river-kayaking expeditions in remote destinations. The ten-night "Ultimate Adventure", from the Maya Mountains to Glover's Reef, Belize, is US$2000; the eight-night "Coral Islands" kayak expedition takes in 50km of the southern Barrier Reef for US$1390. Both include flights within Belize.
Journeys International ☎1-800/255-8735, ⓦwww.journeys-intl.com. Award-winning nature-

and culture-oriented tours to Belize and the rest of Central America, some for women only. Around US$1800–2200 for a week.

Latin American Escapes ☎1-800/510-5999, ⓦwww.latinamericanescapes.com. Adventure and diving holidays in Belize. Eight days inland for around US$1250; four days' diving on Ambergris Caye for US$975.

The Moorings ☎1-800/535-7289, ⓦwww.moorings.com. Luxurious, well-equipped catamaran charters based in Placencia, Belize, enabling guests to explore the pristine southern cayes. Prices range from US$360 to US$1200 per day, depending on size of yacht and time of year; insurance is US$31–36/day extra.

Peter Hughes Diving ☎1-800/932-6237, ⓦwww.peterhughes.com. Luxurious, all-inclusive trips on live-aboard dive boats based in Belize, departing Saturdays. Around US$1900–2100 per week; advanced dive instruction and underwater photography courses available.

Sea Kunga ☎1-800/781-2269, ⓦwww.seakunga.com. Friendly, experienced Canadian company leading good-value small-group sailing, sea-kayaking and jungle trips, mainly in southern Belize: eight days' sea-kayaking US$1600; twelve days' rivers, caves and sea-kayaking US$1800.

Slickrock Adventures ☎1-800/390-5715, ⓦwww.slickrock.com. One of the very best adventure companies, offering sea-kayaking and jungle and river (some white-water) expeditions in Belize: US$2200 for eight-day adventure "week" with caving, jungle hiking and sea- and river-kayaking; US$1900 for a week of kayaking and snorkelling from their base at Long Caye on Glover's Reef.

TMM Bareboat Charters, ☎1-800/633-0155, ⓦwww.sailtmm.com. Superb catamaran charters in San Pedro, Ambergris Caye and Placencia, Belize, from a very experienced company. The fully equipped boats (some have a/c) range in size from 35ft to over 46ft, and sleep six to twelve. Prices, from US$2500 to US$8000 per week (plus US$30/day insurance), vary according to size and season, and you'll usually need to book well in advance.

Victor Emanuel Nature Tours ☎1-800/328-8368, ⓦwww.ventbird.com. The best small-group bird-watching tours you can get, led by dedicated professionals. US$2795 for seven days at Chan Chich and Crooked Tree, Belize; price includes internal flights.

Wildside Birding Tours ☎1-888/875-9453, ⓦwww.adventurecamera.com. Excellent bird-watching and nature trips, with emphasis on photography; US$2300 for nine days including Crooked Tree and Tikal. Also offers educational courses with college credits.

Flights and tours from the UK and Ireland

There are no direct flights from the UK or Ireland to Belize. Flying here always involves a change of aircraft (and sometimes airline), and almost always an overnight stay in a US hub, so ensure you have a machine-readable passport, which will be required to enter the US after October of 2004. From this side of the Atlantic the main destination hubs are Houston, Miami and Charlotte, North Carolina; flying to these cities will offer the least expensive connections to Belize.

Although flying from London gives you the greatest variety of flights to the US and onwards to Belize, you can often get flights from Manchester, Birmingham, Glasgow and other UK airports for the same price. A scheduled return flight to Belize City on American, Continental, US Airways or Virgin (in conjunction with Taca) will cost around £465–555 in the low season (Feb & Nov to mid-Dec), £495–575 in the shoulder season (May, June, Sept & Oct) and £585–695 in the high season (July, Aug, mid-Dec to Jan & Easter); these prices do not include taxes of around £60. There's often some deal available for young people (usually under-26s) and students, but you'll need to book as far in advance as you can, as seat availability at the discount prices is limited. Most tickets are valid for between three and six months, sometimes up to one year (though you will pay more for a budget ticket that allows you to do this); some work out cheaper if you're away less than thirty days.

An alternative to flying direct to Belize is to fly to Mexico and continue overland (see p.16). Many US airlines operating from the UK also have well-priced flights to Mexico via a US hub. It may work out slightly cheaper to fly to Cancún (staying a night or two, perhaps) and take a bus from there to Chetumal, where you can get a bus connection to Belize. From a flight specialist or discount agent you can sometimes get flights to Cancún for around £400, sometimes even less.

From Ireland often the cheapest way to get to Belize is to take one of the numerous daily flights from Dublin or Belfast to London and then connect with one of the transatlantic flights covered above. Fares from

Belfast to Belize (via London and the US) start from £550 low season going up to £700 high season, including add-on flights from Belfast. From Dublin to Belize you can expect to pay around €830 low season, over €1000 high season, plus around €140 tax. Alternatively, you can fly direct from Ireland to the US or Europe (there are many daily departures from Shannon to the US) and connect easily to Mexico to continue overland. Discount fares from Belfast to Cancún range from £490 to £675 return, with BA, Continental and Delta often coming out best. The same airlines also often have good deals on flights from Dublin to Cancún from €700, plus around €100 tax. To sort out the various possibilities contact a reliable travel agent, such as Trailfinders or Usit.

On the Internet, ⓦwww.cheapflights.co.uk has one of the best and fastest fare-finders, allowing some rapid comparisons and best-buy deals on fares to Belize and Cancún from various UK airports. You don't actually book the flight here, though; rather, the site provides a link to the travel agent offering the best price. It's also worth shopping around on ⓦwww.travelocity.co.uk and ⓦwww.expedia.co.uk as well. Frequently, however, no single general travel website is consistently going to give you the best deal, so it's still often the specialist flight agents below, backed by expert first-hand travel advice, who'll offer the best fares. Journey Latin America's website leads the field, closely followed by those of Trailfinders and STA Travel.

Airlines

American Airlines UK ☏08457/789 789, in Dublin ☏01/602 0550, ⓦwww.aa.com. Daily from Heathrow to Miami, then next day to Belize.
British Airways UK ☏0870/850 9850, in Dublin ☏01/800/626 747, ⓦwww.ba.com. Daily to Miami and three flights a week to Mexico City.
Continental ☏08456/076 760, ⓦwww.continental.com. Daily flights from Gatwick to Houston and Newark, then to Belize City next day.
Groupo Taca ☏0870/2410340, ⓦwww.taca.com. Agents for several Central American airlines and their airpasses.
Méxicana ☏020/8492-0000, ⓔsales@mextours.co.uk. Information and reservations only; no Méxicana flights from UK, but they do sell the "Mexipass" airpass.

Flight and travel specialists

Journey Latin America London ☏020/8747 3108, ⓦwww.journeylatinamerica.co.uk, Manchester ☏0161/832 1441, ⓔman @journeylatinamerica.co.uk. The industry leaders for airfares and tours to Latin America, with some of the best prices on high-season flights.
Maxwell's Travel D'Olier Chambers, 1 Hawkins St, Dublin 2 ☏01/677 9479, ⓕ679 3948. Very experienced in travel to Latin America, and Ireland's representatives for many of the specialist tour operators in the UK.
North South Travel ☏01245/608291, ⓦwww.northsouthtravel.co.uk. Small, friendly and competitive agency offering worldwide discounted fares. Profits are used to support development projects in Africa, Asia and Latin America.
South American Experience ☏020/7976 5511, ⓦwww.southamericanexperience.co.uk. Flight and tailor-made itinerary specialists, with very good airfare prices and high-quality, good-value tours to Belize.
STA Travel ☏0870/160 6070, ⓦwww.statravel.co.uk. Student/youth travel specialists with 250 offices worldwide, offering flights, tours, accommodation and many travel-related services, including a help desk if you have problems while abroad. Good website.
Trailfinders London ☏020/7938 3939, Manchester ☏0161/839 6969, Glasgow ☏0141/353 2224, Birmingham ☏0121/236 1234, Bristol ☏0117/929 9000, Dublin ☏01/677 7888, UK ⓦwww.trailfinders.co.uk, Ireland ⓦwww.trailfinders.ie. Airfare specialists and tailor-made packages for independent travellers. Other offices in UK and an excellent travel health clinic in the London Kensington High Street branch.
Usit Dublin ☏0818/200 020, Belfast ☏028/9032-4073, ⓦwww.usit.ie. All-Ireland student travel experts with eighteen offices, mainly on campuses; very useful website.

Tour operators

Adventure Bound ☏0800/316 2717, ⓦwww.adventurebound.co.uk. A range of good budget trips through Mexico and the Maya region of Central America, staying at hotels and using public transport; 22-day "Mayan Circle" for £1405, including airfare.
The Adventure Company ☏0870/794 1009, ⓦwww.theadventurecompany.co.uk. Formerly known as Travelbag Adventures, this company runs small-group hotel-based tours through Yucatán and Central America; has a sixteen-day "Realm of the

Maya" trip, from Mérida through Belize and Guatemala, for around £1300 including airfare, plus a local payment of US$100 for meals.

Dragoman ☎01728/861 133, ⓦwww.dragoman.com. Numerous possibilities of overland camping/hotel expeditions through Mexico and Central America. The 25-day "Temples and Tequila" tour spends six days in Belize and costs around £800, plus US$450 food/hotel kitty.

Explore ☎01252/760 000, ⓦwww.explore.co.uk. Wide range of two- to three-week hotel-based tours to Central America and Mexico. Most tours run year-round. Around £1450, including airfare, for fifteen days in Belize, with a trip to Tikal.

Global Travel Club ☎01268/541 732, ⓦwww.belize-tours.com. Small company specializing in individually arranged diving, adventure and cultural tours to Belize, Mexico and all of Central America.

Journey Latin America ☎020/8747 8315, ⓦwww.journeylatinamerica.co.uk. Wide range of high-standard group tours and tailor-made itineraries from the acknowledged experts. Their three-week "Quetzal Journey" through Guatemala, Chiapas, Yucatán and Belize costs around £1935, including airfare and good-quality accommodation, but not meals.

Kumuka ☎020/7937 8865, ⓦwww.kumuka.co.uk. Several hotel-based group trips (maximum 15 persons) through Mexico and Central America. The 22-day "Mayan Discoverer" takes in Guatemala, Yucatán and Belize for around £1300, excluding airfare and meals.

Naturetrek ☎01962/733 051, ⓦwww.naturetrek.co.uk. Superb bird-watching trips led by expert naturalists, staying at very comfortable jungle and beach lodges in Belize, with a visit to Tikal; £2900 for fifteen days.

Reef and Rainforest Tours ☎01803/866 965, ⓦwww.reefandrainforest.co.uk. Individual itineraries and family holidays from a very experienced company, focusing on nature reserves, research projects and diving in Belize, Honduras and Costa Rica.

Scuba Safaris ☎01342/851 196, ⓦwww.scuba-safaris.com. A knowledgeable, well-organized company, specialists in arranging fully inclusive dive packages. Around £2000 for a week on a live-aboard boat in Belize; £200 less for a week in a luxury dive resort. Prices include airfare, overnight accommodation in Houston, Texas, and six days' diving.

Trips ☎0117/311 4400, ⓦwww.tripsworldwide.co.uk. Friendly, experienced company with an inspired range of high-quality tailor-made itineraries and tours to Belize, Mexico and all of Central America. Does a fifteen-day "Ruins and Rainforest" trip taking in Guatemala's Western Highlands, Tikal and Belize's Cayo District and Ambergris Caye for £1920. Also agents for many other recommended tour operators.

Flights and tours from Australia and New Zealand

There are no direct flights from Australasia to Belize, and consequently you've little choice but to fly to the US first, generally and least expensively via Los Angeles. Flights via Asia are longer and cost more but you do get an overnight in the carrier's home city. For most airlines low season is mid-January to the end of February and October to the end of November; high season is mid-May to the end of August and December to mid-January. Seat availability on some flights out of Australia and New Zealand can be limited, so it's best to book several weeks ahead. Specialist flight/travel agents (see opposite) will offer the best deals on fares and have the latest information on special offers. Flight Centre, Trailfinders and STA generally offer the lowest fares.

Flying to Cancún will save hundreds of dollars over the cost of a flight to Belize. If you are intending to see something of Mexico or other Central American countries en route to Belize you may want to check out the various airpasses on offer that are available with your main ticket. Check with the discount agents listed to help you choose the most suitable airpasses to make the most of your trip.

From Australia, the cheapest fares (from Sydney and most of the eastern state capitals) via Los Angeles to Belize City (on Qantas and Taca via San Salvador or Continental via Houston) start at Aus$2100 low season to Aus$2900 high season, plus about Aus$160 taxes. Perth and Darwin will be anything from Aus$190 to Aus$450 higher. **From New Zealand** (Auckland) the cheapest flights to Belize City are via LA (on Air Tahiti Nui and Continental) from NZ$2190 low season to NZ$2750 high season. Expect to pay an extra NZ$150 for Christchurch or Wellington departures.

Airlines

Air New Zealand Australia ☎ 1800/803 298,
New Zealand ☎ 0800/737 000, ⓦ www.airnz.com.
Daily to Los Angeles from Auckland, either direct or
via Honolulu/Tonga/Fiji/Papeete.
Air Tahiti Nui Australia ☎ 02/9244 2899, New
Zealand ☎ 09/308 3360, ⓦ www.airtahitinui-usa
.com. Daily from Auckland to Los Angeles via
Papeete; code-share with Qantas from Australia.
JAL Australia ☎ 02/9272 1111, New Zealand
☎ 09/379 9906, ⓦ www.japanair.com. Several
flights a week to Los Angeles and Mexico City from
Sydney and major Australian cities and from
Auckland; an overnight stopover in Tokyo is included
in the fare.
Korean Airlines Australia ☎ 02/9262 6000, New
Zealand ☎ 09/914 2000, ⓦ www.koreanair.com.
Several flights a week from Sydney, Brisbane and
Auckland to Los Angeles, with an overnight in Seoul
included in the fare.
Qantas Australia ☎ 13 13 13 or 02/9700 7890,
New Zealand ☎ 0800/808 767, ⓦ www.qantas.com.
Daily to Los Angeles from major Australian cities, either
non-stop or via Honolulu, and daily from Auckland via
Sydney.
United Airlines Australia ☎ 02/9292 4111, New
Zealand ☎ 09/379 3800, ⓦ www.ual.com. Daily to
Los Angeles and San Francisco from Sydney,
Melbourne and Auckland, either direct or via
Honolulu.

Travel agents and flight specialists

Flight Centre Australia ☎ 133 133,
ⓦ www.flightcentre.com.au, New Zealand
☎ 0800/243 544, ⓦ www.flightcentre.co.nz.
Competitive discounts on airfares, plus a wide range
of package holidays and adventure tours.
STA Travel Australia ☎ 1300/733 035,
ⓦ www.statravel.com.au, New Zealand
☎ 0508/782 782, ⓦ www.statravel.co.nz. Discount
fares for students and under-26s, as well as visas,
student cards and travel insurance; good website
and branches throughout Australia and New Zealand.
Trailfinders ☎ 1300/780 122,
ⓦ www.trailfinders.co.au. Discount flights from
superb independent travel specialists.
Travel.com.au ☎ 1300/130 482,
ⓦ www.travel.com.au. Great prices from online
fare-finder and all travel services.

Tour operators

Adventure Associates ☎ 1800/222 141,
ⓦ www.adventureassociates.com. Two- to 12-day
jungle, archeological and cultural tours to Mexico and
Belize.
Contours ☎ 1300/135 391,
ⓦ www.contourstravel.com.au. Specialists in
cultural and archeological tours in Central America,
ranging from short stays to a 27-day expedition
including Mexico, Guatemala, Belize and Honduras.
Geckos ☎ 03/9663 8611, ⓦ www.geckos.cop.au.
Extended overland adventures from southern Mexico
through Guatemala, Belize and all of Central
America.
Intrepid Travel Australia ☎ 1300/360 667 or
03/9473 2626, ⓦ www.intrepidtravel.com. Small-
group tours throughout Belize and the Maya region
with the emphasis on cross-cultural contact and low-
impact tourism.
Kumuka Australia ☎ 1800/804 227, New Zealand
☎ 0800/440 449, ⓦ www.kumuka.com.au.
Australasian offices of the UK-based adventure travel
specialists – see the review opposite for more.

Overland from Mexico

It's a long, two- to three-day haul overland
to Belize from the US and Canada, but if
you'd like to see something of Mexico on
the way, it might be worth considering.
Greyhound buses (☎ 1-800/229-9424,
ⓦ www.greyhound.com) run regularly to all
major border crossings; some even take
you over the frontier and into the Mexican
bus station; you can buy tickets and the
"Discovery Pass" online. From every
Mexican border crossing there are constant buses to the capital (generally 18–22
hours away) and good connections from
there to the border town of Chetumal (a
further 22hr). Once in Chetumal, Belize's
Northern Transport buses leave hourly for
Belize City from 4am. If you've spent less
than three days in Mexico then you should-
n't have to pay the roughly £12/$20 exit
fee – payable only at a bank in Mexico, not
at the border itself.

Travelling south **by car** may give you a lot
more freedom, but it does entail a great deal
of bureaucracy. You'll need a credit card to
pay a bond to ensure you don't sell the car
in Mexico, and separate insurance to cover
your drive through Mexico, sold at the border by Sanborns (☎ 1-800/222-0158) for
about $10 per day; they have a 24hr emer-
gency hotline and can arrange much more
besides, such as legal assistance, road
maps and guides.

US, Canadian, EU, Australian and New Zealand driving licences are valid in Mexico and Belize, but it's a good idea to arm yourself with an International Driving Licence as well (contact your local driving authorities). If you run into problems with the traffic police for any reason, show that first, and if they disappear with it you at least still have your own licence. If you belong to a motoring organization at home you may find they'll offer advice, maps and even help from reciprocal organizations in Mexico. Unleaded petrol/gasoline is widely available in Mexico and Belize. See p.30 for details on driving in Belize.

Entry requirements

Citizens of the US, Canada, the EU, Australia and New Zealand do not need visas to enter Belize as tourists – but see the note at the end of this section for non-US citizens travelling through the States. Swiss, Israeli and South African citizens, as well as most other nationalities, do need a visa (US$25), for which they have to apply to a Belizean embassy or consulate in advance, as visas are not officially obtainable at the border. There is no charge to enter Belize – just fill out the immigration form on the plane or at the border. However, when leaving the country you'll have to pay exit taxes totalling US$18.75 (at land borders) or US$35 (from the international airport).

All visitors are generally allowed a maximum stay of thirty days, though your entry stamp can be renewed for Bz$25 (US$12.50) each month, for a maximum of six months, after which you may have to leave the country for at least 24 hours. If you're flying in on a one-way ticket (in the unlikely event the airline lets you board) be prepared to prove your intention to leave the country, generally by showing a return air ticket to your home country, and to show "sufficient funds" for your stay – estimated at US$35 per day – though these conditions are rarely, if ever, enforced upon arrival. Keep your passport with you at all times, or at least carry a photocopy, as you may be asked to show it at police checkpoints.

The vast majority of foreign **embassies and consulates** are still in Belize City, though the British High Commission (the name for an embassy in a Commonwealth country) is in Belmopan. Addresses of the main ones are given in the relevant chapters, and all current numbers are in the Diplomatic Listings, in the green pages of the Belize telephone directory.

Note: if your journey to Belize takes you through the US, even just for a transit stop, you will need a **machine-readable passport** (one with a bar code) and you may also require a US visa. It's essential you confirm well before you travel that your current passport will permit you to enter the US; allow at least a month, preferably two, if you need to obtain a US visa. For more on this check the latest information on the US Department of Homeland Security website (Ⓦwww.dhs .gov/us-visit).

Belize embassies and consulates

The list below has details of just a few of the Belizean embassies and consulates around the world; for the complete list visit Ⓦwww .belize.gov.bz/diplomats.html. In **New Zealand** and **South Africa** contact the British High Commission, which represents Belize in these countries.

Australia (Honorary Consul) 5/1 Oliver Rd, Roseville, NSW ℡02/9905 8144, Ⓔoutcast@acon.com.au.
Canada (Honorary Consuls) Suite 3800, South

Tower, Royal Bank Plaza, Toronto M5J 2JP ☎416/865-7000, ✉mpeterson@mcbinch.com; in Quebec ☎514/288-1687; in Vancouver ☎604/730-1224.
El Salvador Calle El Bosque Norte, Block P Casa, Col La Cima IV, San Salvador ☎503/248-1423, ✉embassyofbelizeineisal@yahoo.com.
Guatemala (also accredited to **Costa Rica**, **Honduras**, **Nicaragua** and **Panama**) Av La Reforma 1–50, Zona 9, Edificio El Reformador suite 801 & 802, Guatemala City ☎502/334-5531, ✉embelguat@guate.net.
Mexico 215 Calle Bernado de Gálves, Col Lomas de Chapultepec, Mexico DF 11000 ☎555/520-1274, ✉embelize@prodigy.net.mx; there are also Belize consulates in **Chetumal** (the border town

with Belize) on Armada de Mexico 91 ☎983-21803, ✉bzeconsulate@prodigy.net.mx, and in **Cancún** on Av Náder 34, 1st Floor ☎988-78417, ✉nelbel@prodigy.net.mx.
Switzerland 7 Rue du Mont-Blanc, CH140, Geneva ☎22/906-8420, ✉mission.belize@ties.itu.int.
UK (also accredited to **Spain** and **Italy**) Belize High Commission, Third Floor, 45 Crawford Place, London W1H 4LP ☎020/7723 3603, ⓦwww.bzhc-lon.co.uk.
USA 2535 Massachusetts Ave NW, Washington DC 20008 ☎202/332-9636, ⓦwww.embassyofbelize .org; also 5825 Sunset Blvd, Suite 206, Hollywood, CA 90028 ☎323/469-7343.

Information, websites and maps

There's no shortage of information about Belize available from a variety of different sources, much of it online. There are several excellent websites dedicated to Belize and these provide the best place to start and refine your search for facts and practical details. For more in-depth information, especially if Belize is part of an extended trip to the region, it's a good idea to visit one of the organizations or centres that specialize in Central American history, culture and politics. A comprehensive selection of books offering background on all aspects of Belize is listed on p.339 in Contexts; for a broader range of titles, including more academic subjects, contact the specialist publishers detailed there or below. It's also worth looking at the websites of the recommended tour operators and travel agents, both in Basics and throughout the Guide.

Current political analysis and an interesting and informative overview of the society, politics, economy and environment of Belize and all other Central American countries is provided by two specialist, independent publishers: in the US the Resource Center (ⓦwww.irc-online.org) and in the UK the Latin America Bureau (ⓦwww.latinamericabureau.org); both websites are excellent, with superb links. Also in the UK are two very useful resources, open to the public: Canning House Library, 2 Belgrave Square, London SW1X 8PJ (☎020/7235-2303, ⓦwww.canninghouse.com), which has the UK's largest publicly accessible collection of books and periodicals on Latin America,

including a comprehensive section on Belize; and Maya – The Guatemalan Indian Centre, 94 Wandsworth Bridge Rd, London SW6 2TF (☎ & 🖷020/7371-5291, ⓦwww .maya.org.uk), good for anyone planning to visit the Maya areas of Guatemala and Mexico as well as Belize. The Centre also hosts monthly cultural events.

Belize on the Internet

In the early days of the Internet, Belize boasted literally dozens of dedicated sites – but many of those supported by advertising have either faded away or been absorbed into the family of sites owned by Naturalight Productions, a very professional Belize-

The Belize Tourism Board and the BTIA

The **Belize Tourism Board** website, ⓦwww.travelbelize.org, is one of the best in the country, and from the main office in Belize City (see p.60 for address) you can pick up city and regional maps, a bus, boat and domestic airline schedule and a list of hotels. The only other official tourist information offices in the country, in Placencia and Punta Gorda, are listed in the relevant chapters. The **Belize Tourism Industry Association** (BTIA; ⓦwww.btia.org) represents most of the tourism businesses in the country and it produces the annual *Destination Belize* magazine (free from tourist offices and many hotels), packed with good information, lots of ads and a telephone listing of every hotel in the country. There are local representatives of the BTIA in all resort areas.

based Web design and hosting company. Although financed primarily by advertising from tourism businesses, these sites provide some real online highlights. You can check the weather forecast, visit Belize's national parks, look up hotel and tour operators, read the newspapers, surf pages on everything from the Archeology Department to the Belize Zoo, check email addresses in Belize and more.

Planeta (ⓦwww.planeta.com), put together by prolific author and journalist Ron Mader, is the best resource for all aspects of ecotourism and travel in Latin America, with a distinct focus on Mexico and Central America. There are also plenty of quality articles by other writers and concerned travellers, and you're welcome to contribute your views and experiences.

The website of the Latin American Information Center (LANIC; ⓦwww.lanic .utexas.edu) is another great place to look for detailed, authoritative information on Latin America, including Belize. There's a comprehensive, logically laid-out homepage and a seemingly never-ending series of great links; you can reach almost anywhere and anything in Belize connected to the Net from here. Finally, the ever-helpful members of the newsgroup rec.travel.latin-america will answer any query about travel in Belize and the region. Most have been asked already so there's a huge (and generally accurate) information base for you to dip into.

Other useful websites

ⓦ**www.belize.gov.bz** The government's own website is well worth checking – and you can sign up for news reports and press releases.

ⓦ**www.belize.net** The best place to search for links to Belize websites; run by Naturalight Productions who also operate the next listing.

ⓦ**www.belizeaudubon.org** Website of the Belize Audubon Society (BAS), useful for the latest info on the growing number of reserves and national parks and their associated visitor centres. See p.324 in Contexts for more on the BAS.

ⓦ**www.belizefirst.com** The best online magazine dedicated to Belize and featuring accurate reviews and articles about hotels, restaurants and destinations; the travel advice is definitely worth checking out before you go; subscribe to the print version by contacting the editor of *Belize First*, Lan Sluder – his email is ⓔBZEFIRST@aol.com.

ⓦ**www.belize.magazine.com** New online magazine produced in Belize with some worthwhile articles and listings; also available in German.

ⓦ**www.belizenet.com** The best single tourism-related site in the country, with a huge range of accurate listings and links; also see

ⓦ**www.belize.com**, run by same company.

ⓦ**www.belizenet.de** If you're in Germany or you're a German-speaker, International Belize Tourism Marketing, a travel company specializing in visits to Belize, has plenty of worthwhile general information and some good links.

ⓦ**www.channel5belize.com** Daily TV news broadcasts from Belize on an award-winning website.

ⓦ**www.mesoweb.com** Fascinating articles and links, often written by archeologists, on the latest findings in Maya research.

ⓦ**www.revuemag.com** The Guatemala-based site of the free printed tourism info magazine, *The Revue*; some useful pages on Belize and invaluable if you're heading into Guatemala.

ⓦ**www.spearbelize.org.bz** In-depth information on social, cultural, political and economic matters concerning Belize from the Society for the Promotion of Education and Research (SPEAR). Serious researchers can access the Spear resource centre, with an excellent collection of books, journals, newspapers and videos, at the Turton Library on North Front St in Belize City.

Maps

The best map of Belize is the **International Travel Map of Belize** (1:350,000), produced by International Travel Maps of Vancouver (Ⓦ www.itmb.com). It's available online from their website and from Ⓦ www.amazon.com; any good travel bookshop or map outlet, such as the ones listed below, should stock it. It's also available from several bookshops and gift shops in Belize and from *Belize First* magazine (see opposite). Topographic maps produced by Ordnance Survey in the UK are available for Belize: two sheets at 1:250,000 cover the whole country, with 44 sheets at 1:50,000 scale providing greater detail, though many are out of date and not all are readily available; try Stanfords or Elstead in the UK, or, in Belize, the Land Tax Office in Belmopan (see p.151).

Map outlets

In the US and Canada

110 North Latitude US ℡ 336/369-4171, Ⓦ www.110nlatitude.com.
Book Passage 51 Tamal Vista Blvd, Corte Madera, CA 94925 ℡ 1-800/999-7909, Ⓦ www.bookpassage.com.
Distant Lands 56 S Raymond Ave, Pasadena, CA 91105 ℡ 1-800/310-3220, Ⓦ www.distantlands.com.
Globe Corner Bookstore 28 Church St, Cambridge, MA 02138 ℡ 1-800/358-6013, Ⓦ www.globecorner.com.
Map Town 400 5 Ave SW #100, Calgary, AB, T2P 0L6 ℡ 1-877/921-6277, Ⓦ www.maptown.com.
Travel Bug Bookstore 3065 W Broadway, Vancouver, BC, V6K 2G9 ℡ 604/737-1122, Ⓦ www.travelbugbooks.ca.

World of Maps 1235 Wellington St, Ottawa, ON, K1Y 3A3 ℡ 1-800/214-8524, Ⓦ www.worldofmaps.com.

In the UK and Ireland

Blackwell's Map Centre 50 Broad St, Oxford ℡ 01865/793 550, Ⓦ www.blackwell.co.uk. Branches in Bristol, Cambridge, Cardiff, Leeds, Liverpool, Newcastle, Reading and Sheffield.
Elstead Maps PO Box 52, Elstead, Godalming, Surrey GU8 6JJ ℡ 0845/644 1396, Ⓦ www.elstead.co.uk.
John Smith and Sons, 127 Market St, St Andrews, Fife KY16 9PE ℡ 01334/475 122, Ⓦ www.johnsmith.co.uk.
The Map Shop 30a Belvoir St, Leicester ℡ 0116/247 1400, Ⓦ www.mapshopleicester.co.uk.
National Map Centre 22–24 Caxton St, London SW1 ℡ 020/7222 2466, Ⓦ www.mapsnmc.co.uk.
National Map Centre Ireland 34 Aungier St, Dublin ℡ 01/476 0471, Ⓦ www.mapcentre.ie.
Stanfords 12–14 Long Acre, London WC2 ℡ 020/7836 1321, Ⓦ www.stanfords.co.uk. Also at 39 Spring Gardens, Manchester ℡ 0161/831 0250, and 29 Corn St, Bristol ℡ 0117/929 9966.
The Travel Bookshop 13–15 Blenheim Crescent, London W11 ℡ 020/7229 5260, Ⓦ www.thetravelbookshop.co.uk.
Traveller 55 Grey St, Newcastle upon Tyne ℡ 0191/261 5622, Ⓦ www.newtraveller.com.

In Australia and New Zealand

Map Shop 6–10 Peel St, Adelaide ℡ 08/8231 2033, Ⓦ www.mapshop.net.au.
Map World 173 Gloucester St, Christchurch ℡ 0800/627 967, Ⓦ www.mapworld.co.nz.
Map World 371 Pitt St, Sydney ℡ 02/9261 3601, Ⓦ www.mapworld.net.au. Also at 900 Hay St, Perth ℡ 08/9322 5733.
Mapland 372 Little Bourke St, Melbourne ℡ 03/9670 4383, Ⓦ www.mapland.com.au.

Insurance

Travel insurance is essential for a trip to Belize; your cover should include emergency treatment and provision for repatriation by air ambulance, with medical cover of US$2,000,000. Although there is a modern private hospital in Belize City, in emergencies you may well need treatment in a hospital in the US, so ensure that your policy provides you with a 24hr emergency contact number. Consider taking out cover for loss or theft of personal possessions as petty theft is fairly common in Belize; for more on this and how to avoid it see p.43. If you plan to participate in what insurance companies define as "hazardous activities", such as scuba-diving, kayaking, rafting, rappelling or caving using ropes and specialized equipment – all possible in Belize – you may have to pay a premium.

Before shopping around for a policy check first to see what cover you already have. Household insurance policies may cover theft or loss of documents, money and valuables while overseas. Bank, credit and charge cards often have certain levels of medical or other insurance included, especially if you use them to pay for your trip. While this can be quite comprehensive, it should still be considered supplementary to full travel insurance; the medical cover, in particular, is usually insufficient for North and Central America. Canadian provincial health plans typically provide some overseas medical coverage, although they are unlikely to pick up the full tab in the event of a mishap. Holders of official student/teacher/youth cards are entitled to accident coverage and hospital in-patient benefits – the annual membership is far less than the cost of comparable insurance. Students may also find that their student health coverage extends during the vacations and for one term beyond the date of last enrolment; if you need extra cover, check with the student travel specialists STA or Travel Cuts (see pp.11, 13 & 15), though in general policies sold by travel agents are rarely the best value. It's also worth asking if you can extend your cover if you stay abroad longer than planned.

Policies vary: some are comprehensive while others cover only certain risks, such as accidents, illnesses, delayed or lost luggage, cancelled flights, etc. In particular, ask whether the policy pays medical costs up front or reimburses you later, and whether it provides for medical evacuation to your

Rough Guides Travel Insurance

Rough Guides Ltd offers a low-cost travel insurance policy, especially customized for our statistically low-risk readers by a leading British broker, provided by the American International Group (AIG) and registered with the British regulatory body, GISC (the General Insurance Standards Council). There are five main Rough Guides insurance plans: **No Frills** for the bare minimum for secure travel; **Essential**, which provides decent all-around cover; **Premier** for comprehensive cover with a wide range of benefits; **Extended Stay** for cover lasting four months to a year; and **Annual Multi-Trip**, a cost-effective way of getting Premier cover if you travel more than once a year. Premier, Extended Stay and Annual Multi-Trip policies can be supplemented by a "Hazardous Pursuits Extension" if you plan to indulge in sports considered dangerous (for more on this, see above). For a policy quote, call the Rough Guide Insurance Line: toll-free in the UK ☎0800/015 0906 or ☎+44 1392/314 665 from elsewhere. Alternatively, get an online quote at ⌨www.roughguides.com/insurance.

home country. Most North American travel policies apply only to items lost, stolen or damaged while in the custody of an identifiable, responsible third party – hotel porter, airline, luggage consignment, etc. For any policy make sure you know the claims procedure and the emergency helpline number. Note also that very few insurers will arrange on-the-spot payments in the event of a major expense or loss; you will usually be reimbursed only after going home. In all cases of loss or theft of goods, you will have to visit the local police station to have a report made out (make sure you get a copy) so that your insurer can process the claim.

Most companies can also arrange damage waiver and supplemental liability cover for car hire while abroad, often for better value than the rental company insurance.

Health

Belize has a high standard of public health, and most visitors leave without suffering so much as a dose of diarrhoea. Tap water in all towns and many villages (though not in Caye Caulker) is safe to drink, though heavily chlorinated. As a general rule, if you have tap water you're in a potable water area, though check first. In rural areas rainwater is collected; it's usually safe and delicious but you might want to treat it (see box on p.23), especially for children. Restaurants are subject to stringent hygiene regulations, so ice in drinks will almost certainly be made from treated water. Bottled water is also widely available.

Still, it's essential to get the best health advice you can before you set off; always check with your doctor or a travel clinic (see p.25). Many travel clinics also sell travel-related medical supplies such as malaria tablets, mosquito nets and water filters. Regardless of how well prepared you are, medical insurance is also essential (see opposite). You might also want to take a travel medical kit – these range from a box of Band-Aids/plasters to a sterilized medical kit, complete with syringes and sutures; these are available from clinics, pharmacies and specialist suppliers (see "Medical resources", p.24).

If you're pregnant or taking an oral contraceptive you'll need to mention this when you seek health advice on travel medicine, as some vaccines and drugs can have harmful side-effects. Travel health specialists and bookstores stock a number of books advising on health precautions and disease prevention; the best and most up-to-date is The *Rough Guide to Travel Health*, a pocket-size volume packed with accurate health information for all parts of the world.

Vaccinations

The only obligatory inoculation for Belize is yellow fever and that's only if you're arriving from a "high-risk" area (northern South America and equatorial Africa); carry your vaccination certificate as proof. However, there are several other inoculations that you should have anyway, particularly if you intend to spend time in remote rural areas. At least eight weeks before you leave (longer if you plan to be away for more than six months and need several immunizations) check that you are up to date with diphtheria, polio and tetanus jabs and arrange for typhoid and hepatitis A inoculations. Both typhoid and hepatitis A are transmitted through contaminated food and water. The former is very rare in Belize but the hepatitis A virus is common throughout Central

America and can lay a victim low for several months with exhaustion, fever and diarrhoea, and possible liver damage. One dose of vaccine will give protection for up to a year; a further shot, six to twelve months later, gives up to ten years' protection. Although the risk of contracting hepatitis B is low unless you receive unscreened blood products or have unprotected sex, travel clinics often recommend inoculation; a joint hepatitis A and B vaccine is now available from GPs and travel clinics. A course of three injections takes five weeks and gives up to five years' protection.

Though the risk of cholera is considered low in Belize, epidemics occur frequently throughout Central America, though with much less severity in Belize, due to generally good public health education. Spread via food and water, it's an acute bacterial infection recognizable by watery diarrhoea and vomiting. Symptoms (often only mild or even non-existent) are rapidly relieved by prompt medical attention and clean water. The cholera vaccine, which offers only brief and incomplete immunity, is not considered necessary and is no longer generally available from travel clinics.

Rabies exists in Belize, and vaccination (a course of three shots over a month) is recommended for anyone travelling to Latin America for over thirty days. If you're here for less time but intend to travel for days in rural areas you should also have the vaccine. The best advice is, as usual, prevention; give dogs a wide berth, and don't play with any animals at all, no matter how cuddly they look. Treat any mammal bite as suspect: wash any wound immediately with soap or detergent and apply alcohol or iodine if possible. Act immediately to get treatment – rabies is fatal once symptoms appear.

North Americans will have to pay for inoculations, available at any immunization centre or at most local clinics. Many GPs in the UK have a travel surgery where you can get advice and certain vaccines on prescription, though they may not administer some of the less common immunizations; most now charge for the service. Travel clinics (see p.25) tend to be cheaper and you can also get vaccinations almost immediately. In Australasia too, travel clinics tend to be less expensive than doctors' surgeries.

Malaria and dengue fever

Malaria, on the increase worldwide, is endemic in many parts of Central America, especially in the rural lowlands. Though it poses no great threat in Belize's tourist areas – due to an effective nationwide control programme – several thousand cases do occur each year so you should still take all the recommended precautions. The recommended malaria prophylactic in Belize is Chloroquine; you need to start taking the tablets one week before arrival and continue for four weeks after leaving the area. This drug can cause adverse reactions such as nausea; ask your travel clinic about using doxycyline or Malarone as an alternative. Avoiding bites in the first place is the best prevention; sleep in screened rooms or under nets, burn mosquito coils containing permethrin, cover up arms and legs (especially around dawn and dusk when the mosquitoes are most active) and use insect repellent containing over 35 percent Deet (15 percent for children). Other repellents include Avon Skin-So-Soft and natural preparations available from travel health suppliers. Belizeans use smouldering coconut husks or cohune nuts to ward off biting insects, to very good effect. Keeping mosquitoes at bay is doubly important in the case of dengue fever – a viral infection transmitted by mosquitoes also active during the day – for which there is no vaccine or specific treatment. The first symptom is a fever, accompanied by severe joint and muscle pains, which subsides, only to recur a few days later, this time with a rash likely to spread all over the body. After this second outbreak the fever and rash subside and recovery is usually complete. Epidemic outbreaks of dengue fever are frequent in Belize.

Intestinal troubles

A bout of diarrhoea is the medical problem you're most likely to encounter in Belize, generally caused by the change of diet and exposure to unfamiliar bacteria. Following a few simple precautions should help keep you healthy though; be sure to drink clean water (any bottled drinks, including beer and soft drinks, are already purified; for more

Water purification

Contaminated water is a major cause of illness amongst travellers in Central America, due to the presence of pathogenic organisms: bacteria, viruses and cysts. However, in Belize, water in most hotels and resorts will be treated, and bottled water is available pretty much everywhere; you will only need to consider treating the water if you travel to remote areas. Bottled water is also easy to come by in Flores and Tikal. While boiling water for ten minutes kills most micro-organisms, it's not the most convenient method. Chemical sterilization with either chlorine or iodine tablets (or a tincture of iodine liquid) is effective (except in preventing amoebic dysentery or giardiasis), but the resulting liquid doesn't taste very pleasant, though it can be masked with lemon or lime juice. Iodine is unsafe for pregnant women, babies and people with thyroid complaints. Purification, involving both sterilization and filtration, gives the most complete treatment, and travel clinics and good outdoor equipment shops will stock a wide range of portable water purifiers. In the UK the "Aqua Pure Traveller" is the best-value portable water filter and purifier, costing under £30 and capable of treating 350 litres of water; it's available from all the UK travel health specialists listed on p.25, from branches of Boots or from the manufacturer's website, Ⓦwww.thirstpoint.com. The excellent Swiss-made Katadyn filters, produced in a variety of sizes, are expensive but very durable.

advice on water, see box above), steer clear of raw shellfish and don't eat anywhere that is obviously dirty. If you do go down with a dose, the best cure is also the simplest: take it easy for a day or two, eat only the blandest of foods – papaya is good for soothing the stomach and is also packed with vitamins – and, most importantly, ensure that you replace lost fluids and salts by drinking lots of bottled water and taking rehydration salts. If you can't get hold of rehydration salts, half a teaspoon of salt and three of sugar in a litre of water will do the trick. If diarrhoea lasts more than three or four days, is accompanied by a fever or you see blood in your stools, seek immediate medical help.

If you're spending any time in rural areas you're also likely to pick up parasitic infections: protozoa – amoeba and giardia – and intestinal worms. These sound (and can be) hideous, but they're treatable once detected. If you suspect you may have an infestation take a stool sample to a pathology laboratory and go to a doctor or pharmacist with the test results. More serious is amoebic dysentery, endemic in many parts of the region. The symptoms are more or less the same as a bad dose of diarrhoea, but include bleeding. On the whole, a course of flagyl (metronidazole or tinidozole) will cure it; if you plan to visit the far-flung corners of

Central America then it's worth carrying these just in case – but get advice on their usage from a medical professional before you go.

Finally, if you're using the Pill – or any other orally administered drug – bear in mind that severe diarrhoea can reduce its efficacy.

Heat and dehydration

Another common cause of discomfort – and even illness – is the sun. The best advice is to build up exposure gradually, use a strong sunscreen and, if you're walking around during the day, wear a hat and try to keep in the shade. Be aware that overheating can cause heatstroke, which is potentially fatal. Signs are a very high body temperature without a feeling of fever, accompanied by headaches and disorientation. Lowering body temperature (a tepid shower, for example) is the first step in treatment. You should also avoid dehydration by taking plenty of fluids, especially water. If you know you're going to be hiking in the jungle for days you might want to bring oral rehydration tablets or powder, though you'll still need pure water to reconstitute them.

Bites and stings

Apart from malaria-carrying mosquitoes, there are several other biting insects and animals whose nips could leave you in vary-ing degrees of discomfort. Sandflies, often present on beaches, are tiny but their bites, usually on feet and ankles, itch like hell and last for days. Head or body **lice** can be picked up from people or bedding and are best treated with medicated soap or sham-poo. Ticks, which you're likely to pick up if you're walking or riding in areas with domes-tic livestock (and sometimes in the forests generally), need careful removal with tweez-ers – those in a Swiss Army knife are ideal.

Scorpions are common, but mostly noc-turnal, hiding during the heat of the day under rocks and in crevices. You're unlikely to be stung, but if you're camping or sleep-ing in a rustic cabaña, shake your shoes out before you put them on and avoid wander-ing around barefoot. Their sting hurts at first, but the pain usually goes away fairly quickly – though it can cause a severe allergic reac-tion in some people, so you should seek medical treatment if the pain seems signifi-cantly worse than a bee sting.

You're even less likely to be bitten by a spi-der (tarantulas won't bite unless severely pro-voked and even if you are bitten the pain soon dies down) but the advice is the same for scorpions – seek medical treatment if the pain persists or increases, or if the bite becomes infected. You're unlikely to see many snakes and most are harmless in any case; if you're walking through undergrowth, wearing boots and long trousers will go a long way towards preventing a bite – tread heavily and they'll usually slither away. If you do get bitten remember what the snake looked like (kill it if you can), immobilize the bitten limb as far as possible and seek medical help: antivenins are available in most hospitals.

Swimming and snorkelling might bring you into contact with some potentially dangerous or venomous sea creatures. You're extreme-ly unlikely to be a victim of a shark attack (though the dubious practice of shark-feed-ing as a tourist attraction is growing, and could lead to an accidental bite), but jellyfish are common and all corals will sting. Some, like the Portuguese man-o'-war jellyfish, with its distinctive purple bag-like sail, have very long tentacles with stinging cells, and an encounter will result in raw, red welts. Equally painful is a brush against fire coral: in

each case, clean the wound with vinegar or iodine and seek medical help if the pain per-sists or infection develops. See the informa-tion on rabies on p.22 for advice on mammal bites.

Getting medical help

Doctors in Belize will have received training abroad, often in the US, and are generally up to date with current treatments. Your embassy will have a list of recommended doctors, and a doctor is included in our "Listings" for Belize City (see p.73). A visit to a doctor will cost around US$20/Bz$40 and then you'll have to pay extra for medicines and treatment, which can be expensive. However, if you suspect all is not well with your insides, it might be worth heading straight for the local pathology lab (all the main towns have them) before seeing a doc-tor, as he or she will probably send you there anyway. Pharmacists are knowledgeable and helpful and sometimes sell drugs over the counter (if necessary) which are only available by prescription at home. Belize is also a centre for herbal remedies, and if you have confidence in complementary medicine you can seek advice from a number of respected practitioners – see p.171 for details of the Ix Chel Wellness Center.

Many rural communities have a health centre where health care is free, although there may be only a nurse or health-worker available and you can't rely on seeing a doc-tor immediately. Should you need an injec-tion or transfusion, make sure that the equipment is sterile (it might be worth bring-ing a sterile kit from home) and ensure any blood you receive is screened. For anything serious you should go to the best hospital you can reach.

Medical resources for travellers

Whether you're a frequent traveller or this is your first trip to the tropics check the listings below to find the latest travel health advice from the best providers. All the websites usually have excellent links – but by far the best for accurate information, comprehen-sive assessment of the health risks and advice on precautions for anyone travelling to Belize is the website of the **Centers for**

Disease Control (see below) in the US; look here first wherever you live.

In the UK and Ireland

British travellers should pick up a copy of the excellent free booklet *Health Advice for Travellers*, published by the Department of Health and available from GPs' surgeries, many chemists and most of the agencies listed below.

British Airways Travel Clinic Two travel clinics in central London, at 213 Piccadilly and 101 Cheapside. Call ☎0845/600 2236 for an appointment, or visit ⊛www.britishairways.com /travel/healthclinintro for opening hours and more. All travel vaccinations (walk-in service available) and a comprehensive range of travel health items.
Hospital for Tropical Diseases Travel Clinic Mortimer Market Centre, Capper St, London WC1E 6AU (Mon–Fri 9am–5pm; ☎020/7388 9600, ⊛www.thehtd.org); Healthline message service on ☎09061/337 733 (50p/min) with hints on hygiene, illness prevention and appropriate immunizations (after the brief introduction, key in "68" for Belize). All travel vaccinations (usually by appointment only) and travel health products; a visit to a tropical medicine consultant costs £15, which is waived if you have vaccinations at HTD.
MASTA (Medical Advisory Service for Travellers Abroad) ☎09068/224 100, ⊛www.masta.org. Extremely informative and well-organized website with plenty of practical advice on staying healthy abroad, plus information on diseases you might encounter and travel health products. All travel vaccinations available at MASTA-affiliated clinics throughout the country.
Nomad Travel Store and Medical Centre 40 Bernard St, Russell Square, London WC1N 1LJ ☎020/7833 4114, ⊛www.nomadtravel.co.uk; plus other locations in London and Bristol (see website). The Nomad Travel Health Line (60p/min; ☎09068/633 414) lets you speak to a health professional, or you can leave a message and someone will call you back free of charge. One of the best and most experienced travel equipment suppliers in the UK, with a mail and online ordering service. The clinics have some of the best prices for vaccinations, so it's best to call ahead for an appointment.
Trailfinders Travel Clinic 194 Kensington High St, London W8 6BD ☎020/7938 3999. Expert medical advice and a full range of vaccines and travel medical supplies; no appointments necessary and discounts for Trailfinders clients.

Travel Medicine Services PO Box 254, 16 College St, Belfast 1 ☎028/9031 5220. Operates a travel clinic (Mon 9–11am & Wed 2–4pm, only call during these times) which can give inoculations after referral from a GP.
Tropical Medical Bureau Grafton St Medical Centre, Dublin 2 ☎01/671 9200, ⊛www.tmb.ie. Eight specialist travel medicine clinics in the Republic of Ireland; call ☎1850/487 674 for the nearest.

In the US and Canada

Many state and local health departments throughout the US provide travel immunizations; if not, they usually can tell you who in the area does. Go to the website of the **International Society for Travel Medicine** (⊛www.istm.org) for a full list of travel clinics.

Canadian Society for International Health 1 Nicholas St, Suite 1105, Ottawa, K1N 7B7 ☎613/241-5785, ⊛www.csih.org. Non-governmental organization for the promotion of health in the developing world. Distributes a free pamphlet – *Health Information for Canadian Travellers* – containing an extensive list of travel health centres in Canada. Excellent website with very good links.
Centers for Disease Control ⊛www.cdc.gov/travel/camerica.htm. The best travel health website in the world, with current country- and area-specific health information; check here first if you can. Latest information on health risks and precautions, plus links to travel health clinics.
Health Canada ⊛www.travelhealth.gc.ca. Accurate, informative website, in English and in French, produced by the Canadian government; lists travel health clinics throughout Canada, along with lots of other useful links.
Travel Medicine 351 Pleasant St, Suite 312, Northampton, MA 01060 ☎1-800/872-8633. Sells first-aid kits, mosquito netting, water filters and other health-related travel products.

In Australia and New Zealand

The **International Association for Medical Assistance to Travellers** (IAMAT; ⊛www.cybermall.co.nz/NZ/IAMAT) is a non-profit organization open to all; there's no charge for membership, although a donation is requested to help support its work. Membership brings a number of benefits including climate charts, leaflets on various diseases and inoculations, and a list of English-speaking doctors in Central America. The website also has excellent links.

Travellers Medical and Vaccination Centre
☎ 1300/688 844, ⊛ www.tmvc.com.au. Excellent information on travel health; you can also subscribe to the online *Travel Doctor*. Twenty-five TMVC clinics across Australia, with others in New Zealand, South Africa and Southeast Asia.

Costs, money and banks

Belize has the unfortunate but generally well-deserved reputation as the most expensive country in Central America; if you've been travelling cheaply through Mexico to get here, many prices are going to come as a shock. Even on a tight budget you'll spend at least forty percent more than you would in, say, Guatemala. Perhaps as compensation for the general cost of living you can travel in the sure knowledge that, with the exception of some park and reserve entry fees, you'll be paying the same prices as the locals and you'll never have the mysterious (and sometimes illegal) charges levied that are sometimes imposed on foreigners elsewhere in the region.

Currency and exchange

Prices and exchange rates are fairly stable, with the national currency, the **Belize dollar**, very conveniently fixed at the rate of two to the US dollar (**Bz$2 = US$1**). Because of the relatively fixed exchange rate, US dollars (cash and travellers' cheques) are also accepted everywhere – and in some places even preferred – as currency. This apparently simple dual currency system can be problematic, however, as you'll constantly need to ask which dollar is being referred to; it's all too easy to assume the price of your hotel room or trip is in Belize dollars, only to discover on payment that the price referred to was in US dollars – a common cause of misunderstanding and aggravation. Prices in the Guide are usually quoted in Belize dollars – always preceded by the symbol Bz$.

The Belize dollar is divided into 100 cents. Banknotes come in denominations of 2, 5, 10, 20, 50 and 100 dollars; coins come in denominations of 1, 5, 10, 25, 50 cents and 1 dollar. All notes and coins carry the British imperial legacy in the form of a portrait of Queen Elizabeth – and quarters are called "shillings".

For **currency exchange** on arrival, there's a branch of the Belize Bank at the international airport with an ATM that accepts foreign cards. Note that banks generally offer a lower exchange rate for US$ cash than if you simply spent the cash and got your change in Belize dollars. You'll find there's at least one bank (generally Mon–Thurs 8am–2.30pm, Fri 8am–4.30pm) in every town, and there's also one on Caye Caulker and two in Placencia. Cash US$ (very useful for leaving the country) can generally be bought from the banks, though shortages do occur and you're likely to be asked to show your onward ticket before they'll let you have the money.

Officially, the only businesses in Belize other than banks allowed to exchange currency are the licensed **casas de cambio**, and they are often the best places to exchange cash US$ – if you can find them. They were set up in an attempt to control the "black market" in US$ (where you can get higher then the usual Bz$2 for US$1) but the plan has had mixed success and the black market still operates. The casas are dotted around the main towns, often inside another business such as a shop, and they change location regularly so you may have to ask around. Branches of Western Union are also licensed casas de cambio and there are several offices in Belize City and some in other towns. At the Belize land-border crossings licensed moneychangers will exchange US$ cash at slightly higher rates than the standard Bz$2 for US$1, especially for larger sums; anywhere else beware of rip-offs.

Before crossing Belize borders, check with an online currency converter (Expedia has one, and there are several others) to see the going rate for neighbouring countries. Mexican *pesos* and Guatemalan *quetzales* are usually easy to get hold of arriving at airports in those countries, and at land borders you'll be swamped by moneychangers offering fair rates for travellers' cheques and cash. US$ cash will come in handy if you arrive in Puerto Cortés, Honduras, where you'll get better rates for US$ in the market than from the moneychangers at the dockside. Finally, if you're leaving Belize for good (remember to have enough to pay the **exit taxes**, see p.28) make sure you get rid of all your Belize dollars before you go; it's very difficult to change them beyond the border areas.

Travellers' cheques and bank cards

Travellers' cheques, formerly the safest and most popular way to carry your money, are rapidly being superseded by plastic. However, they are still widely accepted and it's always a good idea to have some for emergencies (perhaps 15–20 percent of your spending money). Always check what the charge will be for using your credit or debit card – many places add an extra five or even seven percent for the privilege. Visa is the most useful card in Belize (and throughout Central America) but MasterCard is also accepted fairly widely.

You can use most credit and debit cards at **ATMs** of the Belize Bank and First Caribbean Bank (formerly Barclays) to get cash in Belize dollars at good rates. Other banks will process cash advances on cards at the counter, though at less favourable rates than an ATM. Note that there are currently no ATMs at Belize's land borders, so you'll need travellers' cheques or US$ to exchange.

Charges for using your card in Belize depend on both the card issuers' regulations – most charge a handling fee of one to two percent and perhaps a set fee of a few dollars each time you withdraw cash – and on which bank you use. If you lose your card or it gets stolen, you'll have to get a replacement sent out by courier – the big banks and card issuers can get one to you within two days. A good security policy is to take another card for emergency use only and keep it very safe.

Wiring money

Having money wired from home is never convenient or cheap, and should only be considered as a last resort. Funds can be sent via Western Union (☎1-800/325-6000, ⓦwww.westernunion.com) or American Express MoneyGram (☎1-800/926-9400, ⓦwww.moneygram.com) to several offices in Belize. Both companies' fees depend on the destination and the amount being transferred, but you can expect a charge of around $75 to send $1000. The funds should be available for collection at the office within minutes of being sent. It's also possible to have money wired directly from a bank in your home country to a bank in Belize, although this is somewhat less reliable because it involves two separate institutions: from the UK, Barclays is the best option as they have links with branches of First Caribbean in Belize. If you use this method the person wiring the funds to you will need to know the routing number of the bank in Belize.

Costs

Costs in Belize are generally lower than those in North America and Europe, though not by very much. What you spend will also obviously depend on where, when and how you choose to travel. Peak tourist seasons, such as at Christmastime and around Easter, tend to push hotel prices up, and certain tourist centres are notably more expensive than others. A sales tax (see p.28) increases costs, but the rate of inflation remains relatively low. The few locally produced goods are relatively cheap, but anything imported is overpriced.

As a general rule, a solo budget traveller will need around US$25 per day to cover the basics (accommodation, food and transport); trips such as snorkelling or canoeing will be extra. Travelling as a couple will reduce the per-person costs slightly, but to travel comfortably and enjoy the best of Belize's natural attractions you need to allow at least US$40 per person per day.

A basic room will cost at least US$9 for a single or US$15 for a double, though in many cases you'll pay more than this – a night in an upmarket lodge will set you back anything from US$65 to US$175. Compared with surrounding Central American countries, food and drink are fairly pricey, too, with an average breakfast costing around US$4–5, a simple lunch US$5–7 and dinner US$6–8. A small bottle of Belikin beer costs at least US$1.40 – well overpriced for the region, though imported beer costs over twice as much. Belizean rum, however, is relatively inexpensive, at around US$8 a bottle. Bus travel is also reasonable, with the longest bus ride in the country, Belize City to Punta Gorda, costing only US$11. A taxi ride within a town costs US$3 for one or two people. Travelling by car is expensive: the cost of a rental is higher in Belize than it is in the US – expect to pay at least US$65 per day – as is the cost of fuel, though this is still often cheaper than in Europe. At the time of writing, recent fuel price increases had yet to affect regulated fares on public transport, though some increase is inevitable.

Tax and tipping

In Belize, hotel rooms are subject to a seven percent tax (nine percent come 2005), and this is added to the price quoted. The nine percent sales tax, which applies to most goods and services (including meals in restaurants, though not to drinks), should not apply to hotel rooms; some package operators may try to slap it on anyway, so check carefully to see what you're paying for. Leaving Belize by air you pay a Bz$30 **exit tax** at the international airport, plus an airport development tax of Bz$30, a Bz$2.50 security tax and a Bz$7.50 conservation fee (the PACT; see p.322). At land borders there's a Bz$30 border tax, plus the PACT fee.

Tipping is by no means as commonplace in Belize as it is in North America, and in most budget hotels and restaurants it's certainly not expected. Still, it's a nice gesture to leave some change if the staff have been helpful; tour guides, too, appreciate a tip if you've had a good trip. When you get to the more expensive resorts you'll often find that they will impose a service charge of around ten percent on top of the bill. It's really up to you whether you pay it, as rates are quite high anyway. Check at the time of booking if you can, and only agree to accept this if you're satisfied.

Getting around

Belize has a good public transport network and all main roads are now paved. Buses on the Northern and Western highways are reliable, cheap, frequent and fairly fast; the south has fewer buses but scheduled services are improving all the time. Most places on the mainland are well served by buses; you can get to all the towns and most villages, though naturally it takes a while to reach some of the more distant corners of the country. At some point during your visit you'll probably travel by boat – out to and between the cayes, obviously – but maybe along rivers too, or even further afield to Guatemala and Honduras. There are no trains in Belize.

If you can afford it, flying is a good way to travel around Belize – especially to the south, where buses take a while, or out to San Pedro, when you get superb views of the hills and the clear blue sea, skimming along at low altitude in a small plane. **Car rental** in Belize is very expensive, (US$60–100 per day), but it does enable you to visit more places in a shorter time than you could by bus. Cars and four-wheel-drive trucks are readily available from several companies in Belize City.

By bus

The vast majority of buses in Belize are of the US schoolbus type (equivalent to a second-class service). Luxury express buses operate along all main highways, stopping only in terminals in the towns. Non-express (known as "regular") buses will stop anywhere along their route; tell the driver or conductor where you're heading for and they'll usually know where to let you off. Services usually begin in the very early morning and finish early or mid-evening – there are no overnight buses. For details of bus companies in Belize City and a rundown of the destinations they serve, see pp.74–75; locations, schedules and, where possible, telephone numbers of other bus companies are given throughout the Guide. Note that on Sundays some services are reduced or, in the case of smaller local services, often non-existent.

Along the Northern Highway all buses cross the border and go into the Mexican town of Chetumal. On the Western Highway all buses now terminate in Benque Viejo—you'll need to take a *colectiveo* (shared) taxi the remaining 3km to the Guatemalan border. Services on both these routes are particularly good, with departures half-hourly along the Western Highway and at least hourly to Chetumal. The Hummingbird and Southern highways, to Dangriga, Placencia and Punta Gorda, aren't quite as well served, though there are at least ten daily buses to Dangriga, two to Placencia and seven to Punta Gorda (around seven hours from Belize City).

Heading away from the main highways you'll be relying on the local bus services operated by smaller local companies. In many cases these own just one bus, so a breakdown can bring the whole service to a halt. Travelling by local village buses tends to be a fairly slow business as it caters to the needs of the villagers – taking produce to the market, transporting building materials and so on – but it has its rewards; you're in contact with people who know the area well, and by the time you get to the village you'll have made friends who'll be only too pleased to show you around.

Fares are a bargain in comparison with the cost of most things in Belize: on the regular buses you'll pay Bz$7.50 from Belize City to San Ignacio, Bz$10 to Chetumal and Bz$22 to Punta Gorda (the longest bus ride in the country). Tickets for express buses are about fifteen to twenty percent higher. Note that these fares are regulated by the government, which has not yet permitted increases in fuel prices to filter through to fare prices, though this is certain to change. You'll always get an assigned seat if you board at the bus station; you pay the conductor if you get on along the route. Buses are often very crowded and particularly so during holiday times, so it's a good idea to buy tickets in advance and use express services if you can. However, you'll still usually be able to get a seat most of the time – just get to the bus station half an hour before departure. Luggage usually goes inside the bus, at the back, though some regular buses and most expresses have luggage compartments underneath. Theft of luggage from buses in Belize is very rare indeed, but it still pays to keep your eye on your belongings as people get in and out of the back door.

By plane

The main towns and tourist destinations in Belize are linked by a good network of domestic flights operated by two main scheduled carriers, Maya Island Air (☏223-1140, ⬤www.mayaislandair.com) and Tropic Air (☏224-5671, ⬤www.tropicair.com); there are also several charter airlines. Together, Tropic and Maya Island provide up to eight or nine daily flights on each of the main routes – Belize City to Dangriga (Bz$63), Placencia (Bz$118) and Punta Gorda (Bz$152) – and dozens to San Pedro and Caye Caulker (Bz$52). There are no direct flights from Belize City to Corozal but you can fly there from San Pedro (Bz$70). Maya Island also flies to Belmopan (Bz$118) and San Ignacio (Bz$152). The prices quoted above are one way, including tax, for scheduled flights from Belize Municipal Airport (a few kilometres north of the city centre). All scheduled domestic flights also connect with Belize International Airport; departing from there you'll pay an extra Bz$40 for the destinations listed. Seat availability and reservation changes aren't usually a problem, except during the very busiest days of the peak season.

Flying is also the most convenient way to make side trips out of Belize to neighbouring countries. Domestic airlines operate international flights to Flores (Bz$176) and Taca flies daily from Belize City to its main hub in San Salvador for flight connections throughout Central America.

By boat

Your first experience of water transport in Belize is likely to be aboard one of the fast skiffs that ferry passengers (around 25–35 at a time) from Belize City and other mainland destinations out to the cayes. Mostly open, though some have cabins, they provide a quick (if often bumpy), reliable and safe service. If you're going in an open boat, always take a light, waterproof raincoat – showers can occur at any time of year and you'll chill quickly as you speed along in the rain.

There are many scheduled daily services from the Marine Terminal, next to the Swing Bridge in Belize City, to the most popular destinations, Caye Caulker and San Pedro on Ambergris Caye (see box on p.75); other services to the same destinations also operate from the Fort Street Tourism Village. A regular service operates between these two islands, and most boats on the Caye Caulker/San Pedro run will also call at St George's Caye on request. There's no real need to book tickets in advance for these journeys, though for early departures from the cayes it's worthwhile buying your ticket the day before. From Dangriga there are daily boats to Tobacco Caye (no schedule), while the scheduled boat to Glover's Reef (p.236) leaves Sittee River on Sunday mornings. Times and destinations of all scheduled boats are detailed in the text. Travel to other cayes and atolls is usually done as part of a tour or package, such as the dive boats operating out of San Pedro.

Several daily tour boats leave Placencia for trips up the Monkey River (see p.254) and others ply the New River from Orange Walk to visit the Maya site of Lamanai (see p.91). Alternatively, you could charter a boat for travel along the rivers and amongst the islands. If you're planning to explore the country's river network, then San Ignacio is the ideal base, with canoes readily available to rent for an hour or a week; you can also rent canoes in Bermudian Landing, Placencia, Punta Gorda and a growing number of other locations.

The only **international boat services** are the daily skiffs between Punta Gorda and Puerto Barrios in Guatemala and the weekly skiffs from Dangriga and Placencia to Puerto Cortés in Honduras (see pp.228 & 246); although not essential, it's best to book ahead for international departures by checking with the boat operator the day before.

By car

Although Belize has only four all-weather highways, driving is a popular option among visitors, and these roads offer relatively easy motoring and generally smooth surfaces; if you want to head off the paved roads you'll need high clearance and probably four-wheel drive. Main roads, and even most unpaved side roads, are generally well maintained and usually passable except in the very worst rainstorms, though mud, dust and some massive potholes can be a problem at any time. Under Belize's seatbelt law, you'll be fined US$12.50/Bz$25 for not buckling up, and the speed limit outside towns is 55mph/88kph. Distances in Belize are measured in miles (though throughout the book they're given in kilometres), with some addresses known as "Mile 29, Western Highway", for example. At press time, **fuel** prices were Bz$8.05 per US gallon (which is how it's sold) for super/premium unleaded, Bz$7.91 for regular and Bz$5.54 for diesel; bear in mind when planning your journey that filling stations are scarce outside the towns.

Traffic is generally light outside Belize City but driving standards everywhere are abysmal and fatal accidents are high in relation to traffic density. Road signs are becoming more noticeable along the main highways but you will have to watch out for speed bumps of variable height; these are usually signed but every new driver in Belize is bound to be caught unaware at least once – with potentially disastrous consequences.

The best guide to Belize's roads is Emory King's *Driver's Guide to Beautiful Belize*, updated annually and sold at hotels and filling stations throughout the country. The slim volume contains recommendations heavily weighted towards advertisers, but the sketch maps and distances are accurate and it offers a characteristically Belizean account of the road network. You'll also need a copy of the *International Travel Map* (see p.19).

If you've succeeded in getting your own car to Belize (see p.15) any further problems you face are likely to seem fairly minor, though the traffic police operate regular roadside checkpoints, so keep your licence and other documents handy. **Insurance** is available from an agent just inside either of the land border crossings or in Belize City for a few US dollars per day. Note that some spare parts can be difficult to get hold of.

Car rental

All the main car rental companies offer cars, trucks and vans, including four-wheel drive options, for between US$60 and US$125 a day, plus sales tax at nine percent and another US$13–15 per day for insurance, depending on the class of vehicle; renting for a week may save you a day's rental. They all have offices at the international airport and in Belize City; though there are a (very) few other car rental places in the country you'll almost certainly get a better deal and a better vehicle by renting here.

Avis, Budget, Hertz and Thrifty all have franchises in Belize, and local firm Crystal (which offers some of the best rental prices and is the only company which allows you to take its vehicles to Tikal) can accept advance bookings; there are also other local companies. Advance booking can save

money and gives you the certainty of a car waiting for you on arrival. One-way rentals are not usually available but your rental company will offer a pick-up or drop-off at your Belize City hotel or the airport. See the Belize City "Listings" on p.73 for details of car rental companies.

In most cases you'll need to be 25 to rent a vehicle (between 21 and 25 you might be able to rent by paying a premium) and you'll probably have to leave a credit card imprint as a damage deposit when you pick up the car. Before you belt up and drive off into the sunset, check exactly what the **insurance** covers, examine the car carefully for signs of existing damage (and make sure this is marked on the rental contract) and check what spares and equipment are included. A good spare wheel (and the tools to put it on) is essential – you'll get an average of one puncture a week from some heavy driving on Belize's roads.

By taxi

All taxis in Belize are licensed and easily identifiable by their green licence plates. They operate from ranks in the centres of towns and bus stations and, particularly in Belize City, drivers will call out to anyone they suspect is a foreigner. There are no meters so you'll need to establish a rate in advance, though within the towns a fixed fare of Bz$6 for one or two people usually applies. From the international airport designated airport taxis charge Bz$40 to Belize City; taxis will almost certainly be waiting for all scheduled domestic flights at Belize Municipal Airport.

By hitchhiking

In the more remote parts of Belize the bus service will probably only operate once a day, if at all, so unless you have your own transport, hitching is the only other option. Although locals, including women and children, regularly hitch rides in rural areas, women travellers may prefer to hitch with a friend; hitching in Belize is generally safer than at home or in neighbouring countries but attacks have occurred. Apart from this, the main drawback is the lack of traffic, but if cars or, more likely, pickup trucks do pass, the driver will usually offer you a lift, though occasionally you may be expected to offer some money for the ride. On the plus side, seeing the countryside from the back of a pickup is a wonderful experience – provided you sit on some sort of padding.

By bicycle

Seeing Belize from a bike is fairly straightforward, particularly in the north and west where the roads are well surfaced, and the Hummingbird Highway is marvellous – provided you can manage the hills. Cycling is a popular sport, with regular races along the highways. You'll find cycle repair shops in all the towns and there's even a sponsored "Hike and Bike for the Rainforest" in Cayo every October in which visitors are welcome to take part. An increasing number of resorts and shops have mountain bikes for rent (sometimes free for guests). Two of the best places to rent a bike are San Ignacio, where you can ride along the forest roads in the

Mountain Pine Ridge, and Placencia, for an enjoyable day riding on the flat, smooth, sandy road linking the peninsula's resorts. Renting a mountain bike in Punta Gorda will give you the freedom to get around the Maya villages and hills of Toledo.

Bikes can only rarely be carried on top of buses; few Belizean buses have the roof racks so common in Guatemala. If you're lucky – and there's room – the driver might let you take the bike onto the bus with you.

If you've cycled into Belize from Mexico or Guatemala there's usually no problem bringing your bike over the border, though it may be recorded in your passport and you might then have difficulty leaving the country without it. In the UK, membership of the Cyclists' Touring Club (☎0870/873-0060, ⊛www.ctc.org.uk) enables you to access information and recent trip reports from cyclists who've taken bikes to Belize and around the region before.

Accommodation

Most accommodation in Belize is in the form of hotels and guest houses – generally small family-run places found mainly in towns – or cabaña-style rustic rooms, found in the countryside and on the more isolated parts of the cayes. In each category there is a wide range of choice and prices and it's fairly easy to find somewhere reasonable. Towns in Belize are so small that you can usually walk to the majority of the hotels from the bus stop and see what's on offer; even in Belize City most places are within 1.5km of the Swing Bridge. For much of the year occupancy rates are very low, and you'll have no difficulty finding a room even in the high season. Exceptions, when you'll almost certainly need to book ahead in resort areas, are Christmas, New Year and Easter.

The charming, often somewhat ramshackle two-storey clapboard buildings found throughout the former British Caribbean and the lovely rustic **cabañas**, built of local hardwoods and often roofed with thatch, are among the most appealing places to stay. But for real holiday heaven, it's the small **guest houses**, often in beautifully restored colonial buildings in Belize City or on the cayes, that provide some of the best

accommodation in the country. In some villages and rural areas you can also find inexpensive **bed-and-breakfast** rooms in private houses. Many of these are delightful and you'll be treated more as a member of the family than a guest – the best-value places are mentioned in the Guide. Note that serviceable insect proofing can make the difference here between misery and a good night's sleep. If money's no problem,

Accommodation price codes

All accommodation listed in the Guide has been given a price code according to the following scale. The prices refer to the cost of a **double room in high season** (generally Dec to Easter) in Belize dollars (Bz$) but (unless otherwise stated in the text) do not include the government hotel tax of seven percent (increasing to nine percent in 2005). Note that some establishments also add a service charge: make sure you realize you're agreeing to pay these charges in addition to the quoted price when you take the room. To get the equivalent price in US$, simply divide by two.

❶ under Bz$20
❷ Bz$20–30
❸ Bz$30–50

❹ Bz$50–80
❺ Bz$80–110
❻ Bz$110–150

❼ Bz$150–200
❽ Bz$200–250
❾ over Bz$250

you could try one of the luxurious and delightful **resorts and lodges**, usually set in spectacular locations. Finally, in Toledo, the **Maya villages** run a village guesthouse programme (see p.267), allowing you the opportunity to experience rural Belize in a very different way from most tourists.

The cost of accommodation in Belize is notably higher than that in surrounding countries, but there are bargains available and you'll soon get used to finding what's on offer in your budget. A fairly simple double room usually costs at least Bz$30 (just over half for a single), though you can find a few decent cheaper places. Many of the mid-range and more upmarket hotels are happy to give discounts to visitors using the *Rough Guide*, especially out of season. They may also offer you a discount for booking direct; don't be afraid to ask. Most hotels have an email address and many even have a webpage, which we've given in the listing for the hotel. You can also find links to hotel websites from the recommended websites on p.18.

Arriving early at your destination means you can choose the best room for your budget. A good idea, especially in budget places, is to have a look at the room before you take it; check that the light and fan work, and if you've been told there's hot water, see just what that means. In towns it's sometimes better to get a room at the back, away from the street noise, although people-watching from the front balcony can be fascinating; an upstairs room means you're more likely to benefit from a breeze. Although there's no official hotel rating system in Belize, all hotels are inspected by the Belize Tourism Board before a licence is issued to verify that they meet minimum standards applicable to each type of establishment; this is intended to lead to official ratings in the future. If you have a complaint and the hotel owner or manager doesn't deal with it satisfactorily, you can take it to the BTB (see box on p.18) or the Belize Tourism Industry Association (BTIA), PO Box 62, 10 North Park St, Belize City (☎227-5717, ✉btia@btl.net).

Budget and mid-range hotels

Most small hotels are family-run, and the owners generally take pride in the cleanliness of the rooms. Check-in is typically informal – you'll usually have to pay in advance and sign the register. There may be a place to hand-wash clothes; ask first before you use it.

Budget hotels (❶–❸, see box above) run the gamut of standards. As a rule, a basic room will have a bed, light and fan, and all but the most rock-bottom of places will supply a towel, soap and toilet paper. You'll often have the option of a private bathroom, which is worth paying a little extra for. In most places a fan will be more important than hot water, though nowadays even budget hotels have hot water most of the time (where it's not available, we've indicated this in the text).

In Belize City, you'll pay at least Bz$30 for a simple double room; add about Bz$10 for a private bathroom. Oddly enough, budget rooms in the popular tourist areas of Caye Caulker, San Ignacio and Placencia are usually less expensive, though you'll pay much more in San Pedro. Rooms in mid-range hotels vary from Bz$50 to Bz$150; they'll almost certainly have a private bathroom and probably a private balcony; many will also have the option of air conditioning. In the countryside, especially in Cayo District, you can occasionally get a good-value deal (around Bz$100) on a private cabaña out of season, though most of them belong in the next section.

Resorts and lodges

With more money to spend, you could stay in a very comfortable private cabaña at one of the island resorts, many of which are family-run and have spectacular beach or atoll locations. Alternatively, head inland to one of the beautiful jungle lodges, often in or near national parks and offering private, thatched cabañas, with a balcony overlooking the forest or a river. Expensive they may be, but the extra dollars will soon be forgotten as you watch the sun rise over the reef or hear the rainforest dawn chorus. Several of these luxury lodges have recently added a spa and many others offer massage service.

Resorts and lodges are often used by specialist diving, adventure and nature tour operators (pp.11, 13 & 15) and some only take guests on a complete package, which includes transport, meals and some activities. Rates start at US$75 for a double room per night, and can go up to over US$200 per person on some of the more expensive packages. Watch out for the service charge (see p.28) often added on top of the bill, which, combined with the seven percent hotel tax, can raise the price considerably.

Camping

Formal camping facilities are few and far between in Belize, and the few trailer parks that exist are small and fairly basic in comparison with anything in the US or Canada. Specialist camping supplies are scarce or unobtainable, so don't expect to find camping gas canisters or Coleman fuel, though kerosene is widely available; in most cases cooking will be done over a wood fire. You can only camp in forest reserves and national parks if you obtain special permission from the Forest Department in Belmopan. Two notable exceptions (where you can just turn up and pay the fee) are the Jaguar Reserve and the forestry village of Augustine in the Mountain Pine Ridge (see pp.240 & 179, respectively).

Generally, a tent will only really be of use if you're planning to hike off the beaten track, when you'll probably have a guide who'll lead you to places where you can pitch a tent or sling a hammock. You might also want to take a tent if you're hiking around the Maya villages in southern Toledo, though many villages have a simple guest house. Some of the rural resorts in Cayo and villages throughout Belize (particularly Crooked Tree) do have camping space, but there's none anywhere on Ambergris Caye or Caye Caulker. Places where you can pitch a tent are detailed in the text; the location is usually superb.

Eating and drinking

Belizean food is a distinctive mix of Latin America and the Caribbean, with Creole "rice and beans" cuisine dominating the scene but plenty of other influences playing an important part. Central American empanadas are now as common as pizza, chow mein and hamburgers. At its best, Creole food is delicious, taking the best from the sea and mixing it with the smooth taste of coconut – a favourite ingredient – and spices. The range of international cuisines on offer increases every year and you can find authentic dishes from as far afield as Lebanon and Thailand.

You'll soon become accustomed to the **lunch hour** (noon to 1pm), observed with almost religious devotion. Abandon any hope of getting anything else done and tuck in with the locals. This is often the main meal of the day and, though most places naturally also serve dinner, dining late is not a Belizean custom; generally, getting to your table by around 8pm will mean you'll get a better choice – and possibly better service too.

Where to eat

There's a full range of bars, cafés and smart-looking restaurants around but bear in mind that the quality of the food often bears little relation to the appearance of the restaurant. Out on the islands and in small seashore villages some restaurants are little more than thatched shelters, with open sides and sand floors, though you'll just as often find upmarket places with polished floors, tablecloths and napkins. Belize City, San Pedro, Caye Caulker, Placencia and San Ignacio have the best choice, boasting some surprisingly elegant restaurants, with fast food and snack bars springing up on street corners. Most places in the country, however, lie somewhere between the two, serving up good food but with only a little concern for presentation.

Central American-style streetside **snack bars**, often run by former refugees from El Salvador or Honduras, are now found all over the country, and provide a cheap and delicious fast-food service. You'll find tasty tamales (a savoury cornmeal "pudding", usually with chicken cooked in a lightly spiced sauce inside, wrapped in a banana leaf and steamed), tacos, empanadas (similar to tacos but the tortilla is folded in half after filling, and deep fried) and other Latin staples, adding variety to the range of cuisine on offer. Travelling, you'll find that these snack foods, as well as the usual Belizean standby of "ham" burgers (literally a slice of canned ham in a bun), sometimes come to you as street traders offer them to waiting bus passengers, although the practice isn't nearly as common as elsewhere in Central America.

What to eat

There are few surprises waiting at **breakfast**: you're likely to be offered eggs with ham or sausage, usually accompanied by bread (sometimes toasted) or flour tortillas and stewed or refried red beans, though in tourist areas you'll almost always be offered fresh fruit and pancakes, often served with yoghurt or locally produced honey.

The basis of any Creole main meal is **rice and beans**, and this features heavily in small restaurants. The white rice and red beans are cooked together in coconut oil and flavoured with *recado* (a mild ground red spice) – often with a chunk of salted pork thrown in for extra taste – and usually served with stewed chicken or beef, or fried fish. If you like your flavours full on, there'll always be a bottle of hot sauce on the table for extra spice. Despite the proximity of Mexico, its cuisine has had only a superficial effect on Belizean restaurant food; you might get tamales or *ecsabeche* (a spicy onion soup with chicken), though perhaps without the usual accompaniment of corn (maize) tortillas. Vegetables are scarce in Creole food but on the side of the plate you'll often get a portion of potato salad or coleslaw, and sometimes fried plantain or flour tortillas.

Seafood is almost always excellent. Grouper and red snapper are invariably fantastic, and you might also try a barracuda steak, conch fritters or a plate of fresh (though usually farmed) shrimps. On San Pedro and Caye Caulker the food is often exceptional, with lobster served in an amazing range of dishes: in addition to grilled or barbecued lobster you'll see pasta with lobster sauce, lobster and scrambled eggs, and even lobster chow mein or lobster curry. Note: the closed season for lobster is from mid-February to mid-June, and it will not (or certainly should not) be served then. Turtle is only on the menu in a very few places, in theory only during the short open season, but they're all protected species, threatened with extinction – avoid trying it, or indeed any animal taken from the wild.

When there's little else on offer, Belize's many Chinese restaurants are usually a safe bet and Chinese food will probably feature more in your trip than you anticipated. Other Belizean ethnic minorities are now starting to break into the restaurant trade; many places serve Garífuna dishes, and there are Indian restaurants in Belize City and San Ignacio (where there's also a Sri Lankan restaurant), serving superb curries.

Vegetarians will find the pickings slim and there are few specifically vegetarian restaurants, though many places now offer a couple of vegetarian dishes. Note that in most Belizean restaurants if you say you don't eat meat you're likely to be offered chicken or ham (white meat is often not considered "meat" in the true sense). The fruit is good and there are some excellent locally produced vegetables (thanks mainly to the Mennonites and Central American refugees) but these are rarely served in non-tourist restaurants. Your best bet outside the main tourist areas, where there will usually be a meat-free choice on the menu, is to try a Chinese restaurant.

Drinks

The most basic drinks to accompany food are water, beer and the oversweetened, but familiar, soft drinks. Belikin, the only brewery in Belize, produces almost all the **beer** consumed here. Belikin beer itself comes in several varieties: regular, a tasty, lager-type bottled and draught beer; bottled stout (a rich, dark beer); and Premium and Lighthouse, more expensive bottled beers and often all you'll be able to get in upmarket hotels and restaurants. If you simply ask for a beer at the average bar you'll usually be served a bottled (regular) Belikin. They're all overpriced, with even regular at more than US$1.40 a small bottle (higher out on the cayes); imported European and American beers will cost you twice that. Bottled Guinness is also available – brewed under licence by Belikin; Mexican and Guatemalan beer is virtually unobtainable. The legal age for drinking alcohol in Belize is 18.

Cashew nut and berry **wines**, rich and full-bodied, are bottled and sold in some villages, and you can also get hold of imported wine, though it's far from cheap. On Ambergris Caye the *Rendezvous Restaurant and Winery* (see p.125) produces several varieties of red and white wine from imported grape juice, fermented and bottled at the restaurant; the wine is available at local supermarkets and the airport duty-free shops. Local **rum**, in both dark and clear varieties, is the best deal in Belizean alcohol and there's plenty to choose from. The locally produced gin, brandy and vodka are poor imitations – cheap and fairly nasty.

Non-alcoholic drinks include a predictable range of soft drinks including Sprite, Fanta, Coke and Pepsi. Despite the number of citrus plantations, fresh fruit juices are not always available, though you can generally get orange, lime and watermelon juices. *Licuados*, the thirst-quenching blended fruit drinks, ubiquitous throughout Mexico and the rest of Central America, are only rarely served in Belize. **Tap water**, in the towns at least, though safe, is highly chlorinated, and many villages (though not Caye Caulker) now have a potable water system. Filtered, bottled water and mineral water are sold almost everywhere and pure rainwater is usually available in the countryside and on the cayes.

Coffee, except in the best establishments, will generally be instant. Tea, due to the British influence, is a popular hot drink, as are Milo and Ovaltine (malted milky drinks). One last drink that deserves a mention is **seaweed**, a strange blend of actual seaweed, milk, cinnamon, sugar and cream. If you see someone selling this on a street corner, give it a try.

Communications

Belize's excellent postal services are the best in Central America. Postal rates are relatively inexpensive and mail sent home almost invariably gets through. In contrast, though the country's telephone and Internet services were at one time also the best in the region, now, despite the theoretical opening of telecommunications to competition, they're still a virtual monopoly and becoming less efficient and less responsive to customers' needs almost daily. Many hotels and lodges, particularly in remote areas, increasingly frustrated by the poor service offered by the original provider, Belize Telecommunications Limited (BTL), are turning to satellite systems for communication needs.

Local calls (and many long-distance internal calls) from payphones are fairly cheap, but international calls are comparatively more expensive than at home; you'll find a table of current charges in the Belize phone book, which is clearly laid out and easy to use. Many businesses in Belize are connected to the Internet, and email is one of the best (and cheapest) means of making hotel bookings.

Mail

From Belize, a normal airmail letter takes around four to five days to reach the US (Bz$0.60), a couple of days longer to Canada (Bz$0.60), eight to ten days to Europe (Bz$0.75) and two weeks to Australia and New Zealand (Bz$1). Parcels have to be wrapped in brown paper and tied with string; they may be inspected by customs. You can send parcels via surface mail but this takes literally months. Registration for mail isn't necessary, but it doesn't cost much extra above the postage and you'll get a certificate to give you some peace of mind. Post offices are generally open Monday to Friday 8am–4.30pm. Incoming mail (have it sent to General Delivery) is kept at the main post office in Belize City (or any district town post office) for a couple of months; you'll need some kind of ID, preferably a passport, to pick it up. American Express cardholders can have mail sent to them c/o AMEX at Belize Global Travel, 41 Albert St, Belize City. There's a new branch of Mailboxes Etc. in Belize City (see p.73), where you can send letters and parcels; there are also DHL and Federal Express offices throughout the country.

All towns and most villages have a **post office**, though in the latter it may be in a shop, or even someone's house. These very small ones are likely to be short of stamps, and may not have them in the correct denominations for overseas, so you're better off doing anything important at a main office.

Phones and email

Belize's modern (albeit expensive) phone system is almost always easy to use and payphones are plentiful. At the time of writing the former monopoly of BTL is still the only company with payphones and still controls most access to the Internet. Intelco, the purported competition, is not yet able to provide services for other than their few private users, and the two networks are not interconnected. BTL's main office (for international calls, fax, email and Internet access) is at 1 Church St, Belize City (Mon–Fri 8am–5pm); other offices are given in the Guide.

BTL payphones (good for both local and international calls) are a common sight throughout the country and you'll find them all over Belize City. To use them you'll need a phonecard, which you can also use on any touch-tone phone, pay or private. You can buy phonecards from BTL offices and from many hotels, shops and gas stations; they come in units of Bz$5, Bz$10, Bz$20, Bz$30 and Bz$50. To use, first scratch off the patch to reveal the PIN number, dial the (free) access code, then at the voice prompt dial the PIN number, followed by the number you want to call. The chances are you'll be using phones quite a lot in English-speaking

Useful phone numbers

Calling Belize from abroad

The international direct dialling (IDD) code (also known as the country code) for Belize is ☏501. To call a number in Belize from abroad simply dial the international access code (listed in your phone book), followed by the country code (501) and the full seven-digit number within Belize.

Calling home from Belize

To call the following countries from Belize dial the international access code shown, then the area code and number; access codes for other countries are listed in the telephone directory.

UK   ☏0044 + area code (minus initial zero) and number
US and Canada ☏001 + area code and number
Ireland   ☏00353 + area code and number
Australia   ☏0061 + area code and number
New Zealand   ☏0064 + area code and number

Useful numbers within Belize

Directory enquiries ☏113
Regional operator ☏114
International operator ☏115

Belize, to call hotels and so on, so buy a couple of cards as soon as you can.

There are now no area codes in Belize so wherever you're calling within the country you'll need to dial the full seven-digit number. Domestic call charges inside the local area are cheap at Bz$0.25 per minute; prices increase dramatically the further afield you dial, to between Bz$0.50 to Bz$1.50 per minute. Rural areas are served by community telephones (nowadays often fixed cellular phones) usually located in a private house; you sometimes pay the person who operates the phone, though usually you'll use a phonecard. All villages with community telephones are listed immediately before the pink pages in the telephone directory.

It's simple enough (though expensive) to **dial home direct** using a phonecard: a call to North America costs Bz$2.50 per minute, to Europe Bz$4.50 and to Australasia Bz$5.75, all with a minimum charge of one minute. Taking a telephone charge card with you is a good idea if you need to call home to the US, Canada or the UK; call your phone company to obtain one and have your calls billed to your home number. Calling home collect to these countries is also easy using Home Country Direct, avail-

able at BTL offices, most payphones and larger hotels. Simply dial the access code (posted on some payphones and in the phone book) to connect with an operator in your home country. You can also call toll-free numbers in North America; simply dial ☏001 before the number. **Cellular phones**, both fixed and mobile, cover most of the country and visitors can easily rent one for about Bz$10–12 per day, plus an activation fee – though you'll still need to buy a phonecard to use the phone. BTL cellular and fax numbers and email addresses are listed in the pink pages of the phone book.

Belizean businesses and individuals are also avid users of **email** and the **Internet**, and the number of places visitors can go online increases all the time. Internet cafés and online access locations are listed throughout the Guide, and you can send and surf from BTL's Belize City office (Bz$4.50/30min or Bz$8/1hr). While still technically illegal, satellites are used by many hotels and Internet cafés in Belize for Web access, and these can bring the price down for users. An increasing number of hotels now have a computer or two for guests to use for email. See p.18 for some of the most useful websites covering Belize.

The media

Although Belize, with its English-language media, can come as a welcome break in a world of Spanish, it doesn't necessarily mean that it's very easy to keep in touch with what's happening in the rest of the world. Local news, in the press particularly, but also on radio and television, is reported in a very nationalistic manner, taking pride of place over international stories, which receive little attention.

Newspapers and magazines

The four national newspapers – *The Amandala*, *The Belize Times*, *The Guardian* (no relation to the UK broadsheet) and *The Reporter* – are all published on Friday, but with a dateline of the following Sunday, though *The Amandala* also produces a slim mid-week edition. The first two exhibit racist and xenophobic tones that would make a British tabloid wince and it helps to have an understanding of which newspaper follows which party line: *The Belize Times* is the propaganda organ of the ruling PUP and *The Amandala* also generally supports the PUP, while *The Guardian* is supported by the opposition UDP; *The Reporter* does try to be objective and impartial. That said, they all make entertaining reading, and you'll find some interesting articles in each edition. Belize has no independent, home-produced news magazine along the lines of *Newsweek*. For online magazines covering Belize see the list of recommended websites on p.18.

In Belize City, Belmopan, San Pedro and occasionally some other towns you should be able to get hold of some foreign newspapers and magazines, including *Time*, *Newsweek* and the Caribbean edition of *The Miami Herald*, usually the day after publication (though the top hotels in Belize City get them the same day on the incoming afternoon flights). **The Book Center**, at 4 Church St in Belize City, has the largest selection of magazines in the country.

TV, radio, film and video

There are two more-or-less national **television** stations. Channel 5 is the country's best broadcaster, producing superb news and factual programmes (you can access their daily news output on the Internet at ⓦwww.channel5belize.com). Channel 7, on the other hand, shows an almost uninterrupted stream of imported American shows, mixed in with some local news. Both show some educational programming and both broadcast their main news programmes at 6.30pm. But it's cable TV (mostly pirated from satellite) that gets most of the nation's viewers, with its saturation coverage of American soaps, talk shows, sports, movies and CNN.

All **radio** stations in Belize are privately owned commercial stations. Love FM (89.9, 95.1 and other frequencies around the country), offering easy listening, news and current affairs, has the most extensive network and also runs sister stations Estero Amor (in Spanish) and More FM (youth-oriented). Another major station is KREM (91.1 and 96.5FM) with the emphasis on talk, reggae and punta rock. Belize City's other stations are WAVE FM (105.9) and FM 2000 (90.5), while each major district town also has a local radio station. There's also a British forces radio station BFBS (93.1FM) and in the north you can pick up Mexican stations, and Honduran and Guatemalan ones in the south and west.

There's only one **cinema** in Belize (in the *Princess Hotel*) and, unsurprisingly, no local feature film industry as such, though the country has provided the location for a few well-known films: *The Dogs of War*, *The Mosquito Coast*, *Heart of Darkness* and *After the Storm*. The success of the newly established **Belize Film Festival**, however, has introduced foreign film-makers to local talent and resulted in several film proposals; for more on this event, held annually in March, visit ⓦwww.belizefilmfestival.com.

Great Belize Productions, 17 Regent St, Belize City (☎227-3146, 🔘www.channel5belize.com), produces an excellent series of locally made **videos**, which can make great souvenirs. These include: *The Best of Belize All Over*, showing slices of local life to the accompaniment of great Belizean music; *Belize – The Maya Heritage*, the first of a two-part history of Belize, including interviews with archeologists working in Belize; and *From Invasion to Nation – A History of Belize*, presented by Belizean historian Assad Shoman and diplomat Robert Leslie – all are available in both North American (NTSC) and European (PAL) formats. They also produce several marvellous nature documentaries, the daily Channel 5 news programmes and an annual video anthology of news relevant to Belize.

Opening hours, public holidays and festivals

It's difficult to be specific about opening hours in Belize, but in general most shops are open from 8am to noon and from 1 or 2pm to 8pm. The lunch hour (noon to 1pm) is almost universally observed and it's hopeless to expect to get anything done then. However, a recent edict means government offices are supposed to remain open during the lunch hour, though you'll often find the person you really need is unavailable until after lunch anyway. Some shops and businesses work a half-day on Saturday and everything is liable to close early on Friday. Archeological sites, however, are open 8am to 4pm daily. Public holidays, when virtually everything will be closed – though all public transport operates normally – are given in the box below. Note that if the actual date of a particular holiday falls mid-week then that holiday will usually be observed the following Monday.

You'll generally find plenty of entertainment at any time, as Belizeans are great party people and music is a crucial part of the country's culture. All national celebrations – especially Carnival and Independence Day, both in September, and marked by parades and open-air dances – are the excuse for a fantastic day-long party, with the rhythms of the Caribbean dominating the proceedings.

Dance is very much a part of Creole and Garífuna culture and at these celebrations you'll always be welcome to dance and drink with the locals. The best time to see Garífuna drumming and dance is November 19, Garífuna Settlement Day, and the best places to see it are Dangriga and Hopkins. In the outlying areas, such as around San Ignacio and Corozal and in the Maya villages of the south, you'll find traditional village fiestas, which in many ways resemble their counterparts in Guatemala. For much more on Belizean music and dance see pp.331–338 in Contexts.

Public holidays

January 1 New Year's Day
March 9 Baron Bliss Day
Good Friday varies
Holy Saturday varies
Easter Monday varies
May 1 Labour Day
May 24 Commonwealth Day
September 10 National Day (St George's Caye Day)
September 21 Independence Day
October 12 Columbus Day (Pan-America Day)
November 19 Garífuna Settlement Day
December 25 Christmas Day
December 26 Boxing Day

Some selected annual events

Various sporting events and celebrations take place throughout the year. The following list is just a sample of what's on when and where; check locally for exact dates and venues.

New Year's Day Horse racing, Burrell Boom village.
March (on the Baron Bliss Day weekend) La Ruta Maya canoe race from San Ignacio to Belize City.
April Easter Fair in San Ignacio – and other Easter celebrations throughout the country.
May Cashew Festival, Crooked Tree village; National Agriculture Show, Belmopan.

June Día de San Pedro, San Pedro, Ambergris Caye; Lobster Festival, Placencia.
July Benque Viejo Fiesta, Cayo District; Lobster Festival, Caye Caulker.
August International Costa Maya Festival, San Pedro, Ambergris Caye; Deer Dance Festival, San Antonio, Toledo District.
September Independence Day celebrations, nationwide; St George's Caye Day; Carnival, Belize City.
November Garífuna Settlement Day, Dangriga, Hopkins and other Garífuna communities.
December Boxing Day: parties, dances, cycle race in Belize City and horse races in Burrell Boom.

Sports and outdoor activities

The main spectator sports in Belize are football (soccer) and baseball, which rank about equal as the national games, with avid reporting in the press. Softball is also popular, as is athletics (track and field), while American football and baseball have a devoted following on TV. As in the rest of Central America, cycling is closely followed and there are frequent races in Belize, mainly along the Western Highway. Finally, there are a number of horse-racing meets around Christmas and New Year.

Many of the sports on offer to visitors to Belize are connected to the water in some way, with sailing, windsurfing, diving and snorkelling all extremely popular. Diving courses, for beginners or experts, are run from Belize City, San Pedro, Caye Caulker, many of the other cayes and Placencia. Sea- and river-kayaking, too, is becoming ever more popular and a number of outfits organize trips. Fly-fishing for bonefish on a "catch and release" basis has long attracted dedicated anglers to the shallow, sandy "flats" off Belize's cayes and atolls. Several lodges and other specialist operators can arrange this as well as fishing for permit, tarpon and other sport fish.

Away from the coast, canoeing, rafting and tubing – floating along rivers in a giant inner tube – are extremely popular, particularly in the Cayo district, where there are plenty of people keen to arrange this for you. Back on land, many of the same tour operators can arrange jungle hiking, with anything from a guided walk along a medicinal plant trail or a day's bird-watching in the Jaguar Reserve to very demanding multi-day jungle survival courses. Beneath the jungle, Belize's amazing subterranean landscape is becoming ever more accessible, with highly motivated, very competent caving guides leading tours and organizing specialist expeditions. Caves Branch (see p.221), owned by a founding member of the Belize Cave and Wilderness Rescue Team, makes safety a prime feature of its caving trips; they also offer rappelling and rock climbing.

Horseback-riding and mountain-biking are other possibilities in Cayo and indeed anywhere in rural Belize, with some superb rides through forested hills and to Maya sites. Details of the above activities and the companies organizing them are given on pp.11, 13 & 15 (for international operators) and at relevant places throughout the Guide.

On all these guided trips you'll be led by enthusiastic and highly qualified tour guides. In order to gain a tour-guide licence these men and women have successfully to complete numerous courses, covering everything from archeology and history to geology, biology and presentation skills; all guides are also trained in first aid and CPR. Licensed guides will have a photo ID (which may also state their main field of expertise) and this must be displayed when they're conducting a tour.

Crafts, shopping and souvenirs

Compared to its neighbours, Belize has less to offer in terms of traditional crafts or neighbourhood markets. The latter are purely for food, but in several places you'll come across some impressive local crafts. Craft and gift shops are now found throughout the country – the best ones are covered in the text – but you'll often get better prices from the artisans themselves, on the streets or in the villages.

If time is short, the National Handicraft Center in Belize City (see p.66), run by the Belize Chamber of Commerce, is the best place to buy souvenirs, with a wide range of good-quality, genuine Belizean crafts, including paintings, prints and music, as well as many of the items mentioned below. The craftspeople are paid fair prices for their work and no longer have to hawk it on the streets. Belizean artists often exhibit here too, though the best place for contemporary **Belizean art** is The Image Factory in Belize City (Ⓦ www.imagefactory.org; see p.65).

Wood carvings make beautiful and unusual souvenirs. The wood carvers are often found in Belize City and at the Maya sites; their often exquisitely executed carvings of dolphins, jaguars, ships, etc are made of *zericote*, a two-tone light- and dark-brown wood which only grows in Belize and the surrounding areas. The best wood is kiln-dried – the items you buy on the streets may not be. Also at Maya sites you'll find slate carvers, creating wonderful, high-quality, reproductions of gods, glyphs and stelae; the ceramics aren't as good, but they're improving. In the Maya villages in southern Belize you'll also come across some attractive embroidery, though it has to be said that the quality of both the cloth and the work is better in Guatemala. Maya, Garífuna and Creole villages produce good basketware and superb drums; Dangriga, Hopkins, Gales Point and the Toledo villages are the places to visit if you want to see these.

For superb **videos** of Belizean wildlife, culture or history, have a look at the series produced by Great Belize Productions, which can be purchased from gift shops or from their office (see p.40 for more). Those with a philatelic bent might appreciate a set of wildly colourful Belize stamps; relatively cheap and certainly easy to post home, they often feature the animals and plants of the country. You can get many of them from any post office but the one in Belize City has a special Philatelic Department. One tasty souvenir that everyone seems to want to take home is a bottle (or three) of Marie Sharp's Pepper Sauce, made from Belizean *habañeros* in various strengths ranging from "mild" to "fiery hot". This spicy accompaniment to rice and beans graces every restaurant table in the country – and visits to the factory near Dangriga can be arranged.

For **everyday shopping** you'll find some kind of shop in every village in Belize, however small, and there's a department store and several supermarkets in Belize City. If you have the time to hunt around, most things you'd find in North America and Europe are also available in Belize – at a price. Luxury items, such as electrical goods and cameras, tend to be very expensive, as do other imported goods. Film is more expensive than at home, but easy to get hold of.

Crime and personal safety

Although Central America as a whole has earned a generally justified reputation for criminal activities, violent crimes aimed at tourists were, until relatively recently, extremely rare in Belize. Even now, with a very few deliberate robberies of tourists every year, the crime rate against visitors is still low in comparison with most other countries in the world. In short, you're very unlikely to become a victim – whatever you might hear to the contrary. Although Belize City does have the highest crime rate in the country, the vast majority of victims are the Belizeans themselves and the place is nowhere near as dangerous as you might imagine from its appearance and atmosphere. The regular tourism police patrols provide additional security and have dramatically reduced intimidation by street hustlers. On the whole, petty crime is the only common problem; for more on safety in Belize City see the "Hassle" box on p.59.

That said, it pays to be aware of the dangers. If you've got valuables, insure them properly (see p.20) and always take photocopies of your passport and insurance documents and try to leave them in a secure place. For any travellers the best and most accurate overview of the possible dangers of visiting Belize and Central America can be seen on the UK Foreign Office **Travel Advice Unit** website, ⓦwww.fco.gov.uk. The unit also produces a good advice leaflet for independent travellers, which also explains what a consul can and cannot do for you when you're abroad. The US equivalent is the State Department's Consular Information Service (ⓦwww.travel.state.gov /travel_warnings), which also publishes consular information sheets and lists the main dangers to US citizens.

Crime and avoiding it

The majority of crime in Belize is petty theft such as bag-snatching and minor break-ins at hotels, though there's also a chance (albeit small) of being on the end of something more serious, such as a mugging – so take commonsense precautions everywhere; relax but don't get complacent. During the day there's little to worry about, so whenever possible, try to time your arrival in daylight. At night in Belize City you should stick to the main streets and, for women in particular, it's never a good idea to go out alone. If you arrive in Belize City at night take a taxi to a hotel, as the bus stations are in a fairly derelict part of town. Wherever you are, keep your most valuable possessions on you (but don't wear any expensive jewellery), preferably in a moneybelt under your outer clothes. Trousers with zipped pockets are also a good pickpocket-deterrent. Looking "respectable" without appearing affluent will go some way to avoiding unwanted attention.

Break-ins at hotels are one of the most common types of petty theft – something you should bear in mind when searching for a room. Make sure the lock on your door works, from the inside as well as out. In many budget hotels the lock will be a small padlock on the outside; for extra safety, it's a good idea to buy your own so you're the only one with keys. Many hotels will have a safe or secure area for valuables. It's up to you whether you use this; most of the time it will be fine, but make sure whatever you do put in is securely and tightly wrapped – a lockable moneybelt does the job. In the UK, Catch 22 (ⓦ www.catch22products.co.uk) produces an excellent range of travel securi-

ty products, available from most travel equipment suppliers (see p.25).

If you follow a few simple precautions, you shouldn't experience any trouble at border crossings – the presence of armed officials generally discourages thieves in the immediate area of the immigration post. Nevertheless, it's still advisable to do any transactions with moneychangers out of sight of other people and, once away from the post, be on your guard. Watch out especially for people "helping" you to find a bus and offering to carry your luggage; most of the time they'll just be after a tip, but it's easy to get distracted – never let your belongings out of sight unless you're confident they're in a safe place. When you travel by bus, your main baggage will usually go in the luggage compartment underneath or at the back. It's generally safe (you have little option in any case) but keep an eye on it if you can – theft of bags is uncommon, but opportunist thieves may dip into zippers and outer pockets.

Finally, don't let anyone without the official credentials talk you into being your "guide" – all legal tour guides in Belize are licensed and will have a photo ID. If you have doubts about using a guide, don't, and report the incident to the authorities.

Police and reporting a crime

In addition to a regular police force, Belize has special **tourism police**, operating from local police stations. Easily identified by their

Drugs

Belize has long been an important transhipment link in the chain of supply between the producers in South and Central America and the users in North America, with minor players often being paid in kind, creating a deluge of illegal drugs. Marijuana, cocaine and crack are all readily available in Belize, and whether you like it or not you'll receive regular offers, particularly in San Pedro, Caye Caulker and Placencia. All such substances are **illegal**, and despite the fact that dope is smoked openly in the streets, the police do arrest people for possession of marijuana; they particularly enjoy catching tourists. If you're caught you'll probably end up spending a couple of days in jail and paying a fine of several hundred US dollars. Practically every year foreigners are incarcerated for drug offences – the pusher may have a sideline reporting clients to the police, and catching "international drug smugglers" gives the country brownie points with the US Drug Enforcement Agency (DEA). Expect no sympathy from your embassy – they'll probably send someone to visit you, and maybe find an English-speaking lawyer, but certainly can't get you out of jail.

Police emergency numbers

The police emergency number in Belize is ☎90 or 911; to contact the tourism police or to report a crime in Belize City call ☎227-2210 or 227-2222.

shirts and caps emblazoned with "Tourism Police", they patrol Belize City, San Pedro, Caye Caulker, Placencia and many other tourist destinations around the country. If you have anything stolen it's best to go to the tourist police first, if only to help you through the processes involved in reporting a crime. Police in Belize are poorly paid and, despite the campaign against criminals who prey on tourists, all too often you can't get them to do much more than make out the report – and you may have difficulty getting them to do even that; it helps to have the tourism police aware of your plight.

Always report the crime to your embassy as well if you can – it helps the consular staff build up a higher-level case for better protection for tourists. Not that crime against tourists isn't already treated seriously in Belize; if the criminals are caught they are brought before the courts the next day, which is a much better system than most in the region.

Harassment

Verbal abuse is the most threatening aspect of life on the streets in Belize, though it's only really a problem in Belize City (and occasionally Dangriga), where there are always plenty of people hanging out on the streets, commenting on all that passes by. For anyone with a white face, the inevitable "Hey, white boy/white chick – what's happening?" will soon become a familiar sound. At first it can all seem very intimidating, but if you take the time to stop and talk, you'll find the vast majority of these people simply want to know where you're from and where you're heading – and perhaps to scam you a deal on boat trips, money exchange or bum a dollar or two. Once you realize that they generally mean no harm the whole experience of Belize City will be infinitely more enjoyable. Obviously, the situation is a little more serious for women, and the abuse can be more offensive. But once again, annoying though it is, it's unlikely that anything will come of it and you can usually talk your way out of a dodgy situation without anyone losing face.

Women travellers may initially find the advances from local lotharios a nuisance, particularly in Belize City and on the busier cayes, but there's rarely any real menace. These men think it their duty to pass comments on any woman they consider attractive, but if you make it clear from the outset that you're not interested, they'll generally concentrate their attention on those who are. Women travelling alone shouldn't come across any particular problems, though it's best not to travel or walk urban streets at night. You're almost certain to meet other solo women travellers, or some of the many foreign women who come to Belize to work or to volunteer in NGOs; ask them how they deal with things. It's also a good idea to let other people know of your plans – perhaps call ahead to a hotel, saying roughly when you'll be arriving, for instance. In rural areas, especially in the Maya villages in the south, you'll almost always be treated with great courtesy – as would any outsider.

Voluntary work and study

There's virtually no chance of finding paid temporary work in Belize. Work permits are generally only on offer to investors and those who can prove their ability to support themselves without endangering the job of a Belizean.

There are, however, plenty of opportunities for **volunteer work** – mainly as a fee-paying member of a conservation expedition – or study, at a field study centre or archeological field school. These options generally mean raising a considerable sum for the privilege and committing yourself to weeks (or months) of hard but rewarding work, often in difficult conditions. Many of the expeditions are aimed at students taking time out between school and university – a "gap year" – and arrange work on rural infrastructure projects such as schools, health centres and the like, or building trails and visitor centres in nature reserves. These organizations will usually take expedition members from any country; they also need some experienced technical and administrative staff who, while they may not always get paid, can at least go on the expeditions without raising a large sum first.

At least twenty academic archeological groups undertake research in Belize each year and many of them take paying students (and non-students); for details, see the box on p.310 in Contexts. There are a growing number of Field Study Centres in Belize, aimed primarily at taking college students as part of a degree course, though there are opportunities for non-students to learn about the ecology and environment of Belize; for details, look under "Field Study Centres" in the index. If you want to learn Spanish relatively cheaply you could extend a trip to Tikal by studying at one of the language schools in and around Flores.

If the cost deters you, you could contact the non-fee-paying organizations listed below or even volunteer independently in Belize; the conservation organizations in Contexts (see box on p.324) all have volunteer programmes. And if you want to work with children, the YWCA accepts volunteers

to help teach and organize sports and arts activities in the school they run in Belize City; contact the YWCA Education Director (℡ 501/203-4971, ✉ ywca@btl.net). For any of these options you'll need to be self-motivated and self-supporting – no funding will be available, though you'll probably get food and accommodation.

Volunteer work contacts outside Belize

If you're thinking of working or volunteering in Belize or Central America the best place to begin is on the Internet: try ⊛ www.gapyear.com (UK-based, free membership), with a vast amount of information on volunteering generally, including organizations dealing with Belize. There's also a huge, invaluable database on travel and living abroad. Also well worth looking at is the comprehensive range of books and information published by Vacation Work (℡ 01865/241 978, ⊛ www.vacationwork.co.uk). Titles include *Directory of Summer Jobs Abroad*, *Taking a Gap Year*, *Green Volunteers* and *Work Your Way Around the World*, among many more. Most are updated annually and include work and volunteer opportunities in Central America.

Non-fee-paying organizations

Ecologic Development Fund US ℡ 617/441-6300, ⊛ www.ecologic.org. Founded following the Earth Summit in 1992, Ecologic is a highly respected organization with a great deal of experience in Central America. It aims to conserve endangered habitats by using community-based development and resource management in partnership with local organizations. Internship programmes for volunteers could include training communities in sustainable agriculture or helping local organizations develop environmental advocacy and protected-area management skills.

The Peace Corps US ☏1-800/424-8580, ⓦwww.peacecorps.gov. Sends American volunteers to teach in rural areas. Volunteers are also needed to work in agricultural and environmental education, computer and business-training centres, assisting with women's groups, youth and community outreach and in many health-related areas, including HIV/AIDS and sexual health awareness programmes.

Fee-paying conservation and development projects

Cornerstone Foundation 90 Burns Ave, San Ignacio, Cayo District, Belize ☏501/824-2373 ⓦwww.peacecorner.org/cornerstone.htm. A Belize-based grassroots non-profit organization, offering volunteer placements in areas such as women's development, HIV/AIDS outreach, the environment and youth education. A three-month stay (which can be extended) costs around US$1000, including accommodation and one daily meal. You can also learn about indigenous natural healing methods in a three-week programme for US$650.

Earthwatch ☏1-800/776-0188, ⓦwww.earthwatch.org. Earthwatch matches paying volunteers from around the world with scientists working on marine conservation projects in Belize. Current projects focus on studies of manatees off the coast of Belize; previous ones have included archeological and reef ecology investigations. Projects are reviewed annually, so check the excellent website for the latest information. The cost for a two-week stint is currently US$2150/£1195. Their main office is in the US, though there are other offices in the UK, Australia and Japan.

Trekforce Expeditions, 34 Buckingham Palace Rd, London SW1 0RE ☏020/7828 2275, ⓦwww.trekforce.org.uk. A registered charity established in 1990, Trekforce runs conservation projects in Belize (and other destinations) ranging from surveys of remote Maya sites to infrastructure projects in national parks and village communities. Expeditions last from two to five months, starting from £2750. The longer programmes also involve learning Spanish in Guatemala and teaching in rural schools in Belize.

World Challenge Expeditions Black Arrow House, 2 Chandros Rd, London NW10 6NE ☏020/8728 7274, ⓦwww.world-challenge.co.uk. A youth development organization with sixteen years' experience, taking 18- to 24-year-olds to Belize for three- or six-month placements. Tasks could include teaching in a primary school, joining a conservation project or working in a children's home in Belize City. Around £2000 (which includes a return flight) plus £135 per month for food and accommodation.

Travellers with disabilities

The very nature of Belize's abundant natural attractions often makes much of the country inaccessible to anyone with a disability. Travelling around by public transport (with the possible exception of taxis, which tend to be huge American saloons or estate cars) would be difficult: there's little provision for wheelchairs and much travel is by boat, with the attendant difficulty of getting in and out. Paved streets exist only in the towns, and even there sidewalks are rare; you won't find either in coastal and caye resort locations.

Few hotels in Belize have smooth paths from the road, and even in ground-floor rooms you often have steps to negotiate. Indeed many hotels have all accommodation upstairs – and only two have elevators. However, if you stay in places at the higher end of the range, it's more likely that there will be staff on hand to help out, and if you're determined, you can find a few places that are more suitable for disabled visitors, with accessible ground-floor rooms and other facilities. A very few hotels have specifically adapted rooms and facilities for disabled visitors; the *Radisson Fort George* in Belize City and the *Hok'ol K'in* in Corozal are the best, while *Clarissa Falls* near San Ignacio has wheelchair-accessible cabins (for reviews, see pp.62, 62 & 100, respectively).

Planning well ahead is essential; the organizations listed below may be able to help with general information and advice (nothing specific on travel to Belize, though), and the websites do have extremely good information and links. No tour company specializing in travel for disabled people currently arranges tours that include Belize. *The Disabled Traveller* by Alison Walsh (BBC Books; order from Disabled Traveller, PO Box 7, London W12 8UD), full of information and contacts, is an excellent resource for anyone who wants to plan a trip independently. If you're already a member of any disability organization, they will have good leaflets and advice on travel.

Resources for disabled travellers

In North America

The website ⓦwww.makoa.org/jlubin, built and maintained by Jim Lubin, who is tetraplegic, outshines all others in providing masses of information and links for disabled travellers.

Access-Able Travel Service ☎303/232-2979, ⓦwww.access-able.com. Another very useful

organization for disabled travel generally, with travellers' reports on facilities in destinations; Guatemala and Mexico are mentioned but currently not Belize.

Society for Accessible Travel and Hospitality (SATH) ☎212/447-7284, ⓦwww.sath.org. Nonprofit disability information service with a really well-organized and well-connected website.

In the UK and Ireland

Irish Wheelchair Association Blackheath Drive, Clontarf, Dublin 3 ☎01/833-8241, ⓦwww.iwa.ie. Useful information about travelling abroad for wheelchair-users.

RADAR (Royal Association for Disability and Rehabilitation) 12 City Forum, 250 City Rd, London EC1V 8AF ☎020/7250 3222, ⓦwww.radar.org. A good source of advice on disability organizations, holidays and travel abroad.

In Australia and New Zealand

Both the following organizations provide lists of travel agencies and tour operators for people with disabilities.

ACROD (Australian Council for Rehabilitation of the Disabled) PO Box 60, Curtin ACT 2605 ☎02/6283 3200.
Disabled Persons Assembly 4/173–175 Victoria St, Wellington, New Zealand ☎04/801 9100 (also TTY), ⓦwww.dpa.org.nz.

 # Directory

Addresses In towns, most streets are named. It's easy enough to find your way to a particular address despite there being no grid plan to follow, though numbering may be less prominent. Along Belize's main highways the official addresses are measured (in miles) from the start of the highway.
Contraception Condoms are available from any drugstore in Belize, as are some brands of the Pill, though it's better to bring enough of the latter to last the trip.
Electricity The mains supply is 110 volts AC, with American-style two- or three-pin sockets. Electrical equipment made for the US and Canada should be OK – anything from Britain will need a plug adapter

and possibly a transformer. The electricity supply is generally pretty dependable, but power cuts do occur; if you're bringing any delicate equipment, like a laptop, you'll need a good surge protector. Some small villages have their electricity supplied by local generators and the voltage is sometimes lower and less dependable. Lodges and resorts in remote areas may not be on the grid – in which case they'll have their own generators – and electricity may not be available all night.
Gay and lesbian Belize Homosexuality is still illegal in Belize, and prosecutions for what Belizean law terms "an unnatural crime", though rare, are occasionally brought. Few result in

convictions and so far no visitors have been prosecuted (or even warned), but it's still necessary to be very discreet. Given the legal status, it's no surprise to learn that there's no openly gay community and no exclusively gay bars in Belize.

Laundry Belize City and the main tourist destinations (Caye Caulker, San Pedro, Placencia and San Ignacio) all have excellent drop-off laundry services; addresses are listed in the Guide. Elsewhere you can usually find someone who takes in washing or possibly get away with doing your laundry in your hotel's laundry area.

Time zones Belize is on Central Standard Time, 6 hours behind GMT and the same as Guatemala and Honduras. Belize does not observe Daylight Savings Time, though the US and, more importantly, Mexico, do. This means that when DST is in operation (during the summer) the time in Belize is an hour earlier than in Mexico – something to bear in mind when you're crossing the border.

Toilets Public toilets are still relatively rare, though they are becoming more common. Toilets are usually available for passengers in main bus stations but you'll probably have to pay Bz$.50 to use them. In hotels and restaurants standards are reasonable due to enforcement of health regulations and are improving all the time. Toilet paper is almost always provided, but it's a good idea to travel with your own roll, just in case.

Weights and measures The imperial system is still the main one used in Belize. This book is metric throughout, except when we refer to addresses on main roads outside towns that are commonly referred to in terms of their mile number. Gas/petrol is sold in US gallons, and small bottled drinks (especially beer and Coke) are referred to as "pints", though the measures are in millilitres.

Women in Belize Battling entrenched social and cultural mores of male superiority, the women's movement in Belize has made great strides in recent years. Positive legislation now recognizes women's contribution to national development and many women have asserted themselves as successful business owners and community leaders. However, widespread domestic violence threatens to undermine this progress and there are few resources for abuse victims. In addition, strong religious influences and cultural taboos diminish opportunities to learn about family-planning options, so many women find themselves responsible for large families, a commitment that can limit personal choices. Belize's high-profile Women's Department, part of the Ministry of Human Development, is responsible for monitoring the implementation of policies affecting women, and its Belize City headquarters, at 26 Albert St (T 501/227-7397, E womensdept@btl.net), acts as an umbrella group for the many well-organized and effective women's groups throughout the country. Women travellers to Belize are welcome to make contact.

Guide

Guide

Belize City

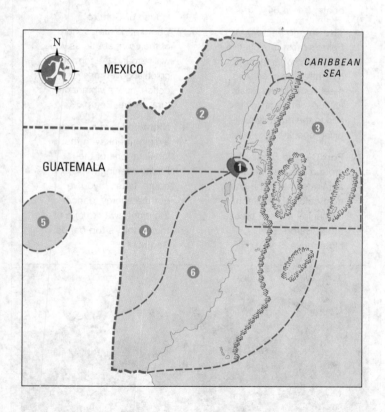

CHAPTER 1 # Highlights

✳ **Swing Bridge and Harbour Mouth** Watch the last manually operated swing bridge in the Americas open at dawn or dusk against a backdrop of neat white-painted wooden fishing boats. See p.64

✳ **The Image Factory** Visit Belize's most provocative art gallery, where you may have the chance to meet some of the artists at work or bag an invitation to the monthly exhibition opening. See p.65

✳ **Fort George** Stroll around this historic area, admire some of the city's best colonial architecture and enjoy the sea breeze at the Baron Bliss Lighthouse. See p.65

✳ **Museum of Belize** Marvel at the astonishing quality of Maya treasures on display in this world-class museum, housed in a beautifully restored former colonial Victorian prison. See p.66

✳ **House of Culture** Capture the atmosphere of the colonial elite as you walk around the former colonial governor's residence, now a vibrant cultural centre. See p.68

✳ **Nightlife** Have an early evening drink with the locals at one of the Friday evening happy hours. Later, if you've got the energy, dance the night away to one of the country's top bands. See p.71

△ St John's Cathedral

Belize City

The narrow, congested streets of **BELIZE CITY** can initially be daunting to anyone who has been prepared by the usual travellers' tales of crime-ridden urban decay. Admittedly, at first glance the city can seem unprepossessing and chaotic. Buildings – many of them dilapidated wooden structures – stand right at the edge of the road, and few sidewalks offer refuge to pedestrians from the ever-increasing numbers of cars and trucks. Narrow bridges force the traffic to cross in single file over almost stagnant canals, which are still used for some of the city's drainage. The overall impression is that the place is recovering from some great calamity – an explanation that is at least partly true. Belize has suffered several devastating hurricanes, the latest in October 1961, when Hurricane Hattie tore the city apart with winds of 240kmph, leaving a layer of thick black mud as the storm receded. The hazards of Belize City, however, are often reported by those who have never been here. In fact, the city has a distinguished history, a handful of superb sights and an astonishing energy.

The 75,000 people of Belize City represent every ethnic group in the country, with the **Creole** descendants of former slaves and Baymen forming the dominant element, generating an easy-going Caribbean atmosphere. As you push your way through the throng you're in no doubt that Belize City is also the business heart of the country. Banks, offices and shops line the main streets, while fruit and fast-food vendors jostle for pavement space with stalls selling plastic bowls or cheap jewellery. Most visitors hurry through on their way to catch their next bus or a boat out to the cayes but if you approach the city with an open mind, meet the inhabitants and take in the new museums and galleries, you may well be pleasantly surprised. One of the very best times to visit is during the "low season", when the **September Celebrations** fill the streets with music, dancing and parades. The highlight, **Carnival**, sees gorgeously costumed dancers shimmer and gyrate through the city to electrifying Caribbean rhythms.

Some history

By the late sixteenth century the Spanish treasure fleets in the Caribbean were attracting British (and other European) pirates, or **buccaneers**, who took advantage of the refuge offered by the reefs and shallows of Belize, using the cayes as bases for plundering raids. Ever the opportunists, the buccaneers made money between raids by cutting the valuable logwood (used for textile dyes) that grew abundantly in the tropical swamps, building a number of camps from Campeche to Honduras. Their settlement at the mouth of the Belize River, constructed by consolidating the mangrove swamp with wood chips, rum bottles and coral, gradually became more permanent. By the 1700s **Belize Town**

BELIZE CITY

ACCOMMODATION

Bakadeer Inn	D
Barrack Road Guest House	I
Belcove Hotel	J
Belize Biltmore Plaza	B
Bellevue Hotel	Q
Caribbean Palms Inn	O
Chateau Caribbean	L
Coningsby Inn	R
Downtown Guest House	G
Freddie's Guest House	F
Grant Residence	C
The Great House	N
Isabel Guest House	K
Mopan	S
North Front Street Guest House	H
Radisson Fort George	M
Seaside Guest House	P
Three Sisters Guest House	E
Villa Boscardi	A

RESTAURANTS

Big Daddy's Diner	8
Bird's Isle Restaurant	16
Chateau Caribbean	L
Gyros and Crepes	3
Harbour View	15
Jambel Jerk Pit	14
Le Petit Café	12
Mar's Restaurant	6
Macy's	13
Marlins	7
Nerie's Restaurant I	4
Nerie's Restaurant II	5
Pepper's Pizza	2
River Side Patio	8
Stonegrill	M
Sumathi	1
Wet Lizard	11

Municipal Airport

Marion Jones Sports Complex

University of Belize

PRINCESS MARGARET DRIVE

BTL Tower

KING'S PARK

Karl Heusner Memorial Hospital

National Library

Bus Stop

Flag Monument

San Cas Shopping Centre

Fire Station

Atlantic Bank

University of Belize

Freetown Road

Cinderella Plaza

Mexico Belize Cultural Institute

Clock Tower

Caesar's Palace Nightclub

Eden Nightclub

Lindbergh's Landing

BTL Park

Princess Hotel & Casino

Princess Marina

BARRACK ROAD

Belize Civic Center

Haulover Creek

NORTHERN HIGHWAY

HAULOVER ROAD

BELCAN BRIDGE

MOPAN ST

ST MATTHEW ST

ST MARK ST

ST LUKE ST

ST JOHN ST

ST CHARLES ST

ST EDWARD ST

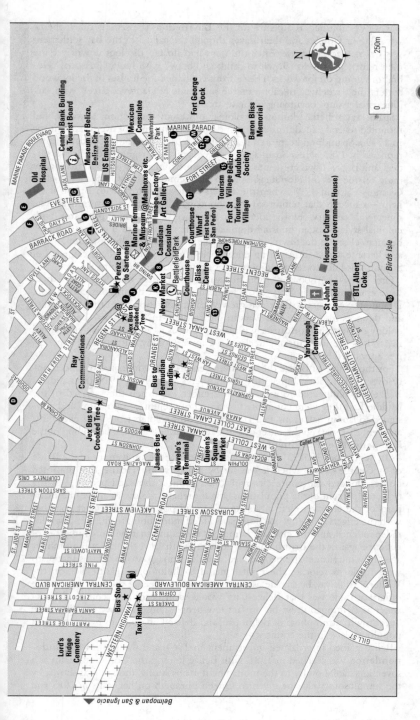

was well established as a centre for the **Baymen** (as the settlers called themselves), their families and their slaves, though the capital of the Bay settlement was on St George's Caye. After the rains had floated the logs downriver the men returned to Belize Town to drink and brawl, with huge Christmas celebrations going on for weeks. The seafront contained the houses of the logwood cutters; the slaves lived in cabins on the south side of Haulover Creek, with various tribal groups occupying separate areas.

Spain was still the dominant colonial power in the region, however, and mounted several expeditions aimed at demonstrating control over the territory. In 1779 a Spanish raid captured many of the settlers and the rest fled, but most returned in 1783, when Spain agreed to recognize the rights of the British settlers, and Belize Town grew into the main centre of the logwood and mahogany trade on the Bay of Honduras. Spanish raids continued until the Battle of St George's Caye in 1798, when the settlers achieved victory with British naval help – a success that reinforced their bond with the British government. The nineteenth century saw the increasing influence of **British expatriates**, with colonial-style wooden housing dominating the shoreline as the "Scots clique" began to clean up the town's image and take control of its administration. Belize also became a base for Anglican missionaries: in 1812 the Anglican cathedral of St John was built to serve a diocese that stretched from Belize to Panamá.

Fires in 1804, 1806 and 1856 necessitated extensive rebuilding, and there were epidemics of cholera, yellow fever and smallpox during this period, too. Despite these reversals, the town grew with immigration from the West Indies and refugees from the Caste Wars in the Yucatán. In 1862 Belize became the colony of **British Honduras**, with Belize City as its administrative centre, and in 1871 Belize was officially declared a Crown Colony, with a resident governor appointed by Britain.

For the people of Belize the twentieth century was dominated by uncertainty over their relationship with the "mother country". In 1914 thousands of Belizeans volunteered to assist the war effort, but when they arrived in the Middle East they were confronted by a wall of prejudice and racism, and consigned to labour battalions. In 1919 the returning soldiers rioted in Belize City, an event that marked the onset of black consciousness and the beginning of the **independence movement**.

On September 10, 1931, the city was celebrating the anniversary of the Battle of St George's Caye when it was hit by a massive **hurricane** that uprooted houses, flooded the entire city and killed about a thousand people – at the time, ten percent of the population. Disaster relief was slow to arrive and many parts of the city were left in a state of squalid poverty. This neglect, together with the effects of the Depression, gave added momentum to the campaign for independence, and the city saw numerous rallies and marches in an upsurge of defiance against the British colonial authorities. In 1961 the city was again ravaged by a hurricane: 262 people died, and the damage was so serious that plans were made to relocate the capital inland to Belmopan. (Hattieville, on the Western Highway, began life as a refuge for those fleeing the hurricane.) The official attitude was that Belize City would soon become a redundant backwater as Belmopan grew, but in fact few people chose to leave for the sterile "new town" atmosphere of Belmopan, and Belize City remains by far the most populous place in the country.

Belize gained internal self-government in 1964, and the goal of **full independence** was reached in 1981, with Belize joining the Commonwealth as a sovereign state. Loyalty to the monarchy remains strong, though – as shown by the tumultuous welcome given to Queen Elizabeth on her visits in 1985 and

1994. Since independence, the rise of foreign investment and tourism has made an impact and Belize City is experiencing a major **construction boom**, reflected in the opening of new museums, galleries and cultural centres.

Arrival, orientation and city transport

Although Belize City is by far the largest urban area in the country (the capital, Belmopan, is one tenth the size), its central area is compact enough to make **walking** the easiest way to get around. The city is divided neatly into north and south halves by **Haulover Creek**, a delta branch of the Belize River. The pivotal point of the city centre is the **Swing Bridge**, always busy with traffic and opened twice a day to allow larger vessels up and down the river. **North** of the Swing Bridge things tend to be slightly more upmarket; here you'll find the most expensive hotels, the majority of the embassies and consulates and – in the King's Park area – some very luxurious homes. **South** of the Swing Bridge is the market and commercial zone, with banks, offices and supermarkets; the foreshore is the prestige area, home to the former colonial governor's residence, now a museum and arts venue. The area south and west of the main thoroughfares of Regent and Albert streets is unsafe after dark.

Getting from the transport terminals to the centre is very easy, and once you arrive downtown you'll find that almost everything you need is within a kilometre of the Swing Bridge. **Taxis**, identified by green licence plates, cost Bz$6 for one or more passengers within the city (usually Bz$8–10 to and from the municipal airport) and Bz$40 to the international airport; for other journeys be sure to agree on the fare in advance. Cars will be waiting for passengers at the main bus terminal and marine terminal, or you can call one on ☏227-2888 or 224-4465; you should definitely take a **taxi** if you arrive anywhere at night. **City buses** operate to outlying residential areas but are of little use unless you know exactly where you're going.

Hassle

Walking in Belize City **during the day** is perfectly safe if you observe commonsense rules. The introduction of specially trained **tourism police** in 1995 made an immediate impact on the level of hassle and this, coupled with the legal requirement for all tour guides to be licensed, drove away most of the hustlers and really reduced street crime. You'll soon learn to spot dangerous situations and in the city centre you can always ask the tourism police (☏227-2222) for advice or directions; they'll even walk you back to your hotel if it's near their patrol route. That said, it's still sensible to proceed with caution: most people are friendly and chatty, but quite a few may want to sell you drugs or bum a dollar or two. The best advice is to stay cool. Be civil, don't provoke trouble by arguing too forcefully and never show large sums of money on the street, especially American dollars. Women wearing short shorts or skirts will attract verbal abuse from local studs.

Even though the chances of being mugged do increase **after dark**, you'll find you can walk around the centre in relative safety, especially if you're not alone, and you'll certainly encounter tourism police in this area. If you're venturing further afield, or if you've just arrived by bus at night, you'd be wise to travel by taxi. For more on security and avoiding trouble see p.43.

Points of arrival

Belize City has two **airports**. **International flights** land at the **Philip Goldson International Airport**, 17km northwest of the city at Ladyville, just off the Northern Highway. Arriving here can be chaotic, with a crush of people waiting anxiously for trolleys to trundle in with their luggage. A recent extension alleviated some of the overcrowding but even this is sometimes swamped by the huge increase in visitor numbers. Belize's **domestic airlines** also make stops at the international airport, so you might want to pick up an onward flight right away (though prices to all destinations are Bz$40 more than from the **municipal airport**, on the seafront a few kilometres north of the city centre).

From the international airport, the only way into the city is by taxi (Bz$40), or by walking out to the Northern Highway (25min) and flagging down one of the frequent passing buses (Bz$1.50 to the centre). From the municipal airport, a taxi to town costs Bz$8–10; walking takes at least 25 minutes.

The main **bus terminal** is on the western side of the city centre, along West Collet Canal, in a fairly derelict part of town known as Mesopotamia. It's only 1km from the Swing Bridge and you can easily walk – or, especially at night, take a taxi – to any of the hotels listed below. Most scheduled **boats returning from the cayes** pull in at the **Marine Terminal**, on the north side of the Swing Bridge, though some use the **Fort Street Tourism Village**, a few hundred metres east along North Front Street, or **Courthouse Wharf**, on the south side of the river; from either it's a fairly short walk or taxi ride to any of the hotels or the bus terminal. If you're arriving by bus or shuttle from Flores or Chetumal, using one of the Guatemala-based services, note that these now stop at the Tourism Village (see above).

Information and tours

The **Belize Tourism Board** (BTB) office is some distance from the centre, inside the Central Bank building on Gabourel Lane (Mon–Fri 8am–5pm; ☎223-1913, ⦿www.travelbelize.org). Although it's not an essential visit, you can pick up free bus timetables, a hotel guide and city map, nature reserve brochures and copies of the (sometimes free) **tourist newspapers**. In the city centre, the Mundo Maya Deli (☎223-1235) in the **Marine Terminal** next to the Swing Bridge has reliable information on **bus and boat schedules**.

Should you want to escape the city for a day or two, you can take one of the **day tours** inland. Most visit at least two of the following: the Belize Zoo, Bermudian Landing Baboon Sanctuary, Crooked Tree Wildlife Sanctuary, Altun Ha ruins and Lamanai ruins. However, all but the last two are very easy to visit independently – though with the exception of the zoo, you'll need to stay overnight if you don't have your own vehicle. Still, even with the extra cost of accommodation, it's likely to work out less expensive than a tour. If time is short and you'd prefer a **guided tour**, contact one of the following independent tour guides: David Cunningham (☎603-6427, ⒺΩcunninghamstours @yahoo.com) or Carlos Gonzalez (☎609-6757); or contact any of the travel agents in "Listings", p.74.

Accommodation

There are over fifty **hotels** in Belize City, around a third of which cost Bz$30–50 for a double room, with at least another half-dozen in the range of Bz$50–75; the selection below covers all price ranges. For the comprehensive list, pick up a copy of *Destination Belize* from the tourism board or most hotels. There's usually no need to book ahead (unless you're eager to stay in a particular hotel), as you'll almost always find something in the price range you're looking for – though a phone call can save time and effort. Most of the city's **budget hotels** are north of the Swing Bridge, and the ones listed have been selected first on the basis of security and then of price – anything cheaper is likely to be unsafe; most of those listed also have good rates for singles. The more **upmarket hotels** (most take credit cards) are generally located in the historic **Fort George area** or along the **seafront** south of the river mouth, where guests can benefit from the sea breezes. If you want a comfortable hotel in a quiet location near the international airport and within easy reach of the city, take a look at the *Belize River Lodge* listing on p.81. To make finding a particular hotel easier the listings below have been divided into accommodation north and south of **Haulover Creek**.

North of Haulover Creek

Inexpensive

Barrack Road Guest House 8 Barrack Rd ☏606-5131. Conveniently located just two blocks from the Marine Terminal and set back from the main road, this quiet, clean and very secure guest house is great value. Rooms are arranged round a tiled courtyard and some have private bath; the rate includes a small breakfast. Helpful owners Molly and Leo Castillo can arrange tickets to Caye Caulker for Bz$12 (normally Bz$15). ❸
Downtown Guest House 5 Eve St, near the end of Queen St ☏223-2057. A good-value, basic budget hotel, clean and secure with a balcony over the street at the front, and a TV and fridge in the sitting room downstairs. Although most rooms are rather small, some do have private bath, TV and a/c. Friendly Chinese owner Miss Kenny will cook a bargain breakfast by arrangement and she sells cold beer and soft drinks. The only drawback is the cat odour in the yard but this doesn't penetrate to the rooms. ❷–❹
Freddie's Guest House 86 Eve St, on the city edge near the waterfront ☏223-3851. Three clean, secure and peaceful fan-cooled rooms with comfortable beds and bedside lamps; the best value in this price range. One room has immaculate private bath and the shared bathroom gleams. ❹
North Front Street Guest House 124 N Front St ☏227-7595, ✉thoth@btl.net. A budget travellers' favourite: friendly, helpful and just two blocks from the Marine Terminal, with a wide balcony overlooking the street. Although the rooms in this 120-year-old building are basic and fairly small and

none has a private bath (cold water only in the downstairs shared bathrooms), it's popular and you may need to book ahead. ❷
Three Sisters Guest House 55 Eve St ☏203-5729. Three large, clean rooms (one with private bath) in a wooden building run by a friendly, mainly Spanish-speaking family. Rooms open onto a spacious upstairs sitting area; tranquil when the TV is off. ❸

Mid-range to expensive

Bakadeer Inn 74 Cleghorn St ☏223-0659. Twelve clean, modern a/c rooms with telephone, TV and private bath with tub, though there's little natural light. Very secure and you can order breakfast. Rates are very good for three or four sharing. ❺
Belize Biltmore Plaza Mile 3, Northern Highway ☏223-2302, ✇www.belizebiltmore.com. A *Best Western* hotel with very spacious, well-furnished a/c rooms (some are wheelchair-accessible and non-smoking rooms are available), offering several levels of comfort and a glorious pool; manager Teresa Parkey and her staff oversee one of the best-run hotels in the country. All rooms have a coffeemaker, some have a king-size beds and, although it's just off the highway, there's no traffic noise in the rooms or among the tranquil grounds, filled with tropical plants. The *Victoria Room* restaurant serves excellent meals, featuring seafood and quality steaks, with daily specials. The *Biltmore* is also is a focal point of the city's nightlife, with a steel band playing during the Friday evening happy hour, a mariachi band on Saturdays and a vibrant Belizean cabaret. There's

1

also a business centre to check email, a well-equipped fitness room and a massage room. ❼–❾

Chateau Caribbean 6 Marine Parade ☎223-3888, ⓦwww.chateaucaribbean.com. Comfortable, colonial-style hotel overlooking the seafront and Memorial Park. Most rooms have been recently renovated, all have spacious tiled bathrooms, a/c and cable TV and some have sea views; the best views are from the two very large, well-furnished rooms with glass-fronted balconies on the top floor. There's also a very good restaurant (see p.70) and a small pool is planned. The *Chateau*, a former hospital, has featured in several movies – the spacious public areas, with wicker furniture and balconies overlooking the sea, are a favourite location for visiting film crews. ❼

Grant Residence 126 Barrack Rd ☎223-0926, ⓦwww.grantbedandbreakfast.com. Four very spacious, individually decorated and extremely comfortable bed-and-breakfast rooms in an impressively maintained guest house, in a quiet seafront location just north of the city centre. Each room has a TV, a well-stocked bookshelf and an immaculate private bathroom. All have sea views and two have a private balcony; smoking is permitted in the rooms. Air-conditioning is being installed but the fans and sea breezes keep the place cool. Owners Ward and P.J. Grant are friendly, helpful and informative, and offer guests a complimentary beer or cocktail each evening. ❼

The Great House 13 Cork St ☎223-3400, ⓦwww.greathousebelize.com. This beautiful four-storey wooden building, originally built in 1927 as the family home of owner Steve Maestre, has been modernized and expanded to become one of the most impressive hotels in the city. Located in the prestigious Fort George area, the sixteen spacious, well-equipped a/c rooms have private bath, coffeemaker, TV, phone and dedicated fax line, gorgeous hardwood floors and a balcony. The *Smoky Mermaid* restaurant (Friday evening happy hour) is located in the courtyard and there's a gallery of upmarket shops and boutiques below. ❽

Radisson Fort George Hotel and Marina 2 Marine Parade, north side of the harbour mouth ☎223-3333, ⓦwww.radisson.com/belizecitybz. The luxurious and extremely well-managed flagship of the city's hotels and, though it's by far the most expensive at around Bz$350 a night, you can expect substantial discounts on the "rack rates" when it's not full. All rooms have a huge cable TV, fridge and minibar and for business travellers, high-speed Internet access. The Colonial Wing has carpeted rooms with views of the sea and the grounds and the ground-floor rooms have bal-

conies; rooms in the Club Wing, reached by the only glass elevator in Belize, have marble floors and unbeatable sea views; and across the road all rooms in the Villa Wing have tiled balconies and some have bathrooms specially adapted for wheelchair-users. There are two excellent restaurants and a great café (see p.70) and the grounds are an oasis of calm on the edge of the sea, with two pools and a dockside marina, used by the larger live-aboard dive boats. ❾

Villa Boscardi 6043 Manatee Drive ☎ & ⒻFAX 223-1691, or ☎614-7734, ⓦwww.villaboscardi.com. Beautiful, spacious, immaculately clean and well-equipped guest rooms with a/c, private bath, TV and telephone in a private house 4km from the city centre, just off the Northern Highway. Owner Françoise Boscardi offers guests free transport from anywhere in the city and will take you to the airport if you're flying out. She will also drop you off if you're going into the city for dinner and generally do all she can to help you enjoy your stay. Breakfast is included in the room rate (other meals can be delivered) and there's a full kitchen for guests; you can use email and send/receive faxes. Françoise runs a women-only mini-spa offering facials and massage, which non-guests may book to use. No smoking in the house; no service charge and no extra charge for using credit cards. ❻

South of Haulover Creek

Belcove Hotel 9 Regent St W ☎227-3054, ⓦwww.belcove.com. Recently renovated rooms, some with a/c and most with private bath, right next to the river with a view of the Swing Bridge. There's a certain thrill of being on the edge of the dangerous part of town, though owner Mirna Harris and her staff ensure that the hotel itself is quite secure. Day (and even overnight) trips to the hotel's private island at Gallows Point, on the reef 15km from the city, can be arranged. ❸–❹

Bellevue Hotel 5 Southern Foreshore ☎227-7051, Ⓔⓜbellvue@btl.net. Fairly large hotel on the seafront south of the Swing Bridge. Most rooms in this former colonial house have been renovated, but it's best to check what you're offered first. All have private bath, a/c and TV, and outside there's a relaxing courtyard, adorned with palms and a pool. There's a restaurant downstairs; upstairs the *Harbour Room* bar is a popular meeting place, especially during the Friday evening happy hour, and in the basement the *Maya Tavern* disco has live music on Friday and Saturday nights. ❻

Caribbean Palms Inn Corner of Regent and King streets ☎227-0472, Ⓔⓜcpalms@hotmail.com. Wonderful new hotel with nine good-value, very comfortable a/c rooms with private bath and TV, run by Belizean/Swiss couple, Albert Dawson and Margrit Steiger. It's tastefully decorated everywhere, with a spacious lounge area and a deck and patio for meals (by arrangement). Internet access for guests and there's a payphone and laundry service. There's also a shared budget room; Bz$30 per person. ⑥

Coningsby Inn 76 Regent St ☎227-1566, ℱ227-3276. Clean, comfortable and very secure rooms, all with private bath, in a quiet part of the city centre. There's a balcony over the street and the upstairs restaurant serves breakfast daily and other meals by arrangement; there's also a small bar for guests. Luggage storage available. ⑥

Isabel Guest House Across the Swing Bridge, above and behind the Central Drug Store ☎207-3019. Small, welcoming, primarily Spanish-speaking guest house with large rooms and private showers, though a little overpriced for a double. Good for groups, as the per person price goes down if more than two share a room. ④

Hotel Mopan 55 Regent St ☎227-7351, ⓦwww.hotelmopan.com. Wood-fronted building with recently renovated rooms at the quiet end of the street near the colonial House of Culture. Run by Tomy and Jeannie Shaw-Wright, son and daughter of the late Jean Shaw, an avid conservationist, it's always popular with naturalists, writers and scientists. The original building is over 200 years old but all rooms have private bath and cable TV, some have a/c and there's Internet access for guests. Great views from the sun roof, also several comfortable verandahs for relaxing and a bar. The restaurant serves good-value breakfasts and you can order lunch and dinner. The hotel is the base for Mopan Travels, which arranges tours throughout Belize. ⑤

Seaside Guest House 3 Prince St, half a block from the southern foreshore ☎227-8339, ⓔseasidebelize@btl.net. A clean, well-run and very secure hotel in a charming wooden building that's a popular meeting place for travellers. The budget room has seven hostel-style dorm beds (Bz$24), there are several private rooms (two with private bath) and the shared bathroom has hot water. The owners are very helpful, and provide an accurate information sheet on Belize City. There's a payphone and Internet access for guests and you get a key for access at all times – a rarity in budget hotels. Relax on the verandah – where you really can see the sea – or in the orchid-filled garden. Breakfast can be ordered and there's a beer and wine licence. ④

The City

Richard Davies, a British traveller in the mid-nineteenth century, wrote of the city: "There is much to be said for Belize, for in its way it was one of the prettiest ports at which we touched, and its cleanliness and order ... were in great contrast to the ports we visited later as to make them most remarkable." Many of the features that elicited this praise have now gone, though some of the distinctive **wooden colonial buildings** have been preserved as heritage showpieces, or converted into hotels, restaurants and museums. Yet even in cases where the decay is too advanced for the paintwork, balconies, carved railings and fretwork to be restored, the old wooden structures remain more pleasing than the concrete blocks that have replaced so many of them. Fires too have altered the architecture of the city, with the worst in recent years claiming the historic Paslow Building, which stood opposite the Marine Terminal.

The fate of the city's historic buildings is not all bad news, however. Two of the very best colonial structures have been carefully restored and are open to visitors; the former city jail, built in Victorian times, is now the **Museum of Belize** and the even earlier **Government House** is a museum and cultural centre. There's a great deal of new construction too, with an enormous **cruise ship terminal** dominating the northern side of the river mouth and beyond here, on the northern foreshore, a massive development is creating new land from the sea.

Before the construction of the first wooden bridge in the early 1800s, cattle and other commodities were winched over the waterway that divides the city

– hence the name **Haulover Creek**. Its replacement, the **Swing Bridge**, made in Liverpool and opened in 1923, is the only manually operated swing bridge left in the Americas. Every day at 5.30am and 5.30pm the endless parade of vehicles and people is halted by policemen and the process of turning begins. Using long poles inserted into a capstan, four men gradually lever the bridge around until it's pointing in the direction of the harbour mouth. During the few minutes that the bridge is open, the river traffic is busier than that on the roads and traffic is snarled up across the whole city.

Emory King

Any sailor shipwrecked on a foreign shore would doubtless be grateful to the land that saved him, but while for many such salvation might leave a lifelong impression, few would be so impressed that they would want to spend the rest of their lives there. Nevertheless, that's exactly what happened to **Emory King**, American-born wit, raconteur, realtor, historian, broadcaster, writer, businessman and film extra, when his schooner *Vagabond* crashed onto the coral off English Caye, British Honduras in 1953. Realizing almost immediately that the colony presented unrivalled opportunities to a young man of limited means but boundless entrepreneurial spirit, he stayed on, convinced he could play a major role in the development of this colonial backwater.

Finding the **Belize City** of the early 1950s much like a nineteenth-century village, with only a handful of cars (which, to his astonishment, drove on the left), a sickly electric power system and a few telephones to represent the twentieth century, he set about trying to change it. Within a year he managed to get appointed as the Secretary of the Chamber of Commerce, and then Secretary of the Tourist Committee – at a time when tourists were counted in dozens rather than hundreds of thousands. Believing that what the moribund colony needed to prosper was investment, and that the best way to attract investors was to offer them a land with low (or no) taxes, he waged a (so far still unsuccessful) campaign to **abolish income tax**. But although he advised investors and found land for American farmers who no longer had a frontier of their own to conquer, Emory King's most enduring gift to his adopted country was persuading the **Mennonites** (see box on p.90) to settle here in 1958; their back-breaking pioneer work is probably Belize's greatest agricultural success story.

Emory King's involvement in Belize extends to **film appearances**: he has had cameo roles in all the Hollywood movies filmed here (see p.39). In perhaps the best-known, *The Mosquito Coast* (1985), based on the novel by Paul Theroux, he played a down-at-heel, drunken landowner offering to sell Harrison Ford a piece of land – a part he claims is not typecasting. In 1998 the government appointed him **film commissioner**, with a brief to attract more cinematic productions to Belize; he soon secured a production of *After the Storm*, based on the Hemingway short story and filmed in Placencia and Ambergris Caye. His success in this role has led not only to "reality television" productions such as *Temptation Island* being filmed here but to the establishment of the **Belize Film Festival** (Ⓦ www.belizefilmfestival.com), held annually in March.

Emory's **books** on or about Belize and Belizean life are sold all over the country; a good one to start with is *Hey Dad, This Is Belize*, a whimsical account of family life (see pp.339–347 for further titles). Most days he can be found in his office, in the forecourt of the *Radisson Fort George*, and will usually have time to sign a book or two – without the markup charged by hotel gift shops. His **website**, Ⓦ www.emoryking.com, provides everything you'll need to know about the man – or at least everything that Emory is prepared to tell.

The north side

Immediately on the **north side** of the Swing Bridge is the **Marine Terminal**, where you can catch boats for the northern cayes (see p.75 for schedule). In the same building – the beautifully restored former Belize City Fire Station, built in 1923 – are two superbly designed museums (both Mon–Sat 8am–4.30pm; Bz$4). The **Coastal Zone Museum** contains fascinating displays and explanations of reef ecology, the highlights being a 3-D model of the entire reef system, including the cayes and atolls, and superb aerial photographs of Belize's marine reserves. Upstairs, the **Maritime Museum** exhibits an amazing collection of model boats and documents relating to Belize's maritime heritage, including personal accounts of the cayes' transition from a fishing-based economy to one centred on tourism. The Mundo Maya Deli, also here, is the best place to find **information** on transport from Belize City; ever-helpful owner Petty Cervantes keeps up-to-date bus schedules for Belize and sells tickets to Flores and Chetumal on the Flores-based buses and for the *Gulf Cruzer* to Puerto Cortés. Another very useful shop is Kaisa International, which sells *pesos* (Mexico) and *quetzales* (Guatemala), as well as tickets to Flores and beyond; both these shops also stock maps and guide-books, including *Rough Guides*. Amazingly, there's no restaurant inside the terminal, but the toilets (Bz$.50) are reasonably clean and there are also some rather expensive **luggage lockers**.

A block east of the Marine Terminal, at 91 N Front St, **The Image Factory** (Mon–Fri 9am–6pm; free but donations welcome), is home to Belize's hottest contemporary artists. The gallery holds outstanding, sometimes provocative exhibitions and you often get a chance to discuss the work with the artists themselves. At the front of the gallery The Image Factory Shop sells Belizean art, books, music and videos; for information on exhibition openings call ⏀223-4151 or visit ⓦwww.belizemall.com/imagefactory.

Continuing east along North Front Street you'll encounter the advance guard of trinket sellers, street musicians, hustlers and hair-braiders, announcing you're near the **Tourism Village**, Belize's new **cruise ship terminal**, often handling thousands of visitors daily – there will almost always be a cruise ship (or five) in view as you look out to sea. The city authorities, in an attempt to improve the area's image, try to keep the streets clear of vendors but the lure of US cash tempts locals to set up improvised stalls, undercutting the "official" shops inside the terminal. The Village itself is little more than a dock for the cruise ship tenders to disembark their passengers, with an attached shopping mall – anyone can go in for a look around. Cruise ship tourism is a new and often controversial phenomenon in Belize, with some stakeholders in the "traditional", low-impact overnight tourism stating that the sheer number of cruise ship tourists (expected to reach one million per year) exceeds the carrying capacity of the sites they visit, leading to irreversible environmental damage.

Beyond the Tourism Village, the road follows the north shore of the river mouth – an area that was Fort George Island until the narrow strait was filled in in 1924 – reaching the point marked by the **Fort George Lighthouse**, beneath which is the tomb of and memorial to **Baron Bliss**, Belize's greatest benefactor (see p.67). Walking around the shoreline you pass the *Radisson Fort George* hotel, in whose forecourt is the office of Emory King, one of Belize's most famous characters (see box opposite). Natural history enthusiasts will benefit from a visit to two of Belize's foremost conservation organizations in the Fort George area: the **Belize Audubon Society**, 12 Fort St (⏀223-5004), has information, books, maps and posters relating to all the country's wildlife reserves and is very prominent in conservation education. Nearby, at 1 Eyre St (☎227-5616), are the offices of the **Programme for Belize**, which manages the Rio Bravo Conservation Area (see p.94); call in for news on access and progress from the enthusiastic staff. For more on these and other conservation organizations in Belize see p.324 in Contexts.

The seafront **Memorial Park** honours the Belizean dead of World War I. In the streets around the park you'll find several colonial mansions, many of the best-preserved now taken over by upmarket hotels and embassies; the *Chateau Caribbean*, *Colton House* and the Mexican embassy are a few fine examples. At 2 Park St, on the south side of the park, is the **National Handicraft Center** (Mon–Fri 8am–5pm), which sells high-quality Belizean crafts and art at fair prices. A little beyond here, at the corner of Hutson Street and Gabourel Lane, set back one block from the sea, is the **US Embassy**; this superb "colonial" building was actually constructed in New England in the nineteenth century from American timber, before being dismantled and shipped to Belize.

Marine Parade, the seaward edge of Memorial Park, marks the beginning of the biggest civil engineering project in the city's history. A massive **seawall**, stretching for hundreds of metres along the shore to Barrack Road, encloses over fourteen acres of shallow sea, now in the process of being pumped dry. Soon this will become a boulevard for traffic and a pedestrian promenade, leading north for over a kilometre to the enormous *Princess Hotel*. Part of the reason for this seaward expansion of the city is to accommodate the ever-growing fleet of tour buses for the cruise ship industry, though it also creates lots of valuable new real estate for development. Beyond the northern end of this development the attractive seafront **BTL Park** was built on reclaimed land and it was in this area that Charles Lindbergh landed the *Spirit of St Louis* in 1927, the first aeroplane to touch down in Belize. The park, with a children's playground, is popular with families and often hosts open-air concerts, with the biggest party taking place during the Independence Day celebrations in September.

The Museum of Belize, Belize City

Just south of the centre of this new development, in front of the Central Bank building at the north end of Queen Street, the Victorian former colonial prison has undergone a remarkable and very beautiful transformation to become the **Museum of Belize, Belize City** (Mon–Fri 9am–5pm; Bz$10; ⓦ www.muse-umofbelize.org). The old city jail, built in 1857 and used to house prisoners until 1993, was reopened as a museum in 2002, the 21st anniversary of Belize's independence. While in use as a jail the building almost certainly didn't appear as impressive as it does today: an elegantly proportioned two-storey structure of clean, sand-coloured brickwork with cream trim, set in lawns and gardens, looking more like a country mansion than a prison.

The lower floor, with plenty of exposed original brickwork and bars on the windows, displays photographs and artefacts celebrating the history and the people of the city as it grew over the last 365 years, from a tiny settlement in the mangrove swamps to the bustling conurbation of today. The building's original role is not glossed over, however; there's a gruesome reconstruction of the condemned (death row) cell. Fascinating though this is, the star attractions are upstairs, in the **Maya Masterpieces** gallery, a permanent, world-class collection of some of the best artefacts recovered from Belize's Maya sites. Well-lit glass cases display fine painted ceramics, representing all periods of Maya history. One of the most striking is the Buenavista Vase, which depicts the mythical Hero Twins dancing, while wearing the costume of the young Maize Gods, after defeating the Lords of Death – the central theme of the Maya creation story, the Popol Vuh (see Books, p.342). If you want to visit the site of Buenavista del Cayo, where the vase was found, see p.175. Other treasures include a replica of the famous jade head from Altun Ha, **jade masks**, pendants and several gorgeous jade necklaces, fantastically executed **eccentric flints**, painstakingly carved from a single piece of flint, and an exceptionally well-preserved wooden figurine, probably of a ruler, from a cave in Toledo District.

The south side

The **south side** is generally the older section of Belize City: in the early days the elite lived in the seafront houses while the backstreets were home to their slaves and labourers. These days it's the city's commercial centre, containing the main shopping streets, banks and travel agencies. Right by the Swing Bridge is the three-storey **new market**, which opened in 1993 on the site of the rather decrepit old market dating from 1820. Though the new one is much cleaner, it's not very popular with either traders or shoppers, many of whom prefer the goods on display on the streets outside or the bustling Queen's Square market, next to the bus terminal.

Albert Street, running south from the Swing Bridge, is the main commercial thoroughfare, with banks, supermarkets and good-value T-shirt and souvenir shops – Sings, at no. 35, has some of the best bargains. On the parallel **Regent Street**, a block closer to the sea, are the former colonial administration and court buildings, known together as the **Courthouse**. These well-preserved examples of colonial architecture, with their columns and fine wrought-iron, were completed in 1926 after an earlier building on the same site was destroyed by a fire. The Courthouse overlooks a square of grass and trees with an ornamental fountain in the centre, ambitiously known as Central Park until it was renamed **Battlefield Park** in the early 1990s, commemorating the heated political meetings which took place there before independence; nowadays most of the noise in the park is generated by the raucous chatter from grackles, roosting in their thousands every night.

Bliss Centre for the Performing Arts

A block south of the Courthouse on the waterfront is the extensively refurbished **Bliss Centre for the Performing Arts** (☎227-2110). A stunning marble-lined entrance hall opens onto a brand-new 600-seat theatre behind, with space for drama workshops and the studios of the **Belize National Dance Company** upstairs. Benefiting from a generous grant from the Mexican government, which provides regular aid to Central American countries, this is the centre of Belizean cultural life, hosting concerts, plays and exhibitions as well as accommodating the country's **National Art Collection**. It's certainly worth a visit to the front desk to see what's on – here and elsewhere – or to enjoy a drink at the *Bliss* café/bar. The cultural programme is spearheaded by the **Institute of Creative Arts** (ICA), also housed here, with a remit to keep alive traditional culture and promote new talent. The organization was originally known as the Bliss Institute, funded by the legacy of Baron Henry Ernest Edward Victor Bliss, a moderately eccentric Englishman with a Portuguese title. A keen fisherman, Bliss arrived off the coast of Belize in his yacht *Sea King* in 1926 after hearing about the tremendous amount of game fish in local waters. Unfortunately, he became ill and died without ever having been ashore, but he must have been impressed by whatever fish he did catch, as he left most of his considerable estate to benefit the people of the colony – meticulously stipulating how the money was to be spent. This became the Bliss Trust, which has been used on various projects, helping to build markets and libraries, improve roads and water supplies and creating the Bliss School of Nursing. In gratitude the authorities declared March 9 (the date of his death) an official public holiday – **Baron Bliss Day** – commemorated by boat races and the La Ruta Maya canoe race (see p.161) from San Ignacio to Belize City, funded partly by his legacy. There's more about him in the Maritime Museum, although mysteriously little is known of how the Baron acquired his wealth. See p.65 for his tomb and memorial.

St John's Cathedral

At the southern end of Albert Street is **St John's Cathedral** (daily 6am–6pm; free), the oldest Anglican cathedral in Central America and one of the oldest buildings in Belize. Work began in 1812 and was completed in 1820, the red bricks for its construction brought over as ballast in British ships. With its square, battlemented tower, it looks more like a large English parish church than anything you might expect to find in Central America. The main structure has survived almost 180 years of tropical heat and hurricanes, though a fire in 2002 destroyed most of the roof, now fully restored. Between 1815 and 1845 the kings of the Mosquito Coast were crowned in the cathedral, amid great pomp, taking the title to a British Protectorate that extended along the coast of Honduras and Nicaragua. The Miskito Indians, keen to keep their links with Britain to avoid Spanish colonial rule, had their kings crowned and children baptized in the cathedral as well.

Just west of the cathedral, **Yarborough Cemetery** was named after the magistrate who owned the land and permitted the burial of prominent people here from 1781 – commoners were admitted only after 1870. Although the graves have fallen into disrepair, a browse among the stones will turn up fascinating snippets of history. At the seaward end of this strip of land, connected to the mainland by a wooden causeway, **Bird's Isle** is a venue for reggae concerts and parties and there's a reasonable restaurant, open for lunch (see review, p.71).

The House of Culture

East of the cathedral, in a beautiful, breezy seafront setting, shaded by royal palms and complete with an immaculate green lawn, is the well-preserved, white-painted colonial Government House, now restored and renamed the **House of Culture** (daily 9am–4.30pm; Bz$10). Built in 1814, it was the governor's residence when Belize was a British colony; at midnight on September 20, 1981 the Belize flag was hoisted here for the first time as the country celebrated independence.

The house has always been used for some official receptions, particularly on Independence Day, but the present governor-general, Sir Colville Young, wanted to make this superb example of Belize's colonial heritage open to everyone, with the result that in 1996 it was designated a **museum**, later becoming the House of Culture. The front door is entered up a flight of steps under the columned portico; inside, a plush red carpet leads down the hall to the great mahogany staircase, and beyond here doors open onto the back porch, overlooking the sea. In the grounds, the carefully restored *Sea King*, the tender of Baron Bliss's yacht of the same name, stands as testimony to the craftsmanship of Belizean boatbuilders. The plant-filled gardens are a haven for birds and it's worth bringing a pair of binoculars.

The building's new role as the House of Culture means that it now hosts painting, dance and drumming workshops, art exhibitions and musical performances. A room off the front porch has a changing exhibition of

△ The Courthouse

contemporary art. In the main room a wide panoramic painting of Belize City in the early 1900s overlooks the collection of colonial silverware, glass and furniture, while one wall is lined with prints of sombre past governors. Another room displays the **Eric King collection**, a fascinating compilation of vintage photographs and postcards of Belize.

Eating

The multitude of **restaurants** in Belize City offer a good deal of variety, though the tasty but humble **Creole** fare of rice and beans still predominates at the lower end. There's plenty of seafood and steaks, and a preponderance of **Chinese** restaurants – usually the best bet for **vegetarians** – as well as very good **Lebanese** and **Indian** restaurants. The big **hotels** have their own restaurants, naturally quite expensive but with varied menus and good service. Generally, vegetables other than cabbage, carrots, onions and peppers are rarely served in the average Belizean restaurant and these are likely to be the main components of any salad. Amazingly the only one of the US-based chains to make inroads into Belize is Subway, with a single branch, though rumour has it that McDonald's is considering opening here. Until then, *HL's Burger*, the self-proclaimed "Burger King of Belize" is the home-grown version, with a growing number of outlets serving standard fast-food fare. Greasy fried chicken is available as takeaway from small stands all over the city: a Belizean favourite known as **"dollar chicken"**, whatever the price.

If you're **shopping for food**, the main **supermarkets** – Brodie's and Romac's – are worth a look; they're on Albert Street, just past Battlefield Park, and their selection of food is good if expensive, reflecting the fact that much is imported. Milk and dairy products, produced locally by Mennonite farmers (see box on p.90), are delicious and good quality. Naturally enough, local **fruit** is cheap and plentiful, though highly seasonal – Belizean citrus fruits are among the best in the world.

In the listings below we have quoted a phone number in places where it is recommended you should **reserve a table** or for those places which offer **delivery service**. You can expect that many smaller places will be closed on Sunday.

North of the river

Chateau Caribbean 6 Marine Parade, above the hotel of the same name. For undisturbed views of blue sea and offshore islands, head up the steps to this cool first-floor restaurant, where prices for Chinese and international dishes are more reasonable than you might guess from the gleaming white linen and cutlery.

Gyros and Crepes 164 Freetown Rd. The best Lebanese food in the country, with delicious tahini, falafel, hummus and kebabs – try the Lebanese plate, which brings together everything above.

Harbour View North side of the harbour mouth, just past the Tourism Village ☏ 223-6420. Fine dining and cocktails on the waterfront in one of the city's top restaurants, featuring East Asian and Belizean specialities, with lots of fresh seafood,

created by the award-winning Filipino chef. Eat indoors in the a/c dining room or at tables on the breezy deck.

Le Petit Café Cork St, in the Villa Wing of the *Radisson Hotel*. The outdoor tables here are the best place in the city to enjoy a genuine café atmosphere, with good coffee and baked treats, including croissants, at reasonable prices. Ideal for a continental breakfast.

Mar's Restaurant 11 Handyside St. Tasty Belizean food at great prices in a spacious, clean, a/c restaurant. Karaoke, and other music, on some Fridays.

Nerie's Restaurant II Corner of Queen and Daly streets. The best Belizean food north of the river and fantastically good value, served in clean, well-run and brightly lit surroundings. Just walk in, find a table and select from the chalkboard menu featuring Creole specialities. Very busy at lunchtimes, when there's always a daily special. Open 7.30am–10pm. On some weekend nights the *La Bodega Lounge* upstairs, features live music and dancing. *Nerie's I*, on Freetown Rd just past Cinderella Plaza, opposite the Belize Technical College, is just as good.

Pepper's Pizza 4 St Thomas St ☏ 223-5000. Decent pizza restaurant with reliable deliveries.

The Stonegrill Cork St, in the Colonial Wing of the *Radisson Hotel*. Poolside restaurant featuring the city's latest dining sensation; select your dish from the menu – seafood, chicken, beef, etc, often on a skewer with vegetables – and get the chance to cook it yourself on a slab of volcanic rock, delivered to your table, that's heated to 350ºC. Great fun and very tasty; you get a range of mild or spicy sauces to accompany your creation.

Sumathi 190 Newtown Barracks Rd ☏ 223-1172. Extremely good north Indian and tandoori food in a quiet, clean restaurant. It's a long way from the centre so you'll need to take a taxi, or call to order and get a taxi to deliver to your hotel room. Closed Mon.

Wet Lizard Fort St, on the waterfront next to the Tourism Village. Capture the feeling of the cayes as you eat at one of the brightly painted tables on a deck overlooking the river mouth. The menu offers an eclectic range of well-prepared and very tasty dishes, including delicately flavoured seafood and tangy spring rolls, with Thai and Mexican specialities; great desserts and cocktails.

South of the river

Big Daddy's Diner Upstairs in the new market, just south of the Swing Bridge. Great breakfasts and Belizean dishes, with a daily lunch special, served cafeteria-style in clean, bright surroundings. The best harbour and bridge views in the city; a pity the windows don't open. Open Mon–Sat 7am–4pm.

Bird's Isle Restaurant Bird's Isle, at the south end of Regent St. Inexpensive Belizean dishes served under a thatched roof by the sea. Usually open only for lunch but sometimes has evening entertainment. There's a happy hour on Thursdays at 3pm.

Jambel Jerk Pit 2B King St ☏ 227-6080. Chef Garnet Brown and his crew cook up very tasty Jamaican-influenced dishes at reasonable prices in this sister restaurant to the long-established *Jambel* in San Pedro, Ambergris Caye (see p.125). Specialities include jerk chicken (obviously), but also worth trying are the delicious spicy fish and other seafood dishes, soups and salads or the daily special. Eat indoors in the a/c or on the palm-shaded patio. Delivery available.

Macy's 18 Bishop St. Long-established, reasonably priced Creole restaurant that's popular with locals and very busy at lunchtime. They also serve traditional game: armadillo, deer and gibnut (a type of large rodent), but thankfully turtle is no longer on the menu.

Marlins 11 Regent St W, next to the *Belcove Hotel*. Good, inexpensive local food in large portions – and you can eat on the verandah overlooking the river.

River Side Patio On the riverside at the rear of the new market. Mexican-style food and snacks served in a great place to relax with a drink as you watch the bridge swing. Sometimes has entertainment on Fri and Sat evenings.

Drinking, nightlife and entertainment

Belize City's more sophisticated, air-conditioned **bars** are found in the most expensive establishments (restos, hotels, nightclubs), and there aren't many of these. At the lowest end of the scale are dimly lit dives, effectively men-only, where, though you might be offered drugs or feel uneasy, it's more likely that you'll have a thoroughly enjoyable time meeting easygoing, hard-drinking locals. There are several places between the two extremes however; on weekend nights try *La Bodega Lounge* upstairs at *Nerie's Restaurant II*, on the corner of Queen and Daly streets; across the road at *Copacabana*, a karaoke bar with pool tables; or any night at *Nu Fenders Bar*, just opposite.

A few of the top-end places tempt the after-work crowd with Friday evening **happy hours** (usually 5–7pm), where you can relax with the city's business elite. The liveliest is the poolside bar of the *Biltmore Plaza Hotel*, accompanied by a fantastic steel band; the *Biltmore* also hosts the jazz/blues band Mango Jam on Thursdays, Mexican mariachi on Saturdays and frequent performances of their own **cabaret**, featuring extravagantly costumed Creole and Garífuna dancers. After the happy hour at the *Bellevue Hotel* you can enjoy **live music** in the basement disco and karaoke upstairs. Other Friday happy-hour venues include the *Radisson Fort George* and the *Calypso Bar* at the *Princess Hotel*, which hold regular dances and frequently host top local bands, and the *Smokey Mermaid Restaurant*, in the patio beneath the *Great House.*

Nightlife, though not as wild as it used to be, is becoming more reliable and there's more variety on offer. An ideal pre-club warm-up is *Aqui Me Quedo,* more commonly known as "Shirley Bar", by the corner of Orange and West Canal streets, with **Garífuna drumming** on Friday nights – though due to the location it's not for the faint-hearted. A relatively safe area of town with a variety of bars and clubs is the strip of Barrack Road either side of the BTL Park – from the *Princess Hotel* to *Caesar's Palace* bar. The latter is a lively bar at weekends from around 10pm, and has a small dancefloor, playing anything from **techno/dance** to **Latin** grooves or punta, **soca** and **reggae**. Next door is *Eden* nightclub, Belize's smartest nightspot, playing a similar mix of music, attracting a more affluent crowd of young people and enforcing a fairly strict dress code. As with any other club here, don't arrive before midnight or you'll find it next to empty. Further along is *MJ's* nightclub, slightly less salubrious, with occasional live punta. Slightly further again are a couple of other bars that have **karaoke**, now very popular across the country. For a more raw experience, very often with punta and **reggae dancehall**, visit *Queen's Club* on Fridays, on Baymen Avenue near St James Street; upstairs at *Archie's* on Saturdays, on Central American Boulevard, south of the Western Highway; or weekend nights at *Paradise 21* (formerly the *Lumba Yard*), on the riverbank just out of town on the Northern Highway. The latter three can all occasionally get out of hand – but they are the best places to catch current bands.

You don't have to be a really high roller to try your luck at the **casino** at the *Princess Hotel*, but you will need a passport or photo ID to gain temporary membership (free) and keep to the dress code: no shorts or sandals. The cash desk changes your Belize or US dollars into tokens for feeding the four hundred slot machines or playing blackjack, Caribbean poker and roulette. Officially there's a Bz$50 minimum to keep out the riff-raff (not always enforced); any tokens you don't use are changed back. Even if you don't win anything a night's entertainment need only set you back around Bz$20–30. Local (as opposed to imported) drinks are free while you're playing and you can enjoy a Las Vegas-style floor show featuring leggy Russian dancers – with a free buffet to follow. The *Princess* has Belize City's only **cinema**, showing the latest releases in (expensive) air-conditioned comfort; this is also the venue for Belize's **Film Festival**, held annually in March.

Listings

Airlines American, corner of New Rd and Queen St ☎223-2522; Continental, 80 Regent St ☎227-8309; Maya Island Air, Municipal Airport ☎223-1140 or 226-2345; Taca, in Belize Global Travel, 41 Albert St ☎227-7363; Tropic Air, Municipal Airport ☎224-5671 or 226-2012; US Airways toll-free to US office ☎0800/872-4700.

American Express In Belize Global Travel, 41 Albert St ☎227-7363.

Banks and exchange The main branches of Atlantic, First Caribbean, Belize and Scotia banks are on Albert St (usually Mon–Thurs 8am–2pm, Fri 8am–4.30pm). Only the Belize and First Caribbean banks have ATMs which accept foreign-issued cards; other will process cash advances over the counter. Cash in US$ is usually only available from the banks if you can show a ticket to leave the country. Casas de cambio, shops, hotels and restaurants change travellers' cheques and accept cash US$. Guatemalan and Mexican currency is often difficult to obtain except at the borders, but Kaisa International and possibly other shops in the Marine Terminal will usually have *quetzales* and *pesos*. For more information see p.26 in Basics.

Books In addition to the shops listed here, many of the larger hotels also sell books, magazines and papers; some budget hotels operate book exchanges. Both The Book Center, 2 Church St, opposite the BTL office (☎227-7457), and Angelus Press, 10 Queen St (☎223-5777) have a wide range of books on Belize, maps and guides including *Rough Guides*.

Car rental The following companies will arrange vehicle pick-up and post anywhere in the city or at the municipal or international airports (where most have offices) at no extra charge: Avis ☎225-2385, ✉avisbelize@btl.net; Budget, Mile 2 Northern Highway ☎223-2435, ⊛www.budget-belize.com; Crystal, Mile 4 3/4, Northern Highway and in the Tourism Village ☎223-1600 or toll-free in Belize ☎0800/777-7777, ⊛www.crystal-belize.com; Hertz, 11A Cork St ☎223-5935. Crystal has by far the largest rental fleet in the country, and is the only outfit that allows you to take vehicles over the Guatemalan border. Owner Jay Crofton, based in his antique-filled courtyard on the Northern Highway, always gives a good deal on rentals and prides himself on service. For more information on renting and driving in Belize see "Getting around" in Basics, p.30.

Embassies and consulates Though the official capital is Belmopan, some embassies remain in Belize City. These are normally open mornings Mon–Fri. Several EU countries have (mainly honorary) consulates in Belize City; current addresses and phone numbers for all embassies are in the Diplomatic Listings, at the back of the green pages in the telephone directory. Canada (cannot issue passports), 83 N Front St ☎223-1060; Guatemala, 8 A St, Kings Park ☎223-3150; Mexico, 18 North Park St ☎223-0194; US Consular Section, 29 Gabourel Lane ☎223-5423.

Film developing For prints, slides and fast passport photos, try Spooners, 89 N Front St, or Titos, 9 Barrack Rd.

Immigration The Belize Immigration Office is in the Government Complex on Mahogany St, near the junction of Central American Blvd and the Western Highway (Mon–Thurs 8.30am–4pm, Fri 8.30am–3.30pm; ☎222-4620). Thirty-day extensions of stay (the maximum allowed) cost Bz$25.

Internet and email There aren't many places to go online in Belize City and finding somewhere out of office hours is difficult, but more places are opening up and increasingly hotels have computers for guests to use; where they do we've indicated this in the hotel listing. The average cost is Bz$7–10/hr. The cheapest place to check email is at Ray Communications, 15 Regent St West, just past the *Belcove Hotel* (Mon–Fri 8am–7pm, Sat 8am–1pm; Bz$4/hr). The most convenient place in the centre is Mailboxes Etc., 166 N Front St, near the Marine Terminal (Mon–Fri 7.30am–6pm, Sat 9am–2pm; Bz$7.80/hr). Also worth trying is M Business Solutions, 13 Cork St (in the gallery beneath *The Great House*) or upstairs in the Turton Library on North Front St; you can also use the computers in the BTL office; see "Telephones" on p.74.

Laundry Central America Coin Laundry, 114 Barrack Rd (Mon–Sat 8.30am–9pm; reduced hours Sun), and in many hotels.

Massage Oltsil Day Spa, 148A Barrack Rd ☎223-7722, ✉oltsil@yahoo.com. Holistic massage, body scrubs, herbal wraps, pedicures and spa treatments using only local products and ingredients from Onelia Palma.

Medical care Dr Gamero, Myo-On Clinic, 40 Eve St ☎224-5616; Karl Heusner Memorial Hospital, Princess Margaret Drive, near the junction with the Northern Highway ☎223-1548.

Police The main police station is on Queen St, a block north of the Swing Bridge (☎227-2210). For emergencies, dial ☎90 or 911 nationwide.

Moving on from Belize City

Moving on from Belize City is easy, with regular departures by bus to all parts of the country, across the border to Chetumal in Mexico and to Benque Viejo in Cayo, for the Guatemalan border. Most transport tends to peter out at dusk and there are no overnight buses. Domestic flights to all main towns leave from the Municipal Airport; boats to the northern cayes leave from the Marine Terminal.

Bus services from Belize City

The main bus company in Belize is Novelo's, with divisions called Northern, Western and Southern Transport, operating the most services to all towns in the country from the large terminal at 19 West Collet Canal. There are several smaller bus companies with regular departures but no contact address or telephone number; most operate from the streets near the terminal and the ones listed below are marked on the city map (pp.56–57).

Although telephone numbers are given (where they exist) you'll be lucky to get a response, even from Novelo's – who don't even have departure times listed inside the crowded terminal.

Bus companies and destinations

Services operate seven days a week unless otherwise stated. **Express services** (Exp) are faster and more expensive than regular services. The abbreviations we've used for the bus companies in the chart below are as follows:

JA = James Bus ⓣ702-2049; for Dangriga and Punta Gorda (via Belmopan); leaves from the Shell station on Cemetery Rd, near Novelo's terminal, at 5.30am, 10am & 2.30pm daily.

JX = Jex Bus ⓣ225-7017; leaves for Crooked Tree from Regent St W (10.50am) and Pound Yard, Collet Canal.

MF = McFadzean's Bus For Bermudian Landing (via Burrell Boom); leaves from Euphrates Ave, off Orange St, near the Novelo's bus depot, at noon and 5pm.

NT = Northern Transport ⓣ207-2025; for the Northern Highway, Orange Walk, Corozal and Chetumal.

PE = Perez Bus For Sarteneja; leaves from the Thunderbolt dock, N Front St at noon & 1pm; also from Courthouse Wharf at 5pm.

RU = Russell's Bus For Bermudian Landing; leaves from Cairo St, near the corner of Cemetery Rd and Euphrates Ave, at noon & 4pm.

ST = Southern Transport ⓣ502-2160; for the Hummingbird and Southern highways and Coastal Road to Dangriga, Placencia and Punta Gorda.

WT = Western Transport ⓣ227-1160; for the Western Highway, Belmopan, San Ignacio and Benque Viejo (for the Guatemalan border).

Destination	Frequency	Bus Company	Duration
Belmopan	at least every 30min 5am–9pm (Exp)	JA, WT, ST	1hr 15min
Benque Viejo (for the Guatemalan border)	every 30min 5am–9pm (Exp)	WT (Novelo's)	3hr 30min

Alternatively, contact the tourism police; see the "Hassle" box on p.59.

Post office The main post office (including parcel office) is on N Front St, immediately north of the Swing Bridge (Mon–Fri 8am–4.30pm).

Telephones There are payphones, which need a phonecard, dotted around the city, or use the main BTL office, 1 Church St (Mon–Sat 8am–6pm), which also has fax facilities and reasonably priced email service. Some hotels have a dedicated phone for guests to use with a phonecard.

Travel and tour agents The following travel agents are the best for information and bookings on flights and connections throughout the region; all can arrange tours within Belize: Belize Global Travel, 41 Albert St (ⓣ227-7363, ⓦwww.belize-global.com), is an agent for most of the international airlines operating in Belize; Belize Travel Adventures, 168 N

Destination	Frequency	Bus Company	Duration
Bermudian Landing	Mon–Sat noon, 4pm & 5pm	MF, RU	1hr 15min
Chetumal, Mexico	hourly 4am–7pm (Exp)	NT	3hr 30min
Corozal	hourly 4am–7pm (Exp)	NT	2hr 30min
Crooked Tree	Mon–Sat 10.30am, 4.30pm & 5.30pm	JX	1hr 30min
Dangriga	12 daily 6am–5pm (Exp)	JA, ST	2hr via Coastal Rd; 3hr 30min via Belmopan
Gales Point	Mon–Sat 5pm	ST	1hr 40min
Maskall (for Altun Ha)	Mon–Sat 4pm	NT	1hr 30min
Orange Walk	hourly 5am–7pm (Exp)	NT	1hr 30min
Placencia	2–3 daily, all via Belmopan; change at Dangriga	ST	6–7hr
Punta Gorda	6–7 daily, all via Dangriga (Exp)	JA, ST	6–8hr
San Ignacio	every 30min 5am–9pm (Exp), all via Belmopan	NT	2hr 30min
Sarteneja	3–4 daily, via Orange Walk;	PE	3hr 30min

By air

See "Listings" p.73 for details of international and domestic airlines.

Domestic flights: Domestic flights originate from Belize City's Municipal Airport, with dozens of scheduled flights to many destinations. Maya Island Air and Tropic Air operate flights to: Caye Caulker (15–20min) and San Pedro (10min from Caye Caulker), at least hourly from 7am to 5pm; Dangriga (8–10 daily; 25min); Placencia (a further 20min); and Punta Gorda (another 20min). See Basics p.29 for further destinations.

International flights: Belize International Airport to: San Salvador (1 daily; 1hr 30min); Flores, for Guatemala City (2–4 daily; 45min); Roatán (1 daily; 1hr 45min); and San Pedro Sula (1 daily; 1hr). See Basics p.29 for further information.

By boat

Scheduled **boats to Caye Caulker** leave from the Marine Terminal on N Front St by the Swing Bridge (roughly every two hours 8am–5.30pm; 45min; Bz$20 one way, Bz$35 same-day return; ☎223-1969); many of these services also continue to **San Pedro, Ambergris Caye**, and will call at St George's Caye on request. Other boats to these cayes leave from Courthouse Wharf and from the Fort Street Tourism Village. For more detail on boat schedules see the boxes on pp.113 & 128.

Note: a van leaves Belize City at 6am on Fridays for Placencia to connect with the *Gulf Cruzer*, a fast boat to **Puerto Cortés**, Honduras (3hr, US$50); to book call ☎202-4506 or check with Petty Cervantes in the Mundo Maya Deli in the Marine Terminal (☎223-1235).

Front St (☎223-3064, ⓦwww.belize-travel.net) is a rep for the Mundo Maya organization, linking tours in the surrounding countries; Belize Trips (☎223-0376 or 610-1923, ⓦwww.belize-trips.com) is run by Katie Valk, a very experienced Belize travel specialist; Maya Travel Services, 42 Cleghorn St (☎223-1623, ⓦwww.mayatravelservices.com), are inbound travel experts, very knowledgeable about tours and hotels within Belize; Travel and Tour Belize, 83 Freetown Rd (☎223-7604, ⓦwww.traveltourbelize.com), is a branch of the San Pedro-based agency, with the same excellent service; and Mopan Travels, in the *Hotel Mopan* (☎227-7351), arranges tours throughout Belize.

Western Union Belize Chamber of Commerce, 63 Regent St ☎227-0014.

The north

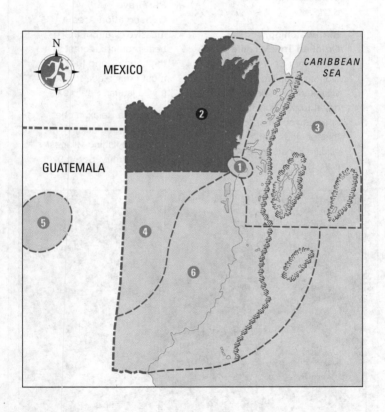

CHAPTER 2

Highlights

✳ **Bermudian Landing**
Guaranteed close-ups
of the black howler
monkey – the largest
primate in the New
World – in this friendly
village on the banks of
the Belize River. **See
p.81**

✳ **Bird-watching,
Crooked Tree Wildlife
Sanctuary** Spend the
night in Crooked Tree
village and get up at
dawn to see how many
species you can spot in
this fabulous wetland
wildlife sanctuary. **See
p.84**

✳ **Lamanai** Take a boat
ride along the tranquil
and beautiful New River
to reach this astonishing
Maya city, with some
wonderfully restored
temples. **See p.91**

✳ **Rio Bravo
Conservation Area** A
massive swath of the
best-protected forest in
the country, and the
most likely place to spot
a wild jaguar. **See p.94**

✳ **Sarteneja** Relax in one
of the few remaining
authentic fishing villages
in the country. **See p.97**

△ Black howler monkey

2

The north

Northern Belize is an expanse of relatively level land where swamps, savannahs and lagoons are mixed with rainforest and farmland. For many years this part of the country was largely inaccessible and had closer ties with Mexico than Belize City – most of the original settlers were refugees from the Caste Wars in Yucatán, and brought with them the sugarcane which formed the basis of the economy for much of the twentieth century. The Indian and Mestizo farming communities were connected by a skeletal network of dirt tracks, while boats plied the route between Belize City and Corozal. In 1930, however, the Northern Highway brought the region into contact with the rest of the country, opening up the area to further waves of settlers.

The largest town in the north is **Orange Walk**, the main centre for sugar production. Further to the north, **Corozal** is a small and peaceful Caribbean town with a strong Mexican element – not surprising as it lies just fifteen minutes from the border. Throughout the north, Spanish is as common as Creole, and there's a distinctive Latin flavour to both of these places.

Most visitors to northern Belize are here to see the **Maya ruins** and wildlife reserves. The largest site, **Lamanai**, features some of the most impressive pyramids in the country; it's served by regular boat tours along the New River and a good road to the nearby village of Indian Church. East of Lamanai, **Altun Ha**, reached by the old Northern Highway, is usually visited as part of a daytrip from Belize City or San Pedro. Other sites include Cuello and Nohmul, respectively west and north of Orange Walk, and Santa Rita and Cerros, both near Corozal.

The four main **wildlife reserves** in the region each offer a different approach to conservation and an insight into different environments. At the **bermudian Landing Community Baboon Sanctuary** in the Belize River valley a group of farmers have combined agriculture with conservation, much to the benefit of the black howler monkey, while at the **Crooked Tree Wildlife Sanctuary** a network of lagoons and creeks offers protection to a range of migratory birds, including the endangered jabiru stork. By far the largest and most ambitious conservation project is the **Rio Bravo Conservation Management Area**, comprising 970 square kilometres of tropical forest and river systems in the west of Orange Walk District. This vast, practically unspoilt area, containing several Maya sites, adjoins the borders with Guatemala and Mexico. The most northerly protected area is the **Shipstern Nature Reserve**, where a large area of tropical hardwood forest, mangroves and wetland is preserved with the help of a Swiss-based conservation organization.

Hattieville (7km) ▼   ▼ Belmopan & San Ignacio

Getting around the north

Travelling around the north is fairly straightforward if you stick to the main roads. Northern Transport operates bus services every hour from 4am to 7pm along the Northern Highway between Belize City and Santa Elena on the Mexican border, calling at Orange Walk and Corozal, and continuing across the border to the market in Chetumal. Smaller roads and centres are served by a fairly regular flow of buses and trucks. Several companies operate tours to the Maya sites and nature reserves, though these can be expensive.

Belize City to Orange Walk

Regular, fast buses run the 88km along the **Northern Highway** from Belize City to Orange Walk in less than an hour and a half. To get to the Bermudian Landing Community Baboon Sanctuary, Crooked Tree Wildlife Sanctuary or the ruins of Altun Ha by public transport, you'll need to take one of the local buses detailed in the text.

The start of the Northern Highway is marked by a roundabout adorned with the flags of the Caricom countries. Leaving Belize City, you pass spreading sub-urbs, where expensive houses are constructed on reclaimed mangrove swamps; look to the east and you'll get a glimpse of the sea. Seven kilometres from the city a metal-framed bridge carries the road over the mouth of the Belize River at the point where the Haulover Creek branches away to the south. For the next few kilometres the road stays very close to the broad river; this stretch is prone to flooding after heavy rain. If you notice a large, brightly painted, concrete building on the right-hand side of the road called Raul's Rose Garden you may care to know that it's not a nursery in the horticultural sense but a brothel. At **Ladyville**, 15km from Belize City, you pass the turn-off to the international airport; another kilometre brings you to the branch road to Airport Camp, now run by the Belize Defence Force, and the main base of the British forces in Belize.

Take either the first or second left turns along the branch road to the airport for a few hundred metres and you'll be on the riverbank, just downstream from the peaceful *Belize River Lodge* (T 225-2022, W www.belizeriverlodge.com; packages only, around US$2600 per week for fishing, room and meals), which was originally built as a fishing lodge in the 1960s. Though the place does still specialize in superb fishing packages, with a renowned reputation for the quality and service of guiding, tours and food, it's also a great base for visiting inland Belize. The neat and spacious wooden cabins have comfortable furniture, panelled walls, private bathroom, a/c and fan, and a huge screened porch with fantastic river views. Owners Mike Heusner and Marguerite Miles know Belize well and do all they can to ensure guests get the most out of a stay here. In addition to several skiffs the *Lodge* has two **live-aboard boats**: the 52ft *Blue Yonder* and the 58ft *Cristina*.

The Bermudian Landing Community Baboon Sanctuary

The **Community Baboon Sanctuary** (W www.howlermonkeys.org), established in 1985 in collaboration with primate biologist Rob Horwich and a group of local farmers (with help from the Worldwide Fund for Nature), is one of the most interesting conservation projects in Belize. A mixture of farmland and broad-leaved forest, the sanctuary stretches along 30km of the Belize River valley – from Flowers Bank to Big Falls – and comprises a total of eight villages and over a hundred landowners. Farmers here have adopted a voluntary code of practice to harmonize their own needs with those of the wildlife in a project combining conservation, education and tourism; visitors are welcome and you'll find plenty of places where you can rent canoes or horses.

The main focus of attention is the **black howler monkey** (locally known as a "baboon"), the largest monkey in the New World and an endangered subspecies of howler that exists only in Belize, Guatemala and southern Mexico. They generally live in troops of between four and eight, and spend the day wandering through the leafy canopy feasting on leaves, flowers and fruits. You're pretty much guaranteed to see them close-up, feeding and resting in the trees along the riverbank and they're often as interested in you as you are in them. At dawn and dusk they let rip with their famous howl, a deep and rasping roar that carries for miles.

The conservation programme has proved so successful that conservationists agreed that the existing troops were stable enough to permit some to be relocated to reserves elsewhere in Belize, with the aim of replacing populations formerly wiped out by hunting or disease. In 1992 eighteen black howler monkeys were successfully relocated to the Cockscomb Basin and in 1996 eight monkeys were transferred to the Macal River valley. Both relocations have resulted in howler monkeys breeding in these former parts of their range, and Belize is now considered to be at the forefront of successful primate relocation techniques. Howler numbers in the sanctuary now stand at around 2500 – almost double the number of the people in the villages here.

The sanctuary is also home to around two hundred bird species, plus anteaters, deer, peccaries, coatis, iguanas and the endangered Central American river turtle. Special trails are cut through the forest so that visitors can see it at its best; you can wander these alone or with a guide from the village, and you can also take a guided canoe or horseback trip.

Bermudian Landing

The village of **BERMUDIAN LANDING**, 43km northwest of Belize City, lies at the heart of the area, a Creole village and former logging centre that dates back to the seventeenth century. The turn-off to the village is 23km along the Northern Highway; the rest of the journey is along a road that's paved as far as Burrell Boom (see below), and is also used to access Hill Bank Field Station (see p.96). Regular buses run from Belize City to the village (see box on p.75), and some of the other villages in the sanctuary now have their own bus services, also departing from Belize City. Bear in mind that returning buses for Belize City leave Bermudian Landing early – between 5.30 & 6.30am.

On arrival at Bermudian Landing you'll need to register at the **visitor centre** (daily 8am–4pm; Bz$10) at the western end of the village. The fee includes a short guided trail walk and entry to Belize's first natural history museum, inside the centre, with excellent exhibits and information on the riverside habitats and animals you're likely to see. The education centre, at the rear of the visitor centre, has a library, satellite Internet access and a new payphone. Sanctuary director Jessie Young, who lives nearby, can advise on how to get the most out of a visit; her husband Fallet is the sanctuary tour director, and he can arrange longer guided walks, or canoe or horse rental for around Bz$50 a day.

You can **camp** at the visitor centre (Bz$10 per person; check in with manager Iola Joseph) and a number of local families offer **bed-and-breakfast** rooms (❸), a wonderful way to experience village life. Booking can be difficult, as few people have phones (try the community phone on ☎209-2001), though you'll always get somewhere to stay if you just turn up. *Nature Resort*, in a wooded field beside the visitor centre (☎610-1378, ✉naturer@btl.net; ❹–❻), has several beautiful cabins (some thatched), most with private hot-water shower, fridge, fan, coffeemaker and hammocks on the porch. All are good value and it's a great place to relax or follow the trails through the woods and along the river.

The **community restaurant** at the visitor centre, run by the village's women's group, serves delicious Creole meals and there are a couple of other restaurants and **bars** in the village. *Russell's Restaurant*, in the centre of the village (also the place where one of the buses parks for the night), has tables under the thatch overlooking the river.

Burrell Boom

On the way to Bermudian Landing, 6km after the Northern Highway turn-off, you'll pass **BURRELL BOOM**, also on the Belize River. In logging days a huge, heavy metal chain (a boom) was placed across the river to catch the logs floating down – you'll see the chain and the anchors that held it by the roadside on the right as you pass through the village. Though not as attractive as Bermudian Landing, Burrell Boom does have a good hotel, *El Chiclero* (☎225-9005, ✉soffitt@io.com; ❻), with large, tiled, air-conditioned rooms, very comfortable beds, a good restaurant and a pool. If you get the chance, have a chat with the owner, Carl Faulkner, an American expat who can regale you with amazing tales of life in Belize. If you have your own vehicle and are heading directly west you can save time and considerable distance by cutting down through Burrell Boom to Hattieville, on the Western Highway, along a newly paved side road.

Altun Ha

Fifty-five kilometres north of Belize City and just 9km from the sea is the impressive Maya site of **Altun Ha** (daily 8am–5pm; Bz$10), occupied for around twelve hundred years until the Classic Maya collapse between 900 and 950 AD. Its population peaked at about 10,000 inhabitants. The site was also occupied at various times throughout the Postclassic, though no new monumental building took place during this period. Its position close to the Caribbean coast suggests that it was sustained as much by trade as agriculture – a theory upheld by the discovery of trade objects such as jade and obsidian, neither of which occurs naturally in Belize and both very important in Maya ceremony. The jade would have come from the Motagua valley in Guatemala and much of it would probably have been shipped onwards to the north.

Around five hundred buildings have been recorded at Altun Ha but the core of the site is clustered around two Classic period plazas, with the main structures extensively restored, exposing fine stonework with rounded corners. Entering from the road, you come first to **Plaza A**. Large temples enclose it on all four sides, and a magnificent tomb has been discovered beneath Temple A-1, **The Temple of the Green Tomb**. Dating from 550 AD, this yielded a total of three hundred pieces, including jade, jewellery, stingray spines, jaguar skins, flints and the remains of a Maya book. Temple A-6, which has been particularly badly damaged, contains two parallel rooms, each about 48m long and with thirteen doorways along an exterior wall.

The adjacent **Plaza B** is dominated by the site's largest temple, B-4, **The Temple of the Masonry Altars**, the last in a sequence of buildings raised on this spot. If it seems familiar, it's because you might already have seen it on the Belikin beer label. The temple was probably the main focus of religious ceremonies, with a single stairway running up the front to an altar at the top; visitors must climb the wooden stairway at the side. Several priestly tombs have been uncovered within the main structure, but most of them had already been desecrated, possibly during the political turmoil that preceded the abandonment of the site. Only two of the tombs were found intact; in 1968 archeologists discovered a carved jade head of **Kinich Ahau**, the Maya sun god, in one of them. Standing just under 15cm high, it is the largest carved jade found anywhere in the Maya world. At the moment it's kept hidden away in the vaults of the Belize Bank, though there is a splendid replica in the Museum of Belize, Belize City (see p.67).

Outside these two main plazas are several other areas of interest which a good guide will point out, though little else has been restored. A short trail through the B Group leads south to **Rockstone Pond**, a literal translation of the Maya name of the site and also the present-day name of a nearby village. The pond was dammed in Maya times to form a

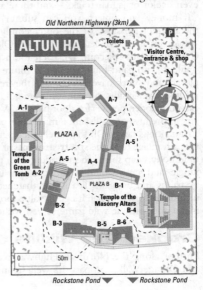

reservoir (today it's home to a large crocodile); at the eastern edge stands Structure F-8 (Reservoir Temple) the oldest building at Altun Ha. Built in the second century AD, it housed a cache that contained green obsidian blades and other offerings imported from the great city of Teotihuacán in the Valley of Mexico. These artefacts have been dated to around 150 AD, evidence of early contact between the lowland Maya and Teotihuacán.

Practicalities

Altun Ha is fairly difficult to reach independently as the track to the site is located along the Old Northern Highway and is not well served by buses. Any travel agent in Belize City will arrange a tour (see "Listings" p.74) and increasing numbers make the visit as part of a day-trip from San Pedro (see p.111). In theory there are buses from Novelo's terminal in Belize City (Mon–Sat, 4pm) to the village of **MASKALL** (where there's a reasonable possibility of getting a room; try calling the community phone on ☏209-1058), passing the turn-off to the site at the village of **LUCKY STRIKE**, 3km from Altun Ha (community phone ☏209-1017), but the service is erratic and unreliable. It's worth calling the community phones above to see if the transport situation has improved – though there is enough traffic to make hitching possible.

The best plan is to **stay nearby** and get to the site before the noise from the tour buses spoils the tranquillity. Despite being a little overpriced, the best accommodation option is *Pueblo Escondido* at Mile 30 1/2, Lucky Strike Village, 3km from the turn-off to the site (☏614-1458, ⓦwww.pueblo-escondido.net; ❹, camping Bz$20 per person); look for the *Fyah Haat* ("fire hearth" in Creole) **restaurant**. The place consists of thatched, screen-sided huts and rooms in a main cabin – all a bit pricey for singles, but owners Lloyd Pandy and Carla Barnett will give a discount for a package with meals. They also offer horse riding on jungle trails and bike rental; you can even ride to the site in a horse-drawn carriage. The name *Pueblo Escondido* is Spanish for "hidden village" (or "hidden people"), and it's a wonderful wildlife haven, complete with lagoons where tapirs bathe. You'll have a good chance of seeing otters and foxes, maybe even ocelot or jaguar tracks – and there are always lots of birds.

If money's no object, you can submit to the hedonistic (and undoubtedly therapeutic) pleasures of the outrageously Californian-style *Maruba Resort and Jungle Spa*, near Maskall at Mile 40, Old Northern Highway (☏322-2199, ⓦwww.maruba-spa.com; ❾). Each room or suite is luxurious, verging on the opulent, with hand-built wooden furniture and feather beds. All rooms have CD-players and suites have DVDs, and they're all decorated individually: some are painted silver inside and out, some are gold – and one does boast larger-than-life carved wooden penises for door handles. With two gorgeous pools, intimate shelters in the lush grounds and a maximum of thirty guests, it's a fabulous place for a romantic getaway. On the purely therapeutic side you'd need to stay a week to take advantage of all the **spa treatments**; if the African honey-bee scrub or mood mud body wrap sound too decadent then perhaps an aromatherapy massage or a jungle sand scrub would be more to your liking. Non-guests can eat surrounded by palms and bougainvillea in the thatched **restaurant**, serving excellent food, including a daily special. It's good value too, considering the setting – though the menu does include wild game, served without the necessary licence.

Crooked Tree Wildlife Sanctuary

Further along the Northern Highway, roughly midway between Belize City and Orange Walk, you pass the well-signposted branch road which heads west

5km to **Crooked Tree Wildlife Sanctuary**, a reserve that takes in a generous area of inland waterways, logwood swamps and lagoons. Founded in 1984 by the Belize Audubon Society and covering twelve square kilometres and four separate lagoons, it was designated Belize's first Ramsar site (after the Ramsar conference on wetlands in Iran) in 1998, as a "wetland habitat of international importance for waterfowl". It's an ideal nesting and resting place for the sanctuary's greatest treasure: tens of thousands of migrating and resident **birds**, including snail kites, tiger herons, snowy egrets, ospreys and black-collared hawks. Representatives of over three hundred bird species (two-thirds of Belize's total) have been recorded here.

The reserve's most famous visitor is the **jabiru stork**, the largest flying bird in the New World, with a wingspan of 2.5m. Belize has the biggest nesting population of jabiru storks at one site; they arrive in November, the young hatch in April or May, and they leave just before the summer rainy season gets under way. The **best time to visit** for bird-watchers is from late February to early June, when the lagoons shrink to a string of pools, forcing wildlife to congregate for food and water. In a good day's bird-watching you can expect to see up to a hundred species. Visitors are welcome to participate in the May jabiru census; contact the Belize Audubon Society (see p.65) for details. If you set off to explore the lagoons you might also catch a glimpse of howler monkeys, crocodiles, coatis, turtles or iguanas.

Crooked Tree village

In the middle of the reserve, connected to the mainland by a causeway, the village of **CROOKED TREE** straggles over a low island in the wetlands. Over 300 years old, it's the oldest inland community in Belize, with an economy based on fishing, farming and, more recently, tourism. The Bz$8 visitor fee is payable in the **Sanctuary Visitor Centre**, at the far end of the causeway. Inside, an amazing diorama displays fantastically lifelike models of the birds, mammals and insects found at Crooked Tree; there's also a good wildlife reference library, with some books for sale. The reserve wardens, Steve and Donald Tillett and Rennie Jones, are excellent guides, hugely knowledgeable about the area's flora, fauna and rural culture. They also have trail maps and give information on accommodation and camping and canoe trips. If you're planning your trip from Belize City, contact David Cunningham, a superb naturalist and avid birder (☎603-6427), who'll take you to Crooked Tree in his air-conditioned van. If you need a guide in the village ask at the visitor centre or at any of the hotels listed on p.86.

Although the main attraction at Crooked Tree – taking guided boat trips through the lagoon and along sluggish, forest-lined creeks – can work out to be quite expensive (upwards of Bz$75 per person, even in a group), it's still worth coming just to enjoy the unbelievably tranquil pace of life in the village. Strolling through the sandy, tree-lined lanes, and along the lakeshore trails you'll see plenty of birds and turtles, to the sound of frogs croaking languidly from the shallows. Villagers are courteous to strangers, and always have time to chat. Guides in the village are supremely knowledgeable, particularly about the many birds you'll encounter in the sanctuary, and impart their expertise with enthusiasm; even the children vie with each other to show off their bird-spotting skills.

Some of the mango and cashew trees here are over 100 years old, and during January and February the air is heavy with the scent of cashew blossom. Since 1993 villagers and visitors have celebrated a **Cashew Festival** during the first week of May; though hardly a tradition in itself (it was started by a US tour company), it does highlight the economic importance of the famous nut, and the music, dance, storytelling and crafts offer a glimpse of village traditions and culture.

Practicalities

There are at least four daily **buses to Crooked Tree** from Belize City. The Jex service (℡225-7017) leaves once daily from Regent Street West (Mon–Sat 10.45am) and thrice daily from the Pound Yard bridge (Mon–Fri 4.30, 5.15 & 8pm); there's usually also a daily Novelo's service (Mon–Fri 4pm); Sunday services are unpredictable but there's enough traffic along the side road from the Northern Highway to make hitching a viable option at any time – any non-express bus along the highway will drop you off at the junction. Returning buses leave early for Belize City (Mon–Sat, between 5.30 & 7am). Phone service is good, with a new **payphone** at the visitor centre and several others around the village. A few stores sell basic supplies (the Jex store, just past the visitor centre, is the biggest) and there are a number of quiet, friendly **restaurants** and **bars** in the village – *3 J's* in the centre serves good Creole meals, while the liveliest bar is the *Riverview*, situated on the lagoon, which has a disco most weekends and occasional live music.

Accommodation

Accommodation at Crooked Tree is either in small family-run hotels or reasonably priced **bed-and-breakfasts** (❸); check at the visitor centre for names. There's also a budget **dorm room** at *Bird's Eye View Lodge* (see below) and all the hotels below have space for camping (around Bz$10 per person). All the places listed can arrange superb guided boat tours through the reserve and have very knowledgeable local guides on site.

Bird's Eye View Lodge ℡205-7027, ⓦwww.birdseyeviewlodge.com. Comfortable rooms in two concrete buildings, right on the lakeshore; rates are higher for upstairs rooms. All rooms have fans and private hot-water bathroom, and some have lake views; there's a dorm room (Bz$30 per person) and family rooms. The food is excellent and the tiny bar on the upstairs deck is a good place to catch the evening breeze. ❺–❻

Paradise Inn ℡225-7044, ⓦwww .adventurecamera.com/paradise. Simple but beautiful thatched cabins with private bath and a deck at the north end of the village just paces from the lake, built by the owner Rudy Crawford, who's now building some larger suites. The bus stops about 500m from the cabins (just let the driver know where you're going); if you call ahead someone will meet you and drive you to the *Inn*.

The hospitality is wonderful and the home-cooked food is great; settle in and relax in a hammock on the deck over the lake. Rudy's sons, Glen and Robert, are two of the best guides in the village. ❺–❻

Sam Tillett's Hotel ℡220-2026 or 614-7920, ⓔsamhotel@btl.net. Near the village centre on the bus route, though not on the lagoon. The best-value hotel in the village, and the garden attracts an amazing variety of birds. Rooms are in a large, thatched cabaña, and have private bath and balcony; the budget room has a shared bathroom. More spacious accommodation is available in two comfortable thatched suites, the wooden Jacana, and the A-frame Jabiru, which has a fridge and a/c; each has a private deck. Sam, known locally as the "king of birds", is a great host. The restaurant serves superb Belizean food. ❸–❺

Around Crooked Tree: Chau Hiix

Visitors to Crooked Tree can benefit from a couple of projects carried out nearby by volunteers from two British-based conservation development organizations, each aiming to promote bird-watching around the lagoon. The first, 3km north of the village, is an amazing 700m-long **boardwalk** supported 1.5m above the swamp on strong logwood posts. You'll need to get there by boat most of the year but in the dry season it's possible to drive. Built in 1997 by a Raleigh team, the walkway allows access through the otherwise impenetrable low forest at the edge of the lagoon and a 7m-high observation tower affords panoramic **views** – a great place to enjoy the sunset.

Chau Hiix ("small cat"), a Maya site on the western shore of the lagoon, has escaped looting and therefore offers potentially revolutionary discoveries to the University of Indiana team currently excavating here. Climbing the nearby **observation tower** (also with a boardwalk), built in 1998 by volunteers from Trekforce Expeditions, will give you a clearer idea of the site, though admittedly much of what you see are just great, forested mounds. A number of burials have been discovered and the findings are currently being analysed. You experience a real thrill of discovery as you wander around the site, particularly if you're with a guide from the village (many of whom have worked on the excavations) as they point out sites of recent finds. Most exposed stonework is covered over at the end of the season, but there are plans to consolidate the structures and make them more accessible to visitors.

Orange Walk and around

With a population approaching 20,000, **ORANGE WALK** is the largest town in the north of Belize and the centre of a busy agricultural region. Though not unattractive, the town itself has only one real attraction – the new House of Culture on the riverbank just north of the centre – and you may prefer to spend the night in Corozal (see p.98), less than an hour to the north. The centre of town is marked by a distinctly Mexican-style formal plaza, shaded by large trees, and the town hall across the main road is called the Palacio Municipal, reinforcing the strong historic links to Mexico. The tranquil, slow-moving **New River**, a few blocks east of the centre, was a busy commercial waterway during the logging days (the Northern Highway wasn't begun until 1925); now it provides a lovely starting point for a visit to the ruins of Lamanai, to which several local operators offer tours (see p.91).

Like Corozal, Orange Walk was founded by Mestizo refugees fleeing from the Caste Wars in Yucatán in 1849, who chose as their site an area that had long been used for logging camps and was already occupied by the local Icaiché (Chichanha) Maya. From the 1850s to the 1870s the Icaiché Maya were in conflict with both the Cruzob Maya, who were themselves rebelling against Mestizo rule in Yucatán (and supplied with arms by British traders in Belize), and with the British settlers and colonial authorities in Belize. The leader of the Icaiché, Marcos Canul, organized successful raids against British mahogany camps, forcing the logging firms to pay "rent" for lands they used, and Canul even briefly occupied Corozal in 1870. In 1872 Canul launched an attack on the barracks in Orange Walk. The West India Regiment, which had earlier retreated in disarray after a skirmish with Canul's troops, this time forced the Icaiché to flee across the Rio Hondo, taking the fatally wounded Canul with them. This defeat didn't end the raids, but the Maya ceased to be a threat to British rule in northern Belize; a small monument opposite the park in Orange Walk commemorates the last (officially the only) battle fought on Belizean soil. Nowadays, the few remaining Icaiché Maya live in the village of Botes, on the Mexican border near the Rio Hondo.

Orange Walk has traditionally thrived on its crops, first with the growth of the sugar (and the consequent rum distillation) and citrus industries, and after the fall in sugar prices, with profits made from marijuana. In the 1990s, however, pressure from the US government forced Belizean authorities to destroy many of the marijuana fields, and today the town has less of a Wild West atmosphere than just a few years ago. The land around the villages of Blue Creek and Shipyard has been developed by **Mennonite** settlers, members of a Protestant religious group many of whom choose to farm without the assistance of modern technology (see box on p.90).

The Banquitas House of Culture

Walk north along Main Street to the imposing bridge over the New River and you'll encounter the **Banquitas House of Culture** (Mon–Fri 8.30am–4pm, Sat 8.30am–1pm; free), another of Belize's excellent new museums and cultural centres. The *banquitas* in the name were the little benches in a riverbank park, used for generations by courting couples and for simply relaxing in the warm evenings. There's still a delightful park here, now with an amphitheatre for outdoor performances, and a pleasant café, but the highlights are in the main building, a renovated former market. A permanent exhibition charts the history of Orange Walk District from Maya times to the present. Well-lit glass cases

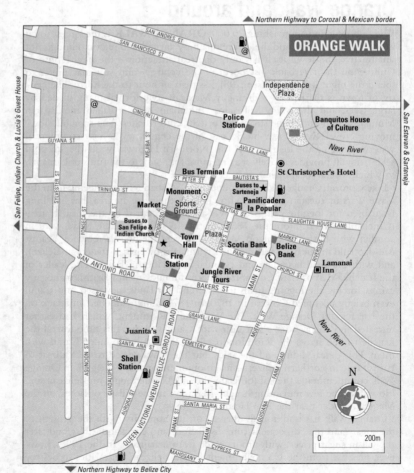

▲ Northern Highway to Corozal & Mexican border

ORANGE WALK

San Felipe, Indian Church & Lucia's Guest House

San Esteven & Sarteneja

SAN ANDRES ST
SAN FRANCISCO ST
CINDERELLA ST
GUYANA ST
SYLVESTER ST
TRINIDAD ST
FONSECA ST
SAN ANTONIO ROAD
SAN LUCIA ST
SANTA ANA ST
ASUNCION ST
GUADALUPE ST
AURORA ST
SANTA MARIA ST
BANAK ST
MAIN ST
MAHOGANY ST
CYPRESS ST
CEMETERY ST
GRAVEL LANE
BAKERS ST
PARK ST
SLAUGHTER HOUSE LANE
MARKET LANE
CHURCH ST
RIVERSIDE ST
FARM ROAD
LOUISIANA
MUEFFEL ST
MAIN ST
DOVER LANE
BEYTIAS ST
BAUTISTA'S
ST PETER ST
SP PETER ST
MEJIBA ST
DUNN ST
PROGRESSO ST
QUEEN VICTORIA AVENUE (BELIZE-COROZAL ROAD)

Independence Plaza

Police Station

Banquitos House of Culture

New River

AVILEZ LANE

St Christopher's Hotel

Bus Terminal

Buses to Sarteneja ★

Monument

Panificadera la Popular

Market

Sports Ground

Buses to San Felipe & Indian Church

Town Hall ★

Plaza

Scotia Bank

Belize Bank

Lamanai Inn

Fire Station

Jungle River Tours

Juanita's

Shell Station

New River

N

0   200m

▼ Northern Highway to Belize City

contain superb artefacts from local Maya sites, and these, together with maps and drawings of the sites themselves, make a visit worthwhile. Other panels display archive material and implements documenting the stories of logwood, mahogany and chicle (the raw ingredient of chewing gum), which tell of the cycles of boom and bust based on extraction of natural resources. Banquitas also hosts art exhibitions and musical events.

Practicalities

Hourly **buses** from Belize City and Corozal pull up on the main road in the centre of town, officially Queen Victoria Avenue but always referred to as the Belize–Corozal Road, and head north on the hour and south on the half-hour. Services to and from Sarteneja (see p.97) stop at Zeta's store on Main Street, two blocks to the east, while local buses to the surrounding villages (including Indian Church, for Lamanai) leave from around the market area, near the centre of town behind the town hall and fire station.

The Belize–Corozal Road is lined with hotels, restaurants and filling stations, so there's no need to walk far. The only recommended **budget hotel**, *Lucia's Guest House*, 68 San Antonio Rd (T322-2244; ❷–❸), has rooms ranging from basic shared bath to private bath with a/c, but by far the best accommodation option in town is the mid-priced *St Christopher's Hotel*, 10 Main St (T322-2420, Erowzbze@btl.net; ❹–❺), which has beautiful, spotless rooms, all with private bath and access to a balcony; some have a/c and fridge. The hotel, set in grounds sweeping down to the river, is run by the friendly Urbina family, who can arrange tours to Lamanai departing from the hotel dock, and there's plenty of secure parking.

The best place to **change money** and get cash advances is the Belize Bank (with ATM) on the corner of Main and Park streets, a block east of the plaza. The **post office** is on the west side of the main road right in the centre of town. **Internet access** in Orange Walk is both cheap and plentiful; K&N Printshop, on the Belize–Corozal Road a block south of the post office, is the most convenient, while Cyberwalk, a kilometre further north, is the fastest.

The majority of **restaurants** in Orange Walk are Chinese, though there are a few Belizean-style places serving simple Creole or "Mexican" food. *Juanita's*, on Santa Ana Street by the Shell station towards the south end of town, has the best Mexican dishes. For Mexican-style *pan dulces* (sweet bread and pastries) and fresh bread, try the *Panificadora la Popular*, on Beytias Street, off the northeast side of the park. The *Lamanai Inn*, on Riverside Street, is a pleasant waterside **bar** with limited food service. Nightlife usually boils down to either the weekend **discos** in the *Mi Amor* or *Victoria* hotels or the numerous bars and clubs dotted around town, some of which serve as brothels. It's also worth checking if there's an event or performance at the House of Culture.

Maya sites around Orange Walk

Although the Maya sites in northern Belize have been the source of a number of the most important archeological finds anywhere in the Maya world, they are not (with the notable exception of Lamanai) as monumentally spectacular as some in Yucatán. The area around Orange Walk has some of the most productive arable farmland in Belize, and this was also the case in Maya times; aerial surveys in the late 1970s revealed evidence of raised fields and a network of irrigation canals, showing that the Maya practised skilful intensive agriculture. In the Postclassic era this region became part of the powerful Maya state of Chactemal (or Chetumal), controlling the trade in cacao beans, which were

Mennonites in Belize

The **Mennonites** arose from the radical Anabaptist movement of the sixteenth century and are named after the Dutch priest Menno Simons, leader of the community in its formative years. Recurring government restrictions on their lifestyle, especially regarding their pacifist objection to military service, forced them to move repeatedly. Having removed to Switzerland they travelled on to Prussia, then in 1663 to Russia, until the government revoked their exemption from military service, whereupon some groups emigrated to North America, settling in the prairies of Saskatchewan. World War I brought more government restrictions, this time on the teaching of German (the Mennonites' language). This, together with more widespread anti-German sentiments in the Dominion and the prospect of conscription, drove them from Canada to Mexico, where they settled in the arid northern state of Chihuahua. When the Mexican government required them to be included in its social security programme it was time to move on again. An investigation into the possibility of settling on their own land in British Honduras brought them to the British colony of Belize in 1958.

They were welcomed enthusiastically by the colonial authorities, eager to have willing workers to clear the jungle for agriculture. Perseverance and hard work made them successful farmers, and in recent years prosperity has caused drastic changes in their lives. The Mennonite Church in Belize is increasingly split between the *Kleine Gemeinde* – a modernist section who use electricity and power tools, and drive trucks, tractors and even cars – and the *Altkolonier* – traditionalists who prefer a stricter interpretation of their beliefs. Members of the community, easily recognizable in their denim dungarees and straw hats, can be seen trading their produce and buying supplies every day in Orange Walk and Belize City.

used as currency and grown in the valleys of the Hondo and New rivers. For a while the Maya here were even able to resist the conquistadores, and long after nominal Spanish rule had been established in 1544 there were frequent Maya rebellions: in 1638, for example, they drove the Spanish out and burned the church at Lamanai.

Cuello and Nohmul

Cuello is a small Maya site 5km west of Orange Walk. It was excavated in 1973 by Norman Hammond, who found structures dating back to 1000 BC, making it one of the earliest sites from the Middle Preclassic Maya lowlands. That said, the site is more interesting to archeologists than the casual visitor; there's not much to look at except for a single small stepped pyramid (structure 350), rising in nine tiers – a common feature of Maya temples – and several earth-covered mounds.

The ruins are behind a factory where Cuello rum is made; the site is on the Cuello family land, so you should ask permission to visit by phoning ☎322-2141. You can also get a tour of the distillery if you ask. Cuello can be reached by simply walking west from the plaza in Orange Walk for a little under an hour; a taxi to the site costs around Bz$15 each way.

Situated on the Orange Walk–Corozal boundary, 17km north of Orange Walk and just west of the village of San Pablo, **Nohmul** (Great Mound) was a major ceremonial centre with origins in the early Preclassic period, perhaps as early as 900 BC. The city was abandoned before the end of the Classic period, to be reoccupied by newcomers from Yucatán during the Early Postclassic period (known here as the Tecep phase, around 800–1000 AD). The ruins cover a large area, comprising the East and West groups connected by a *sacbe* (causeway), with several plazas around them. The main feature (Structure 2) is an acropolis platform surmounted by a later pyramid which, owing to the site's position on a limestone ridge, is the highest point for miles around. As at so many of Belize's Maya sites, looters have plundered the ruins and, tragically, at least one structure has been demolished for road fill – though as it's one of the sites earmarked for tourism, some structural restoration has taken place.

Nohmul lies amid sugarcane fields 2km west of **San Pablo**, on the Northern Highway. Any bus between Corozal and Orange Walk goes through the village. To visit the site, ask around the village for Estevan Itzab, whose land it's on and who lives in the house on the west side of the highway, across from the water tower at the north end of the village; his son Guillermo will probably be your guide.

Lamanai

Extensive restoration of the ancient structures and a spacious new museum make **Lamanai** (Mon–Fri 8am–5pm, Sat, Sun & holidays 8am–4pm; Bz$10) easily the most impressive Maya site in northern Belize. Lamanai is one of only a few sites whose original Maya name – *Lama'an ayin* – is known; it translates as "Submerged Crocodile", hence the numerous representations of crocodiles. *Lamanai*, however, is a seventeenth-century mistransliteration, which actually means "Drowned Insect". The site was continually occupied from around 1500 BC up until the sixteenth century, when Spanish missionaries built a church alongside to lure the Indians from their heathen ways. More than seven hundred structures have been mapped by members of the Lamanai Archeological Project, the majority of them still buried beneath mounds of earth, and the site extends far north and south of the restored area.

Archeological research is undertaken every year here and you can join in the excavations, supervised by archeologist Laura Howard, director of the non-profit **Lamanai Field Research Center** (LFRC; Ⓦ www.lamanai.org). Since students stay at *Lamanai Outpost Lodge* (see "Practicalities", p.93) these courses are fairly expensive, working out to around US$2200 for four weeks. The LFRC also arranges courses at the Las Cuevas Research Station, in the Chiquibul Forest (see p.183).

The site

Lamanai's setting on the bank of the New River Lagoon, in a vast Archeological Reserve which is the only jungle for miles around, give it a special quality that is long gone from sites served by a torrent of tourist buses – though increasing numbers of speedboats now carry cruise ship visitors here. Staying overnight enables you to visit in the quieter times as soon as the site opens and after the crowds have left. Over a dozen troops of **black howler monkeys** make Lamanai their home and you'll certainly see them peering down through the branches as you wander the trails; mosquitoes too, will be ever-present, so you'll need to be armed with a good repellent. Many trees and other plants bear name labels in English, Creole and Maya, and your guide will explain what the ancient Maya used them for.

The most impressive feature at Lamanai, prosaically named N10-43 (informally called the "High Temple", or "El Castillo", the castle), is a massive **Late Preclassic temple**, towering 35m above the forest floor. When first built, around 100 BC, it was the largest structure in the entire Maya world, though one which was extensively modified later. The view across the surrounding forest and along the lagoon from the top of the temple is magnificent – and well worth the daunting climb. On the way to the High Temple you pass N10-27, a much smaller pyramid, at the base of which stands a fibreglass replica of **Stela**

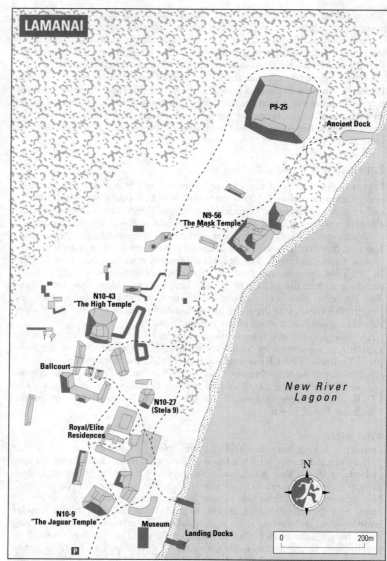

LAMANAI

P9-25

Ancient Dock

N9-56
"The Mask Temple"

N10-43
"The High Temple"

Ballcourt

New River
Lagoon

N10-27
(Stela 9)

Royal/Elite
Residences

N

N10-9
"The Jaguar Temple"

Museum

Landing Docks

0   200m

P

Old Sugar Mill (250m)   ▼ Spanish Colonial Church (200m), Lamanai Outpost Lodge (1.5km) and Indian Church Village (2km)

9, bearing some of the best-preserved carvings at Lamanai. Dated to 625 AD, it shows the magnificently attired Lord Smoking Shell participating in a cere-mony – probably his accession. This glyph has become emblematic of Lamanai and features on many of the T-shirts on sale here. At the northern end of the site, structure N9-56 is a sixth-century pyramid with two stucco masks of a glorified ruler represented as a deity (probably Kinich Ahau, the sun god) carved on different levels. The lower mask, 4m high, is particularly well preserved, showing a clearly humanized face wearing a crocodile headdress and bordered by decorative columns. The temple overlies several smaller, older buildings, the oldest of which is a superbly preserved temple from around 100 BC, and there are a number of other well-preserved and clearly defined glyphs.

The spacious new **archeological museum** at the site houses an amazing collection of artefacts, arranged in chronological order; the majority of these are figurines depicting gods and animals, particularly crocodiles. The most beautiful exhibits are the delicate eccentric flints – star and sceptre-shaped symbols of office – skilfully chipped from a single piece of flint. The most unusual items are a drum the size and shape of a pair of binoculars and a phallus carved from a manatee bone. Traces of later settlers can also be seen around the site: immediately to the south of the museum are the ruins of two churches built by Spanish missionaries, while a short trail behind the museum leads west to the remains of a nineteenth-century sugar mill, built by Confederate refugees from the American Civil War. These refugees settled in several places in Belize, in an attempt to recreate the antebellum South using indentured labourers in place of slaves – but their effort failed, and within a decade most had returned to the States.

Practicalities

Getting to Lamanai is relatively easy. Buses for **INDIAN CHURCH**, 2km from the site (Mon, Wed & Fri, 3.30pm; Bz$5), leave from the street next to the market, behind the town hall, in Orange Walk. The bus is based in the village, leaving for Orange Walk at 5.30am on the same days, so you'll have to stay overnight; you can check bus times by calling the community phone in Indian Church on ☏309-3015. The most pleasant way to get here though is by river, and a number of operators organize **day-trips** for US$40–50 per person, departing around 9am; the price will usually include a picnic lunch at the site. By far the most informative are those by Jungle River Tours, run by Antonio, Wilfrido and Herminio Novelo and based in Orange Walk at the *Lover's Restaurant* (☏302-2293, ✉lamanaimayatour@btl.net), which, unfortunately, is now one of Orange Walk's many brothels. In addition to their extensive knowledge of Maya sites, the Novelos are also wildlife experts, and will point out the lurking crocodiles and dozens of species of birds that you might otherwise miss.

To get to Lamanai by road **in your own vehicle**, head to the south end of Orange Walk and turn right (west) by Dave's Store, where a signpost gives the distance to Lamanai as 35 miles. Continue along the Yo Creek road as far as San Felipe, where you should bear left for the village of Indian Church, 2km from the ruins. *Lamanai Outpost Lodge*, on the lakeshore at the end of the road from the village, has a private **airstrip**, and Tropic Air (☏224-5671) offers flights if there's sufficient demand.

If you want to **stay** in Indian Church (and you'll have to if you're travelling by bus), there are a couple of places offering **rooms** (❸), though they're rather overpriced for what you get. You could try asking in the new Artisan Center, where you can see villagers making attractive jewellery and other craft items, if someone can rent you a room or let you **camp**; you can always eat with the family.

Excellent **upmarket accommodation** is available nearby in the well-run and very comfortable wooden thatched cabañas at *Lamanai Outpost Lodge* (☏223-3578, ⓦwwww.lamanai.com; ❾), set in extensive gardens sweeping down to the lagoon just south of the site. Each cabaña has 24hr electricity, hot water and a private deck; guests enjoy free Internet access in the dining room lobby, where there's also an extensive library. The restaurant, *Bushey's Place*, serves fantastic meals and has a wooden deck overlooking the water. Guests can use the free canoes or take a "moonlight safari" (US$45) to spot nocturnal wildlife; guides here are some of the best in Belize and the lagoon offers superb birding.

The Rio Bravo Conservation Management Area

In the far northwest of Orange Walk District is the **Rio Bravo Conservation Management Area**, a large tract of land designated for tropical forest conservation, research and sustained-yield forest harvests. This astonishing conservation success story actually began with a disastrous plan in the mid-1980s to clear the forest, initially to fuel a wood-fired power station and later to provide Coca-Cola with frost-free land to grow citrus crops. Environmentalists were alarmed, and their strenuous objections forced Coca-Cola to drop the plan, though the forest remained threatened by agriculture.

Following this, a project to save the forest by purchasing it – known as the **Programme for Belize** (PFB) – was initiated by the Massachusetts Audubon Society and launched in 1988. Funds were raised from corporate donors and conservation organizations but the most widespread support was generated through an ambitious "adopt-an-acre" scheme, enthusiastically taken up by schools and individuals in the UK and North America. Coca-Cola itself, anxious to distance the company from charges of rainforest destruction, has donated more than 360 square kilometres of its own land.

Today, rangers with powers of arrest patrol the area to prevent illegal logging and to stop farmers encroaching onto the reserve with their *milpa*s (slash and burn fields). The guarded boundaries also protect dozens of Maya sites, most of them unexcavated and unrestored, though many have been looted.

The **landscape** ranges from forest-covered limestone escarpments in the northwest, near the Guatemalan border, eastwards through the valleys of several rivers, to palmetto savannah, pine ridge and swamp in the southeast around the New River Lagoon. The Rio Bravo area has 240 endemic tree species, and the forest teems with **wildlife**, home to seventy mammal species, including all five of Belize's large cats, tapirs, monkeys and crocodiles, plus four hundred bird species – almost ninety percent of Belize's total. The strict ban on hunting, enforced for over fifteen years now, makes the Rio Bravo and Gallon Jug (see p.96) area the best place in Belize to actually see these beasts; even pumas and jaguars are fairly frequently spotted. Adjoining the Rio Bravo to the south, the privately owned land of **Gallon Jug** also contains a large area of protected land, in the centre of which is the fabulous *Chan Chich Lodge*, regarded as one of the best eco-lodges in the world and an incredibly beautiful place to stay.

There's **no public transport** to the Rio Bravo Conservation Management Area, but if you want to visit or stay at either of the **field stations** see opposite; or, for more information, see the PFB entry in "Conservation", p.324. Getting here from Orange Walk means you have to pass through the modern Mennonite settlement of **Blue Creek**, high up on the Rio Bravo escarpment. Here you'll find one of the most astonishing artefacts in Belize: the fuselage and more of a **Super Constellation**, the world's first real airliner. How it reached its final resting place is a fascinating story; the brief version is as follows. On the Constellation's last flight from Mexico to Guatemala City, in the mid-1970s, it first lost a propeller, then two other engines cut out. The pilot attempted an emergency landing at Belize City but on the final approach the port undercarriage failed to operate and the aircraft skidded off the runway. If you're an aviation buff, call in at Abe Dyck's house, next to the still powerfully evocative remains of the airliner, and he'll show you around and fill you in on the rest of the details.

In the valley below, the Rio Hondo forms the boundary with Mexico. The border crossing here is at present only for use by Belizeans, who pole canoes over to the Mexican village of **La Unión**, where a brisk trade in cigarettes and beer fuels the local economy. There's a customs post but no immigration, though if you stroll down to the riverbank you can join in the negotiations if you have some *pesos*.

La Milpa and Hill Bank field stations

One of the aims of the Programme for Belize is environmental education; as such, **field stations** have been built at **La Milpa** and **Hill Bank** to accommodate both visitors and students – at present these are the only places to stay in the Rio Bravo Conservation Management Area, though more are planned. Both are quite difficult to get to but, with your own vehicle, either could be visited on a day-trip, or you might be able to get a ride in with a ranger or one of the other staff; see below for contact details.

Each field station has comfortable (though expensive) **dorms** (US$88 per person), and the facilities utilize the latest "green" technology, including solar power and composting toilets; La Milpa also has beautiful thatched **cabañas** with private baths and a loft bedroom (sleeps up to six; US$103 per person; discounts for student groups). Prices include three meals and two excursions or lectures a day and each station also has a natural history library. To visit or stay at either station contact the appropriate station manager (Ramon Pacheco at La Milpa, Rudolph Williams at Hill Bank) through the PFB office, 1 Eyre St, Belize City (☎227-5616, ℻227-5635, ✉pfbel@btl.net), who will arrange transport.

La Milpa: the field station and Maya site

Set in a former *milpa* (maize field) clearing in the higher, northwestern forest, **La Milpa Field Station** has a tranquil, studious atmosphere; deer and ocellated turkeys feed contentedly around the cabins, grey foxes slip silently through the long grass and vultures circle lazily overhead. There are binoculars and telescopes for spotting birds and you'll see turtles from the boardwalk bridge over the pond. Guests are mainly students on tropical ecology courses, though anyone can stay. A day-visit to the field station, which includes a guided tour of La Milpa ruins or one of the trails costs US$20, but getting here on public transport is not easy; you'll have to get a bus from Orange Walk to San Felipe, 37km away, and arrange to be picked up there – the PFB office will give details. To get here in your own vehicle, take the road west from Orange Walk via San Felipe to the Mennonite village of Blue Creek. Beyond there the road is paved and in good condition, climbing steeply up the Rio Bravo escarpment, then turning south to the field station and Gallon Jug. Charter flights use the airstrips at Blue Creek and Gallon Jug.

Five kilometres west of the field station is the huge, Classic **Maya city of La Milpa**, the third largest site in Belize. After centuries of expansion, La Milpa was abandoned in the ninth century, though Postclassic groups subsequently occupied the site and the Maya here resisted both the Spanish conquest in the sixteenth century and British mahogany cutters in the nineteenth. The site is currently being investigated as part of a long-term archeological survey by Boston University; recent finds include major elite burials with many jade grave goods. The **ceremonial centre**, built on top of a limestone ridge, is one of the most impressive anywhere, with at least 24 courtyards and two ball-courts. The **Great Plaza**, flanked by four temple-pyramids, is one of the largest public spaces in the Maya world. The tallest structure, the **Great Temple**, rises 24m above the plaza floor, and you can climb the steep, rocky face using roots for handholds and a rope for support. Beyond here are some of the site's *chultunes* – cave-like underground chambers carved out of the rock. For a unique perspective on a *chultun* you can enter one through a collapsed side, view the tightly fitting capstone (similar to a manhole cover) from beneath and ponder what the ancient Maya used them for.

Hill Bank Field Station

At the southern end of the New River Lagoon and 70km west of Belize City, **Hill Bank Field Station** is a former logging camp which has been adapted to undertake scientific forestry research and development. The emphasis here is more on extractive forest use, with the aim of revenue generation on a sustainable basis. Selective logging is allowed on carefully monitored plots; chicle, the base ingredient of chewing gum, is harvested from sapodilla trees; and there's a tree nursery. These and other projects are at the cutting edge of tropical forest management, and there are often students and scientists working here. Some of the Maya sites in the area are currently under investigation by the University of Texas; you can visit them when the archeological teams are working. There's plenty of wildlife around too, particularly birds and crocodiles, and butterflies abound. The **dorms** here (identical to those at La Milpa, p.95) have a screened verandah with table and chairs, overlooking the lagoon. For an even better view, climb the twelve-metre fire tower outside.

There's **no public transport** to Hill Bank, but with your own vehicle you can get here by following the road west and north from Bermudian Landing (see p.82). It's also possible to approach Hill Bank from Lamanai, by boat along the New River Lagoon.

Gallon Jug and Chan Chich Lodge

Forty kilometres south of La Milpa Field Station, the former logging town of **GALLON JUG**, set in neat fenced pastures, is the home of Barry Bowen, reportedly the richest man in Belize. In the 1980s, his speculative land deals led to an international outcry against threatened rainforest clearance. The experience apparently proved cathartic; Bowen is now an ardent conservationist and most of the 500 square kilometres here are strictly protected. The Gallon Jug Estate still has around twenty square kilometres under cultivation and produces the excellent coffee served at the luxurious, world-class **Chan Chich Lodge** (☏223-4419, in US ☏1-800/343-8009, ⓦwww.chanchich.com; ⓞ), the focal point of the estate. The lodge, which regularly wins awards in the travel press, consists of twelve large thatched cabañas (US$200 per double) and suites (US$230 per double) set in the grassy plaza of the Classic Maya site of Chan Chich ("little bird"). It's surrounded by superb forest and there's a refreshing, fully screened pool, complete with waterfall.

The construction of the lodge on this spot (all Maya sites are technically under government control) was controversial at the time, but received Archeology Department approval as it was designed to cause minimal disturbance. Certainly the year-round presence of visitors and staff does prevent looting, which has been a real problem in the past. It is a truly awe-inspiring setting: grass-covered temple walls crowned with jungle tower up from the lodge and the forest explodes with a cacophony of bird calls at dawn. The 14 km of **guided trails** are incomparable and the guides are excellent; day or night wildlife sightings are consistently high, with around seventy jaguar sightings a year, half of them during daylight. You can drive here from Orange Walk (through Blue Creek and La Milpa), but most guests fly in to the airstrip at Gallon Jug; Javier's Flying Service (☎224-5332) has three scheduled flights a week from Belize international or municipal airports.

Sarteneja and the Shipstern Nature Reserve

Until relatively recently, the largely uninhabited **Sarteneja peninsula**, jutting out towards the Yucatán in the northeast of Belize, could only be reached by boat. The entire peninsula is covered with dense forests, swamps and lagoons that support an amazing array of wildlife. The only village is **Sarteneja**, a lobster-fishing centre that's just beginning to experience tourism. The people here are Spanish-speaking Mestizos with close links to Mexico, though most people will also speak English. Although Sarteneja itself, and especially its shoreline, are pretty enough, it's the **Shipstern Nature Reserve**, on the road 5km before you reach the village, which is the main attraction.

Shipstern Nature Reserve

Established in 1981, the **Shipstern Nature Reserve** (daily 8am–5pm; Bz$10 including guided walk) is made up primarily of what's technically known as "tropical moist forest", although it contains relatively few mature trees, as the area was wiped clean by Hurricane Janet in 1955. It also includes some wide belts of savannah – covered in coarse grasses, palms and broad-leaved trees – and a section of the shallow Shipstern Lagoon, dotted with mangrove islands. Taking the superb guided walk along the **Chiclero Trail** from the visitor centre you'll encounter more named plant species in one hour than on any other trail in Belize.

Shipstern, owned and managed by the Swiss-based International Tropical Conservation Foundation, is a bird-watcher's paradise. The lagoon system supports blue-winged teal, American coot, thirteen species of egret and huge flocks of lesser scaup, while the forest is home to fly-catchers, warblers, keel-billed toucans, collared aracari and at least five species of parrot. In addition there are crocodiles, manatees, coatis, jaguars, peccaries, deer, racoons, pumas and an abundance of insects, particularly butterflies. Though the reserve's butterfly farm did not prove as lucrative as hoped, the wardens still tend the butterflies carefully, releasing them into the forest when mature. Visitors can walk around, observing the insect life-cycle from egg to brilliant butterfly – a captivating, reflective experience. Within the reserve, camouflaged observation towers enable you to get good views of the wildlife without disturbing the animals; you'll need to get one of the wardens to guide you to them. All **buses** to Sarteneja (see p.98) pass the entrance to the reserve; the headquarters and **visitor centre** are just 100m from the road.

Sarteneja practicalities

From **SARTENEJA**, guided excursions into the reserve and the surrounding area, either to the many nearby ruins or to seek out wildlife in the lagoons, are easily arranged; ask at where you're staying for the best advice or check Ⓦ www.sarteneja.net. Fernando Alamilla, who runs *Fernando's* (see below) is an excellent fishing guide and can take you across to Bacalar Chico National Park, on Ambergris Caye (see p.123).

Road improvements have made it easier to get to Sarteneja **by bus from Belize City**; the Sarteneja Bus leaves from the Thunderbolt dock on North Front Street at noon and 4pm, Novelo's leaves at 1pm from the main bus terminal and the Perez Bus leaves from Courthouse Wharf at 5pm (all times Mon–Sat; Bz$12). They all pass through Orange Walk ninety minutes later, stopping at Zeta's store on Main Street, where the bus crew takes a break. It's a further ninety minutes to Sarteneja. Novelo's also runs a daily service **from Chetumal to Sarteneja** via Orange Walk, leaving at 1pm. Buses return to Belize City from Sarteneja at 4am, 5am and 6am. The *Thunderbolt*, a skiff running between Corozal and San Pedro on Ambergris Caye, will also stop at Sarteneja if there's sufficient demand (call ☎ 226-2904 to check) and you may be able to get a ride in a sailboat or skiff from Sarteneja to Consejo (see p.102), 13km north of Corozal. Sarteneja's **airstrip** has recently reopened, and flights between Corozal and San Pedro call here on request.

On the seafront, *Fernando's Seaside Guest House* (☎ 423-2085, Ⓔ sartenejabelize@hotmail.com; ❹) is the best **accommodation** option, with very comfortable rooms with private hot-water showers and a thatched rooftop cabaña. *Fernando's* **restaurant** is open if there are enough guests; the thatched *Mira Mar* restaurant on the seafront is the best place to have a **drink**; and several more small bars and restaurants are dotted around the village.

Corozal and around

COROZAL, 45km north of Orange Walk along the Northern Highway, is Belize's most northerly town, just twenty minutes from the Mexican border. Its location near the mouth of the New River enabled the ancient Maya to prosper here by controlling river and seaborne trade, and two sites – Santa Rita and Cerros – are within easy reach. The present town was founded in 1849 by refugees from the massacre in Bacalar, Mexico, who were hounded south by the Caste Wars. Today's grid-pattern town is a neat mix of Mexican and Caribbean, its appearance largely due to reconstruction in the wake of Hurricane Janet in 1955. This is a fertile area – the town's name derives from the cohune palm, which the Maya recognized as an indicator of fecundity – and much of the land is planted with sugarcane.

There's little to do in Corozal apart from visiting the site at Santa Rita, but it's an agreeable place to spend the day on the way to or from the border, and is hassle-free, even at night. There's a breezy shoreline park shaded by palm trees, while on the tree-shaded main plaza, the town hall is worth a look inside for the vivid depiction of local history in a **mural** (recently repainted and updated) in the lobby by local artist Manuel Villamar Reyes. The block west of the plaza was the site of **Fort Barlee**, built in the 1870s to ward off Indian attacks; the brick remains of the fort's corners are preserved as historic landmarks. On October 12, Columbus Day (or Pan-America Day, as it is now known) celebrations in Corozal are particularly lively, Mexican fiesta merging with Caribbean carnival.

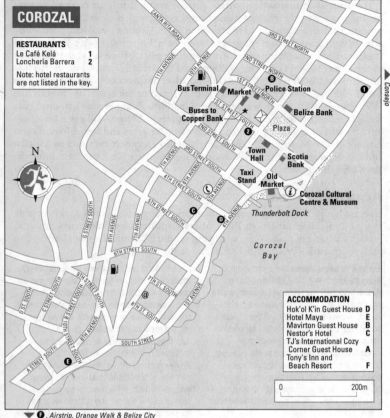

Ruins of Santa Rita (1km) & Mexican border (14km)

COROZAL

RESTAURANTS

| Le Café Kelá | 1 |
| Lonchería Barrera | 2 |

Note: hotel restaurants are not listed in the key.

Bus Terminal
Market
Police Station
Buses to Copper Bank
Belize Bank
Plaza
Town Hall
Scotia Bank
Taxi Stand
Old Market
Corozal Cultural Centre & Museum
Thunderbolt Dock
Corozal Bay

ACCOMMODATION

Hok'ol K'in Guest House	D
Hotel Maya	E
Mavirton Guest House	B
Nestor's Hotel	C
TJ's International Cozy Corner Guest House	A
Tony's Inn and Beach Resort	F

0 — 200m

F, Airstrip, Orange Walk & Belize City

Arrival and information

All **buses** between Belize City and Chetumal pass through Corozal. For the Mexican border (20min) they pass through more or less on the hour from 7am to 9pm; for Belize City (3hr) roughly on the half-hour from 4.30am to 6.30pm. A couple of local companies also operate shuttles to the border, passing the main terminal frequently. The Novelo's bus terminal (☎402-3034) is near the northern edge of town opposite the Shell station, and buses for the surrounding villages (including Copper Bank, see p.103) leave from in front of the market. The skiff *Thunderbolt* provides a **fast boat service** to San Pedro, Ambergris Caye, leaving daily from the dock by the market at 7am (Bz$45 one way/Bz$90 return, 1hr 30min; ☎226-2904). Maya Island Air and Tropic Air operate daily **flights** between Corozal and San Pedro, Ambergris Caye; the airstrip is a few kilometres south of town and taxis (Bz$8 to town) meet all flights. Jal's travel agency (☎422-2163) at the south of town, beyond *Tony's Inn*, can organize both domestic and international flights. If you're in a rush to get to Tikal check at the *Hotel Maya* (see "Accommodation," p.100) for information on the Linea Dorada **express bus from Chetumal to Flores**, which will stop at the hotel if you book ahead.

The **tourist information office** (in the restored former colonial market building just past the present market on the seafront) is closed at the time of writing, though it's scheduled to reopen in 2005. Corozal's well-designed **website**, ⓦ www.corozal.com, produced with help from the town's high-school students, is a good source of information. The **post office** is on the west side of the plaza (Mon–Fri 8.30am–4.30pm) and the Belize Bank, on the north side of the plaza, has an ATM. For broadband **Internet access** visit *Charlotte's Web Cyber Café and Book Exchange*, a few blocks south of the centre at 78 Fifth Ave (Mon–Sat 8.30am–6pm), where owner Charlotte Zahniser also has good coffee, sells maps, books and guides (including *Rough Guides*) and operates a bulletin board. For organized **tours** to local nature reserves and archeological sites, contact Henry Menzies (☎ 422-2725); he's also an expert on travel to Mexico and can arrange tours to the Maya sites in Quintana Roo, the state immediately over the border.

Accommodation

Corozal has plenty of hotel rooms in all price ranges and you'll always be able to find something suitable. At **Four Miles Lagoon**, a few kilometres from the border, a couple of places offer **camping** on the lakeshore; *Lagoon Camping* (no phone) has basic RV sites for Bz$25 and tent sites for Bz$10.

Hok'ol K'in Guest House at the end of 4th St, facing the sea ☎ 442-3329, ⓔ maya@btl.net. Modern hotel near the centre of the seafront with large, tiled private baths and hammocks on the balcony. Some rooms have TV and there's also a shared-bath budget room for Bz$25 per person. The ground floor is completely wheelchair-accessible. Owners Marty Conway and Francisco Puck are very helpful, and the features here, including a restaurant, pleasant gardens, a guest lounge with a book exchange and videos of Belize and a boat for tours, make this a good-value place to stay. ❺

Hotel Maya south end of town, facing the sea ☎ 422-2082, ⓔ stay@hotelmaya.com. Clean, well-run and good-value hotel. All rooms have private bath, some have a/c and cable TV and there's a one-bedroom furnished apartment. Refreshing sea views from the upstairs balcony and a good restaurant downstairs. Owner Rosita May has extensive local knowledge and is an agent for Maya Island Air and the Linea Dorada bus from Chetumal to Flores, which stops right outside. Accepts Visa/MC. ❺–❻

Mavirton Guest House 16 2nd St North ☎ 422-3365, ⓔ mavirton@btl.net. Quiet, family-run hotel with basic rooms, most with private bath. Small bar and restaurant and a payphone for guests. ❸–❹

Nestor's 123 5th Ave South, between 4th and 5th streets ☎ 422-2354, ⓔ nestorshotel@belizemail.net. Acceptable, though fairly basic, rooms, with private baths, but no single rates. Popular sports bar and restaurant downstairs. ❹

TJ's International Cozy Corner Guest House at the end of 2nd St North ☎ 422-0150, ⓦ www.corozal.bz/tj. Six blissfully comfortable, very well-furnished and great-value a/c rooms with private bath, set in beautiful gardens on the edge of town – but still only a 15min walk from the centre. Owners Carlos Mario Bovio and Darlene Bartlett really make you feel at home and have lots of useful information. The restaurant is one of the best in town, and well worth the walk up here. ❺

Tony's Inn and Beach Resort on the seafront, 1.5km south of the plaza ☎ 422-2055, ⓦ www.tonysinn.com. A touch of well-run luxury in a superb location with secure parking. The spacious rooms (most with a/c) with king-sized beds overlook landscaped gardens and a pristine beach bar, and the hotel's *Vista del Sol* and *Y-Not Grill* restaurants are excellent. Internet access for guests and tours and car rental arranged. ❻

Eating

Whatever your budget, most of the best **meals** in Corozal are to be found in the hotels. The popular bar at *Nestor's* serves American and Belizean food, while the *Hotel Maya* serves very good Belizean dishes in a quieter environment. There's a wonderful restaurant at *Tony's*, and *TJ's* serves great American, Belizean and Mexican meals to appreciative locals and expats.

△ Mask at Lamanai

Outside of these places, the *Lonchería Barrera*, just off the southwest corner of the plaza, serves tasty, inexpensive Mexican-style dishes, and there is the usual complement of Chinese restaurants. The best stand-alone restaurant in town is *Le Café Kelá*, on the seafront just north of the centre, run by French couple Stephan and Marguerite Moerman. The food is authentic, delicious and good-value French cuisine, cooked to order and well worth the wait, served beneath a thatched roof in a lovely garden; they also have pizza and Belizean specials. Stephan is also a tour guide and this is a good place to pick up information.

Santa Rita

Of the two small Maya sites within reach of Corozal, the closest is **Santa Rita** (daily 8am–5pm; Bz$10), about fifteen minutes' walk northwest of the town. Follow the main road in the direction of the border and when it divides take the left-hand fork, which soon brings you to the hospital, the power plant and the raised Maya site; the warden will show you around once you've signed in.

Founded as a small settlement around 1800 BC, Santa Rita appears to have been continuously occupied until the arrival of the Spanish, by which time it was in all probability the powerful Maya city known as Chactemal (Chetumal), which dominated the trade of the area. It was certainly still a thriving city in 1531 AD, when the conquistador Alonso Davila entered the town, which had been tactically abandoned by the Maya; he was driven out almost immediately by Na Chan Kan, the Maya chief, and his Spanish adviser Gonzalo Guerrero. Pottery found here has connected Santa Rita with other sites in Yucatán. Structure 1 contained superb Postclassic Mixtec-style murals similar to those found at Tulum, in Quintana Roo, but the building was bulldozed in the late 1970s. Due to this destruction, and the strong possibility that much of the ancient city is covered by present-day Corozal, the only remains of Santa Rita visible today are a few mounds and Structure 7, a fairly small, though attractive, pyramid. Burials excavated here include that of an elaborately jewelled elderly woman, dated to the Early Classic period, and the tomb of a Classic period warlord, buried with the symbols of his elite status.

Consejo

The tiny village of **CONSEJO**, on the end of a peninsula eleven kilometres northeast of Corozal, is perhaps an unlikely site for an upmarket retirement community, which may be why many of the lots in nearby Consejo Shores are still unsold. That said, the few villagers and retirees who are here do live in an idyllic spot on the palm-lined Corozal Bay. Consejo has a few hotels and a couple of simple bars and restaurants, enabling you to experience the utterly peaceful way of life here. The best **place to stay** is right on the beach in one of the comfortable, well-designed and great-value thatched bungalows at *The Smuggler's Den* (☎614-8146, ⓦsmugglersdenbelize.tripod.com; ❹), all with hot-water bathroom, kitchen and TV. The three-storey wood-and-thatch **restaurant** here (Fri, Sat & Sun noon–8pm, other times by reservation), is also the best in the area, serving very tasty Belizean and American dishes and a Sunday lunch special. In the village itself, *Derek's Cozy Corner Bar* provides some local colour in a quiet setting.

Cerros and Copper Bank

On a peninsula jutting from the southern shore of Corozal Bay, the remains of the Preclassic centre of **Cerros** were until recently only accessible by boat.

Though you can still find boats and guides here (ask at one of Corozal's hotels), a new road starting at *Tony's Inn* (see "Accommodation", p.100) and a free cable-winched ferry at Pueblo Nuevo allows cheaper and easier access to the site. The best place to stay for Cerros is **COPPER BANK** village, where there's excellent **budget accommodation** (see below). A **bus** (Mon–Sat 11am, also Mon, Wed & Fri 3.30pm; 30min) leaves for Copper Bank from the market in Corozal, returning at 6.30am Mon–Sat and 1.30pm Mon, Wed & Fri; buses also leave the village for Orange Walk (1hr) at roughly the same times. The bus stops at the end of the village on the shore of the beautiful Laguna Seca and you can easily rent a bike from any of the villagers for the 20min ride through the forest to Cerros along a level road.

Before visiting the site, leave your luggage and have lunch at *The Last Resort* (☎606-1585, ✉donnaflores25@yahoo.ca; ❸–❺), set in shady gardens on the lakeshore 200m along the signposted path from where the bus stops. It's also a wonderfully relaxing place to stay, with clean, simple, whitewashed thatched cabins with electricity, mosquito-netted beds and a hammock on the porch. All cabins have toilet and washbasin, some also have hot showers and one cabin has kitchen facilities. They also have space for **camping** (❶) and RVs, a good restaurant, Internet access and a library/paperback exchange, and the owners can arrange boat trips on the lagoon and along other local rivers and lagoons.

The site

Its strategic position at the mouth of the New River enabled **Cerros** (daily 8am–5pm; Bz$10) to dominate the regional water-borne trade, and it was one of the earliest places in the Maya world to adopt the rule of kings. Beginning around 50 BC it grew explosively from a small fishing village to a major city in only two generations. A kilometre-long canal bordered the central area, providing drainage to the town and the raised field system that supported it. Despite initial success, however, Cerros was abandoned by the Classic period, eclipsed by shifting trade routes. The site includes three large acropolis structures, ballcourts and plazas flanked by pyramids. The largest structure is a 22-metre-high temple, with superb views over to Corozal from the summit. The temple's intricate stucco masks, representing the rising and setting sun, and Venus as morning star and evening star, are presently covered to prevent erosion, but restoration schemes are planned. The **visitor centre** also has good displays and drawings of the structures at Cerros.

The Mexican border crossing

Heading into Mexico, all northbound Northern Transport buses will take you to either the **bus terminal** in Chetumal (with plenty of onward express buses along the Quintana Roo coast to Cancún) or the nearby market. The whole journey from Corozal takes under an hour, including the border crossing. The route takes you to the new **Santa Elena border crossing** on the Belizean side of the Rio Hondo and after you've cleared Belize immigration (paying the Bz$30 exit and the Bz$7.50 PACT conservation tax), the bus carries you to the Mexican immigration and customs posts on the northern bank.

Border formalities for entering Mexico are very straightforward and few Western nationalities need a visa; simply pick up and fill out your **Mexican tourist card**. If you want visa advice, check with the Mexican consulate in Belize City (see "Listings", p.73). There's no fee to pay for entering Mexico, but at the bottom of your tourist card is a section stating how much (in *pesos*) you'll have to pay at a bank in Mexico before you leave – approximately US$20.

Entering Belize from Mexico is also simple: again, no fee to pay, just fill out the Belize immigration form and you'll be given a maximum of thirty days stay. **Moneychangers** on the Belize side will give reasonable rates changing US or Belize dollars for *pesos*; there aren't any on the Mexican side, and the nearest banks are in Chetumal, where there are ATMs you can use.

In between the two border posts but entirely within Belize you'll pass the **Corozal Free Zone**, a seemingly ever-growing and fairly chaotic area of shopping malls and gas stations designed to attract customers from Mexico to part with their US dollars – officially Belizeans aren't allowed in. Once you've left Belize (the guard will look at your passport stamp) you can enter this low-cost temple of Mammon, if only to wonder how so many shops all selling pretty much the same range of cut-price electrical and household goods, clothes and canned food can survive – definitely worth a look if you've got an hour or two to spare.

Travel details

Buses

Bus company addresses and details of services from Belize City to destinations in the north are given in the box on pp.74–75.

Bermudian Landing to: Belize City (2–3 daily Mon–Sat; 1hr 15min), via Burrell Boom.

Chetumal to: Belize City (hourly; 3hr 30min, express services 3hr), via Corozal and Orange Walk; Sarteneja, (1 daily Mon–Sat at 1pm; 3hr 30min) via Orange Walk.

Corozal to: Belize City (hourly; 2hr 30min), via Orange Walk (1hr); Chetumal (hourly; under 1hr); Copper Bank (Mon–Sat 11am, also 3.30pm Mon, Wed & Fri; 30min).

Crooked Tree to: Belize City (at least 4 daily Mon–Sat; 1hr 30min).

Orange Walk to: Belize City (at least hourly from 4am–8pm; 1hr 30min); Corozal (hourly; 1hr); Indian Church, for Lamanai (3 weekly Mon, Wed & Fri at 3.30pm; 2hr).

Sarteneja to: Belize City (3 daily Mon–Sat; 3hr 30min); to Chetumal (1 daily Mon–Sat; 3hr 30min).

Planes

Maya Island Air (☎226-2345) and Tropic Air (☎226-2012) both operate at least four daily flights between Corozal and San Pedro, calling at Sarteneja; there are no domestic flights from Belize City to either Orange Walk or Corozal.

The northern cayes and atolls

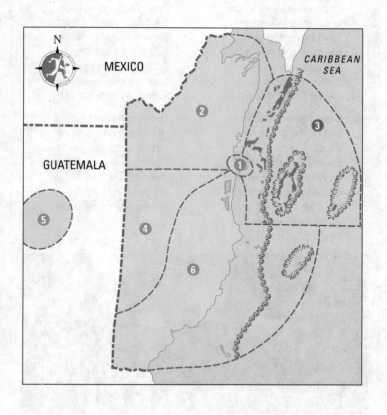

CHAPTER 3 # Highlights

✳ **San Pedro** Sample some of the best food and nightlife in the country in this laid-back former fishing village, made famous by Madonna in her song *La Isla Bonita*. **See p.111**

✳ **Bacalar Chico National Park** Circumnavigate Ambergris Caye on a trip to the remote northern tip of Belize's largest island, visit ancient Maya seaports and enjoy a delicious beach barbecue for lunch. **See p.123**

✳ **Caye Caulker** Go barefoot on the beach, eat delicious, inexpensive meals and snorkel the Barrier Reef offshore; this relaxed island has everything for a perfect Caribbean vacation. **See p.126**

✳ **Lighthouse Reef** Dive or snorkel the unique splendour of the Great Blue Hole, then visit the booby birds on Half Moon Caye, arguably Belize's most enchanting island. **See p.132**

✳ **Sail the Caribbean** Spend a glorious, funfilled day aboard a handsome wooden boat on a sailing trip from Caye Caulker, returning at dusk to enjoy a happy hour drink. **See p.133**

✳ **Turneffe Islands** Take a dive trip during the day or stay overnight on Belize's largest atoll and marvel at the marine life in this nearly pristine environment. **See p.137**

△ San Pedro at Dusk

The northern cayes and atolls

Belize's spectacular **Barrier Reef**, with its dazzling variety of underwater life and string of exquisite islands – known as cayes (pronounced "keys") – is the main attraction for most first-time visitors to the country. The longest barrier reef in the western hemisphere, it begins just south of Cancún and runs the entire length of the Belize coastline at a distance of 15 to 40km from the mainland. One of the richest marine ecosystems on Earth, it's a paradise for scuba divers and snorkellers, the incredible coral formations teeming with hundreds of species of brilliantly coloured fish.

Most of the cayes lie in shallow water behind the shelter of the reef, with a limestone ridge forming larger, low-lying islands to the north and smaller, less frequently visited outcrops – often merely a stand of palms and a strip of sand – clustered toward the southern end of the chain. Though the four hundred cayes themselves form only a tiny portion of the country's total land area, and only around ten percent have any kind of tourism development, Belize has more territorial water than it has land, and the islands' tourism and lobster-fishing income accounts for a substantial proportion of earnings.

In recent years the town of **San Pedro**, on **Ambergris Caye**, has undergone a transition from a predominantly fishing economy to one dominated by tourism. There are still some beautiful spots here, however, notably the protected areas of the island and the reef at either end of the caye: **Bacalar Chico National Park** to the north and **Hol Chan Marine Reserve** in the south. South of Ambergris Caye, **Caye Caulker**, which also has a marine reserve, is less – but increasingly – developed, and very popular with budget travellers. Belize's first capital, **St George's Caye**, occupies a celebrated place in the nation's history and still has some fine colonial houses as well as an exclusive diving resort. **Swallow Caye**, near the tip of Belize City, is now protected as a sanctuary for manatees; visitors can observe these gentle sea mammals on carefully controlled boat trips. Many of the other cayes are populated only by fishing communities, whose settlements fluctuate with the season; a few have just a single upmarket lodge offering diving and sport-fishing to big-spending visitors.

Beyond the chain of islands and the coral reef are two of Belize's three **atolls**: the **Turneffe Islands** and **Lighthouse Reef**. In these breathtakingly beautiful formations the coral reaches the surface, enclosing a shallow lagoon, with some cayes lying right on top of the encircling reef – here you'll find some of the most spectacular diving and snorkelling sites in the country, if not the world. Cayes on the Turneffe Islands have a few resorts, there's a marine research station on **Calabash Caye** and a marine reserve is planned. Lighthouse Reef has beautiful **Half Moon Caye**, where you can view nesting red-footed boobies, and the unique **Blue Hole Natural Monument** – an enormous collapsed cave that attracts divers from all over the world. All are regularly visited on daytrips or live-aboard dive boats from San Pedro or Caye Caulker.

Such is the importance of this astonishing marine ecosystem that virtually the entire barrier reef, the reef surrounding all the atolls and all of Belize's marine reserves were declared a **World Heritage Site** in December 1996. The announcement was greeted with tremendous enthusiasm by Belize's dedicated and influential environmental and conservation organizations. Together, these protected marine areas are designated the **Belize Barrier Reef Reserve System**.

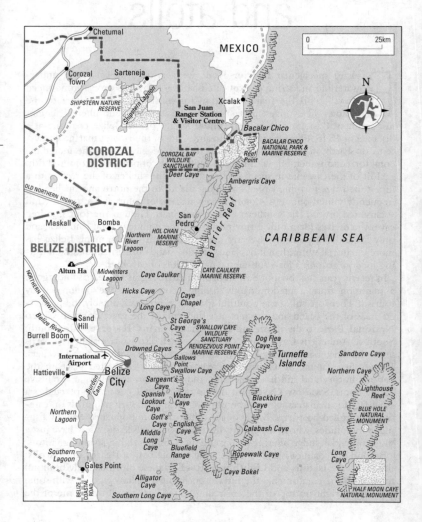

A brief history of the cayes

The earliest inhabitants of the cayes were **Maya** peoples or their ancestors. By the Classic period (300–900 AD) the Maya had developed an extensive trade network stretching from the Yucatán to Honduras, with settlements and transshipment centres on several of the islands. At least some cities in Belize survived the Maya "collapse" and the trade network existed throughout the Postclassic era until the arrival of the conquistadores. **Christopher Columbus** may have sighted the coast of Belize on his last voyage to the "Indies" in 1502; his journal mentions an encounter with a Maya trading party in an immense dugout canoe off Guanaja, one of the Bay Islands of Honduras. Traces of Maya civilization remain on some of the cayes today, especially Ambergris Caye, which boasts the site of **Marco Gonzalez**, near the southern tip, and the remains of a number of ports and trading centres on the northwestern shores. Evidence of coastal trade, such as shell mounds, has also been found on other islands, including Moho Caye, off Belize City.

Probably the most infamous residents of the cayes were the **buccaneers**, usually British, who lived here in the sixteenth and seventeenth centuries, taking refuge in the shallow waters after plundering Spanish treasure ships. In time the pirates settled more or less permanently on some of the northern and central cayes. But life under the Jolly Roger became too hot for them in the late 1600s, after Britain agreed to stamp out privateering under the terms of the Madrid Treaties, and a number of pirates turned instead to logwood cutting. But the woodcutters (aka the **Baymen**) still kept their dwellings on the cayes – specifically **St George's Caye** – as the cool breezes and fresh water offered a welcome break from the steaming swamps where the logwood grew. The population of the cayes remained low during the seventeenth and eighteenth centuries, but the settlement on St George's Caye was regarded by the Baymen as their capital until 1779, when a Spanish force destroyed it, imprisoning 140 of the Baymen and 250 of their slaves. The Baymen returned in 1783 and took revenge on the Spanish fleet in 1798 in the celebrated **Battle of St George's Caye** (see p.290). From then on, however, although the elite of the Baymen still kept homes on St George's Caye, the population of the islands began to decline as Belize Town (later Belize City) grew.

During this period, fishermen and turtlers continued to use the cayes as a base for their operations, and refugees fleeing the Caste Wars in the Yucatán towards the end of the nineteenth century also settled on the islands in small numbers. The island population has increased steadily since, booming with the establishment of the **fishing cooperatives** in the 1960s, which brought improved traps, ice plants (where they make ice for packing lobsters for shipping) and access to the export market.

At around the same time the cayes of Belize, particularly Caye Caulker, became a hangout on the **hippie trail**, and then began to attract more lucrative custom. The islanders generally welcomed these new visitors: rooms were rented and hotels built, and a new prosperity began to transform island life. Luxuries not usually associated with small fishing communities in the developing world – colour televisions, telephones, skiffs with large outboard motors – are all evidence of the effects of tourism. So profound are these changes that fishing has now become a secondary activity; most of the inhabitants of the two largest northern cayes, Ambergris Caye and Caye Caulker, now depend on tourism for their livelihood.

Visiting the cayes

The increasing popularity of Belize as a holiday destination has led to an escalation in land prices, and real estate offices proliferate on San Pedro's main streets, tempting wealthy visitors to invest in a Caribbean island. Luckily, most of the islands are too small and remote to entice large-scale developers. Indeed, getting to many of the cayes and atolls can be difficult, especially if you're limited by time and finances, though access is much easier than it once was. Several organizations have **conservation projects** on the cayes, requiring self-funded volunteers (see pp.324–325), or you could see if a visiting yacht owner needs a crew. Alternatively, **charter catamarans** are available in San Pedro and, if you can get together a group, you might **rent a sailboat** for a few days – easily done on Caye Caulker – and let a local boatman show you the lesser-known parts of the reef.

Life on the cayes is supremely relaxing, tempting you to take it easy in a hammock, feast on seafood and sip rum punch as the sun sets. If you adopt the "no shirt, no shoes, no problem" philosophy of locals and expats alike you'll fit right in. The most accessible and least expensive of the islands is Caye Caulker, and **snorkelling** or **diving** trips to the reef are easily arranged from here or from Ambergris Caye. Dive instruction is also readily available. With either underwater option you can visit sites of almost unbelievable beauty and isolation by joining a group day-trip, visiting three or four different reef sites in a day, or by staying at a lodge on one of the atolls. If you enjoyed the breathtaking aerial view afforded when flying to Ambergris Caye or Caye Caulker (see opposite), you might like to take Tropic Air's **Deep Reef Flying Tour**, a spectacular flight over the northern cayes and atolls that's a perfect way to appreciate your surroundings (minimum of eight people, book at any recommended travel agent; US$125).

Bird-watching, as anywhere in Belize, is fascinating. Over 250 species live in or visit the coastal areas and cayes, from ospreys and sandpipers to flamingoes and finches. Many otherwise rare birds are relatively common here; for instance, there's a sanctuary behind San Pedro to protect nesting roseate spoonbills, while the preservation of the red-footed booby on Half Moon Caye was the main reason for establishing a Natural Monument there in 1982. If you're keen on learning how, when and where to spot birds on the cayes, pick up a copy of *Bird Watching with Bubba*, self-published by expat divemaster Elbert Greer and available on Ambergris Caye.

Catch-and-release **fly-fishing** for bonefish is popular, particularly at the Turneffe Island flats, where a couple of upmarket fishing lodges can fulfil any angler's dream. Fishing trips for species such as snapper, barracuda and grouper are easily arranged, and a local guide can take you to the best spots. Some snorkelling trips can include a chance of fishing using a handline.

Finally, some words of **warning**: in recent years the northern cayes (and other coastal areas of Belize) have suffered direct hits by several powerful hurricanes. The official **hurricane season** begins in June and finishes at the end of November, though the most devastating storms usually occur during September and October – tourist low season. If you are on the cayes during the hurricane season you should keep yourself informed about developing storms by checking Ⓦwww.belizenet.com/weatherix.shtml or The Weather Channel's "Tropical Update", shown at ten minutes to the hour. If there is a hurricane developing *anywhere* in the Caribbean then prepare to leave as quickly as possible or postpone plans for a visit to the cayes. Hurricanes can and do change intensity and direction rapidly, so don't believe anyone who says it won't affect Belize – you can always return once the danger is over.

Safeguarding the coral reef

Coral reefs are among the most complex and **fragile** ecosystems on earth. Colonies have been growing at a rate of less than 5cm a year for thousands of years and, once damaged, the coral is far more susceptible to bacterial infection, which can quickly lead to large-scale irreversible damage. Unfortunately, a great deal of damage has already been caused on Belize's Barrier Reef by snorkellers standing on the coral or holding onto outcrops for a better look. On all the easily accessible areas of the reef you will clearly see white, dead patches, especially on the large brain coral heads. All tour guides in Belize are trained in reef ecology before being granted a licence (which must be displayed as they guide), and if you go on an organized trip, as most people do, the guide will brief you on the following precautions to avoid damage to the reef.

❏ Never anchor boats on the reef – use the permanently secured buoys.
❏ Never touch or stand on corals – protective cells are easily stripped away from the living polyps on their surface, destroying them and thereby allowing algae to enter. Coral also stings and can cause agonizing burns – even brushing against it causes cuts that are slow to heal.
❏ Don't remove shells, sponges or other creatures from the reef or buy reef products from souvenir shops.
❏ Avoid disturbing the seabed around corals – quite apart from spoiling visibility, clouds of sand settle over corals, smothering them.
❏ If you're a beginner or an out-of-practice diver, practise away from the reef first.
❏ Don't use suntan lotion in reef areas – the oils remain on the water's surface. Wear a T-shirt instead to protect your skin from sunburn.
❏ Check you're not in one of the marine reserves before fishing.
❏ Don't feed or interfere with fish or marine life; this can harm not only sea creatures and the food chain, but snorkellers too – large fish may attack, trying to get their share.

Ambergris Caye and San Pedro

Geographically part of Mexico's Xcalak Peninsula, **Ambergris Caye** is separated from Mexico by the narrow **Bacalar Chico** channel, created partly by the ancient Maya. It's the most northerly and, at 40km long, by far the largest of the cayes, though the vast majority of the population is concentrated near the southern end. The island's main attraction and point of arrival is the former fishing village of **SAN PEDRO**, facing the reef just a few kilometres from the southern tip. Development is spreading north from the town, with a number of beach resorts already established and plans for larger hotels and even another airport near the northern end of the caye.

If you fly into San Pedro, which is the way most visitors arrive, the views are breathtaking: the water appears so clear and shallow as to barely cover the sandy seabed, and the mainland and other islands stand out clearly. The most memorable sight is the pure white line of the reef crest, dramatically separating the vivid blue of the open sea from the turquoise water on its leeward side. The aircraft fly at so low an altitude (around 100m – there's no need to go higher on these short hops), that photographs taken from inside the cabin generally turn out well.

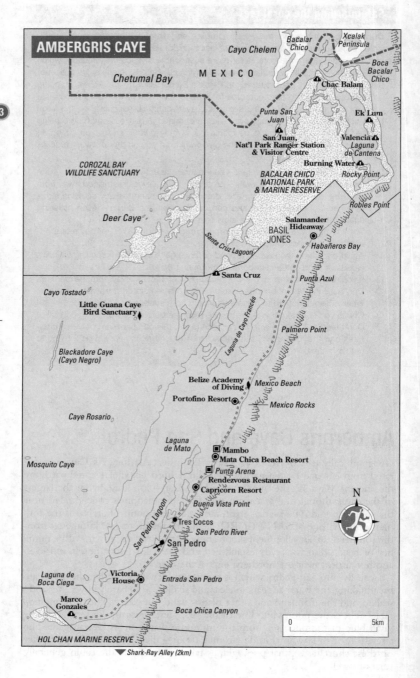

AMBERGRIS CAYE

Chetumal Bay

MEXICO

Cayo Chelem

Bacalar Chico

Xcalak Peninsula

Boca Bacalar Chico

Chac Balam

Punta San Juan

San Juan, Nat'l Park Ranger Station & Visitor Centre

Ek Lum

Valencia Laguna de Cantena

Burning Water

Rocky Point

BACALAR CHICO NATIONAL PARK & MARINE RESERVE

COROZAL BAY WILDLIFE SANCTUARY

Deer Caye

Santa Cruz Lagoon

Salamander Hideaway

BASIL JONES

Habañeros Bay

Robles Point

Santa Cruz

Punta Azul

Cayo Tostado

Little Guana Caye Bird Sanctuary

Palmero Point

Laguna de Cayo Francés

Blackadore Caye (Cayo Negro)

Caye Rosario

Belize Academy of Diving

Mexico Beach

Portofino Resort

Mexico Rocks

Laguna de Mato

Mambo

Mata Chica Beach Resort

Mosquito Caye

Punta Arena

Rendezvous Restaurant

Capricorn Resort

San Pedro Lagoon

Buena Vista Point

Tres Cocos

San Pedro River

San Pedro

Laguna de Boca Ciega

Victoria House

Entrada San Pedro

Marco Gonzales

Boca Chica Canyon

N

0   5km

HOL CHAN MARINE RESERVE

Shark-Ray Alley (2km)

Flying to San Pedro is the easiest and most popular approach. Maya Island Air (☏226-2345) and Tropic Air (☏226-2012) both operate flights from Belize International Airport and Belize Municipal Airport (see p.60 for both) to San Pedro (daily 7am–5.30pm, hourly; 20min from Municipal or International; Bz$52), calling at Caye Caulker on request. Both airlines also operate four or five daily **flights from San Pedro to Corozal**.

From Belize City, most **boats to Ambergris Caye** are operated by the Caye Caulker Water Taxi Association (1hr 20min; Bz$30 one-way, Bz$55 return; ☏226-2194, ⓦwww.cayecaulkerwatertaxi.com) and leave from the Marine Terminal at 8am, 9am, 10.30am, noon, 1.30pm, 3pm and 4.30pm, calling at Caye Caulker on the way. The least expensive boat on the run, the *Triple J* (Bz$24; ☏224-34785), leaves from Courthouse Wharf, south side of the Swing Bridge, at 9am, returning at 3pm; and the *Thunderbolt* (same prices as above; ☏226-2904) leaves from the dock opposite the Holy Redeemer Church on North Front Street (half a block upriver from the Marine Terminal) at 8am, 1pm and 4pm, returning to Belize at 7am, 11am and 4pm. The *Thunderbolt* also runs from **San Pedro to Corozal** (daily at 3pm; 1hr 30min; Bz$45) and back (daily at 7am).

Caye Caulker Water Taxis **leave from San Pedro** to Caye Caulker and Belize City at least every two hours from 7am until 3.30pm (until 5.30pm on weekends and holidays). Travelling from San Pedro to other cayes, any of the above scheduled boats also stop at Caye Caulker, and they'll also call at **St George's Caye** or **Caye Chapel** on request.

As you land at the tiny airport, with the sea to one side and the lagoon to the other, a glimpse at San Pedro shows it taking up the whole width of the island. Still, it's not a large town – you're never more than a shell's throw from the sea – but its population of over five thousand is the highest on any of the cayes. San Pedro is the main destination for over half the visitors to Belize, catering mainly for North American package tours. Almost all prices are quoted in US dollars, which are accepted island-wide. Some of the country's most exclusive and luxurious **hotels**, **restaurants** and **bars** are here; the few budget places are in the original village of San Pedro (ie what existed before tourism development), which is also where most of the action takes place, particularly in the evenings.

During the daytime, for those not shopping, relaxing or enjoying some other land-based activity, it's the **water** which is the focus of entertainment on Ambergris Caye, from sunbathing on the docks to **windsurfing**, sailing, kayaking, **diving** and **snorkelling**, fishing and even taking trips on a glass-bottomed boat. All of the trips described on pp.120–122 can be booked from your hotel or any tour or travel agent.

Arrival, information and getting around

Arriving at San Pedro's **airport**, you're at the north end of Coconut Drive and only 450m south of the centre. It's within easy walking distance of any of the hotels in town, though golf buggies and **taxis** will be waiting if you don't want to hoof it. A taxi in town costs Bz$6 but always check the fare first and never let a taxi driver take you to a hotel of his choosing. Even if you arrive with a booking, call first if you can, as a common taxi-driver **scam** is to tell you the hotel you've booked is actually full, and then take you to one where he earns (or extorts) a fat commission. If you want to, you can **leave luggage** near the

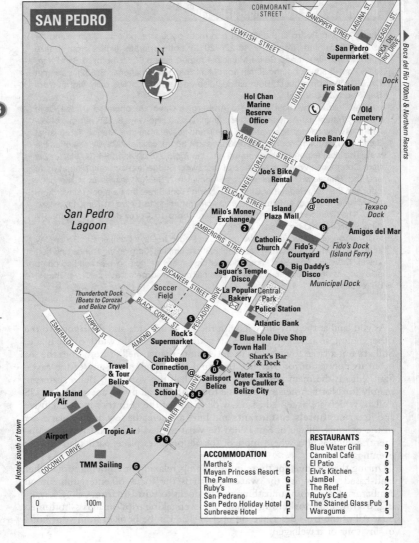

airport while you look for somewhere to stay – see the staff in the Travel and Tour Belize office (☎226-2137, Ⓦwww.traveltourbelize.com), a few steps north of the airstrip. They can give good advice and information on hotels, and indeed anything else in San Pedro; check here, too, for international or regional flights.

Boats usually pull in at the Water Taxi Dock, at the east end of Black Coral Street, on the front (reef) side of the island, or the Texaco Dock, at the end of Caribeña Street. The *Thunderbolt*, however, docks at Cesario's Dock, at the back of the island at the west end of Black Coral Street. All are within a few blocks of the centre of town, marked by the tiny Central Park, on the seafront on Barrier Reef Drive.

There's no official tourist office in San Pedro, but **information** is easy to find. For starters, Ambergris Caye has one of the best **websites** in the country (Ⓦ www.ambergriscaye.com), with good maps and well-designed links to most of the businesses on the island. It's also worth picking up a copy of *The San Pedro Sun* or *Ambergris Today*, the island's **tourist newspapers** (both Bz$1), or the *Green Guide to Ambergris Caye*, a free listings magazine; all three are available from most hotels and restaurants. San Pedro's own **radio station**, Reef Radio (92.3 FM), is worth listening to for both the music and events announcements.

You needn't worry about **changing money** here, as US dollars in cash and travellers' cheques are accepted – even preferred – everywhere. If you do need to get Belize dollars in cash, the Atlantic Bank and Belize Bank (with ATM) are both on Barrier Reef Drive. You can exchange money at Milo's Money Exchange, on Pescador Drive between Ambergris and Pelican streets (open weekdays & Sat mornings; ☎226-2196).

Several **Internet cafés** offer high-speed access and cheap-rate **international phone calls**: on Barrier Reef Drive, *Caribbean Connection* (next to the *Coral Beach Hotel*) has the most modern equipment and serves the best coffee, while *Coconet*, a few blocks north next to *Fido's Courtyard*, also has a lively bar; about 1.5km further south, *Island Internet* offers free coffee while you surf. The **post office** is in the Alijua Building near the centre of Barrier Reef Drive, and the **BTL** office is a few blocks further north.

The town centre is small enough to **get around** on foot; pleasant enough at any time, it's particularly enjoyable on weekend evenings, when the nearest street to the shore, Barrier Reef Drive, is closed to vehicles. However, in recent years, the town has expanded rapidly to the north and south, and some hotels away from the centre have **courtesy bikes** for guests – something you might want to consider when choosing a place to stay. You can also **rent bikes** from Joe's Bike Rental, at the corner of Pescador Drive and Caribeña Street (Bz$14/half-day, Bz$20/full day, Bz$85/week; ☎226-4371).

On some occasions you might need to hire a **water taxi** to visit the more remote resorts and restaurants. The *Island Express* (Bz$10 to places about 5km away, more if further; ☎226-3231) is a regular **fast ferry** running the length of the caye, with departures from Fido's Dock from 7am to 10pm, later at weekends. If you need to charter a boat it's best to ask at your hotel or a recommended tour operator.

Accommodation

With over seventy places to stay, Ambergris Caye has the highest concentration of **hotels** in the country. Many of these, including all the **inexpensive** options, are in San Pedro itself, just a short walk or taxi ride from the airport. Resorts, some very luxurious indeed, stretch for many kilometres along the beaches north and south of town. **Prices** here are higher than the rest of Belize but **discounts** on the quoted rates are often available, especially in the low season, so it's worth asking. All have air-conditioning and private bath (unless otherwise stated) and almost everywhere takes credit cards.

You shouldn't have any problem finding somewhere to stay in the high season (December to Easter), with the exception of Christmas, New Year (when many places hike up the rates even further) and Easter, when it's definitely advisable to **book ahead**. At any time, if you arrive without a booking it pays to call around to a few of the recommended places first; you're likely to get a better price on your room and the hotel owner can advise you as to whether you need a taxi, and how much it should cost – they might even pick you up in their golf buggy.

Ambergris Caye has more **apartments**, condominiums and timeshares than anywhere else in Belize and you can often get good package or long-term deals if you book ahead; check with Caye Management (☎226-3077, ⓦwww.cayemanagement.com) to see what's available. As you walk around the island you may also see "**room for rent**" signs; these are generally for locals (including expatriates) but are worth a try if you plan to stay for a while. There are a couple of places to **camp** but your belongings may not be very secure – and sleeping rough is not recommended.

Hotels in town

Martha's Pescador Drive, across from *Elvi's Kitchen* ☎226-2053, ⓔmiguelperez@btl.net. A bargain in the town centre, offering clean, comfortable fan-cooled rooms with private bath and bedside lamps. ❹

Mayan Princess Resort Barrier Reef Drive, just north of the centre ☎226-2778, ⓦwww .mayanprincesshotel.com. Well-equipped beachfront suites with decent kitchenette and a large balcony overlooking the sea; the best-value suites in town for the price. Daily maid service and free taxi from airport. ❽

The Palms Coconut Drive, just south of the town centre ☎226-3322, ⓦwww.palmsbelize.com. Luxury, well-furnished a/c suites overlooking the beachfront in a quiet location, but conveniently near town. Lots of extras, including fully equipped kitchens, daily maid service and a beautiful private pool. Ground-floor rooms are wheelchair-accessible. US$170 for a one-bedroom; US$250 for a two-bedroom. ❾

Ruby's Barrier Reef Drive, a short walk north from the airstrip ☎226-2063, ⓔrubys@btl.net. Comfortable family-run hotel right on the seafront. The clean rooms (some with a/c) get better views (and increased rates) the higher up you go; all are good value, those with shared bath especially so. *Ruby's* now has more budget rooms in another building a few blocks away, on the lagoon side. *Ruby's Café*, next door, is one of the first cafés to open in the mornings, and the hotel organizes good trips. ❸–❺

San Pedrano Corner of Barrier Reef Drive and Caribeña St ☎226-2054, ⓔsanpedrano@btl.net. Popular hotel in a wooden building with nice rooms, some of which have a/c. Set back slightly from the sea, but with fine views and breezy verandahs. No single rates. ❹

San Pedro Holiday Hotel Barrier Reef Drive, just south of the centre ☎226-2014, ⓦwww.sanpedroholiday.com. San Pedro's first hotel, but with all modern facilities, including fridges and a/c. Rooms face the sea. There's a restaurant, a deli and, on Wednesdays, a beach barbecue with live music. ❽

Sunbreeze Hotel South end of Barrier Reef Drive ☎226-2191, ⓦwww.sunbreezehotel.com. Curving around a sandy courtyard and a pool, this superbly run beachfront hotel has big rooms in three levels of comfort; all have large bathrooms and some have a Jacuzzi bath. Excellent restaurant and very good gift shop. ❾

Hotels south of town

Hotels below are listed in order of distance from town.

Pedro's Backpacker Inn Coconut Drive, almost 1km south of town, opposite *Jade Garden Restaurant* ☎226-3825, ⓔpedroback2000@yahoo.com. Basic and rather bare budget rooms with two single beds and shared showers, though at Bz$25 a night it's the cheapest single rate on the island (but you could end up sharing if it's full). There's a small pool, and some private rooms are being built. ❹

Changes in Latitudes Coconut Drive, almost 1km south of town, near the Belize Yacht Club ☎ & ⓕ226-2986, ⓔlatitudesbelize@yahoo.com. Very friendly B&B set in gardens half a block from the sea – guests can use the Yacht Club dock to swim. Smallish but immaculately clean rooms, with use of common area, including full kitchen, at all times. Owner Lori Reed arranges the best tours and has a book exchange. Rates include a wonderful cooked breakfast; good low-season discounts. ❻

Exotic Caye Beach Resort On the beach, 1km south of town ☎226-2870, in US ☎1-800/201-9839, ⓦwww.belizeisfun.com. Large, well-furnished wood-and-thatch cabaña suites (all with kitchen and some with loft) on a quiet sandy beach; the honeymoon suite (US$225) has a Jacuzzi. There's also a spa, pool and dive shop, plus plenty of food and entertainment. ❾

Corona del Mar On the beach, just over 1km south of town ☎ 226-2025, ⓔcorona@btl.net. Beautiful rooms and suites with full kitchens, TV and phone, with plenty of space and lots of extras. All are very good value; rates include a full breakfast, free rum punch all day and use of the *Coconuts* pool next door. ⑥–⑨.

Coconuts Caribbean Hotel On the beach, just over 1km south of town ☎ 226-3500, ⓦwww.coconutshotel.com. This popular, recently renovated hotel boasts beautifully decorated tiled rooms and suites, a gorgeous pool and hot tub and a great lounge and beachfront restaurant. Excellent service, with free Internet access for guests and a free taxi from the airstrip. The Marauder Suite (US$180 double) has a private Jacuzzi. ⑧

Caribbean Villas Hotel Coconut Drive, just over 1km south of town ☎ 226-2715, ⓦwww.caribbeanvillashotel.com. Large rooms and well-equipped suites, all with ocean views, set in a garden on the beachfront. Plenty of peace and quiet and opportunities to relax; snooze in a hammock or immerse yourself in the hot tub. An observation tower on the grounds gives views of the lagoon; there's also fantastic bird-watching. ⑦–⑨.

Villas at Banyan Bay On the beach, over 1km south of town ☎ 226-3739, ⓦwww.banyanbay.com. New, roomy suites with all possible luxuries, including huge kitchens, fully furnished living and dining areas, Jacuzzi bathrooms and a shady porch, set in immaculately landscaped grounds. Fine dining over the water at *Rico's Restaurant*, and there's also a large pool, a dive shop and a watersports centre. Rack rates are high, at around US$250–300 double, but specials are available. ⑨

Tropica Beach Resort On the beach, next to *Banyan Bay* ☎ 226-2701, ⓦwww.tropicabelize.com. Welcoming, well-appointed (wooden floors, tiled bathrooms) wood-and-thatch cabañas on a lovely beach, with a great pool and a friendly bar and restaurant. Each room has a wooden deck. ⑨

Banana Beach Resort On the Mar de Tumbo Beach, 1.5km south of town ☎ 226-3890, ⓦwww.bananabeach.com. Spacious suites with kitchens and cable TV, rattan furniture and colourful Mexican weavings. All have balconies, some overlooking the pools and courtyard, others facing the ocean. Good weekly rates, and ask about off-season discounts; all rates include a buffet breakfast at the resort's excellent *El Divino* restaurant. Tours can be arranged by the friendly and efficient in-house Monkey Business Travel Shop

(ⓦwww.ambergristours.com). Free taxi from the airstrip. Verandah rooms and courtyard suites ⑧; three-bedroom, three-bath ocean-view suite US$420 a night.

Victoria House On the beach, 3km south of town ☎ 226-2027, in US ☎1-800/247-5159 ⓦwww.victoria-house.com. Award-winning hotel with a wide range of fabulous accommodation in a great location. The luxurious, colonial-style hotel rooms, thatched cabañas, suites and multi-room villas (the latter two options have varnished hardwood furniture and superbly equipped kitchens) are set in spacious grounds resembling a botanic garden. Service is excellent, and there's a beachfront pool and a fine restaurant. Prices start at US$195 for a double ("state") room in high season, and go up to US$825 for a two-bed villa. ⑨

Hotels north of town

Hotels below are listed in order of distance from town.

Caye Casa Just over 1km north of town, before the Boca del Rio ☎ 226-2880, ⓦwww.cayecasa.com. A gorgeous two-bedroom, two-bath pastel-painted house set just back from the beach but with nothing to spoil the sea view. The beautiful bedrooms have queen-size beds and there's a full kitchen/dining room, a sitting room and an outdoor deck. The *Casa* sleeps four and it's a wonderfully relaxing place; the guest rooms (no smoking inside) are on the ground floor, while the friendly owner lives upstairs. Rates are US$175 per night (includes use of golf cart) and there is a three-night minimum stay. ⑨

Capricorn Resort On the beach, 5km north of town ☎ 226-2809, ⓔcapricorn@btl.net. Most people come here for the incredibly good food (see restaurant review, p.125) but there are also three delightful, secluded wooden cabins with porches overlooking a pristine beach; all make perfect hideaways. Breakfast is included as is transport by water taxi from town on arrival and departure. US$175 double. ⑨

Mata Chica Beach Resort On the beach, 7km north of town ☎ 220-5010, ⓦwww.matachica.com. Painted in pastel colours which change with the light, these are the most beautiful and spacious beach cabañas and suites in the country. Each interior is unique, with murals by French artist Lionel Dumas and hand-painted tiles in the bathrooms. There's also a two-bedroom, two-bath luxury villa (US$650) and a three-bedroom, three-bath Beach Mansion (US$950, sleeps six), with stun-

△ Snorkelling off Ambergris Caye

ning views over the reef (just 600m away) from the upper deck. The Jade Spa will pamper and relax you and the food at the hotel restaurant is sublime (see review of *Mambo*, p.125). US$230 for a beach bungalow, US$325 for a double cabaña. ⑨

Portofino On the beach, 10km north of town ☎226-5096, ⓦwww.portofinobelize.com. Set in a glorious location, *Portofino* offers a range of superbly designed thatched beachfront cabañas and suites. The elegant interiors have hardwood floors and furniture, beautiful bamboo beds and Mexican tiles in the bathroom. Service is wonderful, and the resort's *Le Bistro* restaurant is reportedly one of the finest in the country. Rates include free boat transfer from town, free Internet access and continental breakfast. Beach cabaña US$220, treetop suite (on tall stilts) US$270. ⑨

Salamander Hideaway On the beach, 17km north of town ☎602-1713, ⓦwww .ambergriscaye.com/salamander. On secluded Habañeros Bay, this is the most northerly resort on Ambergris Caye, with five simple but exquisite single-storey thatched cabañas, plus two taller jungle cabañas overlooking the littoral forest just behind. The idea here is to create a calm, relaxed and intimate atmosphere – which you can sense has been achieved the moment you arrive – and, appropriately, yoga, massage and meditation are available in the Salamander Spa. There's also a wonderful bar and the food is superb. ⑧–⑨

The Town

San Pedro's main streets are only half a dozen blocks long and the town does not boast any particular sights, but in a place so dedicated to tourist pleasure you're never far from a bar, restaurant or gift shop (see "Shops and galleries", below, for more). Despite this development, the town manages to retain elements of its **Caribbean charm** with a few two-storey clapboard buildings still remaining in the centre. However, lofty concrete structures are an increasingly common feature, and in the built-up area most of the palms have either been cut down, were destroyed by Hurricane Keith in 2000 or are dying from the "lethal yellowing" disease sweeping down from the north. Traffic has increased considerably in recent years, creating deep ruts in the sandy streets, which turn into near-impassable mud holes following heavy rain. To alleviate the worst of this, some of Coconut Drive now has block paving – the only stretch of paved road on the island.

One of the most interesting (and hectic) times to be in San Pedro is during August's **Costa Maya Festival**, a week-long celebration featuring cultural and musical presentations from the five Mundo Maya countries (Belize, Mexico, Guatemala, Honduras and El Salvador). The festival began as a way to drum up visitors during the off season; it's now so popular you may need to book rooms.

Shops and galleries

San Pedro's **gift shops** and **art galleries** offer probably the best shopping selection in the country. Highlights include Belizean Arts, in *Fido's Courtyard*, a large beachfront bar and restaurant on Barrier Reef Drive (ⓦwww.belizeanarts.com), with an unparalleled range of **arts**, **crafts** and **jewellery** from all over Belize, Central America and Mexico. On Pescador Drive, Island Originals Gallery and Ambergris Art Gallery, both display stunning works by Belizean artists, whom you can frequently meet. Look out for artisans of traditional **zericote wood carvings**, many of whom cluster on the beach at the south end of Barrier Reef Drive – you're sure to see their works around town.

In the centre of Barrier Reef Drive, the gallery Ambergris Jade displays superbly executed **carved jade** replicas of Maya originals. Owned by archeologist Pamela Killen, it's also a fascinating jade museum; you're free to browse and watch videos of Maya culture and sights. Some of the best classical and modern **sterling silver jewellery** in the country is on display at the *Caribbean Connection Internet Café*. Meanwhile, for creative and colourful **handmade clothing** go to Isla Bonita Designs, near the north end of Barrier Reef Drive, where Aida Graf and Sami Blouin make their distinctive "Tie-It-On" beachwear designs.

Exploring the caye and the reef

Fifteen hundred metres **north** of the town centre the **Boca del Rio** (usually referred to simply as "The River") is a narrow but widening erosion channel crossed during daylight hours by a tiny, hand-pulled **ferry** (free on foot; golf cart Bz$5). On the northern side of this cut a rudimentary road (navigable by golf cart for perhaps 10km and by bicycle even further) leads to **Tres Cocos** and the northern resorts along miles of gorgeous, mostly deserted beaches. The northernmost section of the caye, now accessible on organized day-trips, boasts the spectacular **Bacalar Chico National Park and Marine Reserve**, as well as several **Maya sites** (see p.123).

Following Coconut Drive **south** of the city, San Pedro merges with **San Pablo**, the semi-official name for this area, with resorts on the beach and houses for the often Spanish-speaking workforce to the west. Set back from the sea, the road runs for several kilometres to the Maya site of **Marco Gonzalez**, though the further you go the swampier and more mosquito-infested the terrain gets. The site is hard to find and there's not much to see, but studies have shown that it was once an important trade centre, with close links to Lamanai (see p.91); archeological teams still conduct excavations here. The southernmost tip of the island is the terrestrial section of the **Hol Chan Marine Reserve**.

Before going **snorkelling** or **diving**, whet your appetite for the wonders of the reef with a visit to the excellent Hol Chan Marine Reserve office and **visitor centre**, in San Pedro on Caribeña Street (Mon–Fri 8am–noon & 1–5pm; ☎226-2247). They have photographs, maps and other displays on the marine reserves, and the staff will be pleased to answer your questions; you may even be able to get a ride with the ranger up to Bacalar Chico. Apart from the Hol Chan office, you can contact Green Reef (☎226-2833, ⓦwww.greenreefbelize.com) for information on the marine reserves and ecology of Ambergris Caye. Founded in 1996 to provide environmental education, they can provide opportunities for self-funded volunteers in education and biological monitoring.

Diving

The reef opposite San Pedro is a heavily used area which has been subject to intensive fishing and souvenir hunting. Heading north, to **Mexico Rocks** for example, or south to **Hol Chan**, you'll find the reef is in much better condition, with fascinating spur and groove formations. Marine life found here can include large **sharks** (hammerhead and tiger, as well as the common and harmless nurse sharks), turtles, spotted eagle rays and even manta rays and whale sharks. To experience the best diving in Belize you really need to take a trip out to one of the **atolls** (see the "Dive operators" box, opposite), for high-voltage excitement in a relatively pristine environment. **Night diving** and snorkelling, a truly amazing experience, is also available.

Open water certification, which takes novices up to the standard of a qualified sport diver, costs around US$350, while a more basic, single-dive **resort**

Several hotels and resorts have their own dive shops and there are plenty of independent operators, too. The best **dive operators** in town are Amigos Del Mar, just north of the centre (☎226-2706, ⓦwww.amigosdive.com) and Blue Hole Dive Center, just south of the centre (☎226-2982, ⓦwww.bluedive.com). They both have fast, comfortable boats for day-trips to the **atolls**: Lighthouse Reef (for the Blue Hole and Half Moon Caye; US$185) and Turneffe Islands (US$165). The Belize Academy of Diving, 11km north of San Pedro (☎226-3170, ⓦwww.belize-academy-of-diving.com), offers very professsional dive instruction and trips to those staying at the northern resorts; they also do free pick-up and return to resorts in the south.

One kilometre south of town, Protech Belize, at the *Belize Yacht Club* dock (☎226-4690, ⓦwww.protechbelize.com), offers all the regular dive trips in small groups, with the best rental gear. They're the only **technical dive centre** in Belize, offering IANTD rebreather technical diving and other courses (including **cave diving**), with oxygen and helium always in stock (they produce all nitrox on the island). Protech also operate San Pedro's only **live-aboard dive boat**, a 43ft, air-conditioned, six-berth SeaRay for overnight trips to the outer atolls. A typical two-day trip costs US$275, including meals and five dives; on a three-day trip you even reach Glover's Reef (see p.236). The boat is equipped with fish- and bottom-finders and is used to host Protech's **advanced expeditions**, such as one proposed for 2005 to descend to the bottom of the Blue Hole.

course (which doesn't lead to PADI certification) ranges from US$90 to 125; both options include equipment. For qualified divers a two-tank local dive costs around US$55, including tanks, weights, air and boat; fins, mask and regulator will be extra. Several dive centres now rent digital or film **cameras**; expect to pay at least US$25 a day for a basic model. In the centre of town on Barrier Reef Drive, the Protech **dive gear shop** (☎226-4660) is the only place in Belize that sells technical equipment; they also have basic cameras, along with a wide range of other scuba and snorkel gear, spares and accessories.

Snorkelling

Almost every dive shop in San Pedro also offers **snorkelling** trips, costing around US$25–50 for about two to four hours (plus about $5 for equipment rental), depending on where you go and whether or not a beach barbecue is included. If you've never used a snorkel before, practise the technique from a dock first. You might also prefer to snorkel in a life-jacket – this will give you greater buoyancy, and help to stop you bumping into the coral. Snorkelling **guides** here (who must also be licensed tour guides) have a great deal of experience with visitors, and they'll show you how to use the equipment before you set off; if they don't seem willing to help novices, go with someone else. Generally, the options available mean you can either head north to the spectacular **Mexico Rocks** or Rocky Point or, more commonly, south to the **Hol Chan Marine Reserve** and **Shark–Ray Alley** (see p.123).

Two of the best local snorkel guides are Alfonso Graniel (☎226-3537) and Dino Gonzalez (☎600-0161). Dino's Ultimate Snorkel Trip (US$50) takes you up to Mexico Rocks with three snorkel stops and a fantastic beach barbecue at Rocky Point featuring freshly caught fish and lobster.

Several boats take snorkellers out for a day-trip to **Caye Caulker**, employing a mix of motor and sail, and comprising two or three leisurely snorkel stops, snacks and drinks on board (lunch on the caye is not included). These return to San Pedro around sunset. A day aboard *Rum Punch II* (US$50;

ⓣ226-2340), a 32ft sailboat with skipper George at the helm, is supremely relaxing, as is a **sunset cruise** (US$25). Large groups can charter Roberto Smith's 72ft, motor-powered *Winnie Estelle* (US$660 for up to twelve people all day, ⓣ226-2934). On board there's a spacious, shaded deck, and the price includes an open bar and fresh snacks and fruit.

Windsurfing, sailing and swimming

The best **windsurfing** and **sailing** rental and instruction on the caye is offered by SailSports Belize (ⓣ226-4488, ⓦwww.sailsportsbelize.com), on the beach in front of the *Holiday Hotel*. SailSports is run by an English couple, Chris and Jo Beaumont, who are both qualified Royal Yachting Association instructors. Sailboard rental costs US$20–25 an hour, or US$65–75 for a seven-hour day, depending on the style of board; sailboat rental is US$25–45 an hour, again with discounts for multiple hours; and **sailing instruction** is US$60, including boat rental. They also offer the exhilarating new sport of **kitesurfing**. The kites range from 3 to 5m in length, allowing high-speed surfing. You'll need two three-hour private sessions (US$150 each) to really get going, as learning kite-control is the hardest part.

Very comfortably equipped **charter catamarans** are a new, expensive and increasingly popular addition to Ambergris Caye's activities. If you're up for it, book a boat in advance from TMM Bareboat Vacations, Coconut Drive, just past the Tropic Air Office (ⓣ226-3026, in the US ⓣ1-800/633-0155, ⓦwww.sailtmm.com). The fleet has one 35ft monohull and the other boats are catamarans, ranging from 38ft, sleeping up to eight, to over 46ft, sleeping up to twelve. All have VHF radio, dinghy, life-jackets, first-aid kit, cruising guide and snorkel equipment. The bareboat price (where you have to be a qualified sailor) ranges from US$200 to US$8000 per week, depending on the boat and the season, and includes an initial briefing lesson. A skipper is US$100 per day and a cook is US$80. In a week you could expect to reach **South Water Caye** (see p.230). TMM has also just opened a new base in Placencia, from where you could reach the Sapodilla Cayes (see p.268) or even the Río Dulce in Guatemala.

If you want to go **swimming**, you should know that **beaches** on Ambergris Caye are narrow and the sea immediately offshore is shallow, with a lot of sea-grass – meaning you'll usually need to jump off the end of a dock or take a boat trip to the reef if you want to swim. A word of **warning**: there have been a number of accidents in San Pedro in which speeding boats have hit people swimming off the piers. A line of buoys, not always clearly visible, indicates the "**safe area**", but speedboat drivers can be a bit macho; be careful when choosing where to swim.

The south: Hol Chan Marine Reserve and Shark-Ray Alley

The **Hol Chan Marine Reserve**, 8km south of San Pedro, at the southern tip of the caye, takes its name from the Maya for "little channel", and it is this break in the reef that forms the focus of the reserve. Established in 1987, its three zones – covering a total of around thirteen square kilometres – preserve a comprehensive cross-section of the marine environment, from **coral reef** through to **seagrass beds** and **mangroves**. All three habitats are closely linked: many reef fish feed on the seagrass beds, and the mangroves are a nursery area for the juveniles. As your boat approaches, you'll be met by a warden who explains the rules and collects the entry fee (Bz$5; combined ticket to Hol Chan and Shark-Ray Bz$8). Note: at the time of writing the fees were set to double, and tour guides will be responsible for ensuring guests have tickets – usually these will be purchased in conjunction with the tour, but if you're getting here in your own boat you'll need to buy tickets from the Hol Chan office (see p.120). The fish here are not fed (as they once were, and still are at Shark-Ray Alley, below), but they're no longer hunted either, so you'll see plenty of **marine life** including some very large snappers, groupers and barracuda. Much damage has already been caused to the **coral** here; see the box on p.111 for more on why, as well as how to avoid causing further damage.

Immediately south of Hol Chan, and now taken under the aegis of the marine reserve itself, is **Shark–Ray Alley** (Bz$5), where you can swim in shallow water with three-metre **nurse sharks** and enormous **stingrays** – an extremely popular (but controversial) attraction. Watching these creatures glide effortlessly beneath you is an exhilarating experience and, despite their reputations, swimming here poses almost no danger to snorkellers, as humans are not part of the fishes' normal diet. Biologists, however, claim that the practice of feeding the fish to attract them alters their natural behaviour, exposing both the fish and humans to danger. In fact, at times the area is so crowded that any hope of communing with nature is completely lost among the flailing bodies of the snorkellers, and there's also the possibility that a shark could accidentally bite a hand – as has already happened. If you do want to experience a close encounter with sharks never offer them food yourself, despite what your guide and other snorkellers do; just look at the sharks and rays from the boat or jump in the water to swim among them.

The north: Bacalar Chico National Park and the Maya sites

A visit to the remote and virtually pristine northern section of Ambergris Caye is an unmissable highlight, not only for the obvious attractions of the **Bacalar Chico National Park and Marine Reserve**, but also for the chance to see a number of previously inaccessible **Maya sites** on the northern coast. On a day-trip from San Pedro you can visit several areas of the reserve and take in two or three of the ten or more Maya sites; the best **guided trips** to Bacalar Chico are run by Excalibur Tours, located at the south end of Barrier Reef Drive (℡226-3235 or 606-8162), and Tanisha Tours, on Pescador Drive between Pelican and Caribeña streets (℡226-2314 or 606-7814).

On trips with either of these companies, you'll travel by boat through the Boca del Rio and up the west coast, stopping briefly to observe colonies of wading birds roosting on some small, uninhabited cayes; **Little Guana Caye** is a bird sanctuary. There are several species of herons and egrets and you might even spot the beautiful and much rarer **roseate spoonbill**, though landing on the islands or disturbing the birds is prohibited. On the way back, you'll navigate **Bacalar Chico**, the channel partly dug by the Maya about 1500 years ago to allow a shorter paddling route for their trading canoes between their cities in Chetumal Bay and the coast of Yucatán. It's so narrow you'll practically be able to touch the mangroves on either side as you sit in the boat. At the mouth of the channel the reef is close to the shore, so the boat will have to cross into the open sea and re-enter the leeward side of the reef as you approach San Pedro – thus completing a circumnavigation of the island.

The national park and marine reserve

Covering the entire northern tip of Ambergris Caye, **Bacalar Chico National Park and Marine Reserve** is the largest protected area in the northern cayes. Its 110 square kilometres extends from the reef, across the seagrass beds to the coastal mangroves and the endangered **caye littoral forest**, and over to the salt marsh and lagoon behind. The area of sea within the reserve is designated a marine reserve and is protected by Belize's Fisheries Department, while the terrestrial area is a national park under the protection of Belize's Forest Department; both are patrolled by rangers based at the head-quarters and **visitor centre** at **San Juan**, on the northwest coast, where you register and pay the Bz$5 park fee. Near the ranger station a seven-metre-high **observation tower**, built by Raleigh volunteers, allows views over undisturbed lagoon and forest – it's also used by rangers to control boat traffic in the reserve.

Despite all the development to the south, there's a surprising amount of **wildlife** up here, including crocodiles, deer, peccaries and, prowling around the thick forests, several of the wild cats of Belize, including even jaguars. Birdlife is abundant and turtles nest on some beaches; contact the Belize Audubon Society (see p.65) or the Hol Chan Reserve office (see p.120) if you want to help patrol the beaches during the turtle nesting season.

Maya sites

Some of the **Maya sites** in the north of the caye are undergoing archeological investigation, meaning there's a real air of adventure and discovery as you explore the ancient ruins now buried in thick bush and jungle. About two-thirds of the way up the west coast of Ambergris Caye, **Santa Cruz** is a very large site, known to have been used for the shipment of trade goods in the Postclassic era, though the precise function of most of the stone mounds here remains uncertain. Further north, the beach at **San Juan** was another transshipment centre for the ancient Maya; here you'll be crunching over literally thousands of pieces of Maya pottery. But perhaps the most interesting site – at least, if archeologists are working there when you visit – is **Chac Balam**, a ceremonial and administrative centre; getting here entails a walk through mangroves to view deep burial chambers, scattered with thousands more pottery shards.

Trips inland

There are increasingly popular **day-trips** inland from San Pedro to the Maya sites of **Altun Ha** (around US$75; see p.83) and even **Lamanai** (US$135; see p.91). Tour prices usually include lunch, soft drinks and beer, entrance fee and rum punch on the way back. Rounding the southern tip of the island in a fast skiff, you head for the mainland at the mouth of the Northern River, cross the lagoon and travel upriver to the tiny village of Bomba. With a good guide this is an excellent way to spot **wildlife**, including crocodiles and manatees, and the riverbank trees are often adorned with orchids. If you like the wood carvings for sale in the gift shops on Ambergris Caye, stop and examine those offered by the people of Bomba; prices here are lower, and the money goes directly to the carver's family. The best naturalist **guides** for these trips are Daniel Nuñez, who runs Tanisha Tours (☎226-2314, ⓦwww.tanishatours.com), and Elito Arceo, who operates Seaduced by Belize (☎226-3221, ⓔseabelize@btl.net).

Eating, drinking and entertainment

There are plenty of places to eat in San Pedro, including some of the best **restaurants** in the country – and at the very top of the range, the quality of food and wine compares favourably with resorts anywhere in the world. **Prices** are generally higher than elsewhere in Belize, though you'll usually get very good service. **Seafood** and **steaks** are on the menu at most restaurants, which tend to reflect the tastes of the town's predominantly North American guests; thus you can also rely on plenty of shrimp, chicken, pizza and salads. Many hotels have their own dining room, and in many cases also do **beach barbecues**. There are several **Chinese** restaurants, the cheaper ones representing the best-value restaurant meals on the island. In the evening several **fast-food stands** open for business along the front of Central Park, serving inexpensive Belizean and Mexican-style dishes. **Buying your own food** isn't particularly cheap: there's no market and the supermarkets are stocked with imported canned goods. The range and quality of groceries is improving all the time, though. At the luxury end of the scale, there's the Sweet Basil deli, just north of the Boca del Rio, with a great selection of imported cheeses, wine and pâté. La Popular bakery, on Buccaneer Street, has a wide selection of bread and buns, including Mexican-style *pan dulces*, and there are some fruit and vegetable stalls dotted around the centre. *Manelly's Ice Cream Parlour*, on Pescador, is the best place in town for a sit-down **ice-cream** treat.

Restaurants

Blue Water Grill At the *Sunbreeze Hotel* ☎ 226-3347. One of the largest and best restaurants in town, serving imaginative seafood (including sushi) and pizza cooked in a wood-fired oven on a deck overlooking the beach; happy hour 4–6pm.

Cannibal Café On the beachfront, just past the *Holiday Hotel*. Tasty, well-priced snacks and light meals on a palm-shaded deck overlooking the sea. Good seafood, tasty tortilla wraps and very good fish and chips.

Capricorn Restaurant 5km north of town, on the beach at the *Capricorn Resort* ☎ 226-2809. Unbeatable gourmet food in a beautiful location; try the French crepes, stone-crab cakes or filet mignon/seafood combo. Great daily brunch from 10am to 2pm; you'll need to book in advance for dinner in high season. Closed Wed.

El Patio Black Coral St, near the *Coral Beach Hotel*. Fine dining on seafood and steaks at very reasonable prices, set in a lovely thatched courtyard.

Elvi's Kitchen Pescador Drive, across the road from *Martha's* hotel ☎ 226-2176. Long an institution in San Pedro, and always serving good burgers and fries, *Elvi's* has now zoomed upmarket, with an expanded menu featuring soups, Caesar salads, steaks, chicken and, of course, lobster and all manner of seafood. The quality is good and the service slick, with prices to match; you may need to book ahead for dinner. Gentle live music in the evenings. Closed Sun.

George's Kitchen Just over 1km south of town, behind the *Corona del Mar* hotel. Large portions of good seafood, Tex-Mex and Belizean dishes, and always a great daily special; a bargain for the island.

Jamel On the park next to *Big Daddy's*. A friendly place serving a very tasty blend of Jamaican and Belizean specialities, such as jerk chicken, pork

and fish, "Jamaicin' me crazy shrimp" and lobster, washed down with Belikin or Red Stripe. Good prices, great fish and chips and always a vegetarian option.

Mambo On the beach 7km north of town ☎ 220-5010. The dining room of the *Mata Chica Beach Resort* and one of Ambergris Caye's top restaurants, with superb food and wine in a classy, romantic atmosphere. The menu changes daily but it's always fabulous; try the exquisite homemade fettuccini (the Italian owner and chef Nadia makes her own pasta) or the "original paella". *Mambo* frequently features Belize's top musical groups for parties and entertainment. Dinner reservations are essential; call for lunch availability.

The Reef Near the north end of Pescador. Really good Belizean food, including delicious seafood, at great prices in a simple restaurant cooled by a battery of fans. Good service and there's usually an offer of free ceviche or a local cocktail to welcome you.

Rendezvous On the beach 5.5km north of town ☎ 226-3426. A delicious and unique fusion of Thai-French cuisine, accompanied by wines from the restaurant's own winery. Try the seafood sour curry, with shrimp, snapper and mussels. Expensive by Belize standards, at around US$17–25 for an entree, but well worth it. Heavenly desserts, too.

Ruby's Café Barrier Reef Drive, next to *Ruby's Hotel*. Delicious homemade cakes, pies and sandwiches, plus freshly brewed coffee. Open at 6am, so it's a good place to order a packed lunch if you're going on a trip.

The Stained Glass Pub Towards the north end of Barrier Reef Drive, opposite the Belize Bank. A convivial blend of an American bar and grill and a British pub. Meals are delicious and the extensive menu includes soups, salads, meatloaf, fish and chips and a range of creative seafood dishes, amply justifying the claim by owners Jim and Marie McGrath to be Belize's only "gastro-pub". **Tastes of Thailand** South of town on Sea Grape Drive, behind the *Barefoot Iguana* disco ☏ 226-2601. Fantastic Thai food (including several vegetarian dishes) from an extensive menu cooked by a friendly English-Thai team. Try the Kaeng Kiew

Wan Goong – king prawns in green curry paste with coconut milk. Closed Sun.
Waraguma Pescador Drive, between Black Coral and Buccaneer sts. A tiny, very inexpensive restaurant serving wonderful Creole, Garifuna, Mexican and Salvadorean dishes to locals and savvy travellers.

Bars and nightlife

San Pedro is the tourist **entertainment** capital of Belize, and the nightlife here becomes more sophisticated every year. At the very least you'll find **live music** on somewhere every night of the week. Many of the hotels have bars, several of which offer **happy hours** – usually two for the price of one on local drinks – while back from the main street are a couple of small **cantinas** such as *Traveller's Cantina* on Pescador Drive, complete with bat-wing doors, where you can buy a beer or a bottle of rum and drink with the locals. The best way to find out what's on where (and what's hot) is to ask at your hotel or check the listings in the local press; what follows is a brief mention of a few highlights. Bars with live music rarely impose a cover charge unless there's a really well-known band playing.

Just north of the park, *Fido's* has a band most nights, with the resident band Category X playing on Saturday; *Shark's Bar*, at the end of the *Coral Beach Hotel* pier, is another good spot to catch local bands. Just over the Boca del Rio, the 4–6pm happy hour on the upper deck at the *Hammock House* is a great place to watch the sunset; and a kilometre or so north, the *Palapa Bar* has its happy hour at the same time. *Palapa* also has a Sunday afternoon jam session, where you should be able to catch San Pedro's best-known singer/songwriter Dennis Wolfe – composer of the expats' anthem "Just Another Gringo in Belize".

For another beachside happy hour (5–7pm), head south to the *Crazy Canuk Bar* at the *Exotic Caye Beach Resort*, where the resident band will get you in the party mood, while *Big Daddy's* **disco**, in and around a beach bar near the park, has the **longest happy hour** on the island, running from 5 to 9pm. *Jaguar's Temple*, opposite the park, usually has a packed dance floor, while the air-conditioned *Barefoot Iguana*, on Coconut Drive just south of the Yacht Club, is San Pedro's biggest disco. A few hundred metres beyond here to the west, the tiny *Black and White Reggae Bar* is the focal point for the island's Garífuna community and a good place to enjoy **drumming** and **punta**. Finally, there's even a small **casino**, The Palace, at the corner of Barrier Reef Drive and Pelican Street.

Caye Caulker

South of Ambergris Caye and 35km northeast of Belize City, **Caye Caulker** – whose name derives from a local wild fruit delicacy, the *hicaco*, or coco plum – has long been a favourite spot for backpackers. It's still the most accessible caye for the independent traveller on a budget, though with new hotels and bars being built (and older ones improved) prices have begun to rise. And, with the building of the airstrip and the ever-growing number of hotels and vehicles, the place is beginning to become more crowded. For the moment, though, Caye Caulker remains relaxed and easy-going, managing to avoid most of the commercialism of San Pedro.

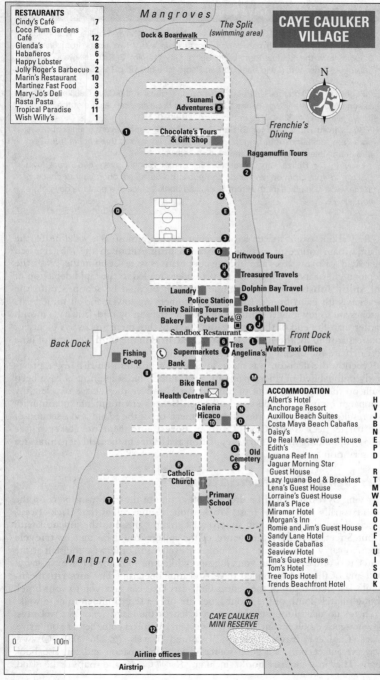

RESTAURANTS

Cindy's Café	7
Coco Plum Gardens Café	12
Glenda's	8
Habañeros	6
Happy Lobster	4
Jolly Roger's Barbecue	2
Marin's Restaurant	10
Martinez Fast Food	3
Mary-Jo's Deli	9
Rasta Pasta	5
Tropical Paradise	11
Wish Willy's	1

CAYE CAULKER VILLAGE

Mangroves

Dock & Boardwalk

The Split
(swimming area)

N

Tsunami Adventures **A** **B**

Frenchie's Diving

Chocolate's Tours & Gift Shop

Raggamuffin Tours **2**

C

E

3

F **G** Driftwood Tours

H

4 Treasured Travels

Laundry **D**

Dolphin Bay Travel

Police Station **5**

Trinity Sailing Tours Basketball Court

Bakery Cyber Café @ **J K**

Sandbox Restaurant **I**

Back Dock **L** Front Dock

Tres Angelina's **6** **7** Water Taxi Office

Fishing Co-op Supermarkets

Bank **8**

Bike Rental **9**

Health Centre ✉

Galeria Hicaco **10** **N**

M

P **O**

11 + +

Q Old Cemetery

Catholic Church **S** **R**

Primary School

T **U**

Mangroves

V
W

CAYE CAULKER MINI RESERVE

12

Airline offices

Airstrip

Barrier Reef (1.5km)

3

THE NORTHERN CAYES AND ATOLLS | Caye Caulker

ACCOMMODATION

Albert's Hotel	H
Anchorage Resort	V
Auxillou Beach Suites	J
Costa Maya Beach Cabañas	B
Daisy's	N
De Real Macaw Guest House	E
Edith's	P
Iguana Reef Inn	D
Jaguar Morning Star Guest House	R
Lazy Iguana Bed & Breakfast	T
Lena's Guest House	M
Lorraine's Guest House	W
Mara's Place	A
Miramar Hotel	G
Morgan's Inn	O
Romie and Jim's Guest House	C
Sandy Lane Hotel	F
Seaside Cabañas	L
Seaview Hotel	U
Tina's Guest House	I
Tom's Hotel	S
Tree Tops Hotel	Q
Trends Beachfront Hotel	K

0   100m

Getting to and from Caye Caulker

Most visitors to Caye Caulker arrive by **boat**: the Caye Caulker Water Taxi Association (☎226-0992) has departures at least every two hours from 8am to 5.30pm from the Marine Terminal in Belize City (45min; Bz$20 one-way, Bz$35 return). All other scheduled boats to San Pedro (see box on p.113) also call at Caye Caulker.

Flights (Bz$52) on the San Pedro run stop on request at the Caye Caulker airstrip, 1.5km south of the village centre. On the island the airline offices are at the airstrip (Maya Island Air ☎226-0012; Tropic Air ☎226-0040).

Boats **from Caye Caulker to San Pedro** (Bz$20) depart every couple of hours from 7am to 5.30pm, returning from San Pedro every two to three hours from 7am to 3.30pm (later on weekends and public holidays).

Leaving for Belize City, boats (Bz$20) depart roughly every two hours from 6.30am to 4pm (5pm on weekends and public holidays). It's often best to check in at the water taxi office (at the Front Dock) and book a place in a boat the day before you leave.

Until about twenty years ago tourism existed almost as a sideline to the island's main source of income, **lobster fishing**. Although the lobster catch increased for many years after fishing cooperatives were set up in the 1960s, the deployment of more traps over an ever wider area led to the rapid depletion of the **spiny lobster**, once so common that they could be scooped onto the beaches with palm fronds. Today their numbers are lower, and in some years catches are so low that the fishermen take the traps in by mid-January, a month earlier than the end of the legal season. Despite this, there are always plenty of lobsters around for the annual **Lobster Fest**, held in the third weekend of June to celebrate the opening of the season.

Recently, the decision was made to allow construction on the larger, previously uninhabited northern part of Caye Caulker, and some houses have been built on the southern point of this section. However, the success of a lengthy campaign by many islanders and others in Belize's environmental community has resulted in the protection of the northern tip of the island and a section of the barrier reef as the **Caye Caulker Forest and Marine Reserve** (see p.131), upholding the country's reputation as a leader in the field of natural area conservation.

Arrival and information

Arriving **by boat**, you'll be dropped off at one of the two main piers on the island: usually the "Front" (east) Dock, though some call at the "Back" (west) Dock. From either dock you simply walk straight ahead to the junction with Front Street, effectively the centre of the village. You'll be met by **tricycle taxis** to carry your luggage (and possibly even you); otherwise the staff at the water taxi office will hold your luggage while you look for a place to stay, as will any of the recommended travel and tour operators. The **airstrip**, meanwhile, is 1.5km south of the centre. Golf-cart taxis can take you to your hotel, though hotels south of the Front Dock are only a ten to fifteen minute walk.

There's no official tourist office, so try to check the island's excellent **websites**, Ⓦ www.gocayecaulker.com and Ⓦ www.cybercayecaulker.com, before you arrive. Caye Caulker's **travel agency**, Treasured Travels (☎226-0083, Ⓦ www .staycayecaulker.com), is a good source of local information and can also book flights. They may also have **books** (including *Rough Guides*) and **maps** of the island.

There are no street names on the caye, but the street running behind the shore at the front of the island is effectively "**Front Street**", with just one or two streets running behind it in the centre of the village. Despite the impression given by some signs, a public right of way exists along the shoreline; walking this route allows you to find hotels right on the water.

The **post office** is south of the centre in the health centre building, while the **BTL** office is off the street leading to the Back Dock; there are plenty of payphones around. Excellent **Internet** access is available at the *Caye Caulker Cyber Café*, just north of the *Sandbox Restaurant*. The Atlantic Bank, just south of the centre, gives **cash advances** (Bz$10 fee); most businesses accept plastic and all take US dollars.

One thing to be aware of in Caye Caulker is the **tap water**; it sometimes smells sulphurous, giving off a rotting odour. This may be the result of natural chemicals in the groundwater, but most places simply use septic tanks for waste disposal, and effluent does seep into the water table. A clean water system is in the planning stage but until this is completed tap water on the caye should be regarded as **unfit to drink**; make sure your hotel gives you rainwater or that you buy bottled water, which is readily available.

Finally, a note about **air-conditioning**: as yet there is little of it on the island, which is fine most of the time when a cooling breeze blows in from the sea, but it can mean some very sticky moments if the breeze dies. On calm days, **sandflies and mosquitoes** can cause almost unbearable irritation, making a good insect repellent essential.

Accommodation

Caye Caulker has an abundance of simply furnished, inexpensive shared-bath rooms in attractive **clapboard hotels**, and there are plenty of more comfortable options with private bathrooms (and some with air-conditioning) – but to arrive at Christmas or New Year without a **reservation** could leave you stranded. Even the furthest **hotels** are no more than ten minutes' walk from the Front Dock and places are easy to find. Almost everywhere now has hot water and many accept credit cards. For some really good **house rentals**, check with Amanda Badger at Vacation Rentals (℡226-0029, 🌐 www .cayecaulkerrentals.com). M&N Apartments (℡226-0229) also have some smaller apartments, and several of the hotels below have an apartment or two for longer stays.

The hotels below are listed in the order you approach them, heading north or south from the Front Dock.

North from the Front Dock

Trends Beachfront Hotel On the beach, immediately north of the Front Dock ℡226-0094, 📧 trendsbze@btl.net. Large rooms in a pastel-painted wooden building with comfortable beds, private baths and tiled floors. Outside, there's a deck with hammocks and there's also a private beachfront cabaña with fridge. Round the corner on Front St (left at *Habañeros Restaurant*) there's another *Trends* with slightly less expensive rooms. ❸–❺

Auxillou Beach Suites 50m along the beach from the Front Dock ℡226-0370, 🌐 www.auxilloubeachsuites.com. Four well-furnished a/c suites with kitchenettes in a glorious location overlooking the beach. The most spacious and comfortable apartments on the island, with living rooms opening onto a wide balcony. Good service, lots of extras and owner Wendy Auxillou can arrange tours throughout the country. ❽–❾

Tina's Guest House 75m along the beach from the Front Dock ℡226-0351, 📧 rastatinabelize@yahoo.com. A relaxing beach house with dorm beds (Bz$20 per person; shared bathroom) and comfortable rooms, some with balcony and private bath. You can cook in the communal kitchen, and there's a book exchange. Outside there's a pretty garden with hammocks and a dock for sunbathing. ❸–❹

Albert's Hotel Front St, above Albert's grocery store ☏ 226-0277. Basic but acceptable wooden rooms – the cheapest on the island – all with shared shower. ❸

Miramar Hotel Front St, past Albert's grocery store ☏ 206-0357 Good-value budget rooms, some with private bath, in a wooden building with a large balcony overlooking the street and the sea. ❸

Sandy Lane Hotel Half a block from the sea, behind the *Miramar* ☏ 226-0117. Small, quiet, clean and inexpensive, with shared-bath rooms in the original building and newer, slightly more expensive cabins in the grounds, with private bath; some have TV. ❸–❹

Iguana Reef Inn At the back (west) of the caye, on the far side of the football field ☏ 226-0213, ⓦ www.iguanareefinn.com. The most luxurious hotel on the island, with thirteen well-furnished, beautifully decorated a/c suites with queen-sized beds, CD player and fridge and great sunset views. Free kayaks for guests to use, and they plan to add a pool. Non-smoking rooms available. ❽

De Real Macaw Guest House Front St, a block past *Oceanside Bar* ☏ 226-0459, ⓦ www.derealmacaw.com. Very comfortable, good-value rooms and thatched cabañas. All have coffeemaker, fridge, cable TV (some have a/c) and porches with hammocks; helpful owners Jessie Benner and Peter Horan make you feel at home. Also a great two-bedroom apartment (usually a three-night minimum stay) for US$110. ❺–❻

Romie and Jim's Guest House Front St, just past *De Real Macaw Guest House* ☏ 600-8411. Some of the best-value private-bath rooms on the island, run by the welcoming Novelo family, who also run the inexpensive restaurant in front of the hotel. The only drawback is the loud music from the beach bar next door. ❹

Costa Maya Beach Cabañas On the beach, towards the Split ☏ 226-0432, ⓔ costamaya@btl.net. Clean, comfortable rooms with bedside lights and private bath in hexagonal cabins, run by a nice family. Also a couple of good-value apartments to rent; US$200 per week. ❺

Mara's Place Just past *Costa Maya* ☏ 226-0156. Six simple, comfortable and good-value wooden cabins facing the sea, with private bath, TV and porch. ❹

South from the Front Dock

Seaside Cabañas Just steps south of the Front Dock ☏ 226-0498, ⓦ www.seasidecabanas.com. Brand-new, very well-designed and -furnished rooms and thatched cabañas, all with a/c, fridge, cable TV and verandah with hammocks. Beautifully decorated inside and out in rich, Mexican-style

colours by British owners Simon and Corinne Morris, these are the best beach cabañas on Caye Caulker, arranged around the island's only pool. There's also a family room and a thatched rooftop bar. ❼–❽

Lena's Guest House On the beachfront ☏ 226-0106, ⓔ lenas@btl.net. Budget rooms in a wooden building by the water, some with private bath. Great sea views from the shady porch at the front. ❹

Daisy's Half a block behind *Lena's* ☏ 206-0150. Set just back from the sea, these simple and delightful budget rooms, all with shared showers, are run by a friendly family. ❸

Morgan's Inn Opposite Galería Hicaco, where you enquire ☏ 226-0178, ⓔ sbf@btl.net. Three quiet, roomy cabins, one with private cold-water bath and one with hot water, set just back from the beach; each sleeps at least three. Perfect for long stays and fine for just a night or two, though only one cabin has cooking facilities. ❹–❺

Edith's On the corner towards the southern end of the town's middle street ☏ 226-0161. Good rooms in a very secure wooden building, all with private bath and better furnishings than most budget places. ❸

Tree Tops Hotel On the beachfront, just beyond the *Tropical Paradise* restaurant ☏ 226-0240, ⓦ www.treetopsbelize.com. The best hotel on the island (indeed the country) at this price, just 50m from the water. Immaculately clean and very comfortable ground-floor rooms with fridge, cable TV and powerful ceiling fans and luxury rooftop a/c suites with fantastic views, set in a small, peaceful garden. Owners Terry and Doris Creasey are extremely helpful, giving reliable tourist information, and will book flights and tours for you. Deservedly popular, so booking ahead is advisable. Rooms ❹ , suites ❻

Tom's Hotel Just past *Tree Tops* ☏ 226-0102, ⓔ toms@btl.net. A large hotel for Caye Caulker, with twenty bargain, clean, tiled rooms (most with private bath) in a two-storey concrete building with all-round balcony. Also has five cabins on the sand. ❹

Jaguar Morning Star Guest House A block behind *Tom's* ☏ 226-0347, ⓔ joanne@btl.net. Two tiled rooms on the third floor with deck and great views and an a/c cabin with a shady porch in the grounds; all rooms have a private shower and a fridge and the cabin has a coffeemaker. A quiet, secure, relaxing place to stay; very good value, too. ❺

Seaview Hotel On the beach, south of *Tom's* ☏ 226-0205, ⓔ seaviewcc@btl.net. Four very comfortable, fan-cooled rooms with private bath and fridge in a concrete house right on the beach.

There's also a one-bedroom wooden cottage with private bath for Bz$700 a week. **⑤**

Anchorage Resort On the shore 300m south of *Tom's* ☎ 226-0304, 🖰 www.anchorageresort.com. Lovely, clean, tiled rooms with comfortable beds, private bath, fridge, cable TV and balconies overlooking the sea in a three-storey concrete building in palm-shaded grounds. Rates for top-floor rooms are higher but they're all great value, with even better prices during the off season. **⑤–⑥**

Lorraine's Guest House Next to the *Anchorage* ☎ 206-0162. A great bargain on the beach. Simple but comfortable wooden cabins with private hot-water showers run by the amiable Alamilla family;

Orlando makes great wooden souvenirs. **③**

Lazy Iguana Bed & Breakfast Follow the signs south from the dock to the back of the island ☎ 226-0350, 🖰 www.lazyiguana.net. The best B&B on the island, with just four beautifully decorated and very comfortable a/c rooms, each with a luxurious private bathroom. The shady gardens are filled with orchids and the top floor has a thatched deck with hammocks to enjoy all-round views over the sea and the lagoon. Friendly owners Mo and Irene Miller prepare a fantastic breakfast and also produce a unique range of perfumes in their own workshop. **⑦**

Exploring the caye and the reef

The **Barrier Reef** lies only 1.5km from the shore, and the white foam of the reef crest is always visible to the east. The entire length of the reef off Caye Caulker was declared a **marine reserve** in 1998 and at the time of writing it's still free (though a reserve manager and wardens have been appointed and there will probably be an entrance fee of Bz$10 by the time you read this). At any rate, visiting the reef is an experience not to be missed, swimming along **coral canyons** surrounded by an astonishing range of fish, with perhaps even the odd shark or two (almost certainly harmless nurse sharks). Here, as everywhere, snorkellers should be aware of the fragility of the reef and be careful not to touch any coral – even sand stirred up by fins can cause damage (see box on p.111).

Caye Caulker is just over 8km long, with almost all the inhabitants living in the section below The Split (where Hurricane Hattie tore through the island in 1961; it's now a great place for swimming and watching the sunset). The narrow northern part is covered in mangroves and thick vegetation that extends right down to the shore; this is the rare and threatened **caye littoral forest** habitat. This area was used as a coconut plantation before Hurricane Hattie in 1961, but has not been in active use since, so the native littoral forest has had nearly 45 years to regenerate. The northernmost forty hectares are now the **Caye Caulker Forest and Marine Reserve**, home to such trees as red, white and black mangroves, gumbo limbo and poisonwood. The mangrove shallows support fish nurseries and small species called "sardines" by the fishermen, who use them as bait to catch snapper. Sponges, gorgonians, anemones and other colourful sea creatures grow on the mangrove roots. As the leaves fall and mud accumulates, some areas rise just above sea level, at least in the dry season. Between these areas are lagoons that remain year-round, serving as excellent habitats for crocodiles, turtles and water birds. American **salt-water croco-diles** are sometimes seen here, but you're more likely to find them in the wild on the Turneffe Islands (see p.137) or in the more remote coastal areas – though if you're really keen to view these magnificent reptiles, head to the garbage dump by the airstrip. The forest is home to many birds rarely seen elsewhere, such as the white-crowned pigeon, the rufus-necked rail and the black catbird. Other native inhabitants of the littoral forest include **boa constrictors**, scaly-tailed iguanas (locally called "wish willies"), geckoes, five species of land crab, hermit crabs and several lizards.

Your trip to the reef or the littoral forest will be more enjoyable if you have some idea of what you're seeing. At the Galería Hicaco, towards the south end of Front Street (☎226-0178), marine biologist Ellen McRae can explain exactly what it is you'll be seeing in this amazing underwater world. As a naturalist guide she can also take you for a really well-informed **tour** of the reef, or for an early-morning **Audubon bird walk**, an introduction to the dozens of bird species of the caye: waders from herons to sandpipers, with pelicans, spoonbills and the ever-present frigate birds swooping down with pinpoint accuracy on morsels of fish.

A small section of the original littoral forest has been preserved in the **Caye Caulker Mini Reserve**, on the beach at the south end of the village (always open; free, but donations appreciated). Walking the cleared paths here will give you some idea of the variety and density of jungle which can grow on bare sand and coral rubble; stray off the path leading down to the southern tip of the island and you'll realize just how spiky and impenetrable this forest really is.

Swimming and snorkelling

Although Caye Caulker has an attractive artificial beach, created by pumping sand from the back of the island, **swimming** isn't really possible from the shore as the water's too shallow; instead you'll have to leap off the end of piers or go to The Split at the north end of the village.

Snorkelling trips to the reef from Caye Caulker are easily arranged and cost around Bz$35–55 per person, depending on where you go. Most last several hours and take in a number of sites, often going to Hol Chan Marine Reserve and Shark-Ray Alley (see p.123) – but these are more expensive and you're actually better off going to the local sites. Most guides take trips to Caye Caulker's own marine reserve but you can also go on trips to Lighthouse Reef and the Blue Hole (see p.138). Keep an eye out for the dolphins that often accompany the boats on the way. You can usually rent decent equipment (around Bz$8–10 for snorkel, mask and fins) from the place where you book your trip; always make sure it fits well and try to practise from a dock before you go to the reef. If you wear glasses check to see if they have masks with prescription lenses – Paradise Down does; see "Diving trips", below.

Other destinations include Swallow Caye Wildlife Sanctuary (see p.139), a mangrove caye and adjacent seagrass beds near Belize City, to view (and not swim with) the manatees. You're almost certainly guaranteed a sighting, often of whole family groups; contact Chocolate (see box opposite) for the best tours (around Bz$75). These trips also usually include a visit to snorkel off Goff's Caye, English Caye or Sergeant's Caye – tiny specks of sand and coral with a few palm trees.

Diving trips and instruction

All the dive shops on the caye offer some great reef diving and visits to coral gardens (two tanks US$60, usually including equipment), as well as **night dives** (US$40). A day-trip to **Lighthouse Reef** and the **Blue Hole**, leaving at 6.30am (three dives, US$150), is an unforgettable experience. The route takes you across the northern tip of **Turneffe Atoll** (which also has some great dive sites), continuing on to Lighthouse Reef. After the unique, slightly spooky splendour of diving over 35m into the depths of the Blue Hole there's the fantastic 80-metre wall off Half Moon Caye. On the island you can meet the red-footed booby birds and the huge hermit crabs face to face, and then it's back in the boat for Long Caye wall.

Dive training is slightly cheaper here than on Ambergris Caye and several dive shops offer PADI **instruction** for around US$250 for an advanced open water course. Some of the best are Belize Diving Services, at the far side of the

Recommended snorkelling tours

A number of offices in the village centre offer snorkelling trips and, as much depends on your guide, there's not really a lot to choose between them. That said, the ones listed in this box consistently offer the best trips and guides; all are on Front Street unless otherwise stated.

Anwar Snorkel Tours Second block north from the main dock ☎226-0327. Carlos Miller, one of the best tour guides on the caye, is based here.

Carlos Eco Tours Near the *Sandbox Restaurant* ☎600-1654, ⒺÞcarlosayala10@hotmail.com. Carlos Ayala is a very conscientious guide who takes small groups on snorkelling or sailing trips, with an emphasis on conservation and education.

Caye Quest Adventures At *Tina's Guest House* ☎226-0351, Ⓔcayequest33@hotmail.com. Run by very experienced guide Mark Leslie, great local snorkelling and tours to observe the manatees at Swallow Caye.

Chocolate's Manatee Tours At Chocolate's Gift Shop ☎226-0151, Ⓔchocolate@btl.net. Lionel "Chocolate" Heredia is Caye Caulker's longest-serving tour guide, and was instrumental in getting Swallow Caye designated a reserve.

Ras Creek By the main front dock, no phone. Ras runs outstanding trips in his boat *Heritage* (Bz$25), leaving from the Front Dock around 11am, taking you out to the reef right in front of the caye. He'll show you nurse sharks and eagle rays in their element as you float above them. Rum punch is provided, and guests help prepare lunch, arriving back as the sun is setting – the perfect end to an utterly relaxing day.

Seagull Adventures On the street leading to the Back Dock ☎226-0384, Ⓔseagulladventures@hotmail.com. Arranges all kinds of snorkelling trips, but specializes in day-trips to the Blue Hole and Half Moon Caye (leaves at 6.30am; Bz$180).

Tsunami Adventures At the *Costa Maya Cabañas* ☎226-0462, Ⓦwww.tsunamiadventures.com. Very professional agency run by Canadian Heather Martin, arranging all snorkelling and diving trips and able to book flights and tours throughout Belize.

---

soccer field (☎226-0217, Ⓦwww.belizedivingservices.com); Paradise Down, whose office is at the front of the *Oceanside Bar* (☎226-0437, Ⓦwww.paradisedown.com); and Frenchie's, towards the northern end of the village (☎226-0234, Ⓔfrenchies@btl.net). You can buy disposable underwater cameras from the dive shops, but higher-quality photographic equipment is not generally available for rent. If you'd like to learn **underwater photography**, get in touch with James Beveridge of Seaing is Belizing (☎220-4079, Ⓔbzvisuals@bvtl.net).

Sailing and other day-trips

Another great way to enjoy the sea and the reef is to spend the better part of a day on one of the caye's **sailboat trips**, costing around Bz$60–75 and usually including several snorkelling stops and lunch, arriving back as the sun goes down; there are also some **sunset cruises** (about Bz$35) on offer. The most tranquil, run by very experienced skipper Juni Zaldivar, is aboard *Trinity* (maximum eight people; ☎226-0414); check at the house across from the basketball court, which is opposite the *Cyber Café*. Other wonderful day-trips are offered by Ragamuffin Tours, near the north end of Front Street (☎226-0348, Ⓦwww.raggamuffintours.com), with several beautiful wooden sailboats. They also operate **overnight trips** to Lighthouse Reef and even go down to Placencia (see p.246). The best bargain has to be Johnny's Tours, on Front Street next to the *Cyber Café*, which offers all-day trips on the sloop *Sexy Chicken* for Bz$60, or a 5pm sunset cruise for Bz$30 – bring your own food and drink.

For **sailboat rental** visit Sayl King, on the beach just north of the centre (☎226-0489, ⓦwww.saylking.com), where you can rent a dingy Bz$20–30 per hour. If you want to go around the southern section of the caye on your own you can rent a **kayak** for around Bz$25–40; try *Daisy's* hotel or ask at the Galería Hicaco, where you can also rent a **sailboard** and receive instruction.

As you walk around town, you'll also see signs for **fishing trips**. Some of the best are operated by Porfilio Guzman (☎226-0152) and Roly Rosado, both of whom live near the north end of the village; ask for them by name – any of the locals will direct you. Several operators (see box on p.133) also offer **day-trips inland** to Altun Ha and Lamanai; see "Trips inland" on p.122 for a description of the route.

Relaxing on land

After a day or two of water-based activity you might feel a need to slow down a little, perhaps get a massage or do some selective **shopping**. Lotus House, near the north end of Front Street (☎608-0009), is an advanced body studio, where Christa Stubbington and Marette Rauet offer a range of **massage and spa therapies**, as well as "aura soma colour readings" and Tarot readings. At the Transcendence Healing Center (☎226-0208), in the Tres Angelinas building next to *Habañeros* restaurant, Eva McFarlane offers massage with aromatherapy and Reiki as well as manicure and pedicure; advance booking is recommended for both. Tres Angelinas also houses the Caribbean Colors Art Gallery (ⓦwww.caribbean-colors.com), where Lee Vanderwalker-Kroll displays her own distinctive and very colourful paintings and photographs alongside the work of talented **local artists** such as Nelson Young; you can also buy CDs of Belizean music, books about Belize and *Rough Guides*.

Eating, drinking and entertainment

Good home-cooking, large portions and very reasonable prices are features of the island's many **restaurants**, half of which you'll pass while looking for a room. **Lobster** (in season) is served in every imaginable dish, from curry to chow mein; other **seafood** is generally good value, accompanied by rice or potatoes and sometimes salad. Along Front Street are a couple of **fast-food** stands, serving tacos and burritos. There's a good **bakery** on the street leading to the football field, which does great cinnamon buns, and many houses advertise banana bread, coconut cakes and other home-baked goodies. As you walk around you'll probably also see children selling bread, pastries and other treats from bowls balanced on their heads – it's always worth seeing what's on offer. If you fancy an ice cream for dessert try the *Lighthouse Ice Cream Parlour*, on Front Street just north of the centre. You can also buy food at several well-stocked **shops and supermarkets**.

Restaurants and cafés

Cindy's Café On Front St, just south of the centre. The best place for filling continental breakfasts, serving homemade bread and bagels, granola, fruit and excellent coffee in a happy atmosphere on a shady deck. Also has a book exchange.

Coco Plum Gardens Café South of the centre, just north of the airstrip. Wholefood café serving great breakfasts – think crepes and homemade granola – as well as gourmet deli sandwiches, pizza and desserts in a lush garden setting, with an art gallery; it's well worth the walk. Also has delicious Belizean fruit jams and wines and sells books and herbal remedies. Open 8am–5.30pm; closed Wed.

Glenda's At the back of the island, south of the main dock. Justly famous for delicious cinnamon rolls and fresh orange juice, this is a favourite breakfast meeting-place.

Habañeros On Front St, near the main dock ☎226-0487. The island's top restaurant, serving fantastic and creative gourmet international meals, with fine wine and slick bar service; it's usually packed, so call for reservations. Closed Mon & Tues.

Happy Lobster On Front St, north of the centre. Inexpensive restaurant serving seafood, rice and beans and local dishes; offers some of the best value on the caye.

Jolly Roger's Barbecue On a beachfront deck north of *Oceanside* (see below). The very jolly Roger Martinez cooks up the island's best grilled lobster and fish in healthy portions at great prices.

Marin's Restaurant Towards the south end of the town's middle street. A long-established locally run restaurant, serving really fresh seafood either indoors or in a shady courtyard.

Martinez Fast Food On Front St, just past the *Miramar Hotel*. Reasonable Belizean food at excellent prices; might also have some basic rooms available.

Mary-Jo's Deli On Front St, a block south of the centre. Great snacks, sandwiches, juices and desserts served on a shady wooden deck. Also rents bikes. Open daily 9am–3pm.

Rasta Pasta On the beach, just north of the centre. A very popular and relaxing place, serving creative seafood and pasta dishes flavoured with owner Maralyn's unique blend of herbs and spices – which you can buy at the bar. Great mixed drinks.

Tropical Paradise At the southern end of Front St. Good-quality Belizean and American-style food at reasonable prices in a comfortable a/c dining room.

Wish Willy's Near the north end of the island; follow the signs from near Frenchie's dock, off Front St. A friendly restaurant in a ramshackle building at the back of the island, where Belizean chef Maurice Moore creates some of the most delicious seafood in Belize in a relaxed atmosphere.

Bars and nightlife

Caye Caulker's **social scene** revolves around its various bars and restaurants, and frequently there's **live music** and **happy hours** to add atmosphere to the evening, especially in the busier places along Front Street. Few places are strictly bars, though the three-storey *I&I's*, between *Tropical Paradise* and *Edith's*, is more bar than restaurant – make sure to take care negotiating the stairs on the way down. Most people are nice enough, but as the evening wears on and drink takes its toll things can get rowdy. Be careful with your money, too – despite the laid-back atmosphere Caye Caulker has a criminal element. Away from the music, evening entertainment mostly consists of relaxing in a restaurant over dinner or a drink, or gazing at the tropical night sky from the end of a dock.

Other northern cayes and atolls

Although Caye Caulker and San Pedro are the only villages anywhere on the reef, there are several **other islands** that you can visit and even stay on. Some of these are within day-trip distance of the main northern cayes or from Belize City and there are a few superbly isolated hotels – usually called **lodges** – on some reefs and cayes. The attraction of these lodges is the "simple life", usually focusing on diving or fishing; staying at them is generally part of a package that includes transfers from the airport, accommodation, all meals and the sports on offer. Buildings are low-key, wooden and sometimes thatched, and the group you're with will probably be the only people staying there. There are few phones (though most are in radio contact with Belize City), electricity comes from a generator and views of palm trees curving over turquoise water reinforce the sense of isolation.

Caye Chapel

Immediately south of Caye Caulker, privately owned **Caye Chapel** stands as a terrible example of a tropical island totally ruined by tourism development. There's an airstrip, hotel and marina, but it's the **golf course** – and the run-off from heavy applications of fertilizer and pesticides required to keep the grass green – which causes the worst environmental problems. Most of the mangroves have been cut down and the daily raking of the shore by tractors to create a beach has caused tremendous erosion. Virtually the whole island is now encased in an ugly concrete sea wall – which you'll see if you're in a boat heading to Caye Caulker. On a historical note, it was on Caye Chapel that the defeated Spanish fleet paused for a few days after the **Battle of St George's Caye** in 1798. According to legend, some of their dead are buried here.

St George's Caye

Tiny **St George's Caye**, around 15km from Belize City, was the capital of the Baymen from the seventeenth century and still manages to exude an air of colonial grandeur; its beautifully restored colonial houses face east to catch the breeze and their lush green lawns are enclosed by white picket fences. The sense of history is reinforced by the eighteenth-century cannons mounted in front of some of the finer houses; for another glimpse into the past you could head for the small graveyard of the early settlers on the southern tip of the island. Today, the island is home to the villas of Belize's elite, an adventure training centre for British forces in Belize and a few fishermen, who live toward the northern end in an area known, appropriately enough, as "Fisherman Town".

There's not much here for the casual visitor, though some fishing and snorkelling trips do call at St George's Caye. If you do come here you may meet Austrian Karl Bishof, who runs Bela Carib, a company that carefully collects and exports tropical fish. The tanks contain a fascinating display of reef creatures and you're welcome to look around. After your visit take a look at the great T-shirts in Karl's Fisherman Town Gift Shop.

Accommodation on the caye is available at the luxurious *St George's Lodge* (T 220-4444, W www.gooddiving.com), an all-inclusive **diving resort** comprising a ten-room main lodge and six luxury wood-and-thatch cottages with private verandahs and a beautiful dining room. The *Lodge* was Belize's first dedicated diving resort and has long enjoyed a reputation as one of the very best in the country, consistently receiving rave reviews in the diving press. The price depends on whether or not you're diving, but rates begin at US$250 per person and go up to US$360 per person. You can get a better deal by paying in advance for a package, which includes airport transfer, diving and meals.

The Bluefield Range

In the **Bluefield Range**, a group of mangrove cayes 35km southeast of Belize City, visitors have the opportunity to stay at a remote **fishing camp**. *Ricardo's Beach Huts* (T 614-4298) offer simple, comfortable accommodation (minimum two nights) right on the water, in huts built on stilts. At US$175 per person for three days/two nights it's not cheap, but the price includes transport to and from Belize City, all meals – including, as you might imagine, fresh fish and lobster – and a fishing or snorkelling trip to Rendezvous Caye, right on the reef; *Rough Guide* readers get a discount. Owner Ricardo Castillo is a reliable, expert fishing guide, scrupulously practising conservation of the reef.

The Turneffe Islands

Though shown on some maps as one large island, the virtually uninhabited **Turneffe Islands** are Belize's largest atoll, an oval archipelago rising over 300m from the seabed and enclosed by a beautiful coral reef. Situated 40km from Belize City, they consist of low-lying mangrove islands– some quite large – and sandbanks around a shallow lagoon. Currently there is no protected land at Turneffe, but there is a proposal for a marine reserve at **Rendezvous Point**, on the northwest edge of the atoll. The islands and reefs can be visited on day-trips from San Pedro or Caye Caulker (see boxes on pp.121 & 133, respectively, for contact info).

Fishing here, for bonefish and permit on the shallow flats, is world-class, and dedicated anglers can expect to fish at least six hours every day, with most of the sport-fishing on a "catch and release" basis. With over eighty logged sites, **diving** is sublime and there's any amount of simply wonderful **snorkelling**. A few places offer all-inclusive **accommodation**, but the construction of resorts on this remote, fragile island has involved cutting down mangroves – the cause of controversy among conservationists.

For all the places below you'll need to book ahead – and, though (with one exception) they are very expensive, most will offer discounts if you book through their websites. Prices include transport from Belize City (and usually from the international airport), all meals and whatever diving and/or fishing package is arranged; all the resorts have electricity and most have air-conditioning. Most guests will be fishing or diving much of the time, but there are always hammocks to relax in; there will usually be kayaks and windsurf boards available to use; and the snorkelling right offshore is superb. Although staying out here has a heavenly, even dreamlike quality, sandflies and mosquitoes can bring you back to earth with a vengeance – so bring repellent.

On **Blackbird Caye**, halfway down the eastern side of the archipelago, *Blackbird Caye Resort* (in US ☎1-800/326-1724, Ⓦwww.blackbirdresort .com), has luxury wood-and-thatch cabañas and rooms (some with a/c) and a beautiful thatched dining room. A week's high-season package, including transfers, all meals, diving/snorkelling and perhaps fishing costs from around US$1650–2400; three- to four-night packages are available from around US$800–900.

Ropewalk Caye (also known as Pelican Caye), on the atoll's southeastern side, has two new resorts. *Zacil Ha* (☎820-4005, Ⓦwww.fivesisterslodge.com) – "Crystal Water" in Mayan – has gorgeous wooden air-conditioned cabañas on a palm-fringed bay sheltered by the reef. It's owned by Carlos Popper, who built the renowned *Five Sisters Lodge* in Cayo (see p.180), and he offers six-day packages for around US$1500. Just a short walk away, *Amigos Dive Camp* (☎824-2553, Ⓦwww.amigosbelize.com) has simpler accommodation, aimed at budget travellers. The one main thatched building is set in a palm grove on the beach, with the kitchen and dining room downstairs and rooms upstairs, and with separate, shared bathroom facilities. It's a bit rustic but very good value for what you get: a five-day package including ocean fishing, some diving and snorkelling is US$700; three days without diving is US$200.

Finally, at the southern tip of the archipelago, **Caye Bokel** boasts the *Turneffe Island Lodge* (in US ☎1-800/874-0118, Ⓦwww.turneffelodge.com), with luxurious air-conditioned cabins on a twelve-acre private island. Catering to upmarket fishing and diving groups, a package costs US$1575–3500 per person for a week, depending on the activity. Half-weeks are also available.

Lighthouse Reef, the Blue Hole and Half Moon Caye

About 80km east of Belize City is Belize's outer atoll, **Lighthouse Reef**, made famous by Jacques Cousteau, who visited in the 1970s. The two main attractions here are the Blue Hole, which attracted Cousteau's attention, and the Half Moon Caye Natural Monument. The **Blue Hole**, now also protected as a Natural Monument, is technically a "karst-eroded sinkhole", a shaft about 300m in diameter and 135m deep, which drops through the bottom of the lagoon and opens out into a complex network of **caves and crevices**, complete with stalactites and stalagmites. It was formed over a million years ago when Lighthouse Reef was a sizeable island – or even part of the mainland. Investigations have shown that caves underlie the entire reef, and that the sea has simply punctured the cavern roof at the site of the Blue Hole. Its great depth gives it a peculiar deep-blue colour, and even swimming across is disorienting as there's no sense of anything beneath you. Unsurprisingly, the Blue Hole and Lighthouse Reef are major magnets for **divers**, offering incredible walls and drop-offs. Several **shipwrecks** form artificial reefs; the most prominent is the *Ermlund*, which ran aground in 1971 and looms over the reef just north of Half Moon Caye.

You can visit the atoll as either a day- or overnight trip from San Pedro (p.121) or Caye Caulker (p.133), and **camp** on Half Moon Caye (see below). The only other place to stay on the atoll is at the amazing *Lighthouse Reef Resort*, an all-inclusive diving and fishing resort on privately owned Northern Caye (in US ☎1-800/423-3114, ⊛www.scubabelize.com). Frequently chosen by dive magazines as the best diving resort in Belize, it really is an exceptional place to stay. After being flown in to the island's private airstrip, guests stay in luxurious colonial-style air-conditioned suites and villas set in splendid isolation on a beach of soft, powdery sand. A package costs US$1700–2200 per person per week depending on activity.

The **Half Moon Caye Natural Monument**, the first marine conservation area in Belize, was declared a national park in 1982. Its lighthouse was first built in 1820 and has not always been effective: several wrecks testify to the dangers of the reef. The medium-sized caye is divided into two distinct ecosystems: in the west, guano from thousands of seabirds fertilizes the soil, allowing the growth of dense vegetation, while the eastern half has mostly coconut palms growing in the sand. A total of 98 bird species has been recorded here, including frigate birds, ospreys, mangrove warblers, white-crowned pigeons and – most important of all – a resident population of four thousand **red-footed boobies**, one of only two nesting colonies in the Caribbean. The boobies came by their name because they displayed no fear of humans, enabling sailors to kill them in their thousands, and they still move only reluctantly when visitors stroll through them. Their nesting area is accessible from a platform and the birds are not in the least bothered by your presence. Apart from the birds, the island supports iguanas, lizards and both loggerhead and hawksbill turtles, which nest on the beaches; this in turn attracts the biggest hermit and land crabs in Belize.

There's no accommodation on the caye, but **camping** is allowed with the permission of the Belize Audubon Society (see p.65), which manages the reserve; many of the overnight diving expeditions camp here. Visitors must register with the rangers on arrival, and pay the Bz$10 **fee**, which also includes the Blue Hole. Some of the overnight dive trips from San Pedro and Caye Caulker and some sea-kayaking trips with Island Expeditions (see "Basics", p.11) include camping on the caye. The **visitor centre**, built by volunteers from Raleigh, will help you understand the ecology of the caye.

Swallow Caye Wildlife Sanctuary

Just a ten-minute boat ride from Belize City, the Drowned Cayes (which include Swallow Caye) form the **Swallow Caye Wildlife Sanctuary** (Bz$10 entry fee), a secure refuge for the area's healthy population of **West Indian manatees**. Belize has the largest surviving population of these gentle giants, which congregate here to feed on the abundant turtle-grass beds, their primary food source, and use the deeper areas near Swallow Caye as resting places. The sanctuary, created in 2002 and covering over 36 square kilometres, sustains an array of other marine life including bottlenose dolphins, American crocodiles and the upside-down jellyfish. It's co-managed by the Friends of Swallow Caye and the Ministry of Natural Resources, and **day-trips** are available, mainly departing from Caye Caulker (see box on p.133). On one of these ventures, the skipper will turn off the motor as you near, quietly pushing the boat towards the manatees in order not to disturb them. Although you're not allowed in the water, you can generally get good photographs – of the head and face at least.

Travel details

For a rundown of **flights** and **boats** to the cayes from Belize City and between the cayes themselves, see the boxes on pp.113 and 128.

Cayo and the west

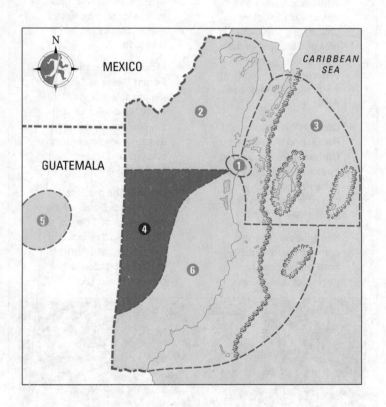

CHAPTER 4

Highlights

✳ **The Belize Zoo** Enjoy close-up sightings of the animals and birds of Central America, notably Panamá the harpy eagle. See p.146

✳ **Actun Tunichil Muknal** Hike across rivers and through jungle before descending to Xibalba, an astonishing cave that was, for the Maya, the underworld and abode of the Lords of Death. See p.154

✳ **Green Hills Butterfly Ranch and Botanic Garden** Relax surrounded by clouds of colourful butterflies in this fascinating and informative botanical garden. See p.157

✳ **San Ignacio** Stay in a comfortable, affordable hotel and choose from dozens of adventure

trips in this charming town, still full of colonial buildings. See p.159

✳ **The Macal River** Observe iguanas in the trees and watch the scenery slide by as you take a tranquil float back to San Ignacio along this gentle jungle river. See p.167

✳ **Mountain Pine Ridge Forest Reserve** Escape the jungle's humidity to enjoy the cooler air of the pine forest, as well as many clear mountain streams and waterfalls. See p.175

✳ **Caracol** The greatest Maya city in Belize, where you can ascend Caana, a 1200-year-old palace and temple complex that's still the tallest building in the country. See p.180

△ Harpy eagle at Belize Zoo

Cayo and the west

Heading along the **Western Highway** to the Guatemalan border 130km away you escape the heat and humidity of Belize City and travel through a wide range of landscapes, from pine savannah and river valleys to rolling hills and tropical forest. It's a fast, paved route that leaves Belize City through mangrove swamps and heads inland across open, sometimes swampy savannah, scattered with palmetto scrub and low pines. Before reaching Belmopan the road passes several places of interest: the **Belize Zoo**, well worth a visit if you're interested in the country's natural history, the **Monkey Bay Wildlife Sanctuary and National Park** and **Guanacaste National Park**. A short detour south (taken by all westbound buses) is the capital, **Belmopan**, established in 1970 and surely one of the smallest capital cities in the world.

West of Belmopan, following the Belize River valley, the road skirts the lush foothills of the Maya Mountains, a beautiful area where the air is clear and the land astonishingly fertile. You're now in **Cayo District**, the largest of Belize's six districts and arguably the most beautiful – a sentiment enthusiastically endorsed by the inhabitants when they declare "The west is the best."

Most of southern and western Cayo, including the entire mountain range, is under official protection in a vast network of national parks, wildlife sanctuaries and forest and archeological reserves – part of Belize's largest continuous area of protected land – stretching from the Caribbean coast to the Guatemalan border. The **Mountain Pine Ridge Forest Reserve**, to the south of the highway, is a pleasantly cool region of hills, pine woods and waterfalls, boasting some of the finest lodge accommodation in the country.

San Ignacio, on the Macal River, and only 15km from the Guatemalan border, is the busy main town of Cayo District and the ideal base for exploring the forests, rivers and ruins of western Belize. A canoe or kayak trip along the **Macal River valley**, as the river tumbles from the Maya Mountains into the calmer waters of the tree-lined Macal gorge, is a highlight of any visit to Cayo, and there are jungle cabins to suit all budgets on the riverbanks. Deep in the jungle of the Vaca plateau, south of Ignacio, lies **Caracol**, the largest Maya site in Belize and a main focus for current archeological research and restoration, while beneath the ground await more astonishing Maya treasures in the many **caves** now open to adventurous visitors.

Between San Ignacio and the Guatemalan border, the road climbs past the hilltop ruin of **Cahal Pech**, then descends following the valley of the **Mopan River**, where there are more delightful riverside lodges. Belize's westernmost Maya site, **El Pilar**, 18km northwest of San Ignacio, actually extends into Guatemala, and is the first International Archaeological Reserve anywhere in

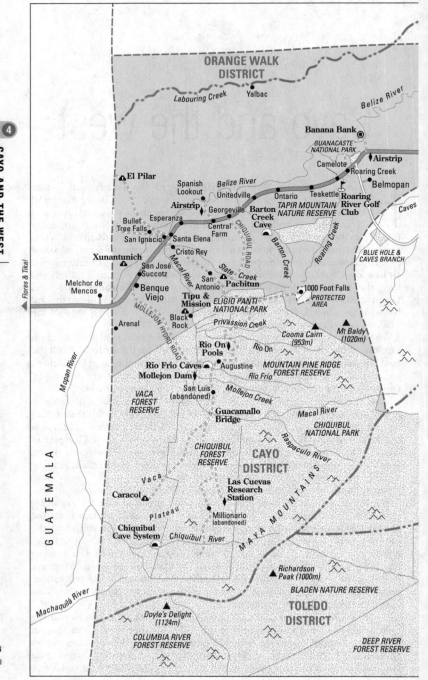

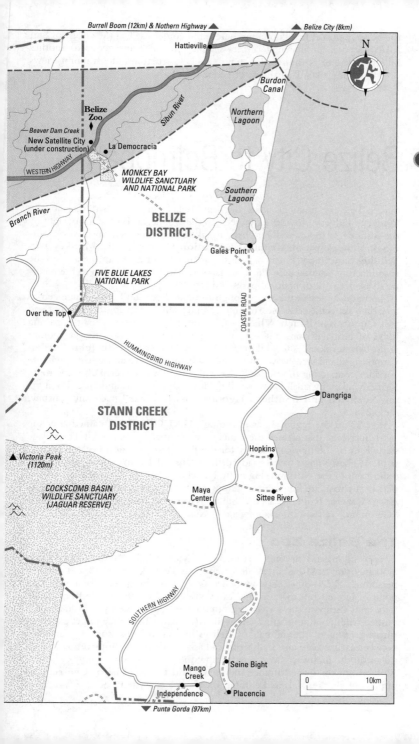

the Maya region. A few kilometres before the border itself, at the village of **San José Succotz**, an ancient ferry crosses the river, allowing access to another hilltop Maya site, **Xunantunich**, whose highest structures offer stunning views over to Guatemala's department of Petén.

Belize City to Belmopan

Served by very frequent buses between Belize City and San Ignacio, the Western Highway provides easy access to the wonderful **Belize Zoo**, right by the roadside, so there's really no need to take a tour; there's inexpensive accommodation nearby at the **Tropical Education Center** and the **Monkey Bay Wildlife Sanctuary**. Further on, at the approach to Belmopan and also on the roadside, tiny **Guanacaste Park** offers a fascinating introduction to the country's vast network of national parks and reserves.

The highway leaves the city through the middle of the Lord's Ridge cemetery, then skirts the coastline, running behind a tangle of mangrove swamps and past **Cucumber Beach Wharf** – until recently a graveyard for the rusting hulks of beached ships but now undergoing transformation to yet another cruise ship terminal. A few kilometres further, you cross the **Sir John Burden Canal**, an inland waterway that serves as a nature reserve and valuable wildlife corridor connecting the Belize River with the **Sibun River**. This is the route formerly taken by small boats travelling down to Dangriga and Gales Point via the **Northern and Southern lagoons** (some tours still make this journey; see p.218).

After 23km the highway passes through **HATTIEVILLE**, named after the 1961 hurricane that created the refugees who initially populated it. The village started life as a temporary shelter for the homeless, but soon became permanent. At Hattieville, a paved road north to **Burrell Boom** (see p.82) provides a short cut to the Northern Highway. The curious steep hills to the left on this part of the road are limestone outcrops, quarried for road-building. The highest is **Gracie Rock**, near the Sibun River, the location of the fictional "Geronimo" in the film *The Mosquito Coast*.

The Belize Zoo

Twenty kilometres beyond Hattieville, at Mile 29, the **Belize Zoo** (daily 8.30am–5pm; Bz$16 adult, Bz$8 for children, Peace Corps, VSO and military personnel; ☎220-8004, ⓦ www.belizezoo.org) is, for most people, the first point of interest out this way and easily visited on a half-day trip from Belize City or as a stop on the way to or from the west. And, unless you're an accomplished wildlife photographer, this is likely to be the best place to get excellent **photographs** of the animals of Belize. To **get to the zoo** take any bus between Belize City and Belmopan and ask the driver to drop you off; there's a sign on the highway and zoo staff know the times of onward buses. A 200m walk brings you to the entrance and the **Gerald Durrell Visitor Centre**, with displays of children's art and exhibits on Belize's ecosystems.

Probably the finest zoo in the Americas south of the US and long recognized as a phenomenal conservation achievement, the zoo originally opened in 1983 after an ambitious wildlife film (*Path of the Raingods*) left Sharon Matola, the film's production assistant, with a collection of semi-tame animals no longer able to fend for themselves in the wild. For locals and visitors alike this means the chance to see the native animals of Belize at close quarters, housed in spacious enclosures which closely resemble their natural habitat. Since the zoo opened no animals have been taken from the wild for display – all are either donated or confiscated pets, injured wild animals brought in for healing and rehabilitation, sent from other zoos (often to take part in captive breeding programmes) or have been born here. The zoo is actively involved in conservation education – all schoolchildren in Belize benefit from a free official trip here – and it has achieved international recognition for its **captive breeding** programmes.

The zoo is organized around the theme of "a walk through Belize", with a trail that takes you into the pine ridge, the forest edge, the rainforest, lagoons and the river forest; witty, hand-painted signs identify what you're seeing. The most famous resident is April, a now venerable **Baird's tapir** (known locally as a "mountain cow") well known to the schoolchildren of Belize, who visit in their hundreds on her birthday (in April) to feed her a huge vegetable birthday cake. Although April has been presented with potential mates, she hasn't produced any offspring; prospects for progeny now rest with Scotty and Bullethead, a pair of younger adult tapirs.

All the Belizean cats are represented and some, including the **jaguars**, have bred successfully; there's even a rarer melanistic (black) jaguar. One of the first aviaries you see houses a flock of vividly colourful **scarlet macaws**, and other birds include toucans, various parrot species, jabiru storks, a spectacled owl and several vultures and hawks. The real avian star of the show, however, is Panamá, a magnificent male **harpy eagle** (originally from Panamá) whose role in an ambitious captive breeding programme is crucial to the planned reintroduction of the largest eagle in the Americas to Belize. When you're on the viewing platform outside his spacious enclosure he'll look at you with seemingly all-knowing eyes – and you can be grateful you're out of reach of his enormous steely talons.

Other zoo inhabitants include deer, spider and howler monkeys, peccaries, agoutis (which sometimes appear on menus as "gibnut") and numerous snakes. Both species of **crocodile** found in Belize thrive here, and you can get great close-ups of open jaws filled with powerful teeth.

In addition to being a dedicated and effective campaigner for conservation in Belize, Sharon has written several excellent and extremely popular children's books with a strong conservation message. These and other souvenirs (including *Rough Guides*) are on sale in the **gift shop**. If you're really keen on supporting the zoo you can become a Friend and receive a regular newsletter. The website is always worth a look for updates about the zoo and current information on conservation issues in Belize.

The Tropical Education Center

Across the highway from the zoo, and a few hundred metres back towards Belize City, the **Tropical Education Center** (T220-8003 or 602-4980, E tec@belizezoo.org) focuses on school, college and tour guide training groups, though it's open to all and has opportunities for overseas students. Study facilities include a classroom with Internet access and a well-equipped library, while outside there are self-guided **nature trails** and observation decks around two small lagoons.

Anyone can stay here and the **accommodation**, all fully screened with electric light, hot showers and flush toilets, arranged in the pine savannah woodland, is wonderful. The three wooden **dorms** with tiled floors (Bz$30 per person) have either double or single beds and shared showers, though for a fraction more money a couple could stay in a comfortable wooden cabin on stilts in the "**camp**" (❹), also with shared showers. Finally, two **guesthouses** (❹; lower long-term rates for researchers) with private bath, stove and fridge, offer seclusion overlooking the lagoon. **Internet** access is available and guests can take a special nocturnal tour of the zoo for Bz$20. If there's no group staying you can cook in the communal kitchen. If you're at the zoo and want to stay, ask at the office and TEC manager Tony Garel will come and pick you up.

Two kilometres beyond the zoo, the **Coastal** (or Manatee) **Road** provides an unpaved short cut (marked by a sign, a gas station and a bar) to **Gales Point** and **Dangriga** (see pp.218 & 223, respectively). The road is in good condition but only served by one bus a day in either direction. The huge construction site just beyond here is the future location of a new town – nicknamed "Satellite City" – which is intended to provide an alternative to both Belize City and Belmopan, though the shoddily built houses haven't managed to attract any serious interest to date. A further 2km past the junction and set back 100m from the highway, *Cheers* is a friendly Canadian-run **bar** where you can get good food at reasonable prices as well as tourist **information**. Should you need to book accommodation somewhere ahead, you can probably use their phone with your phonecard. You can go on guided **bird walks** or follow the **orchid trail** in the bush behind the bar. The **gift shop** has a good selection of maps, books and guides, including *Rough Guides*.

Monkey Bay Wildlife Sanctuary

Half a kilometre past *Cheers* and 400m off to the left of the highway (signposted at Mile 31.5), the **Monkey Bay Wildlife Sanctuary** (Ⓦ www.monkeybaybelize.org) is a 44-square-kilometre protected area extending to the **Sibun River** and offering birding and nature trails through five distinct vegetation and habitat types. The "bay" part of the name comes from a sandy beach on the Sibun River overhung with trees once inhabited by howler and spider monkeys; the monkeys are now returning after a long absence following hurricane disturbance to their habitat. Adjoining the sanctuary across the river is the 9-square-kilometre **Monkey Bay National Park**.

The Sibun River watershed supports abundant birdlife, jaguars, tapirs, howler monkeys, some large crocodiles and the endangered **hawksbill turtle**, which lays its eggs in nests scraped out of beaches at the river mouth. A conservation project has been proposed to protect the entire river valley; the two protected areas covered above already serve as a wildlife corridor spanning the Sibun valley and extending south through karst limestone hills to the Manatee Forest Reserve. Belize government agencies and NGOs are currently working on an ambitious project to expand this corridor to connect protected areas in northern Belize, across the rapidly developing Western Highway, with those in the south.

From Monkey Bay you can arrange guided **canoe, camping, caving and birding trips** on the Sibun River and explore little-visited **caves** in the Sibun Hills to the south, all of which have evidence of use by the ancient Maya. You'll need a guide for the three-day **Indian Creek Trail** to Five Blues Lake (see opposite) and, since Monkey Bay is primarily a field station (see

"Practicalities", below), this and other trips may only be available when student groups are booked in. Anyone can stay here, however, and there's a beautiful swimming spot on the Sibun, a 20min walk from the field station. Monkey Bay is also the contact point for visits to **Cox Lagoon Crocodile Sanctuary**, a 120-square-kilometre private nature reserve north of the highway. This wetland area on the Mussel Creek watershed, home to over one hundred Morelet's crocodiles, also hosts at least a dozen other reptile species, jabiru storks, howler monkeys and jaguars, and visitors can camp, canoe, hike and fish. It's off the beaten track, so you'll usually need to arrange trips well in advance.

Practicalities

The well-signposted Monkey Bay is easily reached by any bus along the highway. The sanctuary headquarters comprises a handsome wooden **field research station** – which serves as library, museum and classroom – a screen-sided dining room and "bunkhouse" dorms. Although the field station specializes in hosting academic programmes in natural history and watershed ecology for students and teachers (it's also the Belize base for Conservation Corridors; see p.324), it's also a wonderfully relaxing **place to stay**, either in the bunkhouse (Bz$15) or camping (Bz$10) on raised platforms under thatched roofs. If there's space available you can also stay in the double rooms or the cabin used by teachers (➍). There are no private bathrooms but the tiled shared showers have hot water and all accommodation has mosquito-netted beds; there's also Internet access for guests. Monkey Bay attempts to be a viable exponent of "off the grid" **sustainable living**, utilizing solar and wind power, rainwater catchment and biogas fuel for cooking; the food, some of it grown in the station's organic gardens, is delicious, plentiful and inexpensive. If you want to hike the Indian Creek Trail contact Marcos Cucul (ⓦwww.mayaguide.bz; see p.220 for more information). To make a **booking** for the field station contact the directors, Matt and Marga Miller (☏820-3032 or 600-3191, ⓔmbay@btl.net), or you can just turn up and ask manager Fiona Martin if there's space available. Next to Monkey Bay, *Amigos Bar* has great **meals** and desserts, a daily happy hour and Internet access.

Banana Bank Lodge

Monkey Bay marks the boundary between the Belize and Cayo districts, and here the open expanse of pine and savannah begins to give way to rich pastures and citrus groves. Twenty-five kilometres beyond Monkey Bay and 2km before the turn-off for Belmopan, opposite the airstrip at Mile 46, a track leads off to the right to **Banana Bank Lodge** (☏829-2020, ⓔbbl@starband.net, ⓦwww.bananabank.com; ➑–➒, including a good breakfast). This 4000-acre working cattle ranch, half of which is still primary forest, is owned by Americans John and Carolyn Carr. They offer great horse-riding, canoeing and swimming, and there are also dozens of Maya mounds to explore. The **accommodation**, with views sweeping down to the Belize River, comprises five spacious, fan-cooled cabañas (two-bed, two-bath), four a/c rooms in the original lodge and new a/c suites with private balconies and Internet access. Tasty, home-cooked meals are served family-style in the thatched dining room.

The *Lodge* is on the north bank of the Belize River; the track ends at the south bank and you cross in a small boat; vehicles can be left safely at the caretaker's house on the riverbank. An alternative route, signposted at the turn-off to the right just beyond **Roaring Creek** village, allows you to drive all the way, crossing the river on an old chain-driven ferry (soon to be replaced by a bridge). Without your own vehicle, call the lodge to arrange a pick-up in Belmopan.

Long before tourists began arriving in Belize *Banana Bank* had been renowned for **horse-riding** – the old racetrack here was popular with the elite from Belize City in the 1920s until the 1970s – and recently the lodge has expanded its equestrian capacity. There are now sixty well-trained horses, a stable block and a training arena. Complete beginners can learn to ride and experts can take some challenging trails. The guides are very friendly, knowledgeable and always ready to help.

The natural history is astonishing: over two hundred bird species have been recorded here, and there's a beautiful **lagoon** with resident Morelet's crocodiles and an observation tower for bird-watching. There's also a small collection of animals at the ranch, including Tika, a tame elderly jaguar. Carolyn is an accomplished artist and her work is exhibited all over the country; if time permits you can visit her studio. She's also very proud of her "**mini observatory**" on the riverbank. The twelve-inch Meade computer-controlled telescope here (which guests can use under supervision) is the best in the country and the absence of light pollution enables you to view galaxies millions of light years away.

Immediately adjacent to *Banana Bank*, *Green Dragon Farm* offers high-speed **Internet access**, a café and bookstore and a swimming pool.

Guanacaste National Park

Right by the highway, 73km from Belize City at the junction for Belmopan and the Hummingbird Highway, **Guanacaste National Park** (daily 8am–4.30pm; Bz$5, includes a short tour with one of the rangers) provides an opportunity to wander through a superb area of lush tropical forest at the confluence of Roaring Creek and the Belize River. This is Belize's smallest national park (only 52 acres), but it's also the easiest to visit – **buses** will stop right outside the park. Sign in at the **visitor centre** near the entrance, which has maps and information on the park ecology (including a superb exhibit on the life-cycle of the leaf-cutter ants, which you'll see all over Belize), and have a look at the orchid display in the courtyard. Outside, four or five short **trails** take you through the park and along the banks of the Belize River, with the opportunity to plunge into a lovely swimming hole after your visit; there's also a large wooden deck for picnicking and sunbathing.

The main attraction here is a huge **guanacaste** (or tubroos) tree, a forty-metre-high spreading hardwood that supports some 35 other species of plants: hanging from its limbs are a huge range of bromeliads, orchids, ferns, cacti and strangler figs, which blossom spectacularly at the end of the rainy season. The hard and partially water-resistant wood is traditionally favoured for use as feeding troughs, dugout canoes and mortars for hulling rice. A good-sized guanacaste can produce two or three canoes; this specimen escaped being felled because its trunk split into three near the base. In season the guanacaste produces ear-shaped fruit, used as cattle feed. Sadly, there's only the one mature tree.

Other botanical attractions include young mahogany trees, cohune palms, a ceiba (sacred tree of the Maya, also known as silk-cotton tree) and quamwood, while the forest floor is a mass of ferns and mosses. As the park is so close to the road your chances of seeing any four-footed **wildlife** are fairly slim, though armadillos, white-tailed deer, jaguarundis, opossums and agoutis have nevertheless been spotted, and howler and spider monkeys use the park as a feeding ground. Birds abound, with around one hundred species, among them blue-crowned motmots, black-faced ant-thrushes, black-headed trogons, red-lored parrots and squirrel cuckoos. Unfortunately mosquitoes are common too, so bring repellent.

Belmopan

From Guanacaste Park the Western Highway pushes on towards San Ignacio and the Guatemalan border, while a paved branch road turns south 2km towards Belize's capital, **BELMOPAN**, beyond which it becomes the Hummingbird Highway, continuing all the way to the coast at Dangriga. For most people, the capital is no more than a break in the bus ride to or from San Ignacio, though if you're heading to Dangriga or Placencia you may have to change buses here.

Belmopan was founded in 1970 after Hurricane Hattie swept much of Belize City into the sea. The government decided to use the disaster as a chance to move to higher ground and, in a Brasília-style bid to focus development on the interior, chose a site in the geographical heart of the country. The name of the city combines the words "Belize" and "Mopan", the language spoken by the Maya of Cayo. The layout of the main government buildings, designed in the 1960s, is loosely modelled on a Maya city, with structures grouped around a central plaza; the National Assembly building even incorporates a version of the traditional roof comb, a decorative stonework and stucco crest. Although these long, grey concrete buildings, set away from the road and surrounded by grass, won their British architect an award, they now present a rather dismal facade, out of line with their importance.

In classic new-town terms Belmopan was meant to symbolize the dawn of a new era, with tree-lined avenues, banks, a couple of embassies and communications worthy of a world centre – a new capital for independent Belize. The population was planned at 5000 for the first few years, eventually rising to 30,000, but few Belizeans other than government officials (who had no option) have moved here. Although the population has now grown to over 7000, the first thing that strikes you is a sense of space. That said, recent **hurricane** scares on the coast – Mitch in 1998, Keith in 2000 and Iris in 2001– are prompting a rethink by those who can afford to buy or build a house here.

Unless you've come to visit a government department, there's no particular reason to stay any longer in Belmopan than it takes your bus to leave. A museum is under construction and until it's ready you can view some interesting Maya artefacts in glass cases at the **Institute of Archaeology**, behind the market; call ☏822-2106 to arrange a visit. The **Archives Department**, 26–28 Unity Blvd (Mon–Fri 8am–5pm; free; ☏822-2247, ⓦwww.archivesbz.org), also welcomes visitors to its air-conditioned reading room, where photographs, documents, newspapers and sound archives provide fascinating glimpses of old Belize. The department also holds regular exhibitions.

Practicalities

Buses from Belize City to San Ignacio, Benque Viejo, Dangriga and Punta Gorda all pass through Belmopan, so there's at least one service every thirty minutes in either direction – the last bus from Belmopan to Belize City leaves at 7pm, to San Ignacio at 10pm. Most buses stop in the Novelo's terminal but the James Bus pulls up across the parking lot, in front of the wooden market cabins – ask at *Dora's Ice Cream*, in the end stall, for times. Heading south along the Hummingbird Highway, the first to leave is the James Bus at 7am, with other, mainly Southern Transport, services roughly hourly until 6pm.

The **market** itself has several good fast-food and fruit stands and vendors will come aboard buses to sell snacks and drinks. The nearest **restaurant** is the *Caladium*, in front of the Novelo's terminal. With air-conditioning, a no-smoking policy and clean toilets, it's easily the best eatery in the centre, serving tasty,

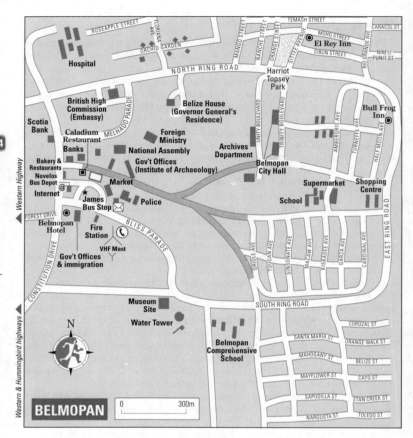

Map of BELMOPAN with labels: ROSEAPPLE STREET, FLORIANA AVE, ORCHID GARDEN, MANGO STREET, NARCHE STREET, ORANGE STREET, SITTEE AVENUE, TEMASH STREET, MOHO STREET, SIBUN STREET, CARACOL ST., NIM LI PUNIT ST., RIO GRANDE AVE, El Rey Inn, Hospital, NORTH RING ROAD, Harriot Topsey Park, British High Commission (Embassy), MELHADO PARADE, Belize House (Governor General's Residence), UNITY BOULEVARD, TRINITY BOULEVARD, AMBERGRIS AVE, TURNEFFE AVE, HALF MOON AVE, Bull Frog Inn, Scotia Bank, Caladium Restaurant, Banks, Foreign Ministry, National Assembly, Gov't Offices (Institute of Archaeology), Archives Department, Belmopan City Hall, Bakery & Restaurants, Novelos Bus Depot, Internet, Market, Police, Supermarket, Shopping Centre, School, James Bus Stop, FOREST DRIVE, Belmopan Hotel, Fire Station, BLISS PARADE, CONSTITUTION DRIVE, Gov't Offices & immigration, VHF Mast, ORIOLE AVE, TOUCAN AVE, SINSONATE AVE, MACAW AVE, KISKADEE AVE, GARZA AVE, CARDINAL AVE, EAST RING ROAD, SOUTH RING ROAD, Museum Site, Water Tower, N, Belmopan Comprehensive School, SANTA MARIA ST, MAHOGANY ST, MAYFLOWER ST, SAPODILLA ST, NARGUSTA ST, CORDZAL ST, ORANGE WALK ST, BELIZE ST, CAYO ST, STAN CREEK ST, TOLEDO ST, BELMOPAN, 0 300m

inexpensive Belizean dishes including a daily special; there's also a takeaway window. Just beyond the market are the **banks** (with ATMs) while the **post office** is to the right of the market square and the BTL **telephone** office is on Bliss Parade, beside the large satellite dish. **Internet** access is available at Techno Hub, in the front of the Novelo's terminal, and at PC Com, behind the *Caladium*. The **immigration** office is in the main government building beside the old movie theatre by the fire station. The **British High Commission** (☎822-2146), equivalent to the embassy, is situated on the North Ring Road, behind the National Assembly building.

Hotels in Belmopan tend to cater for the needs and expense accounts of diplomats and aid officials; San Ignacio, less than an hour away, is far more interesting and much less expensive. If you do have to stay here, the *El Rey Inn*, 23 Moho St (☎822-3438, ✉hibiscus@btl.net; ❸), is a pleasant and reasonably inexpensive option, with clean rooms, bedside lights and private bath. The best place in town is *Bull Frog Inn*, 25 Half Moon Ave (☎822-2111, ⓦwww .bullfroginn.com; ❺–❻). Its comfortable, air-conditioned rooms have cable TV, telephone and balcony, and there's a very good restaurant and bar, frequented by the political elite of Belize.

On to San Ignacio

Beyond Belmopan the scenery becomes more rugged, with thickly forested ridges always in view to the south. Here, although the strictly protected **Tapir Mountain Nature Reserve** is not open to casual visitors, you can get a taste of what's in the reserve by visiting **Actun Tunichil Muknal**, one of the most extraordinary **caves** in the country. The Western Highway stays close to the valley of the Belize River, crossing numerous tributary creeks and passing through a series of villages; Roaring Creek, Camelote, Teakettle, Ontario, Unitedville, Esperanza and finally **Santa Elena**, San Ignacio's sister town on the eastern bank of the Macal River. There's been something of an accommodation boom along this route, with a couple of long-established cottage-style **lodges** now joined by several newer enterprises. Alternatively, with your own vehicle you can turn south at Georgeville, 26km from the Belmopan junction, and take the **Chiquibul Road** to the **Mountain Pine Ridge** (see p.175) and the ruins of **Caracol** (see p.180). Along this unpaved road are several places to stay and the added attraction of Belize's best **butterfly exhibit**.

Roaring River Golf Club

CAMELOTE village, 8km west of Belmopan, holds the first attraction beyond the capital. **Roaring River Golf Club**, at Mile 50 1/4 on the Western Highway (☏ 614-6525), is Belize's only mainland publicly accessible golf course. These immaculately maintained fairways and greens, screened by mature and newly planted trees on the bank of the crystal-clear Roaring River, are the pride and joy of owner Paul Martin. Originally from South Africa, Paul designed and built the nine-hole course himself and it has already gained a fine reputation from both locals and visitors. Here, there's none of the snobbery which can permeate other golf clubs; greens fees are only Bz$40 and it's Bz$20 to rent a set of clubs. Players include the diplomats and other members of the expatriate community that you might expect but you could just as easily find off-duty clerks or Mennonite families swinging their clubs. The abundance of wildlife on the course – testament to Paul's policy of minimal pesticide use – means that it's now a location on the annual Christmas bird count for Belize. And the water hazard on the eighth hole is home to thousands of fish and a crocodile. If you're travelling by bus, get off at the *One Barrel Bar*, at the junction of the three-kilometre track to the course; call from the bar and Paul will come and pick you up.

Tapir Mountain Nature Reserve and Pook's Hill Jungle Lodge

Ten kilometres south of the highway, between Roaring and Barton creeks, **Tapir Mountain Nature Reserve** protects 28 square kilometres of the northern foothills of the Maya Mountains. The reserve, managed by the Belize Audubon Society, is a rich, well-watered habitat covered in high canopy, tropical moist forest and home to all of Belize's **national symbols**: Baird's tapir, the keel-billed toucan, the black orchid and the mahogany tree. Nature reserves are Belize's highest category of protected land and, as one criterion of this is to "maintain natural processes in an undisturbed state", Tapir Mountain can only be visited by accredited researchers and is not readily accessible to the public.

The designation itself however, does not guarantee protection from hunters, and even from farmers encroaching on the reserve.

Although you cannot enter the reserve, you can enjoy spectacular views of it by staying nearby at **Pook's Hill Jungle Lodge** (☎820-2017, ⓔpook-shill@btl.net, ⓦwww.pookshillbelize.com; US$165 double, ⓞ), run by the extremely hospitable Ray and Vicky Snaddon. The turn-off to the lodge is clearly signposted at Mile 52, at the village of **Teakettle**, 8km west of Belmopan. The 9km track up to the lodge is bumpy but in good condition. If you're travelling by bus call ahead – someone will pick you up from the junction, where there's a payphone.

The lodge is set in a clearing on a terraced hillside within a 300-acre private reserve. **Accommodation** is in nine comfortable, thatched cabañas, overlooking the thickly forested Roaring River valley and with breathtaking views across the Tapir Mountain Reserve to the Mountain Pine Ridge beyond. Just below here are two new cabañas, reached by a bridge high over a small creek, and offering even more comfort and seclusion; all have electricity and hot water. This spectacular location clearly held attractions for the ancient Maya, too: the lodge sits on a Maya platform and the cabañas are arranged around a *plazuela* ("small plaza") group with house mounds, an ancestor shrine and other small structures – you can view site plans in the lodge. **Meals** are served in the dining room at the edge of the forest and the food is excellent; upstairs a thatched, open-sided deck with easy chairs and hammocks serves as a bar in the evenings. There's also a small **library** here, with a focus on archeology and natural history.

To see **wildlife**, you don't have to go far. Bird-watching here is in a league of its own and there will almost always be a raptor of some kind, perhaps a **bat falcon**, hunting or feeding in view from the lodge. Every year a pair of spectacled owls raise a brood near the cabins and *Pook's Hill* is also a centre of Belize's green iguana breeding programme. There are wonderful self-guided **nature trails** and superb **horse-riding trails** along farm and forest tracks, and you can hike or ride the lodge's fine horses to more substantial ruins further up the valley (see below). To cool off you can swim or go **tubing** in the river. If you like, a guide can lead you on a hike to Actun Tunichil Muknal.

Actun Tunichil Muknal

A few kilometres higher up Roaring Creek valley, south of the *Pook's Hill Lodge* lies **Actun Tunichil Muknal** ("Cave of the Stone Sepulchre"), one of the most spectacular **caves** in the country. As the cave is also a registered archeological site (entry fee Bz$30), only specially trained guides are allowed to lead groups into the cave – and you'll need to be pretty fit and able to swim to do the trip; for much of the time you're wading knee- or even chest-deep in water. Aaron Juan, of Mayawalk Adventures (☎824-3070) and Emilio Awe of Pacz Tours (☎824-2477), both based in San Ignacio, run excellent, adventurous trips (around US$75).

Actun Tunichil Muknal was discovered in 1986 by archeologist Thomas Miller, who named it for the astonishingly well-preserved skeletons of Maya human sacrifices he found within. A total of fourteen individual skeletons have been identified, including six infants under 3 years old and a child of about 7; the ages of the adults ranged from their twenties to their forties. None was actually buried: they were simply laid in or near shallow pools in natural travertine terraces. Alongside the skeletons are 150 ceramic vessels, probably originally containing food offerings, most of which have been ceremonially "killed" by piercing the base to release the powerful energy or spirit of the vessel.

Although looting has occurred in one chamber, the main chamber, much higher up the cave wall, has not been touched and the **megalithic artefacts** here are absolutely spellbinding: an enormous stingray spine and a huge obsidian blade lean upright against each other, encircled by stones. Carved in slate, these metre-long representations of bloodletting implements are an indisputable indication of the sacred ceremonies performed here over 1200 years ago. Perhaps the most dramatic sight, however, is the skeleton of a young woman lying below a rock wall – and, nearby, the stone axe that may have killed her. To the ancient Maya, caves were the entrances to Xibalba – "Place of Fright" and the abode of the Lords of Death. Yet these victims, and the people who sacrificed them, made the difficult descent over one kilometre underground with only pine torches to light the way: it must indeed have been an apprehensive, even terrifying, journey to an utterly fearful place.

Warrie Head Lodge and Caesar's Place

Beyond Teakettle, just over the Warrie Head Creek bridge at Mile 54, is the entrance to the **Warrie Head Ranch and Lodge** (☎822-3826, ⓦwww.belizenet.com/warrie; ❼), formerly a logging camp and now a working farm offering comfortable wooden cabins and rooms set back a few hundred metres from the road. The lodge is managed by a wonderful couple, Hector and Lydia Wade, while owners Johnny and Elvira Searle have gone to great lengths to provide visitors with a glimpse of Belize's colonial heritage; the rooms, filled with authentic period furniture, including several four-poster beds, have modern facilities and most have private bath. The older building has a full kitchen and living room, complete with library and videos of Belize, and colonial artefacts abound outside, including a restored 1904 steam tractor once used to haul logs, and a working sugarcane mill. Delicious Creole-style meals are taken in the mahogany-panelled dining room, while the outdoor bar, decorated with musical instruments, has a lovely wooden deck shaded by a beautiful old Bay cedar tree, dripping with orchids. The grounds, filled with fruit and native trees, slope down to the creek, where an exquisite series of travertine terraces form turquoise pools – perfect for a cooling dip. You can also arrange tours of the farm trails on horseback or in the ranch's Mennonite buggy.

Further along, on the bank of Barton Creek to the right of the highway at Mile 60, **Caesar's Place** (☎824-2341, ⓔblackrock@btl.net; ❺) is Caesar and Antonieta Sherrard's café and **guesthouse**, with comfortable, attractive and secure rooms with private bath, trailer hook-ups (Bz\$20) and space for camping (Bz\$10). The *Patio Café* is a great place to stop for lunch and serves delicious **home-cooking**, with Belizean and American dishes mingling with the flavours of other Central American countries; you can always get a vegetarian meal here. It's also a renowned **music** venue, featuring local band Mango Jam on the first Saturday of the month. A short trail leads down to a beautiful **swimming** hole on the creek

The **gift shop** here is one of the largest and best in Belize, featuring wood carvings using wood properly dried in a solar kiln, slate carvings reproducing Maya art, a wide selection of Belizean contemporary art, Guatemalan textiles and silver jewellery from Taxco in Mexico. There's also a **mini museum**, authorized by the Institute of Archaeology, exhibiting Maya artefacts from Belize, and the **bookshop** is a good place to pick up information about the Maya, and about travelling in Guatemala and Mexico, with maps and guides, including *Rough Guides*. Caesar's son Julian can organize canoe or caving trips along the Macal River. Caesar runs another place, *Black Rock*, on the Macal River (see p.170).

△ Hawkesworth Suspension Bridge

Beyond *Caesar's*, just over the Barton Creek bridge, two prominent grass-covered **pyramids** mark the unexcavated Maya site of **Floral Park**; you'll see virtually all there is to see as you pass by in the bus. Six kilometres beyond here, you come to the **Georgeville** junction from where (with your own transport) you can head south along the **Chiquibul Road** (see below). A few kilometres further along the highway you pass Central Farm, the University of Belize's Agricultural Research station. On the right, a road leads to **Spanish Lookout**, one of Belize's most successful **Mennonite** farming settlements, its neat, well-maintained farmhouses, white-fenced fields, paved roads, car and tractor show-rooms and the *Golden Corral* diner replicating the American Midwest. The Mennonites here have embraced modern technology enthusiastically – and have the best-stocked auto-parts shops in the country. The Western Highway continues for another 7km to Santa Elena (see p.158) and San Ignacio.

The Chiquibul Road

At the Georgeville junction, an unpaved road leads south to the **Mountain Pine Ridge** (see p.175). This is the **Chiquibul Road** – well used by villagers, foresters and tourists – which reaches deep into the forest and heads for Caracol (see p.180), crossing the Macal River at the Guacamallo Bridge. You could get off at this junction if you're hitching to **Augustine/Douglas Silva**, headquarters of the Mountain Pine Ridge Forest Reserve, though you really need four-wheel-drive, or a mountain bike, to explore this fascinating and exciting area of hills, waterfalls, caves and jungle properly. The road, usually in reasonable condition anyway, is currently being upgraded to enable easier and faster access to Caracol.

Mountain Equestrian Trails

Eleven kilometres along the Chiquibul Road, **Mountain Equestrian Trails** (☎ 820-4041, in the US ☎ 1-800/838-3918, Ⓦ www.metbelize.com; ❽) is unquestionably Belize's premier **horse-riding** vacation centre, with superb riding on nearly 100km of forest trails encompassing various ecosystems. It also offers very comfortable **accommodation** – open to all – in a tropical forest setting on the edge of the Pine Ridge: there are ten rooms in thatched, oil-lamp-lit cabañas and a villa, La Casa Vista, with a private garden. The *Cantina* restaurant here dishes out tasty Belizean and Mexican-style meals in large por-tions. If you want to get even closer to nature there's also an idyllic **tented camp**, *Chiclero Trails* (❹). *MET* can also arrange hiking, birding, kayaking and caving trips into the little-visited interior, and the camp is the base for low-impact wildlife safaris deep into the Chiquibul forest. Jim Bevis, owner of *MET*, led the first commercial crossing of the Maya Mountain divide. He and his wife, Marguerite, are also founder members of the **Slate Creek Preserve**, a privately owned tract of over sixteen square kilometres of karst limestone for-est bordering the Mountain Pine Ridge Forest Reserve. Local landowners, rec-ognizing the importance of conservation and sustainable development, have cooperated voluntarily to establish the preserve, following the guidelines in UNESCO's Man and the Biosphere Programme – one example of how con-cern for the environment in Belize has been translated into practical projects benefiting local people.

Green Hills Butterfly Ranch and Botanic Garden

On the opposite side of the road to *MET*, the **Green Hills Butterfly Ranch and Botanic Garden** (daily 8am–4pm; ☎ 820-4017, Ⓦ biological-diversity.info /greenhills.htm; Bz$10, includes guided tour) is Belize's biggest, best and most professional butterfly exhibit. It's run by Dutch biologists Jan Meerman and Tineke Boomsma, both experts in the field; they have published many scientific and popular articles and books – including a *Checklist of the Butterflies of Belize* – and others on reptiles, amphibians, dragonflies, damselflies and passionflowers; see the excellent website for the full list, where most of the articles can be downloaded free of charge. They've also recorded several species in Belize new to science, including a **tarantula** – *Citharacanthus meermani* – at Green Hills itself.

The main attraction is the enclosed, beautifully landscaped **flight area**, where flocks of gorgeous tropical butterflies flutter around, settling occasionally on the flowers to sip nectar. Over eighty different species have been bred here, though you'll usually see around twenty-five to thirty at any one time, depending on the time of year and the breeding cycle. As this is a breeding centre you can watch one of nature's wonders (particularly in the early morning) as the butterflies emerge from jewelled chrysalises; many of the chrysalises are shipped to approved butterfly exhibits in the US. Fascinating as this is, there's lots more to see, and visitors are given a briefing by an assistant from nearby San Antonio village, who can answer most questions. To rear butterflies you also need to know about their food plants and so there's an amazing botanical garden, home to **Belize's National Passionflower Collection**, as well as a renowned collection of **epiphytes** (air plants), plus cycads, heliconias, orchids and a tropical fruit orchard.

Santa Elena

Before reaching San Ignacio the Western Highway passes through San Ignacio's sister town of **SANTA ELENA**, on the eastern bank of the Macal River. Though quite a large town, Santa Elena has few of the attractions of its sibling, but it is the site of the turn-off to the **Cristo Rey Road** (see p.177) towards Augustine/Douglas Silva and the Mountain Pine Ridge (see p.175). Most visitors choose to stay in San Ignacio, but there is a very good value **hotel** here; the *Aguada* (☎804-3609, ✉aguada@btl.net, ⊛www.aguadahotel.com; ❹), signposted on the right near the town entrance. Run by the very welcoming Bill, Cathie and Shalue Butcher, the hotel has neat, clean, comfortable rooms, all with air-conditioning and private bath. There's a good, inexpensive restaurant, a pool and patio in the landscaped grounds and Internet access for guests.

At Santa Elena the Macal River is crossed by the **Hawkesworth Bridge**, built in 1949 and still the only road suspension bridge in Belize. Traffic from Belize City crosses the river on a low bridge (covered in high water) a little downstream; the suspension bridge is only used by eastbound traffic.

San Ignacio and Cayo District

On the west bank of the Macal River, 35km from Belmopan, **SAN IGNACIO** is a friendly, relaxed town that draws together much of the best in inland Belize. The main town of Cayo District and the focus of tourism in west-central Belize, it offers good food, inexpensive hotels and restaurants and frequent bus connections. However, the town's best feature is its location on the Macal River, in beautiful countryside and close to several reserves. It's an excellent base for day- and overnight trips to the surrounding hills, streams, archeological sites, caves and forests. Several local tour operators run trips south into the **Mountain Pine Ridge** and beyond there to the ruins of **Caracol**. Heading west to the border you pass through the village of **San José Succotz**, where a hand-cranked ferry takes you across the Mopan River, allowing access to the Maya site of **Xunantunich**. A couple of kilometres beyond Succotz, **Benque Viejo** is the last town in Belize and focus of several contemporary art projects, of which the earth-sculpture park of **Poustinia** is the most intriguing.

Meanwhile, the main rivers tumbling down the northern and western slopes of the Maya Mountains, the **Macal River** and the **Mopan River**, join to form the Belize River just downstream from San Ignacio, and the forested hills that begin here roll all the way south to Toledo District and across Guatemala. The evenings are relatively cool and the days fresh – a welcome break from the sweltering heat of the coast – and there's a virtual absence of mosquitoes and other biting insects. The **population** is typically varied: most people are Mestizos – of mixed Spanish and Maya descent – and Spanish is their first language, but you'll also hear plenty of Creole and English and see Creoles, Mopan and Yucatec Maya, Mennonites, Lebanese, Chinese and even Sri Lankans.

Although you can easily use San Ignacio as a base for day-trips, if you'd like to stay in the countryside, numerous guesthouses and ranches in the area offer **cottage- and lodge-style accommodation** and organized trips. On the whole, standards are very high, and most of them cater mainly to upmarket guests on packages who come here after a spell on the cayes – a phenomenon known as a "surf and turf" holiday. However, there are really good-value places in all price ranges, and all are covered in the text. Many are booked up in the peak season (Christmas to Easter) but, if open, can offer reduced prices in low season. Most offer a very comfortable night's sleep and good home-cooking – even gourmet dining – as well as horse-riding, bird-watching, canoeing and various trips into the surrounding area. All can be reached by road and are well signposted from San Ignacio, though to get to a couple of them you'll have to cross the river in a canoe or small boat.

Some history

The name the Spanish gave to this area was **El Cayo**, the same word they used to describe the offshore islands. (San Ignacio town is usually referred to as **Cayo** by locals, and this is the name you'll often see indicated on buses.) It's an apt description of the area, in a peninsula between two converging rivers, and also a measure of how isolated the early settlers felt, surrounded by the forest.

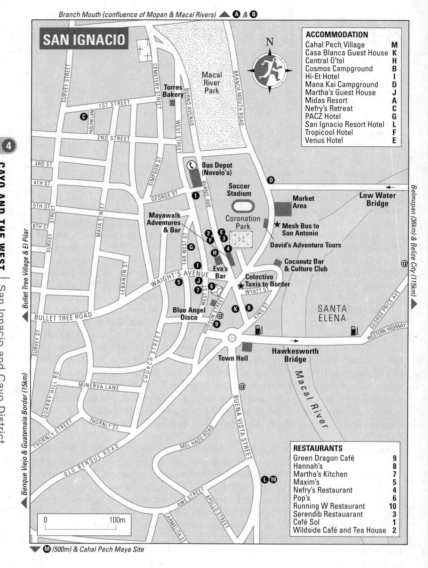

SAN IGNACIO

Branch Mouth (confluence of Mopan & Macal Rivers) ▲ **A** & **B**

N

Macal River Park

ACCOMMODATION
Cahal Pech Village	M
Casa Blanca Guest House	K
Central O'tel	H
Cosmos Campground	B
Hi-Et Hotel	I
Mana Kai Campground	D
Martha's Guest House	J
Midas Resort	A
Nefry's Retreat	C
PACZ Hotel	G
San Ignacio Resort Hotel	L
Tropicool Hotel	F
Venus Hotel	E

Torres Bakery

Bus Depot (Novelo's)

Soccer Stadium

Market Area

Low Water Bridge

Belmopan (36km) & Belize City (115km)

Mayawalk Adventures & Bar

Coronation Park

Mesh Bus to San Antonio

David's Adventure Tours

Eva's Bar

Coconutz Bar & Culture Club

Colectivo Taxis to Border

SANTA ELENA

WAIGHT'S AVENUE

Blue Angel Disco

Town Hall

Hawkesworth Bridge

Macal River

GEORGE PRICE AVE

Western Highway

RESTAURANTS
Green Dragon Café	9
Hannah's	8
Martha's Kitchen	7
Maxim's	5
Nefry's Restaurant	4
Pop's	6
Running W Restaurant	10
Serendib Restauarant	3
Café Sol	1
Wildside Café and Tea House	2

Bullet Tree Village & El Pilar ◄

Benque Viejo & Guatemala Border (15km) ◄

0   100m

▼ **M** (500m) & Cahal Pech Maya Site

It wasn't just the jungle they had to fear; the forest was also home to the inhabitants of a Maya province who valued their independence. **Tipú**, a Maya city that stood at Negroman on the Macal River, about 9km south of San Ignacio, was the capital of Dzuluinicob, where for years the Maya resisted attempts to Christianize them. The early wave of conquest, in 1544, made only a little impact here, and the area was a centre of rebellion in the following decades. Two **Spanish friars** arrived in 1618, but a year later the entire population was still practising idolatry. Outraged, the friars smashed the idols and ordered the native priests flogged, but by the end of the year the Maya had once again driven out the Spaniards. Four years later, Maya from Tipú worked as guides in an expedition against the Itzá (the Maya group who lived in and around present-day Flores, on Lake Petén Itzá in Guatemala; see p.206), and in 1641 the friars returned, determined to Christianize the inhabitants. To express their defiance of the Spanish clerics the Maya priests conducted a mock Mass, using tortillas as communion wafers, and threw out the friars. From then on Tipú remained an outpost of Maya culture, providing refuge to other Maya fleeing Spanish rule, and apparently retaining a good measure of independence until 1707, when the population was forcibly removed to Flores.

Like many places in Belize, San Ignacio probably started its present life as a logging camp. A map drawn up in 1787 simply states that the Indians of this general area were "in friendship with the Baymen". Later it was a centre for the shipment of chicle, the sap of the sapodilla tree and basis of chewing gum. The self-reliant chicleros, as the collectors of chicle were called, knew the forest intimately, including the location of most, if not all, Maya ruins. When the demand for Maya artefacts sent black-market prices rocketing, many of them turned to looting.

Until the Western Highway was built in the 1930s (and the road beyond San Ignacio wasn't paved until the 1980s), local transport was by mule or water. It could take ten days of paddling to reach San Ignacio from Belize City, though later small steamers made the trip. Nowadays, river traffic, which had almost died out, is enjoying a revival as increasing numbers of tourists take river trips. Indeed, a good time to visit San Ignacio is at the start of the La Ruta Maya **canoe race**, held annually in early March to celebrate Baron Bliss Day (see p.161), when teams of paddlers race all the way to Belize City. Anyone can enter but local guides always win.

Arrival and information

San Ignacio's main street is **Burns Avenue**; along here, or nearby, you'll find almost everything you need, including the best produce market in Belize. Novelo's Western Transport **buses** run regular services from Belize City to San Ignacio, stopping at the terminal on Burns Avenue before continuing to Benque Viejo, for the Guatemalan border; a shared **taxi** to the border from San Ignacio costs Bz$4 per person. While looking for a room you can **leave luggage** at *Café Sol*, in the block next to the bus terminal, or in the *Mayawalk Bar*, another block further down Burns Avenue; both places are good for information on hotels, transport and the like.

Although there's no official tourist office in San Ignacio, you'll be bombarded with **information**: Bob Jones, owner of the long-established *Eva's Bar* on Burns Avenue, knows almost everything about Cayo and the walls of the bar are festooned with framed brochures listing what's on offer. *Eva's* also has **Internet access**, as do several other places, but for better value try the *Green Dragon Café* (see p.163) or *Tradewinds*, both on Hudson Street.

The **banks** are on Burns Avenue (the Belize Bank has an ATM). If you need Guatemalan *quetzales* you can save time at the border (but get slightly less favourable rates in town) by using the services of the **moneychangers** who'll approach you. The **post office** is next to Courts furniture store in the centre of town, and the **BTL office** is next to the bus terminal. **Car rental** is available at Cayo Rentals (☎824-2153 or 610-4779); just call and someone will meet you. For domestic and international **air tickets** go to Exodus Travel, 2 Burns Ave (☎824-4400). Arts and Crafts of Central America, two doors down from *Eva's*, sells reasonably priced Guatemalan *típica* **gifts**, books (including

Rough Guides) and maps. Past here, Caesar's Gift Shop sells the same jewellery and wood carvings as at his place on the Western Highway (see p.155); you can also find out about *Black Rock River Lodge*, in the Macal River Valley (see p.170). **Laundry** can be dropped off at *Martha's*, on West Street (see "Accommodation", below).

Accommodation

The **hotels** in San Ignacio offer the best-value budget accommodation in the country, and hotels at all levels are constantly improving in quality and services. You'll almost always find space but you should book ahead if you want to stay at a particular place during busy periods. If rooms are getting full then you could try the *Aguada*, just over the river in Santa Elena (see p.158), or the hotels in nearby Bullet Tree Falls (see p.174). All but the really inexpensive places will take credit cards. The new *Mana Kai Campground*, at start of Branch Mouth Road (☎824-2317), with showers and electricity, has **camping** spaces for Bz$10 for two people in their own tent, or you can rent a tent for Bz$10 per person; for other camping options near town see the *Cosmos* and *Midas* entries below.

Cahal Pech Village On Cahal Pech Hill, just across from the Maya site (see p.166), 2km from town ☎824-3740, ✉daniels@btl.net, ⓦwww.cahalpech.com. A well-designed and good-value "village" of comfortable wood-and-thatch cabañas on a hillside overlooking San Ignacio. Each cabaña (❺) – named after a Belizean Maya site – has a private bath and TV, and the interiors are decorated with Guatemalan textiles; outside there's a wooden deck with a hammock. Above the cabañas, the larger, a/c hotel rooms and suites (❼) are equally comfortable. There's a good restaurant and Internet access for guests; for details ask at *Venus* (see opposite) in town. ❹–❺

Casa Blanca Guest House 10 Burns Ave ☎824-2080, ✉casablanca@btl.net, ⓦwww .casblancaguesthouse.com. A very good-value new hotel with immaculate rooms, all with private bath and cable TV (some with a/c) and a comfortable sitting area with microwave, fridge, coffee and tea – though no stove. It's a bright, friendly place and owner Betty Guerra is quietly proud that her hotel won Belize's "Best Small Hotel" award soon after opening; booking is advisable. ❸–❹

Central O'tel 24 Burns Ave ☎824-3734, ✉easyrider@btl.net. Simple, clean rooms, all sharing a couple of small bathrooms in an old wooden building; one of the best-value budget places in town. The front balcony (with hammocks) is a great place from which to watch the street below. ❷

Cosmos Campground Branch Mouth Rd, a 15min walk north from town ☎824-2116. Campsite with showers and flush toilets (Bz$7 per person) and simple dorm rooms for Bz$10 per person, with shared hot-water showers. The site extends right down to the river, and you can rent canoes,

bicycles and horses at affordable prices – ask at the manager's house, signposted on the left just before the campground. ❷

Hi-Et Hotel West St, behind *Eva's* ☎824-2828. A phenomenally popular and very good-value hotel, in an attractive wooden colonial building with a wrap-around balcony, complete with a seat on a swing. The original rooms, each with its own tiny balcony, share a hot-water bathroom, while the newer, larger rooms in an adjacent concrete building have private bathrooms. Guests can the use fridge in the comfortable sitting room. ❷–❸

Martha's Guest House West St, behind *Eva's* ☎824-3647, ✉marthas@btl.net, ⓦwww.marthasbelize.com. Recent renovations have made the best hotel in San Ignacio even better, but owners Martha and John August have managed to keep the homely atmosphere that made the original hotel so popular, and booking is advised. The rooms are very comfortable and well-furnished, and most have beautiful tiled bathrooms and cable TV; there are also two guest lounges with TV. Each room has either a private balcony or access to a shared one and the suite on the top floor has an enormous, full-width balcony, for views over the whole town; more suites are planned. The restaurant below (see review, p.164) is a favourite meeting place. There's a range of good books on Belize to read (and *Rough Guides* for sale), a gift shop, a good drop-off laundry and a shuttle service to Belize City. ❹–❻

Midas Resort Branch Mouth Rd, a 10min walk from the bus terminal ☎824-3172, ✉midas@btl.net. Set in trees and pasture above the riverbank, *Midas* is the only resort actually in town – and it's one of the best-value cabaña places in Cayo, within walking distance of the town centre but with the peace and quiet of the countryside. Accommodation is in comfortable Maya-style thatched cabañas and newer wooden cabins with porch, all with private bath. There's a restaurant and camping (Bz$8 per person) and trailer hook-ups are available. ❹

Nefry's Retreat 3 Paslow Lane ☎824-4924, ⓔnefrysretreat@yahoo.com, ⓦwww.nefrysretreat.com. A very comfortable new hotel run by the friendly Nancy and Jaime Marin, in a quiet area that's just a 10min walk from the centre. The clean, tiled rooms all have a large private bathroom, a fridge, TV and an a/c option (you get a discount if you can manage with just a fan). They open onto a stone-flagged courtyard with a fountain, across from a shady garden with hammocks. There's also a spa, with massage and other treatments to soothe you after a day's arduous adventure. Breakfast is available if ordered in advance and the family also operates *Nefry's Restaurant* on Burns Ave (see review, p.164). Good-value shuttle service to Belize City and Tikal. ❺

Pacz Hotel 4 Far West St, two blocks behind *Eva's* ☎824-4538, ⓔpaczghouse@btl.net. Five clean, comfortable tiled rooms (some with private hot showers) at bargain rates, especially for three sharing, opening onto a quiet upstairs sitting area. *Erva's Restaurant*, serving excellent Belizean meals, is below; the hotel is also the base for Pacz Tours (see box on p.165) ❸

San Ignacio Resort Hotel 18 Buena Vista St ☎824-2034, ⓦwww.sanignaciobelize.com. In a superb location, just ten minutes' walk uphill from the town centre, with views over the Macal River valley, San Ignacio's premier hotel is renowned locally for hosting Queen Elizabeth on her most recent visit. Most of the spacious, comfortable rooms and suites, some with balcony, have a/c but the fan-cooled economy rooms can save you a lot of money, and there are worthwhile discounts for longer stays. The *Running W* restaurant (see review, p.164) has a terrace overlooking the pool (Bz$10 non-guests), the *Stork Club* bar has a happy hour on Friday, and there's also a business centre with Internet access. The wonderful, tranquil Medicinal Plant Trail, with lots of informative labels, leads down to the river and up to a forested hilltop, ideal for early-morning bird-watching with resident guide Martin Velásquez. ❺ budget, ❽ a/c

Tropicool Hotel Burns Ave, 75m past *Eva's* ☎824-3052, ⓔtropicool@btl.net. Bright, clean (no smoking) and very good-value budget rooms with bedside lights and shared hot-water bathrooms, and wooden cabins in the garden, with private hot showers and cable TV. Ground-floor rooms have level access from the street (meaning wheelchair-accessible); upstairs rooms are bigger. There's a sitting room with TV and a laundry area, and bike rental is available for Bz$25 per day. ❸–❺

Venus Hotel 29 Burns Ave ☎824-3203, ⓔemorfing@btl.net. A two-storey hotel, the biggest in town, with good rates – the best deal around if you want to stay a few days. The modern rooms have clean, tiled bathrooms, a/c and TV, while the rear balcony has views over the market down to the river. Book here for *Cahal Pech Village* (see opposite). ❹

Eating

Along with its budget hotels, San Ignacio has numerous really good **restaurants** in all price ranges, including the only **vegan** café in the country; there are also a number of reliable **fast-food stalls** in the market area. If you have anywhere to cook, then the Saturday **market** is worth a visit; it's the best in Belize, with local farmers bringing in fresh-picked produce. It's also a good place to stock up on provisions for trips; see Chris Lowe at the market for his Fruit-A-Plenty trail mix, granola bars and homemade peanut butter, also available from local shops. For general **groceries**, Celina's Store, two blocks down from the *Venus Hotel* on Burns Avenue, has the widest selection, while the *Green Dragon Café* (see below) is the only **health food store** in the country. In the centre of town there are plenty of **fruit stands** laden with bananas, oranges and papayas. You can pick up good fresh **bread** and baked goods from Torres Bakery, at the end of Far West Street, and most afternoons small boys will be around selling tasty, freshly cooked *empanadas* and *tamales*.

Cafés and restaurants

Café Sol 25 West St. Fresh and attractive vegetarian meals, soups, salads, sandwiches and great desserts, with excellent coffee, served in an atmosphere inspired by similar cafés in Antigua, Guatemala. Always a daily special and you can eat indoors or in the patio garden. Closed Mon.

Green Dragon Café 8 Hudson St. Enjoy a wide

range of excellent coffees, smoothies and delicious snacks in a health food shop that's also San Ignacio's (and the country's) best Internet café and bookshop, run by Dutch couple Miriam and Laurenz Engeln. Relax with a magazine in the tranquil, air-conditioned atmosphere indoors or enjoy beer and wine (with wine tastings on the last Saturday of the month) in the shady patio. Also sells hemp clothing, rechargeable batteries and other environmentally friendly products. Open Mon–Sat 8am–8pm.

Hannah's 5 Burns Ave. A small restaurant with some of the most delicious food in the country at great prices, much of it produced on the owner's farm. Serves everything from Belizean specialities to Burmese curry, all accompanied by freshly prepared salads; get here early or you'll have to wait.

Martha's Kitchen and Pizza Parlour West St, behind *Eva's*. Located below the guesthouse of the same name and just as well run. Great breakfasts with strong, locally grown coffee, and main dishes of traditional Creole food and pizza. There's always a vegetarian choice and delicious cakes for dessert. Good service, too. The patio tables, romantically candle-lit in the evenings, are a popular place to meet tour guides and plan trips.

Maxim's Far West St, behind *Martha's*. The best of San Ignacio's many Chinese restaurants, rapidly serving large portions of Chinese standards.

Nefry's Restaurant Burns Ave, next to Mayawalk Adventures. The best new restaurant in town, serving creative Belizean-style meals and seafood with a Mediterranean influence; try the pork ribs in ginger, honey and plum sauce. The place opens at 6.30am for good-value breakfasts, including potato pancakes, and there's a daily special. Large, shady outdoor seating area to enjoy the street scene.

Pop's West St, across from *Martha's*. A tiny and popular local restaurant, serving very tasty Belizean dishes, including a daily lunch special and all-day breakfast.

The Running W Restaurant At the *San Ignacio Resort Hotel*, 18 Buena Vista St. Excellent food in tranquil surroundings, and not that expensive. Good steaks and seafood (including fish and chips) with a distinctive Lebanese influence, accompanied by real Mediterranean olives. Breakfasts are especially good value.

Serendib Restaurant 27 Burns Ave. Excellent Sri Lankan curries and seafood at very reasonable prices and with good service.

Wildside Café and Tea House 30 Burns Ave, across from the *Venus Hotel*. The only vegan restaurant in the country, with a range of really inexpensive and delicious meals – try the Jamaican coconut stew or the flour tortilla pizza. They also have medicinal herbal teas made from forest vines.

Drinking and nightlife

Most of the restaurants listed above double as **bars**; *Eva's* in particular is renowned as *the* local bar in San Ignacio, and is great place to meet other travellers and tour guides. San Ignacio is also a popular weekend spot for Belizeans and there's a range of **live music and dancing** on offer. For a drink in slightly quieter and more comfortable surroundings, the *Stork Club* at the *San Ignacio Hotel* is the place to be – very popular during the Friday evening **happy hour** – and after that things liven up with a DJ or band. You can also join the **Latin dance classes** here on Wednesday evenings (Bz$10) or belt out your favourite karaoke tunes on Thursdays. Near the riverbank market, the *Culture Club* (above *Coconutz* sports bar) is a typically Belizean **club**, with Latin and Afro-Cuban sounds mixing with Belizean beats. The *Blue Angel* disco, on Hudson Street, has bands at weekends, but has lost its pre-eminent position in the local music scene to the *Cahal Pech Entertainment Center*, on the hilltop next to the Cahal Pech Maya site.

Around San Ignacio

The people of San Ignacio are justifiably proud of their beautiful river valleys and the surrounding countryside, and there are several specific attractions to visit nearby, including the Green Iguana Exhibit at the *San Ignacio Hotel* and the Maya site of **Cahal Pech**. Slightly further afield, the intriguing **Barton**

Independent tour operators in San Ignacio

Numerous independent local operators offer superb guided trips to attractions around San Ignacio. The list below covers a range of adventurous options; there are many more. As always in Belize, make sure anyone offering you a guided trip is a **licensed tour guide**. All the guides named below are either based in San Ignacio or will pick you up there. Not all have an office; if you can't contact them directly then go to the *Green Dragon Café* (T 824-4782, W www.greendragonbelize.com), where they'll do it for you. Most of the tour operators and guides below will accept both US$ and Bz$, whether or not their prices are quoted in one currency or the other.

Operators and guides

Belizean Sun T 823-2781 or 601-2360, W www.belizeansun.com. Former US forester Ken Dart organizes individual trips to the interior of Cayo, and can take you to amazing caves that nobody else visits.

Callego Adventures 4 Bullet Tree Rd T 824-2483. Elmo Richards is a courteous and very knowledgeable guide who'll pick you up at your hotel, drive you wherever you want to go in Cayo and ensure you have the best possible day.

Cayo Adventure Tours T 804-3246, E cattours@btl.net. Customized group tours, in reliable off-road vehicles, to all Cayo attractions. Run by Elbert Flowers and Ces Neal.

David's Adventure Tours At the far side of the park, near the market T 804-3674, W www.davidtours.com. Multilingual David Simpson, the original guide to Barton Creek Cave (around Bz$60), also leads overnight jungle trips and tours to Caracol. See also *Guacamallo Jungle Camp*, p.170.

Easy Rider In Arts and Crafts, on Burns Ave just past *Eva's* T 824-3734, E easyrider@btl.net. Charlie Collins organizes the best-value horse-riding day out in San Ignacio, and she carefully matches riders to the right mount (US$25 half-day, US$45 full day).

Everald's Caracol Shuttle At *Crystal Paradise Resort* (see p.169) T 820-4014. Everald Tut runs good-value daily van tours to Caracol (US$50); he also operates King Tut Tours, for other excursions around Cayo and to Tikal.

Mayawalk Adventures 19 Burns Ave T 824-3070, W www.mayawalk.com. Aaron Juan leads amazing trips to the astonishing sacrificial cave of Actun Tunichil Muknal (see p.154; around US$80) as well as overnight caving and rock-climbing expeditions.

Pacz Tours At *Pacz Hotel* T 824-2477 or 610-3638, E pacztours@btl.net. Specialist archeology guide Emilio Awe arranges expert trips to Actun Tunichil Muknal and other Maya sites in Cayo.

Paradise Expeditions At *Crystal Paradise Resort* T 824-4014, W www.birdingbelize.com. Jeronie Tut runs superb, personalized bird and nature tours throughout Cayo and Belize.

River Rat T 609-6636, W www.riverratbelize.com. Gonzalo Pleitez, who lives up the Macal River, arranges excellent white-water kayak floats and jungle trips (US$45–80).

Snooty Fox Tours Corner West St and Waight's Ave, opposite *Martha's* T 824-2720, E snootyfox@btl.net. Michael Waight has the best-value canoe rental in Cayo (US$30/day, including a cooler for your lunch) and offers drop-off and shuttle service to points along the Macal River.

Toni's River Adventures Ask at *Eva's Bar* T 824-3292, E evas@btl.net. Toni Santiago runs by far the longest-established and best-value guided canoe trip on the Macal River; it's under US$25 for an expert paddle upriver to the Rainforest Medicine Trail (see p.171). Also organizes fantastic overnight camping trips along the river.

Creek Cave is definitely worth a visit, while the **Rainforest Medicine Trail** and the **Belize Botanic Gardens** can be visited on relaxing **canoe trips** along the mostly gentle **Macal River**; resorts along the faster **Mopan River** offer tubing or **kayaking**. The nearby farmland and forest are ideal for exploring on **horseback** or **mountain bike** (you can take a bike on the bus to San Antonio, for the Mountain Pine Ridge; see p.177). For bike rental, check at the *Tropicool Hotel* or the *Crystal Paradise Resort* office on Branch Mouth Road (☎824-2823); for canoes, see Snooty Fox Tours, listed in the box on p.165.

Caving is increasingly popular, but make sure you go with a licensed guide who's qualified in cave rescue. In addition to the people recommended in the box on p.165, you could check with Iain Anderson at Caves Branch and Marcos Cucul of Maya Guide Adventures, both on the Hummingbird Highway; see p.220. Most of the bigger hotels and lodges have their own tour desk but there are several small-scale, independent local operators who offer good-value trips to the many attractions around San Ignacio. Many of these are difficult, even impossible, to visit on your own and it's usually easy enough to join a group.

Branch Mouth

Perhaps the easiest introduction to this region is to take the twenty-minute walk to **Branch Mouth**, where the Macal and Mopan rivers merge to form the Belize River. The track leads north from the football field past clapboard houses on the edge of rich farmland, with thick vegetation, tropical flowers, iguanas and butterflies on either side. At the confluence of the rivers is a huge tree, with branches arching over the jade water. A rusting iron mooring ring in the trunk is a reminder of the past importance of river transport; now there are swallows skimming the surface, parrots flying overhead and scores of tiny fish in the water. The scar of raw earth on the opposite bank is evidence of severe flooding in recent years, when the river has risen within metres of the Hawkesworth Bridge and has even inundated the streets of San Ignacio. Local boys leap off the pedestrian **suspension bridge** across the last stretch of the Mopan River here – but for most visitors just walking along the swaying structure is enough of an adventure.

Cahal Pech

Twenty minutes' walk uphill out of town to the southwest, clearly signposted along the Benque road, the hilltop Maya site of **Cahal Pech** (daily 6am–6pm; Bz$10) has undergone extensive restoration and is well worth a visit. The **visitor centre and museum** has a model of the site, excellent display panels showing paintings of Cahal Pech in its heyday and the history of the Maya in Belize, plus lots of artefacts, such as ocarinas, chocolate pots, projectile points and carved flints, including one which looks remarkably like a modern wrench; if you watch the 50min **video** your tour will be enriched.

Cahal Pech means "place of ticks" in Mopan and Yucatec Mayan, but that's certainly not how the elite who lived here would have known it: this was the royal acropolis-palace of a Maya ruling family during the Classic period. There's evidence of construction from the Early Preclassic, around 1200 BC, after which the city probably dominated the central Belize River valley. Studies of the buildings and ceramics show that the site was continuously occupied until around 800 AD; most of what you see dates from the eighth century AD. Entering the site through the forest you arrive at **Plaza B**, surrounded by temple platforms and the remains of dwellings, and your gaze is drawn to

Structure 1, the **Audiencia**, the site's largest building. If you're used to seeing finely executed, exposed stonework at reconstructed Maya sites then the thick overcoat of lime-mortar on buildings here may come as a bit of a shock. The Classic Maya, however, viewed bare stone facings as ugly and unfinished, and covered all surfaces with a thick coat of plaster or stucco which was then brightly painted. You can climb the steps at the front but the best way to enjoy the view is to walk around the side, through **Plaza D** and through a maze of recently restored ancient corridors and stairways, gradually rising to reveal a surprising and enchanting view of **Plaza A** – a sacred space entirely enclosed by walls and tall buildings. Structure 1 is across the plaza; climb to the front and you can then descend to your starting point. After your visit you can stroll across to the *Cahal Pech Entertainment Center* – a large bar and nightclub – for a cultural experience of an entirely different nature.

Barton Creek Cave

Of the many **cave trips** available in Cayo, one of the most fascinating is to **Barton Creek Cave**, accessible only by river, and only on a tour with a licensed guide (around 4hr; Bz\$60). Like all caves in Belize, Barton Creek Cave is a registered archeological site (entry fee Bz\$20) and nothing must be touched or removed. Although almost everyone now offers trips here, the original and **best guide** to the cave is David Simpson, a multilingual Belizean who runs David's Adventure Tours in San Ignacio (☎804-3674). He'll carefully and responsibly show you the astonishing Maya artefacts in the cave; a trip here also usually includes a visit to Green Hills Butterfly Ranch (see p.157).

To get here you travel east along the Western Highway, turning south onto the Chiquibul Road. After seven kilometres on this road you turn off through farmland, passing the traditional Mennonite settlement of **Upper Barton Creek**, and eventually reaching the cave entrance, framed by jungle at the far side of a jade-green pool. This is where you board a canoe. The river is navigable for about 1600m – though in a couple of places the roof comes so low you have to crouch right down in the canoe – before ending in a gallery blocked by a huge rockfall. If it's been raining, a subterranean waterfall cascades over the rocks – a truly unforgettable sight. Beyond lie many more miles of passageways, only accessible on a fully equipped expedition. The clear, slow-moving river fills most of the cave width, though the roof soars 100m above your head in places, the way ahead illuminated by powerful lamps. Several **Maya burials** surrounded by pottery vessels line the banks, the most awe-inspiring indicated by a skull set in a natural rock bridge used by the Maya to reach the sacred site.

The Macal River

The main tributaries of the **Macal River** rise in the Mountain Pine Ridge and the Chiquibul Forest, and in the upper reaches the water is sometimes fast and deep enough for **white-water kayaking**, though you'll need an expert guide for this (see box on p.165). But if the idea of a gentle day or more on the river appeals, then any of the resorts can rent canoes to paddle on your own (very good value from Snooty Fox Tours; see p.165), though you'll see far more wildlife with a guide than you ever would alone. A very popular choice is to take a **guided canoe trip** upriver to Chaa Creek to visit the fascinating **Rainforest Medicine Trail** and **Chaa Creek Natural History Centre**, two of the premier attractions in Cayo and both in the grounds of *The Lodge at Chaa Creek*; a combined ticket for the two costs Bz\$16, or is free for *Chaa Creek*

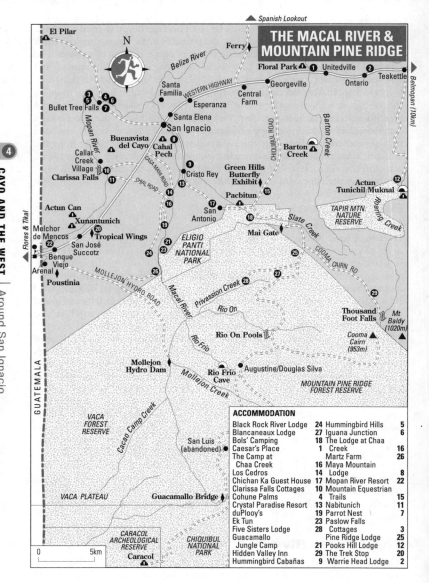

THE MACAL RIVER & MOUNTAIN PINE RIDGE

guests. Further upstream, there's the new and rapidly growing **Belize Botanic Gardens**, at *duPlooy's*. You can also make the trip all the way to Belize City: up to a week of hard paddling, camping on the riverbank each night.

Steep limestone cliffs and forested hills edge the lower Macal valley, and there's plenty of **accommodation** in all price ranges along the river; see opposite for details. On any branch over the river or in the bankside vegetation you can see **green iguanas**, the males resplendent in spring with their orange and brown mating colours. Higher up, you might hear the deep-throated roar of **howler monkeys**, which have been successfully reintroduced to the Macal valley from Bermudian Landing, north of Belize City, and the Monkey River, in Toledo District.

Accommodation

Most accommodation along the Macal River (see map opposite for locations) is in upmarket **cabaña–style resorts**, beautifully located in the forest above the riverbank. There are some budget options, though, and most will give discounts to *Rough Guide* readers. A taxi out here costs around Bz$30, or more for the furthest places. Any of them can organize superb **horseback tours** to nearby Maya ruins and some also have **mountain bikes** and **canoes** for rent. If you'd like a relatively easy but picturesque **canoe float** back to town after your stay they can take your luggage ahead while you drift along and enjoy the scenery.

The listings below are set in the order that you would approach them travelling upriver, though all are accessible by unpaved roads – either along the well-signposted Chial Road turn–off, 10km from San Ignacio along the road to Benque; or by the Cristo Rey Road to San Antonio village. For a couple of places you may also have to cross the river by boat.

Hummingbird Cabañas At the entrance to Cristo Rey village ☎614-7446, ✉ecojungletours@hotmail.com. Simple thatched cabins with private hot shower run by the friendly Madrid family. Good, inexpensive restaurant and canoe rental. For here and *Crystal Paradise* (below) you can get the San Antonio village bus to Cristo Rey. ❸

Crystal Paradise Resort Just beyond the village of Cristo Rey, on the east bank of the river ☎824-2772, ⊛www.crystalparadise.com. Owned by the Belizean Tut family, who built the resort, this is a really welcoming, relaxed place with accommodation in wooden rooms and thatched cabañas; all have private baths with hot water. The deck outside the dining room overlooks the valley (though you can't see the river) and is a tremendous place for spotting hummingbirds. Teresa's in charge of the cooking, Victor built many of the thatched roofs at the resorts in Cayo and sons Jeronie and Everald arrange tours throughout Cayo and over to Tikal; see the box on p.165. Free pick-up in San Ignacio if you call before 4.30pm. Rates include delicious and filling home-cooked breakfast and dinner each day. ❼–❾

Los Cedros On the west bank; turn left off the Western Highway at the police checkpoint, 2km from San Ignacio, then another 5km along the unpaved Casa Maya Rd ☎603-0533, ⊛www.loscedrosbelize.com. Mark and Tracey Langan have three well-constructed jungle-pole houses high above the river, each with a double and single bed, private bathroom and verandah. With a bar and restaurant, a medicinal plant trail, canoeing and swimming in the river, this is a good place for families. The access road passes through the Maya site of Xubin, currently being investigated, and guests can observe (and even help with) the excavation. ❻, including transport from San Ignacio.

The Camp at Chaa Creek On the west bank, just below *The Lodge at Chaa Creek* (see below; same contact details). The brainchild of Mick Flemming of *Chaa Creek*, and managed by Docio and Francelia Juárez, this is camping in comfort, with tents now replaced by neat wooden cabins with tarp roofs. Each has single beds (some sleeping 4) and a porch with a deck overlooking the forest. There's hot water in the clean, tiled bathrooms and romantic oil lamps in the evening. Campers have access to all the *Chaa Creek* trails and attractions and it's often used by adventure tour groups. US$55 per person, including a hearty breakfast and dinner; good group discounts.

The Lodge at Chaa Creek On the west bank, at the end of the Chial Rd ☎824-2037, ⊛www.chaacreek.com. Beautiful, whitewashed wood and stucco cabañas (US$185) and wooden "treetop" Jacuzzi suites (US$285, sleep 4) in gorgeous grounds high above the Macal River, with a justly deserved reputation for luxury and ambiance. One of the first and finest cottage resorts in Cayo, it's won many awards and is often featured in TV travel shows. The cottages have very comfortable beds, tiled floors and large bathrooms, screened windows and a spacious wooden deck. The gorgeous and impressive Orchard Villa (US$285; sleeps 6) has a full-width screened porch, wicker furniture and a loft bedroom reached by a spiral staircase. A detailed trail map guides you through the forest and over the hills in this 340-acre private reserve, leading to several nearby Maya sites; there's a *chultun* (an underground chamber carved out of the rock) right by the gift shop. The stunning hilltop spa is the most modern in Belize, with separate, fully equipped rooms for each treatment. Relax and enjoy the mood music and the views as you sip a herbal tea after a Maya Stone massage; it's so popular you might have to book as soon as you arrive. Naturally there's a fine restaurant and a great bar, with a large outdoor deck. Guests enjoy free guided tours to all the *Chaa Creek* attractions; an early-morning guided bird walk (over 250 species have been recorded here); use of canoes to paddle upstream; and Internet access in the conference centre. ❾, but with good low-season discounts.

duPlooy's Along a signposted road, beyond the *Chaa Creek* turn-off ☎824-3101, ⓦwww.duplooys.com. First-rate accommodation, beautifully located in farmland and forest on the west bank of the Macal River, and home to the Belize Botanic Gardens (see p.172). There are spacious private bungalows with deck, king-size bed and sofa bed, fridge and coffeemaker (US$150); Jungle Lodge rooms, each with queen-size bed and private porch (US$130); and the budget-rate Pink House (which can be rented by groups), with seven rooms, each with a double and single bed (US$50 double), a kitchen and a large, screened porch. La Casita is a large, two-storey house with all-round balcony overlooking the river. Inside are king-size beds and luxurious bathroom with Jacuzzi. The observation deck extending from the bar leads to a walkway into the forest and across to another river overlook that's a superb bird-watching site; there's free coffee and guided bird-watching at 6.30am. ❺–❾

Guacamallo Jungle Camp On the east bank of the river; contact David's Adventure Tours in San Ignacio for transport ☎804-3674, ⓔdavidtours@belizemail.net. Simple cabins high above the river (which you cross in a canoe), located on the edge of a huge and mysterious Maya site; you'll have the pleasure of exploring this on your own. Lots of good food, much of it organically grown near the cabins, and a wonderful sense of timelessness at night as you sit on a Maya mound outside your cabin watching the stars. Bz$55 per person, including transport, dinner and breakfast. ❹

Ek Tun Near the end of the road to *Black Rock* (see below), and across the river ☎820-3002, ⓦwww.ektunbelize.com. The most luxurious stick-and-thatch cabañas in the country; there are only two units, the better to preserve the sublime isolation. Each cottage (sleeping four) is on a terrace

adorned with flowers, and has two bedrooms (one in the loft), a sitting room and beautiful bathroom. Gourmet dinner is served overlooking the river. The turquoise, spring-fed pool is the most beautiful of any resort in the country – and the overflow disappears mysteriously into a cave. Trails lead through the forest and along the river cliffs dotted with more cave entrances, while in the trees above you can hear howler monkeys, and the rare orange-breasted falcon nests on the limestone bluffs opposite; swimming and tubing in the river are idyllic. The 200-acre tract of forest borders the Mountain Pine Ridge Reserve, and there is ample evidence of Maya occupation in the area. Owner Phyllis Lane is a keen member of the Belize Ecotourism Association (see "Contexts", p.323) and everything here is as environmentally friendly as she can make it. No smoking, no singles and no children. US$170 double, US$45 for each extra person; meals are extra and there's usually a three-night minimum stay. ❾

Black Rock River Lodge At the very end of the Black Rock road ☎824-2341, ⓦwww.blackrock-lodge.com. Drive here on your own, or call at *Caesar's Place* on the Western Highway (see p.155) or the gift shop in San Ignacio (see p.162) to make transport arrangements. Set high above the west bank of the Macal River, across from the Eligio Panti National Park (see p.178) and with stunning views of the jungle-clad limestone cliffs of the upper Macal valley, the solidly built deluxe cabañas have a private hot shower and floors made of smooth stones from the river. A couple of equally comfortable shared-bath cabins enable budget travellers to enjoy the adventure, and solar power provides electricity. From the open-sided, thatched dining room you can see the river rushing over the black slate that gives the lodge its name, and you can often see otters playing on the opposite bank. It's a fairly easy hike from here up to Vaca Falls (you can tube back), or to Vaca or Flour Camp caves, containing some amazing Maya pottery; there are also fine horses and mountain bikes to ride. This is the highest easily navigable point on the Macal River, and you can canoe down to San Ignacio; Caesar's son, Julian Sherrard, is a leader in the Belize Canoe Association and can advise on long-distance paddles in Belize. ❺–❽

Martz Farm 13km along the Arenal/Mollejon Hydro road in Benque Viejo ☎614-6462, ⓔmartz-farm@hotmail.com. Run by the grown-up children of the Martínez family, this is far upriver from the other places on the Macal, and difficult to reach on your own – but someone from the *Farm* usually calls in town daily, or check with Bob Jones at *Eva's Bar* in San Ignacio, where guests are met for free transport to the *Farm*. It's well worth the effort to get here, with comfortable thatched cabins perched in trees above a rushing, crystal-clear creek, inexpensive rooms and plenty of home-cooked food. Reaching the river involves a climb down a gorgeous 30m waterfall (by which you can also camp, Bz$10 per person) to a remote beach; across the river the forest beckons and there's great horse-riding. ❹–❺

The Rainforest Medicine Trail

A canoe trip is the best way to visit the **Rainforest Medicine Trail** (daily 8am–5pm; self-guided tour Bz$10, Bz$20 with a guide), winding through the forest above the riverbank to seek out many of the plants and explain their medicinal properties. When first built, the trail was dedicated to Don Eligio Panti, a Maya bush doctor (*curandero*) from San Antonio village who died in 1996 at the age of 103; the naming of a national park after him near San Antonio is fitting tribute (see p.178). At the entrance, there's a large thatched shelter with hammocks to rest in, and visitors can get a refreshing drink during the explanatory talk before going on the trail.

The medical knowledge of the Maya was extensive, and the trail identifies about a hundred species, taking in a wide range of traditional healing plants, many of them now used in modern medicine. It's a fascinating experience: there are vines that provide fresh water like a tap; poisonwood, with oozing black sap; its antidote, the peeling bark of the gumbo limbo tree, always growing nearby; and the bark of the negrito tree, once sold for its weight in gold in Europe as a cure for dysentery. You'll also see specimens of the tropical hardwoods of the jungle that have been exploited for economic reasons. The more mundane, but very welcome, products of the forest range from herbal teas to blood tonic and there's quite a selection available in the **gift shop**. Traveller's Tonic, a preventative for diarrhoea, really works, as does Jungle Salve, for insect bites.

Before his death, Don Eligio passed on his skills to Dr Rosita Arvigo, who founded the Medicine Trail and still lives nearby. She now operates the **Ix Chel Wellness Center** in San Ignacio (open Dec to end of April only), and visitors can benefit from her skills in natural and traditional Maya healing methods and massage. Call ☎820-4031 or 602-1179 for an appointment and visit ⓦ www.arvigomassage.com for details of the classes she teaches in Maya medicine and cooking; she also gives herb walks around San Ignacio. Several plants from the Belize rainforest are being investigated as potential treatments for AIDS; Rosita and the staff at Ix Chel, in collaboration with the New York Botanical Garden, have been at the forefront of this research. Rosita has written about her apprenticeship to Don Eligio (see *Sastun*, in "Books", p.345) and is a founding member of the Belize Association of Traditional Healers; you can purchase their excellent newsletter, *Tree of Life*, and any of Rosita's books in the gift shop.

Chaa Creek Natural History Centre

A visit to the marvellous **Chaa Creek Natural History Centre** (daily 8am–4pm; Bz$10, includes guided tour, every hour on the hour), in the grounds of *Chaa Creek*, next to the Medicine Trail, is the best introduction to Cayo's history, geography and wildlife. If you're spending more than a couple of days in the area try to see this first; call ☎824-2037 to check on the current events programme. The centre has fascinating and accurate displays of the region's flora and fauna, vivid archeological and geological maps, a scale model of the Macal valley and a library with relevant books and journals – all of which make for an engaging visit.

Nearby, at the **Butterfly Breeding Centre** (included in Chaa Creek entry fee), you walk among the enormous and magnificent Blue Morpho butterflies, and even get to watch them emerge from chrysalis most mornings. There's also the **Maya Farm**, where crops such as corn, beans, tomatoes and squash are grown using traditional methods; this produce is incorporated into the meals served at *The Lodge at Chaa Creek* (see p.169).

The Belize Botanic Gardens

South of Chaa Creek, and reached by either road or river (see opposite), the **Belize Botanic Gardens** at *duPlooy's* (daily 8am–5pm; call ahead for a guided tour; Bz$10; ☏824-3101) are an ambitious new project established in 1997 on fifty acres of former farmland and forest. The garden is the brainchild of *duPlooy's* owners and avid plant-lovers, Ken and Judy duPlooy. Though Ken died a few years ago, his knowledge and enthusiasm were held in such high esteem that a new species of orchid has been named after him – *Pleurothallis duplooyii*, with tiny purple flowers. In the gardens there are over four hundred tree species, a nursery with over a thousand seedlings, two ponds with bird hides and several kilometres of interpretive **trails**. The place is well on its way to fulfilling its twin aims of creating a first-class biological educational and study resource and conserving many of Belize's native plant species in small areas representative of their natural habitats. Exploring the gardens, you approach though an avenue of fruit-bearing trees, designed to encourage wild **birds**; you can also be guided around by **expert naturalist** Philip Mai. The magnificent, specially designed **orchid house**, with 160 species, is the largest one in Belize and the best in Central America.

The Mopan River

The main tributary creeks of the **Mopan River** rise in the Maya Mountains, where the river first flows into Guatemala, re-entering Belize at the village of **Arenal**, 5km south of the Benque border post. The international boundary runs right through the middle of this Maya–Mestizo village of stick-and-thatch houses, bisecting the football pitch and with a goalmouth in each country. The river then leaves Belize briefly again, rushing under the bridge just over the frontier, before the final (and perhaps most picturesque) 25km stretch to its confluence with the Macal River at Branch Mouth (see p.166). There are some attractive and not too serious **white-water rapids** along this stretch, and it's easy enough to arrange kayak or rafting trips on the Mopan; check at any of the resorts listed opposite – *Clarissa Falls* or *Trek Stop* (see p.185) are best. Take care when swimming, though, as rapids which appear minor from the bank can present a real danger when you're swept over them – for your own safety you should always wear a **life-jacket** when you're in the river.

Finally, in the vicinity of the river are a couple of captivating **Maya sites**: the extensive **El Pilar** (best visited from the burgeoning village of **Bullet Tree Falls**, west of San Ignacio) and the smaller **Buenavista del Cayo**. These are described on pp.174 & 175, respectively.

Accommodation

There is less accommodation along the Mopan River than there is along the Macal, but what's available is more within the reach of the budget traveller and no less special for it. The first five listed are in **Bullet Tree Falls** village (see p.174), while the rest are listed in order of increasing distance from San Ignacio (see the map on p.160 for locations); see also the *Trek Stop* entry on p.168, with cabins near San José Succotz, just across the road from the river. Most places either have or can easily arrange kayaks, tubes or mountain bikes.

Cohune Palms On a riverbank peninsula in Bullet Tree Falls ☎ 824-2533 or 600-2738, ⓦ www.cohunepalms.com. Four wooden thatched cabins in a beautiful riverbank setting, two with private bathrooms, and some with suspended "hammock" beds. There's a communal kitchen and dining room, and outdoor thatched decks with hammocks to watch the iguanas. Owners Mike and Bevin Waight will provide free pick-up in San Ignacio. ❹–❺

Iguana Junction Near the village centre of Bullet Tree Falls ☎ 829-4021, ⓦ www.iguanajunction.com. Four elevated wooden cabins with private bath and simple rooms with washbasins and shared showers in a riverside setting. The restaurant, serving excellent home-cooked meals, is open to residents by arrangement. ❺–❻

Parrot Nest Bullet Tree Falls, at the end of the track just before the bridge ☎ 820-4058, ⓔ parrot@btl.net Right on the riverbank, six simple, clean, thatched cabins of varying sizes, two sitting very securely up a guanacaste tree. They're all set in beautiful gardens, some have their own verandahs and one has a private toilet and washbasin. The shared bathrooms have hot showers. Owner Pat Barbutti serves good, filling meals and runs free morning and afternoon shuttles for guests from *Eva's* in San Ignacio. ❹–❺

Hummingbird Hills Bullet Tree Falls, on Paslow Falls Rd, turn left before the bridge ☎ 614-4699, ⓦ www.hummingbirdhills.com. Four comfortable cabins, some with private bathroom, in an attractive garden and forest setting. Breakfast and lunch are available and tours can be arranged. ❸

Paslow Falls Cottages Paslow Falls Rd, 1.5km from the village centre ☎ 609-5212, ⓔ marlonwaight @hotmail.com. Four attractive circular white stucco cottages with conical thatched roofs in a secluded forest clearing near the river. Each has a double bed and private bathroom with hot water and is lit by atmospheric oil lamps. No restaurant yet but you can cook in the communal kitchen or eat at the *Riverside* or *Iguana Junction* in the village.

Clarissa Falls 2km along a signposted track to the right off the Benque road, just before the Chial Road turn to the Macal River resorts ☎ 824-3916, ⓔ clarissafalls@btl.net. Although part of a working cattle ranch (ask to help with the round-up), this is a very restful place right by a set of rapids. The original simple, clean, stick-and-thatch cabins have been constantly improved by owner Chena Gálvez. All are now wheelchair-accessible and have private bath, and some have a full kitchen. There's also a "bunkhouse" cabin with shared hot-water showers (Bz$25 per person) and space for

camping (Bz$12.50 per person) and hook-ups for RVs. There are reductions for students. Chena serves great home-cooking and there's a quiet bar overlooking the falls. This is a popular point to take out tubes and kayaks when you put in at Succotz, with a fee of Bz$2 per person. Horse-riding, canoeing, rafting and tubing available. ❺–❻

Nabitunich Mile 71, a couple of kilometres past the *Clarissa Falls* turn-off, along a signposted track on the right ☎ 823-2309, ⓔ bzebike@yahoo.co.au. Maya for "Little Stone House", this was the first and is still one of best resorts on the Mopan River, with comfortable rooms in charming thatched stone cottages set in 400 acres of forest and farmland. The gardens have spectacular views of El Castillo at Xunantunich (see p.184), and the place is deservedly popular with bird-watchers. Horse-riding, canoeing, tubing and tours are organized by the owners Rudy and Margaret Juan's son, Rudolfo. Good, filling meals are served in the restaurant, much of it grown organically on the farm. There's a fantastically good-value student rate (Bz$40, including dinner) but you'll need your student ID card; camping is Bz$10 per person. There is email service for guests. Cabins are Bz$80 per person, including breakfast and dinner. ❻

Mopan River Resort On the west bank of the Mopan River, opposite the park in Benque Viejo ☎ 823-2047, ⓦ www.mopanriverresort.com. Belize's first all-inclusive inland resort, this is the place to be to enjoy some luxurious pampering, staying in some of the most spacious thatched hardwood cabañas in the country. All have comfortable beds and rattan furniture, private bathrooms with tubs, a fridge, cable TV and a large porch. There are also three cabaña suites with fitted kitchens for longer stays. The grounds are beautifully landscaped and there's a refreshing pool. The owners, Jay and Pamella Picon, know Belize well and go to great lengths to ensure a comfortable stay. Pamella (who also speaks French), is licensed to perform marriages and there's a charming wedding chapel by the riverbank. The price is based on a package (minimum stay three nights) which includes accommodation, sumptuous gourmet meals, all drinks (including beer and cocktails), an excellent tour every day (including Tikal and Caracol), use of kayaks and transfers from the international airport. A week in a cabaña costs US$1198 per person (three nights for US$598), while a suite will run you US$1443 for a week. With all the extras on offer it's actually very good value, quite possibly the best deal in the country at this level. No smoking allowed in the cabañas. Closed during the low season, from July to October inclusive. ❾

Bullet Tree Falls

Five kilometres west of San Ignacio (leaving town along the Bullet Tree road) is the village of **BULLET TREE FALLS**, a predominately Spanish-speaking Mestizo farming village spread out along the forested banks of the Mopan River. A bridge crosses the Mopan River at the falls – really just a set of rapids – and several nearby cabaña places offer some very pleasant, good-value **places to stay** on the riverbank. These are listed on p.73, and many of them will arrange transport from San Ignacio for guests; all make a good base from which to visit El Pilar (see below). The village has grown considerably in recent years and its seven bars mean there's quite a busy scene here at the weekend. Right by the bridge the *Riverside Bar and Restaurant* is an agreeable place to enjoy a meal or a drink.

In the middle of the village, immediately before the bridge, is the **El Pilar Cultural Centre**, or *Be Pukte*, which means "road to Bullet Tree" in Mayan (opening hours vary; call Betty Cruz ☎601-2457 to check). Inside there's a good model of El Pilar and you can buy trail guides to all the named trails at the site and other information booklets. A **medicinal trail** has been established along the river, and you can join a guided tour (Bz$10); if you need a **local guide** to El Pilar ask in the village for Teddy Waight. A shared taxi from San Ignacio costs Bz$2.50 per person – catch them at the bus stop at the road junction.

El Pilar

From Bullet Tree Falls you can visit **El Pilar** (daily 8am–4pm; Bz$10), the largest Maya site in the Belize River valley, reached along a rough (motorable and memorable) road climbing the escarpment, 14km northwest of the village. Bullet Tree taxis charge Bz$55 for a carload and the driver will wait for two hours while you visit; caretakers Marcos Garcia or Carmen Cruz will show you around. When the **archeological team** from the University of California is working (usually March–June) you will probably be able to get a lift with them. They also welcome volunteer participation (see Archeology Field Schools, p.310 in "Contexts"). You could reach El Pilar on horseback or by mountain bike – for all these options check at *Eva's* (see p.161) or the hotels in Bullet Tree. **Trail guides** and information on El Pilar are on sale at the *Be Pukte* cultural centre in Bullet Tree (see above); the *Trail of El Pilar* guide details the story of El Pilar by the archeologists who worked at the site.

The Belize River Archaeological Settlement Survey (BRASS; see "Contexts", p.310) has conducted investigation and restoration at El Pilar since 1993. One theory they are investigating is the concept that the forest is a garden, proposing that the Maya cultivated or maintained selected trees from the forest and also grew a number of different food crops on the same plot, while keeping a high level of tree cover – a method known as "forest garden" agriculture, rather than the simplistic picture presented by the inadequate term "slash and burn". Researchers have been recreating this technique in an experimental and educational exhibit that also includes a recreation of a traditional Maya house encountered on the Lakin trail on the east side of the road. The Tzunu'un ("hummingbird" – the guardian of the forest and flowers) residential area of the site was excavated and consolidated in the late 1990s to provide the first (and so far only) view into Maya suburban life that surrounded all the ancient Maya cities.

The site

El Pilar's long sequence of construction began in the Preclassic period, around 700 BC, and continued right through to the Terminal Classic, around 1000 AD, when some of the largest existing structures were completely rebuilt. One reason for such a long period of continuous occupation was almost certainly the presence of numerous springs and creeks in the area – El Pilar is Spanish for "water basin". The most impressive structures – four large pyramids between fifteen and twenty metres high and a ball-court – are grouped around the **Plaza Copal**, from whose west side a flight of steps leads down to a thirty-metre-wide causeway running to **Pilar Poniente** in Guatemala.

The site includes seventy major structures grouped around 25 plazas. Six **hiking trails** lead you around, focusing on both the archeology and natural history of El Pilar, and the site is considered one of the finest bird-watching areas in Cayo. The El Pilar Community Creek Trail provides a historical account of the lives of the people who inhabited the area in the last century. Because of the strong conservation policy at El Pilar most of the structures are still largely covered in forest in order to avoid the severe erosion which can result from removal of this protective covering, though some portions of carved stonework have been uncovered and are on display.

The site's position on the frontier with Guatemala might have led to difficulties of access, or even curtailed further study, but the respective governments, urged on by concerned local leaders and the international archeological community, have overcome generations of mutual suspicion to create the **El Pilar Archaeological Reserve for Maya Flora and Fauna**, covering an area of nine square kilometres on both sides of the border.

The annual **El Pilar Fiesta**, organized jointly by the El Pilar project and the Friends of El Pilar is a joint Belizean–Guatemalan cultural event that's well worth attending – check the dates on El Pilar's very informative and well-organized **website**, Ⓦ www.marc.ucsb.edu/elpilar.

Buenavista del Cayo

On the east bank of the Mopan River, halfway between San Ignacio and the border, the small Maya site of **Buenavista del Cayo** was once the centre of a wider political region of which Cahal Pech is known to have been a satellite. The ruins are on private land and to visit you need permission from the owner, Pablo Guerra, a shopkeeper in Benque. The best way to get here is on horseback – Easy Rider (see box on p.165) runs tours. The site was excavated between 1984 and 1989 by Jennifer Taschek and Joseph Ball, who discovered a palace, ball-courts, carved stelae, plazas and courtyards. A number of important burial items were also found here, including the famous Jauncy vase, now in the Museum of Belize, Belize City (see p.66). There's also evidence that the Maya established workshops to mass-produce pottery on the site. Since excavation, most of the structures have been covered over, but you can still see and visit a small but charming palace structure and arched courtyard in a glade.

The Mountain Pine Ridge Forest Reserve

South of San Ignacio, running roughly parallel to the border with Guatemala, the **Mountain Pine Ridge Forest Reserve** is a spectacular range of rolling hills, peaks and gorges. These heights are formed from some of the oldest rocks in Central America, granite intrusions that have thrust up from below and are part of the bedrock that underlies the entire isthmus. In amongst this there are also some sections of limestone, riddled with superb caves, the most accessible of which is the

The Pine Ridge lives on

Belizeans regard their beautiful pine forest as a national treasure, so news of a very severe infestation of the **southern pine bark beetle** in the Mountain Pine Ridge in early 2000 caused anguish throughout the country. The beetle larvae kill the trees as they feed and these prolific insects can produce a new generation every four or five weeks. The deadly pests swept through the forest, their progress helped by the forest policy of fire suppression, allowing the trees to grow more densely than they would naturally. Initially, it was thought that the entire forest might be destroyed – but a rapidly implemented reforestation programme and abundant natural regeneration means that the forest will eventually recover. The severity of the infestation was exacerbated by human interference – in completely natural conditions the pine forest would periodically be swept by fires, thinning some trees but not killing them all. As you drive around the sandy roads in the Pine Ridge you *will* see large areas of bare, dead pines, stretching to the horizon in places, but already the vigorous young pines are up to two metres tall and growing rapidly. The dead trees themselves provide hunting grounds for woodpeckers and other insect-eaters and as the old trees fall new vistas are opened up. Though the character of the forest has been altered, it's still a beautiful place and, by good fortune, the trees around Thousand-Foot Falls were untouched – you can still see this magnificent sight in all its glory; see p.179.

Rio Frio Cave in Augustine/Douglas Silva. For the most part, the landscape is semi-open, a mixture of grassland and pine forest growing in the nutrient-poor, sandy soil, although in the warmth of the river valleys the vegetation is thicker gallery forest. The pines give way to rainforest south of the Guacamallo Bridge, which crosses the upper Macal River on the road to **Caracol**.

Plentiful rainfall renders the smooth roads in the Pine Ridge difficult to use in the wet season but these rains feed a number of small streams, most of which run off into the Macal and Belize rivers. One of the most scenic is the **Rio On**, rushing over cataracts and forming a gorge – a sight of tremendous natural beauty within view of the picnic shelter. On the northern side of the ridge are the **Thousand-Foot Falls**: actually over 1600ft (490m) and the highest in Central America.

The Pine Ridge is virtually uninhabited but for four or five **tourist lodges** and one small forestry settlement, **Augustine/Douglas Silva**, site of the reserve headquarters. The whole area is perfect for **hiking** and **mountain biking**, but **camping** in the reserve is allowed only at Augustine/Douglas Silva and at the Mai Gate, beyond San Antonio; see Bol's (p.178). Officially you need permission from the Forest Department in Belmopan to camp but in practice you'll almost certainly be allowed to camp if you ask politely when you arrive. It's fairly hard – though rewarding – to explore this part of the country on your own, and unless you have a car, a mountain bike or come on an organized tour, you may have to rely on hitching (but you'd need to be near somewhere to stay in the evening or you could get stuck). To explore the many forestry roads branching off the main reserve road, you really need the 1:50,000 topographic maps of the area, but these are now sold out, though many resorts and attractions do have the relevant sheet on display. See p.168 for a map showing the Macal River valley and the Mountain Pine Ridge.

Getting to the reserve

There are **two entrance roads** to the reserve: the Chiquibul Road, from the village of Georgeville, on the Western Highway (see p.157), and the other from **Santa Elena**, along the **Cristo Rey Road** (see opposite), continuing to the village of **San Antonio**, served by the Mesh buses from San Ignacio. If you're up to it, a good way to get around is to rent a **mountain bike** in San Ignacio; the bus to San Antonio takes bikes, or you could put it in the back of a passing pick-up truck. Any travel agent or resort can arrange **organized tours**: if you're staying at any of the Cayo resorts a full-day tour of the Pine Ridge costs around US$35–50 per person for a group of four, more if you want to go to Caracol (see p.180). Recent road improvements in the Pine Ridge, particularly on the road to Caracol (the last part now has an all-weather surface), make a trip in a **rental jeep** perfectly feasible (most of the year) but always check road conditions first and heed the advice of the forestry officials.

The Cristo Rey Road

The **road to Cristo Rey** village begins in Santa Elena, 450m east of the Hawkesworth Bridge; it's served by all the Mesh buses to San Antonio (see below). Two kilometres along this road is the excellent *Maya Mountain Lodge* (T 824-2164, W www.mayamountain.com; ⑤–⑦), run by Bart and Suzi Mickler. Set in rich tropical forest, it provides a fascinating introduction to the wildlife of Belize. Accommodation is in colourfully decorated individual cabañas, each with a private bath and electricity; the Parrot's Perch Lodge is a larger wooden building with six rooms with private bath and air-conditioning and a huge deck with hammocks. Delicious meals are served in an open-sided dining room, which provides a great opportunity for bird-watching; motmots, aracaris and trogons fly just metres away from the table. The lodge sometimes hosts student groups and has a well-stocked library and a lecture area; after dinner most evenings there's an informed cultural or educational presentation. Families are especially welcome and there are plenty of activities for kids, including a pool and the best illustrated trail guide in Belize. There are great packages available, and if there's space, independent travellers (unless part of a group or in a rented car) can receive a fifty percent discount if carrying this guide.

After another few kilometres you come to **CRISTO REY**, a pretty village of scattered wooden and cement houses and gardens on a high bank above the Macal River. Near the beginning of the village Orlando and Martha Madrid run *Sandals Restaurant* and a few simple, inexpensive **cabins** (see p.169); you can also **rent canoes** at good rates. At the other end of the village, *Crystal Paradise Resort* offers a wider range of accommodation and tours (see p.169).

San Antonio and Pacbitún ruins

In **SAN ANTONIO**, 10km further on from Cristo Rey, the villagers are descendants of Yucatec Maya (*Masawal* is their name in Yucatec) refugees, who fled the Caste Wars in Yucatán in 1847. As a result, most people here still speak Yucatec and Spanish as well as English. Their story is told in a fascinating written account of San Antonio's oral history, *After 100 Years*, by Alfonso Antonio Tzul. Nestled in the Macal River valley, surrounded by scattered *milpa* farms with the forested Maya Mountains in the background, the village is poised to become a base for hiking and horseback tours along old chiclero trails. The Mesh **bus to San Antonio** (Mon–Sat only; 1hr) departs from the market in San Ignacio four times a day between 10.30am and 5pm, returning from San Antonio between 6am and 3pm. San Antonio was the home of the famous Maya *curandero* (healer) **Don Eligio Panti** (see p.171), and his house has become a small, informal museum dedicated to his life and work, and displaying the simple tools he used; opening times are by request. Don Eligio's memory has been further honoured by naming a new national park after him (see below).

The village is a good place to learn about traditional **Maya healing** methods. Go see Don Eligio's nieces, the **Garcia sisters**, who grew up in the village determined not to let their Maya culture be swamped by outside influence. The sisters run the *Chichan Ka Guest House* (☎820-4023; ❸) at the approach to the village, and the bus stops right outside, though the guesthouse has now become rather run-down. The **restaurant** still functions, though, and meals are prepared in the traditional way – often using organic produce from the garden. Maria Garcia is president of the Itzamna Society, a local organization formed to protect the Maya environment and culture, and she also offers courses in the gathering and use of medicinal plants. The sisters are renowned for their **slate carvings**, and the **gift shop** here has become a favourite tour-group stop. Next door is the small **Tanah Museum** (Bz$6), with displays of village life and history and more slate carvings.

Maria Garcia has played a prominent role in the establishment of the new **Eligio Panti National Park**, part of a project to allow the Maya of San Antonio to manage a protected area for conservation and tourism. The park covers over fifty square kilometres of rugged forest, stretching from the boundary of the Mountain Pine Ridge over to the Macal River. Park wardens and guides are being trained, and a visitor centre, trails and campsites are under construction. The new park receives few visitors at present but the landscape is breathtaking and guides from the village can take you to see caves and waterfalls.

Three kilometres east of San Antonio, on the road to the Pine Ridge, lie the **ruins of Pacbitún**, a major Maya ceremonial centre. One of the oldest known Preclassic sites in Belize (1000 BC), it continued to flourish throughout the Classic period, and farming terraces and farmhouse mounds can be seen in the hills all around. Pacbitún, meaning "stones set in the earth", has at least 24 temple pyramids, a ball-court and several raised causeways, though only Plaza A and the surrounding structures are cleared; this is the highest point in Pacbitún, created when the Maya reshaped an entire hilltop. Here, the tombs of two elite women yielded the largest haul of Maya musical instruments ever found in one place: drums, flutes, ocarinas (wind instruments) and the first discovery of Maya maracas. Though the site is not always open to casual visitors, José Tzul, who lives on the right just before the entrance, runs Blue Ridge Mountain Rider (☎824-2322) and can arrange wonderful **horseback tours** of the area (US$50 per day); he can even guide you through little-known trails to the lodges in the Mountain Pine Ridge.

The forest reserve

Not far beyond Pacbitún, the San Antonio Road meets the Chiquibul Road (see p.157) and you begin a steady climb towards the **entrance to the reserve** proper. One kilometre beyond the junction is a **campsite** (Bz$10 per person) run by Fidencio and Petronila Bol, owners of Bol's Nature Tours. It's a good base, on a ridge with views over to Pacbitún and Xunantunich. Fidencio can guide you to several nearby **caves** – the aptly named Museum Cave holds dozens of artefacts, including intact bowls and other ceramics. About 5km uphill from the campsite is the **Mai Gate**, a forestry checkpoint offering information about the reserve as well as toilets and drinking water. Though there are plans to levy an **entrance fee**, for the moment all the guard will do is write your name or that of the tour group in the visitors' book (this is done to ensure there's no illegal camping).

Once you've entered the reserve, the dense, leafy forest is quickly replaced by pine trees. After 3km the often rough Cooma Cairn Road heads off to the left, running for 16km (through an area of dead pines) to a point overlooking the

Thousand-Foot Falls. The setting is spectacular, with rugged, still thickly forested slopes across the steep valley – almost a gorge. The long, slender plume of water becomes lost in the valley below, giving rise to the falls' other, more poetic name: Hidden Valley Falls. The waterfall itself is about 1km from the viewpoint, but try to resist the temptation to climb around for a closer look: the slope is a lot steeper than it first appears and, if you do get down, the ascent is very difficult indeed. Dawn and dusk are perhaps the best times to view the falls, as you'll almost certainly be the only visitors. However, you'd almost certainly need your own vehicle to do this, or be staying at the nearby *Hidden Valley Inn*; see "Accommodation" below. You can't see the river below but this is the headwaters of Roaring River (or Creek) and you can see where it joins the Belize River, at Guanacaste Park (see p.150). There's a shelter with toilets at the viewpoint, and since the site is also a **National Monument** you'll be approached by Pedro Mai, the caretaker, for the entrance fee (Bz$5).

One of the reserve's main attractions has to be the **Rio On Pools**, a gorgeous spot for a swim, back on the Chiquibul Road and 11km further on. Here the river forms pools between huge granite boulders before plunging into a gorge right beside the main road. Another 8km from here and you reach the reserve headquarters at **AUGUSTINE**. This small settlement, now housing only a few forestry workers, was renamed **DOUGLAS SILVA** (after a local politician), but only some of the signs have been changed. If you're heading for **Caracol**, this is where you can get advice on road conditions from the Forest Department. You can **camp** here and there's a small shop for supplies.

The **Rio Frio Caves** are a twenty-minute walk from Augustine, following the signposted track from the parking area through the forest to the main cave, beneath a small hill. The Rio Frio flows right through and out of the other side of the hill here and if you enter the foliage-framed cave mouth, you can scramble over limestone terraces the entire way until you're back out in the open. Sandy beaches and rocky cliffs line the river on both sides.

Accommodation in the reserve

The **resorts** in the Mountain Pine Ridge Forest Reserve include some of the most exclusive accommodation in the interior of Belize. These lodges, mostly cabins set amongst pines, are surrounded by the undisturbed natural beauty of the forest reserve and have quiet paths to secluded waterfalls; they're ideal places to stay if you're visiting **Caracol** (see p.180). The listings below are in the order in which you approach them from the entrance road (see map on p.168 for locations).

Hidden Valley Inn 8km along the Cooma Cairn Rd to Thousand-Foot Falls ☎ 822-3320, in the US ☎ 1-866/443-3364, ⓦ www.hiddenvalleyinn.com. Twelve roomy, well-designed cottages at the highest elevation of any accommodation in Belize, and set in a thirty square kilometre private reserve bordering on Thousand-Foot Falls. Each cottage has a fireplace stacked with logs to ward off the evening chill in the winter. Even the vegetation – pines and tree ferns – appears distinctly untropical, and hiking and 4WD trails take you to mountain overlooks and secret waterfalls. There are so many waterfalls that guests can arrange to have one of several entirely to themselves – a popular option with honeymooners. Meals are served in the spacious main house, with the ambiance of a mountain lodge; wood-panelled walls, a crackling log fire and a well-stocked library. Days are hot enough to swim in the pool and if you do get chilly you can jump in the hot tub. The *Inn* has an impressive list of bird sightings, and you can frequently see the rare orange-breasted falcon. US$150 double. ❾

Pine Ridge Lodge On the Chiquibul Rd to Augustine, just past the Cooma Cairn junction ☎ 606-4557, ⓦ www.pineridgelodge.com. A small resort on the banks of Little Vaqueros Creek, with a choice of simple Maya-style thatched cabins or more modern ones with red-tiled roofs. The grounds and trees are full of orchids, and trails lead to pristine waterfalls. The restaurant is a favourite refreshment stop on tours of the Pine Ridge. Continental breakfast included. ⓲

Blancaneaux Lodge 1km beyond *Pine Ridge Lodge*, then 2km down a signposted track to the right, by the airstrip ☎824-4912, in the US ☎1-800/746-3473, ⓦwww.blancaneauxlodge.com. Owned by Francis Ford Coppola, *Blancaneaux* is the most sumptuous lodge in the Pine Ridge and features a few Hollywood luxuries – not least the prices, though these are considerably lower during the off season. Guests stay in comfortable and very spacious hardwood and thatched cabañas and even more spacious villas overlooking Privassion Creek, and the grounds are beautifully landscaped. Villas (up to US$525, sleeping 4) have two enormous rooms with varnished hardwood floors, and are decorated with Guatemalan and Mexican textiles, and there's a huge screened porch with gorgeous views over the creek. Cabañas (US$175 for garden view, $210 for river view, US$235 for the honeymoon cabaña) are perhaps more affordable. The restaurant boasts a wood-fired pizza oven and an espresso machine, and meals feature Italian specialities served with home-grown organic vegetables and fine Italian and Californian wines. The latest addition to the attractions here is a massage house built entirely with materials from Indonesia. Coppola also owns the equally luxurious *Turtle Inn*, in Placencia (see p.245). ⓳

Five Sisters Lodge 4km past *Blancaneaux*, at the end of the road ☎820-4005, ⓦwww.fivesisterslodge.com. Set on the hillside among the granite and pines, this has the best location in the Pine Ridge. It's also the only Belizean-owned resort here and is the pride and joy of owner Carlos Popper. There are fourteen very comfortable palmetto-and-thatch cabañas and suites, each with hot showers and a deck with hammocks, and less expensive rooms (some with shared bath) in the main building. The grounds are a profusion of flowers, and there's a nature trail through broadleaf forest to Little Vaqueros Falls. Electricity is provided by a small, unobtrusive hydro but the oil lamps are wonderfully romantic and the resort is very popular with honeymooners. The dining-room deck gives tremendous views of the Five Sisters waterfalls cascading over the granite rocks of Privassion Creek. If you don't fancy the climb down – or back up – you can ride in the tiny funicular tram. Below, on a rocky island in the creek, there's a thatched beach bar – and even a small beach. Rates include breakfast; other meals are good value if you're on a day-trip. ⓰–⓳

Caracol

Caracol emblem glyph

Beyond Augustine the main ridges of the Maya Mountains rise up to the south, while to the west is the Vaca plateau, a fantastically isolated wilderness. Sixteen kilometres past Augustine the road crosses the Macal River on the low **Guacamallo Bridge**. The valley here follows a fault line and the vegetation changes dramatically – the pines end at the riverbank and after crossing the bridge you enter the broadleaf jungle of the **Chiquibul Forest**. The turn-off for Caracol is 2.5km past the bridge, and by the time you read this the rest of the road may well have an all-weather surface. A further 18km bring you to the **visitor centre**, where you sign in. Many tour operators in San Ignacio run trips to Caracol (see box on p.165): Everald Tut has a daily **shuttle** van (US$50 per person; ☎820-4014).

Caracol (daily 8am–4pm; Bz$15), the largest and most magnificent Maya site in Belize (and one of the largest in the Maya world), was lost in the rainforest for over a thousand years until its rediscovery by chiclero Rosa Mai in 1937. The site was first systematically explored by A.H. Anderson in 1938: he named the site Caracol – Spanish for "snail" – because of the large numbers of snail shells found there. (Recent research has revealed that the name the ancient Maya gave to their city was **Oxwitzá** – "Three-Hill-Water", pronounced "Osh-witz-ah" – making this one of the few Maya sites where the true name is known.) Anderson was accompanied by Linton Satterthwaite of the University of Pennsylvania in the 1950s, but many early records were destroyed

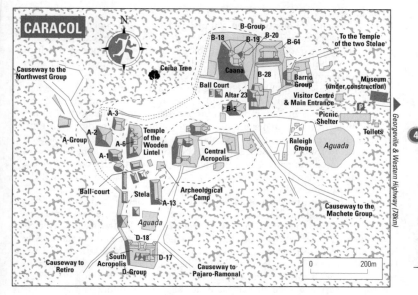

by Hurricane Hattie in 1961, and several altars and stelae were deliberately broken by logging tractors in the 1930s.

In 1985 the first detailed, full-scale excavation of the site, the "Caracol Project", began under the auspices of Drs Arlen and Diane Chase of the University of Central Florida. Initially expected to take at least ten years, research continues to unearth a tremendous amount of artefacts relating to all levels of Maya society. Over a hundred **tombs** have been found, and one of the best preserved is B-19, under the largest temple on the summit of Caana (see p.182). This is almost certainly the tomb of **Lady Batz Ek**, "Black Monkey", who married into the ruling K'an dynasty in 584 AD, and she may even have been a ruler in her own right. Other ceremonially buried caches contain items as diverse as a quantity of mercury and amputated human fingers. There are also many hieroglyphic inscriptions, enabling epigraphers to piece together a virtually complete dynastic record of Caracol's Classic Period rulers from 599 AD to 859 AD.

Apparently there was a large and wealthy middle class among the Maya of Caracol, and dates on stelae and tombs suggest an extremely long occupation, beginning around 600 BC. The last recorded date, carved on Stela 10, is 859 AD, during the Terminal Classic; evidence points to a great fire around 895 AD. At its greatest extent, around 700 AD during the Late Classic period, Caracol covered 88 square kilometres and had a population estimated to be around 150,000, with over 30,000 structures – a far greater density than at Tikal. So far only around ten percent of greater Caracol's full extent has been mapped, and research continues each field season. What continues to puzzle archeologists is why the Maya built such a large city on a plateau with no permanent water source – and how they managed to maintain it for so long.

The site

If you've driven here on your own you may well be accompanied on your visit by one of the site rangers (who know a great deal about recent excavations) or, if excavation is in progress, by an archeology student; this is not so much to inform you (though you undoubtedly will gain from their experience) as to ensure you're not about to damage any recently exposed surfaces or artefacts. So much work is taking place here that new monuments and stucco carvings are discovered almost every week, and many are left under simple thatched shelters until they can be removed to proper storage and laboratory facilities. A new **stela house** is under construction to display these findings but until that's ready you'll learn much more about the latest discoveries from a good tour guide. Despite the presence of the archeology teams and rangers, Caracol is still in an isolated, remote location near the Guatemalan border, and it has been badly looted in the past; the British Army and Belize Defence Force make frequent patrolling visits.

The **visitor centre**, the best at any Maya site in Belize, is an essential first stop. There's a scale model and a map of the centre and some excellent, very informative display panels (follow them from right to left) as well as artefacts from the site. There's also a large, thatched picnic shelter and clean toilets. Only the city's core, covering 38 square kilometres and containing at least 32 large structures and twelve smaller ones around five main plazas, is currently open to visitors – though this is far more than you can effectively see in a day. It's an amazing experience to be virtually alone in this great abandoned city, the horizon bounded by jungle-covered hills, through which it's only three hours on foot to Guatemala.

Towering above the forest, Caracol's largest structure – **Caana**, or "Sky Place" – is, at 43m high, the tallest Maya building in Belize (and still one of the tallest buildings in the country); several others are over 20m high. At the top of this immense restored structure is another plaza, with three more sizeable pyramids above this. When you finally climb B-19, the highest of the three, you'll be rewarded with views of seemingly endless ridges and mountains stretching to the horizon – a perfect environment to contemplate the Maya understanding of the enormity of time while you regain your breath.

Beneath Caana a series of looted tombs still have traces of the original painted glyphs on their walls. Archeological research has revealed other superb tombs, with lintels of iron-hard sapodilla wood supporting the entrances and painted texts decorating the walls. The **B Group**, of which Caana is simply the largest building, is the most massive architectural complex at Caracol, and recent excavations on **Temple B5**, facing Caana across Plaza B, have uncovered fantastically detailed stucco **monumental masks** on either side of the central staircase. These show representations of jaguars and the Witz ("sacred mountain") monster, wearing a headdress of water-lily pads, with small fish nibbling the flowers. In Maya cosmology this symbolizes the evening sun being transformed into the jaguar god of the underworld as he descends into the watery underworld of Xibalba to fight the Lords of Death; according to legend, if successful he will rise again as the sun god.

At the side of Plaza B lies Altar 23 – the largest at Caracol – clearly depicting two bound captive lords from Ucanal and Bital, subdued cities located in present-day Petén; the glyphs above and between them date it to

810 AD. Other glyphs and altars tell of war between Caracol and **Tikal** (see pp.198–206), with power over a huge area alternating between the two great cities. One altar dates Caracol's victory over Tikal at 562 AD – a victory that set the seal on Caracol's rise to power. One of the most awe-inspiring sights in this fantastic city is an immense, centuries-old **ceiba tree** – sacred to the Maya – with enormous buttress roots twice as high as a human being.

Lastly, Caracol is also a **Natural Monument Reserve**, a haven for wildlife as well as archeologists. Bird sightings include the **orange-breasted falcon** and the very rare **harpy eagle** and you may catch sight of ocellated turkeys feeding in the plazas; tapirs dine at night on the succulent shoots growing on cleared areas.

The Chiquibul Cave System

Fifteen kilometres beyond the Caracol turn-off the Chiquibul Road continues to arrive at the vast **Chiquibul Cave System**, the longest cave system in Central America, containing what is probably the largest cave chamber in the western hemisphere. The entire area is dotted with caves and sinkholes, which were certainly known to the ancient Maya and probably used for ceremonies; as yet there has been no cave found in Belize which does not contain Maya artefacts. At present the area is impossible to reach on your own – you'll need to come on a properly organized expedition, with permission from the Forest Department in Belmopan – but some tour operators are planning to run trips in the future, so it's worth checking with those recommended in the Guide (see box on p.165). Further south, **Puente Natural** is an enormous natural limestone arch and the Las Cuevas **rainforest research station** is nearby. Although it's not generally open to the public, visitors on organized tour groups sometimes stay here in the wooden cabins; if you're lucky you could get a lift in with the researchers or a group.

San José Succotz and Xunantunich

Back on the Western Highway, the village of **SAN JOSÉ SUCCOTZ** lies about 12km west of San Ignacio, right beside the Mopan River, just before **Benque Viejo**. It's a very traditional village in many ways, inhabited largely by Mopan Maya, who celebrate fiestas here during the weekend after Holy Saturday (Easter). Under colonial administration, the Maya of Succotz sided with the British, a stance that angered other groups, such as the Icaiché (see p.295), who burnt the village to the ground in 1867. The people here still identify strongly with their Maya culture, and many of the men work as caretakers of other Maya sites in Belize. The Magaña family's art gallery and **gift shop** (signposted from the main road) sells superb wood and slate carvings.

Outside fiesta times, Succotz is a quiet village, and the main reason most people visit is to see the Classic period site of **Xunantunich**, up the hill across the river. Just before the village, *Trek Stop*'s wooden cabins (see p.185) offer some great budget **accommodation**, well-sited for visiting the ruins.

Xunantunich

El Castillo, the tallest building in the impressive Maya city of **Xunantunich** (daily 8am–4pm; Bz$10) dominates the countryside for miles around – you'll see it clearly as you approach from San Ignacio. Pronounced "Shun-an-tun-ich", its name means "the Stone Maiden" in Mopan Mayan – though this is not what the ancient Maya would have called their city, as is the case with many sites. In fact, one of the most significant recent finds at Xunantunich is a chunk of stone frieze bearing the site's original name of **Kat Witz**, or "Clay Mountain".

Xunantunich was first explored in the 1890s by Dr Thomas Gann, a British medical officer, and in 1904 Teobalt Maler of the Peabody Museum took photographs and made a plan of El Castillo. Gann returned in 1924, unearthed (essentially looted) large numbers of burial goods and removed the carved glyphs of Altar 1, the whereabouts of which are now unknown. In 1938, British archeologist J. Eric S. Thompson excavated a residential group and found pottery, obsidian, jade, a spindle, seashells, stingray spines and hammers. Recent excavations have found evidence of Xunantunich's role in the power politics of the Classic period – it was probably allied as a subordinate partner, along with Caracol, with the regional superpower Calakmul, against Tikal. By the Terminal Classic, Xunantunich was already in decline, though still apparently populated until around 1000 AD, shortly after the so-called Classic Maya "collapse".

To **get here**, take any bus or shared taxi running between San Ignacio and the border. You'll be dropped off by the venerable, hand-winched **cable ferry** (daily 8am–5pm; free), which carries foot passengers and vehicles across the Mopan River. From the riverbank, you'll have to walk or drive up a steep 2km road to the site. Your first stop should be the marvellous **visitor centre**, one of the best in Belize. There's a superb scale model of the city, and the labels on exhibits will answer most questions. One of the highlights is a fibreglass repli-

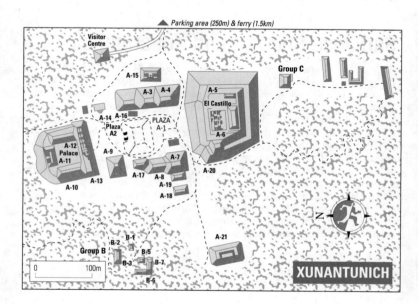

ca of the famous hieroglyphic frieze around El Castillo (see below), from which you get a much better idea of the significance of the real thing. Nearby, the original small **museum** has several well-preserved stelae from the site.

The site
Built on top of an artificially flattened hill, Xunantunich includes five plazas, although the remaining structures are grouped around just three of them. The road brings you out into Plaza A–2, with large structures on three sides.

To the left, Plaza A–1 is dominated by structure A–6, commonly known as **El Castillo**, the city's tallest building at 40m high and a prominent symbol of Belize's national identity. As is so often the case, the building is layered, with later versions built on top of earlier ones. It was once ringed by a decorative **stucco frieze** carved with abstract designs, human faces and jaguar heads, depicting a king performing rituals associated with assuming authority; this has now been extensively restored. The climb up El Castillo is daunting, but the views from the top are superb, with the forest stretching out all around and the rest of the ancient city mapped out beneath you.

To the right as you enter the site, Plaza A–3 is almost completely enclosed by a low, acropolis-like collection of buildings, known as the **Palace**. Artefacts found here in 2003 suggest that this probably was the place where the ruler would meet important officials. The remains of a human sacrifice found in a lower room of the palace may be connected with ceremonies conducted at the same time as the structure was being deliberately filled in and abandoned in the Late Classic – but well before the site itself was abandoned in the Terminal Classic.

Trek Stop and Tropical Wings Butterfly House

Five hundred metres before the village of Succotz and the ferry over the Mopan River (signposted on the left) there's a wonderful budget **place to stay**, *The Trek Stop* (✆823-2265, ✉susa@btl.net, ✇www.thetrekstop.com; ❸). Set in a quiet forest clearing near the road, these eight, simple, clean, non-smoking cabins with comfortable beds, mosquito nets and a porch cost just Bz$20 per person. There's also a **campsite** (Bz$10 per person) and tents are available to rent (Bz$14 per person). Run by American biologists John and Judy Yaeger and Succotz resident Tino Penados, it's an environmentally friendly place, with composting toilets and solar-heated shared showers. Plants here replicate those in a Maya medicinal garden and the excellent library focuses on the Maya and natural history. The **restaurant** serves some of the best-value food and largest portions in Cayo, always with good vegetarian choices, and there's a self-catering kitchen. Bikes (Bz$20 a day), kayaks (Bz$40 a day for one or two people) and tubes (Bz$15 a day) are available for rent, and guided river and nature trips can be arranged. A new activity (popular with visiting school groups) is to have a round on the only **frisbee golf** course in the country.

Also on the site, enter the well-designed **Tropical Wings Butterfly House and Nature Center** (daily 8am–5pm; Bz$5, including an excellent guided tour) and you're suddenly in a delicate, enchanting world full of tropical colour. Native plants arch upwards, pressing against the netting on the roof. About two dozen species of butterflies breed successfully here, laying their eggs on the leaves, and outside you can see the caterpillars at all stages of development.

Benque Viejo and the border

The final town before the Guatemalan border is **BENQUE VIEJO DEL CARMEN**, 13km from San Ignacio. Here Belize and Guatemala combine in almost equal proportions and Spanish is certainly the dominant language, despite the English street names such as Elizabeth and Victoria. Benque, as it's usually known, is a pleasant, quiet town, home to several artists, musicians and writers and has seen a fascinating cultural revival in recent years. Several villagers produce superb **wood and slate carvings**; you'll see them for sale at Xunantunich.

If you're really interested in the cultural aspects of Mestizo traditions, you might want to visit the **Benque House of Culture**, located in the old police station (Wed & Fri 9am–4pm; ☏823-2697). It's supported by the Benque Historical Association, headed up by David Ruiz, whose aim is to revive and promote Maya culture in the area. Inside are displays of old photographs and documents, logging and chicle-gathering equipment, paintings and musical instruments. David and his brother Luis are behind another recent manifestation of this flowering of the arts: Poustinia, a surreal **earth art** sculpture park, 5km south of town on the Mollejon Hydro/Arenal Road; see box below.

Crossing the border, 2km beyond Benque, is straightforward, and there is a constant stream of taxis to and from the border post (Bz$2 per person); full details are given in the box on p.192.

Poustinia Land-Sculpture Park

It is hard to imagine a more impressive and atmospheric venue for an art exhibition than this thirty-acre rainforest setting. The brainchild of Benque-born architect Luis Ruiz – with assistance from his brother David and some British artists – the **Poustinia Land-Sculpture Park** offers a collection of around thirty sculptures from both Belizean and foreign artists, provoking as much as illustrating contemporary Belize. Poustinia seeks to create an awareness of the natural environment, of reforestation and land beautification following human industrial abuse. Some of the sculptures themselves are organic, and thus in time will disappear and be replaced by new exhibits. *Returned Parquet*, by Welsh artist Tim Davies, is a fine example of this philosophy. In Davies's piece, reclaimed mahogany parquet flooring has been relaid as a path through a forest glade; this path will eventually biodegrade and return to the forest whence it came. Other works include installations from David and Luis Ruiz and the schoolchildren of Benque, among other artists.

Given their engaging, thought-provoking mission, it's difficult to see why Poustinia is not better known – but its location 5km south of Benque Viejo on the Arenal Road ensures that it's not on the tourist trail and that it remains the property of the environment around it. On any given day you are likely to have the park to yourself, offering a peaceful place to reflect, a million miles from the usual city art gallery environment. The walk around the park is best enjoyed in sunny weather and at leisure – allow three hours of daylight to complete the route and bring plenty of water. The entry fee is Bz$10 and visitors are provided with maps for a self-guided tour. Bookings and further information can be obtained from David Ruiz at the Benque House of Culture (see above) or by visiting the Poustinia Foundation's website, ⓦwww.poustiniaonline.org. Taxis ply the route from Benque to Arenal so transport shouldn't be a problem unless you're returning late in the day – even then, the 1hr walk back to town is an enjoyable one.

Travel details

Belize City to: destinations along the Western Highway, terminating in Benque Viejo (for the Guatemalan border; 3hr 30min), are served by half-hourly Western Transport (Novelo's) buses (5am–9pm). There is an express service, stopping only in Belmopan, every 3–4hr, saving an hour on the journey time above.

Belmopan to: San Ignacio and Benque (Western Transport runs at least an hourly service Mon–Fri 7am–5pm, fewer services on weekends; some continue to Melchor).

Benque Viejo to: Belize City calling at San Ignacio and Belmopan. (Western Transport buses half-hourly daily 4am–5pm, express service every 3–4hr).

San Antonio to: San Ignacio (Mon–Sat 6am, 7am, 1pm & 3pm; 1hr).

San Ignacio to: Belmopan and Belize City (Western Transport runs half-hourly services, including expresses from 4.30am; last bus to Belize at 6pm); San Antonio (Mesh bus from marketplace Mon–Sat 4 daily 10am–5pm; 1hr); Benque (for the border; every 30min; 20min).

A shared taxi to the border costs Bz$2 per person from Benque, though if you're headed to the border it's often easier and quicker to take a shared taxi for Bz$4 per person from the market area in San Ignacio.

Tikal and Flores

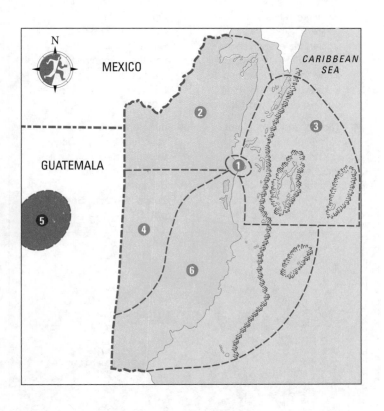

CHAPTER 5

Highlights

* **Laguna Yaxhá** This sublime lake, with the impressive restored ruins of Yaxhá towering above the shore, is one of the best-kept secrets in Petén. See p.194

* **El Remate** Stay overnight in this picturesque, relaxed little village on the eastern shore of Lago Petén Itzá, watch a spectacular sunset and get an early start for Tikal the next day. See p.196

* **Tikal** Spend a couple of days exploring the splendour of this enormous ancient Maya metropolis, set in protected rainforest teeming with wildlife. See p.198

* **Flores** Stroll around the cobbled streets of this tiny colonial capital and enjoy a good, inexpensive meal on the lakeside. See p.206

* **Arcas and Petencito Zoo** Take a *lancha* from Flores to visit Arcas, an inspiring example of wildlife rehabilitation, and then observe the animals of Petén in nearby Petencito Zoo. See p.210

* **Jungle trekking** Extend your Tikal trip by hiking through virtually pristine rainforest to more-distant Maya sites like El Zotz or Río Azul. See p.211

△ Boat approaching Flores

Tikal and Flores

For visitors to Belize, the chance to make side-trips across the western border into **Guatemala**, to see the famous **Maya sites** and spectacular **nature reserves**, is one not to be missed; it's also relatively easily done, either independently or on an organized tour. Here, in the vast northern department of **Petén**, there are literally hundreds of ruins – many of them completely buried in the jungle – but few provide the same combination of intrigue and accessibility as **Tikal**, which is arguably the most magnificent of all Maya sites and situated less than two hours from the border. The monumental temple-pyramids tower above the Tikal rainforest, testament to the fact that Petén was the heartland of the ancient Maya civilization during the Preclassic and Classic periods (around 300 BC–900 AD), and that it was here, during the latter, that Maya culture reached the height of its architectural achievement.

En route to Tikal, there are other Maya sites worth stopping off for, and you'll see signs for several as you head west along the road from the bustling yet nondescript border town of **Melchor de Mencos**. The first major sites are **Yaxhá**, the third largest in Petén, and the much smaller site of **Topoxté**. Both occupy beautiful settings on opposite shores of Laguna Yaxhá, about 30km from the border, and there's camping and cabaña accommodation nearby. At **Macanché**, another 30km beyond the Yaxhá junction on the lake of the same name, **El Retiro** boasts several fine examples of *chultunes* – underground chambers carved out of the limestone whose real function is still a mystery – as well as a serpentarium and a **crocodile sanctuary**.

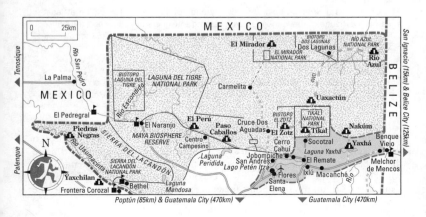

Getting to the border

From Belize City, **buses** leave half-hourly for Benque Viejo (all calling at San Ignacio; see p.74), just 2km from the Guatemalan border. After you disembark at Benque Viejo, you'll need to take a *colectivo* taxi (US$1 per person) the rest of the way to the border. Alternatively (and much more expensively), you could **fly**: Tropic Air and Maya Island Air each have two daily flights from Belize International to Flores/Santa Elena in Guatemala (up to US$88 one-way, plus departure tax totalling US$35). These flights generally depart Belize at 8.30am and 2.30pm, returning at 9.45am & 3.45pm.

Border practicalities

Both the Belizean and Guatemalan border posts are on the eastern bank of the Mopan River, 15km west of San Ignacio. Even if you're leaving Belize for just one day, you'll have to pay the **exit tax** of Bz$30 and the PACT conservation fee of Bz$7.50. Although **visas** are not needed by most nationalities, and most visitors aren't required to pay an entry fee, everyone must fill in the immigration form – and you may still be asked to pay, anything from Q10 to US$10. If you're driving a vehicle from Belize there will a Q50 (about US$6.50) fee, plus smaller, often variable, fees for spraying with insecticide and a bridge toll. At immigration, make sure you request enough time to cover your visit, and ask for the maximum if you're travelling onwards – though the most you're likely to get is thirty days.

Although there is a **bank** just beyond immigration which gives reasonable rates (Mon–Fri 8.30am–6pm; no ATM or cash advances), it's mainly used by truck drivers for paying import charges and doesn't always deal in dollars. It's quicker and easier to use the moneychangers who'll pester you on either side of the border; bargain with a couple and you'll get a fair rate. There's a LADATEL (long distance) **telephone** just past immigration, though the cards it takes are not easy to find nearby. There's no official tourist information office at the border – the closest locations of the Guatemalan Tourist Commission, aka Inguat, are in Flores and at the airport.

If you need **accommodation** at the border (thereby allowing you to get a really early start the next day), the best option is the *Río Mopan Lodge* (☏926-5196, ⒲www.tikaltravel.com; ❸), on the riverbank just past Guatemalan immigration and before the bridge. Swiss owner Marco Gross knows Petén and its archeology extremely well, and he organizes amazing trips to remote Maya sites. You can also safely change money here. The cheap, sleazy hotels in the centre of Melchor are best avoided.

Language

Guatemala is a **Spanish**-speaking country and you'd be wise to acquire at least some knowledge of the language; overcharging foreigners is routine and the better you are at getting by the less likely you are to be ripped off. See p.353 for a quick Spanish-language guide.

Money and costs

The Guatemalan unit of **currency** is the *quetzal* (Q), currently trading at Q7.70–8 to the US dollar. At the border, you can easily exchange money (US or Belize) or cash

---

If you're travelling directly to Tikal by bus from the Belize border, you'll need to change at the village of **Ixlú**, from where it's only a couple of kilometres to the peaceful village of **El Remate** – a good base if you plan to spend more than a day exploring the area. Those with the time for a more extended trip could make for the village and ruins of **Uaxactún**, to the north of Tikal, which also serves as a jumping-off point for expeditions to more remote sites in the

travellers' cheques. If you're not going directly to Flores/Santa Elena (where there are ATMs) make sure you have enough cash (*quetzales* or dollars) to last at least the first day of your trip. Only the more expensive hotels will take credit cards.

Costs are generally much cheaper in Guatemala than in Belize; for transport, accommodation and food they can be as much as forty or fifty percent less. El Remate (roughly on the way to Tikal) and Flores have some of the best budget accommodation in the country; in either town you can get a decent double room for around US$10 – much less for a room with shared bath.

Crime and safety

In Guatemala you'll need to take even greater **safety precautions** than in Belize. The border crossing (and indeed travel to Tikal) is best undertaken in daylight – which is not difficult, as the journey time is short enough to allow you to have an early breakfast in San Ignacio and get to your destination by early afternoon at the latest. In the past, violent robberies and assaults on tourists have taken place in and around El Remate and within Tikal itself, though the introduction of **Tourism Police** – POLITUR – patrols in vehicles and on foot has successfully driven most violent criminals elsewhere. You should check with fellow visitors and with owners of the recommended hotels for information on the security situation where you are. If you see a robbery or are a victim yourself contact POLITUR on ☏226-4835 or 926-1365.

Moving on from the border

The only way to go directly from the border to **Tikal** or **El Remate** is to take a **private minibus** (around US$10–15 per person, depending on the number of people; 1hr 20min), though it's very easy to use public transport and change at the **Ixlú junction** (see p.196) to a bus (or more likely a minibus) that will take you the rest of the way.

All buses to **Santa Elena/Flores** (under 2hr; every couple of hours from 5am to 7pm) pass through the Ixlú junction; these buses can be picked up just over the bridge at the border. If there's not one there you can go to the market in Melchor to find one – a shared taxi from the border will cost a couple of *quetzales* – or take a 15min walk over the bridge and up the hill to the right. The official **bus fare** to Flores is Q15; even if you're only going as far as Ixlú you'll still be asked for at least this by the Pinita bus employees, so get a Rosita or a Fuente del Norte bus if there's a choice. It's worth noting that all public buses will actually drop you off on Calle Principal in Santa Elena, on the mainland opposite Flores. Getting to Flores from here is an easy (if hot) 15min walk across the causeway. Alternatively, you can catch one of the frequent local buses (Q1) from the junction of Calle Principal and the road to the causeway; taxis and tour minibuses go straight there.

New *colectivo* **minibuses** (known locally as *microbuses*) provide an even faster and more frequent service than the public buses; they wait just over the bridge and charge around Q15–20 to Santa Elena. At the border you'll also be approached by *private* **taxi** and **minibus** drivers; they'll charge about US$10 per person to Flores or Tikal – after some bargaining – and leave whenever they have a load (four people). Taking a minibus is generally the quickest and most comfortable way to travel and the best minibus deals are offered by Manuel Sandoval, who runs Transportes Memita, and Hugo Mayén; both are friendly, honest and reliable.

north, such as El Zotz, Río Azul and El Mirador.

But archaeology isn't the only thing to tempt you over the border. Petén is a huge, rolling expanse of tropical forest, swamps, lakes and dry savannahs, stretching into the Lacandón forest of southern Mexico. Tikal itself lies at the centre of a large national park, which forms part of the **Maya Biosphere Reserve**, covering 16,000 square kilometres of northern Petén. As one of the largest tropical forest reserves in Central America, it's extraordinarily rich in **wildlife**, particularly birds, though you're also virtually guaranteed to see **howler** or **spider monkeys**. One of the best places to get an understanding of the forest (apart from Tikal itself) is to visit the **Cerro Cahuí** reserve near El Remate.

Finally, the departmental capital, **Flores**, is a picturesque town set on an island in Lake Petén Itzá, while close by, on the mainland, the growing town of **Santa Elena** is its transport hub.

Melchor de Mencos to El Remate

The sixty kilometres from the **Belize border to the Ixlú junction** takes you through rolling countryside and farmland, past a series of small villages, populated mainly by fairly recent immigrants to Petén, and past the Maya sites of **Yaxhá** and **Topoxté**. The road from Melchor de Mencos is in reasonable condition, with only the first few kilometres beyond the border still unpaved, and runs roughly parallel to a chain of lakes – the largest of which is **Lake Petén Itzá** – used in Maya times as the main route across the region. Other lakes along the way include **Macanché**, with more ruins and a nature reserve, and Sal Petén, where there's another major Maya site. Near the shore of Lake Petén Itzá the Melchor road meets the Flores–Tikal road at the village of **Ixlú**, from where you can continue west to Flores, or north, through **El Remate**, for Tikal.

Yaxhá and Topoxté

Thirty kilometres from Melchor the road passes about 8km to the south of **lagunas Yaxhá and Sacnab**, beautiful bodies of water ringed by dense rainforest. Lake Yaxhá is home to two Maya ruins well worth a visit: **Yaxhá**, on a hill overlooking the northern shore, and **Topoxté**, on an island near the southern shore. The turn-off is clearly signposted and the bus driver will stop if you ask. If you haven't arranged accommodation at *El Sombrero* (see opposite) then you'll probably be faced with a sweltering two-hour walk to get there, though there is some traffic to and from the village of La Máquina, 2km before the lakes. Just before you reach the lakes you pass a **control post** where you may be asked to sign in. From here it's 3km to the site: head along the road between the lakes, then turn left (signed) for Yaxhá.

Yaxhá emblem glyph

Yaxhá, a huge site covering several square kilometres of a ridge overlooking the lake, is primarily a Classic period city. Although a great deal of restoration has been completed in recent years, don't expect the manicured splendour of Tikal. What you can count on here, though, is real atmosphere as you try to discover the many features still half-hidden by the forest. The site is open daily (free at the time of writing); if you're not on a guided trip then one of the guardians will show you around for a small fee. The ruins are spread out over nine plazas and around five hundred structures have been mapped so far, including several huge pyramids and large acropolis complexes. The tallest and most impressive pyramid, **Structure 216**, 250m northeast of the entrance, rises in tiers to a height of over 30m; the recent restoration enables you to climb to the top for spectacular views over the forest and lake.

Topoxté, a much smaller site on the easternmost of three small islands, is best reached by boat from *El Sombrero*. There is a 4km trail to a spot opposite the islands but you still have to get over to them – and large crocodiles inhabit the lake. The structures you see are not on the scale of those at Yaxhá, and date mainly from the Late Postclassic, though the site has been occupied since Preclassic times. Work is in progress to restore some structures.

If you want to **stay** nearby, the wonderful, solar-powered *Campamento El Sombrero* (☎926-5229 or 800-0179, ⓦwww.yaxha.org; ❸–❺), 200m from the road on the south side of the lake, has rooms in thatched wooden jungle lodges, a less expensive shared room and space for **camping**. The thatched restaurant overlooking the lake is a peaceful spot to stop for lunch even if you're not staying here. Gabriela Moretti, the Italian-born owner, is a great source of information about Yaxhá, and can arrange boat trips on the lake and horseback trips to other sites; she'll pick you up from the bus stop if you call in advance. There's another excellent *campamento*, run by locals on behalf of Inguat, on the far side of the lake, immediately below Yaxhá, where you can **pitch a tent** or sling a hammock beneath a thatched shelter for free.

Macanché, Ixlú and El Remate

Beyond the Yaxhá junction the road continues for around another 30km to the village of **MACANCHÉ**, on the shore of **Laguna Mancanché**, where a signed track leads north for 1.8km to another wonderfully tranquil place to stay, the *Santuario Ecológico El Retiro* (☎704-1300, ⓔelretiro7@hotmail.com, ⓦwww.retiro-guatemala.com; ❶–❹). Set in forested grounds on the north shore of the lake are private **bungalows** with hot shower and shady porch for US$30 double, as well as spacious, already-set-up **tents** for US$5.50 per person; you can also **camp** for Q25 per person. There's a good restaurant and a dock for swimming – and the crocodiles are not usually seen at this end of the lake. In the base area is a **serpentarium** where over twenty species of snakes native to Guatemala (including the deadly fer-de-lance) and a venomous beaded lizard – *escorpión* in Spanish – are housed in glass tanks in a very secure building. Owner Miguel Meillon keeps the reptiles under licence from the Guatemalan government and a tour, which can include watching the snakes catch and devour rats, costs Q35; other tours are described below.

On top of the hill behind the base area lie the stone remains of ancient **Maya**

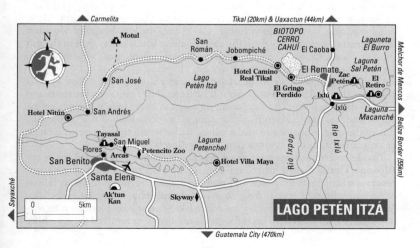

LAGO PETÉN ITZÁ

residential complexes – but far more intriguing are the numbers of *chultunes* found here. A *chultun* is a roughly spherical or gourd-shaped hole carved out of the rock, with a very narrow entrance on top capped by a circular stone. Their exact use is still unknown, though suggested functions include storage chambers, a refuge or a place to conduct ceremonial or religious rites. The best example found so far is just behind the bungalows and this has a main chamber with two or possibly three side chambers accessed by a spiral ramp: anyone brave enough can sleep there.

El Retiro forms part of an extensive private nature reserve and **crocodile sanctuary** which extends along the lake and into two other lakes beyond. Alejandro, the caretaker and guide at *El Retiro* can take you on a 45 minute hike through the forest or a ten minute boat ride to reach the gorgeous **Laguneta** (meaning "small lagoon") **El Burro**, just beyond the north shore of Laguna Macanché, and surrounded by thick rainforest dotted with Maya ruins; use of a canoe to paddle around the *laguneta* is included in the tour. Other trails (each about 45min) lead to another large lake, **Laguna Tintal**, and then on to a *cenote*, a limestone sinkhole 100m across and almost 100m deep. A day tour including lunch, a visit to the serpentarium and all three lagoons costs US$25; a night tour including dinner and a hike and boat trip to spot the crocodiles is US$40.

A few kilometres past Macanché you reach the tiny village of **IXLÚ**, at the junction with the Flores–Tikal road; coming from the Belize border by public transport you'll need to get off here if you want to go to Tikal. Inside the thatched **information** hut you'll find a large map of the area, showing the little-restored **ruins of Ixlú**, 200m down a signposted track from the road, on the shore of Laguna Sal Petén.

El Remate

EL REMATE, 2km north from Ixlú along the shore of Lake Petén Itzá, is a quiet, friendly village and, if you intend to spend more than a day at Tikal, a convenient place to base yourself. The accommodation here is cheaper and better value than at the site itself, and all buses and minibuses to and from Tikal pass through the village. Transportes Hillary and a couple of other companies run regular **minibuses** between Santa Elena (for Flores) and El Remate, passing through Ixlú every couple of hours, and the daily Pinita **bus to Tikal** leaves from the marketplace in Santa Elena at 1pm and passes through Ixlú and El Remate about 45 minutes later, continuing to Tikal and Uaxactún. Many minibuses stop here to allow visitors the chance to buy beautiful **wooden handicrafts**, often directly from the carvers and at better prices than in the gift shops in Flores. One of the best choices is Artesanía Ecológica, where you can see expert carver Rolando Soto at work.

All the hotels now have mains electricity and water, and most have cellular phones – though the networks can still be unreliable. Several **restaurants** and most of the hotels serve meals; the dining room at *Don David* is the one of the largest and you may have to book for dinner. The *Restaurant Cahuí* on the lake side of the road in the centre of the village is also worth trying, serving a range of vegetarian dishes from a wooden deck with relaxing views.

Two kilometres further west along the lakeshore, an unpaved road passes the **Biotopo Cerro Cahuí** (daily 7am–5pm; Q20), a 6.5 square kilometre **nature reserve** with lakeshore, ponds and trails leading through the forest to hilltop Maya ruins. Beyond here is the village of **Jobompiche**, served by buses from Santa Elena, and the road circles the entire lake – great to explore on a mountain bike. A few hotels have bikes for guests to borrow or rent and there's a **bike**

rental outfit just beyond *John's Place* (see below). At the *Hotel Las Sirenas* you can rent bikes (Q50/day) and 100cc **motorbikes** (Q150/day) and they also provide a good **laundry service**. There are plenty of **guides** in El Remate, who can lead you on multi-day trips to remote Maya sites; the best way to find a good one is to ask at the recommended hotels.

Accommodation

In the absence of exact addresses, the **accommodation** below is listed in the order in which you approach it from the village of Ixlú: minibuses will stop outside any of these. There are many more hotels than are listed here and the going rate for a bed in a simple room with shared bath is around Q25–30 (around US$3–4) per person – and this is usually how you'll be charged rather than per room.

Camping Sal Itzá Next to the *Tienda Laura*, 100m down a signposted track opposite the lakeshore ☎701-8300. Simple but comfortable stick-and-thatch cabins with mosquito nets and camping in gardens on a steep hillside with lake views. Run by a very friendly family, headed by Juan and Catalina, who'll cook tasty local food on request. ❶

Las Sirenas In the centre of the village, on the right ☎928-8477/8. Clean, comfortable rooms, some with private bath, in a wooden building with views of the lake. There's a café below and owner Beto Nuñez speaks English and offers guided tours. Telephone and laundry service. ❶

El Mirador del Duende On the right side of the road, high above the lake and reached by a stairway cut into the cliff ☎301-5576, ✉micuchitril@hotmail.com. An incredible collection of whitewashed, stucco cabañas that look like igloos decorated with Maya glyphs. The restaurant serves vegetarian food. ❶

La Mansión del Pájaro Serpiente Just beyond *El Mirador del Duende* ☎702-9434. Set in a gorgeous tropical garden with a pool, these stone-built, thatched, two-storey cabañas provide the most comfortable accommodation in the area, with immaculate baths and superb lake views. When available, the smaller cabañas, usually used by tour guides, are available at a discount. ❺

La Casa de Juan (John's Place) On the right 300m beyond *La Mansión* ☎204-2555. Four very popular budget rooms with shared bath run by the

amiable Juan and family. It has a really good inexpensive restaurant downstairs and a plant-filled deck above. ❶

Posada Felín Immediately behind *John's Place*. Simple rooms with shared bath in a plant-filled garden run by the friendly Norma Figueroa and Luis Oliveros; Luis is an expert on forest lore. ❶

La Casa de Don David At the junction with the road to the Biotopo Cerro Cahuí ☎928-8469 or 306-2190, ✇www.lacasadedondavid.com. Comfortable, spacious and secure wooden bungalows and rooms, all with private bath (most with hot water), set in extensive plant-filled grounds just back from the lakeshore. Owners David and Rosa Kuhn offer great hospitality and wonderful home-cooking; you may need to book for dinner. David can change money, arrange trips and sell bus tickets for Belize and Guatemala City. There are usually a couple of bikes for guests to borrow, and guests can use the Internet. ❸–❹

Casa Roja 500m past *Don David's*, down the road from El Remate to Cerro Cahuí ☎909-6999. A great budget deal right by the lake. The simple, well-constructed stick-and-thatch cabañas, all with shared bath, have great lake views and there's a good, inexpensive restaurant that only serves vegetarian food. Kayaks for rent. ❶

Doña Tonita Just past *Casa Roja*. Quiet, inexpensive thatched dorm room with a lake view and some simple, clean rooms with shared bath. Inexpensive restaurant. ❶

Tikal

Immediately north of El Remate the road climbs a limestone escarpment, and though most peoples' minds are fixed on the mighty ruins of **Tikal**, only 30km ahead, a quick glance behind will reward you with superb views of the lake. The landscape becomes more undulating and the settlements begin to thin out as you approach the entrance to the **Tikal National Park**, a protected area of some 370 square kilometres which surrounds the site. As you get closer, the sheer scale of Tikal as it rises above the forest canopy becomes overwhelming, and the atmosphere spellbinding. Dominating the ruins are five enormous **temples**: steep-sided pyramids that rise up 60m from the forest floor, and around which lie literally thousands of other structures, many still hidden beneath mounds of earth and covered with jungle.

Some history: the rise and fall of Tikal

Tikal emblem glyph

According to archeological evidence, the first occupants of Tikal had arrived by 900 BC, during the **Middle Preclassic**, making this amongst the oldest of Maya sites, though at that time it was little more than a village. It's also one of the few cities where we know the name used by the people who lived there; they called their city **Mutul** – "knot of hair" – found in the city's emblem glyph, which depicts the rear view of a head, with what appears to be a knotted headband around it. The earliest definite evidence of buildings dates from 500 BC, and by about 200 BC ceremonial structures had emerged, including the first version of the **North Acropolis**. Two hundred years later the **Great Plaza** had begun to take shape and Tikal was already established as a major site with a large permanent population. For the next two centuries art and architecture became increasingly ornate and sophisticated, though Tikal remained a secondary centre, dominated by **El Mirador**, a massive city about 65km to the north.

The closing years of the Preclassic (250–300 AD) saw trade routes disrupted and alliance patterns altered, culminating in the decline and abandonment of El Mirador. In the resulting power vacuum the two sites of **Tikal** and **Uaxactún** emerged as substantial centres of trade, science and religion. Less than a day's walk apart, the expanding cities engaged in a heated competition which could have only one winner. Matters finally came to a head in 378 AD, when, under the inspired leadership of Toh Chac Ich'ak, **Great Jaguar Paw**, Tikal's warriors overran Uaxactún, enabling Tikal's rulers to dominate central Petén for much of the next five hundred years.

This extended period of prosperity saw the city's population grow to somewhere between 50,000 and 100,000, spreading to cover an area of around thirty square kilometres. Crucial to this success were Tikal's alliances with the powerful cities of Kaminaljuyú (in present-day Guatemala City) and Teotihuacán (to the north of modern Mexico City); stelae and paintings from the period show that Tikal's elite adopted Teotihuacán styles of clothing, pottery and weaponry. In the middle of the sixth century, however, Tikal suffered a huge setback. Already weakened by upheavals in central Mexico, where Teotihuacán was in decline, the city now faced major challenges from the east, where the city of **Caracol** (see p.180) was emerging as a major regional power, and from the north where **Calakmul** (see "History" in Contexts, p.284) was becoming a Maya "superpower". In an apparent attempt to subdue a potential rival, **Double Bird**, the ruler of Tikal, launched an attack (known as an "axe war") on Caracol and its ambitious leader, Yahaw-te, **Lord Water**, in 556 AD. Despite capturing and sacrificing a noble from Caracol, Double Bird's strategy was only temporarily successful; in 562 AD Lord Water hit back in a devastating "star war", which crushed Tikal and almost certainly sacrificed Double Bird. The victors stamped their authority on the humiliated nobles of Tikal, smashing stelae, desecrating tombs and destroying written records, ushering in a 130-year "**hiatus**" during which no inscribed monuments were erected and Tikal was overshadowed by Caracol, supported by its powerful ally, Calakmul. When research from more recent discoveries at Temple V (see p.204) is published, however, the "hiatus" may come to be viewed in a new light.

Towards the end of the seventh century, however, Caracol's stranglehold had begun to weaken and Tikal gradually started to recover its lost power. Under the formidable leadership of Hasaw Chan K'awil, **Heavenly Standard Bearer**, who reigned from 682 to 723 AD, the main ceremonial areas were reclaimed from the desecration suffered at the hands of Caracol. By 695 AD, Tikal was powerful enough to launch an attack against Calakmul, capturing and executing its king, Ich'ak K'ak, **Fiery Claw/Jaguar Paw**, and severely weakening the alliance against Tikal. The following year, Hasaw Chan K'awil repeated his astonishing coup by capturing **Split Earth**, the new king of Calakmul, and Tikal regained its position among the most important of Petén cities. Hasaw Chan K'awil's leadership gave birth to a revitalized and powerful ruling dynasty: in the hundred years following his death Tikal's five main temples were built and his son, Yik'in Chan K'awil, **Divine Sunset Lord** (who ascended the throne in 734 AD), had his father's body entombed in the magnificent **Temple I**. Temples and monuments were still under construction until at least 869 AD, when Tikal's last recorded date was inscribed on Stela 24.

What brought about Tikal's final **downfall** remains a mystery, but what is certain is that around 900 AD almost the entire lowland Maya civilization collapsed, and that by the end of the tenth century Tikal had been abandoned. Afterwards, the site was used from time to time by other groups, who worshipped here and repositioned many of the stelae, but it was never occupied again.

Getting to Tikal

Coming by bus **from the Belize border** you'll need to change at **Ixlú** (see p.196); look for the *Zac Petén* restaurant on the left. At the junction, local buses to Socotzal and Jobompiche can take you to El Remate (Q3), where there's abundant inexpensive acccommodation. Alternatively, you can just hop on any passing minibus, which will take you directly to Tikal for around Q15–20 per person.

From Flores, any hotel or travel agent will arrange transport in one of the fleet of minibuses leaving at least hourly from 4am to early afternoon; tickets cost Q40 return. Mundo Maya has the best buses on the run, with departures at 5am, 8.30am and 3.30pm. From the **airport**, minibuses to Tikal (via El Remate) connect with flights from Belize City.

From Santa Elena, the daily Pinita bus to Tikal leaves from the marketplace at 1pm, passing through El Remate about 45 minutes later and continuing to Tikal (Q10; 50min from El Remate) and **Uaxactún**, 24km north of Tikal.

Car rental is also available from the airport or from Santa Elena (see "Listings" p.211). Note that if you're **driving to Tikal** you'll be given a timed ticket to ensure you don't break the 30km/hr speed limit in the park; you'll be checked when you arrive at the site and reported to the police if you've taken less than twenty minutes.

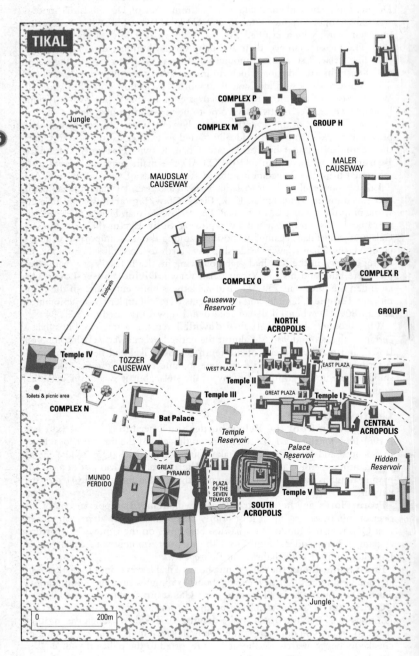

TIKAL

Jungle

COMPLEX P

COMPLEX M

GROUP H

MALER
CAUSEWAY

MAUDSLAY
CAUSEWAY

Footpath

COMPLEX O

COMPLEX R

Causeway
Reservoir

GROUP F

NORTH
ACROPOLIS

Temple IV

TOZZER
CAUSEWAY

WEST PLAZA

EAST PLAZA

Temple II

Toilets & picnic area

GREAT PLAZA

Temple I

COMPLEX N

Temple III

Bat Palace

CENTRAL
ACROPOLIS

Temple
Reservoir

Palace
Reservoir

Hidden
Reservoir

MUNDO
PERDIDO

GREAT
PYRAMID

PLAZA
OF THE
SEVEN
TEMPLES

Temple V

SOUTH
ACROPOLIS

Jungle

0   200m

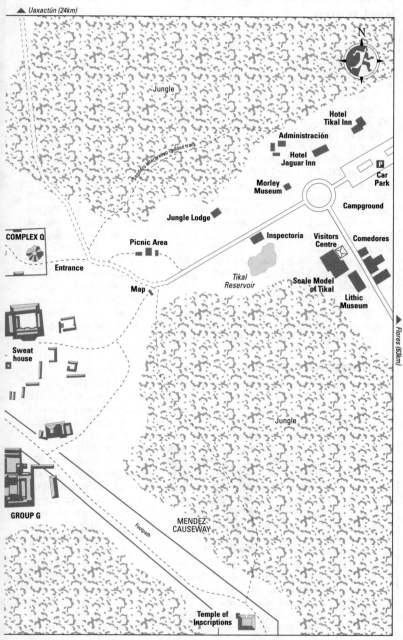

▲ Uaxactún (24km)

N

Jungle

Hotel
Tikal Inn

Administración

Hotel
Jaguar Inn

Sendero interpretivo (guided trail)

Morley
Museum

P
Car
Park

Campground

Jungle Lodge

COMPLEX Q

Picnic Area

Entrance

Inspectoría

Visitors
Centre

Comedores

Tikal
Reservoir

Scale Model
of Tikal

Map

Lithic
Museum

▶ Flores (63km)

Sweat
house

Jungle

GROUP G

Footpath

MENDEZ
CAUSEWAY

Temple of
Inscriptions

Visiting the site: entry fees, information and tours

At the national park entrance barrier, 15km before the site itself, you pay a Q50 **entrance fee** (due every day you stay at the site). If you arrive after 3pm you'll be given a ticket for the next day, which you can also use the day you buy it. The ruins are open from 6am to 6pm; extensions to 8pm can sometimes be obtained from the *administractión* (Mon–Sat 7am–noon & 2–5pm), a complex of bungalows opposite the roundabout at the end of the paved road.

At the entrance to the ruins is a **visitor centre** with the standard overpriced café and gift shop, with a good selection of books. The best guide to the site is William R. Coe's *Tikal, A Handbook to the Ancient Maya Ruins*, while *The Birds of Tikal* is useful for identifying some of the hundreds of species you might come across as you wander round. The highlight here, though, is the **scale model of Tikal** and the **Lithic Museum** (daily 8am–4pm; entry included in site ticket), containing a selection of the finest stelae and carvings from the site. Also at the entrance there is a **post office** and a few stalls selling *tipica* – Guatemalan weavings and handicrafts. A **licensed guide** to show you the site will cost around US$40 for four hours for groups of up to five. Many speak English, and recommended guides include Eulogio López García and José Morales Monzón.

Finally, for something more out-of-the-ordinary, try the **Tikal Canopy Tour** (daily 7am–5pm; US$25; ☎412-7252) if you fancy aping Tarzan: after a 25-minute walk through lovely forest you are strapped into a harness, clipped onto a cable and launched off at tree-height toward the next platform 100m away. You fly suspended through the trees and once you get used to it you begin to look around and enjoy the views, which can include birds and monkeys. The process is repeated ten times, and there are plans to add more platforms.

Accommodation

There are three **hotels** (all with restaurants) near the entrance. They're fairly expensive by local standards (though not compared with prices in Belize) though you can often get discounts out of season; all have hot-water showers. During the winter high season they are often booked up weeks in advance; **reservations** can be made from a recommended travel agent in Belize or Flores. The least expensive hotel, also with the least expensive restaurant, is the *Jaguar Inn* (☎926-0002, ⓦwww.jaguartikal.com), with private bungalows (⑤), a dorm room for US$10 per person or camping (Q25 per person); you can also rent a tent or hammocks for Q40 per person. The *Tikal Inn* (☎926-0065, ⓔhoteltikalinn@itelgua.com; ⑤) has comfortable, attractive thatched bungalows around a very inviting pool and pleasant rooms; this can often be the best-value hotel if you book a package which includes meals. The largest and most luxurious option, the *Jungle Lodge* (☎476-8775, ⓔreservaciones@junglelodge.guate.com), has large, private bungalows in shady grounds (⑥) and some "budget" rooms (④), although the latter are often full. Finally, for a Q25 per person fee you can **camp** or sling a **hammock** under one of the thatched shelters at the **campsite**, in a grassy field across from the entrance. The "cabañas" at the far end of the campsite (Q50 per person) are no more than decrepit sheds; best avoided unless you're really desperate. Hammocks and mosquito nets can sometimes be rented from the camping *administractión*. There's a shower block at the entrance to the campsite, but the water and electricity supplies are sporadic.

There are three **comedores** at the entrance, opposite the Lithic Museum. All offer a limited menu of traditional Guatemalan specialities – eggs, beans and grilled meat and chicken, and a few "tourist" dishes; the best one is the *Comedor Tikal*, at the far end. For longer (and pricier) menus, try the hotel restaurants. During the day cold drinks (*refrescos*) are sold from numerous spots around the ruins, though you should always carry a supply of water.

The Sylvanus G. Morley Museum

At the entrance, between the *Jungle Lodge* and *Jaguar Inn* hotels, is the one-room **Sylvanus G. Morley Museum** (also called **Museo Tikal**; Mon–Fri 9am–5pm, Sat & Sun 9am–4pm; Q10), named after the great Maya scholar who recorded many of the inscriptions at Tikal. It houses some of the stelae found here, including the remains of **Stela 29**, Tikal's oldest carved monument (dating from 292 AD), and many artefacts, including tools, jewellery, pottery, obsidian, eccentric flints and jade. There's a spectacular **reconstruction of Hasaw Chan K'awil's tomb**, one of the richest ever found in the Maya world, containing beautiful polychrome ceramics, 180 worked jade items in the form of bracelets, anklets, necklaces and earplugs, and delicately incised bones, including the famous carved human bone depicting deities paddling canoes bearing the dead to the underworld. A larger bone shows a poignant image of a bound captive with his head bowed – no doubt awaiting a sacrificial death.

The site

The sheer size of Tikal can at first seem daunting. But even if you only make it to the main plaza, and spend an hour relaxing on top of a temple, you won't be disappointed. The **central area**, with its five main temples, forms by far the most impressive section and should be your priority. Outside the main area are countless smaller **unrestored structures**, and though they pale beside the scale and magnificence of the main temples, if you're armed with a good map (the best is in Coe's guide to the ruins, available from the gift shop), it can be exciting to explore some of these rarely visited sections. Tikal is certain to exhaust you before you exhaust it.

Finally, you do need to take great care **climbing the temples**: the steps are narrow and can be slippery after rain – and getting down is always more difficult than getting up. Recent accidents (and one death) caused by visitors falling from the temples mean the authorities may close the taller structures from time to time, especially in the rainy season. Temple I has been closed for many years, though you're almost certain to be allowed up Temple IV.

From the entrance to the Great Plaza

As you walk into the site, the first structures that you come to are the rather unevocatively named **Complex Q** and **Complex R**. Dating from the reign of Hasaw Chan K'awil, these are two of the seven sets of twin pyramids built to mark the passing of a *katun* (a period of twenty 360-day years). Only one of the pyramids (in Complex Q) is restored, with the stelae and altars re-erected in front of it. The carvings on the copy of **Stela 22** (the original is in the Lithic Museum), in the small enclosure set to one side, record the ascension to the throne in 768 AD of Tikal's last known ruler, **Chitam**, portrayed in full regalia, complete with enormous sweeping headdress and staff of authority.

Following the path as it bears around to the left, you approach the back of the recently restored **Temple I**, towering 44m above the **Great Plaza**, the heart of the ancient city. Surrounded by four massive structures, this plaza was the focus of ceremonial activity at Tikal for around a thousand years. Temple I, now the recognizable hallmark of Tikal, was built as a burial monument to contain the magnificent **tomb of Hasaw Chan K'awil**. Within the tomb (a reconstruction of which can be seen in the Morley Museum, see p.203) at the temple's core, the skeleton was found facing north, surrounded by an assortment of jade, pearls, seashells and stingray spines; the latter were a traditional symbol of human sacrifice. Some magnificent pottery was also discovered here, depicting a journey to the underworld made in a canoe rowed by mythical animal figures. The steep pyramid is topped by a three-room building and a hollow roof comb that was originally brightly painted. Unfortunately the stairway on Temple I is now roped off and you're strictly forbidden to climb.

Standing opposite, like a slightly shorter, wider version of Temple I, **Temple II** stands 38m high, although when its roof comb was intact it would have been the same height as Temple I. When open, it's a fairly easy climb to the top, and the view, almost level with the forest canopy, is incredible, with the great plaza spread out below. As an added bonus, you'll almost certainly see toucans in the nearby branches.

The North Acropolis, the Central Acropolis and Temple V

The **North Acropolis**, which fills the whole north side of the plaza, is one of the most complex structures in the entire Maya world. In traditional Maya style it was built and rebuilt on top of itself; beneath the twelve temples that can be seen today are the remains of about a hundred other structures, some of which, including two large **masks**, have been uncovered by archaeologists. One of the masks, facing the plaza and protected by a thatched roof, is clearly visible; the other can be reached by following the dark passageway to the side – you'll need a flashlight. In front of the North Acropolis are two lines of **stelae** carved with images of Tikal's ruling elite, with circular altars at their bases. These and other stelae throughout the site bear the marks of **ritual defacement**, carried out when one ruler replaced another to erase any latent powers that the image may have retained.

On the other side of the plaza, the **Central Acropolis** is a maze of tiny interconnecting rooms and stairways built around six smallish courtyards. The buildings here are usually referred to as palaces rather than temples, although their precise use remains a mystery. The large two-storey building in Court 2 is known as **Maler's Palace**, named after the archeologist Teobert Maler who made it his home during expeditions in 1895 and 1904.

Further behind the Central Acropolis, a wide path leads to **Temple V**, though the best approach is from the Plaza of the Seven Temples – the gleaming, creamy limestone of the newly restored monumental staircase is dazzling as you emerge from the forest. Unfortunately, you can't climb this, though a *very* steep wooden stairway to the left of the stone staircase is sometimes open to visitors and the view from the top is superb. Temple V has been the focus of intensive research (funded by the Spanish government) for much of the past decade. It was once thought to be among the last of the great temples to be built, but findings from the many burials here indicate that it was in fact the earliest, dating from around 600 AD and almost certainly constructed by **Kinich Wayna**, Tikal's governor at the time. This discovery alone overturns most previous views of this era of Tikal's history, as it was built early in the "Mid-Classic hiatus", which followed Tikal's defeat by Lord Water of Caracol in 562 AD. It was previously thought that no new monuments were erected at Tikal during this period: more intriguing discoveries are sure to be announced as the research data is analysed and published.

△ Temple at Tikal

From the West Plaza to Temple IV

The **West Plaza**, behind Temple II, is dominated by a large Late Classic temple on the north side, and scattered with various altars and stelae. From here the **Tozzer Causeway** – one of the raised routes that connected the main parts of the city – leads west to **Temple III**, covered in jungle vegetation. Around the back of the temple is a huge palace complex, of which only the **Bat Palace** has been restored, while further down the causeway, on the left-hand side, is **Complex N**, another set of twin pyramids. In the northern enclosure of the complex, the superbly carved **Stela 16** depicts Hasaw Chan K'awil.

Looming at the end of the Tozzer Causeway, the massive **Temple IV**, at 64m, is the tallest of all the Tikal structures. Built in 741 AD, it is thought by some archeologists to be the resting place of the ruler **Yik'in Chan K'awil**, whose image was depicted on wooden lintels built into the top of the temple. To reach the top you have to ascend secure wooden ladders (one to go up and another to come down). Slow and exhausting as this is, it's always worth it, offering one of the finest views of the whole site. All around you the green carpet of the canopy stretches out to the horizon, interrupted only by the great roof combs of the other temples. At any time this view is enthralling – at sunset or sunrise it's unbeatable.

The Plaza of the Seven Temples and the Mundo Perdido

The other main buildings in the centre of Tikal lie to the south of the Central Acropolis. Here, reached by a trail from Temple III, you'll find the **Plaza of the Seven Temples**, which forms part of a complex dating back to before Christ. There's an unusual triple ball-court on the north side of the plaza, and to the east, the unexcavated South Acropolis. Finally, to the west of here is the **Mundo Perdido**, or Lost World, another magical and very distinct section of the site with its own atmosphere and architecture. The main feature, the **Great Pyramid**, is a 32-metre-high structure whose surface conceals four earlier versions, the first dating from 700 BC. From the top of the pyramid you get awesome views towards Temple IV and the Great Plaza and it's another excellent place to watch the dramatic sunrise or sunset.

Flores and Santa Elena

Although it's the capital of Petén, **FLORES** is an easy-going, sedate place with an old-fashioned atmosphere – quite different from the rough, bustling commercialism of other towns in Petén. A cluster of cobbled streets and ageing houses built around the twin-domed white church of Nuestra Señora de Los Remedios, it sits beautifully on an island in Lake Petén Itzá, connected to the mainland by a causeway; even if you're heading back to Belize, it's worth making the small detour on the way back from Tikal.

The **lake** is a natural choice for settlement and its shores were heavily populated in Maya times. **Noh Petén** (Great Island), the capital of the Itzá on the island that was to become modern Flores, was the last independent Maya kingdom to succumb to Spanish rule – conquered and destroyed in 1697. Cortés, the conqueror of Mexico, passed through here in 1525 and once in a while Spanish friars would visit, though they were rarely welcome. For the entire colonial period (and indeed up to the 1960s) Flores languished in virtual isolation, having more contact with neighbouring Belize than the capital. The modern emphasis lies across the water in the ugly, sprawling twin towns of **Santa Elena** and **San Benito**. Santa Elena, opposite Flores at the other end of the causeway, strung out between the airport and the market, has banks, hotels and buses; you won't need to venture into the chaotic mire of San Benito.

Today, despite the steady flow of tourists passing through for Tikal, Flores retains a genteel air, with residents greeting one another courteously as they meet in the streets, and it offers pleasant surroundings in which to stay, eat and drink. And if you're not going to the Guatemalan highlands but want to

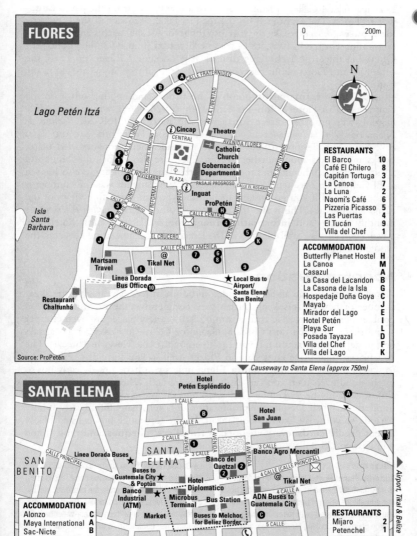

FLORES

Lago Petén Itzá

CALLE FRATERNIDED

Cincap

Theatre

CENTRAL

AVENIDA FLORES

Catholic Church

Gobernación Departmental

PASAJE PROGROSO

CALLE EL ROSARIO

Inguat

ProPetén

CALLE CENTRAL

CALLEJON PEDRITO

AV. 14 DE NOVIEMBRE

Isla Santa Barbara

EL CRUCERO

AVENIDA SANTA ANA

CALLE CENTRO AMÉRICA

Martsam Travel

Tikal Net

Linea Dorada Bus Office

Local Bus to Airport/ Santa Elena/ San Benito

Restaurant Chaltunhá

Source: ProPetén

0   200m

N

RESTAURANTS	
El Barco	10
Café El Chilero	8
Capitán Tortuga	3
La Canoa	7
La Luna	2
Naomi's Café	6
Pizzeria Picasso	5
Las Puertas	4
El Tucán	9
Villa del Chef	1

ACCOMMODATION	
Butterfly Planet Hostel	H
La Canoa	M
Casazul	A
La Casa del Lacandon	B
La Casona de la Isla	G
Hospedaje Doña Goya	C
Mayab	J
Mirador del Lago	E
Hotel Petén	I
Playa Sur	L
Posada Tayazal	D
Villa del Chef	F
Villa del Lago	K

Causeway to Santa Elena (approx 750m)

SANTA ELENA

Hotel Petén Espléndido

1 CALLE

1 CALLE A

Hotel San Juan

2 CALLE

2 CALLE A

SANTA ELENA

3 CALLE

Banco Agro Mercantil

CALLE PRINCIPAL

Linea Dorada Buses

SAN BENITO

Banco del Quetzal

4 CALLE

CALLE PRINCIPAL

Tikal Net

Buses to Guatemala City & Poptún

Hotel Diplomatico

4 CALLE

ADN Buses to Guatemala City

Banco Industrial (ATM)

Microbus Terminal

Bus Station

Market

Buses to Melchor, for Beliez Border

5 CALLE

ACCOMMODATION	
Alonzo	C
Maya International	A
Sac-Nicte	B

RESTAURANTS	
Mijaro	2
Petenchel	1

Airport, Tikal & Belize

buy *tipica* clothing and **gifts**, you'll find shops here have better prices than at Tikal. Flores has its annual **fiesta** from January 12 to 15, celebrated by processions, a fair, beauty contests and fireworks. At midnight on the last day a local wit reads *El Muerto* – a carefully compiled list of gossip detailing the peccadilloes of various townspeople during the previous year, and the drunkest person around (selected from a large cast) is placed in a open coffin and paraded around.

Arrival and information

Arriving by bus from Belize or Tikal, you'll be dropped on or near Calle Principal (aka 4 Calle) in Santa Elena, just a few blocks from the paved causeway to Flores. The **airport** is on the road to Tikal, 3km east of the causeway; **local buses** (*urbanos*) make the trip into town for Q1, but as this entails a time-consuming change halfway, it's easier to take a **taxi** (under $2). The Banco del Quetzal at the airport **changes dollars** at good rates. *Urbanos* run across the causeway into Flores about every ten minutes; they'll stop anywhere along the route.

Inguat has an **information** booth at the airport, and another office on the central plaza in Flores (Mon–Fri 8am–4pm; ☎926-0669), whose staff, while helpful, will probably direct you across the plaza to CINCAP (*Centro de Información sobre la Naturaleza, Cultura y Artesanías de Petén*; Tues–Sat 9am–1pm & 2–8pm, Sun 2–6pm; ☎926-0178), to examine their more detailed maps, books and leaflets about northern Petén. There are also historical exhibits and a shop selling handicrafts and medicinal herbs. This old building is also known as El Castillo de Arismendi (Martín de Ursúa y Arismendi was the conqueror of the Itzá) and if you go upstairs to the café you can enjoy fine views of the island and the lake. This is also the production office of *Destination Petén*, a free monthly listings and **information magazine**, available at most hotels and travel agencies; also available free is *The Revue*, a bigger magazine covering the whole country.

Accommodation

Flores has undergone an accommodation boom in recent years and the sheer number of new **hotels** keeps prices very competitive; the price of a decent double room with private bath is around $10 – a few places are even cheaper – and there are some dorm beds available for Q25 – just over $3. It's always best to get an upstairs room if you can to enjoy the lake views and breezes. The best places in all price ranges are in **Flores** itself so you shouldn't really need to stay in noisier and dirtier **Santa Elena** unless you have a really early bus to catch – and even then you can easily arrange a taxi. Wherever you stay you'll almost certainly be woken by early risers and the pre-dawn departure of their minibuses to Tikal. Despite the proliferation of hotels, many fill up early at busy periods, so you may like to book ahead. All the top-range hotels listed below accept **credit cards**, everywhere takes **travellers' cheques**, and most hotels will change US dollars at a reasonable rate.

Flores

Butterfly Planet Hostel In the centre of town ☎926-0346, ©martsam@itelgua.com. This hostel has a multitude of dorm beds (Q25 per person) and a couple of shared-bath rooms, opening onto a large courtyard. Cooking facilities, too, and the beer is cheap. ❶

La Canoa Facing the south shore ☎926-0853. Above the restaurant of the same name, this is one of the first hotels as you cross the causeway, run by the friendly Alma and Tirso Morales. There are very good-value rooms all with private hot-water bath. ❷

La Casa del Lacandon At the island's far side, overlooking the lake ☎926-3591. One of the best-value hotels, with clean, tiled rooms, all with private hot-water bath and some with a/c. ❷

Casazul Near the northern tip of the island ☎926-1138, ✉reservaciones@corpetur.com. Stylishly converted colonial-style house, tastefully decorated in shades of blue. All rooms have private bath, fridge, a/c and TV, some have balcony, and the spacious lobby is decorated with old photographs of Flores. ❹

La Casona de la Isla Calle 30 de Junio ☎ & ⓕ926-0593, ⓦwww.corpetur.com. An attractive citrus and powder-blue building offering modern rooms with clean, tiled hot-water bath, a/c, telephone and cable TV. There's also a swimming pool and spectacular sunset views from the terrace restaurant/bar. Internet access in lobby for guests. ❺

Hospedaje Doña Goya Calle la Union ☎926-3538. Friendly, family-run budget guesthouse offering clean, well-lit rooms, some with private hot-water bath and balcony, and the best prices on the island for single rooms or dorms. Breakfast available and there's a rooftop terrace with hammocks. ❶

Hotel Petén Calle 30 de Junio ☎926-0692, ⓦwww.corpetur.com. Modern hotel with friendly staff, run by the ever-helpful Pedro Castellanos. The rooms have private hot-water bath, fan, TV and a/c, and most have lake views. There's a small pool in the lobby and the restaurant is on a terrace overlooking the lake for fabulous sunset views. Internet access for guests and kayaks for rent. ❹

Mayab Calle 30 de Junio ☎926-0494. Great little hotel boasting neat, clean rooms with private hot-water bathroom and a terrace at the back to enjoy the lake. ❷

Mirador del Lago I and II Calle 15 de Septiembre ☎926-3276. The best just-above-budget hotels in Flores, with well-furnished rooms with private hot-water bath and fan. Friendly owner Mimi Salguero (who speaks a little English) keeps the lobby fridge stocked with beer and soft drinks, and the restaurant has tables on a lakeshore terrace at which to enjoy them. No. I is

on the lakeshore and No. II is across the street. Great lake views from the roof of either hotel and well-priced meals. ❷

Playa Sur Near the Linea Dorada office ☎926-0351. Some of the cheapest rooms in town, with shared cold-water bath. ❶

Posada Tayazal Calle la Union ☎ & ⓕ926-0568, ✉hotelposadatayazal@hotmail.com. Good budget hotel, with decent rooms, some with private hot-water bath; shared baths have hot water. Prices and views increase as you head upstairs and some rooms have a balcony. Internet available on ground floor. ❷

Villa del Chef Calle la Union ☎926-0926, ✉enrico_ferrulli@yahoo.com. The best-value and most comfortable shared-bath budget rooms in Flores, with a small balcony and sitting area, above the restaurant of the same name. ❶

Villa del Lago Calle 15 de Septiembre ☎ & ⓕ926-0629, ✉hotelvilladelago@itelgua.com. Modern, three-storey building with very comfortable, pretty rooms with private hot-water bath, a/c and TV. The breakfast terraces at the rear are great places to enjoy the sunrise. Good restaurant and laundry service in this well-run hotel. ❹

Santa Elena

Alonzo 6 Ave 4–99 ☎926-0105. Reasonable budget rooms, though always check first; some with a balcony and a few with private hot shower (the shared bathroom is grubby). There's also a restaurant and a public telephone. The Fuente del Norte bus stops right outside. ❶

Maya International 1 Calle ☎334-1818, ⓦwww.villasdeguatemala.com. Set in gardens right over the lakeshore opposite Flores. Good-sized rooms with private bath, TV, phone and a balcony. There's a reasonable restaurant with a pool outside. ❺

Sac-Nicte 1 C A 4–45 ☎ & ⓕ926-0092. Clean rooms with fans and private hot shower; those on the second floor have views of the lake. The well-stocked shop next door is handy if you don't want to venture too far into Santa Elena. ❺

Eating and drinking

There are plenty of good, reasonably priced **restaurants** in Flores and a couple in Santa Elena. Typical Guatemalan meals, accompanied by rice, black beans and corn tortillas are actually quite rare in Flores, many restaurants preferring to serve "tourist dishes", usually spaghetti or other pasta and grilled chicken, fish or beef, pizzas, kebabs (*pinchos*) and other international fare. If you want to try a genuine *comedor* – literally "dining room" – you'll probably have to go to Santa Elena. Several restaurants on the island also serve **wild game**, often listed on menus as *comida silvestre*. Virtually all this has been taken illegally from the reserve and you should avoid ordering items such as *tepescuintle* (paca, a large relation of the guinea-pig), *venado* (deer) or *coche de monte* (peccary, or wild pig).

Flores

El Barco On a flat-decked boat to the left as you cross the causeway. Seafood (*mariscos*), steak and chicken in reasonable portions at good prices, some Guatemalan specialities and vegetarian dishes. Good for the 6–8.30pm happy hour.

Café El Chilero On the unnamed alley leading up from the *urbano* bus stop. Run by an American-Guatemalan couple and offering great breakfasts, sandwiches and salads, served with wholewheat bread. Opens at 4.30am, so you can get a good coffee and homemade cinnamon roll before the early minibus to Tikal.

La Canoa C Centro America. Popular, good-value place, serving pasta, great soups and some vegetarian and Guatemalan food, as well as excellent breakfasts.

Capitán Tortuga C 30 de Junio. Large restaurant, often catering to groups but with a terrace on the lake at the back. Good grills and salads, delicious pizza, good cocktails and excellent service.

La Luna At the far end of C 30 de Junio. The best restaurant in town, and one of the most expensive – though all this means is that a main course of fish, pasta, chicken or steak costs around US$5–6. No wild game. Menus in Italian, English and French as well as Spanish.

Naomi's Café C Centro America. Another good café serving home-baked bread and cakes and a range of local and international food and drinks, including pizza, pastas, cappuccinos and smoothies. Opens early for breakfast, and there's an evening happy hour; also has a book exchange, book sales (including *Rough Guides*) and Internet access.

Pizzeria Picasso C Centro America, opposite the *Tucán* (below) ☎ 926-0637. Wide range of really good pizzas in a popular location. They will also deliver.

Las Puertas Signposted off C Santa Ana. Paint-splattered walls, with live music here and movies across the street. Healthy breakfasts with good coffee and very good pasta, salads and sandwiches. Worth it for the atmosphere; good noticeboard.

El Tucán On the waterfront, a few metres east of the causeway; reached from C Centro America. Good fish, enormous chef's salads, great Mexican food and one of the best waterside terraces in Flores – but prices are now fairly high and there's wild game on the menu.

Villa del Chef C La Unión. A quiet, even romantic, little restaurant with tables on a lakeshore terrace (candlelit in the evenings) serving good cuisine at very good prices, always with vegetarian choices. Book exchange at the bar.

Santa Elena

Mijaro Two locations; one at the top of the road from the causeway, the other round the corner on C Principal. The best Guatemalan restaurant in Santa Elena, with good food at local prices and a daily special. You can usually leave luggage here while you look for a room.

Petenchel 2 C, beyond *Hotel San Juan*, past the park. Simple, good food. You can also leave luggage here.

Around Flores

Local attractions include the **Petencito Zoo**, on the peninsula opposite Flores (daily 8am–5pm; Q20), a surprisingly well-looked-after collection of the local fauna, including jaguars and other cats, monkeys and macaws, housed in generally spacious enclosures in an authentic hilly jungle setting on the lakeshore. A *lancha* to get there will cost around $10 and for this price the boatman will wait for as long as it takes to have a look around. Slightly nearer, the animal rescue center of **Arcas** is open to the public (daily 8am–5pm; Q15); you can even get a free ride in the Arcas boat when it leaves in the morning if you call to arrange it.

At the **Skyway Ixpanpajul**, 10km from Santa Elena, just off the road to Guatemala City (daily 6am–6pm; Q100), an amazing system of suspension bridges and good stone paths connects 3km of forested hilltops in a nine-square-kilometre private reserve. In the middle of the bridges you enjoy a monkey's eye view of the canopy and on top of the highest hill there's an enormous *mirador* with views of virtually the whole of the Petén Itzá basin. It's best to go in the early morning, after mid-afternoon or even at night, when the

Jungle tours and travel agents

Besides Tikal, there are many other Maya sites within the Maya Biosphere Reserve; the agents listed below are the best around for visiting these. The agents will provide a guide (an English-speaking guide can be arranged but this will cost more), food and all equipment, including tents, hammocks and mosquito nets where necessary. In most cases being in a group will cut costs and it's always worth asking for a discount on multi-day trips. Some trips are arduous expeditions, involving hiking through muddy jungle, but the rewards are often spectacular and you can feel a real sense of achievement as you climb to the top of a temple and peer out over nothing but rainforest.

The best travel agent in Flores is the English-speaking **Martsam Travel**, at the western end of C Centro America (☎926-3225, ⓦwww.martsam.com), which runs a daily trip to Yaxhá (p.194) for $20 per person (minimum two people) and also offers overnight jungle trips to El Zotz and El Perú and many other sites. **Explore**, on 1 Calle and 6 Avenida in Santa Elena (☎926-2375, ⓦwww.exploreguate.com), is expert in trips to Ceibal, on the Río Pasión (daily, $25), as well as sites southwest of Flores such as Aguateca and Dos Pilas, on Laguna Petexbatún (overnight $140, including Ceibal). **Conservation Tours**, in the lobby of the *Hotel Mirador del Lago* (☎926-9509, ⓦwww.conservationtours.com), offers kayak, bike and horseback tours around the local lakes and to Uaxactún ruins with English-speaking guides. The tours and guides are excellent but very expensive; you should get a discount with this book.

wildlife really comes to life; allow a few hours so you can take your time and see the trees and orchids. There's a good self-guided trail leaflet (in Spanish only) and you can get there by bike (45min) or any Poptún-bound *microbus* will drop you at the entrance.

Listings

Banks and currency exchange Not all banks in Flores and Santa Elena will change cash dollars, but the Banco Agro Mercantil in Santa Elena, at the junction of the road to the causeway (Mon–Sat 8.30am–8pm), and the Banco del Quetzal do – they also have the best rates. For Visa credit/debit card cash advances use Banco Industrial (24hr ATM), and for Mastercard transactions use the 5B ATM next to the Banco Agro Mercantil. You can also change dollars and cash travellers' cheques at Martsam Travel and many other travel agents.

Bike and motorbike rental Backabush Bike Tours on Avenida Barrios (☎695-7481) has good mountain bikes; rent a bike for Q12/hr or take one of their excellent tours. For motorbikes (Q120 for 2 hrs) see Martsam Travel (☎926-3225).

Car rental Budget, Hertz, Tabarini (which has the widest choice; ☎926-0253) and Koka operate from the airport, and there are some offices in Santa Elena. Rates (usually including insurance) start at around US$50 a day for a small or mid-sized car and go up to over US$65 a day for a double cab pickup with 4WD. It's always worth checking with a recommended travel agent first,

though – they will be able to point you in the direction of reliable small firms.

Communications and Internet LADATEL cardphones are dotted all over and cards are sold everywhere. You can also phone from most travel agents: in Santa Elena try the *Hotel Alonzo*. In Flores the best is Martsam Travel, where there's usually someone who speaks English. There are several places in Flores with Internet facilities; the best service is offered by Tikal Net, on C Centro America (also on C Principal, directly across the causeway in Santa Elena), where you can also make phone calls.

Doctor Centro Medico Maya, 4 Ave near 3 C in Santa Elena, down the street by the *Hotel Diplomatico* (☎926-0180), is helpful and professional, though no English is spoken.

Laundry Lavandería Amelia, behind CINCAP in Flores, or Petenchel on C Centro America (both Q25 to wash and dry).

Post office In Flores, on Avenida Barrios; in Santa Elena, on C Principal, two blocks east of the Banco Agro Mercantil (both Mon–Fri 8am–4.30pm).

Moving on from Flores

Buses to **Melchor de Mencos** (for the Belize border; 2hr 30min; Q10–15) leave from the marketplace in Santa Elena; all pass through Ixlú (for El Remate and Tikal). Most are still crowded "chicken buses" though all companies have some more comfortable "Pullman" services. Pinita (the worst service) leaves at 5am, 8am and 11am; Rosita leaves at 7am, 11am, 2pm, 4pm and 6pm; Fuente del Norte has a Pullman at 4.30pm, leaving from its office on Calle Principal. Mundo Maya in Flores runs daily luxury buses **to Belize City** (terminating at the Marine Terminal; see p.60) at 5am & 8am (4hr; US$16), which continue to Chetumal, Mexico (a further 4hr; US$23 in all) where they connect with a Mexican bus service up the coast to **Cancún** (5hr 30min; first class US$9). *Colectivo* **minibuses** for Melchor (Q20–25) depart every half-hour or so from the terminal on Calle Principal.

All the **Guatemala City** bus companies have offices on Calle Principal in Santa Elena, and there are around thirty departures daily to the capital (8hr). ADN and Linea Dorada offer the best and fastest service, with departures at 8am, 8pm, 9pm & 10pm, from Flores itself, which saves the hassle of getting to the mainland and is much safer; buy tickets (US$20–25) from hotels and travel agencies. Fuente del Norte, much cheaper at around US$10, is the best among the rest.

Tickets for **flights to Belize City** (2 morning and 2 afternoon daily; $80) and **Guatemala City** (at least 8 daily; US$55–75) can be bought at the airport or at any travel agent in Santa Elena and Flores. There are also flights to **Cancún**, with Aviateca (daily at 4.30pm) and Aerocaribe (Mon, Wed & Fri at 8am).

The south

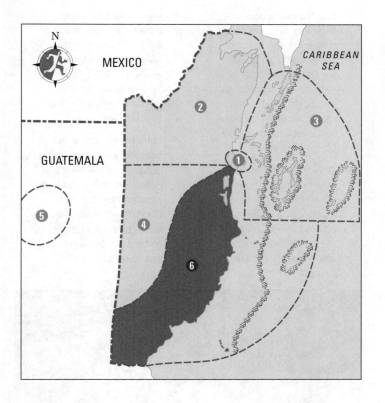

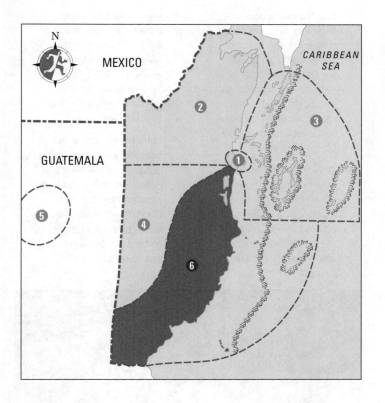

The south

CHAPTER 6

Highlights

✳ **Gales Point** Spend the night in this tiny Creole village, listening to drums in the evening, then rise early to spot manatees and wading birds at dawn. See p.218

✳ **The Hummingbird Highway** Take the most scenic drive in the country, stopping off to visit the Blue Hole National Park, or overnighting on the banks of a crystal-clear river at the wonderful *Caves Branch Jungle Lodge*. See p.220

✳ **Glover's Reef** Indulge your Robinson Crusoe "desert island" fantasy in a cabin on a beach somewhere on the most stunningly beautiful coral atoll in the Caribbean. See p.236

✳ **The Cockscomb Basin Wildlife Sanctuary** Spend a night or two in the world's only jaguar reserve, following the tracks of the largest cat in the Americas. See p.239

✳ **Placencia** The relaxing base for a snorkelling trip to Laughing Bird Caye, swimming with the whale sharks at Gladden Spit, or strolling along the best beaches in the country. See p.246

✳ **Lubaantun** Admire the beautifully restored buildings of the "Place of Fallen Stones" – and wonder if the famous Crystal Skull really did return to the light in this ancient city 80 years ago. See p.271

△ Lubaantum

6

The south

B elize is at its wildest south of Belmopan. Here the central area is dominated by the Maya Mountains, sloping down to the coast through a series of forested ridges and valleys carved by sparkling rivers. As you head further south the climate becomes more humid, promoting the growth of dense **rainforest**, rich in wildlife. The forests here have evolved to cope with periodic hurricanes sweeping in from the Caribbean and have in the past been selectively logged for mahogany. The **coastal strip** south of Belize City is a band of savannah, swamp and lagoon. Large stands of Caribbean pine grow in the nutrient-poor savannah soils, looking strangely out of place in the tropics. Beyond Dangriga the shoreline is composed of sandy bays, peninsulas and mangrove lagoons. In the far south the estuaries of the slow-moving Temash and Sarstoon rivers, lined with the tallest **mangrove forest** in Belize, form the country's southernmost national park, adjoining protected land in Guatemala.

Population density in this part of Belize is low, with most of the towns and villages located on the coast. **Dangriga**, the largest settlement, is the home of the **Garífuna** people – descended from Carib Indians and shipwrecked, enslaved Africans (see box on p.226) – and allows access to a number of idyllic cayes, such as Tobacco Caye and South Water Caye, sitting right on top of the barrier reef and the focus of the **South Water Caye Marine Reserve**. The villages of **Gales Point**, on Southern Lagoon, north of Dangriga, and **Sittee River** and **Hopkins**, on the coast to the south, are worth visiting to experience their tranquil way of life. Further south, the **Placencia peninsula** has become established as the focus of coastal tourism in southern Belize. From here you can visit **Laughing Bird Caye National Park**; the stunning Silk Cayes further east, just inside the reef; and, forming part of the unique **Gladden Spit and Silk Cayes Marine Reserve**, the only sanctuary on the planet established specifically to protect **whale sharks** – the largest fish in the world.

Inland, the Maya Mountains remain unpenetrated by roads, forming a solid barrier to land travel except on foot or horseback. Successive Belize governments, showing supreme foresight, have placed practically the entire mountain massif under some form of legal protection, whether as national park, nature reserve, wildlife sanctuary or forest reserve. The most accessible area of this rainforest, though still little visited by tourists, is the **Cockscomb Basin Wildlife Sanctuary**, a reserve designed to protect the sizeable jaguar population and a perfect base for exploring the forest. You'll come across plenty of tracks – but don't count on seeing a jaguar. The sanctuary is also the starting point for the **Victoria Peak Trail**, an arduous but very rewarding trek to the

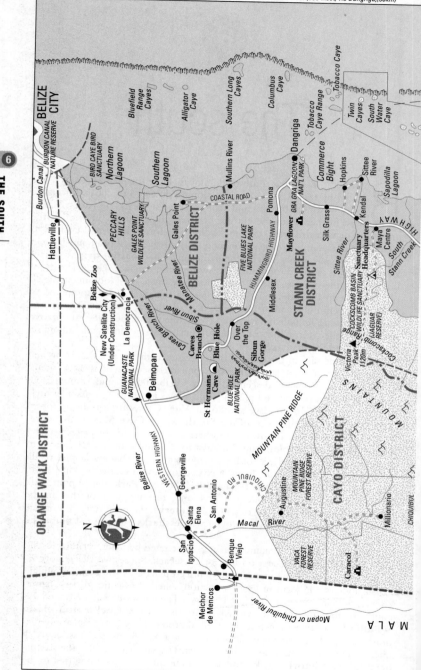

▲ Glover's Reef (see inset; via Dangriga;(50km)

BELIZE CITY

Burdon Canal
BURDON CANAL NATURE RESERVE

Bluefield Range Caves

Alligator Cave

Southern Long Caves

Columbus Cave

Tobacco Cave

Tobacco Cave Range

Twin Caves

South Water Cave

BIRD CAVE BIRD SANCTUARY

Northern Lagoon

Southern Lagoon

Mullins River

Dangriga

Commerce Bight

Hopkins

Sittee River

Sapodilla Lagoon

Hattieville

Belize Zoo

PECCARY HILLS

GALES POINT WILDLIFE SANCTUARY

Gales Point

COASTAL ROAD

Pomona

GRA GRA LAGOON NAT'L PARK

Mayflower

Silk Grass

Kendal

HIGHWAY

New Satellite City (Under Construction)

La Democracia

GUANACASTE NATIONAL PARK

BELIZE DISTRICT

Manatee River

FIVE BLUES LAKE NATIONAL PARK

HUMMINGBIRD HIGHWAY

Middlesex

STANN CREEK DISTRICT

Sittee River

Maya Centre

COCKSCOMB BASIN WILDLIFE SANCTUARY

Cockscomb Range

(JAGUAR RESERVE)

South Stann Creek

Sanctuary Headquarters

Belmopan

Caves Branch

Blue Hole

Over the Top

Sibun Gorge

Victoria Peak 1120m

Sibun River

St Hermans Cave

BLUE HOLE NATIONAL PARK

ORANGE WALK DISTRICT

Belize River

WESTERN HIGHWAY

Georgeville

Santa Elena

San Antonio

Macal River

CHIQUIBUL RD

Augustine

MOUNTAIN PINE RIDGE

MOUNTAIN PINE RIDGE FOREST RESERVE

CAYO DISTRICT

Millionario

CHIQUIBUL

San Ignacio

Benque Viejo

VACA FOREST RESERVE

Caracol

Melchor de Mencos

Mopan or Chiquibul River

MALA

MOUNTAINS

N

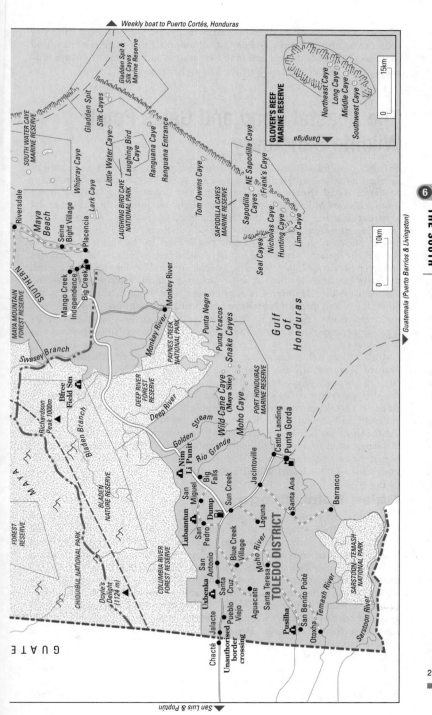

▲ Weekly boat to Puerto Cortés, Honduras

GLOVER'S REEF MARINE RESERVE

Northeast Caye
Long Caye
Middle Caye
Southwest Caye

Dangriga ▼

0   15km

▼ Guatemala (Puerto Barrios & Livingston)

0   10km

South Water Caye Marine Reserve

Riversdale

Maya Beach

Seine Bight Village

Placencia

Whipray Caye

Lark Caye

Little Water Caye

Laughing Bird Caye

LAUGHING BIRD CAYE NATIONAL PARK

Gladden Spit & Silk Cayes Marine Reserve

Gladden Spit

Silk Cayes

Ranguana Caye

Ranguana Entrance

Tom Owens Caye

Sapodilla Cayes

NE Sapodilla Caye

Frank's Caye

Nicholas Caye

Hunting Caye

Lime Caye

SAPODILLA CAYES MARINE RESERVE

Seal Cayes

Gulf of Honduras

Mango Creek

Independence

Big Creek

SOUTHERN

MAYA MOUNTAIN FOREST RESERVE

Swasey Branch

Monkey River

Monkey River

Punta Negra

PAYNES CREEK NATIONAL PARK

DEEP RIVER FOREST RESERVE

Deep River

Punta Ycacos

Snake Cayes

PORT HONDURAS MARINE RESERVE

Bfree Field Stn

Richardson Peak 1000m ▲

Bladen Branch

FOREST RESERVE

BLADEN NATURE RESERVE

Golden Stream

Wild Cane Caye (Maya Site)

Moho Caye

Cattle Landing

Punta Gorda

CHIQUIBUL NATIONAL PARK

COLUMBIA RIVER FOREST RESERVE

Doyle's Delight (1124 m) ▲

Nim Li Punit

Big Falls

San Miguel

Lubaantun

San Pedro

Dump

Sun Creek

Rio Grande

Jacintoville

Santa Ana

Barranco

Uxbenka

San Antonio

Santa Cruz

Santa Teresa

Blue Creek Village

Laguna

Moho River

TOLEDO DISTRICT

Chacté

Jalacte

Pueblo Viejo

Aguacate

Pusilha

San Benito Poité

San Benito Poité

Otoxha

Temash River

Sarstoon River

SARSTOON–TEMASH NATIONAL PARK

Unauthorised border crossing

GUATE

▲ San Luis & Poptun

217

summit of the second highest mountain in Belize. The Southern Highway comes to an end in **Punta Gorda**, a final outpost, from where you can head south to Guatemala or visit **ancient Maya sites** and present-day **Maya villages** in the southern foothills of the Maya Mountains.

The Coastal Road and Gales Point Wildlife Sanctuary

To head south from Belize City you first need to go west; either to Belmopan for the Hummingbird Highway (see p.220) or to the start of the **Coastal** (or Manatee) **Road shortcut to Dangriga**. The unpaved Coastal Road heads southeast from Mile 30 on the Western Highway, skirting the village of **La Democracia** and reaching the Hummingbird Highway at Melinda, 15km from Dangriga. The road is usually in good condition, though it's only served by one bus a day in each direction on the Belize City/Dangriga route. Along the way the scenery is typical of southern Belize: citrus plantations, pine ridges and steep limestone hills covered in broadleaf forest. There is also a route south **by boat** that takes you along some amazing **inland waterways**, travelling upstream on the Haulover Creek, then along the Burdon Canal, across the Sibun River and through **Northern and Southern Lagoons** – though since the completion of the road few villagers use this route. It is, however, used by some tour groups, and if you get a chance to travel this way to Gales Point you should take it.

Much of this rich wetland area is protected as part of the **Burdon Canal Nature Reserve**, and the lagoons are such an essential breeding ground for rare wildlife, including jabiru storks, marine turtles, manatees and crocodiles, that the government has established the **Manatee Special Development Area** to encourage sensitive conservation-oriented development. The area is bounded on the west by the limestone Peccary Hills, riddled with caves, and the shores of the lagoons are cloaked with mangroves. The main beneficiaries this designation is intended to help are the people of **Gales Point**, a tiny village at the tip of a peninsula on Southern Lagoon, with the entire lagoon now protected as **Gales Point Wildlife Sanctuary**.

Gales Point Village

If you want to explore this little-visited area, the tranquil Creole village of **GALES POINT**, straggling along a very narrow peninsula jutting into the Southern Lagoon, is the ideal place to begin. Gales Point was originally settled over two hundred years ago by runaway slaves from Belize City, who founded a *maroon* (meaning "runaway slaves") community among the creeks and shallow lagoons. Today, **scenery** and **wildlife** are the big attractions here: the lagoon system is the largest manatee breeding ground in the entire Caribbean basin, and Belize's main nesting beaches of the endangered **hawksbill** and **loggerhead turtles** lie either side of the mouth of the Manatee River. The villagers have formed the Gales Point Progressive Cooperative to protect their wildlife and encourage tourists to visit, and several of them are licensed **tour guides**. With help from international conservation organizations and volunteers they guard the turtle nesting beaches and have installed signs and buoys warning boatmen to slow down to avoid harming the manatees. Leroy Andrewin, who grew up here hunting turtles but now spends most of his time and practically all his money protecting the turtle nests from predators – both animal and human – is a real conservation hero. For a small donation Leroy will take you out on a night patrol – and you could **volunteer** for a longer stay. Though it can be an uncomfortable experience as you wade through the mosquito-infested mangroves, it's infinitely rewarding if you get a chance to see the adult females laying their eggs or cheer on the newly hatched babies as they race for the sea.

Gales Point is also a centre of **traditional drum-making**. You can learn to make and play drums at the **Maroon Creole Drum School**, run by Emmeth Young and Randolph ("Boombay") Andrewin (Ⓔmethos_drums@hotmail .com); Emmeth often performs elsewhere so it's best to check ahead to see if he's at home. Making a drum costs around Bz$250, including materials and instruction, and it's Bz$15 per hour to learn drumming. You'll also learn a lot about local history, culture and crafts – made even more enjoyable while sipping the home-produced cashew or berry wine in the evenings.

Practicalities

Gales Point is served by only one Southern Transport **bus** daily in each direction on the Coastal Road, leaving Belize City at 5pm and Dangriga at 5am. Other traffic passes the junction, 4km from the village; it's a pleasant walk into town if you're not carrying much luggage, and hitching in is relatively easy.

Walking along the village's only street, you'll see several signs pointing to houses offering simple bed-and-breakfast **accommodation** (❸). Ionie Samuels, who runs Martha's Store, has a room and can arrange other meals and tours; call the community telephone on ☎209-8031 for other possibilities. *Gentle's Cool Spot*, a small bar and restaurant at the point where the buses turn around, also has a few clean, basic rooms in a wooden house with shared bath, fan and electric light (❷), and a room with private bath (❸). You can also **camp** at *Metho's Coconut Camping* (Bz$8 per person), in a sandy spot north of the village centre. The most luxurious accommodation is the *Manatee Lodge* (☎220-8040, in the US ☎1-877/462-6283, Ⓦwww.manateelodge.com; ❼), a two-storey, white-painted wooden colonial-style building with green trim set in lush lawns lined with coconut trees right at the tip of the peninsula. The rooms (all non-smoking) are spacious and comfortable and the meals are superb. On the upper floor a deck with hammocks is an ideal spot to take in a sunrise or sunset over the lagoon; indoors the book and video library has a good collection of Belizean topics. Guests can use the lodge's email and also have free access to canoes and small sailboats to enjoy the lagoon (non-guests can rent them by the day for Bz$20 canoe or Bz$40 sailboat); call ahead and you might be able to arrange the boat trip along the inland waterways from Belize City.

The best **restaurant** in the village is at *Manatee Lodge*, which you'll need to book for if you're not staying there. Otherwise, there's Creole food at *Gentle's Cool Spot*, where owner Raymond Gentle also makes wine, or you could arrange meals with a local family. And, amazingly, you can get a **cappuccino** or a latte at the *Sugar Snack Café*, which also serves snacks and cakes.

As Gales Point is at the centre of a wildlife sanctuary, renting a **dory** (traditionally a dugout canoe) or taking a canoe tour allows you to explore the waterways; rent one either from someone in the village (about Bz$25 per day) or (more expensively) from *Manatee Lodge*. Raymond Gentle has a large motorized dory for trips to **Ben Lomond's Cave**, on the north shore of the lagoon. There are several other guides in the village who can take you fishing or along hiking trails; Delroy Andrewin offers **windsurfing lessons** for Bz$20 per hour.

The Hummingbird Highway

After recent resurfacing work, the **Hummingbird Highway**, heading southeast from Belmopan to Dangriga, offers the most scenic drive in Belize. The scenery is magnificent as the road heads steadily over the hills through lush forest, with the eastern slopes of the **Maya Mountains**, coated in greenery, rising to the right. Until recently, much of this forest was untouched, but here and there Salvadoran or Guatemalan refugees have hacked down a swathe of jungle to plant maize and beans, and you're rarely out of sight of citrus plantations. The hills form part of a ridge of limestone mountains riddled with underground rivers and caves. About 19km out of Belmopan the road crosses the **Caves Branch River**, a tributary of the Sibun River. The upper reaches of this and other nearby valleys hold some of Belize's finest **caves**, carved out of the Cretaceous limestone which covers much of the region. Further on, just past the highest point on the road, is the stunningly beautiful **Five Blues Lake National Park**. Beyond here the road follows the Stann Creek valley (and is renamed the Stann Creek Valley Road), lined virtually all the way to Dangriga with citrus groves.

St Herman's Cave

Just beyond the Caves Branch River, by the roadside on the right, is **St Herman's Cave** (daily 8am–4pm; Bz$8, includes the Blue Hole), one of the most accessible caves in Belize. Any bus between Belmopan and Dangriga will drop you at the cave or the **Blue Hole**, making an easy day-trip (the rangers know the times of onward buses), but to really appreciate the mysteries of caving in Belize you need to stay nearby, preferably at the *Caves Branch Jungle Lodge* (see opposite). Both St Herman's Cave and the Blue Hole (often referred to as the "inland Blue Hole", to distinguish it from the one on Lighthouse Reef) are within the Blue Hole National Park, established in 1986 and managed by Belize Audubon Society (BAS).

You pay the entrance fee at the **visitor centre**, which has good displays of the plant, bird and animal life found here, particularly bats, then follow the marked trail for ten minutes to the cave entrance, beneath a dripping rock face. To enter, down steps that were originally cut by the Maya, you'll need a flashlight. Inside, you clamber over the rocks and splash through the river for about twenty minutes, admiring the stunning formations, before the cave appears to end. To continue beyond, and emerge from one of the other entrances, you need to go on a **tour** – one of the best of them is organized by Marcos Cucul who runs Maya Guide Adventures (☎600-3116, ⓦwww.mayaguide.bz). Marcos is a Kekchí Maya from Toledo, who lives nearby; when not taking a tour he can often be found at the Blue Hole visitor centre. He's very experienced in arranging caving, climbing and jungle survival trips, and can lead you through the amazing **Crystal Cave**, also in the park; first you hike for forty minutes though the jungle, and then you rappel down to the first of literally miles of caves, adorned with fantastic formations (including crystal) and astonishing Maya artefacts. The cost is US$75, including entrance fee, all equipment and lunch. Behind the cave, an **interpretive trail** leads past some unique rock formations, more caves and a spectacular observation platform, arriving after 4km at a **campsite**. For details, enquire at the visitor centre (which also has information on nearby **bed-and-breakfast** accommodation) or call BAS on ☎223-5004.

Blue Hole National Park

From St Herman's Cave, another signposted trail leads 3km over the ridge to the **Blue Hole National Park** (BHNP), which you can also reach by continuing along the highway for 2km; the entrance is right by the road, down a steep flight of steps. The Blue Hole is actually a short, ten-metre-wide oval stretch of underground river – *cenote* in Maya – whose course has been revealed by the collapse of a karst cavern; the river continues to flow on the surface for about 50m before disappearing beneath another rock face. Its cool, fresh turquoise waters, surrounded by dense forest and overhung with vines, mosses and ferns, are perfect for a refreshing dip. Despite the park's small size (only 2.5 square kilometres, though it's adjacent to other protected areas), it boasts an abundance of wildlife. Three of the five species of **cats** found in Belize – the jaguar, ocelot and jaguarundi – have been sighted within park boundaries. Black howler monkeys are occasionally heard, while other mammals include tapir, collared and white-lipped peccaries, tamandua (anteaters), gibnut, coatimundi, opossum, deer, kinkajou and many species of bats. It's also home to more than 175 species of birds, including the slaty-breasted tinamou, black hawk-eagle, crested guan, lovely cotinga, nightingale wren and red-legged honeycreeper. The **Hummingbird Loop**, a 1.5km self-guided trail undulating through the forest, provides a worthwhile glimpse of the park – but to enjoy it comfortably you'll need insect repellent.

Caves Branch Jungle Lodge

The best place to stay near the Blue Hole (and indeed along the whole Hummingbird Highway) is **Caves Branch Jungle Lodge**, at Mile 41 1/2 (T822-2800, Wwww.cavesbranch.com; ❷–❾, no credit cards). It's located 1.5km beyond St Herman's Cave and a few hundred metres before the Blue Hole, 1km in from the main road along a level track, easily accessible and signposted from the highway; all passing buses will stop at the entrance.

The lodge is set in a huge area of superb, high canopy forest on the banks of the beautiful **Caves Branch River** and offers a range of comfortable, rustic **accommodation** to suit all budgets. The highlights are the spacious jungle suites, with a sitting room and wicker furniture (❾), and the bungalows with tiled roofs and all-round verandahs (❽) both these types have private hot showers. Slightly less expensive are the screened cabañas on stilts, with a ceiling fan (❼), and for budget travellers even the screened **bunkhouse** (Bz$30 per person) and **campsite** with hammock space (Bz$10 per person) have clean showers and flush toilets; there's no service charge and you can save money by booking a complete package. Delicious and filling buffet-style meals are served in a simple dining room above the river, and cold beer is always available. Try to plan at least two nights here; even if you don't take any of the trips on offer, one day just won't seem long enough, and the birding is superb.

Caves Branch is run by Canadian Ian Anderson, who, together with some of the most experienced local guides in the country, leads truly amazing guided tours through some of the area's most spectacular caves and along crystal-clear rivers running through the limestone hills. All the caves contain **Maya artefacts** – burials, ceramics and carvings and the like – furnishing abundant evidence of the Classic-period ceremonies that were held in them. Some caves are dry, and you must take great care not to touch the glittering crystal formations as you climb over rocks and around stalagmites. You can float on inner tubes 10km along a subterranean river, your headlamp piercing the intense darkness, or even ascend an underground river several kilometres upstream as it cuts through a limestone ridge, climbing stupendous waterfalls thundering through crystal caverns. Other and perhaps more challenging activities are **rappelling** – descending over the sheer wall of a sinkhole and through the forest canopy to the enormous Actun Loch Tunich cave entrance over 90m below – and **rock climbing**, with walls graded according to your level of experience. All equipment is provided except climbing shoes.

The guides here are experts in natural history, and also lead overnight cave, ruins and wildlife treks in the forest, including a four-day "Jungle Quest" survival course and a nine-day "Lost World Expedition". All the guides are recertified each year in Cave and Wilderness Rescue and Wilderness First Aid (*Caves Branch* were the founders of the Belize Cave and Wilderness Rescue Team; check the website for details if you want to take a course in this), and all expeditions have back-up support. Participants on all expeditions need good hiking boots; the lodge has a good selection if you need to borrow a pair. The cave and river trips are not cheap (beginning at about US$90 per person for a daytrip, including lunch and all equipment except climbing boots), and there are few budget options, but they're well worth the cost, as the guestbook entries testify.

Caves Branch also runs the *Sibun Adventure Lodge* (T 822-2800, W www.adventuresinbelize.com; groups only, US$95 per person per night), 6km further along the highway, in a stunning forest and garden location overlooking the Sibun River. The large, three-storey, thatched lodge is aimed mainly at student groups, with comfortable dorm accommodation and hot showers on the ground floor and classrooms with fantastic views above. It's an ideal place to study tropical ecology, and the private bungalows (currently under construction) will provide even more comfortable accommodation for adult learners. **Kayak trips** on both the whitewater of the upper Sibun and the calmer lower section are available. *Caves Branch* also operates *Almond Beach Resort*, in a beautiful beachfront location near Hopkins; see p.233.

Over the Top and Five Blues Lake National Park

Beyond the Blue Hole the Hummingbird Highway is well paved, undulating smoothly through the increasingly hilly landscape, eventually crossing a low pass. This is the highest point on the road, and the downhill slope is appropriately, if unimaginatively, called Over the Top. On the way down, the road passes through St Margaret's Village, where a women's cooperative arranges bed-and-breakfast accommodation in private houses (community phone T 809-2005; ❸).

A few kilometres past the village, the *Over the Top Restaurant* stands on a hill at Mile 32, overlooking the junction of the track to **Five Blues Lake National Park**, seventeen square kilometres of luxuriantly forested karst scenery, centred around a beautiful lake. Named for its constantly changing colours, the lake is another *cenote,* or "blue hole", caused by a cavern's collapse. Register at the office by the road junction, where you can arrange a guide. It's about an hour's walk to the lake and the road is passable in a good vehicle. Trails enable you to explore the practically deserted park, and canoes can be rented on the lake.

Continuing south for 3km on the Hummingbird Highway from Over the Top, there's more **accommodation** at *Palacio's Mountain Retreat*, at Mile 31 (buses stop right outside; T 822-3683 or 600-2248, W www.palaciosretreat.com; ❺, camping Bz$10 per person). The four simple cabañas with private hot shower and electricity overlook a beautiful river lined with sandy beaches and boulders; it's great for swimming and you can hike to a ten-metre jungle waterfall upstream. The Palacio family who run the place are very proud of their Garífuna culture and guests can enjoy Garífuna food in the restaurant and learn about other customs here.

On towards Dangriga

Palacio's Mountain Retreat marks the start of the **Stann Creek valley**, the centre of the Belizean citrus fruit industry. Bananas were the first crop to be grown here, and by 1891 half a million stems were being exported through Stann Creek (now Dangriga) every year. However, this banana boom came to an abrupt end in 1906, when disease destroyed the crop, and afterwards the government set out to foster the growth of **citrus fruits**. Between 1908 and 1937 the valley was even served by a small railway – many of the highway bridges were originally rail bridges – and by 1945 the citrus industry was well established.

Today citrus comprises a major part of the country's agricultural exports and, despite widely fluctuating prices, is heralded as one of the nation's great success stories – although for the largely Guatemalan labour force, housed in rows of scruffy huts, conditions are little better than on the oppressive coffee *fincas* at home. The presence of tropical parasites, such as the leaf-cutter ant, has forced the planters to resort to powerful insecticides, including DDT. Two giant pulping plants beside the road produce concentrate for export.

The last stretch of the Hummingbird Highway is flat and relatively uninteresting. Ten kilometres before Dangriga, the filling station is a useful place to refuel without going into town; just beyond this is the junction with the now-paved **Southern Highway** heading to Punta Gorda.

Dangriga

DANGRIGA, formerly called Stann Creek, is the capital of Stann Creek District and the largest town in southern Belize. It's also the cultural centre of the **Garífuna**, a people of mixed indigenous Caribbean and African descent, who overall form about eleven percent of the country's population. Since the early 1980s Garífuna culture has undergone a tremendous revival; as a part of this movement the town was renamed Dangriga, a Garífuna word meaning "sweet (or "standing") waters" – applied to the North Stann Creek flowing through the town centre.

The most important day in the Garífuna calendar is November 19, **Garífuna Settlement Day**, when the town is packed solid with expatriate Dangrigans returning to their roots and the town erupts into wild celebration. The party begins the evening before, and the drumming and punta dancing go on all night long. In the morning there's a re-enactment of the arrival from Honduras, with people landing on the beach in dugout canoes decorated with palm leaves. Christmas and New Year are also celebrated in unique Garífuna style. At this time you might see the *wanaragu* or *Jonkunu* (John Canoe) dance, where **masked and costumed dancers** represent figures consisting of elements of eighteenth-century naval officers and Amerindian tribal chiefs wearing feathered headdresses and carrying shell rattles on their knees. Dangriga is also home to some of the country's most popular **artists**, including painter Benjamin Nicolas, painter and guitarist Pen Cayetano, drum-maker Austin Rodríguez and the Warribagaga Dancers and the Turtle Shell Band. Some of the artists have small galleries here, and you may catch a live dance performance. Fine **crafts** are produced as well; distinctive brown and white basketware, woven palm-leaf hats and baskets and dolls in Garífuna costume. The cultural importance of **drumming** is celebrated in the large, attractive "Drums of Our Fathers" **bronze monument**, by Nigerian artist Stephen Okeke (who lives in Dangriga), depicting a group of drums on the roundabout at the southern entrance to town.

During quieter times the atmosphere is enjoyably laid-back, though there's little to do during the day and not much nightlife outside weekends. As the south of the country becomes more accessible, however, Dangriga is becoming increasingly useful as a base for visiting south-central Belize, the cayes offshore and the mountains, Maya ruins and the jaguar reserve inland.

Arrival, orientation and information

In addition to **buses** heading just for Dangriga, all buses between Belize City and Punta Gorda call here (see p.74 for details of bus companies and services in Belize City). Generally there will be a either a James Bus or a Southern

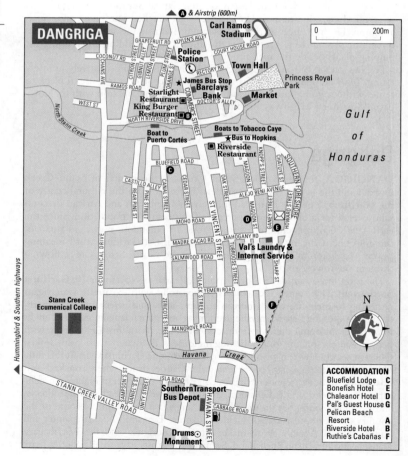

Transport bus passing through Belmopan along the Hummingbird Highway every hour or so from 7am to 6pm. Upon arrival, buses enter Dangriga at the south end of town: Southern Transport has a modern terminal (with luggage storage and clean toilets) about 1km south of the centre, while James buses stop on the street outside the police station. Most buses will in fact continue to the town centre and a **shuttle bus** plies the main street. Dangriga's **airstrip**, served by at least eight daily flights in each direction on the Belize City–Punta Gorda run, is by the shore, just north of the *Pelican Beach Hotel*; you'll need a taxi (at least Bz$6) into town.

The centre of town is marked by the **road bridge** over the South Stann Creek, with the main thoroughfare leading north as Commerce Street and south as St Vincent Street. Almost everything you're likely to need, including **hotels, restaurants, banks** and **transport**, is on or very near this road. There's no official tourist office but you can generally find out all you want to know by asking in the *Riverside Restaurant*, just south of the bridge in the centre of town – especially if you need information on **boats to the cayes** – or at one of the recommended hotels. The Belize Bank, on St Vincent Street just before the bridge, and First Caribbean, near the BTL office a block north of the bridge, have the only ATMs that accept foreign cards. The **post office** is on the corner of Mahogany and Caney streets, in the southern half of town, a block back from the sea. High-speed **Internet** access is available from Val's Laundry, on Mahogany Street, opposite the post office; and of course Val also has a good **laundry** service.

For **bookings and tours** contact Derek and Debbie Jones of Aquamarine Adventures, (☎523-3262, ✉djones@btl.net), independent tour operators dealing with resorts throughout Belize, or Godfrey Young of C&G Tours (☎522-3641, ✉cgtours@btl.net), who has a range of comfortable, air-conditioned vehicles. If you're an experienced paddler you can even rent high-quality **sea kayaks** from Island Expeditions, who have their mainland Belize base in Dangriga (on the Southern Foreshore, next to *Ruthie's Cabañas*; ⊛www.belizekayaking.com). A double kayak costs US$55 per day/US$350 per week and the expedition leaders from Island will arrange a boat charter out to the cayes, camping equipment and everything else you need.

Accommodation

Dangriga has experienced something of a hotel-building boom in the last few years, resulting in a wide choice of places to stay; and – with some real bargains on offer – there's no need to stay in a cheap dive.

Bluefield Lodge 6 Bluefield Rd ☎522-2742, ✉bluefield@btl.net. This small hotel is very clean, secure and well run – everything a budget place should be but rarely is. Owner Louise Belisle is extremely welcoming and has good-value rooms with comfortable beds and bedside lights, while some rooms have private bath and TV. There's a dedicated payphone for BTL phonecards, and Louise maintains a quite reliable information board. ❸–❹
Bonefish Hotel 15 Mahogany St ☎522-2243, ✉bonefishhotelbelize@yahoo.com. Good hotel with cable TV, hot water, carpets and a/c, in a quiet, seafront location. Specializes in fishing trips and is the office for *Blue Marlin Lodge* on South Water Caye (see p.230). Quoted rates include hotel tax. ❺–❼
Chaleanor Hotel 35 Magoon St ☎522-2587, ✉chaleanor@btl.net. Clean, spacious rooms, all

with private bath, run by the very hospitable Chadwick and Eleanor Usher. Next door are some equally clean budget rooms in a wooden building, some with private bath; all rooms are very good value. Free coffee and purified water are available in the lobby, and you can enjoy your meals from the rooftop restaurant. Chadwick's son Elihue is a good guide. ❸–❹
Pal's Guest House 868 Magoon St, by the bridge over Havana Creek ☎522-2095, ⊛www.palbze.net. Good-value accommodation in two buildings: budget rooms (some with private bath and TV) are in the older part; newer beach-front rooms all have private baths and TV. ❷–❹
Pelican Beach Resort On the beach, 2km north of the town, next to the airstrip ☎522-2044, ⊛www.pelicanbeachbelize.com. Dangriga's largest

and most expensive hotel, with the best beachfront location, is also extremely well managed. Rooms at the front are in a wooden colonial-style building, while at the rear is a modern, two-storey concrete building with spacious rooms and large baths with a tub and shower. Most rooms have TV and a/c and some have a balcony over the beach. It's a popular hotel for tour groups, and frequently used by scientists and conservation organizations. The *Pelican Beach* also has some wonderful accommodation on South Water Caye (see p.230); contact the office here for details. Room and package prices do come down out of season and it's worth asking for a dis-

count. The dining room is the best in Dangriga and features a large marine aquarium. ❽

Riverside Hotel Commerce St, right beside the bridge ☎ 522-2168. Clean rooms with shared bath in a good location, with a vantage point over the river. Prices are per person, so it's a good deal for singles. ❷

Ruthie's Cabañas 31 Southern Foreshore ☎ 502-3184. Two bargain thatched cabañas right on the sand, with private bath and porch with hammocks, and some even cheaper rooms in a concrete building, one with bunk beds. Ruthie will cook delicious meals by arrangement. ❸–❹

A Garífuna history

The **Garífuna** (or Garinagu) trace their history back to the island of **St Vincent**, one of the Windward Islands in the eastern Caribbean. At the time of Columbus's landing in the Americas the islands of the Lesser Antilles had recently been settled by people from the South American mainland, who had subdued the previous inhabitants, the Arawaks. These new people called themselves *Kalipuna*, or *Kwaib*, from which the names *Garífuna*, meaning cassava-eating people, and *Carib* probably evolved; St Vincent was *Yurimein*. The natives the Europeans encountered were descendants of Carib men and Arawak women – in fact, a few thousand descendants of the original Caribs still live in Dominica and St Vincent.

In the early seventeenth century, Britain, France and the Netherlands vied for control of the islands, fighting each other and the Caribs. The admixture of African blood came in 1635 when two Spanish ships, carrying **slaves** from Nigeria to their colonies in America, were wrecked off St Vincent and the survivors took refuge on the island. At first there was conflict between the Caribs and the Africans, but the Caribs had been weakened by wars and disease and eventually the predominant race was black, with some Carib blood, becoming known by the English as the **Black Caribs** – in their language they were *Garinagu*, or *Garífuna*. For most of the seventeenth and eighteenth centuries St Vincent was nominally under British control but in practice it belonged to the Garífuna, and with the Treaty of Basse Terre in 1660 the islands of Dominica and St Vincent were granted in "perpetual possession" to the Caribs.

A century later, however, the British attempted to gain full control of St Vincent, and were driven off by the Caribs, with French assistance. Another attempt twenty years later was more successful, and in 1783 the British imposed a treaty on the Garífuna, allowing them over half of the island. The treaty was never accepted, however, and the Garífuna continued to defy British rule, resulting in frequent battles in which the French consistently lent the Garífuna support. The last serious attempt by the Garífuna to establish their independence took place in 1795, when both sides suffered horrendous casualties. The Garífuna lost their leader, Chief Joseph Chatoyer, and on June 10, 1796, after a year of bitter fighting, the French and Garífuna surrendered.

The colonial authorities could not allow a free black society to survive amongst slave-owning European settlers, so it was decided to **deport** the Garífuna population. They were hunted down, their homes (and in the process some of their culture) destroyed, and hundreds died of starvation and disease. The survivors, 4300 Black Caribs and 100 Yellow Caribs, as they were designated by the British, were transported to the nearby island of Balliceaux; within six months over half of them had died, many of yellow fever. In March 1797, the remaining survivors were loaded aboard ships and sent to **Roatán**, one of the Bay Islands, off the coast of Honduras. One of the ships was captured by the Spanish and taken to Trujillo, on the mainland, while barely 2000 Garífuna lived to make the landing on Roatán, where the British abandoned them.

Eating, drinking and nightlife

Despite Dangriga's central position in Garífuna culture, there's no restaurant specializing in Garífuna food – some restaurants in town will occasionally have Garífuna dishes on the menu, but you'll find this cuisine is generally more available in Hopkins (see p.232). **Garífuna dishes** frequently feature fish and vegetables such as yam, plantain, okra and cassava, often served in a rich, thick sauce containing coconut milk – similar in consistency to a chowder – called "sere". This is usually accompanied by rice but above all by the cultural staple of thin, crispy **cassava bread**, baked on a metal sheet over an open fire. The restaurant at the *Pelican Beach* is the top place in town, and the staff there are skilled in preparing all of Belize's cultural specialities.

Perhaps in response to pleas for help from the Garífuna, who continued to die on Roatán, the Spanish Commandante of Trujillo arrived and took possession of the island, shipping survivors to Trujillo, where they were in demand as labourers. The Spanish had never made a success of agriculture here and the arrival of the Garífuna, who were proficient at growing crops, benefited the colony considerably. The boys were conscripted and the Garífuna men gained a reputation as soldiers and mercenaries. Soon they began to move to other areas along the coast, and in 1802, 150 of them were brought as wood-cutting labourers to work in Stann Creek and Punta Gorda. Their intimate knowledge of the rivers and coast also made them expert **smugglers,** evading the Spanish laws that forbade trade with the British in Belize.

In the early nineteenth century small numbers of Garífuna moved up the coast to **Belize** – and although in 1811 Superintendent Barrow of Belize ordered their expulsion, it had little effect. When European settlers arrived in Stann Creek in 1823 the Garífuna were already there and were hired to clear land. The largest single migration to Belize took place in 1832 when several hundred fled from Honduras (by then part of the Central American Republic) under the leadership of Alejo Benji after they had supported the wrong side in a failed revolution to overthrow the Republic's government. It is this arrival which is today celebrated as **Garífuna Settlement Day,** though it seems likely many arrived both before and after.

In 1825 the first **Methodist missionaries** arrived in Belize, and by 1828 they had begun to visit Stann Creek, or "Carib Town" as the settlers knew it. They were outraged to discover a bizarre mix of Catholicism, ancestor worship and polygamy, in which the main form of worship was "devil dancing". They had little success in their struggle to Christianize the Garífuna beyond the adoption of various new rituals such as baptism.

By the start of the **twentieth century,** the Garífuna were well established in the Stann Creek area, with the women employed in bagging and stacking cohune nuts and the men working in agriculture. As in the previous century, the Garífuna continued to travel widely in search of work. To start with they confined themselves to Central America (where they can still be found all along the Caribbean coast from Belize to Nicaragua), but in World War II Garífuna men supplied crews for both British and US merchant ships. Since then trips to the US have become an important part of the local economy, and there are small Garífuna communities in New York, New Orleans, Los Angeles and even in London.

Today, Belize has a National Garífuna Council, and its scholars are attempting to create a written language. The council has already published *The People's Garífuna Dictionary* and school textbooks are available. *The First Primer on a People Called Garífuna*, by Myrtle Palacio, is in English and available in Belize.

Returning **to Belize City** (2–3hr), Southern Transport **buses** (some express services; ☏502-2160) leave every hour or so from 5am to 5pm; most go via **Belmopan** (1hr 45min), though the 5am departure travels the Coastal Road, calling at **Gales Point**. James Bus Line doesn't have a terminal, but departing buses (currently 3–4 daily in each direction) pass along the main street. Buses here are usually very crowded, so buying a ticket in advance (only possible on Southern Transport) *should* guarantee a seat.

If you're **continuing south**, bear in mind that buses to **Punta Gorda** (4hr; up to eight daily, including expresses) don't necessarily originate here and delays are possible. All buses to Punta Gorda stop at **Independence** (under 2hr) – also known as **Mango Creek** – where you can pick up boats to Placencia (see p.246).

There are usually three daily Southern services from Dangriga to **Placencia** (2hr), but departure times are continually changing (they currently leave daily at noon & 5pm, with a 10am departure Mon–Sat); most Placencia buses also call at **Hopkins** (30min) and **Sittee River**. Hopkins also has its own bus, leaving at 10.30am Mon–Sat from near the *Riverside Restaurant*.

Dangriga is also served by **flights** on Tropic Air (☏522-2129) and Maya Island Air (☏522-2659) every couple of hours to and from Belize City (15min to municipal airport; Bz$61) and south to Placencia (20min; Bz$68) and Punta Gorda (40min; Bz$112).

For Puerto Cortes in Honduras a fast skiff leaves each Saturday at 9am (US$50; 3hr) from the north bank of the river, two blocks up from the bridge; be there at 8am with your passport so that the skipper, Carlos Reyes   t522-3227), can take care of the formalitues.

The *Riverside Restaurant*, on the south bank of the river just over the bridge, catering for local boatmen and visitors waiting for boats to Tobacco Caye, is easily the best **place to eat** in the town centre. Owners Ronnie and M.J. Aleman serve tasty Creole and Garífuna food, including great breakfasts and a daily special, and it's the best place to pick up information on the surrounding area. *King Burger* (not what you might think) under the *Riverside Hotel* serves good rice, chicken, burgers, fruit juices, fish and conch soup, a Belizean delicacy. Of the several Chinese restaurants on the main street, the *Starlight* is the best value; and *Dangriga Pizza*, opposite the side of the police station, delivers (☏522-3786).

For picnic supplies you could try the **market** on the north bank of the river, by the sea, but it's very small – for other groceries it's best to head for the supermarket just south of the bridge.

There's no shortage of **bars** in Dangriga, though some, particularly those calling themselves clubs, like the *Kennedy Club*, the *Culture Club* and the *Harlem Club*, are particularly dubious-looking, both inside and out. The best local nightspots are *The Beach Place* and the *Malibu Beach Club*, along the beach to the north of the centre, just before the *Pelican Beach Resort*. Both are good places to meet the locals and dance on the sand, though they're likely to be open only at weekends.

Offshore from Dangriga: Tobacco Range cayes and Columbus Reef

The **Tobacco Range** is a group of mangrove cayes just behind the beautiful **Columbus** and **Tobacco reefs**, about 16km east of Dangriga. The largest caye in the range, **Man-O'-War Caye**, is a **bird sanctuary** named after either the frigate or the man-o'-war birds you'll see hanging on the breeze with outstretched wings. In the breeding season the males develop an immense, bright red balloon on their throats and the island is full of nesting birds; watching the birds from a boat is fine but you can't land on the island. Beyond the superb Columbus Reef, with a scattering of small cayes along its length, including the tiny **Tobacco Caye**, lies Tobacco Reef with the slightly larger **South Water Caye** on the southern end. Each caye has a number of delightful places to stay – sunsets out here can be breathtakingly beautiful, outlining the distant Maya Mountains with a purple and orange aura.

Tobacco Caye

Tobacco Caye, ideally situated right on the reef, is the easiest to reach in this area and has the most accommodation. **Boats** leave every day from near the bridge, but there are no regular departures; check at the *Riverside Restaurant* in Dangriga, where you can meet the boat skippers. The most prompt and reliable service is operated by Captain Buck, though any of the hotel owners on the island will take you, and maybe arrange a package deal. It's a forty-minute trip and the one-way fare is Bz\$35 per person.

The cayes of Columbus Reef were originally visited by turtle fishermen; Tobacco Caye was a trading post where passing ships could pick up supplies, including the tobacco which gave the island its name. The island is tiny, covering just five acres – if you stand in the centre you're only a couple of minutes from the shore in any direction, with the unbroken reef stretching north for miles. On the southern edge a huge storm beach of coral rubble, thrown up by Hurricane Mitch in 1998, encloses a tiny lagoon – creating a lovely natural swimming pool – and the tons of sand dumped on the leeward side provided new beaches. Since the reef is within wading distance you don't even need to take a boat trip for some superb snorkelling and diving; otherwise, the days are spent, eating, drinking or relaxing in a hammock. Some of the resorts have **dive shops** and there's the specialist Tobacco Caye Diving (☎614-9907, ⓦwww.tobaccocayediving.com), with a large selection of equipment, including snorkel gear; owner Andy Muha offers PADI courses, dive packages and trips to the atolls. A local dive (without a boat but including equipment) costs US\$70; an open water certification course is US\$425.

Accommodation

Accommodation here is simple but comfortable, and generally good value; you'll be staying either in wooden buildings on the sand or cabins right over the sea. The price can vary according to demand (bargaining is possible at slack periods) but here more than anywhere it's essential to check what you're paying for – and whether the price is quoted in US or Belize dollars. Unless you've arranged a package in advance the hotels charge per person per night, and the rates we've quoted include all meals; all can also arrange scuba-diving, fishing and snorkelling trips.

Gaviota Coral Reef Resort ☎520-5032 or 509-5032. Five cabins on the sand, and budget rooms in the main wooden building, all with shared bath and all very clean; this place is well run and usually the best value on the caye. There's electric light from a solar panel on a timer, a thatched shelter with hammocks for relaxing and good snorkel equipment for rent. Wonderful food, and rates include meals. ❺–❻

Lana's on the Reef ☎520-5036. Four simple, neat rooms in a lovely wooden house; the upstairs rooms, with private shower and opening onto a balcony, are more expensive. Great food and good coffee, in a romantic atmosphere. ❻–❼

Ocean's Edge Lodge ☎614-9633. Four wooden cabins connected by a walkway in a perfect location overlooking the reef; all have private bath and hot water. The layout inside (and out) makes you feel like

you're in a comfortably furnished ship's cabin. **❼**
Reef's End Lodge ☎ 522-2419, ⓦwww
.reefsendlodge.com. Stay right on the shore in a
room in a large wooden building (upstairs rooms
cost more) or in one of the spacious private
cabañas, all with private hot showers and deck.
The restaurant and bar are over the sea on the tip
of the reef – a fantastic place to enjoy the sunset.
Delicious food, a good dive shop and discounts for
Rough Guide readers. **❼**–**❽**
Tobacco Caye Lodge ☎ 520-5033,

ⓦwww.tclodgebelize.com. The largest area of any
hotel on the island, stretching from the reef at the
front to the lagoon at the back. Accommodation
comprises three spacious, comfortable, two-room
houses with private bath, deck and hammocks, and
there's a good beach bar by the dock. **❽**
Tobacco Caye Paradise ☎ 520-5101. Good-
value, simple rooms in a wooden house, all with
shared bathroom (Bz$50 per person, including
meals) and thatched cabañas over the sea (Bz$35
per person). **❺**–**❻**

South Water Caye

Eight kilometres south of Tobacco Caye and about three times the size, **South Water Caye** is arguably one of the most beautiful and exclusive islands in Belize. Like Tobacco Caye, it sits right on the reef and offers fantastic, very accessible snorkelling and scuba diving in crystal-clear water. The island takes its name from a well in the centre of the island, which made it a fresh-water stop for passing ships – the well still exists today. South Water Caye is now the focus of a large **marine reserve**, which is also a World Heritage Site, and the southern end of the island is part of a small nature reserve. Turtles nest in the sand here, and the reef curves around offshore protecting the pristine beach. Most resorts have their own very good **dive shop** and trips can be arranged to **Glover's Reef** (see p.236). The tiny island off the south end of the caye is **Carrie Bow Caye**, where the Smithsonian Institute has a research station; you can sometimes visit but there's no tourist accommodation.

Accommodation

The island's **accommodation** is mainly upmarket and expensive and has to be booked in advance; rates given are either for groups or for an all-inclusive package. Overnight rates are available, but this may entail paying US$125 one-way for a skiff from Dangriga. Outside of the two places listed separately below, accommodation on the caye is owned and operated by **Pelican Beach Resorts** in Dangriga (☎ 522-2024, ⓦwww.pelicanbeachbelize.com), with a range of idyllic options in a stunning location on the south half of the island; rates include meals and snorkel gear. As the island is a marine reserve electricity is provided by solar cells to minimize the environmental impact and most accommodation has composting toilets. *Osprey's Nest* (US$220 double, including meals; **❾**) is a two-bedroom house with large verandahs, built on stilts over the white sand and shaded by palms; the shower is outside, at the side of the house. *Heron's Hideaway* and *Egret's Escape* (US$220 double, including meals; **❾**) are secluded little houses built in the mangroves, overlooking the reef in the corner of the island – perfect for honeymooners. *Pelican's Pouch* (US$195 double, including meals; **❾**), a former convent, is a two-storey wooden colonial building with five rooms upstairs, each with three beds, and a verandah front and back overlooking the sea. *The Pelican's University* on the west side of the island, designed to house groups, often students, is a two-storey building with five bunk-bedded rooms and shared bathrooms, a large kitchen and recreation area – definitely a fine place to study. It costs US$70 per person per day for groups of 10 to 23, including meals. *Frangipani House*, a separate wooden building, is where the teachers stay.

Blue Marlin Lodge ☎ 520-5104, in the US ☎ 1-
800/798-1558, ⓦwww.bluemarlinlodge.com. The
most luxurious accommodation on the island, set in

a wide expanse of raked white sand under the
coconut trees, and comprising three dome-shaped,
pastel-painted, carpeted a/c cabins, with beautiful

bathrooms, five comfortable wooden a/c cabins with a deck over the sea, and wood-panelled rooms in a typical wooden "caye house". The thatched dining room extending over the sea serves delicious meals. *Blue Marlin* specializes in diving and fishing: there's a fleet of boats with top fishing guides and resident divemaster Martin Green offers PADI certification. Prices (based on two sharing, and including all taxes) are around US$1250 for a week's vacation package including transfers from the international airport, room and all meals, and around US$1600 for a diving package.

Leslie Cottages ℡ 520-5030, in the US ℡ 1-800/548-5843, Ⓦ www.ize2belize.com, Ⓔ izebelize@starband.net. Very comfortable wood-en cabins with private baths, and bunk rooms, all cooled by fans, in a tropical field research station. Although many guests here are on study trips, it's still a wonderful place for anyone to stay. Manager Jennifer Hall is a biologist and the courses focus on reef ecology, with a well-equipped lab and a multimedia classroom. A ten-day student package, which includes a stay at *Blue Creek Rainforest Lodge*, in Toledo District (see p.274), costs around US$998 excluding airfare. A complete package for private guests, including transportation, accommodation, meals and daily boat tour, costs US$135 per person per day; the private cabins have a lounge area and all-round decks, and two are right over the reef. Internet access for guests. ⑨

The Southern Highway to the Jaguar Reserve

To the south of Dangriga the country becomes more mountainous, with settlements mainly restricted to the coastal lowlands. The only road heading in this direction is the recently paved **Southern Highway**, running 170km from Dangriga to Punta Gorda. For its entire length the highway is set back from the coast, running beneath the peaks of the Maya Mountains, often passing through pine forest and vast citrus and banana plantations. Several branch roads lead off to settlements such as **Hopkins**, a Garífuna village on the coast, and the nearby Creole village of **Sittee River**, where you can catch the *Glover's Atoll Resort* boat to Long Caye on **Glover's Reef** (see p.236). From the village of **Maya Centre**, 36km south of Dangriga, a road leads west into the Cockscomb Basin Wildlife Sanctuary (generally referred to as the **Jaguar Reserve**); your first reason to pull off the Southern Highway, however, might be to visit the Late Classic Maya site of **Mayflower**.

Mayflower and Mama Noots Resort

Ten kilometres south of the junction with the Stann Creek Valley Road, an unpaved six-kilometre branch road twists through citrus groves and forest to the foothills of the Maya Mountains and the Late Classic site of **Mayflower**. There are really three Maya sites here: Mayflower, which is near the end of the branch road, Maintzunun ("hummingbird") and T'au Witz ("dwelling-place of the mountain god"), each a short distance through the forest. Apart from a few medium-sized stone mounds and areas which are clearly plazas, the sites have not yet been fully cleared, so there's not that much to see architecturally. The location, however – on a creek where the coastal plain meets the forested mountains – is sublime, rich in tremendous bird and animal life. The sites are currently being excavated by the Mayflower Archaeology Project – see "Archeology" in Contexts, p.310, for details of how to participate in the dig – and the area around them is now protected in the 7000-acre **Mayflower Bocawina National Park** (Bz$10); hiking trails lead to waterfalls tumbling into Silk Grass Creek.

You can stay in the midst of this natural and archeological beauty at **Mama Noots Resort** (℡ 606-4353, Ⓔ mamanoots@lincsat.com, Ⓦ www.mamanoots

.bz.com; ❼), set in a large grassy clearing surrounded on three sides by forest-covered hills. Owners Kevin and Nanette Denny have left most of their fifty acres of primary and secondary forest intact (much of the land is steep hillside anyway) and they make the most of alternative energy, using solar, wind and hydro power. It's an utterly tranquil place, and even the occasional visits by a jaguar only add to the natural atmosphere. All buses heading south from Dangriga pass the side road to the resort; call ahead and they'll pick you up from the junction, 6km away. The accommodation consists of a two-room wood-and-thatch house and six rooms in a wheelchair-accessible concrete building. All the rooms are large, with private baths, fans, 24hr electricity and balconies with hammocks; guests can use the hotel's email facility. Organic vegetables are grown in the garden and served in the thatched dining room; the **restaurant** is open to non-guests. A short trail near the lodge has descriptions highlighting various plants' medicinal properties, while other trails lead to nearby waterfalls, with an easy 35-minute hike to Three Sisters Falls, and a very steep trail to the ridge of the ninety-metre Antelope Falls, visible from the grounds.

Hopkins

Stretching for more than 3km along a shallow, gently curving bay, **HOPKINS** is home to around 1200 Garífuna people, who, until recently, made their living from small-scale farming and fishing, often paddling dugout canoes to pull up fish traps, or using baited handlines. Their houses, traditionally small wood-and-thatch structures, have now mostly been replaced by less visually appealing but more secure concrete buildings. Named after a Roman Catholic bishop who drowned near here in 1923, the village was first settled in 1942, after a hurricane had levelled its predecessor, the community of Newtown, a few kilometres to the north. The population is proud of its traditions (everyone speaks Garífuna as their first language), and **Garífuna Settlement Day** on November 19 is celebrated enthusiastically with singing, dancing and above all the beating of drums – an integral part of the Garífuna culture. Only recently part of the tourist circuit, Hopkins still sees relatively few visitors, and as a stranger you'll be made to feel welcome by the exuberant friendliness of the villagers, particularly the children.

It's a pleasant place to spend a few days relaxing, with food and accommodation in all price ranges. You can rent **kayaks** at *Tipple Tree*, **windsurf** boards at Oliver's (☏601-7818) on the south beach (he also has **Internet access**) and **bicycles** (Bz$20/day) from Tina's Bike Rental, on the road toward the south end of the village. Many hotels can arrange trips to the reef and cayes further out and **diving** here is excellent and uncrowded; check with the resorts beyond the south end or with Second Nature Divers (☏523-7038, ✉divers@starband.net), based in **Sittee River**, a few kilometres south of Hopkins (see p.235). At the north end of the village a small creek gives access to a large, virtually undiscovered lagoon, a good place to take a kayak. The view back towards the village from the sea, with the high ridges of the Maya Mountains in the background, is breathtaking. Unfortunately, the water immediately offshore, while clean, is silty and the coconut trees which once shaded the whole village have been wiped out by the "lethal yellowing" disease advancing inexorably down the coast from Mexico; the disease-resistant variety of trees planted to replace them are growing vigorously but will take a while to mature.

Arrival and orientation

The **bus** service to Hopkins has improved recently, with KC's Bus leaving from the near dock outside the *Riverside Restaurant* in Dangriga (10.30am Mon–Sat, returning at 7am; Bz$5). Most Southern Transport services to Placencia pass through the village, continuing south via Sittee River; see p.246 for details. There are also plenty of trucks between Dangriga and Hopkins, making **hitching** a fairly reliable option; it's also easy enough to catch a bus from Dangriga to the junction with the Southern Highway (where there's a shelter) and hitch in. You might also want to ask around where the **boats** tie up by the bridge in Dangriga and see whether anyone from Hopkins is in town – they may be willing to give you a lift and this is definitely the best way to arrive.

As there are no street names in Hopkins, the best way to locate anything is to describe its position in relation to the point where the road from the Southern Highway enters the village, dividing it roughly into northern and southern halves. The main road from the highway and heading south through the village is paved (as are a couple of other streets in the village) though the asphalt gives way to sand at the southern end; this road continues 5km to **Sittee River** (see p.234).

Accommodation

Hopkins has plenty of **accommodation** in all price ranges, and booking ahead is only really necessary for the days around November 19, Garífuna Settlement Day. That said, it's always worthwhile booking if you want a particular place at Christmas or Easter. There are also several **houses for rent**, and a couple of places to **camp**. An increasing number of hotels also have bicycles for guests to use, which are useful as the village extends so far along the beach. Beyond the southern edge of the village a growing number of luxury resorts line a beautiful beach called **False Sittee Point**; some of these are included in the list below.

All Seasons Guest House Across from the beach at the south end of the village ☏608-3243, ⓦwww.allseasonsbelize.com. Three beautifully decorated rooms, all with private bath, coffeemaker and fridge (with an a/c option), set in a lovely garden with a tranquil, Mediterranean-style patio. Scooter rental (Bz$80/day) also available. German spoken. ➎

Almond Beach Resort On the beach at False Sittee Point, 2km beyond the south end of the village ☏822-2800, in the US ☏1-800/624-1516, ⓦwww .colonialsuitesbelize.com. Beautifully furnished and very spacious suites with full kitchens, at better prices than the other top-end places here. Great views from the roof terrace and guests can use the pool at the *Jaguar Reef Lodge* next door (see below). *Almond Beach Resort* is owned by *Caves Branch* (see p.221), which can arrange a relaxing stay on the beach after a jungle adventure. ➑

Hamanasi Dive Resort False Sittee Point, 1.5km beyond the south end of the village ☏520-7090, ⓦwww.hamanasi.com. One of the top diving resorts in the country, with a range of luxuriously appointed suites (US$250), rooms (US$180) and "treehouse" cabañas on three-metre stilts (US$220), located on a beautiful beach. All accommodation has a/c, ceiling fans, king or queen-size beds, gorgeous Belizean hardwood furniture, colourfully tiled bathrooms and private porches.

The resort has a number of fast, modern dive boats and superb equipment for diving or snorkelling on the reef or any of the atolls. ➒

Hopkins Inn On the beach, south of the centre ☏523-7013, ⓦwww.hopkinsinn.com. Friendly place with four immaculate whitewashed cabins with showers, fridge and coffeemaker. Owners Rita and Greg Duke offer trips on their Super-cat (a small catamaran); they also run snorkel and boat trips and help arrange other activities. Ample continental breakfast included and free bikes for guests. German spoken. ➎

Jaguar Reef Lodge False Sittee Point, 1.75km beyond the south end of the village ☏520-7040, in the US ☏1-800/289-5756, ⓦwww.jaguarreef.com. An expensive luxury resort with large, thatched, two-room cabañas, all with a/c, in beautifully landscaped grounds and in a superb location, often used by top nature tour companies. The restaurant, under a huge thatched roof overlooking the beach and pool, is excellent and so is the service. Kayaks and bikes are available free for guests, and there's a full service dive shop with instruction. US$195 double; prices are reduced considerably in summer. ➒

Kismet Inn On the beach at the north end of the village ☏609-4173, ⓔkismetinnb@hotmail.com. Lovely thatch-roofed and individually decorated stone cabañas with private bathrooms, budget rooms in a wooden house, some with shared bath, and a furnished house to rent for Bz$500/month. *Kismet* is set in beautiful gardens and owner Tricia Martin is a great cook and will prepare meals, or you can use the small guest kitchen. Internet access and use of bike is free for guests, and Garífuna guide Ray Busano (who also speaks German, French and Spanish) can take you on a superb sunrise tour of the lagoon – he's also qualified to give you a massage afterwards. ❸–❺

Ransom's Seaside Garden Cabaña South of the centre. Wonderful, very comfortable two-bedroom cabaña, fully furnished with kitchen and cable TV, and set in a tropical garden. Kayaks and bicycles free for guests. There's usually a two-night minimum stay required. ❹

Sandy Beach Lodge On the beach at the south end of the village. ☎523-7006. Simple, good-value rooms in wood-and-thatch cabins with fan (most with private bath), run by Belize's only women's cooperative. Meals, served at set times, feature seafood cooked in Creole and Garífuna style. ❸

Seagull's Nest Guest House On the beach, south of the centre ☎523-7015, ✉jc-seagulls@yahoo.com. Bargain shared rooms in a wooden house, one with bunk beds for Bz$20 per person, and a separate, two-room, concrete house with tiled floors, kitchen and balcony for Bz$150. There's a free bicycle for guests. ❸

Tania's Guest House South of the centre, on the right side of the road ☎523-7058. Although not directly on the beach, this small, friendly hotel is a great bargain. All rooms have a private shower (most with hot water) and some have bedside light, fridge and cable TV – and there's complimentary coffee. ❷–❸

Tipple Tree Beya On the beach near the south end of the village ☎520-7006, ⊛www.tippletree.com. Good-value, neat, clean rooms in a wooden building with deck and hammocks; one has cold-water shower; others have hot shower and coffeemaker. A very friendly place, run by Patricia Sturman, who provides accurate information and does all she can to ensure you have a good visit. There's also a furnished wooden house to rent, with fridge and microwave, for Bz$100/day, or you can camp for B$10/person. Accepts credit cards. ❸–❹

Whistling Seas Inn On the beach, towards the south end of the village ☎608-0016, ✉whistlingseas@btl.net. Five new, brightly painted cement cabañas with private bathroom and a verandah. Friendly Belizean owners Marcello and Orbita Williams offer great value and run a good restaurant here, too. ❹

Eating, drinking and entertainment

Though the choice can be limited out of the tourist season, Hopkins has a good selection of inexpensive **restaurants** and **bars**. You'll always be able to find simple Garífuna and Creole meals and usually very good seafood. Bear in mind that service can be slow (they might have to send the kids out to buy ingredients), so be prepared to wait for your meal to arrive – at least you'll know it's fresh. For more upmarket dining you could sample the restaurants in the lodges at False Sittee Point, some way beyond the south end of the village. South of the centre, near the end of the village, the *Watering Hole* is one of the best restaurants, serving great seafood, while nearby *Iris's Restaurant* and the *Yugadah* ("coastal village") *Café* both serve good, inexpensive local meals. North of the centre try the *Hideaway Restaurant* or *Tyson's Diner*. For a **drink** with the locals go to either the *Tropical Bar* or *Lebeya* in the north, and for **live music** at weekends check the *King Casava Restaurant*, found where the road from the highway enters the village. The Women's Dance Group sometimes gives performances, and if lucky you'll enjoy **Garífuna drumming and dancing** – certainly around November 19, often too at other times.

Sittee River

A few kilometres south of the Hopkins turn-off is the junction of the road to **SITTEE RIVER**, a pleasant village in its own right, but most useful as a jumping-off point for Glover's Reef (see p.236). The eight kilometre dirt road from the Southern Highway roughly follows the north bank of the river, as does the village itself. On the way in you'll see signs to the ruins of the nineteenth-century **Serpon Sugar Mill**, now preserved as a local park and a good spot for bird-watching.

The road from Hopkins has been raised and improved, though it's still a little rough in places. Sittee River is served by the same **buses** as Hopkins on the Dangriga/Placencia route, and on a **bike** it's about a 25-minute ride from Hopkins. Sittee River and its banks offer great opportunities for spotting **wildlife**; apart from dozens of bird species, there are freshwater turtles and crocodiles. Most visitors here are on their way to *Glover's Atoll Resort* and the bus driver will drop you at the right place (see *Glover's Guest House*, below). Be warned that sandflies in Sittee River can be atrocious, and the screens or mosquito nets provide are essential.

The great-value *Toucan Sittee* (☏523-7039, ✉birdcity@btl.net, ⒲www.toucansittee.info; ❸–❻), signposted at the entrance to the village from the Hopkins road, is the best **accommodation** option in Sittee River, set in a beautiful riverbank location and graced by toucans most mornings. It's owned by the extremely hospitable Neville and Yoli Collins, who offer a wide range of rooms, including some of the best budget accommodation in the country, in solidly built, well-furnished wooden cabins with electric lights and fans; most have a private hot-water bathroom and a fridge. **Rooms** start at Bz$40, and there are also a couple of apartments, each with a small kitchen and fridge (Bz$130, good discounts for longer stays), and very comfortable dorm beds in the "bunkhouse" (Bz$19), or you can camp (Bz$10). The food is really good, with lots of fresh fruit (including sixteen varieties of mango) and organic vegetables, and they also rent **canoes** and **bikes**. Nearby, *Glover's Guest House* (☏520-2016, ✉info@glovers.com.bz; ❸), where you check in for the Glover's Reef trip, has dorm beds for Bz$17 as well as double rooms in cabins (❸). The guesthouse's restaurant is right on the riverbank and the boat to the atoll ties up outside. If you need to stock up on **supplies** for your trip to Glover's Reef there's Hill Top Farm for vegetables and the well-stocked Reynold's Store for groceries. You can go **online** nearby at Sittee River Internet.

A little way downstream from Sittee River, reached by a kilometre-long signposted track from the road between Sittee and Hopkins, there's a range of comfortable, good-value accommodation at *Bocatura Bank* (☏606-4590, ✉bocatura@aol.com, ⒲www.bocaturbank.com; ❹–❼). The main attractions are the spacious whitewashed wooden **cabins** on the riverbank, each with at least one bedroom with queen-sized bed, a living room futon, a kitchenette and a large screened porch with rattan furniture and hammocks; there's also a budget cabin overlooking the river and a "treehouse" cabin on stilts. Meals are US$30 per day and the food's great. Owner Alan Stewart, a biologist from New England, is a keen sailor and not only has a Sunfish sailboat, kayaks and canoes for guests, but also a 40ft catamaran for **sailing charters**. Guests can call ahead for a free ride from Hopkins or Sittee.

Just slightly further down the river, **Possum Point Biological Station** (☏523-7071, ⒲www.marineecology.com) is a tropical ecology field station, run by biologists Paul and Mary Shave. The cabins here are mainly used by student groups, and courses include a spell offshore at the marine ecology lab on **Wee Wee Caye**, a tiny mangrove island 15km off the coast.

The road to *Bocatura Bank* is also the base of Second Nature Divers (☏523-7038, ✉divers@starband.net), where two very experienced dive instructors from England, Janette Melvin and Martin Spragg, offer good-value PADI courses, **dive excursions** and equipment rental. Call ahead and they'll arrange the best-value accommodation for you as well. Day-trip prices are U$75 for a two-tank dive on the reef offshore and US$125 for a three-tank dive on Glover's Reef. Prices include tanks, boat and dive guide, and they have equipment for rent.

Glover's Reef

The southernmost of Belize's three coral atolls, **Glover's Reef** lies between 45 and 55km off Dangriga. Named after British pirate John Glover, the reef is roughly oval in shape, about 35km north to south, and its main cayes are in the southeastern section. Physically, it's the best developed atoll in the Caribbean, rising from ocean depths of 1000m, with the reef wall beginning less than ten metres offshore. At the south end, pinnacles of coral rise up to twenty metres from the sea bed and the atoll offers some of the best **wall diving** in the world – the fantastic Long Caye Wall is less than 100m offshore – offering visibility of over 300m. Inside the beautiful aquamarine lagoon are hundreds of smallish patches of coral, aka **patch reefs** – a snorkelling wonderland. Glover's Reef is also the most biologically diverse atoll in the Caribbean, home to rare seabirds such as the white-capped noddy; all the cayes have nesting ospreys, and Belize's **marine turtles** nest on the beaches. The vitally important snapper spawning grounds on the atoll attract dozens of immense **whale sharks**, which congregate during the late spring full moons to feast on the snapper eggs. These unique features helped to bring about the decision in 1993 to declare the whole atoll a protected area – **Glover's Reef Marine Reserve**. This special status was further enhanced by its designation as a World Heritage Site in 1996. The atoll is divided into management zones and, while no fishing is allowed from any of the cayes themselves, you can fish in the designated zones shown on the map you're given (or should be given) when you pay the Bz$20 **entry fee**, though this may not always be collected.

All of the four main cayes offer some **package accommodation**, mostly in purpose-built camps and cabins; these are often used by **sea-kayaking** and diving groups. Apart from its biological attributes, there's another feature that makes Glover's Reef so unusual among the remote atolls: one of its cayes, Northeast Caye, has accommodation within the reach of budget travellers (see below).

The cayes

Northeast Caye, covered in thick coconut and broadleaf forest, and with evidence of Maya fishing camps, is home to *Glover's Atoll Resort* (☎614-7177 or ☎520-2016, ⓦ www.glovers.com.bz), owned by the French-American Lomont family who have lived here for over 35 years. All accommodation overlooks the sea and the reef, and here more than anywhere else in Belize you can indulge your Robinson Crusoe fantasy to the utmost. The prices quoted below apply year-round (though note the resort may be closed during September and October, the height of the rainy season), and are per person per week, including transport from Sittee River on the resort's boat – either a 55ft motor sailboat, a fast skiff or a diesel-powered catamaran – leaving on Sunday morning and returning the following Saturday. No meals are included, but if you stay for a month the fourth week is free. There are twelve simple wood-and-thatch self-catering **beach cabins** on stilts on the sand or over the water (some cabins have a loft bedroom, ideal for families; US$199), a dorm room in a wooden house (US$149) and space for **camping** (US$99, including the tent and bedding). Kitchens are either downstairs or on the first floor, with cooking done on a kerosene stove or on the barbecue; one evening each week features a potluck supper. You can either bring your own food for the week (fish, lobster, bread and basic supplies are available to buy – bring your own booze) or eat at the thatched **restaurant**. Five gallons of drinking water (stored rainwater) per person is provided free – you pay if you use more – but bear in mind that **coconuts** are free and the green ones contain lots of delicious water.

△ Waterfall, Cockscomb Basin Wildlife Sanctuary

Showers are taken in water drawn from a shallow well. While here you're pretty much left to your own devices and you can choose to enjoy a simple "desert island" experience or you can partake in the **activities** (paid for separately) on offer, including sea kayaking, fishing, snorkelling, scuba diving with PADI certification (less expensive than most other places) and visits to the other cayes.

Long Caye, just across the channel from Northeast Caye, is the base for the wonderful **sea-kayak expeditions** run by Utah-based Slickrock Adventures (ⓦwww.slickrock.com; see Basics, p.12). Guests are picked up in Belize City and transferred by fast launch to the caye, with **accommodation** in sturdy, comfortable, wooden thatched cabins on stilts with a deck and hammock, overlooking the reef, or in tents on a wooden deck under a thatched roof. There's collected rainwater to drink, while varied, filling meals are served in the spacious thatched dining room. Slickrock are very experienced adventure outfitters (they also offer windsurfing, kayak surfing and fishing at the Water Sports Center here, plus river and jungle trips inland) and the base camp is designed to be eco-friendly, with composting toilets and some electricity for lighting provided by wind and solar power. **Diving** on the caye is provided by Jim and Kendra Schofield, who run *Off the Wall Dive Center and Resort* (☎614-6348, ⓦwww.offthewallbelize.com). They offer PADI diving courses, snorkelling and fishing packages for around US$1295–1695 per person per week, depending on the activity, including all meals and boat transfer from Dangriga. Guests stay in charming, rustic wooden cabañas, with separate showers, and if you want a souvenir there's the only **gift shop** on the atoll.

Four kilometres to the southwest, **Middle Caye** is in the wilderness zone of the reserve, with a marine research and monitoring station and laboratory run by the Wildlife Conservation Society (see p.325 in Contexts). This is also the base for the Fisheries Department **conservation officers**, who rigorously patrol the reserve. Only staff and authorized scientists and students stay on the caye but you can visit with permission, and there are some interesting displays on the ecology of the atoll.

Southwest Caye, 5km beyond Middle Caye, is the base for the **sea-kayak** groups of Vancouver-based Island Expeditions (ⓦwww.islandexpeditions.com; see p.11 in Basics), a very experienced adventure outfitter, with superb guides and an exemplary environmental record. Guests are usually flown to Dangriga and taken by fast skiff to the caye, where they sleep in spacious, comfortable white tents with proper beds and eat gourmet meals in the screened dining room. Training is given in paddling and sailing the kayaks, while experienced paddlers can visit the other cayes or even take part in overnight camping expeditions to uninhabited islands. Island Expeditions also offers excellent educational trips (one guide here will always be a biologist) and **scuba diving** is available from *Isla Marisol Resort* (see below).

The original caye was sliced into two islands by Hurricane Hattie in 1961, and on the other part, divided by a narrow channel, is *Isla Marisol Resort* (☎520-2056 or 615-1485, ⓦwww.islamarisol.com), owned and run by Eddie Usher, from Dangriga. He's built eleven attractive, spacious wooden cabañas on stilts on the beach, with queen-sized beds, ceiling fans, private hot-water showers and a shady verandah with hammocks. The food is excellent and the bar is built on a deck over the water. *Isla Marisol* is a PADI dive centre, offering courses from beginner to advanced open-water; a week's **package** in high season, including transport from Dangriga, all meals and seventeen dives (including two night dives) is US$1750. During your stay you could expect to dive on all three of Belize's atolls, depending on the weather conditions at the time; in April, May and June you can dive with the **whale sharks** at Gladden Spit for an extra US$105. A week's fly-fishing is US$3000, or you can just relax and swim off the gorgeous beach for US$1100; three- or four-day packages are also available.

The Cockscomb Basin Wildlife Sanctuary and Maya Centre village

Back on the mainland, the jagged peaks of the **Maya Mountains** rise to the west of the Southern Highway, their lower slopes covered in dense rainforest. The tallest summits are those of the Cockscomb range, which includes Victoria Peak, at 1120m the second-highest mountain in Belize and a dramatic sight on a clear day. In 1888 the Goldsworthy Expedition made the first recorded successful attempt at the summit of Victoria Peak, though it's reasonably certain that the ancient Maya were first to make it to the top. Beneath the sharp ridges is a sweeping bowl, part of which was declared a **jaguar reserve** in 1986. It has since been expanded to cover an area of over four hundred square kilometres – the **Cockscomb Basin Wildlife Sanctuary**.

This area was inhabited in Maya times, and the ruins of **Kuchil Balam**, a Classic period ceremonial centre, still lie hidden in the forest. It was also exploited by the mahogany loggers; the names of their abandoned camps, such as Leave If You Can and Go to Hell, illustrate how they felt about life in the forest. In more recent times the residents of Quam Bank, a logging camp and Maya village, moved out of the Cockscomb when the reserve was established, relocating to the village of **Maya Centre** on the Southern Highway. The sanctuary is managed by the Belize Audubon Society, with some financial assistance from the WWF, the WCS and the Jaguar automobile company. There is an opportunity for a limited amount of **volunteer work** in the reserve, maintaining trails, working on displays in the visitor centre or even tracking howler monkeys; contact BAS in Belize City for information (see p.65).

Maya Centre: arrival and reserve information

All buses heading south from Dangriga pass **MAYA CENTRE** village (35min), from where a rough but reasonable 10km track leads to the sanctuary headquarters. You need to sign in and pay the reserve entrance fee (Bz$10) at the two-storey Craft Centre (daily 7.30am–4.30pm) at the road junction. It's run by the village women's group and there's information here about accommodation in the reserve and good, well-priced slate carvings and embroidery. The Mopan Maya families who live in Maya Centre are a few of the totally genuine proponents of the concept of "eco-tourism", and staying here is a perfect way to learn about the life of the forest and experience Maya culture. You can also spot lots of wildlife along the adjacent Cabbage Haul Creek – it's particularly good for bird-watching.

Although many tour operators will tell you that you can't get into the Jaguar Reserve without going on a tour, you can easily walk in from Maya Centre – it takes a couple of hours or so along the gentle uphill slope, and you can leave any excess luggage at Julio's Store (see p.240). For the best experience, though, don't go it alone – the people of Maya Centre know the reserve intimately, and are by far the best guides around. A guide for the **Victoria Peak Trail** (see box, p.241) will cost upwards of Bz$100 per day and the cost can be shared by groups; if you need help with carrying supplies you'll need to hire porters, too. Greg Sho is the most experienced guide in Maya Centre, and one of the best bush and river-kayak guides in the country, but he's usually booked up; ask in the village for Raul Balona or William Sho. William also has a **butterfly**

exhibit (Bz$10) across the creek from the Craft Centre, featuring a dozen species. Just beyond the Craft Centre, **Julio's Store** sells basic supplies and cold drinks (there's no restaurant or shop in the reserve) and it also has a **bar** and **Internet access**. Owner Julio Saqui runs Cockscomb Maya Tours (☎520-3042, ✉julio_saqui@hotmail.com) and can arrange **guides and transport** into the reserve, as can any of the accommodation places (see below). If you've come by bus and don't fancy the two hour walk up to the reserve, a taxi or truck to the headquarters will cost about Bz$35–40 for up to five people.

Maya Centre: accommodation and eating

Maya Centre village has several good-value **places to stay**, in simple rooms, all with electricity and some with private bathrooms. You can **camp** at any of these for Bz$10 per person, though not all of the places have tents for rent. Each serves good, inexpensive meals, and there's more accommodation at the reserve headquarters (see p.242). Contact *Nu'uk Che'il Cottages* (below) to arrange a "**homestay**" with a family in the village for Bz$40 per person, including dinner and breakfast.

On the highway just before the junction, *Tutzil Nah Cottages* (☎520-3044, ⓦwww.mayacenter.com; ❸) has neat, clean rooms with shared showers in a thatched wooden building. It's run by the Chun family, and the brothers, Gregorio, Julian and Ouscal are really excellent guides and can arrange amazing **kayak trips** along South Stann Creek, which flows through the reserve. The family also runs a store, so you can stock up on supplies.

Set in lovely gardens just behind the Craft Centre, and owned by Liberato and Yoli Saqui, *Mejen Tz'il Lodge* (☎520-3032, ✉lsaqui@btl.net; ❸) has rooms in a thatched cabaña with private bathroom, as well as dorm rooms in a large wooden cabin with a full-length balcony (Bz$16 per person). Yoli serves great **meals** and you can rent **tents** here for use on the Victoria Peak Trail.

Some 500m up the track to the reserve, the *Nu'uk Che'il Cottages* (☎520-3033 or 615-2091, ✉nuukcheil@btl.net; ❸-❹), run by Ernesto and Aurora Saqui, offer simple but delightful rooms with private hot-water bathroom, rooms with shared showers and dorm beds (Bz$16). The **restaurant**, serving Maya and Belizean food, is a great place to get a filling meal on your way to or from the reserve. Aurora is one of the Garcia sisters from San Antonio, Cayo (see p.177), and has developed a medicinal trail (Bz$5) in the forest next to the cottages. A real jack-of-all-trades, Aurora also makes **traditional herbal medicines**, for sale in the H'men Herbal Center and Gift Shop, arranges Maya cultural events, featuring marimba music and dancing, and gives talks on Maya history and healing methods.

The Jaguar Reserve

Heading through towering forest and fording a couple of fresh, clear streams, the road from Maya Centre crosses the Cabbage Hall Gap before reaching the sanctuary headquarters, in a cleared grassy area surrounded by beautiful tropical foliage. Technically, this is a **tropical moist forest**, with an annual rainfall of up to 300cm that feeds a complex network of wonderfully clear streams and rivers, most of which eventually run into the Swasey River and the South Stann Creek; the sanctuary also performs a vital role in watershed protection. The forest is home to a sizeable percentage of **Belize's plant and animal species**. Among the mammals are tapirs, otters, coatis, deer, anteaters, armadillos and, of course, jaguars, as well as all other cat species. Over three hundred species of bird have also been recorded, including the endangered scarlet macaw, the great curassow, the keel-billed toucan and the king vulture. It is particularly important as a refuge for the largest raptors, including the harpy eagle, the solitary eagle and the white hawk eagle. There's also an abundance of reptiles and amphibians, including the red-eyed tree frog, the boa constrictor and the deadly fer-de-lance snake (known as "yellow-jaw tommy-goff" in Belize). The forest itself is made up of a fantastic range of plant species, including orchids, giant tree ferns, air plants (epiphytes) and trees such as banak, cohune, mahogany and ceiba.

The Victoria Peak Trail

Viewed from the sea, the jagged granite peaks of the Cockscomb Range take on the appearance of a colossal recumbent head, whose sloping forehead, eyebrows, nose, mouth and chin have given this profile the epithet of "The Sleeping Maya", **Victoria Peak**, the highest point in the Cockscomb at 1120m (3675ft) and the second-highest mountain in Belize, is no giant by world standards, but the trek to the summit should not be undertaken lightly. You'll need to find a guide in Maya Centre (or contact Maya Guide Adventures; ⓦ www.mayaguide.bz; see p.221 for a very adventurous trip which also involves scaling some of the rock faces below the peak using climbing equipment and be able to carry supplies for three to five days. It's best to begin each day's walk at first light to make the most of the cool morning; **heat exhaustion** is a very real danger and you must carry plenty of water. (Creeks cross the trail at least every couple of kilometres and the water is generally safe to drink, though you may prefer to purify it first.) Simple **shelters**, built with help from Trekforce volunteers, mean it's not absolutely necessary to bring a tent, but if you do have one at least you'll have protection from biting insects. Currently there's no charge for use of the trail itself – you just pay the reserve entrance fee and back-country campsite charges – although there are plans to introduce a **user fee**.

The trail begins at the reserve headquarters, first following a relatively level abandoned logging road through secondary forest for 12km to the first rest point, where the **Sittee Branch River** provides a chance of a cooling swim. On the far bank is the first **campsite**, a sturdy thatched shelter with a kitchen and pit toilets. Beyond here the trail begins to climb steeply – and then descend equally steeply – in a series of energy-sapping undulations until you reach km 17, when you walk up and along a very steep ridge before descending to the second campsite, just before km 19. A **helipad** hacked out of the forest on a tiny patch of flat land at km 18 allows the first real views of the Peak. If you set off early and are fit you can reach this campsite in one day but be warned that the 7km from the first campsite are so rigorous that this section can take as much time as the first 12km. At the campsite you can hang hammocks in an open-sided wooden shelter and your shower is a small waterfall cascading over smooth rocks.

The final stretch to the peak is almost four hours of relentless uphill struggle, with much of the trail along a steep, rocky creek bed – too dangerous to attempt in heavy rain. As the ascent becomes ever more vertical and you rise above the forest canopy the views increase in splendour; closer to the ground, wildflowers cling to rock crevices. Just below the peak you have to haul yourself up through a narrow gully on a rope suspended from a tree. Above here the track along the final ridge passes first though an elfin **cloud-forest**, with gnarled tree limbs draped in filmy moss and tiny ferns, before reaching the summit itself. Low, waxy-leaved bushes and grass offer only scraps of shade and the Belize flag flutters in the breeze. Tethered to the rock which denotes the actual peak is an exercise book inside a screw-topped plastic pipe to record the names of previous successful climbers. Spread beneath you are the rocky peaks of a series of deep green, thickly forested ridges and valleys – on a very clear day you can see the Caribbean – and not a sign of humanity's impact on the environment. The trek down is almost as arduous as the ascent, but takes about an hour less to reach the campsite. With an early start next morning you can walk all the way out to the sanctuary headquarters in one day.

At the headquarters, the excellent **visitor centre** has a relief model of the Cockscomb Basin, displays on the area's ecology and maps and trail guides. You can also pick up a copy of *Cockscomb Basin Wildlife Sanctuary* (see "Books" in Contexts), a superb and detailed guide to the history, flora and fauna of the reserve; the shop also sells drinks and snacks. If you want to really enjoy the Cockscomb experience, you should **stay in the reserve** and listen to the amazing night-time jungle sounds. There's a range of **accommodation** here, aimed mainly at student groups and researchers, but anyone can stay. You can choose from a private furnished cabin (**⑨**), purpose-built wooden dorm rooms (Bz$34 per person) with shared showers and composting toilets, or simple but comfortable dorm beds in more basic "rustic" cabins (Bz$16 per person). There's also space for **camping** (Bz$10 per person, with tents available to rent). You'll have to bring your own food, but the cabins do have a kitchen with a gas stove. Camping at designated sites on the trails is Bz$5 per person and you'll need to get a permit from the reserve ranger at the headquarters.

Although the basin could be home to sixty of Belize's seven-hundred-strong **jaguar population**, your chances of seeing one are very slim. However, it's an ideal environment for plant-spotting, serious bird-watching or seeking out other ever-evasive wildlife, and the trail system in the Cockscomb is the best-developed in any of Belize's protected areas. Several well-maintained short trails lead through the forest to the riverbank or to exquisite waterfalls framed by jungle which you can follow with a self-guiding leaflet, giving you a taste of the forest's diversity. **Ben's Bluff Trail** is a strenuous but worthwhile 4km hike from the riverside to the top of a forested ridge – where there's a great view of the entire Cockscomb Basin – with a chance to cool off in a delightful rocky pool on the way back. **Inner tubes** (Bz$5) are available from the ranger's office; follow the marked trail upstream and float down South Stann Creek for a soothing, tranquil view of the forest. For a longer (or overnight) trip using inflatable kayaks check with the Chuns at *Tutzil Nah* in Maya Centre (see p.240). If you're suitably prepared you can climb **Victoria Peak** (see box, p.241); 3km along this trail a side trail leads to the Outlier Overlook, a challenging day-hike or you can camp overnight.

Kanantik Reef and Jungle Resort

About six kilometres south of Maya Centre a side road heads east to the sea, ending at **Kanantik Reef and Jungle Resort** (☎520-8048, in the US ☎1-800/965-9689, ⊛www.kanantik.com; US$365 per person per day, including meals, activities, tax and service charge; **⑨**), the latest addition to Belize's growing number of all-inclusive luxury resorts. The brainchild of Italian investors Roberto Fabbri and Gianfrancesco Moscatelli, the 25 very spacious, elevated octagonal cabañas with tall, conical thatched roofs are jungle and beach elegance par excellence. Constructed from the finest local materials, decorated with Guatemalan textiles, furnished with four-poster beds, surrounded by a wooden deck and set in tropical gardens, the resort accomplishes the fusion of rustic simplicity with style and sophistication better than anywhere else in the country. *Kanantik* means "to take care" in Mopan Mayan and you're certainly well taken care of here; all the cabañas are air-conditioned and the meals and service are simply superb, but thankfully without the fussy formality of some other luxury places. *Kanantik* is set in 300 acres of beach, jungle, pine forest and wetlands, just south of Sapodilla Lagoon, and the area abounds with wildlife, including jaguars and crocodiles, and there are two towers for bird-watching. The pool is just metres from the sea, and guests can choose from a variety of expertly guided activities, including scuba diving, snorkelling, sailing, canoeing, horse riding and expeditions to Maya sites and the Jaguar Reserve; the only extra charge is for fly-fishing. Most guests arrive by air on scheduled flights on Maya Island Air, landing at the resort's own paved airstrip, but you can be met at the Dangriga airstrip.

The Placencia peninsula

Sixteen kilometres south of Maya Centre, a good dirt road cuts east from the Southern Highway, heading through pine forest and banana plantations, eventually reaching the sea at the tiny settlement of **Riversdale**. This marks the start of the **Placencia peninsula**, a narrow, sandy finger of land separating the Caribbean and Placencia Lagoon. The road then curves down 26km to **Placencia**, a small, laid-back fishing village light years from the hassle of Belize City, and now catering to an increasing number of tourists. The road first passes through a beautiful stretch of coast called **Maya Beach**, halfway along the peninsula, where there are several restaurants and a range of accommodation.

Travelling south down the peninsula you'll pass around twenty resorts and hotels, most of them owned and operated by expatriate North Americans. Accommodation is usually in cabins with private bathrooms and electricity, and Internet access may be available; although they're pricey, most places will give *Rough Guide* readers worthwhile discounts. Meals, if not included in the tariff, come to around US$35 per day, and hotel tax and a ten percent service charge may be added to bills. In addition to the pleasures of a sandy Caribbean beach just a few steps away, most of the resorts also have access to Placencia Lagoon, and can arrange fishing and diving trips offshore, as well as tours inland to the Jaguar Reserve and several Maya sites. Many will have bikes and kayaks for guests and it's a relatively easy paddle to False Caye. Below here, the Garífuna village of **Seine Bight** has several more upmarket places to stay nearby; the majority of the peninsula's budget accommodation is in Placencia village itself. The whole route is served by two or three daily **buses** from Dangriga (see box on p.228), hitching is relatively easy and the sand road is ideal for cycling.

Maya Beach practicalities

The **hotels** here are listed in the order you approach them from the north, and all are right by the road. All the places listed below have mains electricity; more details can be found on Maya Beach's own **website**, ⓦ www.gotobelize.com. Some of them have self-catering kitchens (grocery vans make regular trips down the peninsula and hotel owners know the times and days they call) and there are a few **restaurants** within walking distance. A **taxi** to or from Placencia village costs around Bz$25–30. The *Hungry Gecko*, run by a friendly Honduran family (who also have a store below the restaurant), serves tasty Belizean breakfasts and Central American snacks, plus soups, sandwiches, burgers and seafood at great prices. *Mangos* is a thatched bar and restaurant on the beach, serving burgers and seafood, with a daily special. Imported drinks are expensive but local rum is cheap, especially during the 6–7pm happy hour. You can also enjoy moonlight volleyball and occasional live music – call *Mangos* on ⓣ 532-8022 to check what's happening (open 11am–midnight; closed Mon).

Hotels and cabañas

Green Parrot Beach Houses 13km north of Placencia village ⓣ 523-2488, ⓦ www.greenparrot-belize.com. Six spacious wooden houses (sleeping up to five) raised on stilts and two

secluded thatched wooden "honeymoon" cabins on the beach. Each house has a living room, a loft bedroom with a queen-size and a single bed, a superb kitchen and a deck with hammocks. There's also an excellent restaurant, and the rates include transport from Placencia airstrip, continental breakfast and use of kayaks. ❾

Maya Breeze Inn Immediately south of the *Green Parrot* ☎523-8012, in the US ☎1-888/458-8581, ⓦwww.mayabreezeinn.com. Beautifully furnished and decorated wooden cabins and suites on a gorgeous beach, plus four comfortable hotel rooms back from the road. All the accommodation has a/c, private tiled bathrooms, fridge and balcony or deck; suites have a full kitchen. Owners Buddy and Tressa Olson have put a lot of thought into creating and maintaining their inn, and it shows in the relaxed, friendly service and the fact that everything works. Rates include continental breakfast (full meals available in the *Monarch Café*, open for breakfast and lunch), transfer from the airstrip, bikes and kayaks; no extra credit card fee. ❼–❽

Barnacle Bill's Beach Bungalows 400m south of *Maya Breeze* ☎523-8010, ⓔtaylors@btl.net. Two large, very well-equipped wooden houses on stilts on a beautiful sandy beach, run by Bill and Adriane Taylor. Each house has a double bedroom, bathroom with tub, living room with sofa bed and kitchen with a microwave, stove, coffeemaker, fridge and even a spice and condiment package;

call ahead with a list and they'll even stock up with groceries; kayaks and bikes for guests. ❽

Singing Sands Inn 200m south of *Barnacle Bill's* ☎523-8017, ⓦwww.singingsands.com. Six lovely, ground-level wood-and-thatch cabins, each with a porch, complete with hammock and rocking chair, and a tiny garden in front; there are less expensive rooms overlooking the shady, orchid-filled garden. There's a good restaurant, especially for vegetarians, the only pool in Maya Beach and kayaks, canoes and bikes for guests. Owner Marti Cottrell offers massage service and also has a furnished apartment for longer rentals. ❽

Maya Playa 250m south of *Singing Sands* ☎523-8020, ⓦwww.geocities.com/mayaplaya. Three palmetto-and-thatch A-frame cabañas in a beautiful beachfront location. The main bedroom is upstairs, with a queen-sized bed and a small balcony; on the ground floor the living room has a couch and an extra bed and the spacious semi-circular bathroom has jungle plants growing up the wall. Friendly owner Chuck Meares has built a very tall *palapa* on the beach for his kitchen and dining room, where guests are welcome to cook and eat their meals. There's a fridge in each cabaña, plus free bikes, kayaks, coffee and fruit for guests. ❻

Seine Bight to Placencia

Three kilometres beyond Maya Beach the Garífuna village of **SEINE BIGHT** has several resorts and hotels, some of which look out of place alongside the often dilapidated shacks in the village. That said, the main road has now been paved, and increased prosperity means more people can now afford to build better homes. Reputed to have been founded by privateers in 1629, Seine Bight was possibly given its present name by French fishermen deported from Newfoundland after Britain gained control of Canada. The present inhabitants, numbering about 750, are descendants of the Garífuna settlers who arrived in Seine Bight around 1869.

The village is certainly worth a visit even if you're not staying: Seine Bight has its own **Garífuna band**, Lumalali Beidi ("Voice of the Bight"), who sing and dance accompanied by powerful, evocative drumbeats; the band also teach drumming. The *White Sand Tiki Bar*, a distinctive, two-storey bamboo-and-thatch building on the beach near the centre of the village, plays Garífuna music and Western rock, and often has live music at weekends, when the management runs a shuttle service from Placencia village. You could also check out Lola Delgado's superb (and affordable) oil and acrylic paintings of village life at *Lola's Art Gallery and Cat's Claw Bar and Café*, further south behind the soccer field. Lola is also a great entertainer and a wonderful cook. She serves superb Creole and Garífuna meals most days, and dinners are often followed by **music and drumming** – call ☎601-1913 to check if she's cooking that evening. Lola can also arrange a taxi to pick you up in Placencia.

Resorts from Seine Bight to Placencia

Beyond Seine Bight, another series of resorts offers upscale **accommodation**; the list below is set in the order you approach them from the north. All the places listed also have **restaurants** that are among the best in the country; you'll usually need to book for dinner.

The Inn at Robert's Grove Just over 1km south of Seine Bight ☎ 523-3565, in the US ☎ 1-800/565-9757, ⓦ www.robertsgrove.com. A large luxury resort with spacious, well-designed, a/c rooms and suites, all with cable TV and private balcony overlooking the beach, the sea and a pool. The rooms are decorated with Mexican and Guatemalan art and textiles and there are two pools, two rooftop Jacuzzis and a spa; owners Robert and Risa Frackman ensure that everything here runs smoothly. The *Seaside Restaurant*, with tables on a wooden deck on the beach, serves superb international and local dishes, and has the only temperature-controlled wine cellar in Belize; on the lagoon side *Habaneros Mexican Café* serves Mexican-influenced dishes under a thatched roof. There are plenty of activities on offer, including diving from the PADI dive centre, snorkelling, fishing, sailing, kayaking and canoeing (from a fleet of boats in the marina), windsurfing, tennis courts and a gym; *Robert's Grove* also has three private cayes for guests to enjoy – only Ranguana Caye (see p.253) has accommodation at the moment. Rooms from US$170 to US$190 double; suites from US$225 to US$350. ❾

Miller's Landing 300m south of *Robert's Grove* ☎ 523-3010, ⓦ www.millerslanding.net. Small, secluded resort set among the original vegetation just off a quiet beach, with the added attraction of a fresh water pool. Very laid-back and a bit more rustic than many of the places here, with comfortable rooms in wooden cabins, all with private bathrooms, ceiling fans and a porch; also two "economy" rooms, with a shared bathroom. There's a good bar, and restaurant and owners Gary and Ann Miller are famous for their pizza. Kayaks and bikes for guests. ❺–❼

Rum Point Inn Just north of the airstrip, 4km from Placencia ☎ 523-3239, ⓦ www.rumpoint.com. The giant, mushroom-shaped, whitewashed cabañas, with windows cut into the roof and plants growing inside, are unique, but they're also spacious, cool and very comfortable; the enormous suites have the biggest bathrooms in the country. There's also a pool, to help with dive instruction, and the *Auriga II*, with a highly professional crew, is an excellent dive boat. Massage is available, and the library, with an emphasis on archeology, science and natural history, is the best of any resort in the country. Non-guests need to book for meals. US$165–190 double. ❾

Mariposa Beach Suites 300m south of the airstrip ☎ 523-4069, ⓦ www.mariposabelize.com. Set on a beautiful beach, these gorgeous suites, with tiled floors and a full kitchen, are the best value on the peninsula in their price range. Each has comfortable queen-size beds, a patio under the arches outside and a private *palapa* on the beach. Owners Peter and Marcia Fox pay great attention to detail; the fridges are stocked with basic food and drinks. There are also two brightly painted wooden cottages in the grounds, simpler and less expensive than the suites, but just as comfortable. *Mariposa* is Spanish for butterfly – an appropriate name, as you'll see lots as you wander the paths in the tranquil gardens. ❽

Kitty's Place Just south of *Mariposa* ☎ 523-3237, ⓦ www.kittysplace.com. Conveniently near the village and one of the nicest options in this area, with a variety of accommodation including apartments, beach cabañas, garden rooms and rooms in a couple of colonial-style houses on the beach. The atmosphere is sublime, the grounds and views are unbeatable and every room is really comfortable and beautifully decorated. All rooms have a verandah with hammocks and most have a fridge, a coffeemaker and feature Belizean art. Kitty also rents out several houses and apartments with fully equipped kitchens at US$300–800 per week. There's a lovely new pool in front of the beach bar (Friday evening happy hour), massage is available and the restaurant, upstairs in the main building, serves delicious Belizean and international food. *Kitty's* also offers trips out to French Louie Caye (see p.253). ❾

Turtle Inn 1km north of the village ☎ 523-3244 or 824-4912, ⓦ www.turtleinn.com. Francis Ford Coppola's resort in the Caribbean, set on a gorgeous, palm-lined beach, and as sumptuous and luxurious as his *Blancaneaux Lodge* in Cayo (see p.180). The thatched seafront "cottages" (US$300 double) have lots of varnished wood and Indonesian art and furnishings, plus fabulous tiled bathrooms and a big, screened deck. Other cottages in the garden are just as comfortable and a trifle less expensive, and a two-bedroom, two-bathroom beachfront villa with spacious sitting room is US$400. The atmosphere here is somehow more relaxed than *Blancaneaux*, and there's also a spa to soothe you further, as well as a pool, a dive shop and free kayaks and bikes for guests. ❾

Placencia village

Perched on the tip of the peninsula, shaded by palm trees and cooled by the sea breeze, **PLACENCIA** is a welcome stop after the bus ride from Belize City or Dangriga. It is also one of the few places in mainland Belize with real beaches (making you feel as though you're already on one of the cayes), and this, together with the abundant, inexpensive accommodation, makes it a great place to relax. The villagers enjoy relaxing as much as the visitors – as you'll find out if you're here for the **Lobsterfest**, celebrated over a fun-filled weekend in late June, shortly after the opening of the lobster season. If you're seeking something a little higher on the cultural scale then try to visit during the **Sidewalk Arts Festival**, held around Valentine's Day, when you can meet some of the artists and musicians who create Belize's vibrant arts scene. Placencia's one drawback might be that its remote location and distance from the reef put many of the tours out of the reach of travellers on a low budget, though more options are becoming available.

The easiest way to reach Placencia is on one of the regular Maya Island or Tropic Air **flights** from the international or municipal airports (about 45min). Much cheaper are the direct Southern Transport **buses from Dangriga**, which currently leave at 10am, noon and 5pm. You can also hop over easily on the regular *Hokey Pokey* **boat service** from **Independence/Mango Creek**, the small town just across the lagoon, where residents go to buy supplies and the older children go to school. For full transport details in Independence, see box on p.255.

Arrival and orientation

Buses from Dangriga end up at the beachfront gas station, right at the end of the peninsula (they return at 6am and 1.30pm – but check locally for times of next day's departures; Bz$10; 2hr). If you're looking for budget rooms you should get off the bus when you see the sign for the *Seaspray Hotel*, about halfway through the village, on the left-hand side of the road. Head for "The Sidewalk", a concrete walkway that winds through the village and the palms like an elongated garden path, and you'll be at the centre of a cluster of hotels and restaurants. If you're **flying** in there's usually a taxi (Bz$10) waiting to take you the 3km to the village. If not, it's only a three-minute walk south to *Kitty's* where you can call a **taxi** (Kingfisher ☏601-1903; Percy's ☏523-3202 or 614-7831; or Noel's ☏600-6047). **Flights** to Dangriga (20min) are Bz$61, and Bz$130 to Belize Municipal (45min).

The *Hokey Pokey* **ferry** to and from Independence/Mango Creek (Bz$10), a twenty-minute skiff ride across the lagoon, usually arrives at the main dock, by the gas station, though you can also get on or off at the Kingfisher Dock, on the lagoon side. Independence is on the Dangriga–Punta Gorda bus route and the ferry meets most buses arriving in Independence; see box on p.255 for details of onward travel from Independence. The *Hokey Pokey* leaves Placencia for Independence at 6.30am, 10am, 4pm and 5pm – and sometimes even more frequently.

The *Gulf Cruza*, a large, fast, covered skiff, leaves Placencia for **Puerto Cortés**, Honduras, every Friday at 9.30am (US$50; under 4hr; ☏523-4045 or 202-4506), going first across the lagoon to Big Creek, where passengers often face a lengthy delay to clear immigration: the onward journey from Big Creek to Puerto Cortés is only 2hr 30min. The *Cruza* returns to Placencia from Cortés on Monday around 2pm. If you're **arriving by boat**, walk along the main dock and you're at the end of the road; the Tourism Center is just ahead and The Sidewalk will be to your right.

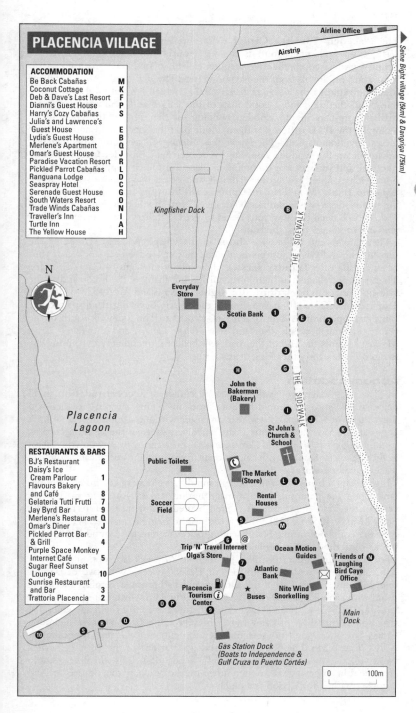

PLACENCIA VILLAGE

ACCOMMODATION

Be Back Cabañas	M
Coconut Cottage	K
Deb & Dave's Last Resort	F
Dianni's Guest House	P
Harry's Cozy Cabañas	S
Julia's and Lawrence's Guest House	E
Lydia's Guest House	B
Merlene's Apartment	Q
Omar's Guest House	J
Paradise Vacation Resort	R
Pickled Parrot Cabañas	L
Ranguana Lodge	D
Seaspray Hotel	C
Serenade Guest House	G
South Waters Resort	O
Trade Winds Cabañas	N
Traveller's Inn	I
Turtle Inn	A
The Yellow House	H

RESTAURANTS & BARS

BJ's Restaurant	6
Daisy's Ice Cream Parlour	1
Flavours Bakery and Café	8
Gelateria Tutti Frutti	7
Jay Byrd Bar	9
Merlene's Restaurant	Q
Omar's Diner	J
Pickled Parrot Bar & Grill	4
Purple Space Monkey Internet Café	5
Sugar Reef Sunset Lounge	10
Sunrise Restaurant and Bar	3
Trattoria Placencia	2

Airline Office

Airstrip

Seine Bight village (5km) & Dangriga (75km)

Kingfisher Dock

Placencia Lagoon

Everyday Store

Scotia Bank

John the Bakerman (Bakery)

St John's Church & School

THE SIDEWALK

THE SIDEWALK

Public Toilets

The Market (Store)

Soccer Field

Rental Houses

Trip 'N' Travel Internet
Olga's Store

Placencia Tourism Center

Buses

Ocean Motion Guides

Atlantic Bank

Nite Wind Snorkelling

Friends of Laughing Bird Caye Office

Main Dock

*Gas Station Dock
(Boats to Independence &
Gulf Cruza to Puerto Cortés)*

0   100m

Information

The **Placencia Tourism Center** (Mon–Fri 9–11.30am & 1–5pm; ☏523-4045, Ⓦwww.placencia.com) is the best tourist information office in the country, with a comprehensive website; call in to find out what's going on locally and call hotels from the payphone here. The staff produce the excellent **local newspaper** the *Placencia Breeze* (Bz$1), which has full local listings and transport schedules, and a good map of the village and peninsula. The **post office** is upstairs in the wooden building on the right at the end of The Sidewalk; the **BTL office** is at the roadside near the soccer field, and there are several payphones around. The *Purple Space Monkey Village*, in the large thatched restaurant on the roadside opposite the soccer field, provides **Internet connection**, and you can also go online in Placencia Office Supply, 150m further on, which is faster, has more terminals and offers many more services. The **Atlantic Bank** (Mon–Fri 8am–2pm), across from the main dock by the filling station, deals swiftly with cash advances. Note: if you're leaving on the *Gulf Cruza* you'll need to show your ticket to get US dollars (to exchange for *lempiras* in Honduras) from the bank.

There are several self-service **shops** in the village; Wallen's Market, by the soccer field, and Olga's, just before the gas station, are the best-stocked. If your hotel doesn't offer **laundry service**, then follow the signs to Cara's Laundry. There's no travel agent as such in the village, but many of the hotels and all the tour operators can book **domestic flights**. Maya Island Air (☏523-3475) and Tropic Air (☏523-3410) have offices at the airstrip. Several **gift shops** provide souvenir opportunities; The Beach Bazaar, next to The Sidewalk south of the centre, has the best selection and sells *Rough Guides*, and the *Purple Space Monkey*, towards the end of the road, sells brilliant oil and acrylic paintings by Ernesto Garica and other local artists.

Accommodation

In Placencia village proper there's a wide choice of **accommodation** in all price ranges, and you should have no problem finding a room provided you don't arrive at Christmas, New Year or Easter without a booking. Possibilities begin at The Sidewalk, famous as the narrowest street in the world according to the *Guinness Book of World Records*, and as you wend your way down it seems as though every family is offering **rooms**. Except where specifically noted all places have **hot water**.

If you want a **house to rent**, bear in mind that plenty of the hotels opposite (and along the peninsula) also manage houses and self-catering apartments. One of the best-value places is offered by Ted Berlin (just before the *Purple Space Monkey*; ☏523-3172), who, in addition to being a qualified acupuncturist, has a couple of simple but charming places to rent for around Bz$250 per week – and they do get booked up quickly.

For something larger, try *Yoli's*, just behind *Merlene's* (see opposite; ☏523-3552, Ⓔyolandaestephan@hotmail.com; Bz$550/week), with two bedrooms, one with queen-size bed, a full kitchen and bathroom, a comfortable living room with cable TV and DVD player and a patio. Also worth trying are *Be Back Cabins* (☏523-3143; Bz$350/week), just before the end of the road, which has two houses on stilts with hot-water showers and a basic kitchen, including fridge. For other good house rentals see the entries for *Lydia's* (opposite) or *Kitty's Place*, p.245. The best-value **rental apartment** in the village is *Colibrí House* (☏523-4046, Ⓔcatalina@btl.net), a beautiful, fully furnished studio apartment in an octagonal wooden house on the beach, with a double bed and a single sofa bed for US$55 per night.

Inexpensive

Deb & Dave's Last Resort On the road in the village centre (the bus will stop outside) ☎ 523-3207, ©debanddave@btl.net. The nicest budget place in the village, with very comfortable wooden rooms with clean, shared hot-water bathrooms, in lovely gardens. You can rent kayaks here and Dave Vernon, who runs Toadal Adventure (see p.252), is a superb tour guide. ❸

Julia's and Lawrence's Guest House In the centre of the village, just south of the *Seaspray* (see below) ☎ 503-3478. Simple, comfortable rooms in a wooden building near The Sidewalk, and newer cabins nearer the beach, all with private bath and a porch; also a small furnished house for rent, Bz$130 per night. ❹

Lydia's Guest House Near the north end of The Sidewalk ☎ 523-3117, ©lydias@btl.net. Quiet, clean, secure and affordable rooms in a great location, all sharing immaculate bathrooms, in two wooden houses, run by the very friendly Lydia Villanueva. There's a fridge for guests' use, and Lydia will cook breakfast on request. Also several good beach houses and kayaks for rent. ❸

Omar's Guest House Opposite the school, on the beach side of The Sidewalk ☎ 503-3033. Bargain rooms, some with private shower (shared ones have hot water), upstairs in a wooden building above a budget restaurant. Enjoy the passing scene from a hammock on the deck. ❸

Paradise Vacation Hotel On the south beach, 250m west of the south dock (turn right at the gas station) ☎ 523-3179, ©pvh@btl.net. Very good-value rooms, most with private hot-water shower and some with a/c (though these have no windows), in a two-storey wooden building with a spacious upstairs deck overlooking the sea. There's a kitchenette with fridge, microwave and coffeemaker; no single rates. ❸–❹

Seaspray Hotel On the beach in the centre of the village ☎ & ⒻⒻ 523-3148, ⓦwww.seasprayhotel.com. A popular, well-run hotel with a range of new or recently renovated accommodation, from budget rooms to a private beach cabin, all with private hot-water bathroom and some with refrigerator, kitchenette, TV and balcony. Owners Jodie and Norman Leslie can arrange tours and give reliable information, and there's *De Tatch* restaurant on the beach for good-value meals and Internet access. ❹–❻

Traveller's Inn On The Sidewalk, just south of the centre ☎ 523-3190. Five basic rooms – the cheapest in the village – with shared bath and a communal porch for relaxing, under Lucille Villanueva's house, who also has some comfortable rooms with private bath in a separate building. ❸–❹

The Yellow House In the centre of the village, between the road and the beach ☎ 523-3481, ©ctbze@btl.net. Bargain rooms with comfortable beds and private, hot-water bathrooms (two also have kitchenette) in a bright yellow wooden building with balcony and hammocks. French spoken. ❸–❹

Mid-range to expensive

Coconut Cottage On the beach south of the centre ☎ 523-3234, ©kwplacencia@yahoo.com. A comfortable, well-decorated and deservedly popular wooden cabin on the beach, with full kitchen; very popular, so you'll need to book in advance. ❻

Dianni's Guest House On the south beach ☎ 523-3159, ©diannis@btl.net. A new and very comfortable two-storey hotel with clean, well-furnished rooms, all with private bathroom, fridge and coffeemaker. The wide, breezy verandahs with hammocks are great for relaxing and you can borrow a cooler to take to the beach. Internet access, laundry service and kayaks and bikes for rent. ❺

Harry's Cozy Cabañas 300m west from the south dock, turn right at the gas station ☎ 523-3155, ©harbaks@yahoo.com. Spacious wooden cabins on stilts with a screened porch on a quiet little beach. Each cabin has a double and single bed, a fridge and coffeemaker and one has a small kitchen. The plant-filled gardens are an iguana sanctuary. According to Harry, relaxing with a Belikin under his "Tree of Knowledge" actually does impart wisdom. Usually a three-night minimum stay. ❻

Merlene's Apartment 225m west from the south dock ☎ 503-3153, ©yolandaestephan@hotmail.com. One of the best studio apartments in the village, with a double and a single bed and a kitchen with a huge fridge and stove. The balcony running along the front allows you to watch the sunrise over Placencia Caye. The restaurant serves the best home-cooking in Placencia, and rates include breakfast. ❻

Pickled Parrot Cabañas Signposted just past the market, towards the south end of the village ☎ 604-0278, ⓦwww.pickledparrotbelize.com. Two varnished wooden cabins with double beds, private bath, fridge and coffeemaker, and a deck with lounge chairs and a hammock, set in luxuriant tropical gardens. Run by Canadian Wende Bryan, the bar and restaurant here (see review, p.250) is a great place to exchange information and arrange trips. There's no credit card surcharge and you'll get a discount if you book using the *Rough Guide*. ❻

Ranguana Lodge On the beach in the centre of the village ☎ 523-3112, ⓦwww.ranguanabelize.com. Five beautiful white cabañas with porches and hammocks, with optional a/c; three are on the beach, and the other two also have sea views. Inside are comfortable beds, bathrooms with tubs, hardwood floors and fittings, a big fridge and a coffeemaker, and there are *palapas* on the beach for relaxing. ⑥

Serenade Guest House On The Sidewalk just south of the centre ☎523-3380, ⓦwww.belize-cayes.com. Good-value rooms with private bath and a/c in a large, white-painted concrete building. There's also a good restaurant upstairs. This is where you book for Frank's Caye (see p.269). ⑥

South Waters Resort On the south beach, 100m west of the south dock ☎523-3308, ⓔsouthwatersresort@yahoo.com. Another spacious and comfortable new hotel, with pastel-painted cement cabañas on the beach, each with fridge, microwave and coffeemaker, and a private patio in front. There are also a/c suites with full kitchen and living room in a two-storey building with wide verandahs and great views. ⑦ & ⑨

Trade Winds Cabañas On the south point ☎523-3122, ⓔtrdewndpla@btl.net. Eight brightly painted cabins (the biggest has a kitchenette and king-size bed; ⑦) and three bargain rooms, all with private bath, fridge, coffeemaker and deck with hammocks, on the largest and sandiest beach in the village. Run by Janice Leslie, Placencia's former postmistress and owner of the *J-Byrd Bar*, who's a mine of local knowledge. ④–⑥

Eating and drinking

There are plenty of good **restaurants** in Placencia; however, even more so than elsewhere in Belize, places here change management fast, so it's always worth asking a resident's advice. There are also a number of good restaurants at the resorts along the peninsula, and it may be worth sharing a cab to try somewhere different. Most places close early; you'll certainly have a better choice if you're at the table by 8pm. Fresh **bread** is available from John the Bakerman, just north of the market, and from a number of local women who bake jonny cakes, Creole bread and buns.

BJ's Restaurant By the road junction just past the soccer field. Some of the best-value Belizean food in the village at genuine Belizean prices, with friendly service in clean surroundings.

Daisy's Ice Cream Parlour Set back from The Sidewalk, just south of the *Seaspray* (see p.249). Long-established and deservedly popular place for ice cream, cakes and snacks, and also serving complete Belizean meals.

Flavours Bakery and Café Near the end of the road, across from the gas station. A great range of filling sandwiches, subs, cakes, pastries, salads and full meals, with daily specials. All-day breakfast, with an ideal "early bird" special, and packed lunches for trips. Eat indoors or on the upstairs verandah. Bike rental available. Open Mon & Wed–Sun 6.30am–5.30pm.

Gelateria Tutti Frutti Near the end of the road. Genuine Italian ice cream, and quite simply the best in Belize; it's available in literally dozens of flavours and you should try at least one every day you're in Placencia.

Merlene's Restaurant Beneath *Merlene's Apartment* (see p.249) ☎503-5013. Great for breakfast, serving good coffee and fantastic homemade bread and fry-jacks. Lunch and dinner are equally good, especially for fish, but the place is small so you may have to book. Merlene is exuberantly friendly and is renowned for her cakes – if you have a birthday to celebrate, ask if she can make one for you.

Omar's Fast Foods On The Sidewalk, just south of the centre. Really inexpensive and sometimes even fast, serving rice and beans, great, filling burritos, seafood and daily specials.

Pickled Parrot Bar & Grill At the *Pickled Parrot Cabañas* (see p.249). Very friendly place under a big thatched roof. Consistently the best restaurant in the village and deservedly popular, serving fresh seafood, great pizza, pastas and salads with a daily special. The bar has wonderful tropical blender drinks and a 5–6pm happy hour. Open Mon–Sat 10am–10pm, Sunday 5pm–10pm.

Purple Space Monkey Village Opposite the soccer field. An Internet café with well-connected computers, serving good coffees and great American/Belizean-style breakfast, lunch and dinner under a huge thatched roof. Also a paperback exchange. Opens early and closes late.

Sunrise Restaurant and Bar On The Sidewalk in the centre of the village. Another really good-value Belizean restaurant, where you can enjoy sea views as you tuck into a filling breakfast or generous portions of rice and beans, seafood, burgers or chow mein under a thatched roof. Sometimes has Garífuna drumming at weekends.

Trattoria Placencia On the beach near the centre of the village. Authentic, good-value Italian meals, including "very nice" salads and a range of handmade pasta accompanied by good wines, in a very relaxed atmosphere. Open Mon–Sat from 5pm.

Nightlife

Evenings in Placencia are as relaxed as the days and, although the restaurants do serve drinks, there are a few places with more of a lively **bar** atmosphere – ideal for drinking rum and watching the sun set – and an increasing number have **live music** to enhance the party mood. Some places in the village and many resorts along the peninsula have regular evening entertainment – happy hours, bar games, music and drumming, a special dinner or barbecue for example; check the *Placencia Breeze* for what's on where. In the village, the *J-Byrd Bar* (with adjacent gift shop), by the south dock and open all day, is a great place to meet local characters, and often has live music at weekends. Much the same can be said for the *Sunrise Bar*, on The Sidewalk. Turn right at the sign by the soccer field for the British-run *Sugar Reef Sunset Lounge* (closed Tues), featuring a daily **happy hour**, bar games, karaoke, a regular DJ and occasional bands.

Around Placencia, offshore and inland

Trips from Placencia can be tailor-made to your preference and perhaps your pocket, and you can arrange anything from a day on the water to a week of camping, fishing, snorkelling or sailing on or around any number of idyllic islands; any of the tour operators listed below can arrange these trips. Diving or snorkelling at the cayes or along the reef is excellent, with shallow **fringing and patch reefs**, and some fantastic **wall diving**. You can visit several virtually pristine protected areas, including **Laughing Bird Caye National Park** and **Gladden Spit and Silk Cayes Marine Reserve**. **Placencia lagoon** is ideal for exploring in a **canoe or kayak**, available from several places in the village; you may even spot a manatee, though it's more likely to be a series of ripples as the shy giant swims powerfully for cover. The reefs and shallows off Placencia are rich **fishing** grounds too, and the village is home to a number of renowned fly-fishing guides.

It's also worth **heading inland** from Placencia – up the thickly forested banks of the **Monkey River** or to the **Jaguar Reserve** (see pp.254 & 240, respectively). Incidentally, although many tour operators offer day-trips to the Jaguar Reserve (around Bz$135), it's quite feasible to do the trip independently by bus, leaving Placencia in the early morning and returning on the afternoon bus from Dangriga as it passes Maya Centre.

If you just want to explore the peninsula by **bike** you can rent one from *Dianni's Guest House* or *Flavours Café* for around Bz$25–35 per day. Finally, after sampling all the activity you might feel in need of some pampering: the Shangri-La Spa, behind The Moorings dock on the south beach (daily 9am–6pm), offers the most complete **spa and massage** service in the village, with over a hundred treatments, employing Asian, European and American techniques.

Diving and snorkelling

The Barrier Reef is wider here than in the north of Belize, and it's not as continuous, breaking into several smaller reefs and cayes, creating even more coral canyons and drop-offs. But it lies about 30km offshore, and this distance means that snorkelling and diving trips are more expensive here than at many other places. There are several smaller mangrove islands and coral heads closer to the shore, however, and you can still see a lot of fish and some coral by snorkelling just offshore. For detailed information on the reefs and all aspects of the ecology of the marine protected areas off Placencia, visit the **Friends of Nature** office, at the south end of The Sidewalk (☎523-3377). FoN co-manages these reserves, and you can support their efforts by becoming a Friend or buying a beautiful and eye-catching whale shark T-shirt.

Day-trips to the cayes (including visits to see **whale sharks** in season) are offered by several operators (the best are listed below), and the choice of dive sites is so wide that during a month-long stay you need never visit the same site twice. PADI open-water certification costs around Bz$700, and a two-tank dive trip is around Bz$150. Snorkelling trips cost from Bz$65 to Bz$85, depending on the location; usually this includes lunch and sometimes snorkelling equipment. If not, you can rent snorkels, masks and fins for around Bz$10. Several resorts along the peninsula have their own **dive shops**; in the village go to Vance Cabral at Advanced Diving, with an office on The Sidewalk (☎523-4037, ⓦwww.beautifulbelize.com), or Brian Young at the Sea Horse Dive Shop on the south dock (☎523-3166, ⓦwww.belizescuba.com) for the best diving instruction, excursions and equipment rental. For **snorkelling** or **manatee-watching** check with Calbert Gardiner at Nite Wind Guides (☎523-3847) or Bernard Leslie at Ocean Motion Guides (☎523-3363, ⓦwww.ocean-motion.com), both at the southern end of The Sidewalk.

Sailing, kayaking and fishing

Sailing among the reefs and cayes off Placencia is, if anything, even more beautiful than from the northern cayes, and the village is a base for top-of-the-range catamaran charter companies TMM and The Moorings; if you'd like (and can afford) a week's sailing you'll usually need to book well in advance; see p.12 in Basics for contact details and prices. Some of the resorts along the peninsula have Hobie Cats (small catamarans) for rent, but other than this the only regular one-day **sailing trip** is aboard the *Next Wave*, a 50ft catamaran operated by British couple Rory and Michelle McDougall. A day-trip to the cayes including buffet lunch and open bar is US$80, while a sunset cruise with drinks and snacks is US$45; to book call ☎523-3391 or 610-5592, or visit ⓦwww.nextwave.com.

The *Talisman*, a wonderful and very comfortable 52ft ketch, is also sometimes available for a day's sailing, but it's often booked for overnight trips. At US$120 per person for a day-trip it's fairly expensive, but this includes snorkelling, kayaking, snacks, a full lunch and an open bar; there are also three staterooms for overnight trips. To book the *Talisman* contact Belize Sailing Charters (☎523-3138, ⓦwww.belize-sailing-charters.com), who can also arrange trips on a number of other sailboats, including catamarans and trimarans, from US$300 to over US$1000 per night. You could also contact Raggamuffin Tours on Caye Caulker (see p.133), who arrange weekly overnight sailing trips from there to Placencia; they may have space aboard for the return journey.

Several places rent **canoes** and sit-on-top kayaks for around Bz$35 per day, and some resorts have free ones for guests; in the village try *Sugar Reef Sunset Lounge* (see "Nightlife", p.251). For top-range double **sea kayaks** (Bz$75 per day) and tours (Bz$120 per person) contact Dave Vernon, who runs Toadal Adventure (☎523-3207, ⓦwww.toadaladventure.com). Dave is one of the best tour guides in Belize, and in addition to his natural history trips he's also a superb river and sea-kayak guide.

World-class **fishing** draws anglers eager to test their skill by catching the permit, tarpon, snook or bonefish which abound in the seas around Placencia, and a day out with a boat and a guide will set you back around US$300; any of the dive or snorkel places can arrange this but one of the best fly-fishing guides around is Earl Godfrey of Southern Guides (☎523-3433, Ⓔlgodfrey @direcway.com), and you should also check with Bernard Leslie, at Ocean Motion Guides (see "Diving and snorkelling", p.251). Fishing flies and tackle are available from a specialist shop in the *Purple Space Monkey Village*.

Laughing Bird Caye

The Bugle Cayes, with a good section of reef, are only a few kilometres away from Placencia, though most operators prefer to take you to uninhabited **Laughing Bird Caye National Park** (Bz$10), about 18km away. The caye itself (named for the laughing gull) is tiny, under 1.5 acres, and the gulls themselves no longer nest here, but the national park protects over 10,000 acres of the surrounding sea as a "no take zone", and it is a World Heritage site. The caye sits on top of a "faro", a rhomboid-shaped limestone reef rising steeply from the sea bed, with an outer rim enclosing a lagoon, and thus similar to (though not the same as) an atoll. There's a ranger station on the caye, and many tours stop for lunch on the beach here, where there's a picnic shelter, tables and a barbecue pit. The northern tip of the caye protects the native vegetation and nesting birds and turtles, and is off-limits to visitors.

Gladden Spit and Silk Cayes Marine Reserve

Twenty kilometres beyond Laughing Bird Caye, the exquisitely beautiful Silk Cayes form part of the **Gladden Spit and Silk Cayes Marine Reserve** (Bz$10), a much larger protected area, designated to safeguard the seasonal visitation of the enormous yet graceful **whale shark**. These migratory fish, found throughout tropical waters, are attracted to Gladden Spit during the full moons of April, May and June by huge numbers of spawning snappers. The sharks are filter-feeders and eat only plankton, so it's the protein-rich spawn they're after, not the fish themselves. Recent research by the University of York and the Nature Conservancy indicates that this is one of the largest and most predictable aggregations of whale sharks in the world. Radio-tracking the sharks has demonstrated that they travel at least as far as Cancún in Mexico and down to Honduras – and it's likely they go even further afield. All **tour guides** in Belize are licensed and anyone taking you to see whale sharks will have undergone special training in how to approach the sharks without harming or disturbing their feeding. Boats should stay 15m away from the sharks and snorkellers and divers must keep at least 3m away.

French Louie Caye

Kitty Fox and Ran Villanueva (from *Kitty's Place*; see p.245) offer a great sea-kayaking or overnight trip to beautiful **French Louie Caye**, a tiny island fringed with mangroves 12km offshore. All around the caye there's great snorkelling, with numerous hard and soft corals, sea anemones and huge schools of tiny fish among the mangrove roots; you can also visit at least half a dozen uninhabited cayes nearby. The caye has a resident pair of ospreys, who nest in a mature white mangrove and successfully rear chicks every year. If you want to stay you can have exclusive use of the caye, sleeping in a two-storey wooden house, with delicious meals prepared and served by the resident cook – or for real isolation you can cook for yourself. This simple paradise costs US$300 double, including transport (you're taken out in a skiff, or you can paddle a kayak if you like), use of a double kayak, a dory and snorkelling gear; camping is half the price. Mosquitoes are not a problem as there's no open fresh water; drinking water (in a rainwater vat) is available, and there are composting toilets.

Ranguana Caye

Ranguana Caye, 35km southeast of Placencia and visited by some snorkel trips from the town, is a jewel of an island just 120m long by 25m wide, surrounded by patch reefs perfect for snorkelling. For divers, the shelf and 800m drop-off begin 750m offshore. The sand on Ranguana is softer than in

Placencia, the palm trees are taller and the sunsets are glorious, silhouetting mountain ranges in Honduras and the Maya Mountains in Belize. It's owned by *Robert's Grove* near Placencia (see p.245), and you can stay here in beautiful wooden cabins facing into the almost constant breeze. Each has an immaculate private bathroom, there's hot water and electricity, and meals are served in a large *palapa*-covered dining area. And, as you might expect, it's expensive, at US$325 per person per night, including transport, meals and local drinks and use of kayaks and snorkel gear; a week's stay is US$1120 per person.

Whipray Caye

Whipray Caye (shown on some maps as Wippari Caye), 13km northeast of Placencia, is another idyllic small caye, surrounded by reef corals and coral heads, and it also has some fine cabin accommodation, a little less expensive than on the previous two cayes. *Whipray Caye Lodge* (☎608-8130, ⓔwhipraycaye @yahoo.com; ❼, meals are US$40 per person per day and transport is US$40 per person each way) has two comfortable wooden cabins with private bathrooms and ceiling fans, and all-around windows, so you can enjoy the views and the breeze. Run by expert fishing guide Julian Cabral with his wife Beverley, it's an ideal base for some serious fishing, or just relaxing, and you'll be eating plenty of fresh fish.

The Monkey River

One of the best inland day-trips from Placencia takes you by boat 20km southwest to the nearly pristine **Monkey River**, teeming with fish, birdlife and **howler monkeys**. Monkey River Magic, in Placencia, runs the best **tours** (US$40, minimum 4 people; contact Trip 'N' Travel, ☎523-343), led by Evaristo Muschamp, a very experienced local guide from Monkey River village. You can also arrange some good packages with accommodation in the village. Tours from Placencia set off by 8am, leaving from the gas station dock. A thirty-minute dash through the waves is followed by a leisurely glide up the river and a walk along forest trails. Binoculars are essential if you want to make the most of the amazing **bird-watching** here and on the journey. Along the river you can see turtles, crocodiles and, of course, howler monkeys. The Monkey River area was badly hit by Hurricane Iris in 2001 (which also caused tremendous damage in Placencia), and the forest will take many years to fully recover. Most of the monkeys survived the ordeal, however, and continue to breed successfully.

If you've brought a picnic, lunch is taken on a sandbank in the river, or you can get a meal in *Alice's Restaurant* in **MONKEY RIVER TOWN** (in reality a small village). There's also time to enjoy a stroll around the village and have a drink at one of the **bars**; *Ivan's Cool Spot*, where the river meets the sea, is one of the best. If you want **to stay**, there's the *Sunset Inn* (❸) on a tiny bay at the back of the village. Rooms are in a two-storey wooden building with comfortable beds, private bath and fan. A wide, shady verandah overlooks the river, and you can get tasty Creole food in the restaurant; owner Clive Garbutt is an excellent guide (contact him on the village's community telephone, ☎609-2069 or 509-3069). Another good guide from the village is Eloy Cuevas, who's also one of the best **fly-fishing guides** in Belize; contact him through the Placencia Tourism Center (see p.248).

Lastly, if you'd rather **drive** to Monkey River, take the 22km dirt road which connects the village to the Southern Highway, south of Independence. The road ends on the opposite bank of the river from the village, but just call out and someone will give you a ride over in a boat.

Just across the lagoon from Placencia, **Independence**, though of little intrinsic interest, is a useful travel hub, served by all **buses** between Dangriga and Punta Gorda (see pp.223 & 261, respectively). Although some maps show **Mango Creek** and Independence as two places, the creek just lends its name to one end of town; Independence begins at the road junction, a kilometre or so away. There's a regular fast **boat to Placencia** – the ironically named *Hokey Pokey* (20min; Bz$10 one-way) – and the boatman usually meets the arriving buses, often with a truck to carry your luggage. The *Hokey Pokey* leaves Independence/Mango Creek at 6.30am, 7.30am, 8.30am, 2.30pm and 4.30pm, returning from Placencia at 6.30am, 10am, 4pm and 5pm – and sometimes there are even more frequent departures. You may be able to get a lift on a boat with a Placencia local; a charter costs at least Bz$45.

Between them, Southern Transport and James **buses** have at least six departures daily in each direction along the Southern Highway (including some express services), heading **north to Dangriga** (under 2hr), Belmopan and Belize City between 6am and 2.30pm, and **south to Punta Gorda** (2hr) from 11am to 7.30pm. Catch the bus where the bus crews take their meal break: Southern Transport at the *Café Hello* and the James Bus at *Sherl's Restaurant* across the road; both serve inexpensive Belizean dishes and snacks.

With all these transport connections you should be able to avoid getting stuck overnight in Independence. If you do, the *Hello Hotel* (T523-2428; ⑥), mainly used by businesspeople, has some a/c rooms. You could also try the clean, simple *Ursula's Guest House* on Gran Main Street (T608-7109; ③).

The far south: Toledo District

South of the Placencia and Independence junctions, the newly paved **Southern Highway** leaves the banana plants and the grim settlements squashed beside the plantation roads, twisting at first through pine forests, and crossing numerous creeks and rivers. This is now the best highway in the country, though it still sees little traffic. People are scarce down here too, with only a few villages along the way, but the neat ranks of new citrus plantations are frequently in view, the trees marching over the hills. The mountains to the west are all part of the country's system of forest reserves, national parks and nature reserves, though conflicts over the status of some protected areas are emerging as **Toledo District** (whose residents often feel they live in Belize's "forgotten district") becomes more developed. Wildlife is abundant but the reserves are often inaccessible, though on the northern border of Toledo, at **Red Bank**, you can see one of the largest concentrations of **scarlet macaws** in Central America, and further south you can stay in a field station on the west bank of the **Bladen River**, surrounded by wild jungle and mountains. As you head south you'll still see scars on the mountainsides and trees with their top branches torn off – evidence of the havoc wreaked on the landscape as Hurricane Iris ripped a narrow but devastating swathe through southern Belize in October 2001. A few more **lodges** have opened their doors in recent years, most of them expensive, upmarket places, but there are also a few more affordable places – the best are covered in the text.

Although the Maya of Belize are a fairly small minority within the country as a whole, in Toledo the two main groups – Mopan and Kekchí – make up about half of the population. For the most part they live in simple villages, very similar in appearance to their Guatemalan counterparts. The verdant, mountainous landscape of the far south resembles that of Guatemala's Alta Verapaz and southern Petén, where the ancestors of most of Toledo's Maya came from. The biggest of the Maya villages are **San Antonio** and **San Pedro Columbia**, reached by a good side road heading west from the highway. These villages have hotels; you can visit many other villages and stay in simple guest-houses.

There's plenty of evidence that the ancient Maya lived here too, with ruins scattered in the hills around the villages. The best-known site is **Lubaantun**, where the famous Crystal Skull was "discovered" (see box on p.273), and **Nim Li Punit**, with some impressive stelae, is an easy visit from the highway; near the Guatemalan border, **Pusilhá** is a little harder to reach, but here you can clearly see the best example of a Maya bridge anywhere. The Southern Highway ends at **Punta Gorda**, the southernmost town in Belize and the only town in Toledo. It's the base for visits both to the inland villages and to the lit-tle-visited southernmost **cayes and marine reserves**. It is connected to **Puerto Barrios** in Guatemala by several daily skiffs.

Red Bank

Fourteen kilometres south of the junction to Riversdale and Placencia, a side road heads 6km west to the small Maya village of **Red Bank**, the focus of a campaign to preserve the habitat of the largest-known concentration of **scar-let macaws** in Belize – if not Central America. These spectacular members of the parrot family, formerly considered uncommon in Belize, congregate dur-ing the winter months to feed on ripe fruit. Knowledge of the flock – which could number over two hundred birds – only came to light when word reached conservation organizations in Belize City that villagers (who had no idea of the macaws' protected and endangered status) were hunting them for food. The Programme for Belize and the Belize Audubon Society immediate-ly devised proposals to establish a tourism project in the hope that income from visitors would save the macaws and bring economic benefits to the people of Red Bank.

Near the village, there's **accommodation** in a four-roomed cabin (Bz$50 per person) with a deck and a separate dining room, overlooking a pretty creek and in sight of the macaws feeding in the surrounding hills. Villagers have been trained to guide visitors to see the macaws and hike along forest **trails** to near-by waterfalls and caves. Keep in mind that the macaws aren't always here, how-ever, so before you visit you should call the contact numbers below to see if the birds are around. There's currently no regular transport to Red Bank, but trucks leave daily from and to Independence. For details on staying or visiting contact the PFB or the BAS in Belize City (see p.65), or telephone Geronimo Sho or Julio Teul on the Red Bank **community telephone** (T 509-3110).

The Belize Foundation for Research and Environmental Education

Twenty-five kilometres south of the Independence junction, and seven kilo-metres south of the bridge over the Bladen River, a track heads west for 10km to the **Belize Foundation for Research and Environmental Education** (Bfree; T 614-3896, W www.bfreebelize.net). Here you can stay in a **field sta-tion** on the riverbank, surrounded by the some of the most magnificent for-est and mountain scenery in the country. Bfree is a research and educational facility, founded in 1994 by biologists Jacob and Kelly Marlin, and the field sta-tion is open to all, though they particularly welcomes **interns** (who pay only

Bz$50 per day, including food and accommodation) to help with tropical forest conservation and research, and to undertake practical tasks such working on the garden and maintaining the buildings; visit the Bfree website for details.

All buses on the Southern Highway pass the turn-off for Bfree (across from and 100m north of the Gomez sawmill, the only building around), which is signposted as "**Bladen Nature Reserve**". Unless you're in your own vehicle (and don't attempt to drive this road without a high-clearance 4WD, preferably one equipped with a winch) you'll have to walk in (under 2hr), and even participants in the study groups who are the main visitors here usually arrive on foot, learning about the local ecosystems on the way. It's a pleasant hike, along level ground, passing first through pine and palmetto savannah, then through the shade and scent of the pines, reaching the broadleaf forest as you approach the riverbank; call out and someone will paddle a canoe over to carry you across.

The location of Bfree is stunning. The field station is set in over 1100 acres of private reserve, at the meeting point of four enormous protected areas: the Cockscomb Basin Wildlife Sanctuary, the Deep River and Maya Mountain Forest Reserves and the pristine Bladen Nature Reserve – the last only accessible to accredited, authorized researchers. The jade-green Bladen River emerges from a steep-sided valley just upstream, and the jungle-clad triangle of **Richardson Peak** – at just over 1000m it's the third-highest peak in Belize – is simply the largest of the range of mountains rising on the western horizon. You can climb this with a guide from Bfree or, suitably prepared, take any route in the fifty-kilometre trail system. The beautiful "**blue pool**", among rocks in the river, is perfect for a swim and canoes are available for river trips. Nearby is a tranquil lagoon, full of fish and overhung by trees laden with bromeliads, where crocodiles lurk, tapirs bathe and monkeys howl, and jaguars and other cats prowl the forest.

There's a range of comfortable, rustic **accommodation**, though generally you'll get a dorm bed in the comfortable wooden bunkhouse (Bz$60 per person, including meals), or you can **camp** (Bz$60 per person, including meals, and tents are available). The private wooden cabins are usually used by researchers. Substantial, delicious meals, often using produce from the organic garden, are served in the thatched dining room. Amazingly, despite the remote location, there's **Internet access** and phone service.

Biodiversity is rich here, with over three hundred bird and 180 reptile and amphibian species, and many of the definitive books on Belizean and regional wildlife have been researched here. With 21 amphibian species in eight families, Bfree is an ideal site for long-term amphibian research, and work undertaken at the field station is vital to the goals of the Maya Forest Anuran Monitoring Project (supported in part by the Wildlife Conservation Society; see p.325 in Contexts). The data collected is particularly relevant and useful in light of concern over the decline in amphibian populations in supposedly undisturbed environments – even if only a visitor or an intern here you could easily share a discovery.

Nim Li Punit to Big Falls

About 58km from the Independence junction, near the Maya village of **Indian Creek**, you pass the entrance to **NIM LI PUNIT**, a Late Classic period Maya site that was probably allied to nearby Lubaantun (see p.271). This site, only discovered in 1976, is home to the largest and one of the best-preserved stelae in Belize, and recent restoration work has revealed many more features. It's only 1km west of the highway and the entrance track is well signposted – making for an easy and very worthwhile visit. The site is often included on tour itineraries, and nearby, two of Toledo's new luxury lodges, *Indian Creek Lodge* and *The Lodge at Big Falls* provide upscale **accommodation** (see pp.259 & 260, respectively). The village of **Big Falls** also has some budget rooms.

Ten kilometres south of Indian Creek, the road to **Silver Creek** branches off to the right (west); with your own transport you can use this route to visit the Maya villages and the site of Lubaantun (see p.271). At the time of writing, paving of the last unpaved stretch of the Southern Highway – the 15km from Golden Stream River to the Silver Creek junction – had just begun, much to the relief of the long-suffering people of Toledo District. The entire highway should be paved by the time you read this.

Nim Li Punit

Nim Li Punit (daily 8am–4pm; Bz$10) occupies a commanding position on a ridge above Indian Creek, with views over the maize fields to the southern coastal plain beyond – a scene largely unchanged since ancient times. **Getting**

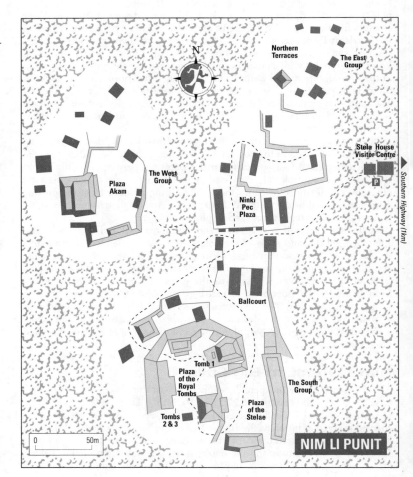

Northern Terraces

The East Group

Stela House Visitor Centre

Southern Highway (1km)

The West Group

Plaza Akam

Ninki Pec Plaza

Ballcourt

Tomb 1

Plaza of the Royal Tombs

Tombs 2 & 3

Plaza of the Stelae

The South Group

0   50m

NIM LI PUNIT

to the site is relatively easy: all passing buses go by the entrance road, so you could head up here from Punta Gorda in the morning and catch a bus back to town in the afternoon. You can leave luggage at the little shop by the roadside, and the family who run it will know the times of onward buses: Pop's, the village bus service, leaves for Punta Gorda at 6am, 7am and 11.30am.

The new **Stela House and Visitor Centre** has a good map of the site, and wall panels provide excellent explanations – in Kekchí and English – of some of the texts carved on the stelae. Nim Li Punit was probably linked politically with all the other sites in southern Belize, and was probably also linked to Copán, in Honduras. The site rangers, Placido Ash or Adriano Mas, may be able to show you around.

You enter the site through a plaza surrounded by walls and buildings of cut stones held together without mortar, a characteristic of sites in southern Belize, and pass through the beautiful **walled ball-court** to the **South Group** – which may have functioned as an observatory to record the sunrise at the solstices and equinoxes. A total of 25 stelae were found here, eight of them carved. **Stela 14**, at almost 10m high, is the tallest in Belize, and one of the tallest anywhere in the Maya world – although it was never erected. Unfortunately, the site was badly looted soon after its discovery and in 1997 several of the stelae were again badly damaged – this time by fire and machete – and the best are now more secure indoors.

Although Stela 14 is now in the Stela House, it's still an impressive sight, with panels of glyphs above and a richly attired ruler below: it's his elaborate headgear that gives Nim Li Punit its name, being Kekchí for "big hat". **Stela 15**, dated to 721 AD and the earliest here, is slightly smaller yet even more impressive. Carvings on this great sandstone slab depict a ruler in the act of dropping an offering – perhaps *copal* incense or kernels of corn – into an elaborately carved burning brazier supported on the back of a monster, in order to conjure up a vision of **Waxaklahun Ubah Kan**, or "Mosaic War Serpent", the ruler's battle standard. To his (or perhaps her – expert opinion differs) right, a smaller figure also makes an offering into the brazier, while on the left side a column of very clear glyphs separates the main figure from an attendant, or guard; all three figures are almost entirely surrounded by panels of glyphs.

Indian Creek Lodge

Across the highway from the track to Nim Li Punit, and set on a hilltop with views over the forest, savannah, and two artificial lagoons, *Indian Creek Lodge* (T 223-6324, W www.belizelodge.com; 9) offers splendid **accommodation** in twelve spacious and very comfortable hardwood and stone cabins. Six are air-conditioned and the interiors of all are richly appointed: the four-poster beds are draped with mosquito nets, the bathrooms are luxurious and each has a large deck to enjoy the views. In the grounds a private zoo houses native birds and animals (including a black jaguar from Mexico) in almost as much luxury as the guests. The *Lodge* is set in the huge, privately owned **Boden Creek Ecological Reserve**, covering 7600 acres from the highway to the coast. Eight kilometres south of the *Lodge* is the *Jungle Camp*, with cabins and a screened dining room overlooking Golden Stream. From here you can take **hiking** trips into the forest and **boat trips** along the river and into Paynes Creek National Park and Port Honduras Marine Reserve with superb naturalist guides. Other boats can take you to the Snake Cayes or Sapodilla Cayes (see p.268), and more accommodation is planned for Moho Caye. Guests are usually flown in to the private airstrip, and most will be here on a package (around US$830 per person for three nights, US$1590 for six nights), which includes a stay at the *Lodge* and the *Jungle Camp*, as well as a choice of numerous excursions on the extensive property and to sites throughout Toledo and to the cayes offshore.

Big Falls accommodation

Just beyond the Silver Creek junction, the village of **BIG FALLS**, with a gas station, a store and a major bridge over the Rio Grande, also has a couple of **places to stay** – one at either end of the accommodation scale. It is not a particularly pretty village (though the river is gorgeous) but it does boast the only **hot spring** in Belize, a luxurious spot for a warm bath. The spring feeds a creek which flows into the Rio Grande just upstream of the bridge in the centre of the village. Just south of the bridge you'll see signs for *Xaiha* ("confluence"), a small, very inexpensive **hotel** a few hundred metres off the highway, run by Alberta and Antonio Shal, who have simple cabins with bunk beds (no phone; ❷) in a garden just above the creek, with only cold water in the showers – but walk down to the garden and you'll find some attractive pools with warm water. Most of the time they're practically deserted, but at weekends the pools are a popular picnic spot.

Just north of the bridge, and signposted 800m off the highway, *The Lodge at Big Falls* (☎722-2878, Ⓦwww.thelodgeatbigfalls.com; ❾, no service charge), run by Rob and Marta Hirons, provides much more luxurious accommodation in very spacious thatched cabañas, set in 29 landscaped and flower-filled acres on a meander bend of the Rio Grande. The six fully screened cabañas, all with tiled floors and cooled by powerful ceiling fans, with roomy bathrooms, hardwood furniture and a large deck with hammocks, offer plenty of comfort and privacy. You'll see lots of nature right here; two hundred species of birds have been recorded and butterflies are everywhere. Trails lead though the lush growth on the riverbank and kayaks are available, and you can be put in at San Miguel, 8km upstream, for a wonderful float back to the *Lodge*. The grounds were once a citrus orchard, with more than enough trees left to provide all the fresh juices served in the restaurant.

Big Falls to Punta Gorda

Seven kilometres south of Big Falls a road branches off west to **San Antonio** (see p.276), from where you can explore the forested southern foothills of the Maya Mountains, dotted with ruins and some delightful riverside Maya villages. This junction goes by the unfortunate name of **Dump**; there's a **gas station** here, selling beer and cold drinks, and if you're driving it's a good place to pick up information. At the time of writing, paving of this branch road is about to begin and eventually it will lead to a **new border crossing** point into Guatemala; until this happens the existing unofficial crossing is not a legal exit point from Belize. The Southern Highway heads east at the Dump junction, smooth and fast all the way into Punta Gorda, 22km to the south. Along the way you'll pass a few small villages, mostly founded and inhabited by more members of Belize's East Indian community, with a few more new places to stay. At **Jacintoville**, 11km from Punta Gorda, a branch road heads south to the Garífuna village of **Barranco**, Belize's southernmost coastal settlement.

At **Sun Creek**, 3km south of the junction, *Sun Creek Lodge* (☎604-2124, Ⓦwww.ibtm.net; ❹, including breakfast) has three beautiful thatched cabañas, all with electricity and one with a private bathroom, owned by Bruno and Melissa Kuppinger. Bruno, originally from Germany, knows Toledo District and the entire country very well, and from here he runs International Belize Tourism Marketing, offering a range of often hard-to-find services for visitors to southern Belize, including tours, **jeep rental** (US$65 per day) and high-speed **Internet** access.

At **Jacintoville**, 7km past Sun Creek, *Tranquility Lodge* (no phone, Ⓔmisspennyl@yahoo.com; ❺, including breakfast), on the bank of beautiful Jacinto Creek, offers air-conditioned comfort at a bargain price in spacious, tiled, en-suite rooms set in orchid-laden gardens. Above the rooms, the fully screened thatched restaurant serves excellent meals, and offers great all-round views of the grounds. *Tranquility's* location, just 300m from the paved highway, at the entrance to the Barranco road (close to the bus route between Punta Gorda and the inland villages), makes it an ideal base for visiting the Maya villages and ruins inland or the southern coast. (If you're travelling by bus get off at the junction, on the south side of the bridge over Jacinto Creek, and follow the signs.) The place is very popular with bird-watchers, with over two hundred species seen along the forested trails here, and the natural, rock-lined pool in the creek is perfect for a refreshing dip. If you want to meet the locals, then stroll along to *Miss Flora's Beer Parlour*, a kilometre from the *Lodge* in the village itself. Flora also serves snacks and simple meals.

Six kilometres beyond Jacintoville a signposted road left (north) leads to another of Toledo's new upscale resorts, *El Pescador Lodge* (☎722-0050, Ⓦwww .elpescadorpg.com; ❾), in a glorious hilltop setting in landscaped grounds high above the Rio Grande and offering wonderful views over the surrounding forest. As the name implies, this is primarily a fishing lodge, with numerous boats to take anglers along the river and out to sea, and a fully stocked tackle shop; it has already received rave reviews in the angling press regarding abundance of snook, tarpon, permit and bonefish in nearby waters. However, due to its location within hundreds of acres of privately protected land and adjacent to Paynes Creek National Park and Port Honduras Marine Reserve, the *Lodge* also attracts visitors who want to get close to nature, and wildlife is abundant here. Guests stay in spacious, beautifully furnished wooden cabañas, each with a private deck shaded by trees; meals are served in the main lodge building. A funicular tram takes you down the steep slope to the river and the waiting boats, and if you're not fishing you can relax in and around the pool on top of the hill or walk the trails through the forest. Overnight rates are US$150 double but most guests are on a package, which costs around US$2500 for five nights for two people, and includes a boat and a guide, plus all meals.

The highway reaches the sea a few kilometres beyond the *El Pescador* junction, at a place called **Cattle Landing**, where you can rent a room for a week or more in *Casa Bonita Apartments* (☎722-2270, Ⓔcba4cnn@btl.net). Here there's a range of good-value furnished private apartments with full kitchens in a concrete building facing the sea – ideal for longer stays. They cost from around US$125–300 per week, there are discounts for students, and meals can be arranged. Beyond Cattle Landing the road continues along the attractive shoreline for the last few kilometres to Punta Gorda.

Punta Gorda

The Southern Highway eventually comes to an end in **PUNTA GORDA** (commonly known as PG), the heart of the still-isolated **Toledo District** – an area that has until recently been hard to reach and largely overlooked by planners and developers. Access is much easier now that the Southern Highway is paved, and visitors who make it out here can be rewarded by spending a few days at the **Maya villages** inland (see p.270), where you can experience a way of life far removed from the rest of Belize. Offshore, the **Sapodilla Cayes** and **Port Honduras** form the focus of Belize's southernmost **marine reserves**. Punta Gorda's position on low cliffs means that cooling sea breezes reduce the worst of the heat and, though this is undeniably the wettest part of Belize, with the trees heavy with mosses and bromeliads, most of the extra rain falls at night, leaving the daytime no wetter than, say, Cayo District.

The town has a population of around five thousand Garífuna, Maya (who make up more than half the population of the district), East Indians and Creoles, with a few Lebanese and Chinese as well, and is the focal point for a large number of villages and farming settlements. The busiest day is Saturday, when people from the surrounding villages come into town to trade. Despite a recent minor building boom, Punta Gorda remains a small, unhurried and hassle-free town – though as a tourist (here and in the villages) you'll constantly be approached by Maya women and girls, imploring you to buy the small and undeniably attractive **decorative baskets** they make from a local vine. These salespeople are polite and utterly charming, and they will take no for an answer, but as you walk on the next group will be entreating you to buy

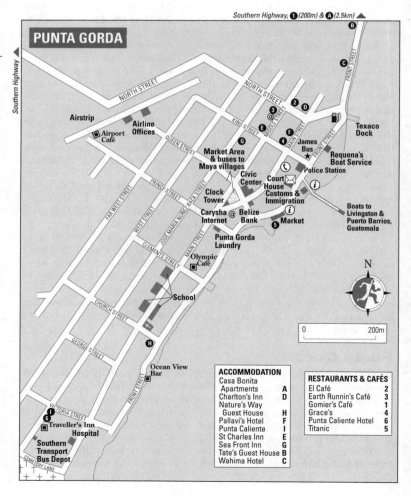

ACCOMMODATION

Casa Bonita Apartments	A
Charlton's Inn	D
Nature's Way Guest House	H
Pallavi's Hotel	F
Punta Caliente	I
St Charles Inn	E
Sea Front Inn	G
Tate's Guest House	B
Wahima Hotel	C

RESTAURANTS & CAFÉS

El Café	2
Earth Runnin's Café	3
Gomier's Café	1
Grace's	4
Punta Caliente Hotel	6
Titanic	5

their baskets; heartbreaking as it is to repeatedly say no to such beautiful children you will probably have to steel yourself.

To the north of Punta Gorda are the remains of the **Toledo settlement**, founded in 1867 by Confederate emigrants from the US. Many of the original settlers soon drifted home, discouraged by the torrential downpours and the rigours of frontier life, but their numbers were boosted by Methodists from Mississippi. The Methodists were deeply committed to the settlement and, despite a cholera epidemic in 1868, managed to clear 160 acres. By 1870 sugar was the main product, with twelve separate estates running their own mills. The settlement reached its peak in 1890, after which it was threatened by falling sugar prices. Most farmers moved into alcohol production, but for the Methodists this was out of the question, and they preferred to feed their molasses to their cattle. By 1910 their community was destitute, although it was largely as a result of their struggle that Toledo was permanently settled.

A fascinating book, *Confederate Settlements in British Honduras*, by Donald C. Simmons Jr (McFarland & Company), tells the story of the defeated Confederates who chose Belize (then the colony of British Honduras) as a location to recreate the antebellum South. You may be able to find a copy in a library or hotel in Belize, if not in a bookstore. Since slavery had been abolished in Belize decades before their arrival (and the few Garífuna and Creoles around at the time had no inclination to work for former slave owners), the settlers brought over indentured labourers from India (then also a British colony). These labourers they called "coolies", and their descendants (now fully assimilated into Belizean culture, and still frequently referred to as "coolies" by other ethnic groups in Belize, though not necessarily in a derogatory way) still live in Punta Gorda and in the first few villages along the Southern Highway.

Arrival and information

Buses from Belize City (all via Dangriga) take around seven hours to reach Punta Gorda, though taking an express service will cut an hour off the journey time. Southern Transport has a terminal at the south end of José María Nuñez Street, while James Bus is based at an office near the dock. Maya Island Air and Tropic Air both operate four or five **flights** to and from Belize City (all calling at Placencia and Dangriga), landing at the small airstrip five blocks west of the main dock. **Skiffs** to and from **Puerto Barrios** (see box on p.265) and Lívingston in Guatemala use the main dock, roughly in the centre of the seafront; the **immigration** office is nearby. See box on p.265 for details of moving on from Punta Gorda.

Despite having relatively few visitors, Punta Gorda has two excellent **information** centres. The Toledo Visitors Information Center (TVIC; ☎722-2470), next to the ferry dock, is run by Alfredo and Yvonne Villoria, who arrange homestay accommodation with families in the Maya villages. The Belize Tourism Board (BTB) has a very informative office on Front Street, just south of the dock (☎722-2531) – staff at either office can help with transportation schedules to the Maya villages and assist in setting up **tours** of the interior of the Toledo District and the outlying cayes. For more information on visiting other places in Toledo see "Around Punta Gorda" on p.266.

The only **bank** is the Belize Bank (with ATM; Mon–Fri 8am–2pm), on the main square across from the Civic Center, though there will usually be a **moneychanger** outside the immigration office when international boats are coming and going, and you can also change money in *Grace's Restaurant*, a block in front of the dock. If you're leaving the country from Punta Gorda, keep in mind that it's best to get rid of your Belize dollars before you cross the border.

The **post office** is in the government buildings a block back from the ferry dock and the **BTL office** is across the parking lot. PG has abundant **Internet access**: there's the long-established *Cyber Café*, just past the *Sea Front Inn* on Front Street (Mon–Sat 8am–8pm); the air-conditioned *Carysha*, on Main Street, opposite the clock tower (Mon–Fri 9am–5pm, Sat 9am–noon); and *Earth Runnin's*, 11 Middle St, PG's only true Internet café (see review, opposite; closed Tues, otherwise daily 7am–11pm).

For **car rental** check at *Charlton's Inn*, below, or contact Bruno Kuppinger, who runs *Sun Creek Lodge* (see p.260; ☎604-2124, ✉ibtm@btl.net). For **bike rental** go to Aba Iseni, on Prince Street, or ask for Elijah in the BTL office (Bz\$20 per day; ☎722-2106).

Accommodation

There has been a spate of **hotel–building** in PG during the last few years and, although visitor numbers have increased, few people spend long here, and there are plenty of bargains, though few places have a/c. For **longer stays** see the entries for the *Sea Front Inn* (below) and *Casa Bonita Apartments* on p.261; for an alternative to staying in town, contact *Nature's Way Guest House* (listed below), which operates an award-winning programme of guesthouse accommodation in surrounding villages in conjunction with the Toledo Ecotourism Association. The only **campsite** near town is *Irie Camping*, 3km away at Cattle Landing (all buses pass by), with tent sites for Bz\$8 per person and some simple cabins (no phone; ❷); it's in a good location near the seafront but there's rarely anyone there, so you may still have to head back into town.

Charlton's Inn 9 Main St ☎722-2197, ✉charlstin@btl.net. Rooms with hot-water showers – some also have a/c – in a two-storey concrete building with safe parking. Owner Duwane Wagner can arrange car rental, and he also sells domestic air tickets. ❸–❺

Nature's Way Guest House 65 Front St ☎702-2119. The best budget place in Punta Gorda and renowned as a meeting-place and information point. Private rooms and clean, comfortable dorm accommodation (Bz\$20), but no private baths and no hot water. Owner William "Chet" Schmidt, a committed environmentalist, has been in PG for over thirty years and is a driving force behind the Toledo Ecotourism Association; he can arrange trips to the villages. You can order good breakfasts and other meals. ❸

Pallavi's Hotel 19 Main St, next to *Grace's Restaurant* ☎722-2414. Clean rooms with private bath and TV in a two-storey concrete building in the centre of town. ❸

Punta Caliente Hotel 108 José María Nuñez St, next to the Southern Transport terminal ☎722-2561. Clean and comfortable en-suite rooms (two with a/c) with cable TV. Owner Alex Arzú is a historian of the Garífuna, and the restaurant – one of the best in town – is virtually a small museum of Garífuna culture. ❹

Sea Front Inn Front St, 600m north of the centre ☎722-2300, ⊕www.seafrontinn.com. A fourstorey stone-and-wood-fronted building, with steep Alpine-style eaves, this hotel is strikingly different from any other in the country. Rooms are spacious, with tiled floors, a/c, TV and balcony; some have a fridge, and there are also furnished apartments from around Bz\$450 per week. The restaurant usually only serves breakfast unless it's booked for a function. Email available for guests. The *Sea Front* is the base for Wild Encounters, who arrange tours in Toledo and throughout Belize. ❼

St Charles Inn 23 King St ☎722-2149. One of Punta Gorda's smartest, best-value options, with clean and quiet rooms with TV (one with a/c) in a charming wooden building with hammocks on the balcony. ❸

Tate's Guest House 34 José María Nuñez St, two blocks west of the town centre ☎722-0007. A very quiet, friendly, family-run hotel with some a/c rooms. ❸–❹

Wahima Hotel Front St, just north of the Texaco gas station ☎722-2542. Inexpensive rooms with private bath, right on the seafront; also some apartments for around US\$150/week. ❸

Eating, drinking and nightlife

Restaurants in Punta Gorda have improved in recent years and it's certainly easy to get a good, filling meal for a reasonable price. **Nightlife** in PG is virtually nonexistent unless a band is playing at the *PG Sports Bar* opposite the clock tower, but there are a few **bars** where you can meet locals and fellow travellers. Visitors wanting a quiet chat over a beer will get a warm welcome from Olympia Vernon in her tiny *Olympic Bar*, near the corner of Main and Clements streets. The equally tiny *Ocean View Bar*, perched over the sea near the south end of Front Street, certainly lives up to its name. *Earth Runnin's* (listed below) is a popular bar among the expat NGO crowd (of whom there are a surprising number in PG). Another good place to enjoy an early-evening drink (and possibly some nightlife) is *Waluco's*, though it's 2km from the centre; follow Front Street north across the metal bridge over Joe Taylor Creek. *Waluco's* is also popular with expats and there's a deck to enjoy the sea breeze, the beers are at normal prices, and you can get meals.

Earth Runnin's Café and Bukut Bar Corner of North and Middle streets. Punta Gorda's most sophisticated dining option, and a bit pricier than the others, with a changing menu that always features good breakfasts, fresh seafood, pasta and delicious vegetarian meals. It's also a popular bar, serving a range of cocktails, and a true Internet café.

El Café North St, behind *Charlton's Inn*. Good, inexpensive Belizean dishes, often including local organic produce; opens for breakfast at 6am, and serves good coffee.

Gomier's Café Front St, 100m north of *Sea Front Inn*. A tiny place serving delicious organic vegetarian, soy and seafood meals, with a daily special.

Moving on from Punta Gorda

Southern Transport **buses** (☎702-2568) leave for **Belize City** (7hr) at 4am, 5am and 10am; the James bus (☎722-2625) departs at 6am, 8am and noon; additionally, at the time of writing, both companies have an **express service** at 4pm, though this is likely to change.

Buses for the **Maya villages** and **Barranco** leave around noon on the market days (Mon, Wed, Fri & Sat), from the streets next to the Civic Center – Leonardo Cal in the Tourist Office will have full details; most village bus companies are literally one-man operations and Sunday is their day off. The only village bus which leaves in the afternoon is Pop's, which leaves PG for **Indian Creek** (near **Nim Li Punit**, see p.258) Mon–Sat at 5pm.

San Antonio is the biggest village and has two daily buses, Chun's and Prim's – at least one of them will continue to **Jalacte** on the Guatemalan border (this is not yet a legal crossing for visitors). If you're visiting **Lubaantun** (see p.271) you need the bus for **San Pedro Columbia**, and you can also usually get there any day with rides in pick-up trucks. If you're heading for **Uxbenka**, the **Rio Blanco** or **Pueblo Viejo waterfalls** (see p.276) you need the **Pueblo Viejo** or **Jalacte** bus. For **Pusilhá**, take the **San Benito Poité** bus. Returning from the villages, all buses leave early, from around 3.30–5.30am.

To Puerto Barrios in Guatemala there are at least two regular daily **skiffs** (Bz$25; 1hr in good weather) and there's usually a boat to **Lívingston** on Tuesday and Friday at 10am. Julio Requena's *Mariestela* leaves at 9am (☎722-2070) and Carlos Carcamo's *Pichilango* leaves at 4pm. There's no need to buy your ticket in advance (though you can); just turn up at the dock half an hour or so before departure so the skipper can get the paperwork ready; you'll have to pay the PACT **exit tax** of Bz$7.50 at the immigration office.

Each domestic airline has four or five daily **flights** from 7am to 4pm to Belize City (1hr 15min; Bz$152), calling at Placencia and Dangriga on the way; check the airlines' offices at the airstrip: Maya Island (☎722-2856) and Tropic (☎722-2008).

Eat inside or at a table beneath a thatched roof and enjoy the sea breeze.

Grace's Restaurant 19 Main St, opposite the BTL office. Inexpensive, tasty Belizean dishes served in very clean surroundings. You can change money here and all buses heading north stop across the road.

Punta Caliente Restaurant José María Nuñez St, beneath the hotel of the same name. One of the best restaurants in town, serving Creole and Garífuna dishes and a daily special. Not open for breakfast and closed Sat & Sun.

Titanic Restaurant Front St, above the market. Good breakfasts and Belizean dishes served on a deck right above the sea. Great ocean and mountain views and the 6am to noon happy hour is the longest – and earliest – in the country.

Around Punta Gorda: Toledo's ecotourism projects

Ecotourism is a buzzword throughout Belize, and several projects in Toledo District are poised to reap the benefits. Their aim is to achieve a balance between the need for economic development and the need to preserve the rich natural and cultural heritage of the area. It is hoped that small numbers of "low-impact" visitors will provide additional income to villages without destroying the communities' traditional way of life. The **Punta Gorda Eco-Trail** incorporates both public and privately owned land in the immediate vicinity of the town, taking in **howler monkey** habitat on nearby forested hilltops, a **green iguana** breeding project and a **medicinal plant** trail; check at *Nature's Way* (see p.264) for details.

Many Maya villages in Toledo are sited in **Indian Reservations**, designated as such in colonial times to protect the Maya subsistence lands. Title, however, remained with the government (which leases logging concessions), not the Maya who actually occupied the reserves. Recent developments in forestry policy have alarmed community leaders, who fear that so-called "conversion forestry", where all trees over a certain size on the reservations are allowed to be cut down for timber production, will cause further severe erosion and silt up previously clear streams used for drinking.

The **Toledo Ecotourism Association (TEA)**, in the BTB office on Front Street in Punta Gorda (☏722-2096, ✉ttea@btl.net), aims to combat the destruction of the forest by offering visitors a **Guest House and Eco-Trail Programme**. Eleven villages in southern Toledo are involved in the project; each has an eight-bed guesthouse (Bz$20 per person) and meals are taken at different houses to allow distribution of the income. Each village has its own attraction, be it a cave, waterfall, river or ruin, and there are guided walks or horse rides (around Bz$8 per hour; 4hr minimum); there may also be canoes to rent. The villagers have an extensive cultural knowledge of the medicinal uses of plants and the ancient Maya myths, and a visit here can be an excellent way to find out about Maya life and culture, experiencing village life without feeling like an intruder. The programme has also raised the consciousness of the villagers themselves as they learn to use both the concept of ecotourism and the political process to protect their forest; these efforts were rewarded in 1997 with a tourism industry prize for "Socially Responsible Ecotourism". The guesthouses detailed in the text on pp.270–274 are part of the programme.

Another interesting commercial project in the villages, with a positive impact on the environment, is the cultivation of organically grown *cacao* (cocoa) beans, to produce **chocolate**; almost all the crop around here is used to make the delicious Maya Gold chocolate sold abroad. The ancient Maya used *cacao* beans as money; Belize was a great centre of production and the beans were traded over great distances. Today you'll often see *cacao* beans drying on special concrete pads as you travel through the villages, and if you've never seen *cacao* growing ask in one of the information offices or the TEA how you could visit a farm.

As an alternative to the guesthouse programme TVIC, the **Toledo Visitors Information Center** (☎722-2470, ✉demdatsdoin@btl.net) promotes the "**host family network**," in which visitors stay in a village with a Mopan or Kekchí Maya family, participate in village work – grinding corn, chopping firewood, cooking tortillas and the like – and sleep in a hammock. In either programme you'll find few modern conveniences like electricity and flush toilets (though most villages have community telephones, operating on a solar panel), but if you go with an open mind you'll have a fascinating and rewarding experience and the villagers will be happy to teach you some Maya words.

TIDE, the **Toledo Institute for Development and Environment** (☎722-2192, ⓦwww.tidetours.org), is an excellent local NGO which manages **Payne's Creek National Park** north of Punta Gorda and **Port Honduras Marine Reserve** offshore, plus 16,000 acres of private lands. The organization is also involved with many practical development and conservation projects, including training net fishermen to become fly-fishing guides. These reserves form part of the continuous corridor of the Maya Mountain Marine Corridor (MMMC), protecting a wide swathe of southern Belize from the cayes to the Guatemalan border. The management of these reserves in Belize is linked with that of other marine protected areas in Guatemala and Honduras, under the umbrella of the **Tri-national Alliance for the Conservation of the Gulf of Honduras** (*La Alianza Trinacional* in Spanish; ⓦwww.trigoh.org), an group comprising prominent NGOs from the three countries dedicated to the conservation of biological diversity and creating sustainable livelihoods for the people living in or near the reserves. If you are interested in **volunteering** in these conservation programmes contact Wil Maheia, TIDE's executive director.

TIDE's subsidiary, Tide Tours, also offers a range of **tours**, including a full-day **kayak** trip along the lower Moho or Rio Grande rivers (around Bz$80–95), **snorkelling** at Moho Caye or the Snake Cayes (around Bz$65–100) and **mountain-bike** trips to all the local attractions. Overnight camping and fishing trips to Payne's Creek and Port Honduras can be arranged; the tiny, isolated seaside community of **Punta Negra**, 30km north of Punta Gorda, has some basic **bed-and-breakfast accommodation**. For tours, contact Erika Diamond, the Ecotourism Coordinator in the TIDE office in Punta Gorda, on Prince Street, near the corner with Main Street.

Tours of the Toledo interior, the coast and the cayes are available from a few other local operators, including Green Iguana Adventures (☎608-0431, ✉southernexplorars@hotmail.com), run by Wilfred Requena and Alex Leonardo, who offer superb bird-watching, fishing, **camping** and **kayaking** trips, in addition to the more usual Maya village and ruins tours.

Out to sea: the cayes and the coast

The cayes and reefs off Punta Gorda mark the southern tip of Belize's Barrier Reef. Though visited by specialist sea-kayaking tours, and becoming more accessible from PG, the whole area gets relatively little attention from international tourism and is very interesting to explore. The closest cayes to Punta Gorda consist of about 130 low-lying mangrove islands in the mouth of a large bay to the north of town, where the shoreline is a complex maze of mangrove islands and swamps. Six hundred square kilometres of the bay and adjacent coast are now protected in the **Port Honduras Marine Reserve**, partly to safeguard the many **manatees** living and breeding in this shallow water habitat. Sport fishing, especially **fly-fishing**, is particularly good in this little-visited region; one of the best local guides is Bobby Polonio (℡722-2135). For others, and for details of how to visit the reserve and the cayes, see the TIDE information on p.267, or TASTE, below.

The cayes and coastline north of Punta Gorda are virtually uninhabited today; in antiquity they were the home of ancient **Maya sea traders** and salt works. Since 1981, archeological fieldwork by Heather McKillop's project through Louisiana State University has documented sea-level rise since the end of the Classic Maya period (900 AD) that submerged ancient sites and created the modern mangrove landscape. The trading port of **Wild Cane Caye**, a mainly mangrove caye 20km north of Punta Gorda, focused on the inland trade of salt (produced in the salt works in nearby Punta Ycacos Lagoon) – a basic biological necessity for the inhabitants of the great Maya cities inland. The salt works were abandoned with the Classic Maya collapse, but Wild Cane Caye continued to participate in long-distance sea trade with cities as far away as Chichén Itzá in Yucatán and other Postclassic cities. The project has also documented unique **coral architecture** at Wild Cane Caye and other islands, in which coral rock was mined from the sea to build platforms for structures of perishable material. The coastal area here is managed by TIDE from Punta Gorda (see p.267) and visitors must check in at the TIDE **ranger station** on **Abalone Caye** (near Wild Cane Caye) in the Port Honduras Reserve before visiting the island site. The ranger station itself is often visited on boat trips, and you can climb to the top deck for spectacular views over the reserve and to the mountains inland.

The first real beaches are found on the idyllic **Snake Cayes**, a group of four main islands surrounded by glorious white coral sand beaches 27km northeast of Punta Gorda, and the easiest to visit from the town. Beyond here the main reef is fragmented into several clusters of cayes, each surrounded by a small independent reef. The largest and most easterly group of islands are the stunningly beautiful **Sapodilla Cayes**, a chain of five main islands – each almost wholly encircled by coral and with gorgeous soft-sand beaches – and several rocky outcrops.

Some cayes already have accommodation and more resorts are planned; all will face increasing visitor pressure in the near future, though a management plan for the Sapodilla Cayes, co-devised by the Fisheries Department and the **Toledo Association for Sustainable Tourism and Empowerment** (TASTE; ℡722-0191, ✉taste_scmr@btl.net), a consortium of local and national NGOs, aims to limit damage to the reserve's environmental base and ensure that local people benefit from the reserve, too. TASTE is very active in environmental education, taking boatloads of local schoolchildren to the Sapodillas to learn about marine ecosystems and participate in beach clean-ups; committed **volunteers** could check at TASTE's office, 53 Middle St in Punta Gorda, if there are any places in the boats for them.

The Sapodilla Cayes

These beautiful islands form the focus of the **Sapodilla Cayes Marine Reserve** and their designation as a reserve means that they receive some protection, though the presence of day-trippers from Guatemala and Honduras can mean a difficult job for the already thinly stretched conservation agencies. Of the five main islands, uninhabited **Northeast Caye**, thickly covered with coconut trees and under government ownership, has been proposed as a **core zone** of the reserve, to be left undeveloped. **Hunting Caye** is where you pay the Bz\$20 fee to visit the reserve, and it has an immigration post to deal with the foreign visitors and has limited camping and picnicking possibilities. The sand at the incredibly beautiful Crescent Moon Beach on the east side attracts hawksbill turtles to nest. **Nicolas Caye** has an abandoned resort and you could **camp** here or ask the caretaker for permission to sleep in a half-finished cabin. The most southerly main island, **Lime Caye**, also has tourism development planned, but for the moment (if you can afford to get here; contact the TASTE office, opposite) you can savour its glorious isolation.

Frank's Caye, a small island flanked by two even tinier ones, is currently the only one in the group to have a functioning tourist resort, the idyllic *Serenade Island Resort* (☎523-3380 or 509-5015, ⓦ www.belizecayes.com; US$200 double, including meals; transport is US$200 return), with comfortable white-painted wooden cabins, each with a private bathroom and a deck with hammocks. Most guests are brought in on a skiff from Placencia (about an hour in good weather), and for details you can contact Carrie Fairweather at the *Serenade Guest House* there (see p.250), who owns both places. Meals are served in the spacious restaurant built over the water, also with a deck and hammocks perfect for relaxing. The fishing is excellent, you can snorkel right off the beach, and the reef is only 200m offshore; rates include use of canoes.

Barranco and the southern coast

From Punta Gorda you can see range upon range of mountains in Guatemala and Honduras, but the Belizean coastline south of here is flat and sparsely populated. Tidal rivers meander across a coastal plain covered with thick tropical rainforest that receives over 350mm of rain a year, forming a unique ecosystem in Belize with a very high biodiversity of plant species, particularly orchids and palms. The **Temash River** is lined with the tallest mangrove forest in the country, the **black mangroves** towering over 30m above the riverbanks, while in the far south the **Sarstoon River**, navigable by small boats, forms the border with Guatemala; the land between these rivers is now the **Sarstoon-Temash National Park**. You can arrange tours from operators in Punta Gorda (see p.267) and the rivers are sometimes paddled on tours run by sea-kayaking companies (see Basics, pp.11–12), this time using inflatable river kayaks.

The only village on the coast down here is **BARRANCO** (community phone ☎709-2010), a small, traditional Garífuna settlement of around 150 people, which you can visit and stay in through the village guesthouse programme (see p.266). A rough road connects the village with the Southern Highway (buses run to Punta Gorda at 6am on Mon, Wed, Fri & Sat, returning to the village at noon on the same days), and the Moho River now has a high-level bridge. Some people, though, still rely on traditional dories, now motor-powered, to get to Punta Gorda. The village is set among forest and savannah, with scattered houses shaded by trees. Many villagers of working age have left to seek opportunities elsewhere, leaving the village populated by children and the elderly, and Garífuna is now only regularly spoken there by older people.

Other aspects of Garífuna culture live on, however: despite virtually all the villagers being Roman Catholics, Barranco boasts the largest *dabuyaba* (a traditional **Garífuna temple**, built of poles with a thatched roof) in the country. It's occasionally used for *dugu* rites, when family members come from far and wide to honour deceased relatives and the spirits of their ancestors. Preparation takes many months and the **ceremonies** – comprising prayers, drumming, singing, dancing and offerings of food – last four days. In the traditional Garífuna belief system the ancestors have a direct influence on the world of the living. From Barranco you can go on foot or horseback along jungle trails and there are **tour guides** in the village; ask for Derek Zuniga, who's an excellent birding guide, or check with village chairman Alvin Lindo.

Towards the mountains: Maya villages and ruins

Heading inland from Punta Gorda towards the foothills of the Maya Mountains, you meet yet another uniquely Belizean culture. Here **Mopan Maya** from Petén are mixed with **Kekchí** speakers from the Verapaz highlands of Guatemala. For the most part each group keeps to its own villages, language and traditions, although both are partially integrated into modern Belizean life and many people speak English. Guatemalan families have been arriving here for the last 125 years or so, escaping repression and a shortage of land at home, and founding new villages deep in the forest. Several families a year still cross the border to settle in land-rich Belize, along routes that have been used for generations. The villages are connected by road and all have a basic bus service

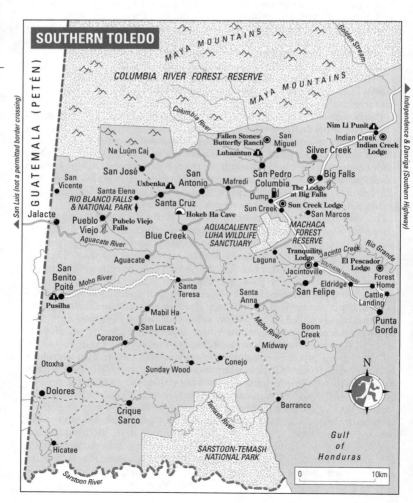

SOUTHERN TOLEDO

from Punta Gorda (see box on p.265), although moving around isn't that easy and in many places you'll have to rely on hitching – despite the fact that there isn't much traffic. A good option is to **rent a bike** from Punta Gorda (ask at *Nature's Way*, TEA or TIDE) and put it on the bus, cycling between those villages in the **guesthouse** programme. The people here are of course used to walking, and the villages are also connected by an intricate network of footpaths. And, when the development plan for Toledo is implemented, the road from the Southern Highway at the Dump junction (see p.260) will be paved to Jalacte on the Guatemalan border, to serve as a feeder road in the **Plan Pueblo–Panamá** – a truly massive infrastructure project which includes upgrading highways throughout southern Mexico and the Caribbean coast of Central America, in part to facilitate the impending implementation of the Free Trade Area of the Americas. This is a controversial proposition, as some Maya communities feel they will be further marginalized as international developers follow in the wake of the highway.

For now though, the existing unpaved road(s) provide access to small villages (almost always on a river) and numerous **Maya sites**, **caves** and **waterfalls** in the surrounding countryside. The area offers wonderful possibilities for hiking (see especially San José, p.276) and you can usually find a guide to lead you on foot or horseback through the lush valleys and over the hills.

Lubaantun and San Pedro Columbia

The Maya site of **Lubaantun**, near the mainly Kekchí village of **San Pedro Columbia**, is an easy visit from Punta Gorda, as the village has its own bus service on market days and there are also many pick-up trucks heading there from the Dump junction. To **get to the site**, head through the village and cross the bridge over the Columbia River, just beyond which you'll see the track to the ruins, a few hundred metres on the left. If you ask around in the village one of the older boys will gladly show you the way; the ruins are about a twenty-minute walk from where the bus drops you. San Pedro itself has limited possibilities for staying overnight (though you might find a room with a local family) but there are a couple of bars and simple restaurants and you should be able to get someone to paddle you to the **"source" of the Columbia River** – a gorgeous spot a couple of kilometres from the village where the river re-emerges from an underground section, gushing forth among the rocks in an enormous, crystal-clear spring, overhung with jungle foliage.

Lubaantun

Lubaantun (daily 8am–5pm; Bz$10) is a major Late Classic city which at one time covered a much larger area than do the remains – impressive though they are – which you see today. The name means "Place of the Fallen Stones" in modern Mayan; the original name is presently unknown. The site is on a high ridge, and from the top of the tallest building you could once (just) see the Caribbean, over 30km away, though climbing on the high pyramids is now not allowed. However, with eleven major structures, five main plazas and three ballcourts with ball-court markers, it's nonetheless a very interesting site – essentially a single acropolis. Lubaantun was brought to the attention of the colonial authorities in 1903, and the governor sent Thomas Gann to investigate. A survey in 1915 revealed many structures, and three ball-court markers were removed and taken to the Peabody Museum at Harvard University. The British Museum expedition of 1926 was joined in 1927 by J. Eric S. Thompson, who was to become the most renowned Maya expert of his time.

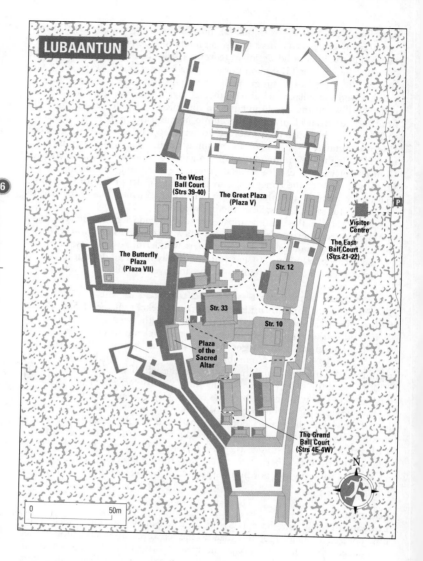

No further excavations took place for over forty years until Norman Hammond mapped the site in 1970, producing a reconstruction of life in Lubaantun which showed the inhabitants' links with communities on the coast and inland. Lubaantun's wealth was created by the production of *cacao* beans, used as money by the civilizations of Mesoamerica.

Sign in at the new **visitor centre** (which, incidentally, has good toilets) where glass cases display some of the finds made at the site – astonishing, eccentric flints (symbols of a ruler's power) and ceramics. Wall panels give accounts of the site's discovery and excavation and show life in a modern Maya village. The very knowledgeable head caretaker Santiago Coc, who's assisted with excavations here for 35 years, or his son Kenan may be able to give you a superb guided tour of the site. Many ocarinas – clay whistles in the shape of animal effigies – were found here and Santiago makes wonderful working replicas; when you hear their evocative notes floating through the ruins you can perhaps imagine the sounds which may have accompanied Maya ceremonies. There are also dozens of mass-produced ceramic figurines, often depicting ball-players – items found nowhere else in such quantities.

Recent restoration has confirmed that the famous Maya corbelled arch was never used here. Instead, buildings were constructed by layering stone blocks carved with particular precision and fitted together, Inca-style, with nothing to bind them. This technique, and the fact that most of the main buildings have rounded corners, give Lubaantun an elegance sometimes missing from larger, more manicured sites. Another anomaly is that no stelae were found here, and it's conjectured that Lubaantun was the regional administrative centre while Nim Li Punit, only 17km away and with numerous stelae, had a more ceremonial or religious function for the same political unit. The relative plainness and monumentality of Lubaantun's architecture is also similar to the later buildings at Quiriguá in Guatemala (another site with numerous stelae), and there may have been some connection between these two sites. It seems that Lubaantun was only occupied briefly, from around 730 AD and abandoned before 880 AD, very near the end of the Classic period.

San Pedro Columbia practicalities

There's currently no guesthouse in San Pedro Columbia (community phone ☎702-2303) but you may be able to find **accommodation** with a local family. However, through the village and 3km beyond the turn-off to the ruins

---

The Crystal Skull of Lubaantun

Perhaps Lubaantun's most enigmatic find came in 1926, when the famous **Crystal Skull** was unearthed here. The skull, made from pure rock crystal, was found beneath an altar by Anna Mitchell-Hedges, the adopted daughter of the British Museum expedition's leader, F.A. Mitchell-Hedges. By a stroke of luck the find happened to coincide with her seventeenth birthday, and the skull was then given to the local Maya, who in turn presented it to Anna's father as a token of their gratitude for the help he had given them. It is possible that the "discovery" was a birthday gift for Anna, placed there by her father who had acquired it on his previous travels, although she strenuously denies the allegation. Anna Mitchell-Hedges still owns the skull; she recalls how she spotted sunlight glinting off it during the excavation of a rubble-filled shaft and promises to reveal more in the course of time.

While mystery and controversy still surround the original skull, London's British Museum has another crystal skull which – according to Dr G.M. Morant, an anthropologist who examined both skulls in 1936 – is a copy of the one found at Lubaantun. He also concluded that both of the life-size crystal skulls are modelled on the same original human head but could give no answer as to their true age and origin. The skull was formerly on display in the Museum of Mankind in London, but when this closed the British Museum decided not to exhibit it, as its origin could not be proved. While on display in the Museum of Mankind, its label was suitably vague: "Possibly from Mexico, age uncertain . . . resembles in style the Mixtec carving of fifteenth-century Mexico, though some lines on the teeth appear to be cut with a jeweller's wheel. If so it may have been made after the Spanish Conquest." There is a similar, smaller crystal skull in the Musée de l'Homme in Paris, and others exist too; all attract great interest from New Age mystics, who believe that crystal has supernatural properties.

(follow the signs), a steeply undulating road leads to *Fallen Stones Butterfly Ranch* (☎722-2167, ⓦwww.fallenstones.co.uk; ❾, including breakfast and service charge), which has comfortable wooden cabins on a hilltop with superb views over the Columbia River Forest Reserve to the Maya Mountains beyond. The cabins all have private showers and electricity, and the dining room juts over a ridge, offering good food and even more gorgeous views at dawn and dusk. The **butterflies** are reared in what amounts to a tiny (and charming) industrial process; every step, from the mating and egg-laying, through the stages of caterpillar development, to the critical packing of the chrysalis for shipping, is governed by meticulous timing – all carefully supervised by the "ranch" workers, who look after their insect babies with tender loving care. Note that at the time of writing *Fallen Stones* was operating but had just been put up for sale, so do check the website for the latest information.

You might also be able to stay as a volunteer or student intern at the **Belize Agroforestry Research Center** (BARC), in a beautiful riverside setting on the outskirts of the village. The Center is located on 150 acres of forest and farmland, and attempts to provide a model of sustainable agroecology, with a tree nursery, dozens of fruit and ornamental trees and organic gardens of raised beds to grow the vegetables eaten here. The study facilities include a classroom, a library and a herbarium collection, and there are several kilometres of trails (you can walk to Lubaantun from here). **Accommodation** is in private rooms, a dorm or camping (all US$15 per person), and all have shared bathrooms. BARC is owned by the Topical Conservation Foundation, PO Box 42, Athens, Ohio 45701. Courses and volunteer projects usually need to be planned well in advance; if you're interested contact the director, Mark Cohen, on ☎614/448-2044 or, in Ohio, 614/767-2638.

Blue Creek

At the tiny village of **Mafredi**, about 9km away from San Pedro Columbia, a branch road (served by buses from Punta Gorda) heads off south and west to **BLUE CREEK**, where the main attraction is the village's namesake – a beautiful stretch of water that runs through magnificent rainforest. The junction is marked by *Roy's Cool Spot*, a well-stocked shop where you can get a snack, a drink and possibly a meal and a room to stay. Four kilometres along the road to Blue Creek is the home of Pablo Bouchub, who runs the tour company Roots and Herbs (☎722-2834 or 608-2879). Pablo is a great **guide** and he can take you to nearby **Aguascalientes Lagoon** for some fantastic bird-watching and he knows fascinating routes to caves and ruins; he and his wife Sonia can also teach you about the medicinal plants of Toledo, and Sonia cooks delicious meals.

Another 3km bring you to Blue Creek itself, with the river flowing through the middle of the village. To get to the best **swimming** spot, walk upriver along the right-hand bank (facing upstream), and in about ten minutes you'll come to a lovely turquoise pool and the wooden cabins of *Blue Creek Rainforest Lodge* (☎523-7076, ⓦwww.ize2belize.com; US$45 per person, including meals) set among the trees. The lodge, used by both student groups and adventure tour groups, is under the same ownership as *Leslie Cottages* on South Water Caye (see p.231), where you should make reservations. It's set in the **Blue Creek Rainforest Preserve**, a 200-acre private reserve, and it's mainly used as a field study centre for students of rainforest ecology, though other visitors can stay at the *Lodge* by arrangement. A student package, including four nights here and five nights on South Water Caye, costs US$998; for non-student prices check with *Leslie Cottages*. Incidentally, since the *Lodge* is privately owned, and you have to pass right by the cabins, the management here sometimes asks you to pay a fee to use the path – so you should know that all rivers and riverbanks in Belize are publicly accessible, and you can in fact walk freely along. The villagers, however, seeing a lucrative source of income, may also wish to charge a small fee for you to use their beautiful river, so you may have to pay up gracefully anyway.

The **source of Blue Creek**, where the water gushes from beneath a mossy rock face, is about another fifteen minutes' walk upriver. Alongside is the entrance to the **Hokeb Ha cave**, which is fairly easy to explore. The entire area is made up of limestone bedrock honeycombed with caves, many of which were sacred to the Maya, and doubtless there are still plenty of others waiting to be rediscovered. If you want to experience the cave in solitude don't come on a Sunday – it can get crowded and you'll be besieged by village children trying to sell you souvenirs, though most other days you'll probably have it to yourself. Sylvano Sho, who lives by the bridge at the entrance to the trail, is the best **guide** in Blue Creek and can take you to Maya altars deep in the Blue Creek cave; he's also a great guide to Pusilhá (below) – and you should not venture there without a local guide. Delphina, Sylvano's wife, serves simple, tasty **meals** in their house.

Pusilhá

About 7km west of Blue Creek is the Kekchí village of **Aguacate**, beyond which the road climbs a ridge leading to the valley of the Moho River, near the border with Guatemala. Further up the valley, almost on the Guatemalan border (and accessed by road via **Santa Teresa**, south of Blue Creek), lies **Pusilhá**, the largest ancient Maya city in southern Belize, where you can view the finest example of an **ancient bridge** anywhere in the Maya world. The site is located in and around the present-day village of **San Benito Poité**, served by a bus on market days from Punta Gorda (up to 2hr, and returning on market days only). At the entrance to the village there's a new bridge over the clear, fast-flowing Pusilhá River, with a lovely **camping** spot nearby. Just downstream from here the Pusilhá and Poité rivers join to form the **Moho River**, the middle stretch of which has some of the best **white-water rapids** in Central America – occasionally paddled by rafting and kayaking expeditions from the US and Canada; see p.11 in Basics.

It's really best to **visit the site** when the archeologists from the **Pusilhá Project** (undertaken by the State University of New York at Buffalo) are working, usually in spring and early summer, as none of the structures here have been fully excavated or restored. Additionally – and even more important – bear in mind that the villagers are not used to seeing outsiders (most speak only Kekchí and a little Spanish), and may view your presence as a threat. You *must* **ask permission** from the alcalde (similar to a mayor) to visit the site as soon as you enter the village and you're strongly recommended to go only with a Kekchí-speaking guide – see if you can get Sylvano Sho, in Blue Creek, above. The alcalde will probably also supply a guide from the village (for whom you'll have to pay a small fee) and he can also arrange food and lodging with a local family. He might also have a copy of the excellent **information sheet** on the site written by Dr Geoffrey Braswell, the project director.

The site

The city, strategically built in the higher land between the confluence of the Poité and Pusilhá (Machaca) rivers, has yielded an astonishing number of carved monuments and stelae, including **zoomorphic altars** (great rounded tablets of stone carved with stylized representations of animals) in a style similar to those at Quiriguá in Guatemala. Initially, this led archeologists to suggest that at some stage Pusilhá may have been under Quiriguá's control, but recent studies indicate a closer connection with Copán, in Honduras.

Although most of the monuments and stelae have been removed (mainly to the British Museum, where they were taken by colonial expeditions in the late 1920s), the **Stela Plaza** – the sacred centre of the ancient city, reached by a *sacbe* (ceremonial road) – still has a few badly eroded stelae and three zoomorphic altars that resemble frogs. Nearby you can also see the remains of an enormous **walled ball-court**. The real highlight, however, is the **Maya bridge**, built at a narrow point over the Pusilhá River. Clearly visible are the remains of the main bridge abutments, solid vertical walls of cut stones several metres high, supported by ramps of rock behind them, and if you look carefully you can still see more large cut stones lining the river bed. In ancient times the bridge supports would have been spanned by beams of sapodilla wood, carrying the road leading to the **Gateway Hill Acropolis** – the residential palace complex of Pusilhá's rulers and administrative centre of the city. Even today you have to admire the Maya architects who designed the bridge and the ability of the artisans who constructed it. During construction the river would have been held back and diverted by a coffer dam upstream, and on either side of the main span are diversion channels, built to take the extra volume of water pouring down the valley during the rains.

The mystery is, why build a bridge at all? The ancient Maya built very few bridges, and rivers were usually crossed by canoe. As such, it would appear this magnificent feat of engineering was constructed solely to provide a suitably impressive **processional route** to the **Acropolis**, the most imposing remains at Pusilhá. Here, a series of pyramidal platforms, terraces and facades, skilfully blended with natural features on the hill slope, have created an awe-inspiring edifice rising 80m above the river – almost twice the height of Belize's tallest free-standing Maya structure, Caana at Caracol, and even higher than Temple IV at Tikal.

San José

Nestled among the southern foothills of the Maya Mountains, **SAN JOSÉ** is one of the northernmost villages in the area. The village bus leaves Punta Gorda for San José at noon on market days (about 1hr) and if you're travelling in your own vehicle the turn-off is about 2km east of San Antonio (see below). To stay at the **guesthouse** here, call the community phone on ☎702-2072. If you're fit, you can take some amazing hikes higher up into the mountains; ask in the village for Valentino Tzub, who can guide you as far as **Little Quartz Ridge**, a steep and isolated plateau with an ecosystem unique to Belize, or even to (at least) the lower slopes of **Doyle's Delight**, the highest peak in Belize. For either of these trips, you'll need camping gear and supplies for at least three days, plus a great deal of stamina. An even more adventurous hike is the extremely arduous five-day **Maya Mountain Divide Trail**, from San José to **Las Cuevas**, at the end of the Chiquibul Road in Cayo (see p.183); if interested, contact Marcos Cucul, who runs Maya Guide Adventures (☎600-3116, Ⓦwww.mayaguide.bz).

San Antonio and Uxbenka

The Mopan Maya village of **SAN ANTONIO**, perched on a small hilltop, is the easiest of the Maya villages to reach, as it's served by daily buses from Punta Gorda, 34km away. It also has the benefit of *Bol's Hill Top Hotel* (community phone ☎702-2144; ❸), which has simple **rooms** with electric light and superb views. There are a couple of shops in the village and you can get **meals** at Theodora's or Clara's house, behind *Bol's*. The area is rich in wildlife, surrounded by jungle-clad hills and swiftly flowing rivers. Further south and west are the villages of the Kekchí Maya, including many fairly recent immigrants who still retain strong cultural links with Guatemala.

The founders of San Antonio were from the Guatemalan town of San Luis just across the border, and they maintain many age-old traditions. Among other things the Indians of San Luis brought with them their patron saint, and opposite *Bol's Hotel* is the beautiful **stone-built church** of San Luis Rey, currently looked after by an American Jesuit order. The church is the third to stand on the site (two previous versions were destroyed by fire) and its most remarkable feature is a set of superb **stained-glass windows**, depicting the twelve apostles and other saints, donated by the people of St Louis, Missouri. The villagers also adhere to their own pre-Columbian traditions and fiestas; the main one takes place on June 13, and features marimba music, masked dances and much heavy drinking.

Seven kilometres west from San Antonio, 1km before the village of **Santa Cruz**, are the ruins of **Uxbenka**, a fairly small Maya site, superbly positioned on an exposed hilltop and with great views towards the coast. Uxbenka's existence only became known to archeologists in 1984 after reports of looting in the area: there's now a site caretaker, who lives in Santa Cruz. As you climb the hill before the village you'll be able to make out the shape of two tree-covered mounds to your left. Though the site has not been fully excavated, you can still make out a couple of pyramids and a plaza, and there are several badly eroded stelae, protected by thatched shelters. There's a **guesthouse** at the entrance to the village, and buses on market days, some of which continue to **Jalacter**, on the border (see below). All around are **trails** through the forest to rivers and waterfalls, and you can walk over to **San José** in about three hours.

On to Jalacte

Continuing west toward the border you can enjoy some wonderful **waterfalls**, within easy reach of the road. Twelve kilometres west of San Antonio, between Santa Cruz and Santa Elena, the **Rio Blanco Falls** tumble five metres over a wide, rocky ledge into a deep pool, perfect for a dip and a picnic. The falls form part of the **Rio Blanco National Park**, and the bus passes right by the (generally deserted) Visitor Centre; walk down the short trail at the side of the building to reach the falls. At **Pueblo Viejo**, 7km further on, an impressive series of cascades on Pueblo Creek provides an even more spectacular sight. Above the falls a steep trail leads through orchid-laden rainforest to a mountaintop overlook; ask in the village for a guide to lead you along the trail. Trucks and buses continue 13km further west to **Jalacte**, at the Guatemalan border, used regularly as a crossing point by nationals of both countries, though it's not currently a legal entry or exit point for tourists.

Travel details

The Southern Highway doesn't have as many buses running along it as the Northern and Western highways, but, with the paving of the road, bus schedules are becoming more reliable, and now express buses cut journey times even further. The main routes are listed overleaf; other buses to the smaller villages are covered in the text. Bus company offices and departure frequencies from Belize City to Dangriga, Placencia and Punta Gorda are covered in the box on pp.74–75.

Buses

Dangriga to: Belmopan (1hr 40min) and Belize City (12 daily; 2–3hr); Hopkins and Sittee River (2–3 daily; 30min); Placencia (2–3 daily; 2hr); Punta Gorda (8–10 daily; 4hr). All buses between Dangriga and Punta Gorda stop at Independence/Mango Creek, where there's a regular ferry to Placencia.

Hopkins and Sittee River to: Dangriga (2–3 daily, first one around 7am; 30min).

Placencia to: Dangriga (2–3 daily; 2hr); all connect with departures to Belmopan and Belize City.

Punta Gorda to: Dangriga (under 4hr) and Belize City (6–7hr; at least 7 daily), all calling at Independence/Mango Creek, for the ferry to Placencia.

Flights

In Belize City, Maya Island Air (☎ 223-1140) and Tropic Air (☎ 224-5671); each have at least four daily flights from Belize City to Dangriga (25min), continuing on to Placencia (a further 20min) and Punta Gorda (20min beyond Placencia).

International boats

Dangriga to: Puerto Cortés, Honduras (weekly skiff, on Sat; 3hr).

Placencia and Big Creek to: Puerto Cortés, Honduras (weekly skiff, on Fri; 3hr).

Punta Gorda to: Puerto Barrios, Guatemala (at least 2 daily; 1hr); to Lívingston, Guatemala (at least 2 weekly; 1hr).

Contexts

Contexts

History

Belize is the youngest nation in Central America, only gaining full independence from Britain in 1981, and its history has been markedly different from the surrounding Latin American republics since at least the mid-seventeenth century. Although the whole region, including Belize, was (to a greater or lesser degree) colonized by Spain in the sixteenth century, it was the colonial entanglement with Britain that gave Belize its present cultural, social and political structures.

Prior to the arrival of Europeans the area now called Belize was part of a vast region known to archeologists as **Mesoamerica**, stretching from north-central Mexico to El Salvador and Honduras. Within this imprecisely defined geographical area the individual cultures shared several common characteristics, including a complex, accurate calendar, hieroglyphic writing, a similar cosmology and religion and a highly organized, stratified society. They may also have shared a common origin, in the **Olmec** civilization, which arose in southern Mexico around 3000 years ago. This definition is designed to exclude the native tribes of North America (whose culture remained largely nomadic) and to group together the pre-Columbian civilizations of their southern neighbours. By far the most important of these (as far as Belize is concerned) are the **Maya**, whose culture began to emerge here as early as 2500 BC and whose cities were at the height of their power between 250 and 900 AD.

Prehistory

Delving further back into the past, archeologists are on uncertain ground, piecing together a general idea on the basis of scattered archeological remains and a handful of written texts. Prior to the advent of Maya civilization very little is known about the area, and the earliest Maya remain fairly mysterious. Set out here is a brief overview of many separate theories, none of which can claim to dominate the academic debate. Over the last few years the situation has, if anything, become even more confused, as excavations of important new sites (especially in Belize) throw up information that casts doubt on many accepted notions. At any moment our whole understanding could be overturned by new discoveries, and there is certainly still a great deal to learn.

Archeological opinions differ as to when the first people arrived in the Americas, but the most widely accepted theory is that **Stone Age hunter-gatherers** crossed the Bering land bridge from Asia in several waves, beginning probably around 25,000 years ago and travelling via an ice-free corridor (and possibly in small boats along the coastline) at a time when sea levels were lowered by advancing glaciers. These early hunters rapidly spread southwards, developing the **Clovis** culture (named after characteristic stone projectile points first identified in Clovis, New Mexico) at least 11,000 years ago; worked stone flakes from this era have been found at Richmond Hill, a site in Orange Walk District. The Clovis people subsisted primarily on hunting the abundant large mammals, including mammoths, mastodons, deer and horses. By 9000 years ago, however, the northern ice sheets were in full retreat, and the big game disappeared during the long period of hot, dry weather that followed.

The scarcity of game, combined with climatic change and altered vegetation patterns, forced the hunter-gatherers to adopt a different way of life, turning to more intensive use of plant foods. During this period (known as the **Archaic** period) the food plants vital to the subsequent development of agriculture, such as peppers, squash, beans and, most important of all, maize, were domesticated. Analysis of pollen grains from that time, found in lake deposits in Petén, Guatemala, reveal that the region (and presumably adjacent Belize too) was an area of savannahs and broad-leaved woodland; the tropical forests did not appear until the Classic period, by which time the Maya could more easily control its profuse growth.

This transition into more settled, primarily agricultural, societies enabled the development of an identifiable culture, which has become broadly known as **Proto-Maya**. There is archeological evidence of Archaic sequences in Belize dating from 7500 BC until later than 2000 BC, though few visible remains from that period can be seen today. An early language, Proto-Maya, was in use in the western highlands of Guatemala, and probably in other places too, including Chiapas in Mexico.

The early Maya in Belize

Somewhere between 2000 and 1500 BC we move into the **Preclassic** (also known as the Formative) period (2000 BC–250 AD). These periods are terms used by archeologists to describe the earliest developments in the history of the culture we recognize as distinctly Maya; each main period is itself usually subdivided into Early, Middle and Late. The boundaries of the different periods are not marked by exact dates, and should be understood as cultural and technological milestones, when particular architectural, artistic and administrative advances were in widespread use; current excavations appear to be pushing back the date when the earliest breakthroughs were made.

The **Early Preclassic** (roughly 2000 BC–1000 BC) marks the beginning of recognizable patterns of agriculture, notably the annual cutting and burning of forest by people living in settled villages in order to plant maize. Crops would have provided part (and increasingly the main part) of their food needs, supplemented by hunting, fishing and foraging for wild plants. There's currently no evidence of structures larger than dwellings for this period, but ceramics were produced; pottery found at **Cuello**, near Orange Walk, dates from around 1000 BC and is among the earliest ceramics in the Maya lowlands.

Elsewhere in Mesoamerica big changes were taking place that were to have a far-reaching impact throughout the region. The first great culture to emerge was the Olmec civilization, originating around 3000 BC in the coastal plain of Veracruz, in Mexico. The Olmecs, often regarded as the true ancestors of Maya culture, developed a complex polytheistic religion, an early writing system and a calendar known as the "long count", later adopted by the Maya (see p.307).

By the **Middle Preclassic** (1000 BC–300 BC) there was a substantial increase in population – evidence of numerous settlements can be found right across the Maya area, from southern Guatemala to northern Yucatán, including almost all of Belize, in particular the main river valleys. Similar styles of red and orange monochrome pottery of the Mamóm style, and stone metates for grinding corn, have been found in all the settlements. It is thought that a common Maya language was spoken throughout the area, and that a universal belief system, practised from a very early date, may have provided the stimulus and social cohesion to build bigger towns. At the same time, as in all early agricultural communities, food surpluses would have eventually freed some to become seers, priests and astronomers. By 750 BC Nakbé, in northern Petén, was a large city, perhaps the first one in the Maya world, evidence that the Maya had progressed far beyond a simple peasant society.

Further advances in architecture and what amounted to an explosion of Maya culture and population came in the **Late Preclassic** (300 BC–250 AD), when the **Chicanel culture** dominated the northern and central areas of the Maya world. The famous Maya corbelled arch (which was not a true arch, with a keystone, but consisted of two sides, each with stones overlapping until they eventually met, and thus could only span a relatively narrow gap) was developed in this period, and the whole range of buildings became more ambitious. Large pyramids with elaborate temples were built at Tikal, El Mirador and Río Azul in Petén. In northern Belize, Cuello, Nohmul, Lamanai and Cerros were the great centres, all featuring major examples of public architecture, some of which can still be seen today. Lamanai and Cerros controlled Preclassic trade routes, and probably continued to do so right through the Classic and into the Postclassic period. The Belize River valley was fully settled, with local centres such as Cahal Pech, Pacbitún and El Pilar expanding and consolidating their power.

The question of what sparked this phase of rapid development is a subject of much debate, though most archeologists agree that the catalyst was the Olmec culture. The Maya adopted and adapted these outside influences, and developed complex administrative mechanisms to feed and control the growing population. As in any advancing society, a hierarchical ruling structure evolved. In the Maya world ultimate military and spiritual power was vested in kings, who established ruling dynasties and communicated with the gods by spilling their own blood at propitious festivals.

The Classic period

The development that separates the Late Preclassic from the **Early Classic** period (250 AD–600 AD) is the introduction of the long count calendar (see p.307) and a recognizable form of writing. This appears to have taken place before the fourth century AD and marks the beginning of the greatest phase of Maya achievement.

Developments in the Maya area were still powerfully influenced by events to the north. The cultural influence of the Olmecs was replaced by that of **Teotihuacán**, which dominated Central Mexico during the early Classic period. Armed merchants spread the power of Teotihuacán as far as Yucatán, Petén and Belize, bringing new styles of ceramics and alternative religious beliefs: complete military invasion and subjugation, however, were a fairly unlikely scenario. Whatever happened around 400 AD, the overwhelming power of Teotihuacán radically altered life in Maya lands. In Petén, **Tikal**'s rise to power must have been helped by close links with Teotihuacán, and both cities prospered greatly: Tikal has a stela (a freestanding carved monument), with inscribed text and dates, depicting a lord of Tikal on one side and a warrior from Teotihuacán on the other.

Most of the cities we now see as ruined or restored sites were built during the Classic period, almost always over earlier structures. Elaborately carved stelae, bearing dates and emblem–glyphs, tell of actual rulers and of historical events in their lives – battles, marriages, dynastic succession and so on. The deciphering of these dates has provided confirmation (or otherwise) of archeological evidence and offered a major insight into the Maya elite. Broadly speaking, the Maya region was made up of independent city-states, bound together by a coherent religion and culture and supporting a sophisticated trade network. The cities jostled for power and influence, a struggle that occasionally erupted into intense warfare. Exactly how the various centres related to one another is unclear, but it appears that three or four main centres dominated the Maya area through an uncertain process of alliances, though no city held sway throughout the entire region. **Calakmul**, in Campeche, Mexico, and Tikal were the nearest of these "superstates" to Belize, and in 562 AD an alliance of Calakmul and Caracol, in southern Cayo District, defeated Tikal, as shown by an inscription on Altar 21 at Caracol. Other detailed carvings on wooden lintels and stone monuments at the site depict elaborately costumed lords trampling on bound captives. It's unclear whether this victory of a previously subordinate city over the dominant regional power was the cause of the major upheaval that followed, but dramatic change was to come.

The collapse of Teotihuacán in the seventh century caused shock waves throughout the civilizations of Mesoamerica as advances were temporarily halted by what is known as the **Middle Classic Hiatus**. No stelae were erected in the Maya cities, and many existing monuments were damaged and defaced. In all likelihood the dominant Maya centres suffered revolts, and warfare raged as rival lords strove to win political power. However, as the new kings established dynasties, now free of Teotihuacán's military or political control, the Maya cities flourished as never before. Architecture, astronomy and art reached degrees of sophistication unequalled by any other pre-Columbian society. Many Maya centres were much larger than contemporary Western European cities, then in their "Dark Ages": Caracol had an estimated 150,000 people.

The prosperity and grandeur of the **Late Classic** (600–850 AD) reached all across the Maya lands: from Bonampak and Palenque in the west, to Calakmul and Uxmal in the north, Altun Ha and Cerros in the east, and Copán and Quiriguá in the south, as well as hundreds of smaller centres. Masterpieces of painted pottery and carved jade (the Maya's most precious material) were created, often to be used as funerary offerings. Shell, bone and, rarely, marble were also exquisitely carved; temples were painted in brilliant colours, inside and out. Most of the pigments have faded long ago, but vestiges remain, enabling experts to reconstruct vivid images of the appearance of the ancient cities.

The Terminal Classic and Postclassic periods

Though it was abrupt when the end came for each Classic Maya centre, it took a century or so (**Terminal Classic**; 800–c.1000 AD) for the Classic Maya civilization to be extinguished in Belize. By 750 AD political and social changes began to be felt; alliances and trade links broke down, wars increased and stelae were carved less frequently. The sacking of Dos Pilas, in the Petexbatún region of southwest Petén by nearby Tamandarito in 761 AD is generally regarded as the first phase of the **Classic Maya collapse**. Warfare became more widespread and destructive, cities gradually became depopulated and new construction ceased over much of Belize after about 830 AD. Bonampak, in Chiapas, was abandoned before its famous murals could be completed, while many of the great sites along the River Usumacinta (now part of the border between Guatemala and Mexico) were occupied by militaristic outsiders. By the end of the Classic period there appears to have been strife and disorder throughout Mesoamerica.

The decline and subsequent collapse of the Classic Maya civilization was probably a result of several factors. There is strong evidence that a prolonged drought in central Yucatán caused competition for scarce resources, with the effects rippling outward. Additionally, the massive increase in population during the Classic period may have put intolerable pressure on food production, ultimately exhausting the fertility of the soil. Finally, the growth and demands of the unproductive elite may have led to a peasant revolt, leading to the abandonment of city life. By the tenth century, the Maya had largely abandoned their central cities and most of those that remained were reduced to a fairly primitive state.

But not all Maya cities were entirely deserted: those in northern Belize, in particular, survived and indeed prospered, with Lamanai and other cities in the area remaining occupied throughout the **Postclassic period** (c.900–1540 AD). The Yucatán peninsula, which appears to have escaped the worst of the depopulation, came under the influence (possibly by outright conquest) of the militaristic **Toltecs**, who came from central Mexico in 987 AD, creating a hybrid of Classic Maya culture.

From around 900 AD to the time of the Spanish Conquest the Yucatán peninsula and northern Belize consisted of over a dozen rival provinces, bound up in a cycle of competition and conflict. Northern Belize was part of the Maya province of **Chactemal** (later known as Chetumal), covering an area from around Maskall, near the site of Altun Ha to Laguna Bacalar in southern Quintana Roo in Mexico, and with Santa Rita, near Corozal, as its possible capital. Chetumal was a wealthy province, producing *cacao* and honey; trade, alliances and wars kept it in contact with surrounding Maya states up to and beyond the Spanish conquest of Aztec Mexico. Further south, the forests were thicker and the ridges of the Maya Mountains intruded across the land. To the Maya of Chetumal this area was known as **Dzuluinicob** – "land of foreigners" – whose capital was Tipú, located at Negroman, on the Macal River south of San Ignacio. The Maya here controlled the upper Belize River valley and put up strenuous resistance to attempts by the Spanish to subdue and convert them.

The first Europeans

The general assumption that Belize was practically deserted by the time Europeans arrived is now widely discredited. In 1500 AD the native population in the area which was to become Belize is estimated to have been around 200,000 – almost as high as it is today – and the Maya towns and provinces were still vigorously independent, as the Spanish found to their cost on several occasions.

The first **Europeans** to set eyes on the mainland of Belize were the Spanish sailors Pinzón and de Solis in the early sixteenth century, though they didn't attempt a landing. The first, accidental, contact occurred in 1511, when a small group of shipwrecked Spanish sailors managed to reach land on the southern coast of Yucatán: five were immediately sacrificed, the others became slaves. At least one of the slaves must have escaped and regained contact with his fellow countrymen, because when **Cortés** reached Cozumel in 1519 he knew of the existence of two other enslaved survivors of the shipwreck, and sent gifts to their masters for their release. Geronimo de Aguilar immediately joined Cortés, but the other survivor, **Gonzalo Guerrero**, refused: Guerrero had married the daughter of Na Chan Kan, the chief of Chactemal, and preferred life among his former captors. Because of his knowledge of Spanish tactics he became a crucial military adviser to the Maya in their subsequent resistance to Spanish domination: the archeologist Eric Thompson calls him the first European to make Belize his home.

In the early years of the conquest few reports were made of contact with the Maya in Belize, probably because the Spanish heard no stories of gold or treasure – their overriding obsession. In 1525 Cortés himself almost certainly passed through southern Belize on his epic march from Veracruz in Mexico to punish a rebellious subordinate in San Gil de Buena Vista, near the mouth of the Río Dulce on the Bay of Honduras. The course of his march took Cortés and his retinue of 140 Spanish soldiers and 3000 Indians across the unknown territory of the Maya heartland, which still contained many thriving towns and cities. At Tayasal on Lake Petén Itzá, he was welcomed by Can Ek, chief of the Itzá, who had heard of Cortés' cruelty in conquering Mexico and decided not to oppose him. The expedition continued southwards, to the valley of the Sarstoon River, the present boundary with Guatemala. After reaching and pacifying the rebels Cortés sailed north to Mexico, without apparently realizing that Yucatán was not an island.

Attempted conquest

For the Spanish it proved relatively simple to capture and eventually kill the "living god" leaders of such militaristic, unified and highly organized empires as the Aztecs and Incas. However, at the time of the conquest, the Maya of present-day Yucatán and Belize were not united into a single political entity and the rulers of the Maya provinces were accustomed to dealing with enemies either by fighting or forming temporary alliances to retain their independence – one reason why the Spanish found this region so difficult to subdue.

In 1528 **Francisco de Montejo**, granted permission by the Spanish Crown to colonize the islands of Cozumel and Yucatán, established a settlement called Salamanca, on the mainland coast south of Cozumel. At the same time his lieutenant, **Alonso Dávila**, led an overland expedition south. Neither was particularly successful: both groups encountered hostile Maya, and Dávila was forced to turn away from Chetumal (Chactemal) by Maya under the command of Gonzalo Guerrero. A second attempt by Dávila to found a town at Chetumal, in 1531, was marginally more successful but nevertheless short-lived. This time (on the advice of Guerrero, who realized they could not defeat the Spanish outright) the Maya had abandoned the town; it was then occupied by Dávila and renamed **Villa Real** – the first attempt by Spain to conquer and settle the area which later became Belize. Once established, however, Dávila and his troops were continually harassed by the Maya and were driven out eighteen months later, fleeing south along the coast of Belize, eventually reaching Omoa in Honduras. For some years after Montejo and Dávila's unsuccessful attempts to conquer Chetumal, the Maya in Belize remained largely free from Spanish interference. Chetumal regained its important trading links and was also a powerful military ally, sending fifty war canoes to Omoa in 1542 to assist the local chief fighting the Spanish.

Montejo's vision of ruling a vast province of the Spanish empire comprising the whole of Yucatán, Belize and Honduras was not to be fulfilled. His son, Montejo the Younger, completed the conquest of Yucatán, establishing his capital at Mérida in 1542: Montejo himself was occupied in settling Honduras. In theory, the area of the Montejos' colonial administration initially stretched from Honduras to Yucatán, and would have included Belize, but in practice the interior was never completely pacified nor were administrative boundaries clearly defined.

Late in 1543, however, **Gaspar Pacheco**, his son Melchor and his nephew Alonso began another chapter in the sickeningly familiar tale of Spanish atrocities, advancing on Chetumal, destroying crops and food stores and ruthlessly slaughtering the inhabitants. In a letter to Spain, cleric Fray Lorenz de Bienvenida wrote: "Nero was not more cruel [than Alonso Pacheco]. He passed through and reached a province called Chetumal, which was at peace. . . . This captain with his own hands committed outrages: he killed many with the garrotte, saying 'This is a good rod with which to punish these people'."

By 1544 the Pachecos had subdued Maya resistance sufficiently to found a town on Lake Bacalar, and claim *encomienda* (tribute) from villages around Chetumal. It is likely that the Pachecos also conquered parts of Dzuluinicob to the south, though for a time Tipú was the centre of an alliance between the two adjacent Maya provinces, showing that there was still armed resistance to Spanish domination.

During the second half of the sixteenth century missions were established, including one at Lamanai in 1570, and the Spanish, with difficulty, strengthened their hold over northern Belize. However, the Maya resentment that was always present beneath the surface boiled over into total rebellion in 1638, forcing Spain to abandon the area of Chetumal and Tipú completely and more or less permanently.

In the mid-seventeenth century the nearest permanent Spanish settlements to Belize were Salamanca de Bacalar in southern Yucatán and Lago de Izabal in Guatemala. Records are scarce, but it is likely that the Maya of Belize were under some form of Spanish influence even if they were not under Spanish rule. Perhaps the determination of Maya resistance deterred Spain from attempting to fully colonize the area; perhaps the Maya fled to inaccessible forests in an attempt to retain their independence. Repeated **expeditions** were mounted by Spanish friars and colonial leaders during the seventeenth century in an attempt to bring the heathen Maya of Tipú into the fold of the Catholic Church, though these were never more than partially successful.

In 1695 a Spanish mission met leaders of the Itzá to discuss the **surrender of the Itzá**. The negotiations were fruitless, and in 1697 Spanish troops attacked Tayasal, the Itzá capital on Lake Petén Itzá (near the site of modern Flores), bringing Maya independence in Petén to an end – at least in theory. At Tipú the struggle was to continue with simmering resentment until 1707, when the population was forcibly removed to Lake Petén Itzá. This cruel act effectively ended Spanish attempts to settle the west of Belize, as it would be impossible to establish a successful colony without people to work for the Spanish landowners.

In the late seventeenth century Bacalar was abandoned after years of **Maya and pirate attacks**. Spain's forces were simply too stretched to cope with securing the vast (and relatively gold-free) territory from Campeche on the Gulf of Mexico to Nicaragua. English, and later British, trade and territorial ambitions now focused on America and the Caribbean, resulting in almost continuous conflict with Spain. The capture of Jamaica in 1655, after 150 years of Spanish rule, gave England a base in the Caribbean from which it could harass Spanish shipping and support the growth of its own colonies.

The arrival of the British

The failure of the Spanish authorities to clearly delineate the southern boundary of Yucatán subsequently allowed **buccaneers** or pirates (primarily British) preying on the Spanish treasure fleets to find refuge along the coast of Belize, and ultimately led to Guatemala's claim to British Honduras and refusal to recognize Belize's independence. Had Spain effectively occupied the area between Yucatán and Honduras it is unlikely that British influence – and a British colony – would have been allowed to become established. When Spain attempted to take action on various occasions to expel the British pirates and woodcutters there was confusion over which Spanish captain-general maintained jurisdiction in the area. Consequently the pirates were able to flee before the Spanish arrived and could return in the absence of any permanent Spanish outposts on the coast.

British incursions along the Bay of Honduras were first made by buccaneers, resting and seeking refuge after raids on Spanish ships and settlements. Some of the great Elizabethan sailors, such as Raleigh, Hawkins and Drake, may have landed on the coast of Belize, though there are no records to prove this. Indeed records of any kind concerning settlements or even temporary camps until the 1700s are scarce; while the dates of the establishment of other British colonies in the Caribbean are known, there was no attempt on the part of the British government to colonize Belize itself.

Other European powers, notably **France** and **the Netherlands**, were also keen to establish a foothold in the Caribbean. Companies were set up to equip privateers, who were really government-sanctioned pirate ships, to raid the Spanish treasure fleets. Treasure wasn't always easy to come by and sometimes they would plunder the piles of **logwood**, cut and awaiting shipment to Spain. The wood itself, hard and extremely heavy, was worth £90–110 a ton, and the trade was controlled by Spain. Back in Europe logwood was used in the expanding textile industry to dye woollens black, red and grey. Naturally such an abundance of convertible wealth attracted the attention of the buccaneers, once they learned of its importance. By the mid-seventeenth century (possibly as early as 1638) British buccaneers had settled on the coasts of Campeche and the Spanish Caribbean.

The various treaties signed between Britain and Spain from the late seventeenth to the mid-eighteenth century, initially designed to outlaw the buccaneers, eventually allowed the British to establish logwood camps along the rivers in northern Belize. However, this was never intended to legitimize permanent British settlement of a territory which Spain clearly regarded as its imperial domain. Thus, the British settlements in Belize periodically came under attack whenever Spain sought to defend its interests. But the attention of the European powers rarely rested long upon the humid and insect-ridden swamps where the logwood cutters, who were becoming known as **Baymen**, worked and lived. The British government, while wishing to profit from the trade in logwood, preferred to avoid the question of whether or not the Baymen were British subjects. For the most part they were left to their own devices.

Life in the logwood camps was uncomfortable, to say the least. Though the wood was mainly cut in the dry season, it was too heavy to float, and the men had to build rafts to float it down to the river mouth in the rainy season, where it was stored awaiting shipment. The Baymen lived in rough huts thatched with palm leaves (known as "Bay leaf", and still seen today, mainly in tourist cabañas), surviving on provisions brought by ships from Jamaica. These ships also brought rum, which the Baymen drank with relish whenever it was available. An English merchant (writing in 1726) reports: "Rum Punch is their Drink, which they'll sometimes sit for several Days at . . . for while the Liquor is moving they don't care to leave it."

Though many of the woodcutters had "voluntarily" given up buccaneering, raiding of Spanish ships still occurred in the later years of the seventeenth century, only to be punished by Spain whenever it had the will and opportunity. One such reprisal against British woodcutters in the Bay of Campeche left the survivors imprisoned in Mexico and led to Belize becoming the main centre for logwood cutting.

As the gangs of woodcutters advanced further into the forests in search of **mahogany** (which had overtaken logwood as the principal export by the 1760s and was increasingly valuable for furniture-making) they came into contact with the Maya of the interior. Although the Baymen had no wish to colonize or convert the Maya they did capture some for slaves, and records show that the early buccaneers took Maya captives to trade in the slave markets of Jamaica. By the mid-eighteenth century the Maya had been so weakened by disease and depopulation that they could offer only limited resistance to British incursions into their territory.

Spanish attacks on the settlements in Belize occurred throughout the eighteenth century, with the Baymen being driven out on several occasions. Increasingly though, Britain – at war with Spain from 1739 to 1748 (the War of Jenkins' Ear) and France from 1743 to 1748 (the War of the Austrian Succession) – began to admit a measure of responsibility for the protection of the settlers. For the British there was little to lose.

In 1746, in response to requests from Belize, the governor of Jamaica sent troops to aid the Baymen, but this assistance didn't stop the Spanish laying waste to the settlement in 1747 and again in 1754. The **Paris Peace Treaty** of 1763 was the first (of many) to allow the British to cut logwood, but since it did not define boundaries the governor of Yucatán sent troops from Bacalar to ensure that the cutters confined themselves to the Belize River. In 1765 Admiral Burnaby, the British commander-in-chief at Jamaica, visited Belize to ensure that the provisions of the treaty, vague though they were, were upheld. As so often in the reports of naval officers concerning the condition of the settlers, he found them "in a state of Anarchy and Confusion". The admiral, recognizing that the Baymen would benefit from some form of British law and regulation, drew up a simple set of laws concerning the maintenance of justice in a remote and uncouth area where the British government did not care to become too closely involved. These rules, known as **Burnaby's Code**, gave authority to a bench of magistrates, supported by a jury, to hold quarterly courts with the power to impose fines. The Baymen attached an importance to the Code (though they apparently rarely obeyed it) beyond that which Burnaby had intended, and even voted to increase its scope a year later.

A century of antagonism, boundary disputes and mutual suspicion between the Spanish colonial authorities and the woodcutting (ex-buccaneering) Baymen meant that relations were never secure: the Spanish feared raids on their treasure ships, and the Baymen feared being driven out of what was ostensibly Spanish imperial territory. Spanish reprisals and animosity to Britain had fostered in the settlers a spirit of defiance and self-reliance, and led to the realization that British rule was preferable to Spanish, as long as they could choose which of its institutions to accept.

The Baymen's tenure in Belize was still very uncertain, however. In 1779 Spain (then allied with France on the side of the American colonies fighting for independence from Britain) sent a fleet from Bacalar to Belize and captured all the inhabitants of St George's Caye – the capital of the Baymen – imprisoning them in Mérida and Havana. The **Versailles Peace Treaty** (1783) did little to resolve the question of the Bay settlement, but a convention signed three years later allowed timber to be cut as far south as the Sibun River. The clause that rankled with the independent-minded settlers most was that no system of government could be established without approval from Madrid. True to their "turbulent and unsettled disposition", the Baymen ignored the strictures of the convention, cutting wood where they pleased and being generally unruly. After 1791 the settlement was without even the little-regarded authority of a superintendent appointed by the governor of Jamaica.

The Battle of St George's Caye

The final showdown between the waning Spanish empire and the Bay settlers (supported this time by a British warship and troops), the **Battle of St George's Caye**, came as a result of the outbreak of war between Britain and Spain in 1796. Field Marshal **Arthur (Don Arturo) O'Neil**, an Irishman and the captain general of Yucatán, assembled ships and troops, determined to drive out the British settlers and this time to occupy Belize. The Baymen appealed to Lord Balcarres, the governor of Jamaica, for help, and a **Lieutenant-Colonel Barrow** was despatched to Belize as superintendent, to command the settlers in the event of hostilities. At a vital Public Meeting held on June 1, 1797, the Baymen decided by 65 votes to 51 to defend the settlement rather than evacuate. A few companies of troops were sent from Jamaica, and slaves were released from woodcutting to be armed and trained. The sloop **HMS Merlin**, under the command of Captain John Moss, was stationed in the Bay, local vessels were armed, gun rafts built and an attack was expected at any time. Throughout the next year the mood of the defenders vacillated between aggression and despair. Under the supervision of Colonel Barrow the men of Belize, now under martial law, prepared for war – albeit grudgingly in some cases. The Baymen (and their slaves) would have to defend themselves with the scant resources at their disposal.

The **Spanish fleet**, reported to consist of 32 vessels, including sixteen heavily armed men-of-war and 2000 troops, arrived just north of St George's Caye in early September 1798. On September 3 and 4, several of the Spanish warships attempted to force a passage over Montego Caye Shoals, between Long Caye and St George's Caye, but were repulsed by the Baymen's sloops. Stakes put down by the Spanish to mark the channels through the shoals were removed by the defenders, who knew these waters well. Colonel Barrow and Captain Moss correctly guessed that the Spanish would now try to seize St George's Caye. The *Merlin* and part of the Baymen's tiny fleet sailed there on the evening of September 5, securing it just as twelve of the heaviest Spanish warships were attempting to do the same.

The next few days must have passed anxiously for both sides: the Spanish with their massive firepower severely restricted by the shallow water; and the Baymen with their small but highly manoeuvrable fleet awaiting the impending attack – with the Baymen's slaves apparently at least as eager to fight the Spanish as were their masters. On the morning of **September 10, 1798**, fourteen of the largest Spanish ships sailed to within 2.5km of St George's Caye, keeping to the deep water to the east, and began firing. Captain Moss of the *Merlin* held his fire – the Spanish broadsides were falling short. At 1.30pm he gave the order to open fire. Guns blazing, the *Merlin* and the Baymen's fleet swept forward, wreaking havoc among the heavy and crowded Spanish ships. The Spanish fleet, already weakened by desertions and yellow fever, suffered heavy losses and fled in disorder to Caye Chapel. There they remained for five days, burying their dead on the island. On the morning of September 16 the defeated fleet sailed for Bacalar, still harassed by the Baymen.

Though a victory was won against overwhelming odds, the Battle of St George's Caye was not by itself decisive. No one in Belize could be sure that the Spanish would not once again attempt to remove the Baymen by force. The legal status was as before: a settlement where the inhabitants could cut timber but which did not constitute a territory of the British empire. Sovereign rights remained, nominally at least, with Spain.

However, in purely practical terms the power of the Spanish empire was waning while the British empire was consolidating and expanding. But in Belize the slaves were still slaves, though they had fought valiantly alongside the Baymen: their owners expected them to go back to cutting mahogany. Emancipation came no earlier than elsewhere in the British empire. Indeed controversy still exists within Belize over the fact that the battle was fought between two European powers to establish rule over a colony. It created the conditions for Belize to become an integral part of the British empire and enabled the slave owners to claim that the slaves were willing to fight on behalf of their masters. Whatever its legacy, the 1798 expedition was the last time that Spain attempted to gain control over Belize; Britain gradually assumed a greater role in the government of the settlement.

Settlers and slaves

A report by a Spanish missionary in 1724 mentions the ownership of **slaves** by English settlers, and it's possible that slaves were brought in (from Jamaica and Bermuda) before that time. The British population of the settlements in the Bay of Honduras during the century and a half following the arrival of the first buccaneers had never been more than a few hundred, their livelihoods dependent on the attitude of the authorities in the adjacent Spanish colonies. In order to gain concessions from Spain favourable to the Belize settlement, Britain had agreed to relinquish claims to the Mosquito Shore (a British protectorate along the coasts of Honduras and Nicaragua) in the **Convention of 1786**. Many of the aggrieved inhabitants displaced by the convention settled in Belize, and by 1790 the population had reached over 2900, of whom over 2100 were slaves.

Over the years the view that slavery in Belize was somehow less harsh than elsewhere in the Caribbean has emerged. It's a misconception that may have arisen because of the differences between plantation slavery as practised in the West Indies and the southern United States, and the mainly forest labour that slaves in Belize were required to perform. The misconception has evolved into a myth, skilfully manipulated by apologists for colonialism, who maintain that during the pivotal Battle of St George's Caye slaves voluntarily fought "shoulder to shoulder" with their white masters, and thus preferred slavery over the freedom offered by the Spanish authorities to any slave who escaped to Spanish territory. Although some slaves did fight alongside their masters in 1798, they also continued to escape: in 1813 fifteen slaves belonging to Thomas Paslow, one of the heroes of the battle, escaped "because of ill-treatment and starvation", their desperation evidence enough to refute the myth. Records of **slave revolts** from 1745 to 1820 are further indication that relations between master and slaves were not as amicable as some would like to believe.

The whites in the settlement, always vastly outnumbered by their slaves, feared rebellion at least as much as they feared attack by the Spanish. The biggest (and arguably most successful) revolt occurred in 1773 when six white men were murdered and at least eleven slaves escaped across the Hondo River, where they received asylum from the Spanish authorities. This was not a display of altruism on the part of the Spanish, since encouraging slaves to flee the British settlement was calculated to weaken its economy.

The *nature* of slavery in Belize was, however, very different from that on the sugar plantations in the West Indies. The cutting of mahogany involved small gangs working in the forest on their own or on a fairly harmonious level with an overseer. The slaves were armed, with firearms in some cases, to hunt for food and for protection against the Maya. Skills developed in searching for the trees, cutting them down and transporting them to the coast gave the slaves involved a position of trust that their masters depended on for the continuation of their own way of life. **Manumission**, whereby a slave might purchase freedom or be freed as a bequest in a will, or simply a gift, was much more frequent in Belize than in the Caribbean islands, perhaps as an indication of the greater informality of Belizean society. However, treatment could still be harsh and little protection was offered by the law. Owners could inflict up to 39 lashes or imprison their slaves, and if a slave was hanged for rebellion the owner could be compensated for the loss of property.

Ironically, it was the **Abolition Act of 1807** – which made it illegal for British subjects to continue with the African slave trade but not to transport slaves from one British colony to another – that gave the settlers in Belize recognition as **British subjects**. If Belize was not a colony (which it clearly was not) then slaves could not be transported between Jamaica and the settlement. Superintendent Arthur, the British government's representative and upholder of the law in Belize, decided that the settlers in Belize were British subjects and therefore forbidden to engage in the slave trade. The **Abolition Act of 1833** ended slavery throughout the British empire, and contained a special clause to include Belize. The passing of the Act, however, did not end slavery immediately: "freed" slaves were to be called "apprentices", required to work for their masters for forty hours per week with no pay before being allowed to work for payment. This abuse continued until 1838, when the former slaves were fully and legally free. Despite the inherent immorality in the institution of slavery the Act provided for **compensation** to be paid to the owners for the loss of property, rather than to the former slaves for the suffering they had undergone for so long – and, at £53 per slave, the compensation paid was higher than in any British colony.

The settlement becomes a colony

The consolidation of British logging interests in the eighteenth century and the grudging, tentative steps towards recognition from Spain, led to a form of **British colonial government** gradually becoming established in the Belize settlement. The **Public Meeting**, with its origins in the early 1700s, was the settlers' initial response to the need for some rudimentary form of government. At first informal, the meetings slowly assumed greater importance, and by the 1730s were electing magistrates with powers to hold courts and impose fines, though in the democratic spirit of the time only property-owning white men could vote. Free black men were allowed to vote at the Public Meeting after 1808, though their franchise was limited by burdening them with higher property requirements than that of whites. **Burnaby's Code** in 1765 reinforced and enlarged the jurisdiction of the magistrates, and allowed the laws passed at the Meeting to be enforced by the captain of a British naval ship, though reports by visiting naval officers almost invariably commented on the lamentable inability of the settlers to keep their own laws.

These early examples of Britain's acceptance of some form of responsibility to the settlers led to the appointment in 1784 of the first **Superintendent**, Captain Despard, who took up his post in 1786. The office of superintendent, always held by an army officer, appears to have been a difficult one. They often faced an unsupportive Public Meeting, which wanted to run the settlement without "interference" from London. Gradually though, the powers of the superintendent grew, while those of the magistrates lessened. The election of magistrates ceased altogether in 1832, after which they were appointed by the superintendent. The office of superintendent was moving towards the role (though not the title) of a lieutenant-governor of a colony, and in 1854 an elected **Legislative Assembly** was formed, establishing the beginnings of colonial-rule parliamentary democracy. The assembly began petitioning for recognition as a colony, arguing that the settlement was in fact, if not in law, already a British colony. Earl Grey, at the Colonial Office, supported the assembly and Palmerston, the British prime minister, agreed. On May 12, 1862, the Belize settlements, with the boundaries that still exist today, became the **Colony of British Honduras**.

Partly as a result of arguments about raising finance, the Legislative Assembly dissolved itself in 1870 and was replaced by a Legislative Council. This enabled the British government to establish a **Crown Colony** form of government in 1871, in line with colonial policy throughout the West Indies. Now under the control of a governor appointed by the Colonial Office, the self-determination of the settlers was effectively reduced.

Mexican and Guatemalan claims

After the Battle of St George's Caye in 1798 Spain continued to maintain its claim to Belize, and the **Treaty of Amiens** in 1802 required Britain to hand back to Spain the territory captured during the war. Spain took this to include Belize, though the Baymen had no intention of leaving. But in the face of gathering difficulties throughout the Spanish empire, and Britain's willingness to assist the settlers in the defence of Belize, Spain's claim became increasingly insupportable.

Although **Mexico's independence**, achieved in 1821 and followed two years later by the colonies in Central America, marked the end of the Spanish empire on the mainland of the Americas, it didn't signal the end of external claims to Belizean territory. The years between the collapse of the Spanish empire and the close of the nineteenth century were filled with claim and counter-claim and with treaties made and broken – a situation not entirely resolved today.

Mexico's claim to at least the northern part of British Honduras as an extension of Yucatán was unacceptable to the British government, and eventually, after numerous diplomatic exchanges, an **Anglo–Mexican Treaty** was ratified in 1897. However, Mexico stated at the time that should Guatemala successfully revive any of its claims to British Honduras then Mexico would press a claim to the area north of the Sibun River.

Guatemala's claim has been the source of more belligerent disagreement with Britain, and there's no doubt that the British government shares much of the blame for the confusion. In treaty after treaty Britain regarded Belize as a territory under Spanish sovereignty, and long after Spain's expulsion from the area, Britain maintained the fiction of Spanish sovereignty, which only complicated relations with the independent Guatemala. The Guatemalan claim to the territory of Belize rested upon the acceptance in international law of *uti possidetis* – the right of a colony which successfully gains independence from a colonial authority to inherit the rights and territory of that authority at the time of independence. For this to be valid, however (even if Britain accepted the premise of *uti possidetis* – which was doubtful), the entire territory of Belize would have had to have been under Spanish control in 1821. Since this was clearly not the case the British position was that Guatemala's claim was therefore invalid.

In a vain attempt to reach a settlement Britain and Guatemala signed the **Anglo–Guatemalan Treaty** in 1859: the interpretation of this treaty and its various clauses has been the source of controversy and dispute ever since. The treaty, which in the British view settled the boundaries of Guatemala and Belize in their existing positions, was interpreted by Guatemala as a disguised treaty of cession of the territory outlined – if the crucial and controversial Article 7 of the treaty was not implemented – and not a confirmation of the boundaries. Under the provisions of Article 7, Britain agreed to fund and build a road from Guatemala City to the Atlantic coast and in return Guatemala would drop its claim to Belize. If the road was not built then the territory would revert to Guatemala. Although a route was surveyed in 1859, Britain considered the estimated cost of £100,000 to construct the road too high a price to pay to secure the territory of Belize, and for this and other reasons the road was never built. The disputes were no nearer resolution when the settlement became the colony of British Honduras in 1862. The provisions of this article continued to be a cause of rancour and disagreement between the two countries for decades, and despite conventions and negotiations no agreement was reached. Finally, in 1940, Guatemala repudiated the treaty on the grounds that the provisions of Article 7 were not fulfilled, and the new constitution of 1945 declared Belize – *Belice* in Spanish – to be the 23rd department of Guatemala. In 1948 Guatemala made the first of several **threats to invade** Belize to "recover" the territory; Britain responded by sending cruisers and troops, the first of many military deployments required to counter this threat over the next four decades. With hindsight, £100,000 in 1859 would have been a comparative bargain.

The Caste Wars of Yucatán

The terrible, bloody **Caste Wars** of Yucatán began with a riot by Maya troops at Valladolid in 1847. They sacked the town, killing whites and spreading terror throughout the peninsula, and came within a hair's breadth of capturing the capital, Mérida, and throwing off white rule completely. From 1848, as Mexico sent troops to put down the rebellion, thousands of Maya and Mestizo

refugees fled to Belize, increasing the population of Orange Walk and Corozal and clearing the land for agriculture. The superintendent in Belize encouraged them to stay as they brought sugarcane and much-needed farming skills.

The rebellious **Cruzob Maya** (taking their name from a sacred "talking cross") occupied a huge, virtually independent territory in the east of the Yucatán peninsula. They established their capital at Chan Santa Cruz ("little holy cross" in English), the modern town of Felipe Carillo Puerto, well to the north of Belize, giving them their alternative name – the **Santa Cruz Maya**. At this time, the border between Belize and Mexico was not clearly defined, and the Belize woodcutters came into conflict with the Santa Cruz Maya, who attacked the mahogany camps and took prisoners for ransom. The alarm spread throughout Belize and eventually a compromise was reached, whereby the settlers would pay a ransom to secure the prisoners' release, and would furthermore pay royalties to the Santa Cruz for the rights to cut wood in the Maya territory. In fact British merchants in Belize profited from the war by selling the Santa Cruz Maya arms, provoking strong protests from Mexico.

The story is further complicated by suspicion between the Santa Cruz and another Maya group, the **Icaiché**, who were not in rebellion and consequently were not trusted by the Santa Cruz. In 1851 the Icaiché were attacked by the Santa Cruz Maya, leading the Mexican government to propose an alliance between themselves and the Icaiché against the Santa Cruz. The Icaiché leaders requested British help in their negotiations, and since the woodcutters wanted to enter Icaiché lands to log mahogany, the Belize timber companies were also signatories to the treaty. In the **treaty of 1853** the Icaiché were granted virtual autonomy in the lands they occupied in return for recognizing the authority of Mexico, and the British were allowed to cut wood under licence in the Icaiché lands, in what was to become the northwest of Belize. The British woodcutters viewed the agreement as a means to expand their territory at the expense of both the Icaiché and a weakened Mexico.

It was now the turn of the Icaiché to demand rent from the British loggers; again this was only paid after **Maya attacks** on the camps. The continuing British arms trade with the Santa Cruz Maya incensed the Icaiché, and the flames were fanned further when they were attacked by the Santa Cruz. After years of broken agreements and betrayal the Icaiché, supported by Mexico and led by **Marcos Canul**, attacked mahogany camps on the Rio Bravo and the New River in 1866, capturing dozens of prisoners and spreading panic throughout the colony. The lieutenant governor declared martial law and sent for reinforcements from Jamaica. Raids and counter-raids continued for years, as the Maya sacked villages in Belize and colonial troops destroyed Maya villages and crops in reprisal. Canul briefly occupied Corozal in 1870, and even his death following a battle at Orange Walk in 1872 did not put an end to the raids. Corozal became a fortified military base, and, although the violence diminished, the danger of Maya attacks wasn't over until 1882 when the Icaiché leader, Santiago Pech, met the governor in Belize City to recognize British jurisdiction in the northwest.

The twentieth century: towards independence

By 1900, free for the moment from worries about external threats, Belize was an integral, if minor, colony of the British empire. The population in the census of 1901 was 37,500, of whom 28,500 were born in the colony.

Comfortable complacency set in, and the predominantly white property owners could foresee no change to their rule. The workers in the forests and on the estates were mainly black, the descendants of former slaves, known as "Creoles". Wages were low and the colonial government and employers maintained strict controls over workers, with the power to imprison labourers for missing a day's work and stifling any labour organizations.

Belizeans rushed to defend the "mother country" in **World War I** but the black troops from Belize were not permitted to fight a white enemy and were instead placed in labour battalions in British-held Mesopotamia. On their return in 1919, humiliated and disillusioned, their bitterness exploded into violence, and the troops were joined by thousands of Belize City's population (including the police) in looting and rioting, an event which marked the onset of **black consciousness** and the beginnings of the independence movement. The ideas of **Marcus Garvey**, a phenomenally industrious and charismatic black Jamaican leader, and founder of the Universal Negro Improvement Association (UNIA), were already known in Belize – the colonial government's ban on *Negro World*, the UNIA's magazine, contributed to the severity of the 1919 riot – and in 1920 a branch of the UNIA opened in Belize City. Garvey believed that the "Negro needs a nation and a country of his own" – a sentiment which found increasing support among all sectors of black society in Belize. Garvey himself visited Belize in 1921.

The status of workers had improved little over the previous century, and the Depression years of the 1930s brought extreme hardship, the disastrous hurricane of 1931 compounding the misery. The disaster prompted workers to organize in 1934 after an unemployment relief programme initiated by the governor was a dismal failure. **Antonio Soberanis** emerged as a leader, founding the Labourers and Unemployed Association (LUA), and holding regular meetings in the "Battlefield" – a public square outside the colonial administration buildings in Belize City. Soberanis was arrested in October 1934 while arranging bail for pickets at a sawmill who had been arrested. He was released a month later, and the meetings resumed. The colonial government responded by passing restrictive laws, banning marches and increasing the powers of the governor to deal with disturbances.

World War II gave a boost to forestry and the opportunity for Belizeans to work abroad, though conditions for the returning soldiers and workers were no better than they had been following World War I. Even in 1946 political power lay with the tiny wealthy elite who controlled the Executive Council and with the governor, a Foreign Office appointee. The devaluation of the British Honduras dollar at the end of 1949 caused greater hardship. A cautious report on constitutional reform in 1951 led to a new constitution, and in 1954 a **general election** was held in which all literate adults over the age of 21 could vote. These elections were won with an overwhelming majority by the **People's United Party** (PUP), led by **George Price**, and ushered in a semblance of ministerial government, though control of financial measures was retained by the governor. Belize became an **internally self-governing** colony in 1964, a step intended to lead to full independence after a relatively short time, as was the policy throughout the Caribbean. Until then, however, the British government, through the governor, remained responsible for defence, foreign affairs and internal security. The National Assembly became a bicameral system with an appointed Senate and an entirely elected House of Representatives.

The delay in achieving independence was caused largely by the ongoing **dispute with Guatemala** as to its still unresolved claim to Belize. At least twice, in 1972 and 1977, Guatemala moved troops to the border and threatened to invade, but prompt British reinforcements were an effective dissuasion. The situation remained tense but international opinion gradually moved in favour of Belizean independence.

Independence and the border dispute

The most important demonstration of worldwide endorsement of Belize's right to self-determination was the **UN resolution** passed in 1980, which demanded secure independence, with all territory intact, before the next session. Further negotiations with Guatemala began but complete agreement could not be reached: Guatemala still insisted on some territorial concessions. On March 11, 1981, Britain, Guatemala and Belize released the "Heads of Agreement", a document which, they hoped, would eventually result in a peaceful solution to the dispute. Accordingly, on September 21, 1981, Belize became an independent country within the British Commonwealth, with Queen Elizabeth II as head of state. In a unique decision British troops were to remain in Belize, to ensure the territorial integrity of the new nation.

The new government of Belize, formed by the PUP with George Price as premier, continued in power until 1984, when the United Democratic Party (UDP), led by **Manuel Esquivel**, won Belize's first general election after independence. The new government encouraged private enterprise and foreign investment, and began a programme of neo-liberal economic reforms which meant privatizing much of the public sector. The next general election, in 1989, returned the PUP to power.

In 1988 Guatemala and Belize established a joint commission to work towards a "just and honourable" solution to the **border dispute**, and by August 1990 it was agreed in principle that Guatemala would accept the existing border with Belize. The only sticking point preventing full recognition by Guatemala was a geographical anomaly in the extreme south, where the territorial waters of Belize and Honduras formed a common boundary, making it theoretically possible for Guatemalan ships to be excluded from their own Caribbean ports. The PUP government's response was to draft the **Maritime Areas Bill** in August 1991, which would allow Guatemala access to the high seas by restricting Belize's territorial waters between the Sarstoon River and Ranguana Caye, 100km to the northeast. This measure proved acceptable to Guatemala's President Serrano, and on September 11, with just ten days to go before the celebrations for Belize's tenth anniversary of independence, Guatemala and Belize established full diplomatic relations for the first time.

The air of euphoria soured somewhat during 1992 as opposition to Serrano's controversial recognition of Belize became more vocal and was ultimately challenged in Guatemala's Constitutional Court. Eventually the court decided that the president had not actually violated the constitution, and in November 1992 Congress (albeit with thirteen abstentions) conditionally approved Serrano's actions. The Guatemalan president's remaining time in office was short, however: in May 1993 he attempted to rule without Congress, and by June was overthown in exile. Belize's premier, George Price, hoped to gain from the confusion this caused and, with the opposition UDP deeply divided, called a snap general election in July 1993. To his astonishment the gamble failed, and Manuel Esquivel's UDP was allowed a second term of office.

Eventually negotiations between the two countries resumed, and in 2002 both governments agreed that the territorial dispute – now called the "**border differendum**" – could at long last be resolved by Belize ceding a tiny sliver of land in the far northwest (the result of an incorrectly positioned survey marker in 1931), and by establishing a joint-use area in the southern territorial waters. Almost everyone in Belize realized this was a golden opportunity: a few square kilometres of unoccupied land (which had never actually belonged to Belize in the first place) and joint use of sea lanes and seabed (together with the creation of an international protected area) and the Guatemalan claim would be over. The problem in implementing what was, on the face of it, a proposal where both parties had everything to gain and neither lost face, was that in order to ratify the agreement a referendum would have to be held in each country, with the electorate voting in favour. This would not be difficult to arrange in Belize, but holding a referendum in Guatemala, where most people have only a vague idea (if any) of the border dispute and of the attempts to resolve it, would require such a massive education programme to inform voters that the government is making no moves to hold one.

And so, despite agreement between the two governments, the border issue remains a stumbling block in relations between the two countries. The dispute simmers on as Guatemalan peasant farmers clear land just inside Belize and small groups of soldiers from each country stray across the other's border. One positive outcome of the 2002 agreement is the setting up of an **adjacency zone** a few kilometres either side of the border, where potentially inflammatory cross-border disputes can be referred to an impartial committee under the jurisdiction of the Organization of American States. Thus, despite the failure to reach a completely watertight agreement, the outlook is probably brighter than at any time in history; both countries continue to exchange ambassadors and are committed to resolving the dispute through **negotiation**.

Belize's **democratic credentials** are beyond dispute: at each general election since independence (until the most recent) the voters have kicked out the incumbent government and replaced it with the opposition. This has meant that the nominally left-of-centre **People's United Party (PUP)** has alternated with the more market-led **United Democratic Party (UDP)**. At the general election of March 2003, however, the PUP under the leadership of Prime Minister **Said Musa** won an unprecedented second term in a second consecutive landslide victory.

The booming **tourist industry**, bringing in around US$250 million a year out of Belize's US$1.25 billion GDP and employing almost a third of the country's workforce, is now the mainstay of Belize's **economy**, pushing agriculture and fisheries into a close second place. Annual growth is around 5 percent, with inflation at 2.6 percent, while unemployment hovers around 10 percent. Figures are obviously not available for Belize's income from the lucrative drug transshipment business, but this illicit economy is certainly a sizeable fraction of the official one. **Per capita** income is high for Central America, at almost US$5000, boosted by the remittances many Belizeans receive from relatives abroad, mainly in the US. This apparent advantage is somewhat offset by the fact that many of the brightest and most highly trained citizens leave Belize, fitting in well in English-speaking North America, though increasingly many graduates do return as more skilled and managerial positions become available within Belize.

Though Belize's traditional links with Britain and the Commonwealth countries in the West Indies remain strong, the **United States** is by far its largest trading partner and supplies much of the **foreign aid** on which Belize still depends. Britain's position as the former colonial power and a major aid-provider following independence is gradually being replaced by aid channelled through multilateral organizations, including the EU.

Belize is currently participating in the negotiations for the **Free Trade Area of the Americas** (FTAA), with January 2005 set as the target date for the agreement to come into force, though this is unlikely to be achieved. This agreement would establish the largest free trade area in the world, an idea viewed with alarm by many Belizean workers, who fear that an end to all tariffs will further depress agricultural prices and drive the small manufacturing base into bankruptcy. Even worse in many eyes, such proposals might signal an end to the **fixed rate of exchange** with the US$, leading to a potentially catastrophic devaluation of the Belize dollar. A leading opponent of the FTAA describes it as "an economic onslaught on national sovereignty". Regardless of the populist rhetoric of the PUP government and domestic popular sentiment, however, Belize is firmly linked to the US-dominated international financial structures and will have to face increasing challenges from global competition in the future.

Chronology of the Maya

25,000 BC ▶ **Paleo-Indian** First waves of nomadic hunters from Siberia.

10,000 BC ▶ **Clovis culture** Worked stone tools found at many sites in North and Central America.

7500 BC ▶ **Archaic period** Beginnings of settled agricultural communities throughout Mesoamerica; maize and other food crops cultivated.

4500 BC ▶ **Proto-Maya period** First Maya-speaking groups settle in western Guatemala; Proto-Maya speakers probably spread throughout extent of Maya area.

2000 BC ▶ **Preclassic** or **Formative period** Divided into: Early: 2000–1000 BC; Middle: 1000–300 BC; Late: 300 BC–250 AD.

The Maya begin building centres which would develop into the great cities of the Classic period. Trade increases, and contact with the **Olmec** on the Gulf coast of Mexico brings many cultural developments, including the calendar and new gods. **Kaminaljuyú** dominates highland Guatemala, **El Mirador** is the most important city in Petén and by 1000 BC Lamanai is a large city.

200 BC ▶ Earliest carved stela found in Belize: Stela 9 at Cahal Pech.

250 AD ▶ **Classic period** Divided into: Early: 250–600 AD; Late: 600–850 AD; Terminal: 850–c.1000 AD.

During this period Maya culture reaches its height. Introduction of the **long count calendar**, used to mark dates of important events on stelae and monuments. The central lowlands are thickly populated, with almost all of the sites now known flourishing. The great monumental architecture associated with the Maya mainly dates from the Classic period. **Caracol** is the largest Classic Maya city in Belize.

800 AD ▶ **Terminal Classic period** Decline (some say collapse) of Classic Maya civilization for reasons which remain unclear. Population decline and abandonment of many Maya cities, though some in Belize – notably **Lamanai** – survive throughout the Terminal Classic period.

987 AD ▶ Yucatán sites show strong evidence of **Toltec culture**, possibly a result of invasion. Toltec culture grafted onto the region's Maya culture, possibly also extending into Belize.

1000 AD ▶ **Early Postclassic period**

Re-focus of populations. Some centres, such as **Xunantunich**, which survived the Terminal Classic, are now abandoned, but many centres in Belize continue to thrive. Toltec domination of the Guatemalan highlands.

c. 1250 ▶ Rivalry and trade among the city-states of Petén, Yucatán and Belize. New, competitive, power structures formed by centres along the trade routes. **Tayasal** (near Flores) rises to dominance in Petén. Cities in the river valleys of Belize grow rich controlling trade routes.

1511 ▶ First **Spanish contact with Maya** in Yucatán; Spanish sailors are captured.

1521 ▶ Aztec capital Tenochtitlán falls to Spanish troops commanded by **Cortés**.

1531 ▶ **Alonso Dávila** makes first attempt to capture and settle at Chetumal.

1543 & 1544 ▶ Gaspar and Melchor **Pacheco** brutally conquer southern Yucatán and northern Belize.

1570 ▶ **Spanish mission** established at Lamanai; eight others built in northern Belize.

1697 ▶ **Conquest of the Itzá Maya** of Noh Petén (present-day Flores), the last independent Maya kingdom.

Chronology of Belize

1618 ▶ Spanish priests Fuensalida and Orbita visit **Tipú**, on the Macal River, where they punish the Maya for worshipping "idols"; the Maya burn the church in defiance.

1630–1640 ▶ Led by Tipú, the **Maya revolt against Spanish rule**. First pirate attacks on Bacalar, just north of Hondo River.

1640s ▶ First **buccaneer** (pirate) settlements at mouth of Belize River.

1670 ▶ **Treaty of Madrid**, under which European powers begin to restrict piracy. Buccaneers start to cut logwood in the swamps of Belize. Spain claims sovereignty over Belize (but had never effectively colonized the area).

1716 ▶ First **Spanish attacks** on British woodcutters (**Baymen**) in Belize. These attacks continue until 1798; at times the whole population of the settlement is driven off or captured, but the Baymen always return. African slaves brought from Jamaica to cut wood.

1763 ▶ **Treaty of Paris** allows British to cut and export wood in Belize; Spanish continue to maintain sovereignty but Britain increasingly prepared to defend settlers' rights.

1786 ▶ **Convention of London** allows Baymen to cut wood, but not to establish plantations, fortifications or government. First **British superintendent** in Belize.

1798 ▶ **Battle of St George's Caye**: settlers and slaves under the command of British army and with support from the Royal Navy defeat a Spanish invasion fleet.

1821–1824 ▶ Mexico and the **Central American republics gain independence** from Spain. Both Mexico and Guatemala claim sovereignty over Belize.

1832 ▶ Main date of arrival of **Garífuna** from Honduras, though some were already in Belize.

1838 ▶ Emancipation of slaves (four years later than in Britain).

1847–1900 ▶ **Caste Wars in Yucatán** Maya refugees flee to northern Belize; other groups of Maya raid towns and settlements in Belize until 1880.

1859 ▶ **Anglo-Guatemala Treaty** and other agreements aim to end dispute over sovereignty of Belize, but no real conclusion reached.

1862 ▶ Belize becomes part of the British empire as the colony of **British Honduras**.

1871 ▶ Status of British Honduras changed to **Crown Colony**.

1919 ▶ Belizean troops riot on return from World War I. Start of **nationalist sentiment** and beginning of calls for independence.

1931 ▶ **Hurricane** (unnamed) devastates Belize City and the entire coast.

1945 ▶ New Guatemalan constitution defines "*Belice*" as a department of Guatemala.

1950 ▶ **PUP** formed.

1954 ▶ New constitution introduces universal adult suffrage. PUP wins the **general election**.

1964 ▶ Belize gains **full internal self-government**. Independence delayed by Guatemala's claim to Belize. Guatemala threatens to invade in 1972 and 1977.

1979 ▶ First of 40,000 **refugees** from Guatemala and El Salvador arrive in Belize.

1981 ▶ Belize gains **independence** on September 21. **George Price** of PUP is prime minister.

1984 ▶ First general election after independence. UDP wins; **Manuel Esquivel** becomes prime minister.

1989 ▶ **PUP wins general election**; George Price is again prime minister.

1991–1993 ▶ Guatemala's President Serrano agrees to recognize Belize. Diplomatic relations are established but no final agreement signed. George Price and PUP lose the general election. Manuel Esquivel and **UDP are elected**.

1998 & 2003 ▶ PUP wins landslide general elections; **Said Musa** is prime minister.

2002 ▶ Organization of American States (OAS) sponsors agreement to settle border dispute agreed to by Belize and Guatemala, but neither likely to hold the necessary referendum leading to ratification.

The Maya achievement

For some three thousand years before the arrival of the Spanish, Maya civilization dominated Central America, leaving behind some of the most impressive and mysterious architecture in the entire continent. At their peak, from 200 to 900 AD, Maya cities were far larger and more elaborate than anything that existed in Europe at the time. Their culture was complex and sophisticated, fostering the highest standards of engineering, astronomy, stone carving and mathematics, as well as an intricate writing system.

To appreciate all this you have to see for yourself the remains of the great centres. Despite centuries of neglect and abuse they are still astounding, their main temples towering above the forest roof. Stone monuments, however, leave much of the story untold, and there is still a great deal we have to learn about Maya civilization. What follows is a brief introduction to the subject, hopefully just enough to whet your appetite for the immense volumes that have been written on it.

Maya life and society

While the remains of the great Maya sites are a testament to the scale and sophistication of Maya civilization, they offer little insight into daily life in Maya times. To reconstruct the lives of ordinary people archeologists have turned to the smaller **residential groups** that surround the main sites, littered with the remains of household utensils, pottery, bones and farming tools. These groups are made up of simple structures made of poles and wattle-and-daub, each of which was home to a single family. The groups as a whole probably housed an extended family, who would have farmed and hunted together and may well have specialized in some trade or craft. The people living in these groups were the commoners, their lives largely dependent on agriculture. Maize, beans, *cacao*, squash, chillies and fruit trees were cultivated in raised and irrigated fields, while wild fruits were harvested from the surrounding forest. Much of the land was communally owned and groups of around twenty men worked in the fields together.

Maya **agriculture** was continuously adapting to the needs of the developing society, and the early practice of slash-and-burn farming was soon replaced by more intensive and sophisticated methods to meet the needs of a growing population. Some of the land was terraced, drained or irrigated in order to improve its fertility and ensure that fields didn't have to lie fallow for long periods, and the capture of water became crucial to the success of a site. The large cities, today hemmed in by the forest, were once surrounded by open fields, canals and residential compounds, while slash-and-burn agriculture probably continued in marginal and outlying areas. Agriculture became a specialized profession, and a large section of the population would have bought at least some of their food in markets, although all households still had a kitchen garden where they grew herbs and fruit.

Maize has always been the basis of the Maya **diet**, in ancient times as much as it is today. Once harvested it was made into *saka*, a corn-meal gruel, which was eaten with chilli as the first meal of the day. During the day labourers ate a mixture of corn dough and water, and we know that *tamales* were also a popular speciality. The main meal, eaten in the evenings, would have been similarly maize-based, although it may well have included vegetables, and occasionally meat. As a supplement to this simple diet, deer, peccary, wild turkey, duck, pigeon and quail were all hunted with bows and arrows or blowguns. The Maya also made use of dogs, both for **hunting** and eating. Fish were also eaten, and the remains of fish hooks and nets have been found in some sites, while there is evidence that those living on the coast traded dried fish far inland. As well as food, the forest provided firewood, and cotton was cultivated to be dyed with natural colours and then spun into cloth.

The main sites represent larger versions of the basic residential groups, housing the most powerful families and their assorted retainers. Beyond this these centres transcended the limits of family ties, taking on larger political, religious

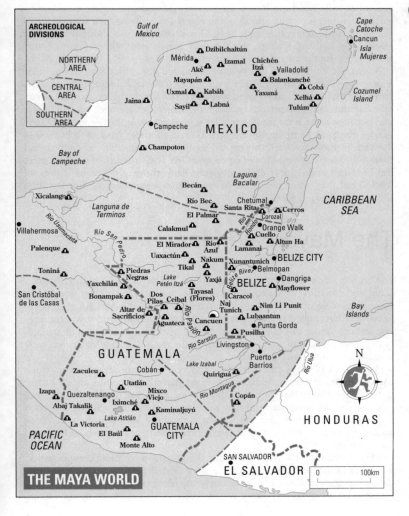

THE MAYA WORLD

and administrative roles, and as Maya society developed they became large cities. The principal occupants were members of royal families and the nobility, but others included bureaucrats, merchants, warriors, architects and assorted craftsmen – an emerging **middle class**. At the highest level this hierarchy was controlled by a series of hereditary positions, with a **king** (occasionally a queen) at its head; these figures also occupied the role of religious leader. At certain times in the calendar cycle kings (and probably other members of the ruling class) communicated with gods and illustrious ancestors by performing acts of ritual **blood-letting** upon themselves, often accompanied by the sacrifice of important captives who may have been kept alive for years, awaiting the ceremonial celebrations.

The relationship between the cities and the land, drawn up along feudal lines, was at the heart of Maya life. The **peasant farmers** supported the ruling class by providing labour – building and maintaining the temples and palaces – food and other basic goods. In return the elite provided the peasantry with leadership, direction, protection and above all else the security of their knowledge of calendrics and supernatural prophecy. This knowledge was thought to be the basis of successful agriculture, and the ruler-priests were relied upon to divine the appropriate time to plant and harvest.

In turn, the cities themselves became organized into a hierarchy of power. At times a single city, such as El Mirador, Tikal or Calakmul dominated vast areas, controlling all of the smaller sites, while at other times smaller centres operated independently. The distance between the larger sites averaged around 30km, and between these were myriad smaller settlements, religious centres and residential groups. A complex, shifting structure of **alliances** (and rivalries) bound the various sites together in an endless round of competition and conflict, and there were frequent outbursts of **open warfare**. The structure of these alliances can be traced in the use of emblem-glyphs. Only those of the main centres are used in isolation, while the names of smaller sites are used in conjunction with those of their larger patrons.

The Maya calendar

For both practical and mystical reasons the Maya developed a highly sophisticated understanding of arithmetics, calendrics and astronomy, all of which they believed gave them the power to understand and predict events. All great occasions were interpreted on the basis of the **Maya calendar**, and it was this precise understanding of time that gave the ruling elite its authority. The majority of carving, on temples and stelae, records the exact date at which rulers were born, ascended to power, sacrificed captives and died.

The basis of all Maya **calculation** was the vigesimal counting system, which used multiples of twenty. All figures were written using a combination of three symbols – a shell to denote zero, a dot for one and a bar for five – which you can still see on many stelae. When calculating calendrical systems the Maya used a slightly different notation known as the head-variant system, in which each number from one to twenty was represented by a deity, whose head was used to represent the number.

When it comes to the Maya **calendar** things start to get more complicated, as a number of different counting systems were used, depending on the reason the date was being calculated. The basic unit of the Maya calendar was the day, or *kin*, followed by the *winal*, a group of twenty *kins* roughly equivalent to our month,

Maya time – the units

1 *kin* = 24 hours
20 *kins* = 1 *winal*, or 20 days
18 *winals* = 1 *tun*, or 360 days
20 *tuns* = 1 *katun*, or 7200 days
20 *katuns* = 1 *baktun*, or 144,000 days
20 *baktun* = 1 *pictun*, or 2,880,000 days
20 *pictuns* = 1 *calabtun*, or 57,600,000 days
20 *calabtuns* = 1 *kinchiltun*, or 1,152,000,000 days
20 *kinchiltuns* = 1 *alautun*, or 23,040,000,000 days

but at the next level things start to get more complex, as the Maya marked the passing of time in three distinct ways. In an ideal vigesimal system (as the Maya arithmetic system was) the next level would be 400 *kins* – but for marking the passing of a period approximating a year the Maya used the *tun*, comprising 18 (rather than 20) *winals*, plus a closing month of five days, the *Uayeb*, a total of 365 days. This so-called "**vague year**", or *haab*, made it a very close approximation of the annual cycle, though of course the Maya elite knew that the solar year was a fraction over 365 days. Beyond this unit however, the passing of time was ordered in multiples of twenty, with the *katun* being twenty *tuns*.

The 260-day **sacred almanac** was used to calculate the timing of ceremonial events and as a basis for prophecy. Each day (*kin*) was associated with a particular deity that had strong influence over those born on that particular day. This calendar wasn't divided into months but had 260 distinct day names. (This system is still in use among the Cakchiquel in the highlands of Guatemala, who name their children according to its structure and celebrate fiestas according to its dictates.) These first two calendars weren't used in isolation but operated in parallel so that once every 52 years the new day of the solar year coincided with the same day in the 260-day almanac, a meeting that was regarded as very powerful and marked the end of one "**calendar round**" and the beginning of the next.

Finally the Maya had another system for marking the passing of history, which is used on dedicatory monuments. The system, known as the **long count**, is based on the "great cycle" of 13 *baktuns* (a period of 5128 years). The dates in this system simply record the number of days that have elapsed since the start of the current great cycle – dating from 3114 BC and destined to come to an end on December 21, 2012 – a task that calls for ten different numbers, recording the equivalent of months, years, decades, centuries, etc. In later years the Maya sculptors obviously tired of this exhaustive process and opted instead for the **short count**, an abbreviated version.

Astronomy

Alongside their fascination with time, the Maya were interested in the sky and devoted much time and energy to unravelling its patterns. Several large sites such as Copán, Uaxactún and Chichén Itzá have **observatories** carefully aligned with solar and lunar sequences; in all probability, a building or buildings in each city was dedicated to this role.

The Maya showed a great understanding of **astronomy** and with their 365-day "vague year" were just a quarter of a day out in their calculations of the solar year, while at Copán, towards the end of the seventh century AD, Maya astronomers had calculated the lunar cycle at 29.53020 days, just slightly off from our current estimate of 29.53059. In the Dresden Codex their calculations extend to the 405 lunations over a period of 11,960 days, as part of a pattern that set out to predict eclipses. At the same time they had calculated with astonishing accuracy the movements of Venus, Mars and perhaps Mercury. Venus was of particular importance to the Maya as they linked its presence with success in war; there are several stelae that record the appearance of Venus prompting the decision to attack.

Religion

C

CONTEXTS | The Maya achievement

Maya **cosmology** is by no means straightforward, as at every stage an idea is balanced by its opposite and each part of the universe is made up of many layers. To the Maya, this is the third version of the earth, the previous two having been destroyed by deluges. The current version is a flat surface, with four corners, each associated with a certain colour; white for north, red for east, yellow for south and black for west, with green at the centre. Above this the sky is supported by four trees, each a different colour and species, which are also sometimes depicted as gods, known as *Bacabs*. At its centre the sky is supported by a ceiba tree. Above the sky is a heaven of thirteen layers, each of which has its own god, while the very top layer is overseen by an owl. Other attested models of the world include that of a turtle (the land) floating on the sea. However, it was the underworld, *Xibalba*, "the Place of Fright", which was of greater importance to most Maya, as it was in this direction that they passed after death, on their way to the place of rest. The nine layers of the Maya "hell" were guarded by the "Lords of the Night", and deep caves were thought to connect with the underworld.

Woven into this universe, the Maya recognized an incredible array of **gods**. Every divinity had four manifestations based upon colour and direction and many also had counterparts in the underworld and consorts of the opposite sex. In addition to this there was an extensive array of patron deities, each associated with a particular trade or particular class. Every activity from suicide to sex had its representative in the Maya pantheon.

Religious ritual

The combined complexity of the Maya pantheon and calendar gave every day a particular significance, and the ancient Maya were bound up in a demanding **cycle of religious ritual**. The main purpose of ritual was the procurement of success by appealing to the right god at the right time and in the right way. As every event, from planting to childbirth, was associated with a particular divinity, all of the main events in daily life demanded some kind of religious ritual and for the most important of these the Maya staged elaborate ceremonies.

While each ceremony had its own format, there is a certain pattern that binds them all. The correct day was carefully chosen by priestly divination, and for several days beforehand the participants fasted and remained abstinent. The main ceremony was dominated by the expulsion of all evil spirits, the burning of incense before the idols, a sacrifice (either animal or human) and blood-letting.

In divination rituals, used to foretell the pattern of future events or to account for the cause of past events, the elite used various **drugs** to achieve altered states of consciousness. Perhaps the most obvious of these was alcohol, made either from fermented maize or a combination of honey and the bark of the balche tree. Wild tobacco, which is considerably stronger than the modern domesticated version, was also smoked. The Maya also used a range of hallucinogenic mushrooms, all of which were appropriately named, but none more so than the *xibalbaj obox*, "underworld mushroom", and the *k'aizalah obox*, "lost judgement mushroom".

Archeology

L ike almost everything in Belize, archeology has made leaps and bounds in the last couple of decades as researchers have unveiled a wealth of new material. The main text that follows was originally written by the late Winnel Branche, former Belize Museums Director, and illustrates the problems that faced Belizean archeology in the past, as it emerged into the limelight under siege from foreign expeditions and looters. At the beginning of the twenty-first century, Belize is taking control of its own archeological heritage; as such, this section has been brought up to date with help from Dr Jaime Awe and staff of the Belize Institute of Archaeology.

Archeology field schools and projects in Belize

Many of the sites under investigation in Belize accept paying students (and often non-students): the average two- to four-week stint at a field school costs in the region of US$1100–2600. It's fascinating work, but be prepared for some pretty arduous conditions. In addition to the schools and projects listed below it's worth looking in the Archaeological Institute of America's website (ⓦwww.archaeological .org) for details of fieldwork opportunities, or check out *Archaeology Magazine* (ⓦwww.archaeology.org). Earthwatch (see p.47 for details) frequently has archeological projects in Belize and throughout the region. Check also *Lamanai Outpost Lodge* (see p.93) for details of their field study centre. Finally, the websites ⓦwww.mesoweb.com and ⓦwww.famsi.org (Foundation for the Advancement of Mesoamerican Studies, or FAMSI) have myriad useful links.

The Belize Fieldwork Program of Boston University undertakes research at a number of sites in Belize, including La Milpa, in the northwest (see p.95) and Xibun, in the Sibun River valley, Cayo. Directed by noted Maya scholars Norman Hammond and Patricia McAnany, these programmes are very highly regarded and places are in great demand. Contact the directors by visiting ⓦwww.bu.edu/archaeology.

The Belize Postclassic Project of SUNY-Albany is a long-term regional programme of research to understand processes of social transformation of Maya populations living in northern Belize after the "collapse" of Classic period city-state civilizations, from AD 1000 until the Spanish colonial era. Research takes place at Progresso Lagoon, in northern Belize, an inland waterway surrounded by the Freshwater Creek Forest Reserve. Contact Dr Marilyn Masson, SUNY-Albany, New York (ⓔmassonma@albany.edu, ⓦwww.albany.edu/anthro).

The Belize River Archaeological Settlement Survey (BRASS) has been working in the Belize River valley area since 1983 and at El Pilar since 1993. El Pilar, a major Maya centre straddling the Belize–Guatemala border (see p.174), forms the core of the new El Pilar Archaeological Reserve for Maya Flora and Fauna. Preference is given to those with experience and skills in ceramics, drafting, computers and photography. Contact Dr Anabel Ford, MesoAmerican Research Center, University of California, Santa Barbara (ⓔelpilar@btl.net, ⓦwww.marc.ucsb.edu/elpilar).

The Belize Valley Archaeological Reconnaissance Project (BVAR) has been conducting long-term research at several sites in the Belize River valley, particularly at Baking Pot and recently at Pook's Hill (see p.153). Students are involved in all aspects of archeological investigations, from the excavation of Maya architecture to the illustration of the artefacts recovered from the site. No previous experience is required, though participants will need to be in good physical condition. Email ⓔarchaeology@bvar.org, or visit ⓦwww.bvar.org.

The ancient Maya sites of Belize have seen activity since the late nineteenth century. During these early times British amateur archeologists and both **British and American museums** kept up a lively interest in artefacts from these sites. Preservation of monuments was not yet "in", and techniques were far from subtle. In some cases dynamite was used to plunder the sites and Belizean artefacts often found their way, unmonitored, into museums and private collections worldwide.

Since 1894 the ancient monuments and antiquities of Belize have had loosely structured legislation to protect them, but it was not until 1957 that the **Belize Department of Archaeology** (now called, since 2003, the **Institute of Archaeology**) was formed to excavate, protect and preserve these remains. Since then, scientific excavation of hundreds of sites in Belize has been carried out by universities, museums and scientific institutions from the US, Canada and, to a lesser extent, Britain, always with prior agreement from the institute.

Blue Creek Archaeological Project of the Maya Research Program (MRP) has been conducting excavations at Blue Creek (see p.94) in northwestern Belize for 14 years. Their research attempts to learn about the growth of Blue Creek and understand its role in the region. Contact John Lohse (©lohse@utexas.edu, Ⓦwww.mayaresearchprogram.org).

Mayflower Archaeology Project in Stann Creek District covers three Late Classic sites: Mayflower, Maintzunun and T'au Witz (see p.231). The area was surveyed over twenty years ago but, until fairly recently, excavations have been virtually nonexistent; much of the site is still covered in tropical forest. Students stay in Hopkins (see p.232). Contact Wendy Brown or Jeffrey Stomper, Social Sciences Division, College of Lake County, Grayslake, IL 60030 (Ⓣ847/543-2608, ©wbrown@clcillinois.edu, ©stomper@clcillinois.edu, Ⓦclcpages.clcillinois.edu).

Minanha' Archaeology Project of the Social Archaeology Research Program (SARP) of Trent University, Canada, focuses on ancient Maya sociopolitical interaction, investigating how centres of different hierarchical rank interacted with one another, and what life was like on the borders of political units. Research is carried out at Minanha', on the Vaca plateau in Cayo District, a site located between two major Classic period cities, Caracol and Naranjo; students stay at *Martz Farm* (see p.170). Contact Dr Gyles Iannone, Dept of Anthropology, Trent University (Ⓣ705/748-1011 ext. 1453, ©giannone@trentu.ca, Ⓦwww.trentu.ca/anthropology /Belize/Belize1.html).

The University of Texas Archaeological Field School undertakes research at several Maya sites in the Rio Bravo Conservation Management Area (see p.94), including La Milpa and Dos Hombres, where a royal tomb has been discovered. You can take part either as a volunteer for a minimum of one week (US$640) or enroll as a student. Contact Dr Fred Valdez, Dept of Anthropology, University of Texas at Austin (©fredv@mail.utexas.edu, Ⓦuts.cc.utexas.edu/~marl).

The Western Belize Regional Cave Project, under the direction of Dr Jaime Awe of the Belize Institute of Archaeology, has undertaken research at several caves in Cayo District (including Actun Tunichil Muknal; see p.154), collecting and analysing data in order to understand the use of caves by the ancient Maya. Current investigations include Actun Chap ("The Cave of the Centipede") and other recently discovered caves. Due to the strenuous and dangerous nature of cave reconnaissance, volunteers/students must be in excellent physical condition. Prior archeological field school or caving experience is preferred. Contact Cameron Griffith (©belizemaya @aol.com, Ⓦwww.indiana.edu/~belize).

The institute's main role is to monitor fieldwork and excavations carried out by foreign researchers in the country, though it has lately expanded into other areas: it now trains Belizeans to carry out archeological work in the country, still in conjunction with foreign researchers, and it also performs small-scale salvage excavations in emergencies.

With the wealth of Maya remains in the country, it is hardly surprising but most unfortunate that **looting** of sites and the sale of antiquities on the black market is still prevalent. Since any immovable manmade structure over 100 years old and any movable manmade item over 150 years old are considered ancient monuments and artefacts respectively, the institute is also in charge of all the **non-Maya historical and colonial remains**. The responsibility of maintaining archeological sites, especially those open to the public, falls to the institute, as does the safekeeping of the vast national collections.

In Belize, all ancient monuments and antiquities are owned by the state, whether on private or government land or under water. Residents are still allowed to keep registered collections under licence, but the sale, purchase, import or export of antiquities is illegal. Excavation and other scientific research can only be done with permission from the Commissioner of Archaeology, under agreed conditions. While intended to prevent looting and destruction, this law is also meant to keep the remains intact and within the country so that Belizeans and visitors can see the evidence of this splendid heritage.

Extensive **cave systems** form a vast network under much of inland Belize, and the Chiquibul Cave System (see p.183), the longest cave system in Central America, contains the largest cave room in the western hemisphere. All caves discovered so far in Belize contain Maya artefacts, making them archeological sites only visitable with prior permission from the Institute of Archaeology or with a licensed tour guide. Cave tourism in Belize increases every year, and the **caves visitation policy** sets out regulations for both tourists and tour guides. Ancient Maya **maritime trade routes** are also a focus of recent research, with coastal sites and those on the cayes receiving more attention.

Since 2003 the Institute of Archaeology has become responsible for overseeing all archeological investigation in Belize, issuing site-excavation permits only to those scholars whose proposals conform to their policies and will be of demonstrable benefit to Belize. The Institute also carries out **educational programmes** including lectures, slide shows and travelling exhibitions in an attempt to interest the public in this part of their heritage. It also hosts the **Belize Archaeology Symposium**, held annually in July, where all the archeological teams excavating in Belize present their latest findings – a fascinating and well-organized event which anyone can attend; email ✉ia@nichbelize.org for details.

At least sixteen archeological research teams visit Belize annually (see box on pp.310–311), illustrating the fact that the Maya of Belize were not on the fringe of the Maya civilization, as was once thought, but were in fact a core area of the Maya culture. Evidence has been found of extensive raised-field agriculture and irrigation canals in northern Belize, and the oldest known site so far found in the Maya world is at Cuello, near Orange Walk. Even Tikal in Guatemala, once thought to have been the centre of power of the lowland Maya, is now known to have been toppled by Caracol, the largest Maya city in Belize.

Landscape and wildlife

For its size, Belize has a diverse range of environments: from the coral reefs and atolls of the Caribbean coast, through lowland swamps and lagoons, up the valleys of pristine tropical rivers, to the exposed ridges of the Maya Mountains. Physically, the land increases in elevation as you head south and west; the main rivers rise in the west and flow north and east to the Caribbean.

Away from the coast, which is entirely low-lying and covered by marine sediments for 10–20km inland, the country can be roughly divided into three **geological regions**: the **northern lowlands**, a continuation of the Yucatán Platform, with Cretaceous limestone overlain by deposits of alluvial sand; the **Maya Mountains**, where Santa Rosa quartz with granite intrusions rises to over 1000m to form the highest peaks in the country; and **southern Belize**, where more Cretaceous limestone hills with an impressive range of wonderfully developed **karst features** – including caverns, natural arches and sinkholes – give way to foothills and the coastal plain.

The **wildlife** is correspondingly varied; undisturbed forests provide a home to both temperate species from the north and tropical species from the south, as well as a number of indigenous species unique to Belize. In winter, the hundreds of native bird species are joined by dozens of migrant species from the eastern seaboard of North America. With its variety of tropical land and marine ecosystems Belize is increasingly a focus of scientific research.

The tropical forest

Belize still has over fifty percent of its **primary forest**, and across most of the country the natural vegetation is technically **tropical moist forest**, classified by average temperatures of 24°C and annual rainfall of 2000–4000mm; the only true **rainforest** lies in a small belt in the extreme southwest. More than four thousand flowering plant species can be found in Belize, including around seven hundred species of tree (about the same number as the whole of the US and Canada) and over two hundred varieties of orchid. So diverse is the forest that scientists have identified seventy different types, though these can be placed into three broad groups: 13 percent is fairly open **pine savannah** (known in Belize as "pine ridge", regardless of the elevation); 19 percent is **mangrove and coastal forest** (which includes the rarest habitat type in Belize, **caye littoral forest**); with the remaining 68 percent **broadleaf forest** and cohune palm forest – the type commonly referred to as rainforest.

While temperate forests tend to be dominated by a few species – for example, fir, oak or beech – it's **diversity** that characterizes the tropical forest, with each species specifically adapted to fit a particular ecological niche. This biological storehouse has yet to be fully explored, though it has already yielded some astonishing discoveries. Steroid hormones, such as cortisone, and diosgenin, the active ingredient in birth control pills, were developed from wild yams found in these forests, while tetrodoxin, derived from a species of Central American frog, is an anaesthetic 160,000 times stronger than cocaine.

But despite its size and diversity the forest is surprisingly **fragile**, forming a closed system in which nutrients are continuously recycled and decaying plant matter fuels new growth. The forest floor is a spongy mass of roots, fungi, mosses, bacteria and micro-organisms, in which nutrients are stored, broken down with the assistance of insects and chemical decay, and gradually released to the waiting roots and fresh seedlings. The thick canopy prevents much light from reaching the forest floor, ensuring that the soil remains damp but warm, a hotbed of chemical activity. The death of a large tree prompts a flurry of growth as new light reaches the forest floor and seedlings struggle towards the sunlight. However, once a number of trees are removed the soil is highly vulnerable – exposed to the harsh tropical sun and direct rainfall, an area of cleared forest soon becomes prone to flooding and drought. Recently cleared land will contain enough nutrients for three or four years of crop growth, but soon afterwards its usefulness declines rapidly and within twenty years it can become almost completely barren. If the trees are stripped from a large area soil erosion will silt the rivers and parched soils disrupt local rainfall patterns.

Belize's forests are home to abundant **birdlife** – 574 species at the last count, with several species "new" to the country discovered each year. In fact, birds are the most visible of the country's wildlife, and a big draw for many visitors. Even if you've never had much of an interest in them, you'll be astonished at the sheer numbers of birds you can see just by sitting by a cabin in any one of the jungle lodges in Belize. Parrots, such as the **Aztec** and **green parakeets**, are seen every day, and if you're an expert you'll be aware of a range of otherwise scarce species that you might catch a glimpse of here, from the tiny **orange-breasted falcon** to the massive **harpy eagle**, the largest of Belize's raptors. Watching a jewel-like **hummingbird** feed by dipping its long, delicate bill into a heliconia flower as it hovers just inches in front of your eyes is a wonderful experience. Hummingbird names are as fascinating as their colours: the rufous-tailed, the little hermit, the white-bellied emerald and the violet sabrewing, to mention just a few.

Although Belize has 60 species of **snakes**, many of which occur widely throughout the country, only nine are venomous and you're unlikely to see any snakes at all. One of the commonest is the **boa constrictor**, which is also the largest, growing up to 4m, though it poses no threat to humans. Others you might see are **coral snakes** (which are venomous) and **false coral snakes** (which are not); you'd need to be quite skilled to tell them apart. **Frogs and toads** (collectively anurans) are plentiful, and at night in the forest you'll hear the characteristic chorus of frog mating calls. You'll also frequently find the **red-eyed tree frog** – a beautiful pale green creature about 2–3cm long – in your shower in any rustic cabin. Less appealing perhaps are the giant **marine toads**, the largest toad in the Americas, weighing in at up to 1kg and growing to 20cm. These are infamous as the "cane toad", which caused havoc with the native species when introduced into Australia; it eats anything it can get into its capacious mouth. Like most frogs and toads it has toxic glands and the toxin of the marine toad has hallucinogenic properties – a characteristic the ancient Maya employed in their ceremonies by licking these glands and interpreting the resultant visions.

Finally, one thing you'll realize pretty quickly is that you're never far from an **insect** in Belize. Mostly you'll be trying to avoid them or even destroy them, particularly the common (though by no means ever-present) mosquitoes and sandflies. But the **butterflies** are beautiful, and you'll frequently see clouds of them feeding at the edges of puddles on trails; the caterpillars are fascinating and sometimes enormous. The largest and most spectacular are the gorgeous, electric-blue **blue morpho** and the **owl butterfly**, and you can see many more on a visit to one of a number of **butterfly exhibits** around the country. **Ants** are the most numerous insects on the planet – something you can easily believe here. Perhaps the most impressive are the **army ants**, called the "marchin' army" in Belize, as the whole colony ranges through the forest in a narrow column voraciously hunting for insects. Rest assured that, unlike their Hollywood movie counterparts, they can't overpower you and rip the flesh from your bones – though they will give you a nasty bite if you get too close. People in rural areas welcome a visit, as the ants clear pests from their houses. **Leafcutter ants** ("wee-wee ants" in Kriol) have regular trails through the forest along which they carry bits of leaves often much larger than themselves – which is how they get the name "parasol ants". The leaves themselves aren't for food, but they provide a growing medium for a unique type of fungus that the ants do eat.

   Spiders are also very common: take a walk at night with a flashlight anywhere in the countryside and you'll see the beam reflected back by the eyes of dozens of **wolf spiders**. **Tarantulas**, too, are found everywhere – the sharp fangs may look dangerous but, despite their reputation, tarantulas won't bite unless they're severely provoked.

The Maya Mountains

The main range of the **Maya Mountains** runs southwest to northeast across the whole of south-central Belize and straddles the border with Guatemala. This wild region, covered in dense forest and riddled with caves and underground rivers, has few permanent residents. The mountains form part of the great swathe of **national parks** and **forest reserves**, the most accessible of which are the **Mountain Pine Ridge** (p.175) and the **Cockscomb Basin Wildlife Sanctuary** (p.239), home to the world's only **jaguar reserve**.

   The flora and fauna, though similar to those found in the tropical forests of Guatemala, are often more prolific here as there's much less pressure on the land. Though rarely seen, the **scarlet macaw** is occasionally found in large flocks in the southern Maya Mountains and the Cockscomb Basin. All of Belize's cat species are found here, too. **Jaguars** ("tigers") range widely over the whole country, but the densest population is found in the lower elevation forests of the west, while **pumas** ("red tigers") usually keep to remote ridges. The two smaller species of spotted cats – the **ocelot** and the smaller **margay** (both called "tiger cat" in Belize and slightly larger than a domestic cat) – are also found here, as is the **jaguarundi**, the smallest and commonest of Belize's cats – you might spot one on a trail since it hunts during the day. Belize's largest land animal, **Baird's tapir** ("mountain cow"), weighing up to 300kg, is usually found near water. Tapirs are endangered throughout most of their range, but are not that rare in Belize, though you're unlikely to see one without a guide.

   On the northern flank of the Maya Mountains, the **Mountain Pine Ridge** is a granite massif intruded into the sedimentary quartz and resulting in a ring of metamorphic rock around the granite. Many of the rivers rising here fall away to the Macal and Belize river valleys below, in some of the most spectacular waterfalls in the country. On this nutrient-poor soil the dominant vegetation is the **Caribbean pine**, which covers sixty percent of the area in the largest stands anywhere in its range; bromeliads and orchids adorn the trunks and branches. It's a unique habitat in Belize, and home to several endemic species, including two frogs and a fish known only by their Latin names. Currently, the forest is recovering from a very severe outbreak of **pine bark beetles** (see p.176).

Lowland Belize

The forests of Petén, Guatemala, extend into northwestern Belize, where the generally low-lying topography is broken by a series of roughly parallel **limestone escarpments**. The main ones – the Booth's River and Rio Bravo escarpments – each have a river below that drain north to the Rio Hondo. Here the **Rio Bravo Conservation Management Area** (see p.94) protects a huge area of forest. Further east, the plain is more open; pine savannah is interspersed with slow-flowing rivers and lagoons, providing spectacular wetland habitats that continue to the coast. In the centre, **Crooked Tree Wildlife Sanctuary** (see p.84) covers several freshwater lagoons, protecting over three hundred bird species, including the nesting sites of the rare jabiru stork. The tiny village of Sarteneja is the only settlement between Belize City and Corozal on the northeast coast – an important wetland area for wading birds, crocodiles (Morelet's and American) and several species of turtles, protected in the **Shipstern Nature Reserve** (see p.97). In addition, almost all of the mammals of Belize – with the exception of monkeys but including jaguar, ocelot and tapir – can be found in this mosaic of coastal lagoons, hardwood forest and mangrove swamp. Other forest mammals you might see signs of include the collared and the white-lipped peccaries ("warries"), brocket and white-tailed deer, opossums, weasels, porcupines and armadillos. At the **Bermudian Landing Baboon Sanctuary** in the lower Belize River valley (see p.81), visitors can be almost guaranteed views of troops of black howler monkeys ("baboons"); you'll certainly hear the deep-throated roar of the males.

In the south there's only a relatively narrow stretch of lowland between the Maya Mountains and the coast, but heavy rainfall ensures the growth of lush rainforest. Along the coast and navigable rivers much of the original forest has been selectively logged for mahogany and some is in varying stages of regrowth after hurricane damage; around human settlements the original forest has been replaced by patches of agricultural land and citrus plantations. A boat journey along the **Burdon Canal Nature Reserve** (see p.218), which connects the Belize and Sibun rivers to the Northern and Southern lagoons, and on into the **Gales Point Wildlife Sanctuary** (see p.218), where manatees congregate, is a good introduction to the wildlife to be found in the inland mangrove forests and lagoons.

Take a trip along almost any **river** and you'll see green iguanas, which, along with their very similar cousin the spiny-tailed iguana ("wish-willy"), are probably the most prominent of Belize's reptiles; despite protection these are still hunted for their meat and eggs. Rarer, but still fairly frequently seen in protected-area rivers, the Central American river otter is much larger than its European cousin. Along the New River and in many lagoons you'll see (or more likely be shown) Morelet's crocodiles, which can be found in almost any body of water, and are of no danger to humans unless they're very large – at least 3m long. Previously hunted to the brink of extinction, they've made a remarkable comeback since being protected, and are now frequently spotted in the mangroves of Haulover Creek, immediately west of Belize City. Rivers also offer great bird-watching, including several species of kingfisher. One of the most common, the belted kingfisher, is also Belize's largest – it's widespread, too, and features on the Canadian $5 bill. You'll also see many species of herons and egrets, including the tri-coloured heron, the boat-billed heron, the great egret and occasionally the two-metre tall jabiru stork.

The Caribbean coast and the Barrier Reef

Belize's most exceptional environment is its **Caribbean coastline** and off-shore barrier reef, dotted with hundreds of small islands and three atolls. Much of the shoreline is still largely covered with mangroves, which play an important role in the Belizean economy, not merely as nurseries for commercial fish species but also for their stabilization of the shoreline and their ability to absorb the force of hurricanes. Each kilometre of mangrove shoreline is valued at several thousand dollars per year. The dominant species of the coastal fringe is the red mangrove, although in due course it undermines its own environment by consolidating the sea bed until it becomes more suitable for the less salt-tolerant black and white mangroves. The cutting down of mangroves, particularly on the cayes, exposes the land to the full force of the sea and can mean the end of a small and unstable island.

Just inland from the mangroves along the coast and on the cayes the **littoral forest** occupies slightly higher ground. The vegetation here is salt-tolerant, and many plants are characterized by their tough, waxy leaves which help conserve water. Species include red and white gumbo limbo, black poisonwood, zericote, sea grape, palmetto and of course the coconut palm which typifies Caribbean beaches, though it's not actually a native and is now threatened by the lethal yellowing disease spreading down the coast from Mexico. The littoral forest supports a very high density of fauna, especially migrating birds, due to the succession of fruits and seeds, yet it also faces the highest development pressure in Belize due to its slightly higher coastal elevation; the limited extent of **caye littoral forest** is the most endangered habitat in the country.

The basis of the shoreline food chain is the nutrient-rich mud, held in place by the mangroves, while the roots themselves are home to mangrove oysters and sponges. Young stingrays cruise through the shallows adjacent to the tangle of mangrove roots, accompanied by juvenile snappers, bonefish and small barracudas; you'll see the adult versions on the reef and around the cayes. The tallest mangrove forests in Belize are found along the Temash River, in the **Sarstoon–Temash National Park** (see p.269), where the black mangroves reach heights of over 30m. From a canoe among the mangrove cayes and lagoons you can easily spot the brown pelican, white ibis or roseate spoonbill. You might even see the American salt-water crocodile, rarer and much larger than the Morelet's crocodile.

The mangrove lagoons are also home to the West Indian manatee. Belize has the largest manatee population in the Caribbean, estimated to be somewhere between three hundred and seven hundred individuals. Several large areas have been set aside for their protection, including the **Corozal Bay**, **Gales Point** and **Swallow Caye** wildlife sanctuaries. Manatees can grow up to 4m in length and 450kg in weight, but are placid and shy, moving between the freshwater lagoons and the open sea. Once hunted for their meat, they are now protected, and the places where they congregate are tourist attractions. In shallows offshore, "meadows" of seagrass beds provide nurseries for many fish and invertebrates and pasture for conch, manatees and turtles. The extensive root system of seagrasses also protects beaches from erosion by holding the fragments of sand and coral together.

The **Western Caribbean Barrier Reef** is the longest in the western hemisphere, an almost continuous chain of coral that stretches over 600km from northern Quintana Roo in Mexico to the far south of Belize. For centuries the reef has been harvested by fishermen. In the past they caught manatees (and they still take some turtles), but these days the spiny lobster and queen conch are the main catch, though numbers of both species have declined and are now protected during the breeding season.

East of the barrier reef are the **atolls** (see p.107), roughly oval-shaped reefs rising from the seabed surrounding a central lagoon. **Glover's Reef** atoll is considered by the scientific community to be one of the most pristine and important coral reef sites in the Caribbean. Whale sharks, the largest fish in the world, are sometimes found here, gathering in large numbers to gorge on snapper eggs at **Gladden Spit**, offshore from Placencia. Beneath the water is a world of astounding beauty, with fish and coral in every imaginable colour. Resembling a brilliant underwater forest, each coral is in fact composed of colonies of individual polyps, feeding off plankton wafting past in the current. There are basically two types of coral: hard, calcareous, reef-building corals, such as brain coral and elkhorn coral (known scientifically as the hydrocorals), and soft corals such as sea fans and feather plumes (the ococorals). On the reefs you'll find the garish-pink chalice sponge, the appropriately-named fire coral, the delicate feather-star crinoid and the apartment sponge, a tall thin tube with lots of small holes in it. Coral bleaching occurs when the polyp loses some or all of the symbiotic microalgae (zooxanthellae) which live in its cells, usually in response to stress. The most common cause is a period of above-average sea temperatures – a major coral reef bleaching event occurred throughout the Caribbean in 1995, midway through what is reported to have been the hottest decade on record. Temperatures continue to be above the average of previous decades, almost certainly indicating that **global warming** is taking place.

The reef teems with **fish**, including **angel** and **parrot fish**, several species of **stingrays** and **sharks** (the most common the relatively harmless **nurse shark**, frequently seen on reef trips), **conger** and **moray eels**, **spotted goatfish**, the striped **sergeant-major** and many, many more. The sea and islands are also home to **grouper**, **barracuda**, **marlin** and the magnificent **sailfish**. Dolphins are frequently seen just offshore, and will mostly be of the Atlantic **bottle-nosed** variety, though further out large schools of the smaller **spotted dolphin** are sometimes seen.

Belize's three species of **marine turtles**, the loggerhead, the green and the hawksbill, occur throughout the reef, nesting on isolated beaches. These are infrequently seen as they are still hunted for food during a limited open season.

Above the water, the cayes are an ideal nesting ground for birds, providing protection from predators and surrounded by an inexhaustible food supply. At **Half Moon Caye**, right out on the eastern edge of the reef, there's a reserve designed to protect a breeding colony of over four thousand **red-footed boobies**. Here you'll also see magnificent frigate birds, ospreys and mangrove warblers, among a total of 98 species.

Conservation

Recent additions to Belize's already impressive network of national parks, nature reserves and wildlife sanctuaries bring over 46 percent of the land under some form of legal protection, an amazing feat for a developing country with a population of only 275,000. With such enlightened strategies to safeguard the nation's biodiversity, Belize has gained recognition as the most conservation-conscious country in the Americas. That said, the success of these protected areas is due as much to the efforts of local communities to become involved in conservation as it is to governmental decisions.

Conservation strategy

Following independence in 1981, the conservation of natural resources was the main plank in the government's declared policy to make "**ecotourism**" a focus of development and marketing in the nation's tourism industry. Ideally, this is a community-based form of tourism, inspired primarily by the wildlife and landscape of an area and showing respect for local cultures. The theory is that by practising small-scale, nonconsumptive use of the country's natural resources, visitors will be contributing financially both to the conservation of protected areas and to local communities; it is hoped that this will aid sustainable development not only locally but in Belize as a whole. However, the recent and rapid growth of the **cruise ship industry**, creating massive visitor pressure on fragile sites, now threatens to undermine this policy. Calls from environmentalists within Belize to set limits to cruise-ship visitor numbers have prompted only token responses from a government unwilling to halt the ever-increasing flow of dollars the industry generates.

Legislation

In 1928 the southern tip of Half Moon Caye was established as a Crown Reserve to offer protection to the rare red-footed booby (*Sula sula*); other bird sanctuaries were established in the 1960s and 1970s. The **Forestry Act** of 1960 focused on forest reserves established by the colonial government to provide areas for timber exploitation. This law was passed primarily as an instrument to protect the country's timber industry, and was not meant to be a tool for conservation. In the period since the country's independence the government has taken numerous measures which have significantly increased the area of land and sea under protection. The passing of the **National Parks Systems Act** in 1981 provided the legal basis for establishing national parks, natural monuments, wildlife sanctuaries and nature reserves; and the **Wildlife Protection Act** of 1981 (amended in 1991) created closed seasons or total protection for various endangered species, including marine and freshwater turtles, dolphins and manatees.

Hunting, which has long been a means of supplementing diet and income, remains a real problem in almost all reserves and protected lands; the most popular species include iguana, armadillo, *hicatee* (freshwater turtle), deer and the gibnut, or *tepescuintle*, a large rodent sometimes seen on menus. Needless to say, you should avoid ordering these beasts in restaurants.

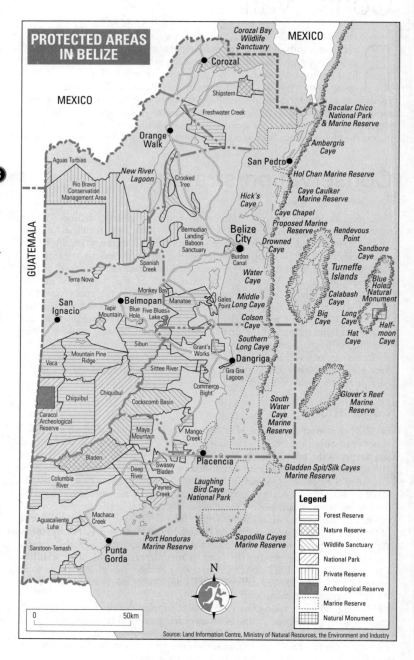

PROTECTED AREAS
IN BELIZE

MEXICO

Corozal Bay
Wildlife
Sanctuary

MEXICO

Corozal

Shipstern

Freshwater Creek

Bacalar Chico
National Park
& Marine Reserve

Orange
Walk

Ambergris
Caye

San Pedro

Hol Chan Marine Reserve

Aguas Turbias

New River
Lagoon

Rio Bravo
Conservation
Management Area

Crooked
Tree

Hick's
Caye

Caye Caulker
Marine Reserve

GUATEMALA

Bermudian
Landing
Baboon
Sanctuary

Belize
City

Caye Chapel
Proposed Marine
Reserve

Rendevous
Point

Spanish
Creek

Burdon
Canal

Drowned
Caye

Sandbore
Caye

Terra Nova

Water
Caye

Turneffe
Islands

San
Ignacio

Monkey Bay

Belmopan

Tapir
Mountain

Manatee

Gales
Point

Middle
Long Caye

Calabash
Caye

Blue
Hole
Natural
Monument

Blue
Hole

Five Blues
Lake

Colson
Caye

Big
Caye

Long
Caye

Half-
moon
Caye

Sibun

Grant's
Works

Southern
Long Caye

Hat
Caye

Mountain Pine
Ridge

Vaca

Sittee River

Dangriga

Chiquibul

Chiquibul

Cockscomb Basin

Gra Gra
Lagoon

Glover's Reef
Marine
Reserve

Caracol
Archeological
Reserve

Maya
Mountain

Mango
Creek

South
Water
Caye
Marine
Reserve

Bladen

Swasey
Bladen

Placencia

Columbia
River

Deep
River

Paynes
Creek

Laughing
Bird Caye
National Park

Gladden Spit/Silk Cayes
Marine Reserve

Aguacaliente
Luha

Machaca
Creek

Legend

Forest Reserve

Sarstoon-Temash

Punta
Gorda

Port Honduras
Marine Reserve

Sapodilla Cayes
Marine Reserve

Nature Reserve

Wildlife Sanctuary

National Park

Private Reserve

Archeological Reserve

Marine Reserve

Natural Monument

N

0   50km

Source: Land Information Centre, Ministry of Natural Resources, the Environment and Industry

Another step in the right direction came with the 1992 **Environmental Protection Act** (EPA), intended to control pollution and promote environmental health by requiring companies to carry out an Environmental Impact Assessment (EIA) before undertaking any potentially polluting development. The law utilizes the "polluters pay principle" and recent amendments to the EPA increased penalties for contravention and have resulted in more stringent enforcement.

Belize has also signed, ratified and actively implements twenty important **international environmental agreements**, including the Ramsar Convention on Wetlands of International Importance, the UNESCO World Heritage Convention, the Convention on the International Trade in Endangered Species (CITES), the Convention on Biodiversity and the Cartagena Convention on the Protection of the Marine Environment. Seven reserves on the Belize Barrier Reef, totalling over 90 square kilometres, were declared World Heritage Sites in 1996: Bacalar Chico National Park and Marine Reserve, Blue Hole and Half Moon Caye Natural Monuments, South Water Caye Marine Reserve, Glover's Reef Marine Reserve, Sapodilla Cayes Marine Reserve and Laughing Bird Caye National Park. All of these can be visited, and details are in the relevant chapters of the Guide (check the index for quick reference). These and other protected areas form the **Belize Barrier Reef Reserve System**, which has the ultimate aim of forming a continuous corridor of marine reserves from Mexico to Honduras. An important step towards this was taken in 1997 when the leaders of Belize, Guatemala, Honduras and Mexico signed the **Mesoamerican Caribbean Coral Reef System Initiative** (the Tulum Declaration) to promote conservation and sustainable use of the coral reef system shared by these four nations.

These countries are also members of the **Central American Commission on Environment and Development** (CCAD), an organization that encompasses all seven Central American nations and is now planning the implementation of an even more ambitious project: the **Mesoamerican Biological Corridor** (visit ⓦwww.biomeso.org for more information), which aims for an unbroken corridor of parks and wildlife refuges stretching from southern Mexico to Panamá. It is hoped that international cooperation in linking the reserves will create a network of protected areas spanning the isthmus and safeguarding the entire region's biodiversity.

The role of government

Three government ministries in Belize (and various departments within them) shoulder between them most of the responsibility for drafting and implementing legislation relating to conservation, and ensuring compliance with the relevant laws: the **Ministry of Agriculture, Fisheries and Cooperatives**, the **Ministry of Natural Resources, the Environment, Commerce and Industry** and the **Ministry of Tourism and Culture**. They are staffed by very able, dedicated professionals, and Belize's reputation as a leader in protected areas management owes much to their expertise.

The **Department of the Environment** has overall responsibility for management of the country's natural resources and control of pollution, and is tasked with identifying and developing solutions for environmental problems facing Belize. It implements and enforces the Environmental Protection Act.

The **Fisheries Authority** is charged with not only monitoring and enforcing fishing regulations, but also managing the country's increasing number of marine reserves and the responsible exploitation of commercially viable species. The Ecosystems Management Unit and Conservation Compliance Unit carry out these tasks. The **Coastal Zone Management Authority and Institute** is responsible for implementing and monitoring all policies that affect the use and development of the coastal zone in Belize and for fostering regional and international collaboration in marine conservation.

Belize's timber reserves (including all mangroves) have always been under the compass of the **Forest Department** (part of the Ministry of Natural Resources, the Environment, Commerce and Industry), though it now has a much greater role in forest conservation than the provision and regulation of hardwoods for export. The department's **Protected Areas Management Division** also has overall responsibility for the management of all terrestrial protected areas and the coordination of biodiversity management, including implementing plans to establish the Mesoamerican Biological Corridor (see p.321). Its **Wildlife Management Programme** is responsible for the enforcement of the Wildlife Protection Act, and conservation officers have been appointed to all the country's forest reserves.

Apart from attracting tourists to Belize and providing them with information, the **Ministry of Tourism**, together with the **Belize Tourism Board**, licenses and trains the country's tour guides; you'll find the guides in Belize are highly motivated guardians of the environment. The **National Institute of Culture and History** (NICH) manages all cultural and historical features, including all **archeological sites** (which are also reserves), and has responsibility for developing appropriate tourism packages for all historic sites.

In general, these government agencies have proved extremely successful in coordinating protection of the nation's reserves, almost always with the cooperation of the private sector and expert assistance from a range of local and international NGOs (see opposite). However, the dramatic increase in the amount of protected land has posed the question of how such protection is to be financed by a developing nation. Following years of discussion between the government and various NGOs as to how best to raise conservation funds, the **Protected Areas Conservation Trust (PACT)** was established in 1996 and has since become a model for other developing countries. The primary source of income is a **conservation exit fee** of Bz$7.50 per person, payable at all departure points and totalling around Bz$2,500,000 a year. PACT also receives twenty percent of entrance fees to protected areas and fees from cruise ship passengers; a percentage of the money raised is invested in a trust fund to provide a long-term buffer against the vicissitudes of government funding. Other revenue generated is shared between the government departments and voluntary organizations responsible for conservation, according to a pre-arranged formula, but it is not allowed to be used for salaries or recurrent expenses. For more information visit PACT's superb website, Ⓦwww.pactbelize.org.

A thorough overview of Belize's environmental and wildlife protection policies and legislation, undertaken by both government and conservation NGOs, the **National Protected Areas Systems Plan** identifies areas where critical habitat was not protected and recommends a comprehensive, yet practical, system to protect viable examples of all Belize's ecosystems, whether on public or private land. Although the government has not yet approved or endorsed all the plan's recommendations, present progress on protected areas management has largely been enacted in accordance with them.

NGOs and voluntary organizations

Various national and international **non-governmental organizations** (NGOs) have been active in conservation in Belize for many years, building up experience through practical work in the country and by attending and hosting environmental conferences. Most conservation organizations are members of the **Belize Association of Conservation NGOs** (BACONGO), believing that a united front presents their cause to government more effectively. This unity was successfully demonstrated in the Lamanai Room Declaration (see below), which called into question the then-government's environmental and conservation policies. In recent years, however, member organizations' differing attitudes toward several controversial development proposals have opened a rift in BACONGO, resulting in key players withdrawing from the association.

Despite this setback, Belize continues to demonstrate innovative and successful methods in protected areas funding and management. The PACT (see opposite) is one example, and **co-management agreements** between the relevant government departments, national NGOs and local conservation organizations play an increasingly important role in involving local communities in managing nearby protected areas. The Belize Audubon Society (see p.324) already manages several reserves (all covered in the Guide) and others, including the Sapodilla Cayes Marine Reserve, Port Honduras Marine Reserve, Gales Point Wildlife Sanctuary and Laughing Bird Caye National Park, have co-management agreements in place.

The tourism industry also plays a part in raising environmental awareness. The **Belize Eco-Tourism Association** (BETA, ⓦwww.bzecotourism.org) is a small but growing band of hotels and other tourism businesses whose members agree to a code of ethics promoting sustainable tourism management. One of the agreed aims is to reduce (and eliminate) the use of disposable products from their businesses. A longer-term goal is to develop an accredited "**Green Listing**" system, which will rate the environmental efforts and credentials of members on a sliding scale. If you're concerned about your hotel's impact on the environment ask if they're a member of BETA.

If it sounds as if the Belize authorities and the NGOs are too closely linked to enable the latter to undertake proper scrutiny of proposals that might adversely affect the environment, the outcome of the **Lamanai Room Declaration** of August 1997 should put your mind at ease. Signed by over thirty NGOs, the declaration sent a strong message to the government of the time that it could not ignore their concerns, which, at that point, related to certain existing and proposed developments that they claimed indicated "disregard for the principles of sustainable development", and were "a possible violation of Belizean legislation . . . and international agreements relating to the environment". These included damage to the reef by cruise ships and the sale of logging concessions on Maya lands in Toledo District. But it was the proposal by a Mexican company to build a "dolphin park attraction" at Cangrejo Caye, southwest of San Pedro, that caused alarm nationwide. Dolphins (imported from Mexico, as they are a protected species in Belize) were to be held in "semi-captivity" – a term no one was able to define satisfactorily – and resort cabañas built around the enclosure. So vehement was the opposition that the government never issued the necessary licence and all other proposals that had triggered the protests were dropped.

Conservation organizations in Belize

The following are some of the national and international organizations either directly involved in conservation projects in Belize or providing support and funding to various projects. Several of these organizations welcome **volunteers** to help carry out a huge range of conservation work, from constructing trails and camping facilities in national parks to undertaking wildlife surveys. If you're interested, contact the organizations directly, but have a look first at the general information on volunteering in Belize given on p.46.

The Belize Audubon Society (BAS), founded in 1969, is the country's pre-eminent conservation organization and extremely well-respected both in Belize and internationally. While the name might suggest bird-watching as its main focus of activity, BAS is active in all aspects of nature conservation and manages nine of the country's protected areas. It also publishes a range of books, guides and fact sheets on the reserves it manages. Members receive an excellent quarterly newsletter about the progress of wildlife conservation in Belize. Call in at the office to find out how to get to the various nature reserves. For details write to BAS, 12 Fort St, Belize City, call ☏223-5004 or visit ⊛www.belizeaudubon.org.

The Belize Zoo and Tropical Education Center (see p.146; ⊛www.belizezoo.org) is renowned throughout the conservation world for the quality of its educational programmes. The zoo encourages Belizean schoolchildren to understand the natural environment by visits and the Outreach Programme. If you wish to support its aims, individual membership is available.

Conservation Corridors (CC) is a UK-based charity that works directly with the Belizean organizations involved in the Mesoamerican Biological Corridor (see p.321). It places volunteers with participating organizations, arranges fieldwork research for students and has opportunities for professional volunteers with management skills. In the UK, contact Conservation Corridors of Central America (☏020/8964-5325, ℮richardwotton@conservcorridor.u-net.com).

Friends of Nature (FoN) co-manages Laughing Bird Caye National Park and Gladden Spit and Silk Cayes Marine Reserve, off Placencia (see p.251), and provides an environmental education programme for students from the village and four other local communities. The FoN office is at the south end of The Sidewalk in Placencia; call ☏523-3377 for volunteer opportunities.

Green Reef is dedicated to the promotion of sustainable use and conservation of Belize's marine and coastal resources, particularly in San Pedro on Ambergris Caye, Belize's busiest tourist destination. Green Reef is actively involved in implementing management plans for bird sanctuaries on the leeward side of Ambergris Caye, and aims to incorporate these into new extensions to existing protected areas. The organization also provides educational programmes for schools in Belize, and can accept volunteers to help with many aspects of its work. Contact Mito Paz, 100 Coconut Drive, San Pedro, Ambergris Caye (☏226-2833, ⊛www.greenreefbelize.com).

The Programme for Belize (PFB), initiated in 1988 by the Massachusetts Audubon Society and launched in Britain in 1989, manages over 250,000 acres in the Rio Bravo Conservation Management Area (see p.94). The programme has bought land, to be held in trust for the people of Belize, and is now managed entirely by Belizeans. For information on visiting the sites in Belize contact the PFB in Belize City (☏227-5616, ⊛www.pfbelize.org). In the UK, the former PFB is now the **World Land Trust** (⊛www.worldlandtrust.org), which raises funds for conservation in Belize under the title Friends of Belize and has volunteer opportunities.

The Siwa-Ban Foundation (SBF) was formed in 1990 for the purpose of establishing a multi-habitat reserve on Caye Caulker. Years of dedicated campaigning by the Siwa-Ban members and the whole community bore fruit in 1998 when the Caye Caulker Forest and Marine Reserve (see p.131) was established, with the northern tip of the caye forming the terrestrial element, connected to several kilometres of the reef offshore. Self-funded volunteers are needed to work on educational projects and biological surveys. In Belize, contact Ellen McRae, *Morgan's Inn*, PO Box 47, Caye Caulker (☎226-0178, ✉sbf@btl.net); in the US, contact Susan Scott, 185 Gates, San Francisco, CA 94110.

The Toledo Association for Sustainable Tourism and Empowerment (TASTE) is an NGO formed in 2000 to assist with plans for sustainable development of Toledo District; in 2001 they signed an agreement with the Fisheries Authority to co-manage the Sapodilla Cayes Marine Reserve (SCMR; see p.268). TASTE is active in local and international conservation efforts to protect the SCMR and runs environmental education programmes in the reserve. Contact TASTE chairman Jack Nightingale at 53 Main Middle St, Punta Gorda (☎722-0191, ✉taste_scmr@btl.net).

The Toledo Institute for Development and Environment (TIDE) was formed in 1997 to focus resources and attention on the conservation of a network of protected areas in southern Toledo District, linking the Maya Mountains to the Sapodilla Cayes. TIDE, with support from The Nature Conservancy (TNC), also promotes Integrated Conservation and Development Projects (ICDPs), providing alternative sources of income for local people through conservation-based tour-guiding activities such as fly-fishing and kayaking. TIDE co-manages Paynes Creek National Park and the Port Honduras Marine Reserve (see p.267). Visit ⊕www.tidetours.org for more information.

The Wildlife Care Center of Belize (WCCB), established in 1998, operates a holding facility for confiscated and rescued native wildlife, many of which have been kept illegally as pets. It has successfully repatriated some creatures which would survive in the wild, including howler monkeys and parrots. WCCB works in collaboration with the Forest Department's Conservation Division to raise public awareness of Belize's wildlife protection laws and to discourage the acquisition of wild animals as pets in the first place. The WCCB is not open to the public but there are opportunities for volunteers; you'll need zoo experience, be self-funded and be able to commit for at least three months. If you're interested, email the director, Robin Brockett, at ✉wildlifecarecenter@yahoo.com.

The Wildlife Conservation Society (WCS) works with all the countries involved in the Mesoamerican Biological Corridor project (see p.321) to strengthen and improve management of parks and conservation lands, and to restore degraded habitat for migratory wildlife. Instrumental in developing plans to establish marine reserves throughout the barrier reef, it maintains a research station on Middle Caye, Glover's Reef, working closely with the Belize government to develop a coordinated research and management programme for the whole atoll. Inland, in reserves in the Maya Mountains and at Gallon Jug (see p.94), researchers are developing guidelines to preserve biodiversity. Visit ⊕www.wcs.org for more information.

The World Wide Fund for Nature (WWF) works closely with the BAS (see opposite) and is also helping the Belize government to raise its capacity for environmental regulation and protected-area management. WWF has for many years provided initial support for a number of projects in Belize, from the Community Baboon Sanctuary at Bermudian Landing (see p.81) to the Cockscomb Basin Wildlife Sanctuary (see p.239) and Gladden Spit and Silk Cayes Marine Reserve (see p.253). One current project works with farmers in the buffer zones adjacent to the Maya Mountains to develop new technologies for profitable and sustainable agricultural systems. The excellent and well-organized website (⊕www.panda.org) is packed with useful information.

The Ya'axché Conservation Trust (YCT), an NGO established in 1997 and based in Toledo District, aims to promote biodiversity and provide sustainable economic opportunities for the Maya communities bordering the Golden Stream watershed. These include making furniture using wood salvaged from trees felled by Hurricane Iris in 2001. With financial and technical support from Flora and Fauna International (⊕www.fauna-flora.org), YCT co-manages the Golden Stream Corridor Preserve. For volunteer opportunities call ☎722-0108, or email ✉yct_ffi@btl.net.

Current conservation issues

Until very recently, the most vociferous and contentious "conservation or development" debate focused on the **Chalillo Dam project**, where a proposed hydro-electric dam on the upper Macal River threatened to flood a beautiful valley which is not only ideal habitat for Baird's tapirs and a threatened subspecies of the scarlet macaw but also contains unexcavated and undocumented Maya sites. Flooding the area would damage legally designated protected areas and may also contravene international conservation conventions to which Belize is a signatory. After years of determined and often bitter opposition by BACONGO, the dam proposal was given the go-ahead in 2004, despite the developers, Fortis, having been shown in court to have erased fault lines on a map submitted as part of the Environmental Impact Assessment (EIA). Although this environmental battle appears to have already been lost, BACONGO has promised to monitor the construction of the dam, and report any violations of the EIA; for the latest news visit ⓦwww.stopfortis.com.

Today the hottest topic on the conservation agenda is the growing opposition to the meteoric rise in the number of cruise ships and their passengers to Belize's shores – described by one activist as "mobile mass tourism". The scale of increase in these arrivals is literally staggering: from just a few hundred per year in the late 1990s to a forecast of over 700,000 for 2004. Although the government's **Cruise Ship Policy Document** states a recommended upper limit of eight thousand cruise ship visitors per day, this limit (which was arbitrarily set by the BTB without reference to any scientific study) is regularly exceeded with impunity. Visitor pressure at many archeological sites and certain cayes already exceeds carrying capacity many times over, leading to destructive trampling and environmental degradation from the sheer numbers involved. Additionally, as word of the numbers of cruise ship visitors spreads, many overnight tourists are stating they do not want to visit sites scheduled for cruise-ship tours. The Belize Ecotourism Association is strongly opposed to the unrestricted growth of the cruise ship industry, claiming that, in addition to the reasons outlined above, this growth undermines the very principles of ecotourism. BETA is calling on the government to limit, regulate and monitor the cruise ship industry.

Other current issues include the de-reservation of protected areas, such as took place recently in Payne's Creek National Park to provide a cruise ship dock in Punta Negra village, and the proposal to build a large tourism facility on Tom Owen's Caye, a tiny outcrop of rock in the Sapodilla Cayes Marine Reserve. BETA, BACONGO and several other conservation and tourism organizations are joining forces to resist these and other potentially damaging and unsustainable developments which may hurt Belize's world-renowned record of sound environmental stewardship.

Human rights and democracy

Despite the absence of the kind of political turmoil and mass human rights abuses that have characterized much of Latin America – and while tourists remain largely unaffected – there are nonetheless grounds to doubt the extent and depth of human rights protection and political participation in Belize.

On the face of it, this relaxed idyll of Latin America and the Caribbean – with a constitution and multi-party democracy built on the British system – might appear to be a model state as far as the protection of **fundamental human rights** is concerned. However, delving just below the surface reveals a majority with little knowledge of their rights and subject to a historical system of **political patronage** where local affiliation to one of the two political parties (PUP or UDP) can seriously undermine full **freedom of expression**. In other words, contesting the party line in your constituency could find you without land or services, or worse.

Awareness of potential victimization by higher authority is a concrete part of Belizean social life, and maintains a population careful not to speak out. **Freedom of the press**, too, has its problems. The only paper independent of political affiliation, the *Reporter*, regularly notes a lack of transparency across the media and the intimidation of journalists into withdrawing from publication articles against government or party favour.

In this respect, for the Belizean majority, human rights are hardly seen as universal, being viewed instead as being granted: the higher up the socio-economic ladder you are, the more rights you're deemed to have. Ask most Belizeans, and a regular reply perceives rights as belonging to the rich, powerful, white and male. At the opposite end of the scale you'll find the poor, black and female; and it's worth remembering that thirty percent of Belizeans live in abject poverty.

A contributing factor to the political climate may well be the **abuse of power by police**. For many years the Belize Defence Force (BDF) has joined the police on the streets in response to increased gang, often drug-related, violence. Tourists probably notice little difference between the two groups of law enforcers, and this increased **militarization** adds to a general atmosphere of intimidation and danger. The **checkpoints** on roads across the country have been a subject of further dispute, as have the increasing numbers of killings at them by police shooting, both on the mainland and the cayes.

Recent issues

A number of recent incidents remind us of the fragility of law enforcement – but perhaps most serious were the police shootings at a peaceful protest in **Benque Viejo** in 2003 against an increase in bus fares. PUP and UDP supporters were marching together on the streets of this small border town when police responded to a few youngsters throwing stones by opening fire on demonstrators. Over thirty were injured as police fired indiscriminately and used tear gas. Declaring it a riot so as to legitimize violent repression, police continued with **arbitrary arrests** and excessive beatings for three days after the event. The government's failure to condemn the police action further demonstrated its attitude towards protest and freedom of expression.

Another issue that has come to the fore in recent years is that of indigenous **Maya land rights**. In 1998, the Indian Law Resource Centre and the Toledo Maya Cultural Council issued a petition to the **Inter-American Commission of Human Rights**, alleging the state be responsible for violations of Mopan and Kekchi Maya rights to land and resources. This requested the suspension of licenses for logging and resource extraction in Maya areas, which are deemed to have adversely affected the local environment and culture. In response the government contends that petitioners have presented insufficient evidence, and that they failed to take advantage of domestic judicial processes when able to do so. In spite of this, it appears that some headway has been made on the issue, with a ten-point agreement signed by both government and Maya groups. Other **minorities** continue to suffer abuses of rights, including large numbers of **immigrants** from El Salvador, Nicaragua, Guatemala and Honduras, who are frequently denied the same rights as nationals and are very often referred to as aliens.

Many visitors will encounter Maya children from Guatemala and Belize selling their wares on the cayes and in the south of Belize, and should be aware that, despite financing their families in this way, they really should be in school. The immigrant issue increasingly manifests itself in the business of **people trafficking** – very often of women and children for the sex industry; a 2001 study commissioned by UNICEF reported that 35 percent of prostitutes in Belize were under 18 and the majority of them from Honduras, El Salvador and Guatemala.

The death penalty

Corporal punishment and the **death penalty** remain highly popular in Belize, despite the fact that no one has been executed since 1985. General disputes are often solved through violence – lashings in schools and at home are common for children, and flogging by tamarind whip was reintroduced around three years ago in the Hattieville prison, though there are no reports of recent floggings. The unknown level of **domestic abuse of women** is also cause for growing concern by human rights groups.

The popular campaign to replace the British-based **Privy Council** with a **Caribbean Court of Justice** as the highest court of appeal may owe itself largely to the perception that more executions would be approved. In 2002 the Belize government introduced a fifth amendment to the constitution, lowering the level of coherent justice through the prevention of the right of appeal to the Privy Council for capital punishment cases. If it had been passed, this bill would have built discrimination into the constitution; now, a move towards a regional court seems almost inevitable. While on the face of it removing that last bastion of direct colonial authority and replacing it with a regional court seems a positive step forward, the fear in some quarters is of a lower standard of justice. The Privy Council could well be in a better position to look at individual rights and representations; in the context of the region's growing **drug economy**, alongside the downsizing of the state through structural adjustment programmes and the high level of **external debt** (in Belize around US$500 million), it may be harder to uphold democratic principles and fundamental freedoms at a state or regional level than ever before.

Ethnic Belize

Belize has a very mixed cultural background, with the two largest ethnic groups, Creoles and Mestizos – forming 75 percent of the total population (currently 275,000) – being the descendants of very different ancestors. In total, thirteen ethnic groups are recognized in Belize, the vast majority being members of one of the groups described below. There is also a great deal of ethnic mixing between the groups.

The largest ethnic group (just under fifty percent) are **Mestizos**, descended from Amerindians and early Spanish settlers, many of whom speak Spanish as their first language. They are mainly located in the north and on Ambergris Caye and Caye Caulker, with a sizeable population in Cayo. Many of the ancestors of the present population fled to Belize during the Caste Wars of the Yucatán (see p.294). In the 1980s many thousands of refugees (see p.330) from conflicts and repression in El Salvador, Guatemala and Honduras have settled in Belize, adding permanently to the numbers of Spanish-speaking Mestizos – though many of these people refer to themselves as Ladinos.

Creoles, descended from Africans brought to the West Indies as slaves and early white settlers, comprise just under a quarter of the population. They make up a large proportion of the population of Belize City, with scattered settlements elsewhere. Creole is the common language in Belize, a form of English similar to that spoken in areas of the West Indies that were once part of the British empire. Belizean spoken Creole is undergoing a formalization similar to that taken by the Garífuna in the 1980s, with a more or less standardized written Creole (referred to as "Kriol") used in some academic writing, newspaper articles and published folklore tales; for more on this see "Language", p.351. Occasionally, controversy rages in the press over whether or not Kriol should become the country's official language and be taught in schools, alongside English.

The **Maya** in Belize are from three groups – the Yucatec, Mopan and Kekchí – and make up around eleven percent of the population. The Yucatecan Maya also entered Belize to escape the fighting in the Caste Wars, and most were soon acculturated into the Mestizo way of life as small farmers. The Mopan Maya came to Belize in the 1880s and settled in the hills of Toledo and the area of Benque Viejo in the west. The last and largest group, the Kekchí, came from the area around Cobán in Guatemala to work in *cacao* plantations in southern Belize. Small numbers still arrive in Belize each year, founding new villages in the southern district of Toledo.

The **Garífuna** (see box on p.226) form just over six percent of the population and live mainly in Dangriga and the villages on the south coast. They are descended from shipwrecked and escaped African slaves who mingled with the last of the Caribs on the island of St Vincent and eventually settled in Belize. A Garífuna dictionary, published by the National Garífuna Council, is available within the country.

Another significant group is the **East Indians**, with a relatively large population in southern Toledo District. These are the descendants of indentured labourers brought over in the late 1860s by a small number of Confederate refugees seeking to re-establish the plantocracy following their defeat in the American Civil War.

Though the white, German-speaking **Mennonites** (see box on p.90) form only around four percent of the total population, they contribute to Belizean agriculture out of all proportion to their actual numbers. Over the past several centuries their opposition to government interference in their religious beliefs – particularly their utter rejection of military service – has forced them to move on to other lands. In Belize, however, they appear to have found a secure and permanent home at last.

Without a doubt, the greatest shift in Belize's demography for centuries has been the recent Hispanic influence. During the 1980s, the arrival of an estimated 40,000 **Central American immigrants**, refugees from war and poverty, boosted Belize's population to more than 200,000. Those granted refugee status were settled in camps, mostly in Cayo, and allowed to farm small plots, though many, especially the undocumented refugees, provide convenient cheap labour in citrus and banana plantations. The immigrants are tolerated, if not exactly welcomed – few countries could absorb a sudden twenty percent increase in population without a certain amount of turmoil – and the official policy is to encourage them to integrate into Belizean society. Despite the signing of peace accords ending the civil wars in their countries of origin, there is no question of enforced repatriation for these former refugees. Their children born in Belize are Belizean citizens, and the vast majority of the original refugees have since received Belizean nationality.

The former refugees are industrious agriculturists providing a variety of crops for the domestic market. Nevertheless they are often referred to as aliens and blamed for crimes. Their presence means that Spanish is now the most widely spoken first language in Belize, causing some Creoles to feel marginalized. Additionally, Guatemalan peasant farmers continue to clear land just inside Belize's western border, but these are regarded as illegal immigrants and official policy is to remove them – creating tensions between the two governments.

An excellent TV **documentary series** entitled *Simply Belize*, which will eventually cover all thirteen ethnic groups, is currently in production, and the first three programmes, each featuring a different Maya group, have already been screened. This series is available on video in the Belize City Museum and some gift shops; for more information visit Ⓦwww.simplybelize.org.

Music

F or such a tiny country, Belize enjoys an exceptional range of musical
styles and traditions. Whether your tastes run to the wind melodies and
percussion of the Maya, the up-tempo punta rock of the Garífuna or to
calypso, marimba, brukdown, soca or steel pan, Belize is sure to have
something to suit. Some visitors still complain about the noisiness of Belizean
society and the volume at which the music is played, but if you can get into
it, it's one of the quickest ways to the heart of Belizeans and their culture.

Roots

Until the demise of the Maya civilization and the arrival of the Spanish, the
indigenous **Maya** of Belize played a range of instruments drawn almost entirely from the flute and percussion families. Drums were usually made from hol-
lowed logs covered in deerskin, with rattles, gourd drums and turtle shells providing further rhythmic accompaniment. Trumpets, bells, shells and whistles
completed the instrumentation. However, as befits a nation of immigrants, each
new group arriving – the Europeans, the Creoles, the Mestizos and the
Garífuna – brought with them new styles, vigour and variety which today
inform and influence popular culture.

Mestizo music combined elements of its two constituent cultures: Maya ceremonial music and new instruments from Spain, such as the classical guitar and
violin, and later brass band music. Mestizo communities (including the Mopan
Maya) in the north and west of the country continue to favour **marimba**
bands: half a dozen men playing two large, multi-keyed wooden xylophones,
perhaps supported by a double bass and a drum kit. Up to half a dozen bands
play regularly in Cayo District: Eligio Panti presides over the nation's pre-eminent marimba group, **Alma Beliceña**, and **Los Angeles Marimba Band** is
another popular group. Leading marimba bands frequently pop over from
Flores in Guatemala, and Mexican **mariachi** bands occasionally make an
appearance, too. Nonetheless, traditional Mestizo music remains under threat as
the youth turn to rock, rap and punta.

Europeans introduced much of the hardware and software for playing
music: "Western" musical instruments and sheet music, and, much later, record
players, compact discs and massive sound systems. From the mid-nineteenth
century onwards, British colonial culture, through church music, military bands
and the popular music of the time, was able to exert a dominant influence over
what was acceptable music in Belize.

An exciting melange of **West African rhythms** and melodies, as well as
drums and stringed instruments, arrived in Belize as a result of the slave trade
during the eighteenth century. However, given that the Baymen purchased
slaves from **Jamaica** rather than directly from Africa it should be remembered
that African influences arrived indirectly.

A new, syncretic style, nurtured in the logging camps and combining Western
instrumentation with specifically African musical inflections, emerged in the
late nineteenth century to create a specifically Belizean musical tradition
known as "**brukdown**". Featuring a modern line-up of guitar, banjo, accor-
dion, drums and the jawbone of an ass (rattling a stick up and down the teeth!),

brukdown remains a potent reminder of past **Creole** culture. Although the style is slowly fading, as Creole society itself changes, there are a few active practitioners. The style's most prominent figure, master accordionist **Wilfred Peters** (now in his seventies and still playing), is the founder of the nationally celebrated **Mr. Peters and his Boom and Chime**, and has composed countless classics and performed to audiences in festivals around the world. Generally, though, brukdown is recreational music best enjoyed in the Creole villages of Burrell Boom, Hattieville, Bermudian Landing and Isabella Bank.

Brad Patico, an accomplished guitarist and singer-songwriter, similarly does his best to keep the Creole folksong tradition alive from his base in Burrell Boom – his recordings can still be found in Belizean record stores. Originating from the same cultural roots, and equally conscious of a disappearing musical past, is Brother David Obi, better known as **Bredda David**, the creator of **kungo music**, a mixture of musical styles that includes the traditional Creole music of Belize and the pulsating drum rhythms of Africa. A skilful musician and songwriter, David still plays occasionally in Belize City with his **Tribal Vibes** band. Currently the best-known singer seen to preserve traditional Creole folksong is **Leela Vernon** from Punta Gorda, who plays to highly appreciative audiences at national festivals, often appearing with long-standing pop bands, including **Youth Connection**, **Gilharry 7** and **Santino's Messengers**. Her most famous song, "Who say Creole gat no culture?" is a national favourite amongst older people and a reminder of pride in Belizean society.

More recently, the African elements in Creole music have been expressed through wider **pan-Caribbean** styles like calypso, reggae, soca and rap. **Calypso** enjoyed a brief period of pre-eminence – Belize's most famous calypsonian **Lord Rhaburn** is still occasionally to be seen as a special guest at official functions, increasingly rare performances that shouldn't be missed.

Punta rock

If traditional Maya, Mestizo and Creole styles retain only a fragile hold on popular musical consciousness, it is the **Garífuna** who have been catapulted to centre-stage over the last two decades with the invention and development of **punta rock**. The key musical developments that led to punta rock were the amplification of several traditional **drum rhythms** originally associated with courtship dances, while keeping faith with other traditional instruments such as the turtle shell – and initially the almost universal aversion to singing in anything but Garífuna. Although many master musicians and cultural nationalists (both from Belize and the other Garífuna communities across Central America) pushed Garífuna culture forward, particular recognition must go to master drummer and drum-maker **Isabel Flores** and the enigmatic singer, guitarist and artist **Pen Cayetano** in Dangriga. Pen pioneered popular Garífuna music, widening the scope of punta with the introduction of electric guitars and helping to spark a new cultural assertiveness that saw dozens of younger musicians take up the challenge. His **Turtle Shell Band** set the standard, and within a few years other electric bands – including **Sounds Incorporated**, **Black Coral**, **Jeff Zuniga**, **Titiman Flores**, **Mohubub** and, above all, **Andy Palacio** (see box on p.334) – consolidated punta's popularity. Palacio's brainchild, the seminal compilation *Punta Rockers* (1988) featured recordings by himself and several other punta rock pioneers. Credit should also be given to Dangriga-based **Al Obando** in the development of the punta rock sound. As Belize's preeminent sound engineer, Obando produced the hugely popular band the **Punta Rebels** through the 1990s and is still relied upon for studio recordings today.

Guardians of more orthodox arrangements **Lugua and the Larubeya Drummers** marked their debut with the release of *Bumari* (1997). Covering the full range of Garífuna drumming styles alongside powerful call and response vocals, their music is a telling reminder of the African influence in Garífuna history; their live shows should on no account be missed. Recently there has also been a resurgence of the traditional Garífuna style of **parranda,** performed with acoustic guitars, drums and shakers. This was marked by the international release of the eponymous album, recorded by various *parranderos* living in Belize, Honduras and Guatemala. It is recognized as being one of the best collections to come out of Central America. This movement looks set to continue with two forthcoming releases – the first by Belize-produced Honduran **Aurelio Martínez**, who blends parranda with Latin influences and Spanish vocals, and the second by **Andy Palacio & The Garífuna All-Star Band**, featuring other Garífuna stars such as **Paul Nabor**.

Additionally, several young Garífuna stars from Dangriga have emerged to take the nation by storm, combining fast infectious punta with reggae dance-hall and soca in highly energized performances. This is punta for the young generation, relying largely on **sound-systems**, often at the expense of live musicians. Former Punta Rebels **Super G** and **Lloyd & Reckless**, alongside favourites the **Griga Boyz**, are the main exponents and can be found performing regularly throughout the country. Showing an awareness of the wider market potential in Guatemala and Mexico, Super G now also sings in Spanish and includes **cumbia** numbers on his albums – a Latin style highly popular amongst young mestizos. Increasingly often these punta rock stars make the trip across the borders to rapturous audiences in Chetumal and Flores, demonstrating the position of Belize both as a major regional music producer and as a bridge between Caribbean and Latin American styles.

Venues and other artists

The wide ethnic diversity of Belize ensures a music scene of equal variety (there's much more to hear than punta) and most people will find something to enjoy. Thursday evening is widely considered to mark the start of the **weekend**, which is the best time to catch bands and other entertainment in **Belize City**. The **radio** is the best place to hear about forthcoming gigs and events, with Krem, Wave and Love FM being the main Belize City stations. *Paradise 21, Queens, MJ's* and *Archie's* **nightclubs** cater to the younger generation with live punta, while the *Princess Hotel* regularly has live entertainment for a more mature audience. Bigger venues like the Civic Centre and *Bird's Isle* host longer variety bills and foreign (very often Jamaican) artists. The larger **hotels** (here and throughout the country) usually have something on offer as well: Fridays at the *Bellevue* attract a young crowd, while most week nights at the *Radisson* you'll find live jazz and other styles. Just out of town on the Northern Highway, the *Biltmore Hotel* has live music most evenings – currently jazz on Thursday, steel band on Friday and Mexican mariachi on Saturday. Look out also for the excellent daytime **Belizean Cabaret** (see "Dance", p.338). The newly refurbished **Bliss Centre for the Performing Arts** is the main theatre and concert hall, sponsoring performances by both contemporary and classical musicians.

San Pedro, as the major tourist destination in Belize, guarantees a range of

Andy Palacio

For two decades **Andy Palacio** has influenced, dominated and even helped produce the modern Belizean sound. Although he performs less often than he did in the 1990s, he remains the country's only truly professional star and music ambassador to the rest of the world. Over the years Palacio has succeeded in incorporating an enormous diversity of national and regional styles into a unique popular sound that appeals to all sections of the music market.

Born in Barranco, he grew up in the rural cosmopolitanism of Garífuna, Maya and Mestizo communities, integrating a diversity of linguistic and cultural influences from an early age. As a teenager in the 1970s he experienced first-hand the new Belizean cultural nationalism of the PUP party, which brought the country to independence, introducing a broader ideological dimension to his inevitable cultural affinity with the Garífuna musical tradition. The break came in 1987 when, on an exchange visit to London, he spent a year picking up the latest recording techniques and honing his compositional skills. He returned triumphantly to Belize a year later with enough equipment to open a studio, also bringing with him several London recordings of the songs that would become huge hits back home and transform the music scene.

The biggest song was undoubtedly the 1988 hit **Bikini Panti** – an English-Garífuna, punta-rock satire on Belize's burgeoning tourist business – which set a new musical and lyrical standard for the entire country. But if *Bikini Panti* was the dancefloor killer, it was **Me Goin' Back** that provided the clear ideological expression of the new national sensitivity, as the almost calypsonian lyrics demonstrate:

Set up the line for the Dangriga posse
Play a little rhythm for the Stann Creek posse
Mash up the place with the Cayo posse
Bruk down the house with the Belize posse
Control the area for the Orange Walk posse
Mek them know that me fresh and ready
Mek them know, me have the authority

Now don't burst your brains wondering what
I'm goin back to
So I'll mention just a few
Some old and some new

Rice n Beans and a Belikin
Friends FM and a dollar chicken
Pine Ridge and a Swing Bridge
Brukdown, Punta Rock
Sunshine and a cashew wine
Belize Times and Amandala
Maya, Creole and the Garífuna

Palacio's longstanding collaboration with Stonetree Records has seen two releases to date (see the discography box on pp.336–337), and his new project with the **Garífuna All-Stars** band from across Central America included a tour of Europe in 2003 before the release of the new album in 2004. More comfortable in his national superstar status, he has established an enviable reputation as a musician capable of producing catchy melodies accompanied by articulate, astute and entertaining lyrics, underpinned by unique Garífuna rhythms.

entertainment – check at *Fido's*, the *Barefoot Iguana* and the *Crazy Canuks* bar, as well as in the relevant section of this book for more information. **Caye Caulker** now offers almost as much choice and frequently plays host to the latest punta rockers, as does **Placencia** with live music at *White Sands* (Seine Bight) on weekends and *Jungle Juice* on weekdays. In **Belmopan** check out *The Roundabout* club – though for better choice, **San Ignacio** presents far livelier options. Punta artists and Latin favourites regularly perform at the *Cahal Pech Entertainment Centre*, Sam Harris and his original **World Culture Band** often play roots reggae and ska at the *Culture Club*, and the *San Ignacio Hotel* also features occasional live acts and Latin dance classes. Also in Cayo District, *Caesar's Place* is a great venue to catch live jazz and blues the first Saturday of every month. Another highly talented Belizean artist is **Pablo Collado** of Benque Viejo; influenced strongly by traditional Mayan music he now has six beautiful and evocative flute and guitar albums to his credit. His regular live shows at several resorts in Cayo and the Mountain Pine Ridge also feature dancing and more up-tempo instrumentals. In **Dangriga,** *Club 2000* and *Malibu Beach* provide regular live music. Rural areas also occasionally come up with the best live shows, often unexpected and informal: Hopkins, Succotz, Bullet Tree, Ladyville, Burrell Boom, Consejo and Maskall all still entertain in the traditional way.

Special events

Perhaps the best times to hear and see the full panoply of Belizean musical culture are the various national events that regularly punctuate the social calendar. Biggest and best are **National Day/St George's Caye Day** (Sept 10) and **Independence Day** (Sept 21) – dates that mark almost two weeks of festivities as Belize City comes close to the spirit and atmosphere of Caribbean carnival. In fact, between these dates there's a genuine **Carnival**, established only since independence but a hugely popular event, with an enormous street parade, floats, a carnival queen attended by a bevy of princesses and of course bands and sound systems. Block parties, "jump-ups" and late-night revelry characterize what are popularly known as the "**September Celebrations**". On Independence Day, Eve Street (leading to the BTL Park) is closed to traffic and the country's top bands and sound systems line the parade route and perform on stages in the park.

The **Costa Maya Festival**, held in San Pedro during the third week of August, is a celebration of dance, music and culture that attracts performers from Mexico and throughout Central America. **Garífuna Settlement Day** (Nov 19) brings huge crowds to Dangriga, with 2003 marking the first Puntafest – a long weekend of late nights, rum and rhythm. The **National Agricultural Show**, held just outside Belmopan in May, gathers together up to 50,000 people over three days for all things agricultural and recreational. Almost all the country's top artists, bands and sound systems will appear at some stage during the weekend.

Mestizo communities celebrate with a number of Latin-type **fiestas**: bands, funfairs, sports and competitions, usually held around Easter. The week-long **Flores Fiesta**, held in mid-January across the border in Guatemala, is also great fun, with many Belizean artists performing alongside Guatemalan acts.

For a current list of the best of Belize's recorded music, check out **Stonetree's website**, ⓦ www.stonetreerecords.com.

Andy Palacio *Keimoun* and *Til Da Mawnin* (Stonetree) Two great albums displaying a mastery of punta and a widening of scope to incorporate Latin and Anglophone Caribbean influences. New release with the **Garífuna All-Stars** features *parranderos* **Aurelio** and **Paul Nabor**.

Bredda David & Tribal Vibes *Raw* (Stonetree) Rock guitars overlaid on new-generation Belizean rhythm and lyrical wit combine to produce a satisfying run around the kungo kingdom.

Caribbean Pulse *Stand-Up* and *Unity* (Irie Records) Two albums from this US-based Belizean reggae group present well-produced conscious music. Visit ⓦ www.caribbeanpulse.com.

Florencio Mess *Maya K'ekchi' Strings* (Stonetree) One of the few remaining harpists to maintain this centuries-old Maya tradition.

Leroy Young the Grandmaster *Just Like That* (Stonetree) Impressive musical debut from Belize's own dub-poet presents a powerful commentary and new Creole style, featuring a wide range of roots rhythms and strings.

Lugua and the Larubeya Drummers *Bumari* (Stonetree) Roots Garífuna music at its strongest, a new chapter in the history of Garífuna percussion.

Maria Reimer *Maria* (Digitrax/EMI) Belizean country/Latin singer demonstrates a powerful voice.

MKL and others *Three Generations Walking* (Spiritual Life Music) This project from Belizean MKL and others showcases a highly original blend of dub, jazz and modern electronic music. See ⓦ www.spirituallifemusic.com.

Mr. Peters and his Boom and Chime *Weh Mi Love Deh* and *Rub Mi Belly* (Stonetree) Two excellent releases from the undisputed king of brukdown. A musical journey through Creole culture and the ideal introduction to this genuine Belizean art form.

The Original Turtle Shell Band *Beginning* The first-ever punta rock recording from 1982 features Pen Cayetano, Mohubub and the band, remastered here in 2000. See ⓦ www.cayetano.de.

Belizean musicians abroad

No review of Belizean music would be complete without considering the impact of the Belizean diaspora on the national scene. A number of Belize-born bands and artists from a diversity of musical genres are now experiencing fame in their respective styles both in the US and back home.

The wider Garífuna community in the US, from both Belizean and Honduranan origins, sustains a growing market for punta rock in North America and crosses over into the wider Latin music market. Artists such as **Aziatic**, **Garífuna Legacy**, punta-rap group **Garífuna Kidz**, **Punta Cartel** and the more traditional **Del and the Sensations** all make annual trips to Belize and are well worth a listen. On a different musical note, but nonetheless wholeheartedly Belizean, is country-Latin singer **Maria Reimer**, born in Cayo to Mennonite and Mestizo parents, and recently having recorded for EMI in Nashville. You may well hear her melodic country tones while travelling in Cayo and the north, or catch her live performances at national festivals. California-based Belizean conscious-reggae outfit **Caribbean Pulse** is also making good headway with two albums to date and tracks featuring such reggae luminaries as Tony Rebel and Damian Marley.

Pablo Collado *Naturaleza Despierta* and *Amanecer* (Derechos Reservados, Guatemala) Two of the best from this Maya-Mestizo master flautist/guitarist.

Super G *Unity* and *Unlock* (Love Entertainment) Two recent albums showcasing Spanish, English and Garífuna lyrics from this punta favourite, although often using backing tracks in preference to live drumming.

Titiman Flores *Fedu* (Stonetree) A punta rock party album from beginning to end. The recent *Stop Crime* (Love Entertainment) shows Titiman still controlling the dancefloor.

Various Artists *Celebration Belize* (Belize Arts Council) Includes contributions from Andy Palacio, Mr. Peters, Leela Vernon, Florencio Mess and many others in this colourful musical journey.

Various Artists *PARRANDA: Africa in Central America* (Stonetree/Warner Classics) Three generations of Garífuna together for the first time on this landmark recording. Imagine African drumming, American blues, Cuban son and West African guitar all wrapped into one.

Various Artists *The Rough Guide to Central America* (World Music Network) Covering music from six countries, the album includes five well-known Belizean artists from the cross-section of styles – an ideal introduction to the music of the whole region.

Other punta artists and recordings to look out for are **Aziatic** with *Most Wanted* (Stonetree), *The Re Birth* (Sta-tic Productions) and, together with **Griga Boyz**, *Crazy Fi We* (Stonetree); **Mohubub**'s self-titled album (Stonetree), with conscious lyrics; the **Punta Rebels** *Gial DePan Fiya*; and *Desire* (Love Entertainment), from former Rebels **Lloyd and Reckless**.

Forthcoming on Stonetree are *Garífuna Women Voices*, featuring the songs from coastal villages in Belize, Guatemala and Honduras; Honduranan **Aurelio**'s Belizean debut, demonstrating a powerful voice over Latin, punta and parranda rhythms; and *The Creole Experience – Music from the Riverbanks*, based on traditional Creole songs with an eclectic mix of acoustic instruments.

Apart from traditional Caribbean and Latin musical territory – and proving that Belizean musicians are breaking boundaries beyond drums and roots – is Belize City-born **MKL**, alias Michael Lopez. Based in New York, his highly original musical project entitled *Three Generations Walking* (see the discography box) encompasses soul, jazz, dub, laid-back electronics and female vocals, alongside live congas and guitars. Outside the studio, MKL occupies himself as a global touring DJ, and may yet find his niche in the Belize music scene.

Original text by Ronnie Graham. Fully revised by Rob Coates, with additional material from Ivan Duran and Hector Martinez.

Dance

Alongside the growth in music production since independence, Belize has witnessed the formation and development of an active dance scene. Most visitors will notice a vibrant dancing culture among the different ethnic groups – but since the inception of the Belize National Dance Company in 1990, a countrywide programme has been established.

Under the leadership of director-choreographers **Gregory Vernon** and **Althea Sealy**, and with initial assistance from Eduardo Rivero of the Caribbean Dance Theatre of Santiago de Cuba, the **Belize National Dance Company** was created in an effort both to promote a collective cultural identity and to preserve the traditional dances of the Belizean people. Amalgamating the various dances from across the country, the **Belize modern technique** draws from Afro-folkloric dances including traditional Garífuna movements and expression and Creole brukdown and bram dance, alongside Cuban technique and creative modern and contemporary styles. Traditional dances such as the punta, Jonkunnu (John Canoe) and chumba all still feature strongly. In addition to performance, the BNDC also includes the promotion of dance countrywide as part of its vision. Its members give regular dance workshops in schools, and a summer camp is held each year to bring together young dancers for training and skill development. The company's recent choreographic work *Wind Fire on Earth* demonstrated the national sensitivity through the use of entirely Belizean choreographers alongside the compositions of local musicians, touring Belize to popular acclaim from Punta Gorda to Corozal.

Another dance group that performs regularly – both in Belize and internationally – is the **Ugandani** ("happiness" in Garífuna) group led by **Charles Flores**, which encourages the promotion of traditional Garífuna dances, music and language.

Venues and festivals

With its home now at the **Bliss Centre for the Performing Arts** (see p.67), the BNDC also performs regularly at international festivals across Europe and the Americas, while maintaining an annual dance concert at home and a bi-annual **International Dance Festival** that includes foreign dance groups. Perhaps the best place to get a feel for Belizean dance is at the *Biltmore Hotel* in Belize City, which hosts the excellent **Belizean Cabaret** (currently three times weekly at lunchtimes) featuring Ugandani and BNDC dancers alongside live drumming and a voice-over describing the history of the dances of the different ethnic groups – from Maya and Mestizo to Creole and Garífuna. The annual **Children's Festival of Arts**, which takes place all over the country in May/June, showcases the latest young talent. With active dance companies and training in Belize City, Belmopan, San Pedro, San Ignacio and Dangriga, Belizean dance looks set for a great future.

Books

Belize under British rule didn't inspire much literature, but independence has prompted a handful of writers to publish works based on the transition to independence and the emergence of a national identity. There are a number of excellent wildlife guides and studies, and also several good travel accounts covering Belize. Books on the ancient Maya increase in number and quality of information every year.

Cubola Productions is Belize's pre-eminent specialist publishers, with a wide range of fiction and non-fiction on all subjects related to Belize, including many of the archeology and wildlife books listed below; check their website, ⒲ www.cubolabelize.com, for full details. The Angelus Press in Belize also publishes an impressive list of titles by Belizean authors and books about Belize, and they offer an online and mail order service; visit ⒲ www.angeluspress.com. See also the box on p.17 for specialist publishers outside Belize. Where possible we have given both the US and UK publishers (listed after the book title), with the US publisher first. Many books are published only in Belize; o/p means a book is out of print. Books that are especially recommended are preceded by a ☒ symbol.

Travel

Thor Jansen *Belize, Land of the Free by the Carib Sea* (Bowen and Bowen, Belize). Published by the company which produces Belikin beer, this lavishly illustrated coffee-table travelogue through modern Belize makes a perfect souvenir.

Aldous Huxley *Beyond the Mexique Bay* (Flamingo, UK; o/p). In 1934, Huxley's travels took him from Belize through Guatemala to Mexico, swept on by his fascination with history and religion, and sprouting bizarre theories on the basis of what he saw. There are some great descriptions of Maya sites and Indian culture, with superb one-liners summing up people and places, including the classic "If the world had any ends British Honduras would surely be one of them."

Jeremy Paxman *Through the Volcanoes* (Paladin, UK; o/p). A political travel account investigating the turmoil of Central America and finding solace in the calm of Costa Rica. Paxman's travels take him through all seven countries, includ-

ing Belize, and he offers a good overview of the politics and history of the region in the mid-1980s.

John Lloyd Stephens *Incidents of Travel in Central America, Chiapas, and Yucatán* (Dover; Prentice Hall). Stephens was a classic nineteenth-century traveller. Acting as American ambassador to Central America, he indulged his own enthusiasm for archeology: while the republics fought it out among themselves he was wading through the jungle stumbling across ancient cities. In Belize he dines with high society and is given a naval gun salute from the superintendent, though he doesn't venture inland. His journals, written with superb Victorian pomposity, punctuated with sudden waves of enthusiasm, make great reading. Some editions include fantastic illustrations by Frederick Catherwood of Maya ruins overgrown with tropical rainforest.

☒ **Ronald Wright** *Time Among the Maya* (Grove Press, US). A vivid and sympathetic account of

339

Wright's travels in the late 1980s from Belize through Guatemala, Chiapas and Yucatán, meeting the Maya and exploring their obsession with time. The book's twin points of interest are the ancient Maya and the violence that occurred throughout the 1980s. Certainly one of the best travel books on the area, and the author's knowledge is evident in the superb historical insight he imparts throughout the book.

Literature

★ **If Di Pin Neva Ben: Folktales and Legends of Belize** (various authors; Cubola, Belize). A vibrant collection of traditional Belizean folklore. Includes a host of colourful characters, ranging from creatures who enforce the preservation of nature to figures who allow storytellers to explore otherwise taboo subjects. Gathered by folklorists during the late 1970s, these short tales capture the richness of a society that fluidly blends the cultures of its many ethnic groups. Other anthologies of Belizean literature published by Cubola include *Snapshots of Belize*, a collection of short stories by major Belizean writers, and *Ping Wing Juk Me*, six short plays reproduced in an attempt to revive the strong theatrical tradition which thrived prior to the advent of television; both of these contain some writing in Creole (see "Language", p.351).

Zee Edgell *Beka Lamb* (Heinemann). A young girl's account of growing up in Belize in the 1950s, in which the problems of adolescence are described alongside those of the Belizean independence movement. The book also explores everyday life in the colony, describing the powerful structure of matriarchal society and the influence of the Catholic Church. *In Times Like These*, also by Edgell, is a semi-autobiographical account of personal and political intrigue set in the months leading up to Belize's independence.

Zoila Ellis *On Heroes, Lizards and Passion* (Cubola, Belize). Seven short stories written by a Belizean woman with a deep understanding of her country's people and their culture.

Felicia Hernandez *Those Ridiculous Years* (Cubola, Belize). A short autobiographical book about growing up in Dangriga in the 1960s.

★ **Emory King** *Belize 1798, The Road to Glory* (Tropical Books, Belize). Rip-roaring historical novel peopled by the characters involved in the Battle of St George's Caye. King's enthusiasm for his country's history is supported by meticulous research in archives on both sides of the Atlantic. Wonderful holiday reading. King is something of a celebrity in Belize (see box on p.64): his first book *Hey Dad, This Is Belize*, a hilarious account of family life in Belize, became something of a minor classic and was followed up with *I Spent It All In Belize*, an anthology of witty, lightly satirical articles gently but effectively pricking the pomposity of officialdom. These and other books by King are usually only available in Belize, though you can order online from the Angelus Press.

Carlos Ledson Miller *Belize – A Novel* (Xlibris, US). Fast-paced historical saga of a Central American father and his two sons – one American and one Belizean – who struggle against a forbidding land, and often with each other. The story opens in 1961, on the eve of Hurricane Hattie, then transports the reader across forty years from the unrest of colonial British Honduras to the turbulence of present-day Belize. A good read.

History, politics and society

A History of Belize – A Nation in the Making (Cubola, Belize). Straightforward and simple historical accounts, written for use in schools but providing a good, accurate background; available within Belize.

The Maya Atlas (North Atlantic Books, US; o/p). As much a collection of personal accounts of contemporary Maya life as a geography book, this is a fascinating co-production between university researchers and the Maya of Toledo in southern Belize. Trained by Berkeley cartographers, teams of villagers surveyed their lands, completed a census and then wrote a history of each community. The regional maps accurately show the position of each village, and drawings and photographs show scenes from everyday life.

★ **Readings in Belizean History** (various authors; St John's College Press, Belize). Recently updated version of a highly acclaimed textbook, comprising essays by noted Belizean scholars on all aspects of Belize's history. Will interest anyone looking for a broader and deeper insight into Belize.

O. Nigel Bolland *Colonialism and Resistance in Belize: Essays in Historical Sociology* (Cubola, Belize/UWI Press) This revised (2003) edition of the 1988 text is the most comprehensive and academic study of Belizean history there is. Covering both the early colonization of the Maya, the growth of slavery and progress of Creole culture, through to the development of nationalism over divergent ethnic identities, Bolland places particular emphasis on labour control and resistance – providing a broadly Marxist analysis that is both compelling and convincingly argued.

Sebastian Cayetano *Garífuna History, Language & Culture of Belize, Central America & the Caribbean* (Angelus Press, Belize). A brief, simply written history of the Garífuna. Mainly aimed at children, it also mentions the great changes the Garinagu are experiencing as they adapt to modern life.

Byron Foster *Heart Drum* and *Spirit Possession in the Garífuna Community of Belize* (Cubola, Belize). These two slim volumes focus on the importance of spirituality in the lives of the Garífuna and the experience of spirit possession as described to Foster, an anthropologist. Another of Foster's books, *The Baymen's Legacy: A Portrait of Belize City* (Cubola), is a school text but offers an approachable and interesting history of the city.

Emory King *The Great Story of Belize* (Tropical Books, Belize). Four slim, large-format volumes from a master raconteur. The meticulously researched narrative, full of events great and small and packed with larger-than-life characters, presents a vivid account of Belize's history from the first Spanish contact to the 1990s.

Gerhard S. Koop *Pioneer Years in Belize* (self-published; available in Belize). A history of the Mennonites in Belize, written in a style as stolid and practical as the lives of the pioneers themselves. A good read nonetheless.

Ian Peedle *Belize in Focus* (Resource Center; LAB). A relatively up-to-date, easily digested overview of Belizean society and politics. Worth taking along if you're there for more than a few days.

★ **Assad Shoman** *Thirteen Chapters of a History of Belize* (Angelus Press, Belize). A treatment of the country's history written by a Belizean who's not afraid to examine colonial myths with a detailed and rational analysis. Primarily a school textbook, but the style will not alienate non-student readers. Shoman, active in politics both before and since independence, also wrote *Party Politics in Belize*, a short but highly detailed account of the development of party politics in the country.

Ann Sutherland *The Making of Belize: Globalization in the Margins* (Bergin and Garvey, US). A fairly recent study of cultural and economic changes in Belize, based on the author's experiences as a visitor and her observations as an anthropologist. The result is an enjoyable mixture of academic research, anecdotal insights and strong, even controversial, opinion; Sutherland reserves her strongest criticism for conservationists, whom she castigates as "ecocolonialists [who] totally disregard the interests of the Belizean people".

Colville Young *Creole Proverbs of Belize* (Cubola, Belize). A wonderful compilation of oral folk-wisdom from Belize, written by the present governor general, who's also a distinguished linguist. Each saying or proverb is written in Creole, translated into English, and then has its meaning explained. A primer for street life. Other books by Young include *Pataki Full*, a slim anthology of Belizean short stories and folk tales, and two volumes of poetry, *From One Caribbean Corner* and *Caribbean Corner Calling*, which bring Belize and its Creole language to life.

Archeology

⭐ **The Popol Vuh** (Touchstone; Scribner). The great creation myth poem of the K'iche' (Quiche) Maya of the Guatemalan highlands, written shortly after the conquest and intended to preserve the K'iche' people's knowledge of their history. Although not directly connected with Belize and strictly speaking a work of literature not archeology, the characters and images in the book are directly relevant to an understanding of the ancient Maya anywhere. It's an amazing swirl of fantastic gods and mortals who become gods, particularly the Hero Twins and their battle to overcome the Lords of Death in Xibalba. There are several versions on offer, though many of them are half-hearted and include only a few lines from the original. The best is translated by Dennis Tedlock.

Jamie Awe *100 Questions and Answers about the Ancient Maya of Belize* (Factory Books, Belize). Written by Belize's Director of Archaeology and designed primarily for schoolchildren, this slim book is ideal for anyone interested in the basic facts about the Maya.

⭐ **Michael Coe** *The Maya* (Thames & Hudson). Now in its seventh edition, this clear and comprehensive introduction to Maya archeology is the best on offer. Coe has also written several more weighty, academic volumes. His *Breaking the Maya Code* (Thames & Hudson), a very personal history of the decipherment of the glyphs, owes much to the fact that Coe was present at many of the most important meetings leading to the breakthrough. While his pointed criticism of J. Eric S. Thompson – much of whose work he describes as burdened with "irrelevant quotations", and his role in the decipherment of the Maya script as "entirely negative" – may provoke controversy, this book demonstrates that the glyphs did actually reproduce Maya speech.

William Coe *Tikal: A Handbook to the Ancient Maya Ruins* (University of Pennsylvania, US). Superbly detailed account of the site, usually available at the ruins. The detailed map of the main area is essential for in-depth exploration.

David Drew *The Lost Chronicles of the Maya Kings* (University of California Press; Weidenfeld and Nicolson). Superbly readable and engaging; the author draws on a wealth of material including some of the very latest findings to deliver an excellent account of ancient Maya political history. The alliances and rivalries between the main cities are skilfully unravelled, and there's a particularly revealing analysis of late Classic Maya power politics.

Byron Foster (ed.) *Warlords and Maize Men – A Guide to the Maya Sites of Belize* (Cubola, Belize; o/p). An excellent handbook for fifteen of the most accessible sites in Belize, compiled by the Association for Belizean Archaeology and the Belize Department of Archaeology.

Thomas H. Guderjan *Ancient Maya Traders of Ambergris Caye* (Cubola, Belize). Interesting details about the original inhabitants of Belize's most popular tourist destination. Fifteen hundred years ago this was one of the busiest places in the Maya world, with even higher numbers of locals and visitors than there are today.

Peter D. Harrison *The Lords of Tikal* (Thames and Hudson). Outstanding study of the great Maya metropolis, based on more than thirty years of research and the latest hieroglyphic readings. There's a tremendous amount of detail about the city's monuments and artefacts, and the rulers who commissioned them.

Grant D. Jones *The Conquest of the Last Maya Kingdom* (Stanford University Press). A massive academic tome that's also a fascinating history of the Itza Maya and a gripping tale of how the Spanish entered and finally defeated the last independent Maya kingdom, at Tayasal, site of present-day Flores.

Joyce Kelly *An Archaeological Guide to Northern Central America* (University of Oklahoma). Detailed and practical guide to 38 Maya sites and 25 museums in four countries; an essential companion for anyone travelling purposefully through the Maya world. Kelly's "star" rating – based on a site's archeological importance, degree of restoration and accessibility – may affront purists but it does provide a valuable opinion on how worthwhile a particular visit might be. Still the most detailed single-edition guide available to the Maya sites of Belize, though recent developments make it somewhat dated in certain areas.

Diego de Landa *Yucatán Before and After the Conquest* (Dover, UK). A translation edited by William Gates of the work written in 1566 as *Relación de las Cosas de Yucatán*. De Landa's destruction of almost all original Maya books as "works of the devil" leaves his own account as the chief source on Maya life and society in the immediate post-conquest period. Written during his imprisonment in Spain on charges of cruelty to the Indians (remarkable in itself, given the institutional brutality of the time), the book provides a fascinating wealth of detail for historians. Although (as far as is known) Landa did not visit Belize, the vivid descriptions of Maya life and ceremony are applicable to the Maya of Chetumal, a province then extending into northern Belize.

★ **Simon Martin and Nikolai Grube** *Chronicle of the Maya Kings and Queens* (Thames & Hudson). Highly acclaimed work based on exhaustive new epigraphic studies, and the re-reading of previously translated glyphic texts. The historical records of eleven key Maya cities – including Tikal and Caracol – complete with biographies of 152 kings and four queens, plus full dynastic sequences and all the key battles and dates. As Michael Coe, author of *The Maya* says, "There's nothing else like this book. It supersedes everything else ever written on Maya history."

Heather McKillop *Salt: White Gold of the Ancient Maya* (University Press of Florida). Salt, essential to life and a precious resource, was traded throughout the Maya world. This groundbreaking work overturns earlier theories, demonstrating that much of the salt consumed in the great lowland cities of Belize and Petén was produced on the coast of Belize. These previously unknown sites also show evidence of rising sea levels in the Postclassic Period, as many are now underwater. The author's latest book, *The Ancient Maya: New Perspectives* (ABC–CLIO, US) is a comprehensive account of the ancient Maya, incorporating the most recent findings and theories from current research.

★ **John Montgomery** *Tikal: An Illustrated History of the Ancient Maya Capital* (Hippocrene Books, US). Easily the most readable book on the subject and sure to become a classic. In addition to being a detailed history of Tikal, it's packed with fascinating information about the Maya in general, and the comprehensive chronology gives an overview of what was happening elsewhere in the Maya world. The author is a noted scholar and his other books (same publisher), including *A Dictionary of Maya Hieroglyphs* and *How to Read Maya Hieroglyphs*, are well worth reading.

Mary Ellen Miller *The Art of Mesoamerica: From Olmec to Aztec* (Thames & Hudson). An excellent, wonderfully illustrated survey of the artisanship of the ancient cultures of Mexico, whose work reflects the sophistication of their civilizations.

Miller is the acknowledged expert on Mayan and Mesoamerican art; her more recent *Maya Art and Architecture* (Thames & Hudson) provides fascinating and well-illustrated background reading, though little specifically on sites in Belize.

Mary Ellen Miller and Karl Taube *The Gods and Symbols of Ancient Mexico and the Maya: An Illustrated Dictionary of Mesoamerican Religion* (Thames & Hudson). A superb modern reference on ancient Mesoamerica, written by two leading scholars. Taube's *Aztec and Maya Myths* (British Museum Press, UK) is perfect as a short, accessible introduction to Mesoamerican mythology.

Jeremy A. Sabloff *The New Archaeology and the Ancient Maya* (Scientific American Library). Sabloff explains the "revolution" which has taken place in Maya archeology since the 1960s, overturning many firmly held beliefs and assumptions on the nature of Maya society, and stating how the study of archeology relates to current environmental problems.

Linda Schele and David Freidel (et al.) *A Forest of Kings: The Untold Story of the Ancient Maya* (Quill, US). The authors, at the forefront of the "new archeology", have been personally responsible for decoding many of the glyphs. Their writing style, which frequently includes "recreations" of scenes inspired by their discoveries, is controversial in some areas, but has nevertheless inspired a devoted following. This book, in conjunction with *The Blood of Kings* (Thames & Hudson, US; Braziller, UK), by Linda Schele and Mary Ellen Miller, shows that far from being governed by peaceful astronomer-priests, the ancient Maya were ruled by hereditary kings, lived in aggressive city-states and engaged in a continuous entanglement of alliances and war. *The Maya Cosmos* (Quill, US) by Schele, Freidel and Joy Parker is perhaps more difficult to read, dense with copious notes, but continues to examine Maya ritual and religion in a unique and far-reaching way. *The Code of Kings* (Scribner, US), written in collaboration with Peter Matthews and illustrated with Justin Kerr's famous "rollout" photography of Maya ceramics, examines in detail the significance of the monuments at selected Maya sites (Tikal is included, though none are in Belize). This, Schele's last book (she died in 1998), is a classic of epigraphic interpretation.

⭐ **Robert Sharer** *The Ancient Maya* (Stanford University). A comprehensive (and weighty) account of Maya civilization, now in a completely revised and much more readable fifth edition, yet as authori-

tative as ever. Required reading for archeology students, it also provides a fascinating reference for the non-expert.

J. Eric S. Thompson *The Rise and Fall of the Maya Civilization* (University of Oklahoma). A major authority on the ancient Maya, Thompson has produced many academic studies – this is one of the more approachable. *The Maya of Belize – Historical Chapters Since Columbus* (Cubola, Belize) is a very interesting book on the first two centuries of Spanish colonial rule – a little-studied area of Belizean history – and casts some light on the groups that weren't immediately conquered by the Spanish.

Wildlife and the environment

Belize has a range of superb wildlife books and pamphlets, written by specialists with visitors, teachers and students in mind. Unfortunately, many are difficult to obtain outside the country; the best ones might be available from Cubola (see p.339) or the Belize Audubon Society (BAS; see p.324), who offer a mail-order service.

Rosita Arvigo with Nadia Epstein *Sastun: My Apprenticeship with a Maya Healer* (HarperCollins). A rare glimpse into the life and work of a Maya *curandero*, the late Eligio Panti of San Antonio (see p.171). Dr Arvigo has ensured the survival of generations of healing knowledge, and this book is a testimony both to her perseverance in becoming accepted by Mr Panti and the cultural wisdom of the indigenous people. Arvigo has also written or collaborated on several other books on traditional medicine in Belize. *Rainforest Remedies: One Hundred Healing Herbs of Belize* (Lotus Books, US), co-authored with Michael Balick of the New York Botanical Garden, is a detailed account of some of Belize's commonest medicinal plants and

their uses. Both books are widely available in Belize.

Les Beletsky *Belize and Northern Guatemala – The Ecotraveller's Wildlife Guide* (Academic Press, UK). Although other, specialist wildlife guides may cover their own subjects in more detail, this is the only reasonably comprehensive single-volume guide to the mammals, birds, reptiles, amphibians and marine life of the region. Helpfully, the illustration of each creature is given opposite its description, avoiding confusing page-flicking.

Louise H. Emmons *Neotropical Rainforest Mammals* (University of Chicago, US). Highly informative and very detailed, with colour illustrations by Francois Feer, a book written by experts for non-scientists. Local and scientific names are given, along with plenty of interesting snippets. Emmons is also the principal author of *The Cockscomb Basin Wildlife Sanctuary* (Producciones de la Hamaca, Belize; Orang-Utan Press, US), a comprehensive guide to the history, flora and fauna of Belize's Jaguar Reserve. Though aimed at teachers and students, it's incredibly useful to any visitor and is available from the sanctuary and the BAS.

Carol Farnetti Foster and John R. Meyer *A Guide to the Frogs and Toads of Belize* (Kreiger, US). Great book with plenty of photos and text to help you identify the many anurans you'll see – and hear – in Belize.

Tony Garel and Sharon Matola *A Field Guide to the Snakes of Belize* (Cubola, Belize). Slim guide to all 60 species of snakes in Belize, most illustrated with a colour photograph.

Idaz Greenberg *Guide to Corals and Fishes of Florida, the Bahamas and the Caribbean* (Seahawk Press, US). Great, easy-to-use guide to 260 species that you're most likely to encounter in Belize. Inexpensive and widely available on the cayes; it's waterproof, so you can take it with you on a snorkel trip.

Steve Howell and Sophie Webb *The Birds of Mexico and Northern Central America* (Oxford University Press, UK). The result of years of research, this tremendous work is the definitive book on the region's birds. Essential for all serious birders.

Paul Humann and Ned Loach *Reef Fish Identification: Florida, Caribbean and Bahamas* (New World, US). This guide is for real enthusiasts; it's the one the professionals use, with sturdy bindings, detailed drawings and 825 colour plates. *Reef Creatures* and *Reef Corals*, by the same publisher, are the definitive guides in their respective fields.

Kimo Jolly and Ellen McRae *The Environment of Belize* (Cubola, Belize). Intended as a high-school textbook, this is still an excellent introduction to the ecosystems of Belize. Clearly and intelligently covers all relevant issues from environmental laws to energy cycles.

★ **H. Lee Jones** *Birds of Belize* (University of Texas Press). A long-awaited, comprehensive guide to all 574 species so far recorded in Belize. Already receiving the highest praise from the experts, this excellent book is written by a biologist who's lived in the country for over ten years. At over three hundred pages it's a fairly weighty volume, but the text is very well organized, with 234 range maps, and the superb colour illustrations by Dana Gardner help you easily identify the birds you're looking for. The author, with A. C. Vallely, also has written the *Annotated Checklist of the Birds of Belize* (Lynx, US).

★ **John C. Kricher** *A Neotropical Companion* (Princeton University, US). Subtitled "An Introduction to the Animals, Plants and Ecosystems of the New World Tropics", this book contains an amazing amount of valuable information for nature lovers. Researched mainly in Central America and recently updated, there's plenty that's directly relevant to Belize.

Julian C. Lee *A Field Guide to the Amphibians and Reptiles of the Maya World* (Cornell UP, US). The definitive guide to the herpetology of Yucatán, northern Guatemala, with 180 photographs and 180 drawings covering all 188 species found in the region, with much of the research undertaken in Belize. Excellent range maps and there's even a guide to identifying tadpoles of different species of frogs and toads.

Alan Rabinowitz *Jaguar* (Anchor/Doubleday). A personal account of the author's experiences studying jaguars for the New York

Zoological Society in the early 1980s, while living with a Maya family in the Cockscomb Basin. Rabinowitz was instrumental in the establishment of the Jaguar Reserve in 1984.

Stephen B. Reichling *Tarantulas of Belize* (Kreiger, US). The best guide to these fascinating and often falsely maligned creatures, telling you all you need to know about their habits and habitats, illustrated with plenty of photos and great anatomical drawings by Norma B. Reichling. A real gem for aracnophiles.

Fiona A. Reid *A Field Guide to the Mammals of Central America and Southeast Mexico* (Oxford University Press). The first comprehensive guide to the mammals of the region, written by a truly dedicated researcher who also drew the colour illustrations based on live specimens she caught herself, many of them in Belize. Reid also has written and illustrated *Mammals of Belize* (Hopscotch Interactive, Canada), a booklet widely available in Belize.

Victoria Schlesinger *Animals and Plants of the Ancient Maya* (University of Texas). Part field guide, with illustrations by Juan C. Chab, and part author's observations and vignettes, this book covers around a hundred commonly seen species, giving for most of them their Maya name as well as their common and scientific name.

Peter J. Stafford and John R. Meyer *A Guide to the Reptiles of Belize* (Academic Press, UK). Superb, comprehensive and thoroughly detailed guide to the 120 species of crocodiles, turtles, lizards and snakes found in Belize; the colour photographs really help with identification.

Specialist guides

For field guides to plants, animals, birds, reptiles and the marine fish of Belize, look under "Wildlife", above.

Emory King *Emory King's Driving Guide to Beautiful Belize* (Tropical Books, Belize). Worth a look if you're driving around the country. The maps are perhaps a little too sketchy for complete accuracy, but the book is typically Belizean: laid-back and easy-going.

Freya Rauscher *Cruising Guide to Belize & Mexico's Caribbean Coast* (Wescott Cove Publishing, US; o/p). Although aimed primarily at yachting visitors, this very detailed book offers fascinating insights into the cayes and the entire Belize Barrier Reef; you'll find it in some island resorts and on larger boats.

A single cookbook

Mmm... A Taste of Belizean Cooking (various authors; Cubola, Belize). A compilation of successful recipes and mixed drinks from chefs in restaurants and resorts all over Belize, illustrated by young artists from St John's College, Belize City.

Everything from rice and beans with coconut milk from *Elvi's Kitchen* in San Pedro on Ambergris Caye to shrimp and feta pasta from Chef Whiz at *Tranquility Lodge*, Toledo District.

Language

Language

Language

E nglish is the official language of Belize (the only English-speaking
country in Central America) and naturally enough it's spoken everywhere. However, it's really the first language of only a small percentage of Belize's multilingual population, since seven main languages are
spoken here. For at least half the population, mainly the Mestizos in
the north and the west, Spanish is the language spoken at home and in the
workplace. In fact, the last 25 years have seen a significant increase in the speaking of Spanish, largely due to immigration from neighbouring Central
American countries. Likewise, for many Maya communities their first language
is Mopan, Kekchí or Yucatec Mayan.

For one third of the population – mainly the Creole people – the first language is **Kriol** (the modern spelling favoured by linguists, though still usually
spelt "Creole"), a language partly derived from English and similar to the languages spoken in other parts of the Caribbean colonized by the British.
Uniting the different ethnic groups of Belize, it is the **most widely spoken**
language. English and Kriol are the languages used in public or official situations and for speaking to outsiders. That said, listening to any conversation can
be confusing, as people switch from, say, English to Kriol to Spanish to
Garífuna and back – often in the same sentence.

Many **Garífuna** continue to speak their own tongue as their first language,
although the only community where *everyone* does this is the village of
Hopkins (see p.232). The Belizean **Mennonites** add to the linguistic cocktail
with their old form of High German, spoken in many of their communities.
The jigsaw is completed by recent immigrants from Asia speaking Chinese and
south Asian languages. Unless you spend a lot of time in the Maya or Garífuna
communities you're unlikely to pick up more than a word or two of those languages. If you plan to cross the border into **Guatemala** to visit Tikal, some
Spanish will be essential.

Kriol

Kriol is the *lingua franca* of Belize, spoken by every native Belizean: whether
their first language is Maya, Spanish, Garífuna or English, they can all commu-
nicate in Kriol. It may sound like English from a distance and as you listen to
a few words you'll think that their meaning is clear, but as things move on
you'll soon realize that complete comprehension is just out of reach. It's a
beautifully warm, expressive and relaxed language, typically Caribbean, with a
vocabulary loosely based on English but with significant differences in pronunciation and a grammatical structure that is distinctly West African in origin.
One characteristic is the heavy nasalization of some vowels, for example
waahn (want) and *frahn* (from).

Written Kriol, which you'll see in some newspaper columns and booklets,
is a little easier to get to grips with, though you'll need to study it hard at first
to get the meaning. A booklet designed for use by Peace Corps volunteers
explains the grammar; this is available from some bookstores. A dictionary is
also available, though Kriol will always be much more of a spoken language
than a written one.

Some history

Only in recent years has Kriol begun to be **recognized** as a separate language. There is still much debate and controversy among Belizeans as to whether it is a language or just a dialect of English, and whether it deserves official status as one of the national languages of Belize. In **colonial times**, Kriol was not accepted as a legitimate language and was regarded as bastard English, its usage prohibited in schools, although in practice teachers often lapsed into Kriol. But for all intents and purposes this was (and remains) the language of the people at all levels both at home and work, clearly an integral part of their culture and identity. **Independence** brought a growing pride in the language and today a movement is under way to formalize Kriol as a language and for it to be recognized as one of Belize's national languages, alongside English and Spanish.

For a long time Kriol was an **oral language** with no written form. However, by the 1970s some writers and poets were beginning to write in it, using ad hoc forms of spelling. In 1980 Sir Colville Young – at that time a school principal and today Governor General of Belize – published his *Creole Proverbs of Belize* (see p.342), and in 1993 a group of educators and enthusiasts started the **Belize Kriol Project** to work on developing Kriol into a written language. In 1995 the **National Kriol Council** was formed with the principal aim of promoting the culture and language of the Creole people of Belize. A standardized writing system using a phonemic system has since been developed and, despite some controversy, is gradually gaining acceptance.

The Kriol Council's **website**, ⊛www.kriol.org.bz, has a great deal of useful information on the Kriol language, including a mini-dictionary and information on the history and culture of the Creole people.

Phrases and proverbs

To give a taste of Belizean Kriol, here are some useful phrases:

Excuse me, where is the post office?	Eksyooz mi, weh di poas aafis deh?
Where do I catch the bus to Dangriga?	Weh fu kech di bos tu Dangriga?
Do you have any rooms free?	Yu gat eni room fu rent?
How much is a single room?	How moch wahn singl room kaas?
I have some dirty laundry for washing.	Ah gat sohn doti kloaz fu wash.
Is there a restaurant near here serving Creole food?	Weh sel Kriol food kloas tu ya?

And some proverbs:

Proverb	Literal translation	Meaning
Mek di man weh loos taiga tai ahn bak.	*Let the man who loosed the tiger tie it back.*	Let the man who created a dangerous situation deal with it.
Fish geh kech bai ih own mowt.	*A fish gets caught by its own mouth.*	Guilt often gives itself away.
Kyaahn kech Hari, kech ih shot.	*If you can't catch Harry, catch his shirt.*	If you can't get what you want, get the next best thing.

Publications and media

For more of these fantastic **proverbs** arm yourself with a copy of *Creole Proverbs of Belize*, written by linguist Sir Colville Young, the present Governor General, available from bookstores and the Angelus Press in Belize City. Several **publica-**

tions in Kriol have been produced, including *A Bileez Kriol Glossary an Spellin Gide* (a Kriol–English dictionary), *Rabbit Play Trik Pahn Hanaasi*, a traditional folk tale, and *Kenti an Ih Pah Mek Wahn Doary*, a children's story about constructing a canoe. The *Kriol Kalinda 2004* was a great success and rapidly sold out.

Kriol is increasingly seen and heard in **radio and TV** advertising and on hoardings – for example, *Dis da fu wi chikin* (This is our chicken) seen on delivery vans, and *Da paynt yu waahn?* (You want paint?). *The Reporter* newspaper has a weekly Kriol column *Weh Wi Gat fi Seh* (What we have to say). An **anglicized Kriol** can often be heard on radio and TV, much easier for foreigners to understand.

The Kriol section was supplied by John Pirie.

Spanish

The **Spanish** spoken in both Guatemala and Belize has a strong Latin American flavour to it, and if you're used to the dainty intonation of Madrid or Granada then this may come as something of a surprise. Gone is the soft "s", replaced by a crisp and clear version. If you're new to Spanish it's a lot easier to pick up than the native version.

The rules of **pronunciation** are pretty straightforward and, once you get to know them, strictly observed. Unless there's an accent, words ending in d, l, r and z are **stressed** on the last syllable, all others on the second last. All **vowels** are pure and short.

A somewhere between the "a" sound of back and that of father.

E as in get.

I as in police.

O as in hot.

U as in rule.

C is soft before "e" and "i", hard otherwise: *cerca* is pronounced serka.

G works the same way, a guttural "h" sound (like the *ch* in loch) before "e" or "i", a hard "g" elsewhere: *gigante* becomes higante.

H always silent.

J the same sound as a guttural "g": *jamón* is pronounced hamon.

LL sounds like an English "y": *tortilla* is pronounced torteeya.

N as in English unless it has a tilde (accent) over it, when it becomes "ny": *mañana* sounds like manyana.

QU is pronounced like an English "k".

R is rolled, RR doubly so.

V sounds more like "b", *vino* becoming beano.

X is slightly softer than in English – sometimes almost "s" – except between vowels in place names where it has an "h" sound – ie Mexico (Meh-hee-ko) or Oaxaca (Wa-ha-ka). Note: in Maya the English letter "x" is pronounced "sh", thus *Xunantunich* is Shunan-tun-eech.

Z is the same as a soft "c", so *cerveza* becomes servesa.

Although we've listed a few essential words and phrases, some kind of dictionary or **phrasebook** is a worthwhile investment: the *Rough Guide to Mexican Spanish* is the best practical guide, correct and colloquial, and certainly acceptable for most purposes when travelling in Guatemala. One of the best small Latin-American Spanish dictionaries is the University of Chicago version (Pocket Books); the Collins series (published by HarperCollins) of pocket grammars and dictionaries is also excellent.

Basics

please, thank you	por favor, gracias
where, when	dónde, cuando
what, how much	qué, cuanto
here, there	aquí, allí
this, that	este, eso
now, later	ahora, más tarde
open, closed	abierto/a, cerrado/a
with, without	con, sin
good, bad	buen(o)/a, mal(o)/a
big, small	gran(de), pequeño/a
more, less	más, menos
today, tomorrow	hoy, mañana
yesterday	ayer

Greetings and responses

Hello, goodbye	¡hola!, adios
Good morning	buenos días
Good afternoon/night	buenas tardes/noches
How do you do?	¿Qué tal?
See you later	Hasta luego
Sorry	lo siento/disculpeme
Excuse me	Con permiso/perdón
How are you?	¿Cómo está (usted)? *(formal)* ¿Cómo estás? *(to someone you know)*
Not at all/ You're welcome	De nada
I (don't) understand	(No) Entiendo
Do you speak English?	¿Habla (usted) inglés?
I (don't) speak Spanish	(No) Hablo español
What (did you say)?	¿Mande?
My name is...	Me llamo...
What's your name?	¿Como se llama usted?
I am English	Soy inglés(a)
...American	americano(a)
...Australian	australiano(a)
...Canadian	canadiense(a)
...Irish	irlandés(a)
...Scottish	escosés(a)
...Welsh	galés(a)
...New Zealander	neozelandés(a)

Needs, hotels and transport

I want	Quiero
Do you know...?	¿Sabe…?
I'd like....	Quisiera... por favor
I don't know	No sé
There is (is there?)	Hay (?)
Give me...	Deme...
(one like that)	(uno asi)
Do you have...?	¿Tiene...?
...the time	...la hora
...a room	...un cuarto
...with two beds	...con dos camas
...with a double bed	...con cama matrimonial
It's for one person (two people)	Es para una persona (dos personas)
...for one night (one week)	...para una noche (una semana)
It's fine, how much is it?	¿Esta bien, cuánto es?
It's too expensive	Es demasiado caro
Don't you have anything cheaper?	¿No tiene algo más barato?
Can one...?	¿Se puede...?
...camp (near) here?	¿...acampar aquí (cerca)?
Is there a hotel nearby?	¿Hay un hotel aquí cerca?
How do I get to...?	¿Por dónde se va a...?
Left, right, straight on	izquierda, derecha, derecho
Where is...?	¿Dónde está...?
...the nearest bank	...el banco más cercano *(ATM is cajero automático)*
...the post office	...el correo
...the toilet	...el baño/sanitario
Where does the bus to... leave from?	¿De dónde sale el... camión para?
What time does it leave (arrive in)...?	¿A qué hora sale (llega en)...?
What is there to eat?	¿Qué hay para comer?
What's that?	¿Qué es eso?
What's this called in Spanish?	¿Cómo se llama este en español?

Numbers and days

1	un/uno/una	60	sesenta
2	dos	70	setenta
3	tres	80	ochenta
4	cuatro	90	noventa
5	cinco	100	cien(to)
6	seis	101	ciento uno/una
7	siete	200	doscientos/as
8	ocho	500	quinientos/as
9	nueve	700	setecientos
10	diez	1000	mil
11	once	2000	dos mil
12	doce	1999	mil novocientos noventa y nueve
13	trece		
14	catorce	first	primero/a
15	quince	second	segundo/a
16	dieciséis	third	tercero/a
17	diecisiete	fifth	quinto/a
18	dieciocho	tenth	decimo/a
19	diecinueve		
20	veinte	Monday	Lunes
21	veintiuno	Tuesday	Martes
30	treinta	Wednesday	Miércoles
40	cuarenta	Thursday	Jueves
50	cincuenta	Friday	Viernes
		Saturday	Sábado
		Sunday	Domingo

Rough
Guides

advertiser

Rough Guides travel...

...music & reference

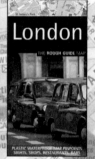

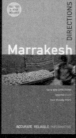

small print and
Index

A Rough Guide to Rough Guides

In the summer of 1981, Mark Ellingham, a recent graduate from Bristol University, was travelling round Greece and couldn't find a guidebook that really met his needs. On the one hand there were the student guides, insistent on saving every last cent, and on the other the heavyweight cultural tomes whose authors seemed to have spent more time in a research library than lounging away the afternoon at a taverna or on the beach.

In a bid to avoid getting a job, Mark and a small group of writers set about creating their own guidebook. It was a guide to Greece that aimed to combine a journalistic approach to description with a thoroughly practical approach to travellers' needs – a guide that would incorporate culture, history and contemporary insights with a critical edge, together with up-to-date, value-for-money listings. Back in London, Mark and the team finished their Rough Guide, as they called it, and talked Routledge into publishing the book.

That first *Rough Guide to Greece*, published in 1982, was a student scheme that became a publishing phenomenon. The immediate success of the book – with numerous reprints and a Thomas Cook prize shortlisting – spawned a series that rapidly covered dozens of destinations. Rough Guides had a ready market among low-budget backpackers, but soon also acquired a much broader and older readership that relished Rough Guides' wit and inquisitiveness as much as their enthusiastic, critical approach. Everyone wants value for money, but not at any price.

Rough Guides soon began supplementing the "rougher" information about hostels and low-budget listings with the kind of detail on restaurants and quality hotels that independent-minded visitors on any budget might expect, whether on business in New York or trekking in Thailand.

These days the guides – distributed worldwide by the Penguin group – offer recommendations from shoestring to luxury and cover more than 200 destinations around the globe, including almost every country in the Americas and Europe, more than half of Africa and most of Asia and Australasia. Our ever-growing team of authors and photographers is spread all over the world, particularly in Europe, the USA and Australia.

In 1994, we published the *Rough Guide to World Music* and *Rough Guide to Classical Music*; and a year later the *Rough Guide to the Internet*. All three books have become benchmark titles in their fields – which encouraged us to expand into other areas of publishing, mainly around popular culture. Rough Guides now publish:

- Travel guides to more than 200 worldwide destinations
- Dictionary phrasebooks to 22 major languages
- History guides ranging from Ireland to Islam
- Maps printed on rip-proof and waterproof Polyart™ paper
- Music guides running the gamut from Opera to Elvis
- Restaurant guides to London, New York and San Francisco
- Reference books on topics as diverse as the Weather and Shakespeare
- Sports guides from Formula 1 to Man Utd
- Pop culture books from *Lord of the Rings* to Cult TV
- World Music CDs in association with World Music Network

Visit www.roughguides.com to see our latest publications.

Rough guide credits

Text editor: Hunter Slaton
Layout: Dan May
Cartography: Jai Prakesh Mishra, Karobi Gogoi & Miles Irving
Picture research: Harriet Mills
Proofreader: Jennifer Speake
Production: John McKay

....

Editorial: London Martin Dunford, Kate Berens, Helena Smith, Claire Saunders, Geoff Howard, Ruth Blackmore, Gavin Thomas, Polly Thomas, Richard Lim, Lucy Ratcliffe, Clifton Wilkinson, Alison Murchie, Fran Sandham, Sally Schafer, Alexander Mark Rogers, Karoline Densley, Andy Turner, Ella O'Donnell, Keith Drew, Andrew Lockett, Joe Staines, Duncan Clark, Peter Buckley, Matthew Milton; **New York** Andrew Rosenberg, Richard Koss, Hunter Slaton, Chris Barsanti, Steven Horak, Amy Hegarty, AnneLise Sorensen
Design & Pictures: London Simon Bracken, Dan May, Diana Jarvis, Mark Thomas, Jj Luck, Harriet Mills; **Delhi** Madhulita Mohapatra, Umesh Aggarwal, Ajay Verma,

Jessica Subramanian
Production: Julia Bovis, John McKay, Sophie Hewat
Cartography: London Maxine Repath, Ed Wright, Katie Lloyd-Jones, Miles Irving; **Delhi** Manish Chandra, Rajesh Chhibber, Jai Prakesh Mishra, Ashutosh Bharti, Rajesh Mishra, Animesh Pathak, Jasbir Sandhu, Karobi Gogoi
Cover art direction: Louise Boulton
Online: New York Jennifer Gold, Cree Lawson, Suzanne Welles, Benjamin Ross; **Delhi** Manik Chauhan, Narender Kumar, Shekhar Jha, Rakesh Kumar
Marketing & Publicity: London Richard Trillo, Niki Smith, David Wearn, Chloë Roberts, Demelza Dallow, Kristina Pentland; **New York** Geoff Colquitt, Megan Kennedy, Milena Perez
Finance: Gary Singh
Manager India: Punita Singh
Series editor: Mark Ellingham
PA to Managing Director: Julie Sanderson
Managing Director: Kevin Fitzgerald

Publishing information

This third edition published October 2004 by
Rough Guides Ltd,
80 Strand, London WC2R 0RL.
345 Hudson St, 4th Floor,
New York, NY 10014, USA.
Distributed by the Penguin Group
Penguin Books Ltd,
80 Strand, London WC2R 0RL
Penguin Putnam, Inc.
375 Hudson Street, NY 10014, USA
Penguin Books Australia Ltd,
487 Maroondah Highway, PO Box 257,
Ringwood, Victoria 3134, Australia
Penguin Books Canada Ltd,
10 Alcorn Avenue, Toronto, Ontario,
Canada M4V 1E4
Penguin Books (NZ) Ltd,
182–190 Wairau Road, Auckland 10,
New Zealand
Typeset in Bembo and Helvetica to an original design by Henry Iles.

Printed in Italy by LegoPrint S.p.A

384pp includes index
A catalogue record for this book is available from the British Library

ISBN 1-84353-276-X

Help us update

We've gone to a lot of effort to ensure that the third edition of **The Rough Guide to Belize** is accurate and up-to-date. However, things change – places get "discovered", opening hours are notoriously fickle, restaurants and rooms raise prices or lower standards. If you feel we've got it wrong or left something out, we'd like to know, and if you can remember the address, the price, the time, the phone number, so much the better.

We'll credit all contributions, and send a copy of the next edition (or any other Rough

Guide if you prefer) for the best letters. Everyone who writes to us and isn't already a subscriber will receive a copy of our full-colour thrice-yearly newsletter. Please mark letters: **"Rough Guide Belize Update"** and send to: Rough Guides, 80 Strand, London WC2R 0RL, or Rough Guides, 4th Floor, 345 Hudson St, New York, NY 10014. Or send an email to **mail@roughguides.com**

Have your questions answered and tell others about your trip at
www.roughguides.atinfopop.com

Acknowledgements

Peter: Firstly, as always, thanks to Maureen for her support over the years. And thanks to everyone at Rough Guides, especially my editors in New York, Hunter Slaton and Andrew Rosenberg, who've seen this edition through some trying times and whose efforts have made it an even better book than before. In the London Rough Guides office, thanks to Katie Lloyd-Jones, Dan May, Ed Wright, Harriet Mills, Mark Thomas, and Julia Bovis; also thanks to the Delhi cartography team. And thanks of course to fellow authors Mark Whatmore, whose original idea it was all those years ago to produce The Rough Guide to Guatemala and Belize, and to Iain Stewart for his help and contacts in Guatemala.

In the UK I'd like to say thanks once again to the consultants and staff of the Hospital for Tropical Diseases for some interesting diagnoses and superb treatment. Thanks, too, for the support and help from everyone at the Belize High Commission in London, especially High Commissioner Alexis Rosado and First Secretary Joseph Aguilar. Thanks also to Johno at Journey Latin America for his expert help with UK flights information, and to Wendy Angrove of eXito Travel for the US flights.

In Guatemala, thanks to Lorena Artola and everyone at Dos Lunas in Guatemala City for boundless help and hospitality; in Antigua thanks to Laura and Nissim for the books and to Peter Stone and family for the hospitality; in Flores, thanks to Lileana and Benedicto Grijalva for all the help and advice; in Macanche thanks to Laura for the first aid and to Miguel, Virgilio and Alfonso for the medical advice and arranging the hospital visit.

To select just a few from the literally hundreds of people in Belize, from archeologists to zoologists and typists to taxi drivers, who've provided so much help, advice and assistance, and made my visits both fascinating and fun is always a difficult task. Most of you know who you are and many of you are already mentioned by name in the Guide, so to all of you many, many thanks and I'll be seeing as many of my friends and colleagues in Belize as I can during the coming year. Thanks of course to Steve Schulte and everyone at Tropic Air who've helped (and continue to help) me to get around Belize.

A very special mention once again to John Pirie, whose witty and erudite reports from even farther-flung places has improved the ever-expanding text, and thanks to Rob Coates for researching and producing the new Art section, for overhauling and updating the Music section in Contexts and for his diligent, even exhaustive, research into Belize City's cultural scene and nightlife. Rob and Peter would also like to say many thanks to Ivan Duran of Stonetree Records, Yasser Musa of NICH, John Morris and Gilvano Swasey of the Museum of Belize, and Lita Krohn at the House of Culture for their assistance and support in researching all aspects of cultural life in Belize. Thanks again to Andy Palacio of the Institute of Creative Arts for the song lyrics.

I'd also like to thank Dr Jaime Awe, George Thomson, Allan Moore, Brian Woodye, Teresa Batty and everyone at the Institute of Archaeology for providing insight into the past and allowing me a glimpse of recent discoveries. Many thanks to Beverly Wade of Fisheries, to Diane Wade-Moore, Valdemar Andrade and everyone at the BAS, to Noreen Fairweather of Lands and to everyone in both government departments and the conservation movement for their help in my conservation and environmental research. Thanks also to Bruno and Melissa Kuppinger for welcoming me into their home and office, and to Lee Anne Hasselbacher of the Cornerstone Foundation, for her prompt and enthusiastic responses and her book review. And of course thanks to all those who speedily and accurately answered my last-minute email enquiries, including (but not limited to) Anabel Ford at El Pilar, Jason Yeager, Geoffrey Braswell at Pusilhá, Marty Casado on Ambergris Caye, Annie Seashore on Caye Caulker, Ellie Dial and Laura Godfrey in Placencia and Jerry Shaver in Punta Gorda.

Finally, a fond farewell to Cheney Roberts, a very special person who loved her river and gardens in Toledo District and who is greatly missed by all those who loved her.

The editor: Thanks to Peter, whose enthusiasm for Belize knows no bounds; to the cartography team in Delhi; Katie (KT Boundary) Lloyd-Jones; Harriet Mills and Mark Thomas; Dan May; Ed Wright; and Andrew Rosenberg.

SMALL PRINT

Readers' letters

Thanks to all the readers who have taken the time and trouble to write in with comments and suggestions. Listed below are those who were especially helpful: apologies for any errors, ommissions or misspellings.

Michael Van Zee, Allan M. Gathercoal, Lt Col Colin Draper, Emma Curnow, Sid and Mary Thornhill, Mary Weerts, Fred Midtgaard, Patricia San Miguel, Jane Bryce, Jonathan Gore, Casey DeMoss Roberts, Rae Calladine, Sarah Dickens, Emily Fisher, Carlos Montoro, Becky Harris, Liz Parke, Ingrid Lagerberg, Mafalda Carvalho, Stuart Torrie, Alice Lucy Hawa, Robert Shepard, Leighton Cheal, Ellen Boliek, Dawn Kaiser, Florence Reed, Cindy Blount, Robert and Ann Tasher, Veronique McKenzie, Jonathon Gore, Anthea Rawlings, Suzanne Lehr, Rosalind Incledon-Webber, Lizzie Evans, John Biskovitch and Ken, Ann and Laura Hastings.

Photo credits

Cover credits

Main front Cushion Starfish © Getty
Small front top Jaguar © Getty
Small front lower Maya ruins © Getty
Back top Tropical foliage © Alamy
Back lower Aerial shot of Belize © Alamy

Colour introduction

Blue morpho butterfly © Gail Shumway/Taxi/Getty Images
Jungle river view © Belize, Island Expeditions.com
Mopan mask maker, Maya Center © Chloe Sayer
Scarlet macaw © James Beveridge
Painting by Nelson Young © James Beveridge
Queen angelfish © James Beveridge
Sunset over Victoria Peak © James Beveridge
Top of Caana, Caracol ruin © Tony Rath/www.trphoto.com

Things not to miss

1. Blue Hole, aerial view © Ron Watts/CORBIS
2. Pottery artefacts, Museum of Belize © James Beveridge
3. Belize City Carnival © James Beveridge
4. Snorkelling and kayaking © Belize, Island Expeditions.com
5. Hiking, Cayo District © Cindy Blount/Naturalight Productions Ltd
6. Newly discovered frieze, Caracol © James Beveridge
7. Sailing off Caye Caulker © Nick Hanna
8. Jaguar, Belize Zoo © Tony Morrison/South American Pictures
9. Paddling on the Upper Macal River © Belize, Island Expeditions.com
10. Lamanai © Juan-Carlos Cuellar/Naturalight Productions Ltd
11. Garífuna Drumming © David Sanger/Alamy
12. Toucan © Belize, Island Expeditions.com

13. Hawksbill turtle © Doug Perrin/naturepl.com
14. Tikal © Robert Francis/South American Pictures
15. Five Sisters Falls, Mountain Pine Ridge © Carlos Popper
16. Beach, Ambergris Caye © Peter Menzel/Impact Photos
17. Flower seller, San Ignacio © Lynsey Addario/ Corbis
18. Swimming at coral reef © Tony Rath/www.trphoto.com
19. Actun Tunichil Muknal Cave © Tony Rath/www.trphoto.com
20. Glover's Reef © Belize, Island Expeditions.com
21. Lobsterfest, Caye Caulker © James Beveridge

Black and white photos

St John's Cathedral, Belize City © Tony Morrison/South American Pictures (p.54)
The courthouse, Belize City © Tony Morrison/South American Pictures (p.69)
Monkey in tree © James Beveridge (p.78)
Mask from Mask Temple, Lamanai © Chris Sharp/South American Pictures (p.101)
San Pedro at dusk, Ambergris Caye © Bob Krist/CORBIS (p.106)
Bird's eye view of snorkellers © James Beveridge (p.118)
Harpy eagle, Belize Zoo © Tony Morrison/South American Pictures (p.142)
Hawkesworth Suspension Bridge, San Ignacio © Chris Sharp/South American Pictures (p.156)
Flores © Chris Sharp/South American Pictures (p.190)
Tikal © Tony Morrison/South American Pictures (p.205)
Boy at Lubaantun © Macduff Everton/CORBIS (p.214)
Waterfall at Cockscomb Basin Wildlife Sanctuary © James Beveridge (p.237)

SMALL PRINT

Index

Map entries are in colour

INDEX

INDEX

Map symbols

maps are listed in the full index using coloured text

-----	International boundary		@	Internet
---	Chapter boundary		☏	Phone office
═══	Major road		ⓘ	Tourist office
═══	Minor road		▣	Restaurant
....	Road under construction		◉	Accommodation
-----	Path		★	Bus stop
───	River		⛽	Fuel station
⌇⌇⌇	Reef		🅿	Parking
⅍⅍⅍	Escarpment		⊠	Post office
⌃⌃	Mountain range		⛳	Golf course
⌇⌇	Gorge		Ⓐ	Campsite
▲	Peak		✈	Airport
⌂	Cave		▬	Building
⚱	Waterfall		✚	Church
◆	Place of interest		⬭	Stadium
✚	Immigration post		✛✛✛	Christian cemetery
⚒	Inca ruin		▦	Park
⛲	Lighthouse		▨	Beach
🌳	Tree		▧	Jungle/forest